Sixth Edition

THE MAGNIFICENT PENINSULA
The Comprehensive Guidebook To Mexico's

CALIFORNIA

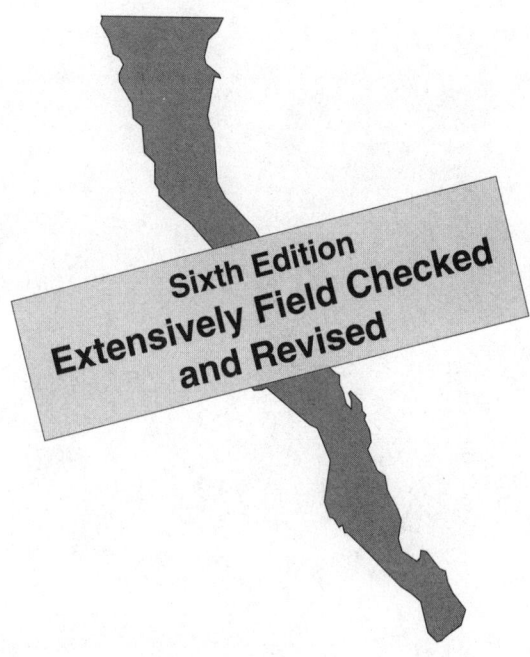

Sixth Edition
**Extensively Field Checked
and Revised**

Jack Williams and Patty Williams

With Fieldwork Assistance by Barbara Williams

1

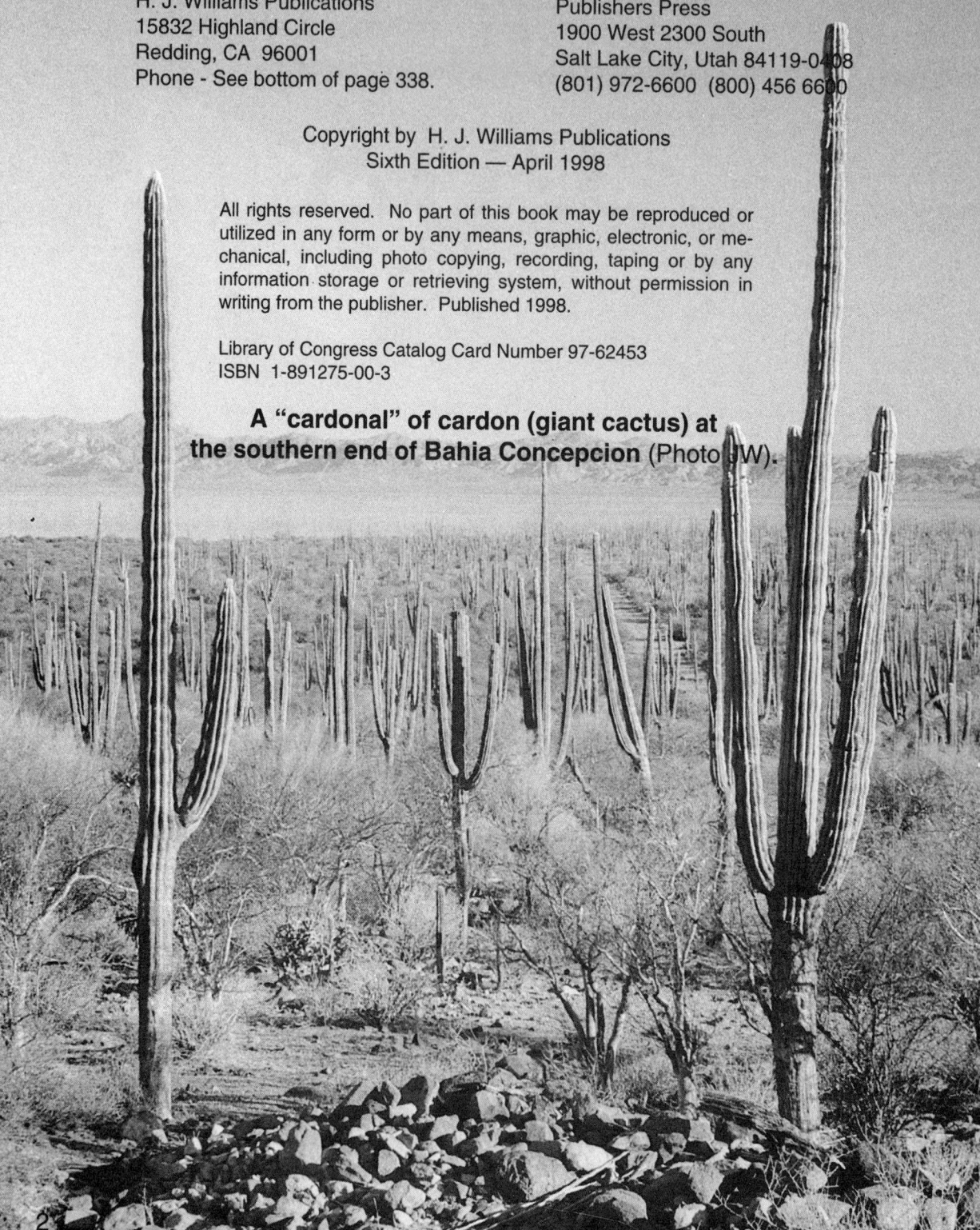

Published by
H. J. Williams Publications
15832 Highland Circle
Redding, CA 96001
Phone - See bottom of page 338.

Printed by
Publishers Press
1900 West 2300 South
Salt Lake City, Utah 84119-0408
(801) 972-6600 (800) 456 6600

Copyright by H. J. Williams Publications
Sixth Edition — April 1998

Library of Congress Catalog Card Number 97-62453
ISBN 1-891275-00-3

A "cardonal" of cardon (giant cactus) at the southern end of Bahia Concepcion (Photo JW).

CONTENTS

AUTHOR'S PREFACE

The Author's Preface in the original edition of *The Magnificent Peninsula* presented my qualifications for producing the book. It was essentially an apology for my having had the audacity to become an author in that my past experience in writing had been limited to business letters and the reports and other assorted jargon of the world of bureaucracy. As *The Magnificent Peninsula* has now met with some modest success, I am perhaps justified in withdrawing the apology. However, still included here is some background material about myself as many readers have expressed interest in the pedigree of their guide.

Initially, I love to travel, and this activity is one of the driving forces of my life. I submit that having such an affliction is the basic requirement for writing a travel guide. By quick tally I find I have expended some 29 months traveling in Mexico, with over three-quarters of this time spent on the Baja peninsula or over its surrounding waters. Perhaps, more importantly, I am a rover, not lingering long in any one haunt. I frequently talk to other people whose knowledge about a particular place in Baja exceeds my own, but perhaps the nature and breadth of my wanderings have provided an overall perspective of Baja shared with only a relative few.

By training and experience I am a forester, although I have now retired from that calling. Being a specialist in trees and forests may seem a strange qualification for delving into the almost totally desert environment of the Baja peninsula. In practice, many foresters find themselves engaged in the far broader task of managing land with all its surface and subsurface resources. We are fortunate in becoming familiar with geology, wildlife, botany, soils, and a variety of other outdoor-oriented subjects. In addition, many of us become keen observers and interpreters of what we see, whether it be forest or desert.

At the core of my view of travel book writing is the concept that travelers need a source of information concerning the land and all its natural and man-made attributes as a basis for enjoying and appreciating what they see. As a purveyor of such material, I am an expert in very little, but in keeping with my name, I am perhaps a "Jack" of all trades concerning the great outdoors.

My post-retirement activities in Baja started in 1983 gathering data to assist another author in republishing his out-of-print boating guide. *The Magnificent Peninsula* was written as an act of frustration as I waited for this individual to produce his book. As his project still did not materialize, I produced my own *Baja Boater's Guide* in 1988. During this five year period from 1983 to 1988 I conducted two complete circumnavigations of the peninsula in my sailboat, retraced this same terrain by aircraft taking over 1,000 aerial photos, and traveled approximately 20,000 miles over Baja's roads and highways.

In presenting these credentials I have so far omitted what may be most important. I have a love affair with Mexico and the Baja peninsula. This is the catalyst that has led me to the perilous task of authorship. Hopefully, this infatuation will not overly cloud my objectivity. It is my sincere wish that these efforts will enhance your ability to plan, and to savor traveling in Mexico's Magnificent Peninsula. If perchance it does, or if you can offer the path to improvement, it would be a pleasure to hear from you.

Jack Williams, Redding, California.

Sixth Edition Notes -- Field work for this 6th edition was accomplished in October and November, 1997 by Jack Williams and Barbara Williams. We found scores of places where modest changes in Baja required revision of the book. Material concerning golf, motorcycles, off-road racing, and a new port-of-entry at Mexicali have been added. Also new are several maps and many photographs taken by Barbara Williams.

In a broader sense, the 6th edition fieldwork found no major new changes in travel related conditions and facilities other than continued development of several existing Cape Area resort areas. The transportation system was essentially unchanged with recent improvements limited largely to streets in the peninsula's ever growing communities. In any case, we have done our best to bring you what we hope is the best and most up-to-date Baja guidebook on the market.

ACKNOWLEDGMENTS

Where does one begin? I have no big names to drop, but many people have made big contributions to *The Magnificent Peninsula*. My thanks go to:

My daughter, Barbara Williams, who was the first to review the manuscript in the office and who sat at my side as we checked the original GRAND TOUR in the field. The changes made at her suggestion were immense. Now with this 6th edition she has again been my companion in the field with the anticipation that she will take over full responsibility for field investigations for the book's next edition; ——— Gene Kira, who has produced an outstanding 6th edition cover at a truly modest cost; ——— Ken Reimer, for contributing the poetry, a welcome touch of class; ——— Alan Lamb, a true friend and excellent companion during La Patricia's circumnavigation of the Baja peninsula and for his office and field review of the original manuscript. (Putting up with the vile moods of the skipper takes a special kind of person;) ——— June Siringer, for a masterful job of editing the original manuscript where the spelling was inspired by the political philosophy of Abraham Lincoln: "Some of the words were spelled wrong all of the time, and all of the words were spelled wrong some of the time, but mercifully all of the words were not spelled wrong all of the time;" and where the author looked upon commas as a cook looks on salt, "something to be sprinkled on at random in the process of preparation."

And a special tribute to my wife, Patricia Williams, for endless hours of help and understanding in many forms. Without her, there would have simply been no La Patricia, no *The Magnificent Peninsula*, and perhaps, no Jack Williams. She has become the books editor, index maker and on and on. H. J. Williams Publications is truly a joint endeavor for the two of us and her name has been added as the book's coauthor.

My thanks also to Lyn Gladstone for hunches, and counsel, (my thin skin will never be the same); to Peter Schultz for guidance through the strange and wonderful world of printing; to Ellie Lamb for reviewing the original manuscript in the field; to my parents, Henry and Margaret Williams whose energy and frugality produced the initial financial resources to publish the book; and to Leland Lewis, who provided the motivation and opportunity for my venture into writing. Sometimes it is not what you do, but what you don't do that is important. Thus it was with Leland.

My gratitude to the late Chet Sherman, President of the Vagabundos del Mar for extensive cooperation in bringing this book to the attention of the members of his fine travel club. Chet passed away in 1997.

Finally, thanks to an endless number of travelers in the Magnificent Peninsula who have offered their counsel; to Mexican officials who have struggled with my poor Spanish in answering my questions; and to the wonderfully warm and friendly Mexican people who share their land with we travelers from the north.

Thank you all -- Jack Williams

PHOTO CREDITS

The Cover -- The photos on the front and back covers are mixture of those taken by Jack Williams, Barbara Williams and the cover's designer, Gene Kira.

Internal Photos -- With this 6th edition we have added or changed many of the photos. With a few exceptions the ground level photos are by Jack Williams or Barbara Williams. The aerial shots are by Jack Williams. The initials JW or BW in the photo's captions indicate the photographer.

BAJA CALIFORNIA
By Ken Reimer

Baja California...legendary land
Of the warrior women,
Of precious pearls...;
Stepchild appendix
Of a great continent...,
Where the sands of time
Mark the ages languidly,
as she dreams on and on
In her siesta 'neath the sun.

On October 15, 1524, Hernan Cortez wrote the king of Spain. The conqueror of New Spain reported on a legendary island that was populated only by women. It was also said to be rich in pearls and gold. These reports no doubt inspired Cortez to dispatch expeditions in search of this romantic land. They also provide the background for Ken Reimer's poem. (More poems by Ken are found later in this book.)

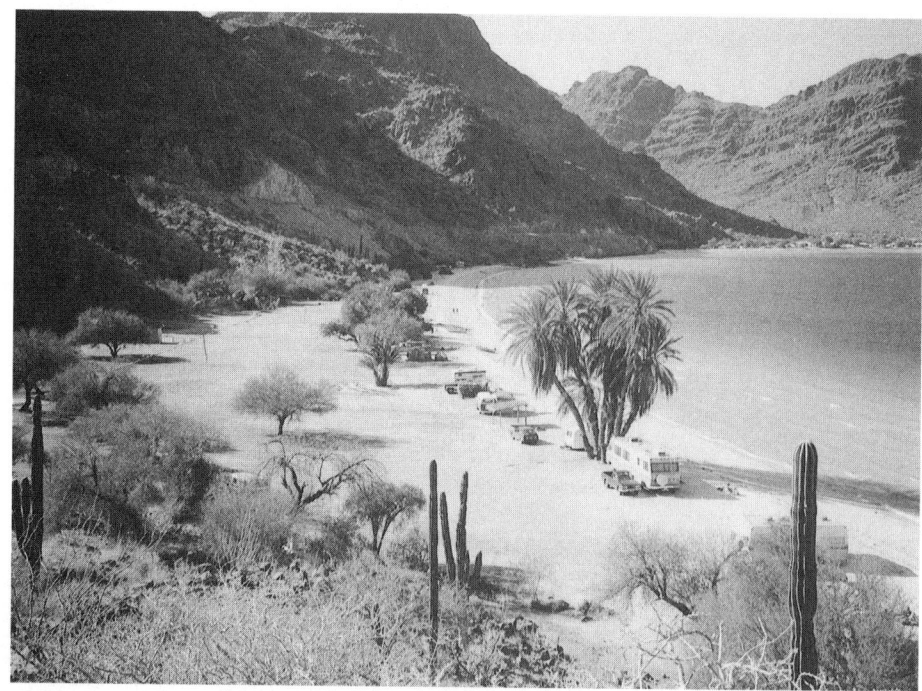

"Siesta 'neath the sun" at Playa el Coyote. Photo JW.

THE GREAT WEST

A Traveler's Guide To

HISTORY

Of Western United

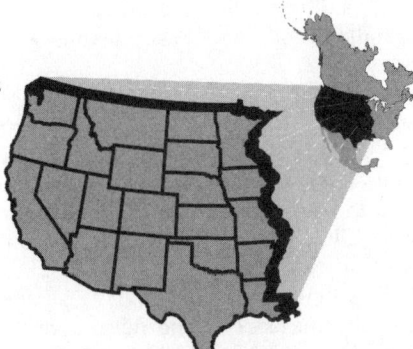

A Partial List of Contents

Prehistoric Indian Sites
    Pueblo sites of the Southwest
    The Earthlodge People
Spanish Expeditions, & Settlements
    Francisco Coronado (**1540**)
    The Settlement of New Mexico
    Missions in Texas
French Expeditions and Settlements
    La Salle
    New Orleans
The War of 1812
The Texas Revolution
Mexican-American War
Civil War in the West
Lewis and Clark Expedition
Fur Trappers and Trading Posts
The Mountain Men
The Mormon Story

The Mining Era
Missions in the Northwest
Pioneer Roads and Trails
    Santa Fe Trail
    Oregon Trail
    California Trail
Transportation Enterprises
    Butterfield Overland Mail
    The Pony Express
    The Transcontinental Railroad
Farming the Frontier
The Great Cattle Era
The American Indian and the
Frontier Conflict
    Apache - Navajo - Kiowas &
    Comanches - Dakota Sioux
    Pacific Northwest - Nez Perce
    Plains Tribes - The Plains Wars
    Battle of Wounded Knee (**1890**)

By **Jack Williams & Patty Williams**

author's of two of Baja's great guidebooks

The Magnificent Peninsula and **Baja Boater's Guide**

Patty and I have been working on THE GREAT WEST since 1992 and have driven 38,000 miles doing field investigations. This first volume about history will be joined by others covering Geology and Vegetation in the months to follow. Many of you have expressed kind words concerning our Baja guidebooks. In all honesty, producing them has been child's play compared to THE GREAT WEST. We sincerely hope that this first book about history will add enjoyment to your recreational travel in the 22 western states.

Jack Williams

Price $19.95 + $3.50 shipping + $1.30 tax for books mailed to addresses in California. (VISA or MASTERCARD)

Order from the Baja Bookshelf in the Appendix
Phone (800) 355-8635
or see note bottom
of page 338

Travel Information for 370 Historic Attractions -- 97 Historic Maps -- 32 Photos
288 Pages -- 7"x 9" Format -- Extensive Text About Western History

The Guide that Links History with Places to Visit

CHAPTER 1
INTRODUCTION

Few places in the world so perfectly fit Webster's definition of a peninsula: "A portion of jutting land nearly surrounded by water." From the United States-Mexican border to Baja's tip at Cabo San Lucas is a straight-line distance of nearly 700 miles, a length greater than that of two of the world's other well-known peninsulas, Florida and the Italian boot.

This enchanting land is also unique in another manner. Baja is largely a wilderness. Except for La Paz, the border towns and the resorts at the peninsula's tip, it is little developed and lightly visited. It has always amazed me that such an area is located adjacent to one of the most densely populated metropolitan centers in the world. It is as if there were a magic line separating the two, and of course there is, the international border. There can be little doubt that the face of the peninsula would bear slight resemblance to what one finds today if it were a portion of the United States. Those of us who love Baja are unanimous in expressing gratitude for the presence of that border.

THE COMPREHENSIVE GUIDEBOOK

It is perhaps a bit brazen for an author to maintain that his book is THE COMPREHENSIVE GUIDEBOOK

Many things are modernizing in Baja but people riding donkeys and other signs of the past are still commonplace. Photo BW.

when several other volumes on the same topic may be readily acquired. Making such a statement is a good marketing technique, but in the final analysis it will succeed only if it is true. I submit here the reasons why I believe the claim is correct, and at the same time tell you how the volume is organized and present the basic ideas on which it is founded.

Most of the space in many travel books provides descriptions of specific attractions and locales. Relatively little space is devoted to more broadly based background material concerning the total area under consideration. *The Magnificent Peninsula* devotes approximately equal attention to these two arenas. PARTS I and II provide the background. PART III, a GRAND TOUR through the entire peninsula, stresses and relies upon the PARTS I and II information. I believe it is the nature and use of this background material that makes the book comprehensive.

We will now move to a brief discussion of the three parts of this book.

PART I -- BACKGROUND AND PLANNING

It is one of my principal objectives to paint the big picture rather than to provide overly finite details that may be of limited value. I hope to bring Baja alive so that you can visualize it as a whole and obtain a grasp of its major attributes and recreational attractions. But don't be misled. This does not mean you will be reading a cluster of broad generalities. As in many subjects, even the big picture can be quite complex. So it is with Baja.

The seven chapters in PART I are designed to provide BASIC background information that every visitor to Baja should know. I suggest you use PART I as a planning tool to help decide <u>if</u> you want to go, <u>where</u> you want to go, <u>how</u> you will travel, and in <u>what</u> activities you will engage. Obviously it should best be read before undertaking a visit to the Magnificent Peninsula.

In PART II we will move on to a HIGHER level of background material.

PART II -- HIGHER NEEDS

Psychologists have long recognized that all human animals share certain BASIC needs for things such as food, safety, protection, care, gregariousness, love, respect, standing, status, and self-respect. Famous psychologist Abraham Maslow stresses that these elements seem to arrange themselves in a hierarchy of importance and that the demand to fulfill a particular need usually rests on some prior satisfaction of those that fall lower on the scale. Maslow also contends that at the apex of this hierarchy there is a still HIGHER group of needs which relate to the sheer quest for knowledge, understanding, and such aesthetic factors as beauty, symmetry, simplicity, and order.

As before, it appears that these HIGHER needs only come into prominence when the BASIC list has been adequately serviced. I submit that it would be relatively easy to defend the proposition that most American and Canadian citizens who have the leisure and financial resources to visit Baja California have their BASIC needs reasonably well in hand. It follows that the fulfilling of Maslow's HIGHER needs is an important objective for many of Baja's visitors.

It is the objective of PART II of *The Magnificent Peninsula* to provide the data needed to gratify this human quest for knowledge, understanding, and the search for beauty. It does this by discussing subjects that relate to what is in plain view when one travels through Baja: land, vegetation, wildlife, places of historic interest, the people and their works. I suggest that its five chapters

be read or reviewed a few days prior to making your trip so that its material will be fresh in mind. You can ignore PART II and still have a fine trip to Baja, but I urge you to absorb its contents in your quest for Maslow's higher ground.

NOTE — In writing the above paragraphs in the 1st edition of this book I was fearful that many readers would not share my enthusiasm for the subject matter in PART II. To my pleasant surprise, these pages have proven to be the book's most popular segment. Maslow was right.

PART III -- THE GRAND TOUR

The long, craggy finger of the Baja peninsula is dominated from a transportation standpoint by the Transpeninsular Highway (Highway 1) which extends over 1,000 miles from the international border to within a mile of the famous arch at the tip of Cabo San Lucas. In PART III, the reader is taken on a GRAND TOUR of the Baja peninsula along the highway from north to south and is directed to dozens of side trips along the way. It also includes tours of the border towns, the San Felipe area, and numerous other highways and roads.

The GRAND TOUR is packed with elements of real interest which will enhance your trip. Often these items are based upon background material presented in PARTS I and II. PART III goes well beyond simply keeping you from getting lost and recommending where to spend the night. It features a thirty stop POINTS OF SPECIAL INTEREST Tour and other unique features which are outlined in more detail in the INTRODUCTION to PART III.

PART III is designed to be read as you make the GRAND TOUR. Of course, it may be perused as part of the planning phase prior to departure.

THE MAGNIFICENT PENINSULA'S HIERARCHY OF NEEDS

The Five Chapters In PART II

HIGHER NEEDS INFORMATION

The Seven Chapters In PART I

BASIC NEEDS INFORMATION

At work on the book above the beach on the El Migrino Loop, south of Todos Santos. -- Tough work, but somebody has to do it. Photo JW.

history chapter provides the principal exception to this rule, but even there a special effort has been made to relate the historical account to the sites where events took place and which you may visit.

It has been a constant temptation to refer to citizens of the United States as *Americans*. I am aware that Canadians and Mexicans rightly consider that they too are Americans. To avoid offending these people, the term *North Americans* is frequently used when referring to everyone who visits Baja from *north of the border*. These terms apply to the two peoples and countries of Canada and the United States collectively.

A FEW GROUND RULES

Preparation of *The Magnificent Peninsula* has been based on two cardinal rules.

1. I REPORT WHAT I HAVE SEEN. — This book has been written almost exclusively from my own notes and observations, supplemented in a few cases by those of trusted associates. I have reviewed the works of the authors who have preceded me but I have not pirated their accounts. In some instances I have visited coastal areas by boat but have not traveled the back roads to reach these same locations. I will alert you to these situations. In all other cases I have personally seen or investigated everything that is described. In preparing PART II, it has been necessary to base the background for much of the material on scientific literature relating to the subject in question. This is particularly true for the chapter on history. However, the specific points of interest that are noted in relation to these subjects all reflect my own observations.

2. I CONCENTRATE ON WHAT THE TRAVELER CAN SEE. — A majority of the information presented relates to objects that can easily be seen while traveling in the Magnificent Peninsula. I have refrained from relating lenghty accounts of the geologic past, the activities of nocturnal or rare desert animals or other phenomena that no one is likely to see. The

Use of the word *California* also presents a problem. For several centuries California was everything *over there* west of the mainland of New Spain (Mexico). With the establishment of the Franciscan missions in what is now California in the United States, the northern area became *Alta California* and the name *Baja California* was applied to the peninsula itself.

The Magnificent Peninsula refers to the present State of California as Alta California, or California in the United States, in deference to our Mexican friends who might otherwise feel that the name of their land has been usurped. The peninsula as a whole is usually referred to as *Baja*, as this is a term universally used north of the border. I apologize to those in Mexico who feel that the full name Baja California is more appropriate. Also, the names Baja and the Magnificent Peninsula are used interchangeably. *The Magnificent Peninsula* is printed in italic when it refers to this book.

It has recently come to my attention that some individuals refer to Baja California as "The Baja," meaning "The Lower." I am sure most true Baja lovers would join me in endeavoring to discourage this practice.

Finally, place names in Baja are presented in Spanish. Thus, *Bahia Escondido* is not referred to as *Escondido Bay* or *Hidden Bay*. The exceptions to this rule are the

BAJA TRAVEL CLUBS

There are two full-service travel clubs that concentrate their activities on Baja California. Both have approximately 5,000 family memberships. I recommend you consider membership in one or both of these organizations. There are also two other clubs whose membership is more broadly based. All offer discount auto insurance to their members along with a variety of other services.

The oldest is the VAGABUNDOS DEL MAR, 190 Main St, Rio Vista, CA 94571 (800) 474-BAJA. They offer a monthly newsletter and feature a variety of highly enjoyable social events. See notice on page 12 of this book.

The DISCOVER BAJA TRAVEL Club offers a full range of services including planning assistance to its members. 3065 Clairemont Dr., San Diego, CA 92117, (800) 727-BAJA. See notice on page 13 of this book.

The BAJA BUSH PILOTS specializes in services for the private flyer. It is described in more detail in Chapter 3 under Air Travel.

The two broader based clubs that provide services concerning Baja California are: (1) The AUTOMOBILE CLUB OF SOUTHERN CALIFORNIA, 2601 South Figueroa Street, Los Angeles, CA 90007 which publishes an excellent road map for the peninsula along with many other services, and (2) the RECREATION VEHICLE ASSOCIATION OF BRITISH COLUMBIA, P.O. Box 2977, Vancouver, B. C. V6B 3X4. (604) 581 0745. They publish the RV Times and sponsor rallies and other special events.

Pacific Ocean and the Sea of Cortez because they are so well known in their English versions. A list of words such as cape, bay, and beach, which are frequently used in geographical place names, is given in both Spanish and English in the GLOSSARY.

SOME PERSONAL OPINIONS

Travel book authors, as a breed, tend to paint enchanting pictures of the realms they are describing. Their third person descriptions sometimes take on the tone of indisputable truths or natural laws laid down by the gods. "The place has a magic charm and is a veritable heaven on earth" not because the author says so, but because that's the way it is. Descriptions and advertisements concerning Mexico frequently fall in this category. They describe a carefree land of fiestas, mariachi music, swimming pools, luxury hotels and never ending balmy weather.

With a title like The Magnificent Peninsula before one, a discerning reader might conclude I have fallen victim to this same sleight of hand. Please, forgive me, one must have a catchy title or no one will notice his book. In my defense I draw attention to the fact that I have chosen to write in the first person so it will be clear "from whence comeith the word" in this volume. And now that you have been enticed into purchasing the book, and hopefully cannot retrieve your money, let me present a few personal comments aimed at

bringing a note of realism to the Baja peninsula.

First of all, I sincerely believe that the Baja peninsula is magnificent. Its mountains, unique desert vegetation, coastline, people, and culture appeal to thousands of Baja Buffs. Others may not find it so. Baja is largely a desert. This is an inescapable reality. If deserts are an uncomfortable environment for you, magnificent may seem overly generous. If you have become addicted to all the finely tuned luxuries of the 20th century that are commonplace north of the border, you may be less than enchanted with Baja. What is charming, unique, or challenging to one individual may be an inconvenience to others.

It is also inescapable that the living standards in Mexico are considerably below what many of us are accustomed to in the United States and Canada. A great majority of the Mexican people you will meet are fully engaged with activities lower on Maslow's scale of needs than those at its summit. The traveler can simply overlook this situation or, preferably, will adapt a frame of mind that accepts what one encounters as part of a culture that provides a foreign country with its charm. Regrettably, I know people who find what they view as poverty in Mexico is personally offensive, even when seen from the window of a luxury hotel. Should you be one of these, your travel plans might best be directed at places other than Mexico or other developing countries.

Finally, I wish to direct your attention back to a comment presented in the opening lines of this introduction. It concerns the fact that except for selected areas, Baja is relatively unvisited. Thousands of vacationers visit Baja every year. Many return over and over, the true *Baja Buffs*. But their numbers are astonishingly small when one considers the enormous population living next door in the Los Angeles-San Diego area. Why isn't Baja simply overrun with tourists? I believe I know the major answer. It can be expressed in only one word. *Fear.*

I have given considerable thought to bringing forth this subject. Is it wise for a travel book author to raise the potential of something negative about the area he is promoting? Obviously I have decided to do so. Proceeding otherwise would be to ignore what is all too apparent; that is, that many people are frightened to travel in Mexico. Some may fear the language barrier or the potential for becoming ill. But many more are concerned with the potential for crime and harassment from dishonest public officials. To deny that there are such officials, or to proclaim that there is no crime in Baja, would be inaccurate and I am personally aware of several unfortunate incidents that have occurred in the past year. But the level of anxiety experienced by the North American public is blown far out of proportion with reality.

Many negative events concerning Mexico have been in the news the past several years. There have been two prominent political assassinations, high officials have been accused of political corruption, and the former Mexican President has been exiled from his country. There are ongoing problems related to the drug trade. U.S. concern about illegal immigration has reportedly angered Mexico. All these reports increase the anxiety of North Americans toward traveling in Mexico.

Those of us whose task is to promote travel to Mexico often point out that fear-provoking events in the United States and other parts in the world are far, far more frequent than anything ever experienced in Baja. This is true, but, what the reader wants to know is "is it safe to travel in Baja?" I must make it clear that I can guarantee nothing. But, my many journeys to Baja support my long held belief that the peninsula must be the safest place to travel in the two American continents. My 1997 6th edition field trip disclosed nothing to alter this view. It was as if none of the above noted events had even taken place.

I have discussed the fear issue with *Baja Buffs* camped on the beaches and otherwise absorbed in the beauty and remoteness of the Magnificent Peninsula. Many concur that there is a fear problem, but I have been universally and firmly requested not to do anything to remedy the situation. They well know that their favorite haunts will become overwhelmed with tourists if this conceptual barrier is removed.

In closing this issue, I must note that I have stayed the night alone or with a single friend in scores of the most remote coves, beaches, and villages in Baja. I have never been treated with anything but friendship and courtesy, a remarkable record considering that I sport an often unkempt beard and have never been nominated as a candidate for Mr. Neat. Thousands of foreign visitors go to Mexico without fear. I hope you will join us, but please don't tell many others. Those *Baja Buffs* will crucify me.

INFORMATION ABOUT BAJA

You may wish to consider the task of obtaining advance information about Baja as falling into three categories; Guidebooks, Newsletters, and Speciality Books. Each of these is noted below. In addition you

See the
BAJA BOOKSHELF
in the Appendix

BAJA BOOKSHELF

See the
BAJA BOOKSHELF
in the Appendix

The BAJA BOOKSHELF offers the Baja Buff an array of publications concerning Baja California. Some were written about the peninsula. Others are the best available books dealing with subjects related to Baja such as wildlife, Spanish, etc. Each represents my choice as the best title available on the subject. -- Order books by mail, phone or FAX (Visa or Mastercard) from the BAJA BOOKSHELF in the Appendix.

Jack Williams

will find a wide array of printed advertising material in tourist oriented establishments after you arrive south of the border. These include several English language newspapers including the very informative *Baja Sun*.

TRAVEL GUIDEBOOKS -- This guidebook, *The Magnificent Peninsula*, is all that most people will need to travel in Baja. It covers a wide variety of subject matter, and it is updated through field investigation prior to each new edition. But it is impossible to prevent changes from occurring in Baja between this field work and your reading of these pages. The best way to bridge this time-gap is through obtaining newsletters published by one of two travel clubs covering the Baja beat.

NEWSLETTERS -- The Discover Baja Travel Club (notice on page 13) and *Vagabundos del Mar* (notice on page 12) travel clubs each produce excellent monthly newsletters which report current developments and conditions in the peninsula as well as news about club activities. I recommend you join one or both of these organizations.

SPECIALITY BOOKS -- It is impossible for this guidebook to provide in-depth coverage of all subjects related to Baja. Those desiring more detailed information on specific subjects are directed to THE BAJA BOOKSHELF in the Appendix. Here you may obtain mail or phone order delivery of publications concerning - Boating - Fishing - Camping - Natural History - Backroad Travel - and many other subjects.

THE INTERNET -- Over the years Baja California has been the subject of an enormous number of books. Even I wrote this one. Now the computer era has spawned a similar explosion of Internet sites concerning the peninsula.

Many of these sites are little more than the ego trips of individuals airing their views or experiences about Baja. Others are highly informative. I was planning on listing some of the better sites at this point when I was informed of BajaLinks, a site produced by Richard VanBree and Paula McDonald. As a service to the Baja public, these folks have gathered together in one place the URL's (Universal Resource Locators or Internet addresses) of some 300 Internet sites that they judged have some reasonable merit. BajaLinks URL is **http://www.bajalinks.com/**. Once you call up BajaLinks on your computer you can easily transfer to any of the 300 other sites with the click of a mouse button. The sites are arranged in categories as follows:

Airlines, Cruises & Ground Transportation
Baja Maps, Road & Weather Conditions
Books, Newspapers, & Publications
Businesses
City Guides
Events
Fish 'net
The Governments of Mexico
Health and Medicine
Home Pages of Baja
Real Estate Sales & Rental
RV, Caravans, & Camping
Resorts, Hotels & Accommodations
Restaurant & Winery Guide
Sports
Surfing, Diving, & Watersports
Travel Agents, Outfitters, & Baja Tours
Weddings in Mexico
Whales of Baja

I will call attention to several useful sites during the balance of this book. In particular, Chapter 6 will alert you when one the hotels it lists has an Internet site.

PHOTOGRAPHS

Several years ago I encountered a young lady in Baja who was using an earlier edition of this book. She complemented the book as a whole but noted that the photos were substandard. In the same breath she offered her services for hire as a photographer. I had to tell her that the financial realities of the guidebook business precluded me from paying someone else to do all the little niceties at which I personally was not overly proficient. *The Magnificent Peninsula* is a do-it-yourself project and past readers have had to settle for my own meager efforts.

But, with this 6th edition I stumbled upon a gold mine. My daughter Barbara who accompanied me on this edition's field investigations is an above average photographer complete with fancy film and cameras. I found it relatively easy to get many excellent new photos by simply bringing our van to a frequent halt and yelling "Get out there and shoot that" while staying comfortably inside or walking the dog. Her work is identified with the initials BW.

Even with this improvement, the book's photos are not normally artistic masterpieces as they are in-

Chapter 1

Signs of Distinction

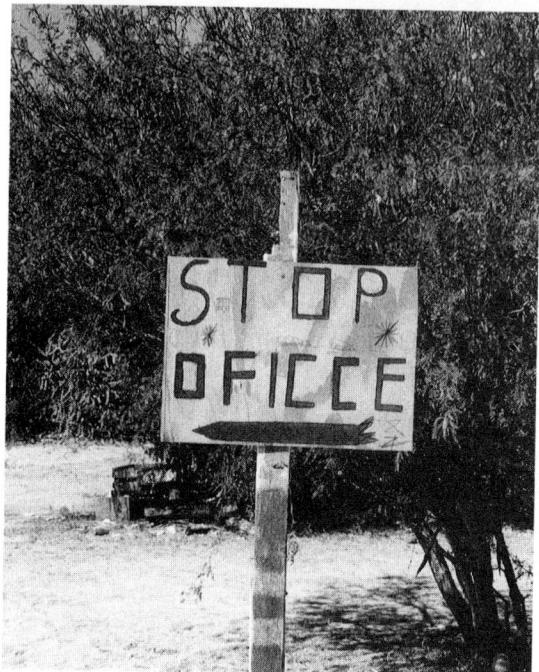

There is something the matter here. It reminds me of my skills as an author. After six editions I can now usually spell the words well enough so that the computer spell-checker can figure out what I have in mind. I would make an effective sign painter in Baja. Photo JW.

tended primarily as illustrations of conditions in Baja. There is nothing artistic about the photo of the rear end of a truck as shown in Chapter 3 on *Transportation*, but it depicts the narrowness of Baja's highways far better than can be done with words.

And then, I have indulged myself by including a variety of photos which my warped sense of humor has concluded are funny. Among these are some bearing the heading *Signs of Distinction* as Baja is a good place to hunt for interesting signs. Some are the work of enterprising Mexican's who are having a bit

of trouble with the English language. Others may be credited to persons of Gringo extraction who have liberated signs from captivity north of the border and transplanted them into more exotic locations in the Magnificent Peninsula or who's own sense of humor has been lavished on projects spawned by an excessive availability of leisure time. In any case, they are a reflection of what you yourself will find in Baja. The first of these is included on this page.

Signs of Distinction

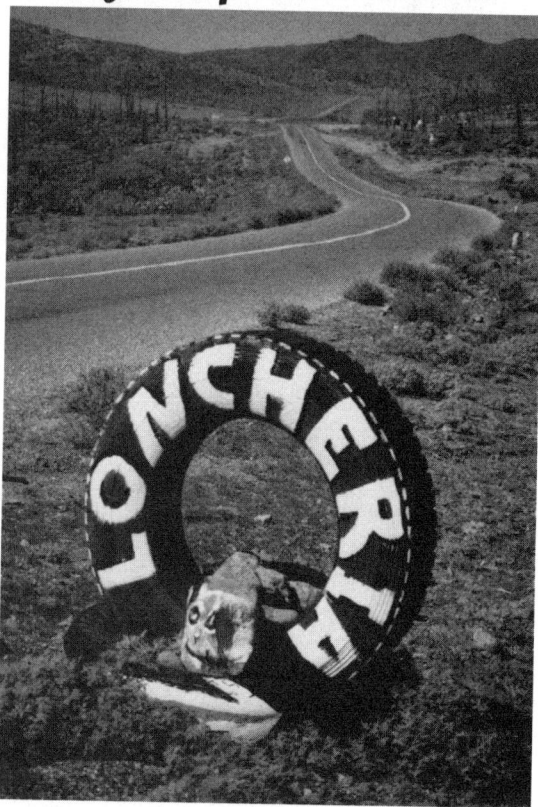

Signs are painted on anything that is handy in Baja. Here along the Transpeninsular Highway two tires announce an upcoming loncheri (cafe). Photo BW.

PART I
BACKGROUND
AND PLANNING

BAJA'S FASCINATING CIRIO BACKED BY OTHER SONORAN DESERT VEGETATION. Photo JW.

CHAPTER 2
THE BIG PICTURE

Much of the world's information is best understood if presented through the art of classification. For this reason, I will be continually breaking Baja and many of its principal subjects into segments or areas. The first of these will be a vertical slice in which we will examine four zones that run more or less north-south. I say more or less because in reality, the Baja peninsula extends closer to northwest-southeast than true north and south. The four zones are: (1) Baja's Pacific coast, (2) Baja's Sea of Cortez coast, (3) the interior, and (4) Mexico's mainland coast (north half). The last zone may come as a surprise because it isn't a part of Baja. The reason for its inclusion will be explained in due course.

THE VERTICAL SLICE

BAJA'S PACIFIC COAST — Measuring a line drawn along the edge of the many projections of Baja's interface with the Pacific Ocean would disclose a largely deserted coastline of approximately 1,000 miles. Inclusion of the many bays and lagoons would add hundreds of additional miles. The startling fact is how little of this shore is readily accessible to tourists who travel to Baja by conventional two-wheel-drive vehicles and whose temperaments require them to stay on the main roads. This description fits the majority of those who visit Baja by road.

Traveling from the international border to Cabo San Lucas over Highways 1 and 19 is a trip of approximately 1,025 miles. I have inventoried this route in terms of coastal accessibility and found that only some 230 miles of highway provide access to the Pacific Ocean. (See COASTAL ACCESSIBILITY Map.) If anything, these estimates are generous. In most places the ocean is not visible from the highway, and side roads must be used to reach the water's edge. Conditions are similar on the Sea of Cortez coast. As the great majority of tourists traveling to Baja by road are destined for seashore areas, it is important to understand this situation.

There are several sizeable villages and many *fish camps* along those sections of the Pacific coast that are not readily accessible from the main highway. These are regularly visited by yachts making the Baja Passage and by a few land-based travelers whose equipment and interests lead them to explore the hundreds of miles of secondary and lower standard roads. These communities provide a fascinating contrast with life as we know it north of the border. Visiting them, one finds it hard to believe they are so close to the metropolitan centers of southwestern United States.

Several other subjects must be presented to complete the big picture of the Baja peninsula's Pacific coast. The first concerns the weather. Most travel south of the border towns in Baja takes place in late fall, winter, and

Typical section of Baja's Pacific Coast where the surf pounds on rocky, sparsely vegetated cliffs. — Photo taken north of Playa los Cerritos. (See Chapter 24.) Photo JW.

COASTAL AREAS ACCESSIBLE FROM PRINCIPAL HIGHWAYS

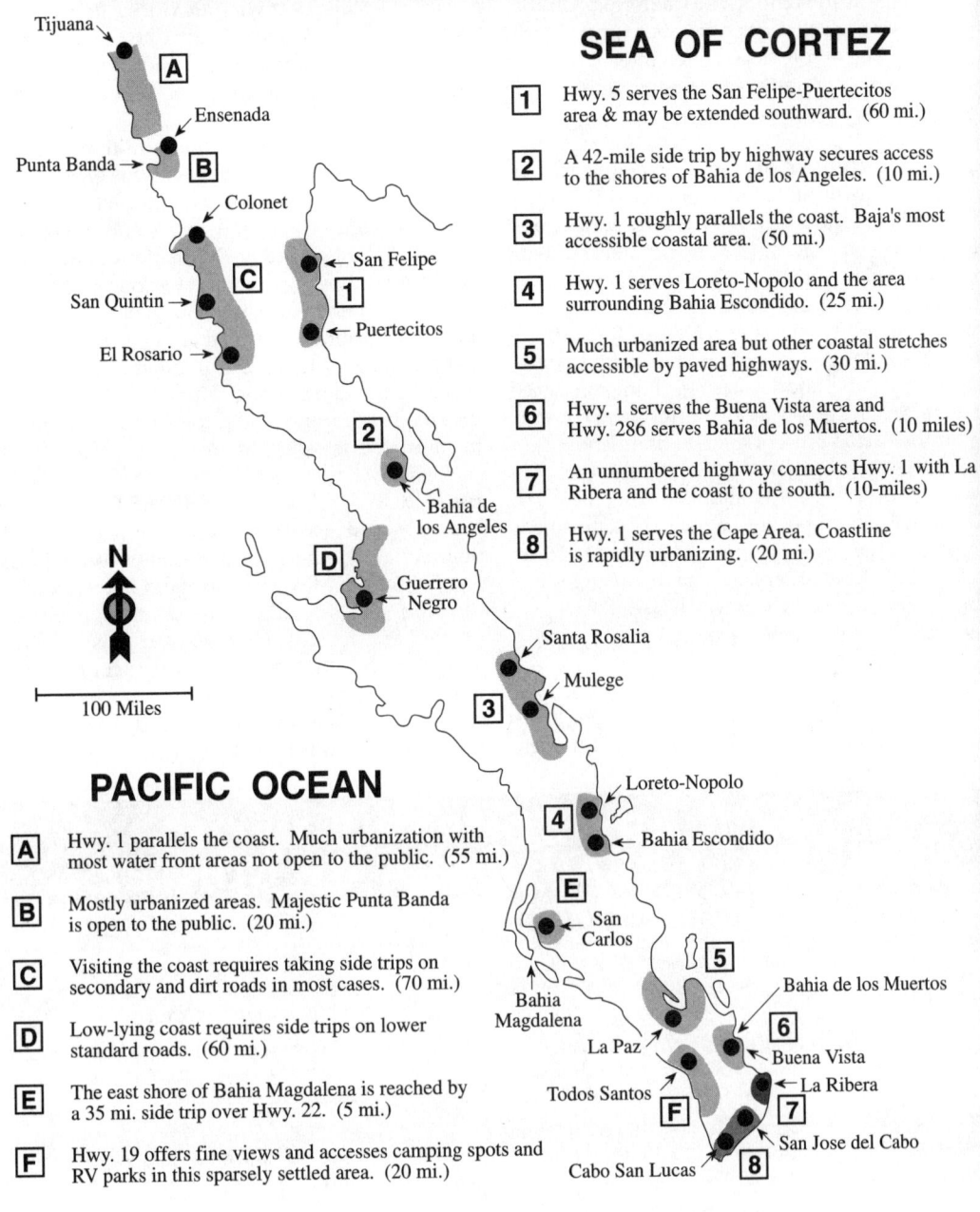

SEA OF CORTEZ

1 Hwy. 5 serves the San Felipe-Puertecitos area & may be extended southward. (60 mi.)

2 A 42-mile side trip by highway secures access to the shores of Bahia de los Angeles. (10 mi.)

3 Hwy. 1 roughly parallels the coast. Baja's most accessible coastal area. (50 mi.)

4 Hwy. 1 serves Loreto-Nopolo and the area surrounding Bahia Escondido. (25 mi.)

5 Much urbanized area but other coastal stretches accessible by paved highways. (30 mi.)

6 Hwy. 1 serves the Buena Vista area and Hwy. 286 serves Bahia de los Muertos. (10 miles)

7 An unnumbered highway connects Hwy. 1 with La Ribera and the coast to the south. (10-miles)

8 Hwy. 1 serves the Cape Area. Coastline is rapidly urbanizing. (20 mi.)

PACIFIC OCEAN

A Hwy. 1 parallels the coast. Much urbanization with most water front areas not open to the public. (55 mi.)

B Mostly urbanized areas. Majestic Punta Banda is open to the public. (20 mi.)

C Visiting the coast requires taking side trips on secondary and dirt roads in most cases. (70 mi.)

D Low-lying coast requires side trips on lower standard roads. (60 mi.)

E The east shore of Bahia Magdalena is reached by a 35 mi. side trip over Hwy. 22. (5 mi.)

F Hwy. 19 offers fine views and accesses camping spots and RV parks in this sparsely settled area. (20 mi.)

N

100 Miles

Tijuana
Ensenada
Punta Banda
Colonet
San Felipe
San Quintin
Puertecitos
El Rosario
Bahia de los Angeles
Guerrero Negro
Santa Rosalia
Mulege
Loreto-Nopolo
Bahia Escondido
San Carlos
Bahia Magdalena
Bahia de los Muertos
La Paz
Buena Vista
La Ribera
Todos Santos
San Jose del Cabo
Cabo San Lucas

early spring. (Most of the principal tourist areas are a bit hot during summer and early fall.) These travelers are seeking escape from a variety of adverse weather conditions north of the border. Unfortunately Baja's Pacific coast north of about Bahia Magdalena does not present a significant contrast to the weather in coastal areas of southern and central Alta California. Clearly, rain decreases as one travels south, but temperatures remain cool. Fog or low clouds often prevail. It is not the warm *swimsuit-lie-in-the-sun* weather most people are seeking in sunny Mexico.

The next big picture subject for the Pacific coast concerns the ocean itself. While the coast is largely deserted, there is much activity on the surface and within the ocean waters. Each year thousands of yachtsmen cruise from San Diego to Cabo San Lucas and beyond. Mexican fishing vessels in the 70-foot class are numerous, and these in turn are far outnumbered by shorter range, outboard-powered *pangas* engaged in fishing and lobstering. I am convinced that there is considerably more traffic on these waters than off the Pacific coast of the U.S. mainland.

Below the surface there is abundant fish life. The ocean off the central portion of the Baja peninsula is the most productive fishing area of the entire Mexican Pacific coast. These waters are also the winter home of the California gray whale which uses Baja's protected lagoons as its calving grounds.

South of the Ensenada area there is an almost total absence of the small, tourist-owned, sportfishing boats which are commonplace in the Sea of Cortez. The reasons for this situation are the lack of launching ramps and swell and surf conditions which make launching over the beach and use of the ocean itself a bit hazardous. Swells sweep onto the peninsula from the northwest unobstucted for thousands of miles. While they severely limit the use of small boats, they make the Pacific coast a fine area for surfing. It is also a scenic coast with its rocky outline and pounding surf. You will find the small boating and surfing situations reversed on the calmer waters of the Sea of Cortez.

Finally, as a by-product of the conditions just mentioned, the Pacific coast between Ensenada on the north, and Todos Santos on the south, has few tourist-oriented facilities. The few hotels and trailer courts are usually not visited as destinations in themselves but only as stopping points on the journey to the east coast or the peninsula's tip. The people in the towns along the Pacific side make their living from farming, cattle raising, fishing, and mining. Relatively few serve the traveling public. These towns offer little of the architectural and landscaping charms common in the more tourist-oriented areas.

BAJA'S SEA OF CORTEZ COAST — We will now proceed across to the eastern coast of the peninsula. The body of water between Baja California and the Mexican mainland is referred to as the Gulf of California on most maps, even those printed in Mexico. However, to most Mexicans and many North American tourists it is known as the Sea of Cortez (Mar de Cortez) in honor of conquistador Hernan Cortez, and that is what it will be called in this book.

ITEM	PACIFIC OCEAN	SEA OF CORTEZ
SUMMARY COMPARISON OF PACIFIC OCEAN & SEA OF CORTEZ		
OCEAN WATERS	Heavy northwest swells. Boat launching difficult. Good surfing. Water is cold.	Seas flat except in high winds. Easy boat launching. Good wind surfing and swimming.
HOTELS & RV PARKS	Numerous from Ensenada north. Few south of Ensenada and little visited as destination points.	Numerous at San Felipe and in the southern half from Santa Rosalia to Cabo San Lucas.
TOURIST SEASON WEATHER	Cool north of Bahia Magdalena, warmer to the south. Some fog. Northwest winds.	Generally warmer and dryer than the Pacific Coast. Winds from the north.
CAMPING	Some camping spots, but most are lightly used due to cool ocean and weather conditions.	Numerous camping spots. Many heavily used because of good ocean and weather conditions.

Traveling south to Cabo San Lucas entirely on the Transpeninsular Highway (Highway 1) is 34 miles longer than is the combination of Highway 1 and Highway 19 through Todos Santos. Taking the former route provides access to the Sea of Cortez. An inventory of accessibility, as was done for the Pacific side, shows that 145 miles of coast are made accessible by the main highways. An additional 60 miles can be reached in the San Felipe area and this will be increased if paving of Highway 5 ever continues southward from Puertecitos. Fortunately, many additional miles of the coast are made accessible by secondary and lower standard roads. Also, on the positive side is the fact that hundreds of miles of unroaded peninsular and offshore-island coast is available to boaters as a result of good boating conditions in the Sea of Cortez.

Because of the differences in the two coasts, the mileages presented are of minimal value when compared directly with each other. The key point is that relatively few miles of the main highways provide direct coastal access on either shore. Obviously the traveler needs to know where the principal tourist areas are located. This information is presented later in this chapter.

One shoreline condition applies to both coasts. Baja is a mountainous land. Where these mountains meet the sea both coastlines are rocky, steep-faced, and majestic. Beaches are small but picturesque. This situation is typical of some 75-80 percent of the Baja coasts. Vegetation is sparse and there is little soil. The mountains stand out sharply with their geologic features clearly visible. The colors and textures of their rocks are readily apparent. These coastal sections are beautiful to behold, particularly when viewed from the sea itself.

The remaining 20-25 percent of the two coasts consists of low coastal plains fronted by scores of miles of deserted beaches. Most of these are seldom visited and are on the Pacific side. In any event, you may be assured that there are miles of beautiful, although generally smaller, beaches at all of the popular tourist areas.

It is important for the traveler to realize that there are marked differences in the surf conditions between the two coasts. The Sea of Cortez lacks the pounding swells which are an ever-present condition on the Pacific side. The peninsula's picturesque rocky tip at Cabo San Lucas is generally considered to be the dividing point between the Pacific Ocean and the Sea of Cortez. The Pacific swells dissipate rapidly easterly from the cape and disappear completely approximately 50 miles to the NE. With few swells in the Sea of Cortez, it is relatively easy to launch small boats over the beach, swimming is far safer than on the Pacific side and wind surfing is a common activity. While this is good news for those enjoying these watersports, wave-surfing enthusiasts will be disappointed along with those travelers who enjoy the picturesque breaking of waves on a rock-bound coast. Except during high wind conditions, the water's edge on Baja's east side takes on the characteristics of a large inland lake.

From what has been presented, you may have concluded that the Sea of Cortez coast provides home for most of the principal tourist areas in Baja; if so, you are correct.

THE INTERIOR — A prominent backbone of mountains dominates the entire western edge of the continents of North and South America, with large bellies of flatter lands to the east. The mountains of Baja parallel these ranges, but in Baja the terrain is mostly backbone with relatively little belly.

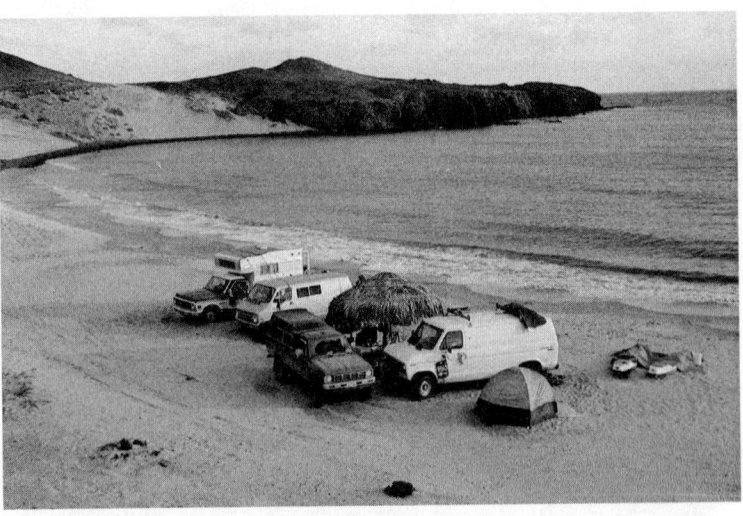

Campers on the beach north of Punta Chivato on the Sea of Cortez. — Photo taken on a windy day at an exposed location but wind-waves are low and gentle compared to Pacific coast swells. Photo JW.

One more or less continuous chain of mountains runs the full length of the peninsula with only one brief interruption, near La Paz (See GEOLOGIC PROVINCES map in Chapter 9). The crest of this chain rims the eastern side of the peninsula with most of the flat land found along the southern half of the Pacific coast. It is, however, important to qualify these remarks for those of you who plan to drive to Baja. While the peninsula is mountainous, traversing Baja's highways is not an arduous task for a variety of reasons that will be discussed in Chapter 3. Many of you will be exposed to artists' renditions of the peninsula's mountains on the covers and pages of maps and guidebooks. A considerable number of these are badly exaggerated and could easily frighten the faint of heart into staying home. There are many highways in the United States and Canada that traverse far more difficult terrain.

Almost all of Baja's significant cities and towns are located within a few miles of the coasts. Few are in the interior. This area's most dominant feature is manmade; the Transpeninsular Highway. By North American standards it is a modest accomplishment, but its completion in 1973 was of monumental importance for the future of Baja. It is the principal way for the tourist to travel by land to the peninsula's primary destination areas along the southern portion of the Sea of Cortez.

The interior of the peninsula also provides habitat for the best of Baja's outstanding desert vegetation. Neither coast can match the higher lands in this regard.

MEXICAN MAINLAND COAST / NORTH HALF -- The area under consideration here lies directly opposite the Baja peninsula and is the eastern shore of the Sea of Cortez. It is shown on the TRANSPORTATION Map in Chapter 3.

Any map that depicts topography will show that most of this coastal area is composed of flat terrain. This condition extends south from the mouth of the Rio Colorado for about 1,000 miles to near the town of Tepic, south of Mazatlan. While sailing along this coast, one is confronted with hundreds of miles of deserted and monotonous sandy beaches backed by sparsely vegetated, low coastal plains and marshes. From a scenic standpoint, the two Baja coastlines are hands-down winners over their mainland neighbor. The mainland highway from the United States, Highway 15, offers almost no views of the coast or the Sea of Cortez.

Still, there are some scenic areas on the mainland, the principal ones being at Bahia Kino, Guaymas, and Mazatlan. These three areas, along with Puerto Penasco to the north, attract almost all the North American tourists. Guaymas, more accurately the town of San Carlos just to the north, has a large winter tourist population. It is a Mexican Phoenix, a haven for retirees and others escaping the northern winter. Mazatlan also is a fine town with excellent beaches and many tourists.

Why do so many people choose the mainland instead of Baja? It is partly a matter of transportation routes. It is closer to the mainland than to Baja from the United States intermountain west. Its cities are large and provide abundant trailer courts and hotels. Because people are attracted to other people, they feel more secure in such places. Perhaps, most importantly, Baja is remote, unknown, and *over there*.

The point of this discussion is to give you the information needed to make a choice. I don't wish to downgrade the mainland, but alas, the scenery in Baja is better, the boating and camping areas are far more extensive, the choice of destination points is larger, the hotels are more charming, etc., etc., etc. However, should you crave the company of large numbers of your fellow North Americans in a trailer court atmosphere or at highrise hotels, and the amenities of large nearby cities, the mainland may be best for you.

SIX PRINCIPAL TOURIST AREAS

Having sliced Baja vertically, we will now reassemble it and classify the peninsula into six principal tourist areas. (See SIX PRINCIPAL TOURIST AREAS Map). These are:

1 — Tijuana-Ensenada Area
2 — San Felipe-Puertecitos Area
3 — Bahia de los Angeles
4 — Central Coast
5 — La Paz
6 — The South Coast

1 TIJUANA / ENSENADA AREA — Poised at the international border and eager to entice North American tourists are the city of Tijuana and the smaller town of Tecate. Ensenada lies sixty-eight miles south along the Pacific coast. Between Tijuana and Ensenada are numerous tourist-oriented subdivisions and other developments. The number of visitors to these com-

SIX PRINCIPAL TOURIST AREAS

Tijuana
Tecate
Mexicali
①
Ensenada
Punta Banda

STATE OF BAJA CALIFORNIA
① Tijuana -- Ensenada Area
② San Felipe -- Puertecitos Area
③ Bahia de los Angeles

San Felipe
②
Puertecitos

PACIFIC OCEAN

Baja California

Bahia de los Angeles
③

28th Parallel (State Line)

San Ignacio
Santa Rosalia
Mulege
Bahia Concepcion
④
Loreto

Baja California Sur

N

100 Miles

SEA OF CORTEZ

⑤

Buena Vista
La Paz
La Ribera
Todos Santos
San Jose del Cabo
Cabo San Lucas
⑥

STATE OF BAJA CALIFORNIA SUR
④ Central Coast
⑤ La Paz
⑥ The South Coast

munities is very sizeable. Tijuana boasts of being visited by more people from a foreign country than any other city in the world.

The large city of Mexicali also lies on the international border. Many people living and working in adjoining areas in the United States visit here, but it would appear that much of their activities are not related to tourism. At least in my view, Mexicali is not a tourist-oriented city.

Here are the highlights of this area:

(a) The most accessible area from the United States. Many visitors walk across the border to visit Tijuana. The place to go if you have only a day or two. Otherwise, head south.

(b) A bonanza for buying gifts and Mexican handicrafts of all kinds. Many of these items are typical tourist fare, but there is also much quality merchandise available.

(c) Excellent party-boat sportfishing and assorted night life at Ensenada.

(d) Thousands of second, and some first, homes for North Americans lie along the coast south to Punta Banda.

(e) In recent years several excellent hotels, golf courses and fancy trailer courts have been constructed along the coast between Tijuana and Ensenada. This "Between the Cities" area is thus becoming a tourist area in itself. There are very few places left for camping outside the developed trailer courts.

2 SAN FELIPE-PUERTECITOS AREA — San Felipe is the northernmost communitiy along the Sea of Cortez. The town is modest in size but heavily tourist oriented and provides all essential services. There are several good hotels. There are miles of beachs lined with housing developments, trailer courts and more modest *campos*. Visitation to this area will greatly increase if the paving of Highway 5 is completed south to Highway 1 (See discussion at the beginning of Chapter 15).

(a) The quickest way for most North Americans to hit the beach on the Sea of Cortez. It is 127 miles by highway from the border at Mexicali.

(b) Winter temperatures not as balmy as farther south, and it is hot in the summer.

(c) Many long-term trailer sites, but also a good spot for the long weekender.

(d) Puertecitos, a small town of Norte Americano homes 48 miles south of San Felipe, is accessible over a paved highway.

(e) A few low hills near San Felipe provide a scenic coast, but much of the shoreline is one continuous long sandy beach backed by low coastal plains. The desert vegetation is relatively unattractive. Thus the scenery is not as good as other areas to the south, although the towering Sierra San Pedro Martir mountains are in view to the west.

(f) No nearby offshore islands, and tidal differences of up to 20 feet make small boat launching difficult.

3 BAHIA DE LOS ANGELES — Located here is a sizeable

Signs of Distinction

<u>We always try to obey the law.</u> Here on the washboarded road from San Felipe to Highway 1 a sign warns us, "DOGS ON LEASH." The fact that there is no evidence of civilization for miles in any direction prompts one to think, "surely they must jest." But there it is, so we simply had to walk the dog. On his leash of course. Photo JW.

The islands lying in the Bahia de los Angeles area make it one of Baja's best boating and fishing locations. Photo BW.

bay with miles of beaches protected by several offshore islands. A small village offers modest services.

(a) Several hotels and RV parks. There are also many miles of undeveloped beaches north of the village offering camping sites.

(b) Reaching the area requires a 42 mile side trip from the Transpeninsular Highway. The total distance to Tijuana is 415 miles, making it a very long one-day trip from the border.

(c) A scenic mountainous area with a good mixture of beaches and rocky coast but with relatively unattractive desert vegetation. The nearby coast and offshore islands contain many coves and provide good boating and fishing.

(d) The least visited of the six principal tourist areas except over the Spring Break-Easter Weekend when it receives heavy visitation from north of the border.

4 CENTRAL COAST — This is one of the principal destination areas in Baja. It features three coastal, and one inland town. (Santa Rosalia, Mulege, Loreto, and San Ignacio.)

(a) Each town has its charms and all are worth exploring.

(b) The late winter and spring weather is balmy. This is what you came to Baja to experience.

(c) Several first-class hotels and other more modest ones, but fewer than farther south. Served by an international airport at Loreto.

(d) Many trailer courts and minimum facility beach parking areas. Bahia Concepcion is the most popular RV and camping area in Baja.

(e) Good combination of beaches and rocky coast backdropped by the most scenic mountains in Baja. Numerous offshore islands and coves. Fine area for fishing and overnight trips by small boat.

5 LA PAZ — A fine, large, modern community and the capital city of Baja California Sur. Thought by many, including myself, to be the finest large city in Mexico. Its tourist facilities are slowly increasing but at a much slower rate than at the Cape Area.

(a) Several fine luxury hotels served by an international airport, but not as fancy as at the Cape Area

(b) City fronts the beach on a protected bay, but the main attraction here is the weather and the city itself.

(c) There are several trailer courts, but the central and south coasts are superior if your objective is to enjoy the beach and the out-of-doors.

(d) Excellent modern stores. The only really good shopping area south of the towns near the border although there are many tourist oriented shops at Cabo San Lucas.

(e) Good, but sometimes windy, winter weather. Winter weather not as good as in the Cape Area.

(f) Sportfishing boats are available, many based at nearby Bahia de los Muertos. You can use your own small boat but other areas are better suited for such craft.

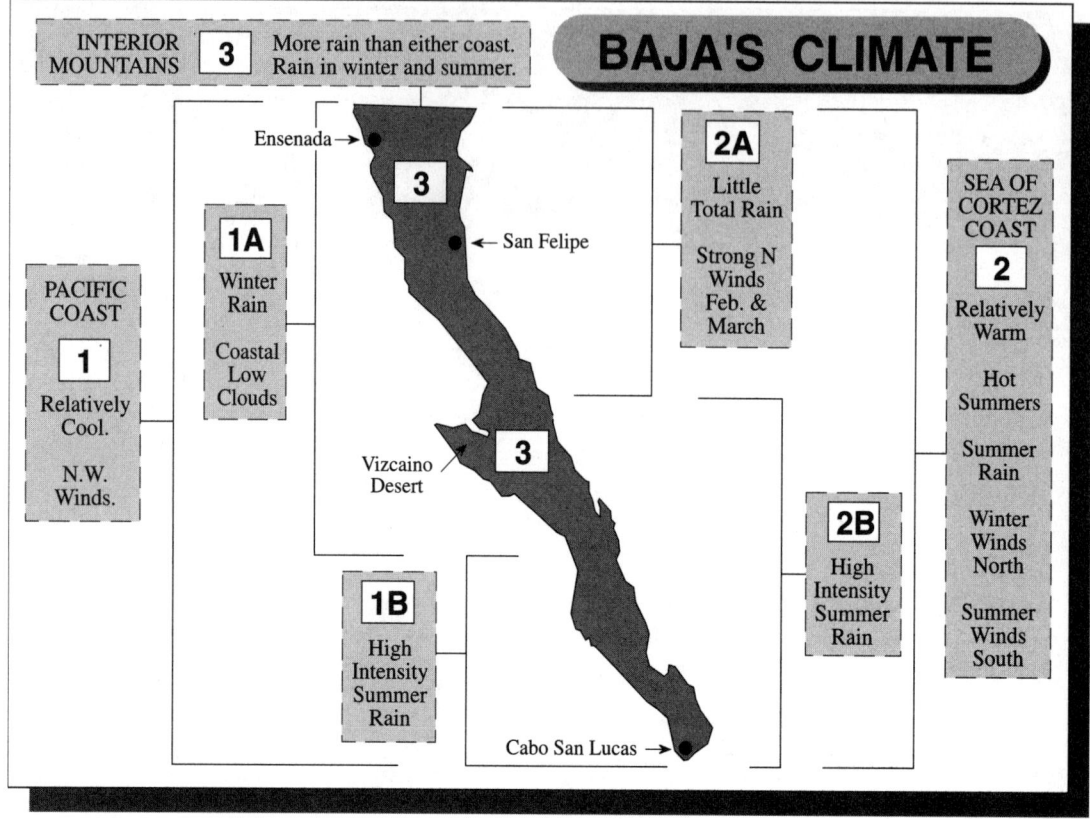

BAJA'S CLIMATE

INTERIOR MOUNTAINS **3** — More rain than either coast. Rain in winter and summer.

Ensenada →

3

San Felipe ←

1A — Winter Rain / Coastal Low Clouds

PACIFIC COAST **1** — Relatively Cool. N.W. Winds.

2A — Little Total Rain / Strong N Winds Feb. & March

SEA OF CORTEZ COAST **2** — Relatively Warm / Hot Summers / Summer Rain / Winter Winds North / Summer Winds South

Vizcaino Desert

3

2B — High Intensity Summer Rain

1B — High Intensity Summer Rain

Cabo San Lucas →

6 THE SOUTH COAST — The U-shaped area capping the peninsula's southern tip has developed into three distinct zones. These are;

THE CAPE AREA -- At the peninsula's tip and between the small communities of Cabo San Lucas and San Jose del Cabo is Baja's principal hotel, condominium, and golf course area. Many of these developments are world-class. Construction has been going on for some 20 years and it continues at a rapid pace. It is served by an international airport. There are several good trailer courts but only one is on the beach. On-your-own camping on the beach is a thing of the past.

THE EAST CAPE -- On the right side of the South Coast-U is the East Cape. There are several good but modest-sized hotels, and trailer courts at and near Buena Vista. It is the place to go to experience the older Baja hotel charm without the jet-set-bustle that has developed at the Cape Area. There are many undeveloped camping sites south of Buena Vista and an oiled highway has been completed some 10 miles south from the small town of La Ribera. Eventually it will be completed south to San Jose del Cabo a development which will change the complexion of the area.

Both the Cape Area and the East Cape are famed for their marlin and other big-game fishing. This fishery is amongst the best in the world.

THE WEST CAPE -- This section of coast was basically undeveloped until Highway 19 was completed in 1984. There is one small hotel in Todos Santos and several trailer courts and fine beach camping areas between there and the Cape. This is the area to go for free-lance beach campers who have been forced out of the Cape Area by urban development.

BAJA'S CLIMATE

Two circumstances dominate the climate of Baja California. As is obvious to any visitor, the peninsula is an arid land. The reasons for this situation are discussed in the BAJA'S DESERT LANDS Section in Chapter 10 VEGETATION. The low level of precipitation is key in determining vegetational characteristics.

Of equal but less apparent importance is the variability of the climate from one area to another, from season to season, and from year to year. Most of the time the peninsula receives no rainfall because it lies outside the normal influence of any of the major weather systems in this part of the world, but by a twist of geographic fate, it lies near the outer edge of several such systems. It is the occasional impact from these entities that creates climatic variability in Baja.

Baja lies (1) at the southern edge of the winter storms that bring plentiful rainfall to the west coast of the United States and Canada, (2) at the western perimeter of the monsoons formed over the Gulf of Mexico that bring precipitation to northern Mexico and southwestern United States in the summer, and (3) at the northeastern fringe of the region of tropical storms and hurricanes that form off the west coast of the Mexican mainland in late summer and fall. A separate section on these tropical storms is included later in these chapter.

The overall effect of these systems is summarized on a graphic labeled BAJA'S CLIMATE. The following statements relate to the zones that it depictes.

1. The air temperature along the full length of Baja's Pacific coast is relatively cool as the result of prevailing northwest winds which move inland over the cool waters of the Pacific Ocean.

1A. The northern segment of the Pacific coast receives its rainfall during winter from the southern edges of the same storm systems that impact the coast of the United States and Canada. The average annual rainfall at Ensenada is about eleven inches, but from here south to Bahia Magdalena records show only three to four inches per year. The vegetation in the Vizcaino Desert at the midpoint of the peninsula is extremely scant.

1B. Rainfall picks up along the southern Pacific coast with Cabo San Lucas receiving an average of over nine inches per year. In contrast to area 1A, this precipitation comes mostly from high-intensity tropical storms that breed in the warm waters to the south during late summer and fall.

2. The Sea of Cortez coast is much warmer than that on the Pacific side. Some of the hotels in the Cape Area close during summer. To the north, San Felipe has the highest summer temperature of any of Baja's tourist areas.

2A. During the winter, temperatures at San Felipe are almost as chilly as at Ensenada. This coolness is aggravated by strong northerly winds funneling down the Sea of Cortez from southwestern United States. This is Baja's driest area, but what little rain does fall comes in the winter.

2B. As on the Pacific coast, most of the rainfall comes from high-intensity tropical storms in the late fall and summer. Winter months are windy.

3. Baja's interior mountains receive considerably more rainfall than either coastal area. Also, they are battered by storms in both winter and summer. The winter systems are the same as those that dampen area 1A. The summer rain comes from systems in the Gulf of Mexico that also pass over the Mexican mainland and SW United States.

A final note concerning El Nino, an unusual warming of Pacific ocean waters off Central and North America every few years.

The winter of 1991-92 was an El Nino year. Southern California in the United States received near record rain storms and the Baja peninsula received abundant winter precipitation. This occurred not only in the northern area but in the southern portions which normally receive their rainfall in the late summer.

The result was a less than fully desirable vacation to Baja for tourists seeking endless sunshine. Travel on back roads was also hazardous due to muddy conditions. On the bright side was a wonderful display of lush desert vegetation and flowers. So keep alert to the occasional occurrence of El Nino and brace for unusual weather conditions in Baja.

In evaluating all this material, keep in mind the key

MONTHLY AND ANNUAL AVERAGE NUMBER OF STORMS PER YEAR												
Month	Jan	Feb	Mar	Apr	May	Jun	Jul	Aug	Sep	Oct	Nov	Dec	Annual
Tropical Storms (34-63-knots)	—	—	—	—	—	1.5	2.8	2.3	2.3	1.2	0.3	—	9.3
Hurricanes (Over 64-knots)	—	—	—	—	0.3	0.6	0.9	2.0	1.8	1.0	—	—	5.8
Tropical Storms & Hurricanes	—	—	—	—	0.3	2.0	3.6	4.5	4.1	2.2	0.3	—	15.2

AVERAGE NUMBER OF TROPICAL STORMS & HURRICANES PER TIME PERIOD BY 5-DEGREE SQUARE

factor of variability. One can only hope that you will not find yourself recovering from a trip through the arid desert one day and struggling with the runoff from a tropical storm the next. And remember, I am not in charge of the weather. Contact *You Know Who*.

TROPICAL STORMS AND HURRICANES

In past editions of this book I have made no reference to tropical storms and hurricanes other than what has just been noted above. The hurricane season of fall

1997 convinced me that the tropical storm information contained in my *Baja Boater's Guide* should also be made available to those who travel to Baja by land. During 1997 (an El Nino year) Hurricane Nora passed some 200 miles south of Cabo San Lucas on September 23rd resulting in heavy rains, high winds and much flooding in the Cape Area. Later in the month a lesser hurricane crossed the entire peninsula from west to east. It caused relatively minor damage but again it brought heavy rain and high winds. Such conditions are not conducive to happy holidays.

AVERAGE NUMBER OF TROPICAL STORMS & HURRICANES PER TIME PERIOD BY 5-DEGREE SQUARE

AVERAGE NUMBER OF TROPICAL STORMS & HURRICANES PER TIME PERIOD BY 5-DEGREE SQUARE

TROPICAL STORMS — Tropical storms are generated over warm ocean waters in six parts of the world. One of these is off the west coast of Mexico from about Puerto Vallarta south to the Guatemalan border. It is referred to as the Eastern North Pacific Area. While Baja is situated at the southern extremity of the NE-Pacific storm systems, it is at the northern fringe of this tropical storm area. <u>The main storm season is from June to October, but with significant occurrences in May and November.</u>

Meteorologists have established three intensities of the cyclonic disturbances under discussion. These are:

<u>Tropical Depression</u> - Wind speed below 34 knots.
<u>Tropical Storm</u> - Wind speeds from 34-to-63 knots.
<u>Hurricane</u> - Wind speeds 64 knots or greater.

A table accompanying this discussion indicates the average number of tropical storms and hurricanes by month which have been generated in the Eastern

AVERAGE NUMBER OF TROPICAL STORMS & HURRICANES PER TIME PERIOD BY 5-DEGREE SQUARE

North Pacific Area. Also presented are charts showing the average number of tropical storms and hurricanes observed for twelve time periods in the vicinity of the Baja peninsula. They reflect observations made from 1949 to 1970. These data are taken from *Mariner's Worldwide Climatic Guide to Tropical Storms at Sea*, published in March of 1974 by the Naval Weather Service Command. Unfortunately, it is out-of-print at this writing.

Note the chart for June 1 - 30. On the average, one could expect to encounter 0.29 storms with wind velocities in excess of 34 knots in the 5 degree square lying SE of the tip of the Baja peninsula during June. Thus, there is about a three percent chance of experiencing such a storm during June of any one year.

The arrows shown on each chart represent the most common storm track for the period in question. The tropical storms formed off the Mexican mainland initially move westward and then pole-ward from their area of generation. Some of the storms then "recurve" eastward. It is this tendency to recurve which brings tropical storms to Baja California. Recurvature is readily apparent from August 21 until October 15. These tropical storms are normally accompanied by torrential rain.

The above noted charts indicate that the chances of experiencing a tropical storm in a given area are very low. However, storms occurring anywhere in the general area south of the Baja peninsula can result in heavy rain, high winds and flooding. It does not require a direct hit or even a near miss to have a tropical storm cause total disruption to ones vacation plans. Please keep these facts well in mind when planning when to visit southern Baja.

WHEN TO VISIT

I am often asked, "When is the best time to visit Baja?" This question is best answered by asking another question, "Why do you want to visit Baja?" There are three principal answers to this latter question. They are discussed below.

1 -- TO ESCAPE BAD WEATHER TO THE NORTH
— Most tourists visit Baja in the winter months (November through March). That is not when the peninsular weather is at its best, but it is when conditions at home north of the border are at their worst,

and when escape is most needed. After Easter, there is a dramatic drop-off of tourism in Baja.

2 -- TO VISIT BAJA FOR ITS OWN SAKE — I
recommend April, May, and June as the best months to visit Baja. Temperatures are warm, and the often chilly winter winds that sweep down the Sea of Cortez have ceased. Many beaches and other camping areas are uncomfortably cool and windy in the winter months. And there are far fewer other tourists with whom to contend after Easter. These months are also outside of the tropical storm season noted above.

3 -- TO GET THE BEST FISHING — If fishing is your
primary goal, go south in the summer (July through October). Air temperatures are hot, and sea waters warm. The latter condition induces the game fish to migrate north into the Sea of Cortez. Summer is also the time to visit the many isolated camping and fishing areas along the cooler Pacific shore south of Ensenada. But keep in mind that the summer months bring with them the risk of tropical storms.

BAJA'S TWO STATES

There are two states in the Baja peninsula. The dividing line is the 28th parallel of northern latitude. (See SIX PRINCIPAL TOURIST AREAS Map.)

There is little question that the southern state is *Baja California Sur* (south). Its capital city is La Paz. In contrast, there is much confusion about the name of the northern state with its capital in Mexicali. I have investigated this matter in considerable depth and can guarantee with absolute certainty that its name is *Baja California* (probably). This is the name used on state documents, stationery, license plates, and many other places. Government officials have assured me that this is the proper name.

Other officials firmly attest that the name is *Baja California Norte* (north). I have seen this title on the doors of government offices and in official publications, travel guides, and numerous other places. You may call it what you choose. I believe Baja California is correct.

I am advised that many Mexican citizens of Baja have solved this name complication by referring to the two states as Baja Norte (north) and Baja Sur (South). Why not.

CHAPTER 3
TRANSPORTATION

By now, the reader will have little difficulty in forecasting that it is possible to travel to Baja by land, sea, or air. These alternatives will be discussed in that order.

LAND TRAVEL

The Magnificent Peninsula provides information concerning all methods of transportation, but the great majority of its readers are looking for data on the land itself and how to travel to Baja by road. Thus, much of the remainder of the book is devoted to these subjects.

THE TRANSPENINSULAR HIGHWAY — The Transpeninsular Highway is Mexican Federal Highway 1 and 1-D. Officially it is La Carretera Transpeninsular Benito Juarez. It traverses the full length of the peninsula from the international border to Cabo San Lucas, a distance of 1,057.468 miles to the inch. How do I know so accurately? I have consulted five references to the length of the highway, each of which is different. I have added all these offerings together and divided by five, a method I'm sure will be understood by my high school mathematics instructor who gave me a D in his subject.

Photo shows a typical section of the Transpeninsular Highway in hilly terrain. Note that the truck is crowding the center of the road. Will he get over? See next photo for the answer. Photo BW.

The five sources provide answers from 1,042 as a low to a high of 1,067. For the balance of this book I will use 1,059 miles as this is the distance given on the widely used map distributed by the Auto Club of Southern California. It has to be close.

Baja's citizens waited through many decades of promises by Mexico's presidential candidates before witnessing completion of the Transpeninsular Highway. At long last, on December 1, 1973, President Luis Echeverria Alvarez fulfilled his promise to build the road and dedicated its completion at the 28th parallel near Guerrero Negro. The actual completion had taken place when road building crews from north and south met the previous October near what is now named Catavina in the plateau lands some 75 miles south of El Rosario. The President was apparently motivated to action after being treated to a trip over the old road, known to its travelers as "The Trail." By all accounts such a trip was an adventure. The new highway is a monumental leap forward.

Prior to describing Highway 1, I will repeat an opinion expressed in this book's introductory chapter. There I promised to be realistic in my descriptions of the beauty and charms of Baja, as I feel that many authors stray from reality in their use of adjectives and in their efforts to achieve literary merit. Even more disconcerting to me are those authors who create literary horror stories when providing cautionary advice. This often becomes the case when they are describing the Transpeninsular Highway. I have seen articles which would frighten even the most stout-hearted traveler into staying home. What are, in truth, reasons for caution become blown out of proportion by overly poetic adjectives and a sense of the dramatic. I will steer for the middle ground.

31

TRANSPORTATION

Mexicali

Tijuana

2

5

Ensenada

23

3

Puerto Penasco

San Felipe

Puertecitos

1?

1

— HIGHWAYS

1

···· FERRY ROUTES

✝ INTERNATIONAL AIRPORTS

? Four places where new highway construction is occurring with timing and ultimate locations uncertain. See text under Highway Standard (Not Paved).

Bahia Kino

Isla Cedros

Guerrero Negro

San Ignacio

Bahia de los Angeles

San Carlos

Guaymas

Bahia Tortgugas

2?

Santa Rosalia

7 Hours

Airport Unused Fall 1997

Mulege

3?

PACIFIC OCEAN

La Purisima San Isidro

Loreto

SEA OF CORTEZ

Topolobampo

8 Hours

Ciudad Insurgentes

22

Ciudad Constitucion

N

1

11

16 Hours

100 Miles

286

To Mazatlan

La Paz

19

4

Cabo San Lucas

Los Cabos Airport

Cabo San Lucas to Puerto Vallarta ferry was discontinued in 1989.

The Transpeninsular Highway is paved its entire distance. It is well engineered. Appropriate banking and curves allow for adequate visibility if you drive at reasonable speeds. Some 44 percent of its length is over hilly terrain but grades (steepness) are modest and not overly demanding for vehicles that are adequately powered. The remaining 56 percent passes over level ground. The highway is generally well maintained. One frequently sees crews doing everything from cutting roadside weeds to applying new oiled surfacing.

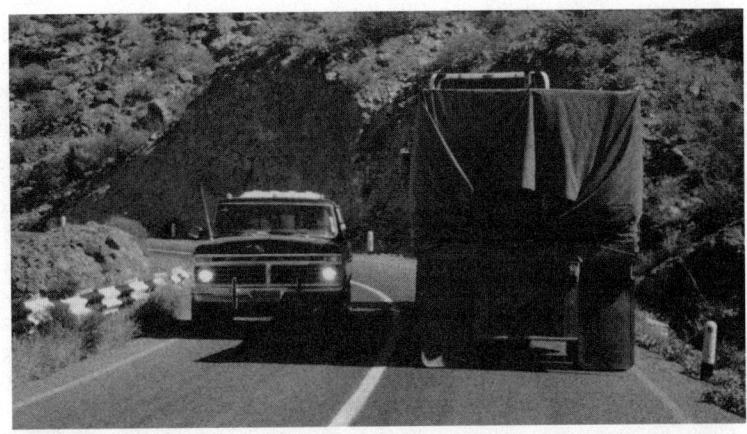

He got over, but the driver of a big RV would not find much room to spare. Photo BW.

Sections of the highway may be seen in several photos in this and other chapters.

But Highway 1 does have its shortcomings, any of which can result in serious accidents or inconvenience if you violate one of two cardinal rules. These are, (1) don't drive at high speeds and (2) don't drive at night. Here is a list of the negative features:

1. — With the exception of the northerly most 80 miles, the highway is narrow. Most of it has a travel surface only 24-feet wide. Its narrowness is heightened by the almost total lack of a shoulder. There is little margin for error and if you slip off the travel surface you face the very serious threat of rolling over, particularly if you are in a recreation vehicle with a high center of gravity. Thus what is otherwise a fine highway is compromised by its lack of width.

2. -- Small portions of the edge of the paving tend to fall away in spots resulting in a narrowing of the travel surface. Thus, the highway will not be a full two-lanes wide in some spots. My recent surveys indicate that this condition has been corrected in many places with a variety of edge protecting techniques. However, it is still the number one safety problem on Baja's highways. My 1997 survey disclosed that erosion along the edge of Baja's highways was the primary damage that occurred from the passage of a hurricane over the peninsula in October of that year.

3. — A large part of Baja is open range. Thus the roadside is not fenced, and cattle and other animals may be encountered, particularly at night when they are attracted by the warmth of the road surface. I almost hit a goat during my 1995 field trip.

4. — There are few turnouts or other places to move off the travel surface. It is not uncommon to come upon a vehicle blocking one lane of the highway while the driver is engaged in some roadside activity or correcting a mechanical problem.

5. — The major arroyo crossings have been bridged; however, hundreds of the lesser crossings are designed to let water flow over the highway during storms. These dips *(vados)* provide no problem most of the time, but they can be full of water, rocks, and soil during and after heavy storms.

6. — There are occasional sections of potholes which can be very hard on tires if hit at high speeds. I have found that areas of potholes encountered one year have been repaired the next, but others take their place. Also, with the passage of time much of Highway 1 has received two or more layers of oiled paving. In these places the potholes only break through to the layer below and the resultant hole is only about 1 inch deep.

My 1997 survey disclosed two promising conditions. (1) Highway 1 was almost totally free of potholes. In contrast several of the secondary paved highways are often badly pitted. This condition seems to be a chronic problem with the roads into Puerto San Isidro and Bahia de los Angeles. (2) For the first time I observed Highway 1 being resurfaced with *plant-mix* asphalt some 3 inches thick. This material is applied using a *Barber Green* machine and results in a far more satisfactory, smooth and long lasting surface. Some 50 miles of road had already been treated in November 1997 with work in progress at several locations. The days of the potholes on Highway 1 may be coming to a close.

Cows? What cows? I don't see any cows! Besides they're small ones and I'm going fast in my big RV. No Problema. Photo BW.

7. — Finally, for the person of environmental sensitivity, there is one unfortunate problem with the Transpeninsular Highway. All new roads in Baja are constructed by first clearing the right-of-way of all vegetation with a bulldozer or grader. In most places various plants are returning but there is an almost total lack of the larger and more picturesque species that make the Baja desert spectacular. The vegetation is often outstanding but unfortunately is a few yards removed.

Traveling Highway 1 can be a safe and rewarding experience if it is driven at reasonable speeds during daylight hours. Insurance industry data indicate that some 80 percent of the accidents on Baja's highways occur at night. And, what are safe speeds? A travel time estimate provided by one of the Mexican insurance companies indicates that it would take 23-3/4 hours to drive the 991 miles from Ensenada to Cabo San Lucas. This equates to 42 miles per hour. I would have estimated 40 miles per hour. You can do it faster, but you should not.

BAJA'S OTHER ROADS —
From 1973 until about 1983 there were few paved roads other than the Transpeninsular Highway. The location of this road appears to have been planned to connect the peninsula's

Note that the edge of the road has been eaten away by erosion and again the truck driver is taking his half near the middle. Photo BW.

principal communities over the most cost-effective route. As stressed in Chapter 2, it provides little direct access to the seaside areas most sought after by tourists.

From 1983 until about 1989 many additional miles of unpaved, but otherwise highway standard roads, were constructed along with hundreds of miles of gravel-surfaced secondary roads. This time period was clearly Baja's era of road construction. My inspection of the peninsula in spring 1995 disclosed that little new highway or secondary road construction of interest to the tourist has taken place since 1989 and that continues to be the case. However, there has been much road paving and landscaping in many of the peninsula's communities. As a result their appearance has been much improved. Also, sections of Highway 5 south of Mexicali and the southern most section of Highway 1 have been upgraded to four lane divided highways. ------ Baja's roads may be classified rather neatly into four classes. These are described below.

HIGHWAYS (PAVED) — There are approximately 800 miles of main paved highways in Baja in addition to the Transpeninsular Highway. Roughly 550 miles are in the northern state of Baja California, with the remaining 250 in Baja California Sur. These figures do not include a considerable additional mileage of paved roads within the Valle de Mexicali agricultural area adjoining the international border and occasional short roads in other places.

I have driven all 800 miles of these highways and have concluded that they have all been engineered to approximately the same standards as the Transpeninsular Highway. Thus, they are all adequate facilities and in general are safer than the Transpeninsular Highway as there is often less traffic and fewer wide trucks, buses, and recreational vehicles. Most of these 800 miles of highway are shown on the TRANSPORTATION Map in this chapter.

The only totally new recreation-oriented section of paved highway to appear since 1989 is the extension of Highway 11 (north of La Paz) from Pichilingue to Tocolote.

HIGHWAY STANDARD (NOT PAVED)

In Baja, all construction work up to final paving is usually completed several years before surfacing is applied. At the end of my earlier 1989 survey there were about 250 miles of these roads, constructed to highway standards, but still awaiting finished grading and their oiled surface. These are the four projects shown as numbered question marks on the TRANSPORTATION Map. Following is a brief 1997 status report on these four areas:

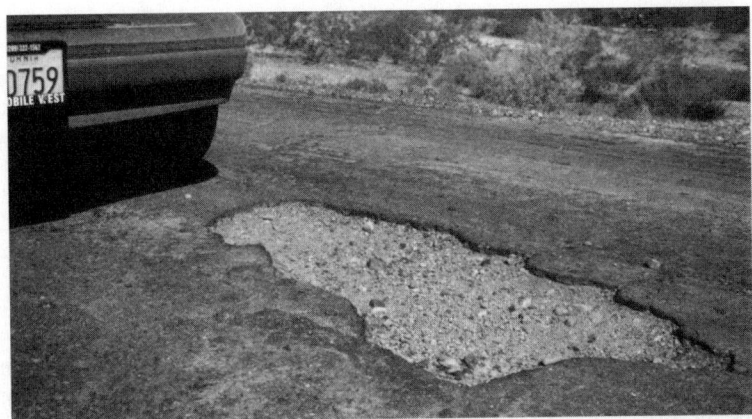

A pothole that will make a beliver out of you. Note that the road here has only had one application of oiled surface so the pothole will continue to grow deeper. Happy landings. Photo BW.

1 -- San Felipe south to Highway 1 -- This highway has been paved south to Puertecitos for several years and is well maintained. The remaining portion has had no further improvement and has deteriorated in some places. It is very washboarded and suffered more damage during the October 1997 hurricane.. If it is eventually completed it will provide a major new alternative route of travel from the United States to southern Baja.

2 -- Highway 1 to Bahia Tortugas -- The oiled surface was extended westerly from Highway 1 for 22 miles some years ago, but no further extension has occurred. The balance of the road is smoother than most of Baja's's other unpaved roads.

3 -- Ciudad Insurgentes Northward -- In 1995 the oiled surface had been completed from Ciudad Insurgentes to the town of San Isidro. I am informed that a highway toll road may eventually be constructed further northward to San Ignacio, but it is not an imminent project.

4 -- The East Cape -- The paved surface has been completed from Highway 1, southward for 10 miles passed La Ribera. The remainder of the road south to San Jose del Cabo is often in rough condition. I was advised that this section was scheduled to be completed and paved by 1996 but that did not happen. Time will tell.

The pit-run gravel used for the subsurface of these projects is often quite coarse, as it is not intended as the final surface. Thus, some unpaved sections of these roads quickly become very rough and badly washboarded. Travel speeds are usually substantially less than over much lower-standard dirt roads. One of my traveling companions once noticed a dump truck loaded with 8-to-10 inch diameter stones destined for someone's rock wall. He said, "There goes a

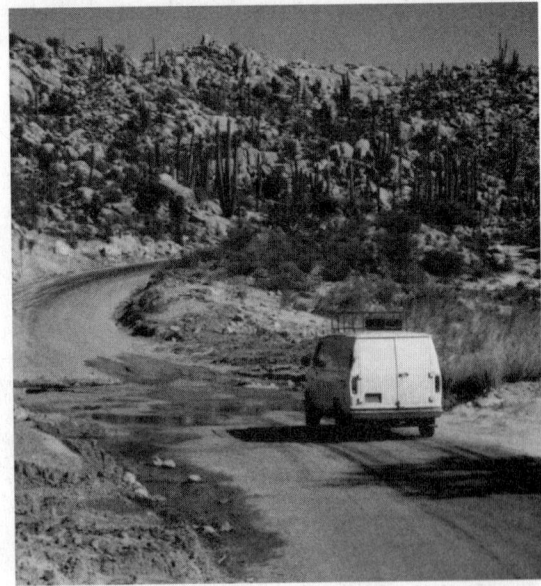

One of the hundreds of low-water-crossings (Vados) along Highway 1. Most of them are normally dry. This one in the Catavina Boulder Fields always carries some water. Photo BW.

load of road gravel." It's not that bad, but be prepared for a bumpy ride. As with the secondary roads described below, this class of roads are best suited for pickups and vans.

SECONDARY ROADS (UNPAVED) — A decade or so ago, one could say that there were only two standards of roads in Baja (1) the paved highways and (2) all the others, which were of the *two tracks in the desert* variety. As previously noted, this is no longer the case. There are now hundreds of miles of dirt and gravel-surfaced roads of intermediate standard. The majority have been built to provide improved road access to Mexicans living in small towns or ranches. In many cases they also serve the needs of the recreational traveler who wants to get away from the more heavily used areas. As these areas become more and more crowded, these secondary roads will become increasingly important.

These roads are 1 1/2-to-2 lanes in width. Some sections are wider and some are narrower. In most places, you can pass an oncoming car, but slowing down and keeping well to the right are often necessary. The surface is sometimes composed of native soil and gravel; in other places, a better grade of gravel has been imported. In all cases, the travel surface has been constructed by earthmoving equipment and is free of large rocks and similar obstacles. With few exceptions, secondary roads are those shown as "Graded Dirt Road" on the widely-used road map produced by the Southern California Automobile Association.

Secondary roads are infrequently graded. When recent maintenance has occurred, one can travel in the

The Pothole Crew. The barrel at the right is placed over a fire of dry brush used to heat the patching material. One sees many modern improvements in Baja but highway maintenance is not one of them. Photo BW.

20-40 mph range. More often you will be greeted by miles of washboarding and occasionally by rutting caused by erosion and wet weather use. As this rough road surface is common, consider letting some of the air out of your tires to soften the washboard shock.

You will also be faced with a choice dictated by the 4-40 rule. That is, drive slowly (4 mph) to cooperate with the surface, or fly over the tops of the ridges at 40 mph. Most owners of the vehicle they are driving will choose the former alternative. (You actually will average in the 10-20 mph range.) However, brace yourself for meeting some of the local citizens flying low with the fishing-co-op pickup .

These secondary roads have been *engineered*. By that I mean that the surface may have been built-up (turnpiked) above the natural terrain and there are often hard surfaced arroyo crossings and an occasional culvert. Also, there are sometimes kilometer posts and usually directional signs where these roads join the main highways. Curves and grades are modest; in most cases these roads have been constructed in areas of gentle topography. If you become alert to these characteristics of an engineered road, you can be reasonably assured that you are on the type of facility that I am describing and that washboarding will be the worst of your troubles. Be careful after storms, however, as even these engineered roads will become slick and sometimes impassable when wet.

My impression of such roads is the same as for the main highways; that is, that they all seem to have been constructed to about the same standard. To a large degree, when you have seen one, you have seen them all, and you can develop confidence in using them for recreational travel. Keep in mind that while the chief problem with the main highway system is lack of width, the weak points of secondary roads are washboarding and slick or muddy surfaces after storms.

The GRAND TOUR in PART III provides maps and details concerning such roads and the places they serve. These routes will be referred to as *secondary roads*. This term will not be used for lower standard facilities.

OTHER ROADS (DIRT SURFACE) — There are thousands of miles of lower-standard dirt roads in Baja. Some have been built by a bulldozer pushing its way through the desert. Typically, the surfaces of such roads are lower than the surrounding terrain. They are not built-up as indicated for the secondary roads. Other roads simply developed as the result of vehicular use. Such roads provide access to scores of isolated ranches, fish camps, and miles of coastline. They are generally unsuitable for sedans and large recreational vehicles; however, for those with vans and lightly loaded pickups, these roads offer endless possibilities. Often their travel surfaces are smoother than are those of secondary roads and unpaved highways, but they will be narrow and harbor steep trouble spots at arroyo crossings. Directional signs are rare. These roads will be referred to as *dirt roads*.

A portion of the secondary road in steep mountain country between Loreto and the famous mission at San Javier. Most secondary roads are located on far more level terrain. Photo JW.

BACK COUNTRY TRAVEL — This section concerns traveling on Baja's many secondary and lesser standard roads. In this regard I am often asked, "Do you need four-wheel-drive in Baja?" The answer is "No." I have visited scores of isolated villages and ranches by land and sea and seeing a Mexican with a four-wheel-drive vehicle is very unusual. The workhorse of the economy is the standard pickup truck and, until recently, all of my investigative work has been done with such a vehicle. One can go <u>almost</u> everywhere with two-wheel-drive. But keep in mind that I just said <u>almost</u> everywhere. If you have a 4x4 vehicle, by all means take it to Baja, as it will add a positive new dimension to your travels.

The comments that follow have been prepared in consultation with Bob and Jean Evans, longtime members of the Vagabundos del Mar, and 4x4 travelers in Baja since 1965. They report that 98 percent of their off-highway travel in Baja is in standard drive, but it is that remaining two percent that makes the difference for them. With only standard drive one must frequently stop just short of that special place to camp. A 4x4 vehicle allows one to travel onto the beach, out on rocky ledges overlooking the sea, or into sandy arroyos seeking the shade of the desert's only trees. Four-wheel power allows for a steady climb up steep pitches where other vehicles have scraped deep ruts while spinning their tires. But most importantly to the Evans is the peace of mind they have in knowing that their vehicle will take them to the places they really want to go.

<u>BOB AND JEAN BACKROAD</u> -- Accompanying these comments is a table showing Bob and Jean's recommendations for nine backroad adventures that provide a cross section of the type of experiences that Baja has to offer. They vary from a very short side trip at Morro Santo Domingo to a loop trip along the Pacific shore of over 100 miles. These trips will be noted in further detail when they are encountered in PART III of this book. (I have not personally traveled these routes.) Each will be highlighted by the "BOB & JEAN BACKROAD" logo shown in the upper corners of the table. With few exceptions they involve travel over existing roads. I do not recommend cross-country travel which frequently results in damage to Baja's sensitive desert environment.

<u>BACKROAD BAJA</u> -- Also featured here is a graphic illustrating nineteen back country trips featured in a book entitled *Backroad Baja* by Patti and Tom Higginbotham. Patti and her husband Tom are Americans who live much of the time in Mulege on the Sea of Cortez. It contains maps and mileage-logs of each trip along with background material on history and points of interest. The book is available in the BAJA BOOKSHELF in the Appendix.

Chapter 3

Some of Patti and Tom's trips are over roads for which brief road logs are also provided here in *The Magnificent Peninsula*. Others are really rough 4x4 routes not even shown on most Baja maps. In each case their book provides more information than it has been possible to present in these pages.

REPAIRS AND FUEL — Two problems concerning travel in Baja do not relate directly to the roadways. These are vehicle repairs and fuel supplies.

REPAIRS -- Except when driving in the heat of summer, there is little reason why a vehicle should have more repair problems in Baja than north of the border. The difficulty arises when something does happen. With the exception of Ensenada, Ciudad Constitucion, La Paz, and the border cities, full service repair facilities and parts stores are few and far between. The prudent driver will always carry spare belts, hoses, filters, and a tool kit. But, sadly, our modern cars contain little under the hood that most of us can repair.

During our 1995 field trip, our transmission died. We had to be towed 100-miles to La Paz where we spent 18-days waiting for a new transmission from the US of A. It never arrived and we settled for a rebuilt model fashioned from parts from our deceased edition and those from a convenient wreck. All of this in La Paz, a city of 160,000 people which has an authorized agency for our make of vehicle.

I recommend that you obtain the name and phone number of an authorized dealer in the San Diego area for your make of vehicle, before leaving for Mexico. Should you have a serious breakdown and need parts not available in Baja, call this agency. If they are experienced in shipping parts to Baja and can assure you of help, let them assist you. If not, your best course of action is to travel to San Diego, acquire the needed parts and bring them back to Baja personally.

On one of our previous trips, my wife and I gave a lift to a young lady whose car had serious engine trouble. We delivered her to the machine shop (*taller mecanico*) in Loreto. Its floor was the native surface and there was very little roof. Its benches and the surrounding area were littered with tools and the remains of automotive disasters of previous decades. These wrecks serve as the "parts department." We did our best for our friend but do not know how she fared.

At a similar facility in another town, I was in need of a tire pressure gauge and asked the owner if I might borrow one. When he headed for the refrigerator I thought I had been misunderstood. Alas, the refrigerator had long outlived its original calling and now served as a tool cache, the only place in the entire facility that would remain dry in the event of rain.

The favorable news is that I have found the Baja mechanics to be good at their trade. They have to be, in a land where new cars in top running order are relatively few in number. I have also found them to be friendly and eager to help, in sharp contrast to what one often finds you-know-where. The other saving feature is the Green Angels (*Angeles Verdes*), a service of the Mexican government. They patrol the Transpeninsular, and other main highways, in their green-and-white pickup trucks. There is usually a crew of two, one of whom speaks English. They carry a limited supply of spare parts, gasoline, oil, and water and perform minor repairs at no charge. Parts are sold at cost. While you may have to wait a few hours, help is always on the way.

FUEL -- Mexico's fuel supplies are another subject where some travel authors rejoice in painting an

BOB & JEAN BACKROAD	**BACKROAD RECOMMENDATIONS** By Bob and Jean Evans	BOB & JEAN BACKROAD

1 Diablo & Diabalito - Ch 15 — Rugged canyons with waterfalls, pools, & entrancing vegetation.
2 Pacific Coast Loop - Ch 19 — An isolated section of coast - Puerto Catarina to Santa Rosalillita.
3 El Volcan - Ch 19 — Crystal forming spring near the famous El Marmol onyx mine.
4 Mission Santa Maria - Ch 19 — One of Baja's least visited mission ruins in a lovely palm canyon.
5 Morro Santo Domingo - Ch 19 — A short 4x4 trip provides spectacular camp spots along the Pacific.
6 Candelaria - Ch 21 — Prehistoric cave paintings at Candelaria.
7 Punta Concepcion - Ch 21 — Drive eastern shore of Bahia Concepcion to Punta Concepcion.
8 San Luis Gonzaga - Ch 22 — Visit 1737 stone mission plus numerous rugged mountian roads.
9 Agua Caliente - Ch 23 — Hot spring & camping by a large pool at the foot of the mountains.

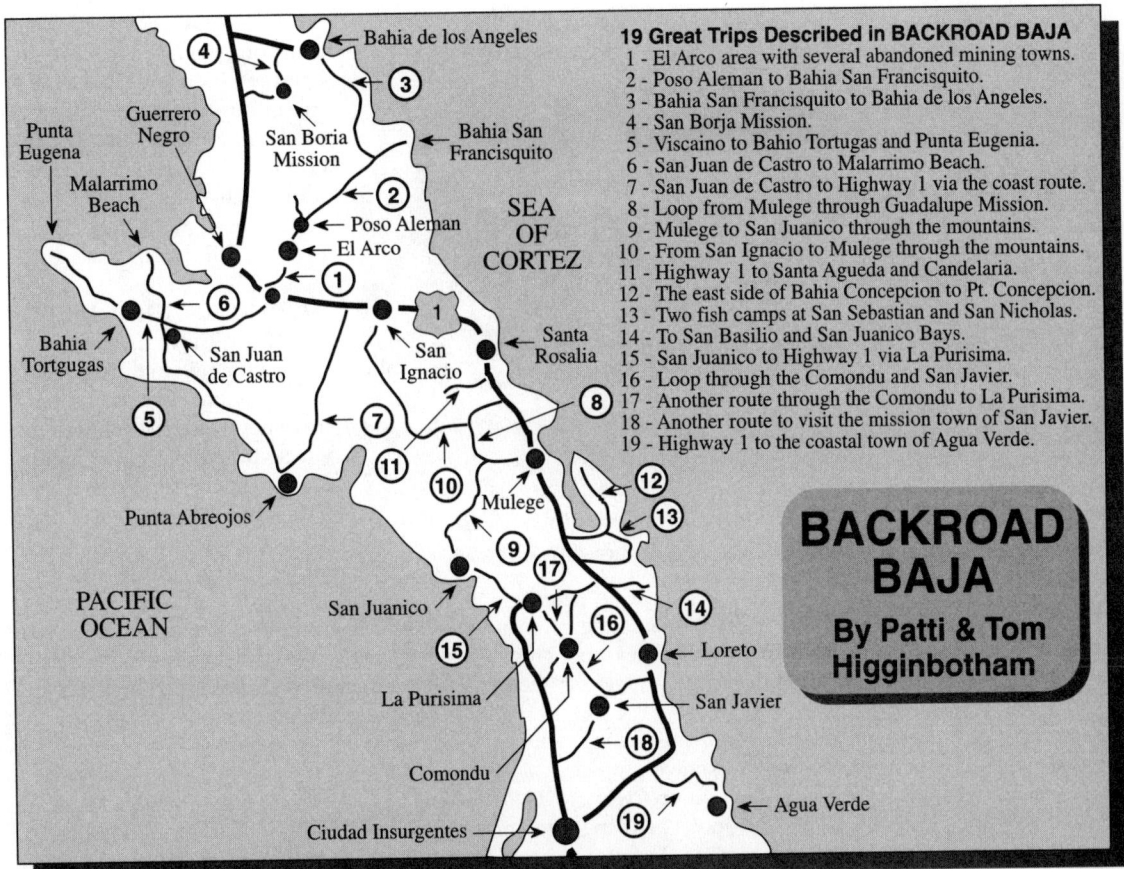

19 Great Trips Described in BACKROAD BAJA

1 - El Arco area with several abandoned mining towns.
2 - Poso Aleman to Bahia San Franciscuito.
3 - Bahia San Francisquito to Bahia de los Angeles.
4 - San Borja Mission.
5 - Viscaino to Bahio Tortugas and Punta Eugenia.
6 - San Juan de Castro to Malarrimo Beach.
7 - San Juan de Castro to Highway 1 via the coast route.
8 - Loop from Mulege through Guadalupe Mission.
9 - Mulege to San Juanico through the mountains.
10 - From San Ignacio to Mulege through the mountains.
11 - Highway 1 to Santa Agueda and Candelaria.
12 - The east side of Bahia Concepcion to Pt. Concepcion.
13 - Two fish camps at San Sebastian and San Nicholas.
14 - To San Basilio and San Juanico Bays.
15 - San Juanico to Highway 1 via La Purisima.
16 - Loop through the Comondu and San Javier.
17 - Another route through the Comondu to La Purisima.
18 - Another route to visit the mission town of San Javier.
19 - Highway 1 to the coastal town of Agua Verde.

BACKROAD BAJA

By Patti & Tom Higginbotham

unrealistically pessimistic picture. I sometimes feel that the poor conditions that were present in the past are copied from one author to the next and passed on like old wives' tales. Their most common accusation is that Mexican fuel is filled with impurities. I am sure some drivers have experienced this problem, but I have motored my diesel-powered sailboat over 10,000 miles on Mexican fuel and changed a filter only once. I have never had to change a filter in my pickup. It stands to reason that the highways would be lined with stalled vehicles if unclean fuel was a serious problem.

Also good news is the fact that gasoline and diesel prices are the same almost everywhere because fuel is sold through a government marketing monopoly. Each station bears the same sign, PEMEX (*Petroleos Mexicanos*). If all else fails, look for the pumps.

<u>Previous Edition Conditions</u> -- The green pump is for MAGNA SIN, a 92-octane unleaded fuel. The blue pump dispenses NOVA, which is an 82-octane regular gas containing tetraethyl lead. Diesel fuel, spelled

the same in English and Spanish, comes from the red pumps.

In the past, gas stations were not always open for a variety of reasons and there was difficulty obtaining fuel along the 221-mile section of Highway 1 between El Rosario and Guerrero Negro. In recent years both of these problems have been greatly reduced but it is still wise to never let your fuel supply drop below the halfway point. Also, in past years, many Baja gas stations did not carry unleaded gas. However, our 1995 survey found that all but only the most remote stations had MAGNA SIN pumps.

Occasionally some one will attempt to overcharge you at a PEMEX station. Beware of pumps with inoperable or taped over price gauges. The attendant will tell you what you owe by multiplying the number of liters pumped by the price per liter; or perhaps his version of the price per liter. Check him out.

<u>1997 Update</u> -- The above three paragraphs have been presented in past editions of this book. Condi-

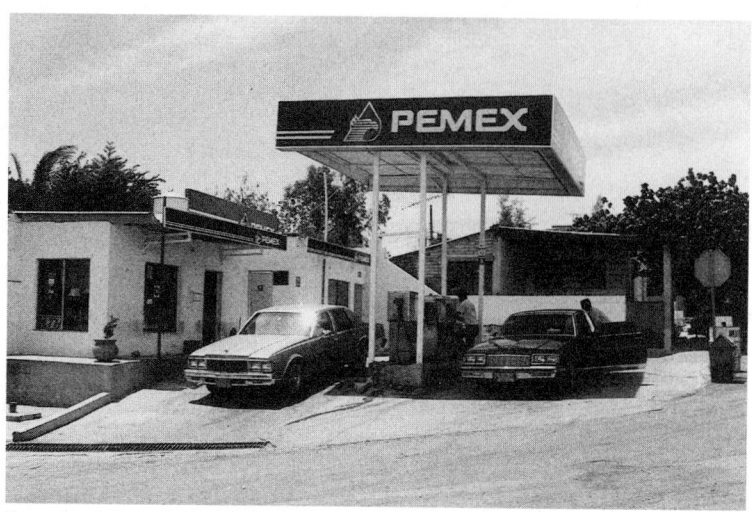

A typical Baja gas station (this one at the small town of Santiago south of La Paz). The logo on the sign is the same at every station in Baja. Photo JW.

stations. Young boys also often climb on your hood to wash the windows for a few pesos. Contribute to the cause. Also get used to the word "lleno," pronounced "yay-no." It means "full." The attendant will often yell it at you to determine if you want to "Fill it up."

MAPS AND ROAD DIRECTIONS — The maps and directions contained in this book are fully adequate for recreational travelers using the main highways and principal secondary roads. However, I strongly recommend that you obtain the *Baja California Road Map* published by the Automobile Club of Southern California (AAA). This is an outstanding publication that is available at club offices as a free service to its members. This map shows all four classes of roads described in this chapter. Obtain road maps before going to Baja as they are hard to find once you are in the peninsula.

tions changed with our 1997 survey but I am leaving in the old material as I am not certain as to whether the new findings will be universal.

It appeared that most if not all of the stations along the main travel routes had recently received new pumps. The stations that did not have new pumps were closed and appeared abandoned. It looks as if the word was "Upgrade or get out of business." The new pumps are fancy electronic ones little different than those found north of the border. This takes the guess work out of how much gas has been pumped and the attendant has less opportunity to cheat you. I am informed however, that the station owners can and do adjust the internal settings so that less fuel is delivered than the pump indicates. The only way to combat this is to avoid pumps that don't have some local Mexican customers. The locals soon learn what is going on.

There was also a change in what fuel was available. In the past many stations did not carry unleaded gas (Sin Plumo). Now the situation is reversed. The newly equipped stations have no leaded gas (Con Plumo) and have two grades of unleaded gas. The green pumps have Magna (Sin Plumo), the red pumps have Premium (Sin Plumo) and the black pumps have diesel. Except for the colors, its just like north of the border. What will they think of next?

Finally, you may be happy to find that station attendants actually pump gas for you, the self-service era has penetrated south of the border at only a few

RAILROADS — Baja was linked to the Mexican mainland by railroad in 1948. This line now proceeds north from Mexicali into the United States and eventually returns to Baja at Tecate and then to Tijuana. Most of this Tecate to Tijuana segment appears to receive very little use. However, in recent years, vintage railroad passenger cars have been used to run from the US town of Campo southwest to Tecate. This 45-minute train ride terminates at the Tecate brewery where it is reported that passenger's spirit's are revived with samples of the brewer's output. Campo is located on California Highway 94 east of San Diego.

Trains from Mexicali make regularly scheduled runs southeastward to the Mexican mainland. The Mexicali train links up with the main line from Nogales to Mexico City at Benjamin Hill. The trip to Mexico City is scheduled to take about 48 hours, although I am advised that connection problems in Guadalajara add an extra day. En route, it passes through Guaymas, Mazatlan and Guadalajara. The line then continues east from Mexico City to the Yucatan peninsula and its Mayan ruins.

I have made this run from Mexicali as far as Guadalajara, and can recommend it for the not too faint of heart. I have also made, and can thoroughly recommend, a related side rail trip from Los Mochis to Creel near Copper Canyon. The Pullman and other passenger cars are of 1940 vintage, which actually allow you to open up the windows; no choking from the air conditioning. You won't see much of Baja, but Mexicali is the starting point for these railroad adventures. Train reservations may be acquired through Romero's Mexico Service, 1600 West Coast Highway, Newport Beach CA 92663, (714) 548-8931.

BUSES — Several bus companies provide frequent service between Tijuana, Mexicali, and mainland Mexico along Highway 2. They operate from the Central de Autobuses (Central Bus Terminal) located near the airport in Tijuana. (See Tijuana map in Chapter 14). Two of these lines, Tres Estrellas de Oro (Three Stars of Gold) and ABC (Autobuses Baja California) also traverse Highway 1 from Tijuana to La Paz. The trip takes about 26 hours. During our 1995 and 1997 surveys the most commonly observed bus line in Baja was Autotransportes Aguila.

Bus service in Mexico is rated as super deluxe, deluxe, first, second, and third class. The third-class buses are affectionately referred to as *chicken buses* as they often are used to transport members of the animal kingdom other than man. Tourists are advised to utilize only the first class or higher services. Seats on these buses are reserved, but you must acquire your reservations and tickets in person.

There are usually two drivers on the longer runs. One drives while the other rests. I have found the service and quality of Mexican buses to be very good. If I were asked to compare the overall deportment and other characteristics of the people on Mexican buses with those in the United States, I would cast my vote for south of the border.

RENTAL CARS — Rental cars are available in Tijuana, Mexicali, Loreto, La Paz and at the Cape. In 1997 the Los Cabos airport boasted four different car agencies. The major companies are the same as those serving the United States and Canada. Reservations may be made by calling these firms' 800 telephone numbers. It is not normally possible to rent a car in Tijuana and drop it off in the southern part of the peninsula.

Tourists renting a car at La Paz or the two Cape communities can easily make the Hwy 1- Hwy 19 loop and return their car at the point of origin.

OCEAN LINERS — Thousands of people make the passage to Baja each year in pleasure craft of various types and sizes. This fascinating means of seeing the world will be examined in some detail in Chapter 5. At the opposite end of the ocean travel spectrum is the growing number of tourists who can now experience a few hours stopover at Cabo San Lucas while their ocean liner lies at anchor in the bay. As it has been for centuries, Cabo is a natural stopover point for vessels plying the sea. Its inner harbor provides tourist facilities at the water's edge but is too small and shallow for the large cruise vessels. Passengers make the trip to and from the anchorage in ships' launches.

During a trip to Cabo San Lucas my wife and I encountered an elderly lady who had arrived in this manner. The lady asked how we had made our journey. We replied that we had driven in our camper. Her response was, "You mean there is some kind of giant bridge to this island?" My wife provided a brief geography lesson. In an act of great restraint, I refrained from advising her that the Spanish explorer Francisco de Ulloa discovered that the Baja peninsula was not an island in 1539.

In contrast to Cabo San Lucas, Baja's Pacific coast port city of Ensenada can accommodate ocean liners at dockside. In recent years, liners have made the run from San Pedro (near Los Angeles) to Ensenada on a regular basis. Our 1997 survey disclosed plans to build a new cruise ship dock on the inner side of the Ensenada harbor within easy walking distance from the main tourist area. The present dock is some distance away.

In 1991 a passenger dock and terminal suitable for large ocean liners was completed within the harbor of Pichilingue 10 miles from the city of La Paz in an effort to lure the ocean cruising trade to that community. To date it has had little or no use and was being used as a tuna clipper dock in 1995. Contract your travel agent for details concerning ships to both Ensenada and La Paz .

The 143 foot, 80 passenger *Pacific Northwest Explorer* provided cruises into the Sea of Cortez in past years. This service was discontinued at press time but it may reappear in the future.

FERRY SERVICE — The Sea of Cortez ferry routes are shown on the TRANSPORTATION Map in this

RENTAL CARS IN BAJA

AVIS INT'L 1 (800) 228-4369
  Los Cabos Airport
  La Paz and La Paz Airport
  Mexicali
  Tijuana Airport
BUDGET INT'L 1 (800) 472-3325
  Tijuana
  Loreto
  La Paz
  San Jose del Cabo
  Cabo San Lucas
DOLLAR INT'L 1 (800) 800-6000
  Cabo San Lucas
  San Jose del Cabo
  Los Cabos Airport
  Tijuana

HERTZ INT'L 1 (800) 654-3001
  Cabo San Lucas
  Ensenada
  La Paz
  Los Cabos Airport
  Mexicali
  Tijuana
THRIFTY 1 (800) 367-2277
  Cabo San Lucas
  La Paz
  La Paz Airport
  Loreto Airport
  Los Cabos Airport

chapter. The FERRY SCHEDULE shown nearby summarizes the overall operation of the system. Keep in mind that this schedule changes from time to time. It has been different in each of the last four editions of this book and the system offers more frequent service in the winter than it does during the summer. Also, there may be lengthy delays and cancellations of reservations when the ferries do not operate due to storm conditions or mechanical breakdowns. Fog at the entrance to the Topolobampo harbor on the Mexican mainland, and constricted entrance conditions at Santa Rosalia often cause delays in the run between these two ports. Wise travelers will maintain a flexible schedule when planning to use the ferry system.

The Santa Rosalia ferry terminal is located inside the man-made harbor at this community. The La Paz ferry docks within the natural harbor of Pichilingue located 17 Km (10.5 miles) from downtown La Paz over a blacktop highway. There is also a ferry terminal inside the man-made harbor at Cabo San Lucas but the service from there to Puerto Vallarta was

discontinued in 1989. About 1990 the ferry system was sold by the Mexican government to private interests now doing business under the name SEMATUR TRANSBORDADORES. As a result the formerly subsidized prices have risen sharply.

There are four passenger classes. Salon Class passengers are entitled to one of the numerous seats located throughout the ferry. Reservations are given for this general seating area. Advance reservations are required for Turista Class (cabins with toilet facilities outside the room) and Cabina Class (cabins with toilets). There is also a new Especial Class for the luxury minded. Recent prices quoted in new pesos are noted below. For Internet information contact (http.//www.trybaja.com/ferry.html).

BETWEEN MAZATLAN and LA PAZ -- Passengers -- Salon N$ 64.60 -- Turista N$128.90 -- Cabina N$193.20 -- Especial N$257.60. Vehicles -- Autos to 5 meters N$ 450.50 -- Autos 5.1-6.5 m. N$ 586.00 -- w trailers to 9 m. N$ 811.80 -- 9.1-17 m. N$1533.30 -- Motorhomes N$ 765.40 -- Motorcycles N$ 58.20.

BETWEEN TOPOLOBAMPO and LA PAZ -- Passengers -- Salon N$ 42.90 -- Turista N$ 85.90 -- Cabina ????? -- Especial N$171.80 -- Vehicles -- Autos to 5 meters N$274.55 -- Autos 5.1-6.5 m. N$356.60 -- w trailers to 9 m. N$494.50 -- 9.1-17 m. N$933.00 -- Motorhomes N$469.50 -- Motorcycles N$ 34.50.

BETWEEN GUAYMAS and SANTA ROSALIA -- Passengers -- Salon N$43.00 -- Turista N$85.90 -- Vehicles -- Autos to 5 meters N$316.20 -- Autos 5.1-6.5 m. N$411.20 -- w trailers to 9 m. N$569.30 --

FERRY SCHEDULE

Schedule effective November 1997				
ROUTE		DEPARTURES		TRAVEL TIME
FROM	TO	DAYS	TIME	
Guaymas	Santa Rosalia	Tues. and Fri.	11 AM	7 Hours
Santa Rosalia	Guaymas	Sun. and Wed.	8 AM	7 Hours
Topolobampo	La Paz	Daily except Sun.	10 PM	10 Hours
La Paz	Topolobampo	Daily except Sun.	11 AM	8 Hours
Mazatlan	La Paz	Wed. & Fri.	3 PM	18 Hours
La Paz	Mazatlan	Tues & Thurs.	3 PM	18 Hours

The Cabo San Lucas to Puerto Vallarta ferry was discontinued in 1989.

Motorhomes N$539.30 --
Motorcycles N$ 46.40.

The ferry system has become the lifeline for southern Baja California. Food and endless other commodities are carried on large trucks, and truck containers transported from the mainland by ferry. It is thus becoming increasingly more difficult to secure ferry reservations for recreational vehicles. Passenger traffic has also increased and I have had reports of tourists having to buy tickets from scalpers at dockside.

The *La Paz*, a typical vessel in the ferry system serving Baja. Here she is docked at Pichilingue near La Paz.

Procedures for using the La Paz ferry are a bit complex as the ferry terminal and the La Paz reservation office are not at the same location. Using the system at Santa Rosalia is simpler as the two facilities are in one building. (See Santa Rosalia and La Paz maps for locations of the ferry offices.)

A temporary export permit is required for any vehicle using the ferry system. It is best to take care of this procedure at Tijuana or the other ports-of-entry. In La Paz, it may be obtained at the office of the Registro Federal de Vehiculos located near the corner of Belisario Dominguez and 5 de Febrero.

AIR TRAVEL

Air travel has both increased and decreased in importance as a means of transportation to Baja since the early 1970s. This seeming contradiction is explained by the fact that commercial jet travel has substantially grown due to the construction of international airports and many new hotels in the peninsula's southern half. In contrast, the completion of the Transpeninsular Highway in 1973 has considerably lowered the tourist industry's reliance on travelers who transport themselves in small private aircraft.

COMMERCIAL AIR TRANSPORTATION -- Commercial aviation has gained in importance as the hotel industry has expanded.

AIRPORTS — There are five airports that serve modern jet aircraft. A sixth has been constructed south of Santa Rosalia but has yet to be utilized. (See TRANSPORTATION Map.) Two of these accommodate the border area at Tijuana and Mexicali, but these two cities are seldom the destination points of North Americans traveling to Mexico for recreational purposes.

The three airports in the peninsula's southern half receive nearly all the airborne tourist traffic from the United States and Canada. The La Paz airport has been in existence for some time, while those at Loreto and Los Cabos were constructed since 1975 in tandem with new resort facilities sponsored by FONATUR, a government tourist development agency. The Loreto terminal is small with only one flight per day in 1997. While larger, the other two facilities are small in comparison to the terminals in the world's major cities. Passengers exit their aircraft on portable stairways, walk in one door and out another. The only hassle I have observed is at the Los Cabos airport where taxi drivers, car rental agents, real estate salesmen and similar folks can give first time visitors some uneasy feelings. Relax, they are harmless.

Almost all of Baja's cities and towns have airstrips, and several of these are served by propeller-driven aircraft on a scheduled or nonscheduled basis. The more prominent of these places are Ciudad Constitucion, Ensenada, Guerrero Negro, Bahia Tortugas, Mulege, Santa Rosalia, Isla Cedros, and several of the larger southern hotels. Relatively few tourists travel using these facilities, but it is comforting to know that they are available in case of emergencies.

AIRPORT TAX — As in most places in the world, there is an airport tax. In flying into Mexico, it somehow is magically taken care of in the cost of the ticket; however, in leaving the country one must pay the tax at an airport ticket stand, and the price may be quoted only in pesos. This system causes considerable distress to some tourists who do not understand Spanish, have spent all of their pesos, and suspect that the whole process may be a local extortion operation. It is best to find out the amount of the tax in advance and save a few pesos for that purpose. It's all quite simple, although why they don't combine the tax with the ticket price is a great mystery, except perhaps to the ticket seller's union.

AIRLINES — Mexican-operated, Mexicana, AeroMexico and Aero California are the principal regularly scheduled jet-equipped airlines serving Baja's resort areas from points in the United States. U.S. carriers join in the peninsular market from time to time. My 1997 survey found the following airlines serving the Los Cabos Airport. AeroMexico, American, Allegro, Sun Country, Mexicana, Continental, Alaska and America West. The Mexican airlines fly a variety of American-made aircraft, and the service is as good or better than it is north of the border. See your travel agent for details.

There are also several air charter companies based in Southern California which serve Baja. Among these are Air Charter Express, 6714 Avenida Andorra, La Jolla, CA 92037 (619) 993 5861.

AIRPORT GROUND TRANSPORTATION — Most air travelers know that getting to and from the airport is often more complex and tiring than the flight itself. At the three southern Baja airports there is ample van-type transportation to all tourist facilities. Prices are moderate and are often included in hotel accommodation packages. Taxis also are plentiful and one is required to use them to return to the airports as a concession to the taxi unions. As a result both taxis and vans run empty during half of the airport round

trip. One hotel operator informed me the government has refused permission for him to provide the hotel's own airport shuttle but several hotel mini-buses were observed using the Los Cabos airport.

The Loreto airport is only three miles from the main resort areas. From Los Cabos airport it is about ten miles to the San Jose del Cabo resorts and 27 miles to Cabo San Lucas. The La Paz airport is about five miles from the downtown area.

PRIVATE FLYING — People flying to Baja in small private aircraft share with the ocean cruisers a means of savoring the peninsula's truly unique features. Unfortunately their choice of landing strips has been greatly reduced in recent years as the Mexican government has closed many of the smaller landing fields as a means of combatting drug traffic.

For many years the pilot's bible for flying in Baja was a detailed book entitled *Airports of Baja California and Northwest Mexico* by Arnold Senterfitt. Arnold also operated the *Baja Bush Pilots* . This organization is now operated by Jack McCormick at 1255 W. Baseline Road, Mesa, AZ, Suite 138, 85202. To my knowledge this is the best source of information on general aviation flying and Mexican aircraft insurance. A notice for the Airports book may be found with the Baja Bookshelf in the Appendix. I also recommend the 2 tape video set by Rick Roessler which is described in a nearby notice.

Some of the peninsula's hotels and resorts have nearby landing strips, although their number has decreased in recent years. Several of these are noted under Fly-in-hotels in Chapter 6. The traveler's aircraft can often be tied down within a few yards of their lodging, and management takes special pains to attend to those who fly in. Virtually all Baja towns have a community airstrip; thus almost all of the peninsula's hotels and resorts are readily available to the small plane pilot.

CHAPTER 4
RECREATION VEHICLES
AND CAMPING

This chapter was entitled *Camping* in earlier editions of this book. I have adapted the present title as the passage of time in Baja has made it evident that camping with tents and minimum facility vehicles, and the use of motor homes and larger recreation vehicles, are two quite different activities. Likewise, for the most part, they take place at different places and provide different recreation experiences.

RECREATION VEHICLES

Recreational vehicles make up a significant portion of the traffic one sees on Baja's highways. While increasing numbers of tourists are traveling to Baja in private automobiles, such vehicles do not dominate the scene as they do north of the border. Recreational vehicles that travel south include bicycles, motorcycles, sport-utility vehicles, vans, pickup campers, trailers, and motor homes of all sizes. Most of you will travel to Baja in the vehicle you already own and will not venture forth to buy one based on reading this book. However, you do need to understand the relationship of your particular RV to conditions in Baja.

All of life is a compromise. The owner of an RV must choose between <u>accessibility</u> and <u>accommodations</u>. Smaller, lighter vehicles can go to far more places than their larger cousins. Obviously there are more creature comforts in the larger motor homes and trailers. While

these conditions are also true in the U.S. and Canada, the contrast is considerably greater in Baja. This is why the marked differences between the different classes of roads were stressed in the previous chapter.

Most users of larger RVs do not stray far from paved highways and tend to congregate in developed RV parks. The risk of an accident is also increased when these large, top-heavy rigs have to pass oncoming vehicles on Baja's narrow highways. In contrast, the smaller vehicles commonly use all classes of roads. As a result, their owners can access much more of the Magnificent Peninsula and can escape the more heavily used areas that are close to the paved highways.

Remember, also, that the principal negative feature of unpaved highways and secondary roads is their rough surface. If you are willing to subject your motor home, its passengers and contents to washboard shock treatment, there is little other reason why larger rigs cannot be driven on many of these roads in dry weather. In fact, one occasionally finds them in the strangest places, although it is very unusual to see a trailer on such roads.

To complete this discussion, I need to convey a definition of *smaller RV* and *larger RV* as these terms will be used frequently throughout the book. Motorcycles, sport-utility vehicles, vans, and pickup trucks with low, shell-type campers clearly fall into the former group. Most single-purpose motor homes and trailers are clearly in the latter. My early travels in Baja used a 3/4-ton pickup truck with a powerful 454-cubic-inch engine and equipped with a 8-foot cab-over camper. Such an arrangement falls midway between the small and large RV groups.

In the past I frequently used this pickup-camper combination on secondary and unimproved dirt

Baja offers a variety of camping conditions. For those who like lots of company, there are many beaches like this one at Caleta San Lucas where campers and their boats line the shore. Photo BW.

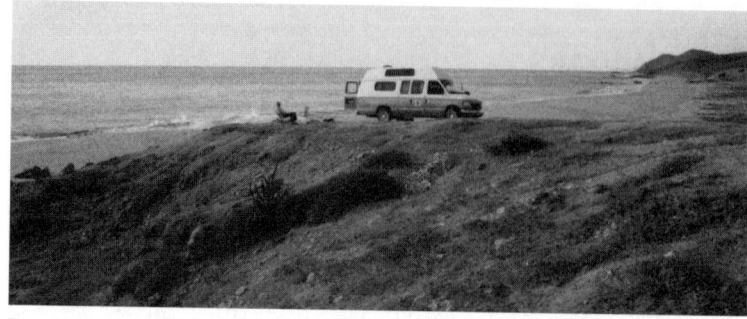

For those who like a little more space, there are many places like this isolated spot at the north end of the El Migrino Loop (See Chapter 25) only a few hundred yards from Highway 19. Photo BW.

roads but occasionally found myself in places where I wish I had not ventured, due primarily to the top-heaviness of the camper. I simply could not drive over many other unimproved roads which I wanted to explore. For these reasons I switched to a lightweight shell-type camper. This allowed travel almost everywhere where I could enjoy camping in secluded settings. Obviously creature comforts are minimal and when I have to stay at a trailer court I am ill at ease sitting on my tailgate while large motor homes tower over me on either side. Finally I have moved to a custom van camper to secure an upgrade in creature comforts (It is shown in the photo of the El Migrino Loop in this chapter). These comments clearly illustrate the decision you need to make between <u>accessibility</u> or <u>accommodations</u> for camping in Baja.

The above remarks relate to those vehicles our society has come to refer to as Recreation Vehicles or RVs. They usually contain some form of on board sleeping accommodations. Obviously many people travel to Baja for recreational purposes in other types of vehicles. Prominent among these are motorcycles and bicycles. Material concerning both of these is contained at the end of this chapter.

RV PARKS AND CAMPING AREAS

MAP AND TABLES -- A four-page-long table in this chapter lists the principal RV parks and camping areas in Baja. Their locations are shown in an accompanying map. (Most are also shown on larger scale maps in PART III THE GRAND TOUR.) The site numbers on the map correspond to those in the table. For those desiring additional information on these areas, I strongly recommend Fred and Gloria Jones' *Baja Camping* book. It provides information in much greater detail than space allows here in *The Magnificent Peninsula*.

CHANGING TIMES -- There were almost no RV parks in Baja for the first few years after the completion of the Transpenisular Highway in 1973. It was a glorious era of camping for both tenters and those with larger RVs. One could simply pull up near the beach at many places along the highway and do one's thing, which of course included substantially degrading the area's sanitary conditions. Those days are largely gone if you have a larger RV and don't wish to travel on the back roads. There are still many *Glory Days* beach camping spots but you must travel farther off the highway, usually using smaller vehicles.

Most of the good places near the highway are now occupied by (1) developed RV parks, or (2) camping areas. These two types of facilities are considered separately below.

RV PARKS -- In Baja, the term *RV park* applies to several types of facilities. These are:

1. — Permanent mobile home subdivisions. Many of these are decades old. They lie along the Sea of Cortez from the San Felipe area south to Puertecitos, and along the Pacific coast from Tijuana south to La Jolla. In these places North Americans have leased a small site and moved in a recreation vehicle, usually adding a roof of some kind along with a variety of other attached structures. The result has usually been a community that is considerably less than luxurious. In most cases, the structures are now permanent. These are de facto recreation-vehicle second-home tracts.

In more recent years, similar places have developed farther south in Mulege, Puerto Escondido, Los Barriles, Cabo San Lucas and Todos Santos. Some of these developments are more pleasing to the eye than those in the north. Most started out as transient parks and gradually converted to all permanent residents. Where there is a mixture of permanent and transient sites, the better spots usually go to the permanent people. This arrangement best serves the economic interests of the land owner. Unfortunately the result is that the best properties are occupied most of the time by vacant improvements while the current tour-

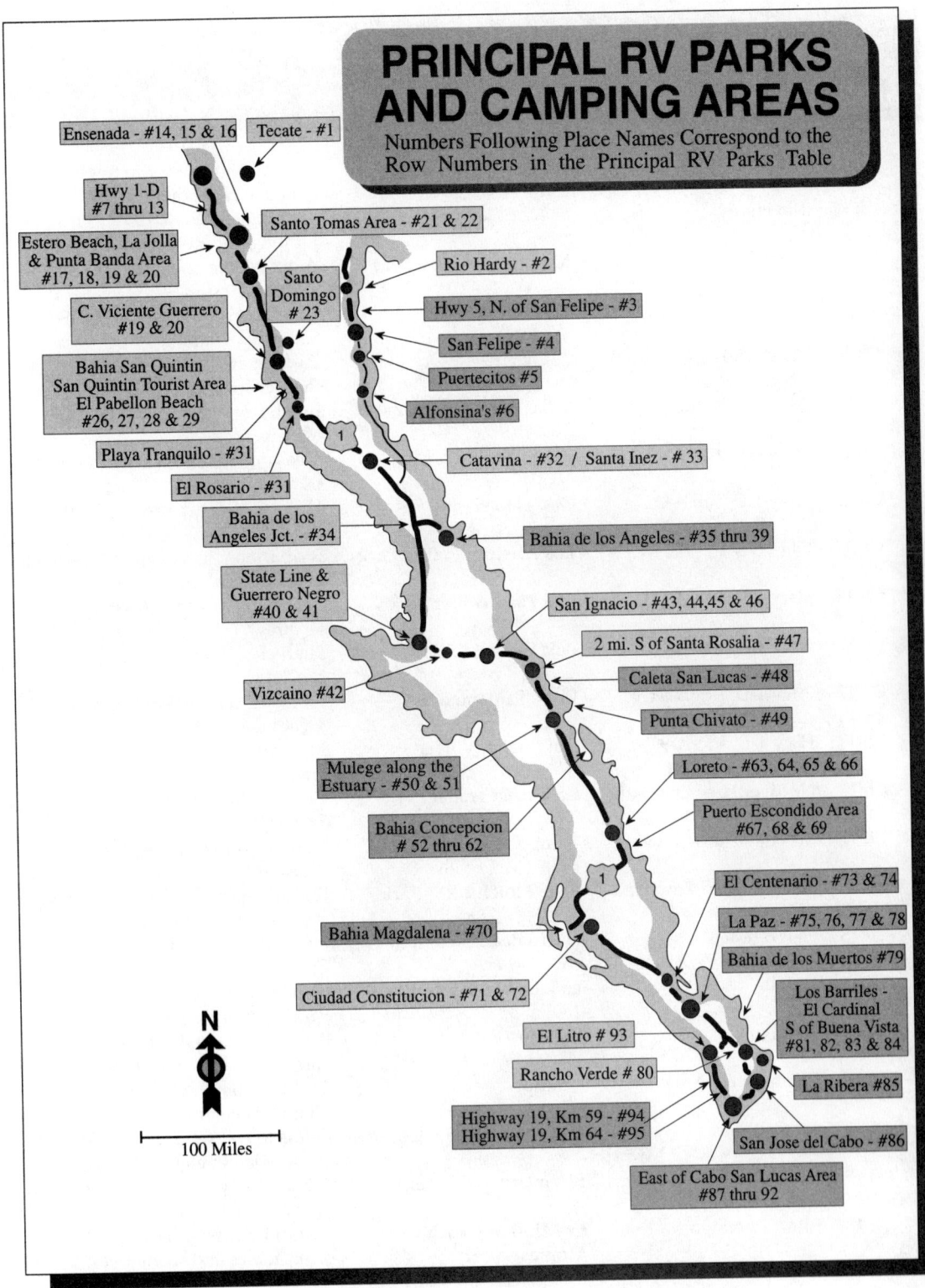

PRINCIPAL RV PARKS AND CAMPING AREAS

Numbers Following Place Names Correspond to the Row Numbers in the Principal RV Parks Table

Ensenada - #14, 15 & 16

Tecate - #1

Hwy 1-D #7 thru 13

Santo Tomas Area - #21 & 22

Estero Beach, La Jolla & Punta Banda Area #17, 18, 19 & 20

Santo Domingo # 23

Rio Hardy - #2

Hwy 5, N. of San Felipe - #3

C. Viciente Guerrero #19 & 20

San Felipe - #4

Puertecitos - #5

Bahia San Quintin San Quintin Tourist Area El Pabellon Beach #26, 27, 28 & 29

Alfonsina's #6

Playa Tranquilo - #31

Catavina - #32 / Santa Inez - # 33

El Rosario - #31

Bahia de los Angeles Jct. - #34

Bahia de los Angeles - #35 thru 39

State Line & Guerrero Negro #40 & 41

San Ignacio - #43, 44,45 & 46

2 mi. S of Santa Rosalia - #47

Vizcaino #42

Caleta San Lucas - #48

Punta Chivato - #49

Mulege along the Estuary - #50 & 51

Loreto - #63, 64, 65 & 66

Puerto Escondido Area #67, 68 & 69

Bahia Concepcion # 52 thru 62

El Centenario - #73 & 74

Bahia Magdalena - #70

La Paz - #75, 76, 77 & 78

Bahia de los Muertos #79

Ciudad Constitucion - #71 & 72

Los Barriles - El Cardinal S of Buena Vista #81, 82, 83 & 84

El Litro # 93

Rancho Verde # 80

La Ribera #85

Highway 19, Km 59 - #94 Highway 19, Km 64 - #95

San Jose del Cabo - #86

East of Cabo San Lucas Area #87 thru 92

N

100 Miles

PRINCIPAL RV PARKS & CAMPING AREAS
* Indicates Full Hookups

No	Ch	Location	Name	Comments
1	Ch 14	13 miles E of Tecate	**Rancho Ojai RV Park**	100 yds N of Hwy 2 in trees & part of active cattle ranch. Pleasant.*
2	Ch 15	Rio Hardy	Several Campos	Used mostly as camps for bird hunting and Rio Hardy fishing.
3	Ch 15	Hwy 5, N of San Felipe	Many Campos on Beach	A mixed bag of beach camping and permanent sites.
4	Ch 15	San Felipe	12 Trailer Courts	11 in town, 1 south of town. See San Felipe map.*
5	Ch 15	Puertecitos	Puertecitos Resort	Parking areas adjoining the Puertecitos Motel.
6	Ch 15	Alfonsina's Village	Villas Mar de Cortez	Beach front palapa area near new airstrip.
7	Ch 17	Hwy 1-D, Km A-22	KOA Trailer Park	Pleasant hillside location. Lots of transient spaces.*
8	Ch 17	Hwy 1-D, Km A-25	Oasis Hotel - RV Resort	High-class & expensive. On the beach.*
9	Ch 17	Old Hwy 1	**Los Alistros Trailer Park**	RV parking. Great views overlooking beach but minimum facilities.
10	Ch 17	Hwy 1-D, Km A-71	Mal Paso Trailer Park	Parking on beach but with poor facilites.*
11	Ch 17	Hwy 1-D, Km A-72	Baja Seasons	High-class & expensive. On the beach.*
12	Ch 17	Hwy 1-D, Km A-94	Playa Saldamando	A steep road leads to sites with great views of the Pacific.
13	Ch 17	Hwy 1-D, Km A-99	San Miguel Village	Minimum faciltity parking on level area near beach.
14	Ch 17	North edge of Ensenada	California Trailer Park	Good park, Part of California Trailer Park and Motel.*
15	Ch 17	Ensenada, downtown	Campo Playa	Only court in downtown Ensenada. Pleasant.*
16	Ch 18	South edge of Ensenada	Joker Hotel & RV Park	Pleasant park along the highway adjoining the motel.
17	Ch 18	Estero Beach	Estero Beach Resort	First-class court adjoining hotel. On lagoon near ocean.*
18	Ch 18	La Jolla	La Jolla Beach Camp	Permanent leased sites but with parking area for transients.
19	Ch 18	La Jolla	Villarino RV Park	Permanent leased sites but with parking area for transients.
20	Ch 18	Punta Banda Area	4 camps	See Punta Banda Area Map. Minimum facility camps.
21	Ch 18	Santo Tomas	El Palomar Trailer Court	Caters to weekend groups. Pleasant spot in olive grove.*
22	Ch 18	Ejido Urnapan	**Ejido Urnapan Camp**	Adjoins Hwy 1. Community camp under live oak trees.
23	Ch 18	Santo Domingo	**La Mission Rancho Montes**	Pleasant camp with two pools, picnic tables and shade trees.

PRINCIPAL RV PARKS & CAMPING AREAS
* Indicates Full Hookups

No	Ch	Location	Name	Comments
24	Ch 18	C. Vicente Guerrero	Don Pepes	Restaurant. A mixture of permanent and transient sites.*
25	Ch 18	C. Vicente Guerrero	Posada Don Diego	Restaurant. A large area used as a stopover by caravans.*
26	Ch 19	Bahia San Quintin	Old Mill Motel	Large area next to the Old Mill Motel.*
27	Ch 19	Bahia San Quintin	Muelle Viego	On bluff overlooking the bay. Pleasant - minimum facilities.
28	Ch 19	San Quintin Tourist Area	Rancho Cielito Lindo Mtl.	Poor facilties near beach. Better park adjoining motel.
29	Ch 19	El Pabellon Beach	El Pabellon	Minimum facility area on the beach.*
30	Ch 19	Hwy 1 at Pla.Tranquilo	**Playa Tranquilo**	On bluff overlooking cobble beach. Being developed 1997.
31	Ch 19	El Rosario	Sinai Motel	A simple parking area behind the Sinai Motel in town.*
32	Ch 19	Catavina	Government Court	A pleasant, safe, landscaped place to park but no facilities.
33	Ch 19	Santa Ines near Cativina	Rancho Santa Ines	A cleared area for parking near small motel and cafe.
34	Ch 19	Bahia de los Angeles Jct.	Government Court	A pleasant, safe, landscaped place to park but no facilities.
35	Ch 19	Bahia de los Angeles	Villa Vitta RV Court	Unaesthetic court (no vegetation) but on the beach.*
36	Ch 19	Bahia de los Angeles	Guillermo's Trailer Court	Unaesthetic court (no vegetation) but on the beach.*
37	Ch 19	Bahia de los Angeles	Brisa Marina RV Park	Old government park near beach. No facilities.
38	Ch 19	Bahia de los Angeles	Tony Resendiz	Adjoining #37. On the shore of Bahia de los Angeles
39	Ch 19	Bahia de los Angeles	Playa la Gringa	At Punta la Gringa north of Bahia de los Angeles village.
40	Ch 20	State Line	Government Court	A pleasant, safe, landscaped place to park. Modest facilities.*
41	Ch 20	Guerrero Negro	Serveral courts in town	Parking areas adjoining motels N-side of highway into town.*
42	Ch 20	Vizcaino	Kaadekaman	Court under development adjoining Highway 1.*
43	Ch 20	San Ignacio	Government Court	A landscaped parking area. Modest facilities. Near PEMEX.
44	Ch 20	San Ignacio	**Don Chon's Camping**	Pleasant parking area in palms adjoining a pond on road into town.
45	Ch 20	San Ignacio	Manual Quezada RV	Pleasant parking area in palms on road into town.
46	Ch 20	San Ignacio	El Padrino RV Park	Pleasant park in palms on road into town.*

PRINCIPAL RV PARKS & CAMPING AREAS
* Indicates Full Hookups

No	Ch	Location	Name	Comments
47	Ch 21	2 mi. S of Santa Rosalia	RV Park Las Palmas	Well landscaped park along highway with small restaurant.*
48	Ch 21	Caleta San Lucas	San Lucas RV Park	Little landscaping but directly on the water.*
49	Ch 21	Punta Chivato	Punta Chivato Resort	On beach east of the Punta Chivato Hotel.
50	Ch 21	Mulege along the estuary	Orchard Vacation Village	Pleasant court in palms between highway and the estuary.*
51	Ch 21	Mulege along the estuary	Maria Isabel Court	Pleasant court in palms between highway and the estuary.*
52	Ch 21	Bahia Concepcion	Playa Punta Arena	RV parking directly on the beach. No hookups.
53	Ch 21	Bahia Concepcion	Los Naranjos	RV parking directly on the beach. No hookups.
54	Ch 21	Bahia Concepcion	Playa Santispac	RV parking directly on the beach. Restaurant - no hookups.
55	Ch 21	Bahia Concepcion	Posada Concepcion	A few transient sites adjoining a RV subdivision.*
56	Ch 21	Bahia Concepcion	Los Cocos	RV parking directly on the beach. No hookups.
57	Ch 21	Bahia Concepcion	La Burra	RV parking directly on the beach. No hookups.
58	Ch 21	Bahia Concepcion	Playa El Coyote	RV parking directly on the beach. No hookups.
59	Ch 21	Bahia Concepcion	Playa Buenaventura	Nice court and palapas directly on the beach. Restaurant.*
60	Ch 21	Bahia Concepcion	El Requeson	RV parking directly on the beach. No hookups.
61	Ch 21	Bahia Concepcion	Playa la Perla	RV parking directly on the beach. No hookups.
62	Ch 21	Bahia Concepcion	Playa Armenta	RV parking directly on the beach. No hookups.
63	Ch 21	Loreto	Loreto Shores Villas	Pleasant court among many palms directly on the water.*
64	Ch 21	Loreto	Loremar RV Park	Little landscaping, directly on the water.*
65	Ch 21	Loreto	Villas de Loreto RV Park	Well landscaped area behind the Villas de Loreto Hotel.*
66	Ch 21	Loreto	El Moro RV Park	Poorly landscaped area in center of town.*
67	Ch 22	N. of Puerto Escondido	El Juncalito	RV parking directly on the beach. No hookups. (Popular)
68	Ch 22	Puerto Escondido	Tripui RV Resort	Small transient area next to permanent sites in RV Resort.*
69	Ch 22	S. of Puerto Escondido	Ligui (Ensenada Blanca)	RV parking directly on the beach. No hookups.
70	Ch 22	Bahia Magdalena	SE of San Carlos, No name	RV parking directly on the beach. No hookups.

PRINCIPAL RV PARKS & CAMPING AREAS
* Indicates Full Hookups

No	Ch	Location	Name	Comments
71	Ch 22	Ciudad Constitiucion	Manfred's RV Trailer Park	Nicely landscaped park with Austrian restaurant.*
72	Ch 22	Ciudad Constitiucion	Camperstre La Pila	Parking area near grassy pool area adjoining working farm.
73	Ch 22	El Centenario	City View RV Park	An old government court with desert plants.*
74	Ch 22	El Centenario	Oasis de Aripes	A pleasant court on the water 10 miles NW of La Paz.*
75	Ch 22	La Paz	Casa Blanca Trailer Park	A pleasant court with pool on the hwy entering La Paz.*
76	Ch 22	La Paz	El Cardon	A pleasant court with pool on the hwy entering La Paz.*
77	Ch 22	La Paz	Aguamarina Trailer Court	A pleasant court with pool in residential area of La Paz.*
78	Ch 22	La Paz	La Paz Trailer Court	A pleasant court with pool in residential area of La Paz.*
79	Ch 23	Bahia de los Muertos	No Name	RV parking overlooking the beach. No hookups.
80	Ch 23	Hwy 1 N of San Bartolo	**Rancho Verde**	A pleasant court in Arid Tropical Forest.*
81	Ch 23	Los Barriles	Martin Verdugos	Very good shaded park on the beach.*
82	Ch 23	Los Barriles	Juanito's Garden	Fair park across road from the beach.*
83	Ch 23	El Cardonal	El Cardonal Resort	Park on bluff overlooking the sea. Restaurant.*
84	Ch 23	South of Buena Vista	Capilla Trailer Court	Good park on the beach in rural area.*
85	Ch 23	La Ribera	La Ribera Trailer Court	Pleasant court in mango orchard. Short walk to the beach.*
86	Ch 24	San Jose del Cabo	Brisa del Mar	Pleasant court, pool, restaurant on the beach.*
87	Ch 24	East of Cabo San Lucas	Villa Serena	Near water with fine view of the Cape. Pool, etc.*
88	Ch 24	Edge of Cabo San Lucas	Vista Bonita	On the Hwy entering town from the E. Not finished in 1997.
89	Ch 24	Edge of Cabo San Lucas	El Arco	On the Hwy entering town from the E. Pool, etc.*
90	Ch 24	Edge of Cabo San Lucas	Cabo Cielo (closed 1997)	On the Hwy entering town from the E. Pool, etc.*
91	Ch 24	Edge of Cabo San Lucas	Vagabundos del Mar	On the Hwy entering town from the E. Pool, etc.*
92	Ch 24	Edge of Cabo San Lucas	Club Cabo	A small park behind the Vagabundos del Mar. Pool*
93	Ch 25	Town of Todos Santos	**El Litro RV Park**	Under development 1997.
94	Ch 25	Highway 19, Km 59	San Pedrito RV Park	Good park on fine beach. Pool in palm grove.*
95	Ch 25	Highway 19, Km 64	Government Court	On fine beach. Desert landscping

The Complete Guide
BAJA CAMPING

The Jones' book provides 288-pages (5 1/4 x 8 1/2) of detailed information concerning Baja's RV parks and camping areas. Included are data on camping fees, number of units, restroom facilities, access directions and notes on each areas good and bad points. Personal comments by the author's concerning their many years of traveling in Baja are also included.

Fred and Gloria are longtime members of the Vagabundos del Mar Travel Club. Fred is currently its Excutive Vice President and Editor of the club's monthly newsletter.

By Fred & Gloria Jones

Get your copy from the BAJA BOOKSHELF in the Appendix

ist has difficulty finding a nice place to stay. This type of RV park is not shown on this chapters map and tables nor are they identified in PART III, THE GRAND TOUR. Many are covered in Fred and Gloria Jones' *Baja Camping* book noted earlier in this chapter.

2. — During the mid-1970s the Mexican government built nine trailer courts at various places. They were nicely landscaped with desert vegetation and were enclosed with chain-link fences. Water lines were enclosed in concrete structures that made these parks look like grave yards. There were large wooden restroom buildings. Most of these parks were promptly abandoned. Today, many of them are maintained on a hit-and-miss basis by local Mexicans who often live in the restroom buildings. These parks are referred to as "Government Camps" in the *Principal RV Parks and Camping Areas* Tables. Additional such parks are located at San Agustin NW of Cativina and at the south end of Bahia Concepcion. They are usually closed.

3. — Over the years, a sizeable number of additional RV parks have been constructed throughout Baja so that travelers are never far from a place to stay. They range in quality from super deluxe to scroungy, with most falling some where in the middle of this range. Our 1997 survey found six new parks all of them pleasant places in pleasing locations. Their names are shown in **Bold Type** in the *Principal RV Parks and Camping Areas* Tables.

CAMPING AREAS -- One of Baja's most popular tourist regions lies along the eastern shore of Bahia Concepcion south of Mulege (see Chapter 21). In this area are located several beaches that become lined with recreation vehicles each winter season. There are few facilities except rather primitive pit toilets and trash barrels. But the RV people love them because everybody gets to park directly on the beach and the camping fee is low. I am categorizing these areas as Camping Areas as, in spite of their popularity, they fall below the development standards most people expect in an RV park. They are numbers 52 through 62 on the Tables. There are similar places at other locations (numbers 67, 69, & 79).

WHERE DO I STAY? -- RV parks, deluxe or scroungy, are not among my favorite places. I have been known to refer to them as "Parking lots with sewers." If you find me in one in the United States or Canada you will know I am desperate and could not reach a national, state or local public campground that offers a little elbow-room. In Baja, some RV parks are really very nice, but I am an isolationist and seek out a place under a tree away from the crowds. The sound of a generator in one of those large RVs with the television running is, shall we say, disturbing. So where do I stay in Baja? My list is a secret, so I will disclose it only with the explicit understanding that you will not share it with others. We must keep it a secret. Knowing that you are honorable people, here it is. The numbers are those on the *Principal RV Parks and Camping Areas Tables*. Some are not on the table. Each of these places is noted in the Index at the back of this book so you can look them up if necessary. Remember, don't tell any body else!

1 - #12. Playa Saldamando. Great views of the Pacific.
2 - #20. One of the Ejido camps overlooking the Pacific.
3 - #27. Muelle Viejo. Most of the gringos stay at the

Old Mill.

4 - #33. Rancho Santa Inez.

5 - El Tomatal. Under a few palm trees about 100 yards from the beach

6 - San Ignacio. The place by the pond used by the locals as a swimming hole.

7 - Under a couple of Acacia trees east of the abandoned government RV park at the south end of Bahia Concepcion.

8 - #69. Ligui. There is a little hill 100 yards east of the town of Ensenada Blanca with a great view of the water. Everybody else wants to be on the beach. So let them.

9 - #79. Bahia de los Muertos on the floor of the old warehouse. Everybody else is over by the beach.

10 - El Migrino Loop north of Cabo San Lucas.

BACK COUNTRY CAMPING

By the term *camping*, I am here referring to staying overnight in a natural setting with the use of tents or minimum facility vehicles such as vans and pickup trucks with camper shells.

If one visits Baja's main RV parks and beaches it is easy to conclude that the camper is now far outnumbered by the owners of larger RVs. But one still sees many smaller rigs on the highways indicating that there are still many true campers around hiding out in the lesser known and harder to reach areas. The balance of this chapter is dedicated to these people.

If you are a veteran camper you will know that in most places north of the border you are not permitted to camp because you are on private land or are restricted to developed sites on public lands. In the latter areas, you will be accustomed to graceful loop roads and parking spurs all neatly lined with barriers to keep you in your place. These facilities come complete with camp tables, stoves, restrooms, and a sign, or an attendant at the gate who will tell you in great detail the rules of the camp and how to pay your fee. In Baja, forget all that. Camping here is a unique experience and the rules are quite simple. They are: (1) find campsite, (2) camp.

Much of the land in Mexico is federally owned, and in all cases the shoreline is open to the public. Even where the land is privately owned, no one will bother you unless you are in their front yard. Exceptions are the cities and towns and the waterfront area between San Jose del Cabo and Cabo San Lucas. In the latter place the beaches themselves are open to the public but camping is no longer possible. In other places, unless there is some obvious reason why you should not camp, you are free to do so. If someone is authorized to charge a fee, they will seek you out.

I have frequently camped in close proximity to remote seaside fish camps. One waves at the fishermen on the way in and out, but unless I initiate it, there is usually no other contact. If someone does come by, it is simply out of curiosity and to say hello. Travelers from north of the border may expect to be told "you are on private property, get out." I have never had this happen.

Campgrounds north of the border are almost always built some distance from the feature you came to see. Camping at the edge of the stream, on the beach, or at the rim of the canyon is next to impossible. Much of this practice is justifiable, but I am also convinced that campground planners take great pleasure in separating the public from what they came to enjoy. In Baja, you may camp as near as you like to the shoreline. You may need plenty of sea water for dish washing and the sensible camper will not expend excess energy in carrying it too far.

Beach camping at Santispac on Bahia Coyote. It is one of the most heavily used beaches in Baja as it directly adjoins Highway 1 and is used as a overnight stopover point. Photo JW.

Camping on the sand spit at El Requeson on the west shore of Bahia Concepcion.

On a recent trip to Baja's Pacific shore, I pulled my camper to within 10 feet of the edge of a cliff overlooking the surf pounding over a rock-lined coast. There were majestic views for 20 miles in both directions. Baja is one of the few places in North America where you can camp in this manner. I believe it is this freedom to spend time in such sites, free from the restraints placed on us by more civilized portions of our continent, that make travelers to Baja return again and again. On the same trip I met a Canadian lady camping in this type of isolated area. She was obviously enthralled by Baja. I asked her why. She said, "I really don't know, there's just something about the place!"

There are still countless uncrowded shoreside camping sites on the peninsula, but many are accessible only by secondary and lower standard dirt roads. Thus, as in many parts of the world, true campers must search out the lesser known and harder to access spots to fill their needs.

NOTE -- During our 1995 Baja survey we encountered the Canadian owner of a new RV Park. In his pitch to encourage me to advertize his facility he noted that it is contrary to Mexican law to camp on the beach. Perhaps he is correct, but it is a law that is enforced in the breach.

THE LAST 100 YARDS

What follows is a discussion of the fine art of getting stuck in the sand, followed by some suggestions on how to reverse the process. As noted above, many camping spots are undeveloped, and foremost among

the features that are missing are adequate roads for the last few yards to that spot that you are simply in love with only 20 feet from the ocean. In many places, you will be driving on the natural surface that has not been compacted adequately to support a vehicle. The problem is compounded by the fact that shoreline camping spots will usually be at a lower elevation than the main road. Thus, you drive downhill to your campsite but must return uphill. Spin-outs in loose sand are a frequent result, followed by "Henry, I told you this would happen."

Most people camp in one location for many days, weeks or even months, so the pain of extracting one's vehicle from a place that has provided so much pleasure may be a small price to pay. Many veterans know full well what will happen and are well versed in the extraction process.

The prudent traveler to Baja's beaches will carry a shovel and tow chain or nylon line. Others are equipped with several buckets for carrying sea water to wet down the surface on which the drive wheels will travel. This should be done prior to moving a vehicle; however, the best method of which I am aware is to let some, or nearly all, of the air out of your tires. The increase in traction is miraculous. For this reason, don't travel in Baja without some means of pumping up your tires after returning to firmer ground. Most U.S. auto parts stores carry small, inexpensive tire pumps that operate by plugging into your vehicle cigarette lighter. Others function from engine compression and require the temporary removal of one spark plug. Don't leave home without one.

Obviously use of four-wheel-drive vehicles is the ultimate answer to the problem of "The Last 100 Yards," although sometimes even drivers of these vehicles overextend themselves and become mired down. Then one really has trouble.

CAMPFIRES

If you are expecting to hear that firewood is scarce in Baja you would be in error. As long as the land is covered with woody desert vegetation, there will be plenty of firewood. This is the situation in most of Baja. Unfortunately, the individual pieces of wood are small, and they will be well picked over near camping areas. The keys to success in gathering firewood in Baja are one or more large cloth or canvas sacks and a pair of gloves. Before you reach your camping site, stop near an area of heavy vegetation, wander through the desert, and fill up your sacks. Wear the gloves for protection from the ever-present thorns.

Many desert plants have dead branches near their bases, and the inside skeletal structure of dead cactus is excellent firewood. I have never had to use an axe in Baja. In most places, it's only a matter of a few minutes work to gather all the wood needed for several days. The pieces will be small, but they will be dry, full of energy, and easy to gather.

Finally, keep in mind that wildfires do occur in Baja. The brushy areas in the California Vegetative Region of northern Baja are as highly flammable as similar places in southern California in the United States. Deserts can also burn, and I have seen several large devastated areas in Baja where centuries will have to pass before revegetation occurs. PLEASE BE CAREFUL WITH FIRE.

MOTORCYCLES and BICYCLES

MOTORCYCLES -- Several months ago I was contacted by Bob Keough of Richland, Washington. He is a 62 year old retired scientist from the nuclear energy field who has made some 20 trips to Baja mostly on back roads utilizing dual purpose bikes. What transpired was his willingness to provide the following material concerning motorcycling in Baja. Much of it is in response to specific questions which I had posed to him. Bob lives at 1811 McPherson, Richland, WA 99352 and may be contacted at (509) 943-3507 or rkeo@3-cities.com.

How do Baja conditions fit with enjoying motorcycling? -- First, there are several ways to enjoy Baja on motorcycles. The street riders have no problems in Baja

as long as they keep to the paved roads and watch for the possibility of chuck holes. The common tourist complaint about Baja's narrow roads don't apply to motorcycles although many large trucks and RV's may want to have a bit more than half of the road. The hard core dirt bikers on their 2-stroke racing bikes can go just about anywhere there is a track as well as on some boring pavement if required. In between are the dual purpose bikers who are comfortable everywhere except the very worst of the trails. Riding on beaches is not common for the touring rider, even those on dirt bikes. It isn't a good idea for anyone because of the salt corrosion problem. Of course in northern beach communities like San Felipe, its a Way-Of-Life.

Dirt bikers enjoy bad roads and are bored by the graded and graveled roads that have replaced many of the old, natural-surface roads. A good dirt biker can go places a good four-wheeler can't. And bikes are a lot faster in the rough stuff, even when the riders are being careful. But the range is gas-limited and they can't carry a cooler of iced beer as can a jeep. Baja dirt riding is roughly equivalent to riding the logging roads in the western states in that there is very little "cow trail" or off road riding. Because of the spinney vegetation, it is imprudent to attempt cross country travel. There are still plenty of interesting back roads.

I would have to say that I ride in Baja because I love motorcycling, especially dirt biking, and I enjoy Mexico immensely. The two fit together very well. To get to Baja from the state of Washington I generally truck my bike down through Nevada to Calexico. I pass at least 500 miles of country that looks much like Baja

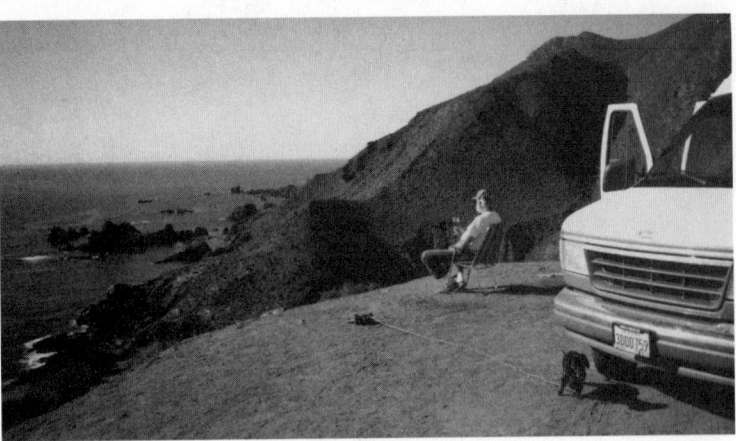

A great camping spot at one of the ejido camps near La Bufadora (See the *Punta Banda Area* map in Chapter 18). In view are some of the many rocks lying off Punta Banda. Photo BW.

but I never give a thought to riding there. It's just not the same.

<u>What about Mexican gasoline and gasoline supplies?</u> -- Most bikes seem to run just fine on Magna Sin gasoline (See *Repairs and Fuel* in Chapter 3) if they can use regular unleaded fuel in the United States. Fuel additives can be purchased in Mexico at auto-part stores if necessary although some would question their effectiveness. A few riders retard the spark advance and accept the reduction in power. The biggest problem for most bikers is carrying enough fuel. While some street bikes have a range of 300 miles, off road bikes typically have three gallon tanks which carry only enough fuel for 90 to 130 miles. Many bikers carry a gallon or so extra strapped on in one of those red plastic gas "cans" ($4.00). Some install oversize fuel tanks ($150-$250). I have seen riders with two, one gallon Clorox bottles of gas attached to their belts. Not a good idea! For a price, it seems you can almost always get gas from a farmer or fisherman if he has any. It also pays to have a siphon hose along.

<u>How many people take bikes to Baja?</u> -- I asked several local Mexicans about the number of motor-cycles that came through each year. South of Bahia San Luis Gonzaga, Coco (at Coco's Corner - See Chapter 15) estimated 1,000 bikes excluding those involved in races (some races have over a hundred). He said that most dirt bikers come in winter and spring but that in June-July there are quite a few Harley, BMW and other street bikes. I can't understand what these people are doing 40 miles from the pavement on a rough, gravel road in 100 degree weather. Looking for a cool beer I suppose. At Punta San Francicito, a hundred miles south, the owners of the "resort" say they get about 500 dirt bikes per year. Two days before we were there in April 1997 they had a pre-planned lunch visit by an organized tour of some 70 riders.

In Loreto, a gas station attendant said that while a lot of gringos were riding bikes, most brought them down in trucks or on trailers. He estimated two per day came into the station but felt that many riders bypass Loreto as a fueling stop. It appears that the bulk of bikes ridden as far south as Loreto are the standard, multi-cylinder, street bikes. It's interesting that the Mexicans hardly ever ride motorcycles, par-ticularly in Baja.

<u>Are there bike tours available as there are for RV owners?</u> The professional packaged tour is getting popular in Baja. Most of these operate in the northern half of the peninsula. They provide bikes, guides, hotels, meals, support trucks, everything for a few hundred dollars a day. I understand the tours are getting popular with Europeans and the Japanese market is regarded as a gold mine just waiting.

I normally talk to 10-15 "touring" bikers on an average trip. By "touring" I mean spending each night in a different place. Most are staying in motels and most have been to Baja before. They generally cite showers as a main reason for motels versus primitive camping. The La Pinta Hotels (See Chapter 6) apparently will allow camping on their property with use of showers although I haven't seen public showers in evidence. Could be the group rents one room for the shower access and the others sleep out-side. Dirt oriented riders have very limited carrying capacity for such luxuries as sleeping bags or tents. I camped a few times on my first trip (1971) but now it is easy to plan a trip around gas and room availabil-ity. I might note that most Baja bikers seem to be able to afford motels. My impression is that most bikers are rather affluent and choose not to burden them-selves with camping gear just so they can suffer sleeping on

Here a group of motorcyclists stops for gas at the PEMEX station near Tourist Row in Ensenada. Photo BW.

the ground all night. I would suggest that first timers plan staying at motels; especially if they are not on street bikes. Street bikers pulling trailers are not common in Mexico. Certainly a trailer would be an additional problem in dodging chuck holes.

<u>Have you had any problems with Baja's legendary Banditos or other crime problems?</u> -- I read of the Banditos on the internet and in AAA publications occasionally so I guess they are alive and well. However, it was my impression that they had all moved to the United States. I have never had a problem of any kind in Mexico. And I don't personally know of anyone who has. However, when traveling by cycle, your gear is rather exposed and could be a temptation, especially to kids. If practical, I park at restaurants, etc. where I can watch my bike. That's about it. What bothers me more than anything is the concern most Mexican business people have about theft of my property. I can't remember how many upscale motels/hotels have had me park in their lobby or patio. In Playa del Carmen last year we parked our Harleys in the hotel dining room at the manager's insistence.

<u>What about safety considerations?</u> -- It's downright dangerous to go into remote areas of Baja by oneself. It's impractical to carry enough water on a bike to

Two bicyclists heading south along Highway 1 in the Catavina Boulder Fields. Photo BW.

survive more than a single summer day if you get lost, injured or breakdown. Off road riders are prone to crashing (they do it too often to call it "accidental") and injuries are commonplace. Riders should slow down a bit and keep aware of the remoteness in Baja and the seriousness of a broken leg or similar accident in that environment.

Two high tech items useful to dirt bikers are: helmet mounted, 2-way radios for bike to bike communication. These allow two or more bikes to spread out to reduce riding in the leaders dust and while still keeping track of each other. GPS (global positioning system) navigators allow you to quickly find your location within less than a mile with an AAA map. These instruments are the size of a small phone and cost about $200. In contrast to cell phones, they work just about anywhere.

BICYCLES -- I have not observed many bicycles being used by tourists on Baja's highways but there are a few. And, during our 1997 survey we encountered a group of some 25 Canadians who were biking the entire peninsula in company with a supply truck. There are now adequate RV parks and motels along Highway 1 to allow most bikers to have a developed place to stay at the end of each days ride.

Man and his dog, such as they are. We took this photo at our camp on a shingle beach at Punta la Gringa to illustrate that there is almost nothing to mar one's solitude here on the shore of Bahia de los Angeles. Photo BW.

It would be my concern that the worst problem for bicyclists would be the narrowness of Baja's highways. There is not room enough for two motor vehicles and a bicycle at

Potty of Distinction

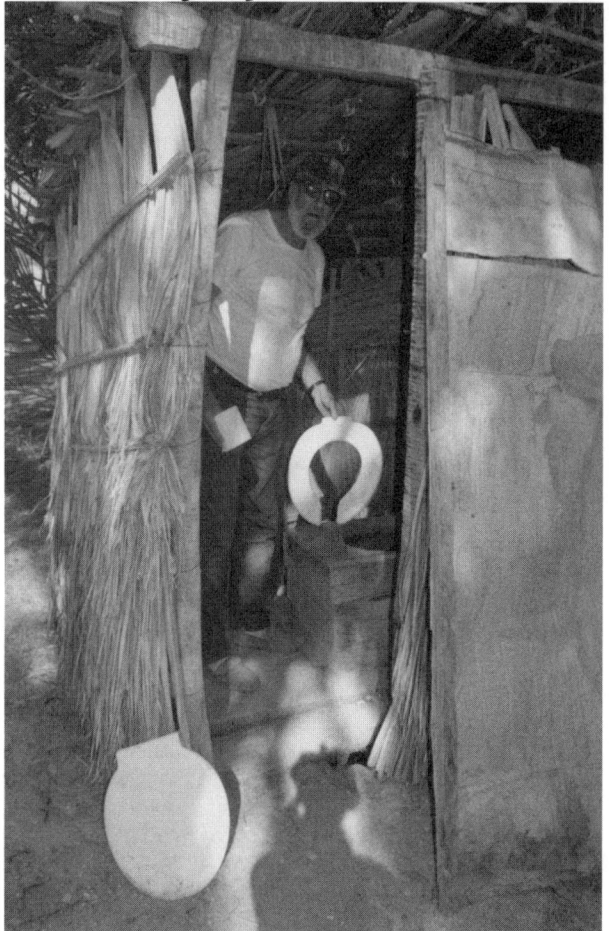

The RV parks in Baja offer a variety of restroom standards. Some are as nice as anything to be found north of the border. But, in this spot we found the two parts of the seat lid lying unattached on top of the hole and the door propped up against the wall. And, as I recall it, I almost fell through the floor. As we entered the camp the proprietor was drinking beer with his cronies. The fee was $3.00.

On our return trip we stayed at the same spot and escaped paying a fee as the proprietor was drinking beer elsewhere that day. $1.50 per night for such a delightful spot in the palms adjoining the pond is a steal. It was then that we discovered the camp's other restroom; the deluxe model. The entire top of the seat was covered with carpet which extended down the sides of the diminutive hole. I asked my daughter to take its photo. She declined. Photographers have high ethical standards for their work. So you will have to seek it out on your own. Photo BW.

the same point at the same time. Thus, bikers must have to frequently endure mini-traffic jams when two vehicles are approaching their position at the same time from opposite directions. It would be an unusual place where a biker could pull off the road and continue to move forward.

CULTURE SHOCK IN THE POTTY

I have always declined to report this item of interest, but now is the time. In many restrooms in Baja you will find an ominous looking waste basket sitting along side the toilet. In places frequented by gringo types there will be a hand printed sign asking that you place used paper in the basket (Mexicans know what the basket is for and don't need instructions). Do they mean newspapers you are reading? No, they mean toilet paper.

At one of Baja's better RV parks I asked the Canadian owner "Do they really mean that, and if so why?" He answered "I am a plumber and 95% of the time I was called to unplug a toilet it was the paper forming the blockage. Yes, they mean it." So, except in the better hotels, brace yourself for *potty basketball*. Two points if you hit the basket. Missing is a foul. No bankshots. There is one other exception. At Manfred's RV Park in Ciudad Constitucion we found different signs, each in English, Spanish and German. They read "Please flush used toilet paper down the toilet. Don't leave it outside." Any questions? Austrian bred Manfred will have no part of this disgusting practice. Lets hear it for Manfred!

CHAPTER 5
WATERSPORTS

I really do not exaggerate in telling you that Baja, and in particular the coast of the Sea of Cortez, is a paradise for watersports. This is especially true for windsurfers and the owners of small trailerable or car-top boats who are confronted at home with the bone-chilling temperatures and heavy swells of the Pacific Ocean off the United States and Canada. North of the border the use of small boats is limited almost exclusively to inland lakes, reservoirs, rivers, and protected ocean bays. In the Sea of Cortez deep-sea fishing and other watersports can be enjoyed in ocean waters that have mild temperatures and light swells.

BOATING

BAJA BOATER'S GUIDE — My interest in writing about Baja California started in 1983 when I circumnavigated the peninsula in my sailboat gathering data to assist in the revision of the out-of-print *Baja Sea Guide*. The first edition of the book you are reading, *The Magnificent Peninsula*, was written as an act of frustration while I waited for the *Sea Guide*'s author to prepare his new edition. Alas, it never appeared. I thus set about producing my own *Baja Boater's Guide*, having had my fill of joint endeavors.

The *Baja Boater's Guide* was designed to be by far the most comprehensive marine guide ever produced for the Baja peninsula. It evolved into a two volume production totaling 476 pages, with 178 charts and 455 photographs, most of them aerial views. Both volumes are still available in revised editions. I recommend them for the serious boater and for surfing enthusiasts and fishermen needing detailed information about Baja's coast. Both are available from the BAJA BOOKSHELF in the Appendix. They are further described a notice in this chapter. Because of the availability of these detailed guides, only a broad overview of boating is presented in this chapter.

BOAT CLASSIFICATION — It is important to understand the relationship of several different classes of boats to conditions in Baja. The message is that not all

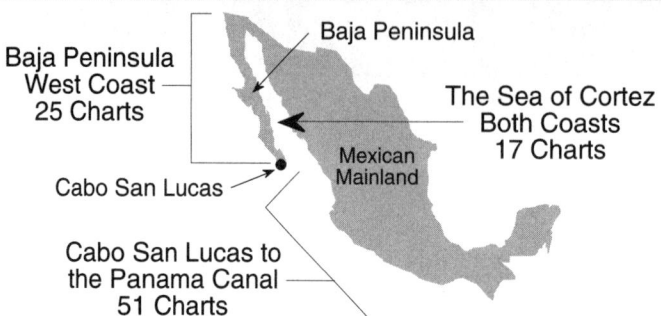

YACHTSMAN CHART BOOK
93 Charts For All of the Mexican West Coast

Baja Peninsula West Coast
25 Charts

Baja Peninsula

The Sea of Cortez
Both Coasts
17 Charts

Mexican Mainland

Cabo San Lucas

Cabo San Lucas to
the Panama Canal
51 Charts

An outstanding collection of U.S. Government nautical chart reproductions. These are identical to the original government charts except for reduced scale. Suitable for navigation.

The collection is printed in full color where the government charts contain color. Even the black and white pages have color "trimmings" making the overall product very attractive. A plastic spiral binding allows charts to lie flat for easy use. Size is 16" by 22 1/2" with a hard plastic cover. Good quality paper although not waterproof.

Shocked at the price. Don't be. The original government charts now sell for 14.95 each, if you can find them (many charts in this collection are not generally available). That's $14.95 x 93 = $1,390.35. (A former collection entitled ChartGuide Mexico West is now out-of-print.)

boats may be transported to, or used in Baja. Here are the details. (The four-boat classification system is my own creation. See BOAT CLASSIFICATION Table.)

BOAT CLASSIFICATION

1	Ocean-going sail and powerboats having the capabilities for travel by sea.	LONG RANGE Great experience. Travel almost anywhere.
2	Boats without long range ocean capabilities, but too big to trailer safely.	UNUSABLE IN BAJA
3	Heavy trailer boats that require a launching ramp to enter the water.	MEDIUM RANGE Sea access limited due to shortage of launching sites.
4	Light trailer or car-top boats which can be launched over the beach.	SHORT RANGE Maximum flexibility due to ease of launching.

CLASS 1 — Sail and power vessels that have the fuel capacity, crew capabilities, and design characteristics for ocean conditions can make the Baja Passage from San Diego around the peninsula's southern tip and into the Sea of Cortez. Hundreds make this trip every year. See the OCEAN-CRUISING Section in this chapter for further discussion concerning the use of such boats.

CLASS 2 — An unfortunate problem lies in the fact that the marinas of the United States and Canada are overflowing with boats that are either too small, have insufficient fuel capacity, or are under designed for the ocean passage. At the same time, they are too large to be easily trailered or launched under Baja conditions. The majority of such vessels are powerboats in the 20-to-35-foot cabin cruiser category. They should not be taken to Baja. Please read the material to follow concerning ocean-cruising and review the description of the Transpeninsular Highway if you are inclined to ignore this advice.

CLASS 3 — Two classes of boats (Classes 3 and 4) can be transported to Baja by highway. First are those that because of their weight must be floated from a trailer into the water by use of a launching ramp. There are now a sizeable number of places in Baja that have ramps but many of these have one or more shortcomings. (See BOAT LAUNCHING RAMPS Table in this chapter.)

Once in the water, these larger vessels enjoy distance and water condition capabilities greater than lightweight class 4 boats, so I don't discourage your taking them south. Simply keep in mind that they can only be launched at a limited number of locations and that you must face the risks of towing engendered by the narrowness of the Transpeninsular Highway.

CLASS 4 — Finally, there are those boats which are light enough to be manhandled over the beach. In most cases, this involves carrying the outboard motor separately. Inflatable rubber dinghies and lightweight aluminum boats in the 13-to-17-foot range make up the majority of this class. My observation is that the great majority are carried in or on top of vans or on pickup truck racks. A few are transported by trailer.

Various types of inflatable boats are also common and in the final analysis may be the best and safest way to enjoy the water.

SMALL BOATS — By small boats, I am referring to the class 3 and 4 vessels just described.

SMALL BOAT LAUNCHING — Since first publishing this book in 1986, the number of boat launching ramps in Baja has significantly increased. Details are shown in the BOAT LAUNCHING RAMPS Table in this chapter and much greater detail is available from Mike Bales' *Launch Ramps of Baja California* book available from the BAJA BOOKSHELF.

The ramps at about half of these locations have rough concrete surfaces which have rather obviously been poured by hand. A ready-mix concrete truck in Baja is not a common sight. Because of the difficulty in getting concrete to set after the tide comes in, some of these ramps do not extend far enough toward the water to be effective at low tide.

As previously noted, those boaters with craft that are light enough to be manhandled over the beach will be able to use their boats in far more places than those who require a ramp. Boats 18 feet and larger usually require a hard-surfaced ramp.

Other boaters abandon the boat-trailer method altogether and, after lowering their boat to the ground, maneuver it in and out of the water by hand or on various types of rollers. Also, rolling devices can be purchased that attach directly onto the hull of small boats. Many veteran Baja fishermen rely solely on lightweight 13-15 foot aluminum boats because of the ease of launching such craft over the beach.

SMALL BOAT CRUISING — I approach this subject with a considerable degree of trepidation, fearing that

BOAT LAUNCHING RAMPS

LOCATION		COMMENTS
General	Specific	
San Felipe	Ramps located at Ruben's RV Park - Motel el Cortez - Club de Pesca. See San Felipe Map Ch 15.	Ramps used only at high tide due to extreme fluctation of water level.
Puertecitos Area	Near north entrance to Puertecitos Cove & at the Papa Fernandez Resort some distance to the south. See map Ch 15.	Both are concrete ramps but they are usable only at high tides.
Ensenada	A concrete ramp near the sportfishing piers within the harbor. See Ensenada Map Ch 17.	Good concrete ramp but access may be constricted by new building construction.
Ensenada	Ramp is located within grounds of the Ensenada shipyard. See Ensenada Map in Ch 17.	Good contrete ramp used to haul sizeable commercial fishing boats. Inquire at the shipyard.
Estero Beach	Ramp is at the Estero Beach Hotel, 6 miles S of Ensenada. See Punta Banda Map in Ch 18.	Contrete ramp. After launching, boats must cross estero entrance bar to access the ocean.
La Jolla	2 ramps at La Jolla Beach RV camps 8 miles W of Maneadero. See Punta Banda Map Ch 18.	Directly on Pacific Ocean. Concrete ramps are unusable in windy weather or low tide.
La Bufadora	Near the head of the cove E of the La Bufadora blowhole. Punta Banda Map Ch 18.	Steep, concrete ramp leading to gravel beach. Constructed in bottom of a short, narrow arroyo.
Puerto Santo Tomas	In arroyo bottom at the W end of the fish camp. See Ch 18 Map.	A steep concrete ramp. Unusable when ocean swells are heavy. Ask for help at the nearby fish camp.
Puerto San Isidro	Concrete ramp is at the small fish camp & resort area N of Ejido Erendira. Ch 18 Map.	Ramp enters directly into the Pacific Ocean but the site is partially protected by a rocky reef.
San Quintin	There are two ramps located at the Old Mill Motel & the Pedregal subdivision. See San Quintin Area Map Ch 18.	Old Mill ramp is hard-packed natural surface plus new concrete ramp. It is widely used.
Bahia de los Angeles	3 neighboring concrete ramps run by hotels & RV parks. See Bahia de los Angeles Map Ch 19	Hotel VIlla VIta ramp built from a rock breakwater & reaches deeper water than the other two.
Campo Rene	Campo Rene resort on the shore of shallow Estero Coyote. See Punta Eugenia Area Map Ch 20.	A natural-surface (sand & shell) beach. Fishing inside the bay or access to the open Pacific.

Ramps shown on maps with this symbol. ▄▄▄▟.

what I write might encourage the use of small boats in waters beyond their capabilities. I am proceeding simply because the cruising of small class 3 and 4 boats in the Sea of Cortez is already a common practice. These adventures range from a simple overnight camping trip to extended voyages involving many weeks and hundreds of miles. Some utilize the heaviest possible trailer boats with on-board sleeping and cooking facilities. At the other extreme, lengthy voyages are undertaken in kayaks and small, centerboard sailboats not over 12 feet in length.

Few owners of ocean-cruisers would trade their vessels for such craft, but the little fellow does have some clear advantages over the bigger boats. Most small powerboats have a greater speed than the 4-to-8 knots of the average ocean-cruiser. They can thus traverse a considerable distance in a short time taking advan-

BOAT LAUNCHING RAMPS

LOCATION		COMMENTS
General	**Specific**	
Caleta San Lucas	Ramp is inside the grounds of the San Lucas RV Park. See Caleta San Lucas Map Ch 21.	A natural surface launch area, but well protected inside the cove at Caleta San Lucas.
Punta Chivato	200 yards NW of the Hotel Punta Chivato. 16 mile dirt road E from Hwy 1. See Ch 21 Map.	Rock & concrete ramp. The hotel staff will help out if a problem arises.
Mulege	3 ramps at RV parks & hotel on S side of estuary + ramp near lighthouse. Mulege Map Ch 21.	Concrete ramps (lighthouse ramp is packed sand). There is no water in river when tide is out.
Playa Buenaventura	Plays Buenaventura RV park on Bahia Concepcion. Km F-94 on Hwy 1. See Ch 21 Map.	A wide concrete ramp run by the RV park. Plenty of parking & easy approach.
Loreto	2 ramps. In breakwater lined harbor & on the open water at Las Palmas RV Resort (closed 1997). Loreto Map Ch 21.	Good concrete ramp. There is a large public parking area adjoining the breakwater lined harbor.
Puerto Escondido	At S end of inner harbor adjacent to the entrance channel. See Loreto-Puerto Escondido Area Map Ch 22.	Good concret ramp accessible by oiled hwy. One of the most heavily used ramps in Baja.
Bahia Magdalena	1 mile S of San Carlos on a Bahia Magdalena side lagoon. See San Carlos Map Ch 22.	A concrete ramp. Does not extend far enough at low tide & floods at high tide. try mid-tide.
La Paz	5 ramps. Fedepaz, Aquamarina RV, Marina de La Paz, Palmira Marina (2). La Paz Map Ch 22.	All are good concrete ramps leading into the quite waters of Canal de La Paz.
El Sargento	El Sargento is on a spur road off Hwy 286 E of La Paz. Ramp was reported to me by its owner. I have not seen it.	Reported to be a concrete ramp with nearby boat storage area.
Pichilingue	In small cove N of Puerto Pichilingue. Off Hwy 1, N of La Paz. See La Paz Area Map Ch 22.	Two good double concrete ramps on both sides of protected cove. South ramp at Baja Diving Service Marina.
Buena Vista Area	Over the beach launching at RV parks & hotels. See Los Barriles Buena Vista Area Map Ch 23.	Launch over the beach using 4x4 trucks owned by the RV parks & hotels.
Cabo San Lucas	Ramp is at the N end of the inner harbor next to the marina office.	A good concrete ramp operated by the marina. The former ramp at the south end of the harbor is no longer present.

Ramps shown on maps with this symbol.

tage of windless periods. During some months, the wind blows heavily during all but a few hours per day. Also, small shallow-draft boats can be easily hauled onto the beach almost anywhere if the weather kicks up, and they can be anchored in coves too small or shallow to offer protection to larger vessels. These advantages open up the potential of isolated camping in scores of charming and pristine hideaways.

For the very adventuresome, I need to note that some skippers of large trailer boats launch their vessels at Kino Bay on the Mexican mainland and make the 100-plus mile crossing of the Sea of Cortez to Bahia de los Angeles. Others launch at San Carlos and cross to Bahia Concepcion. The former trip is the safer as the Midriff Islands lie en route and offer wind and sea protection and potential

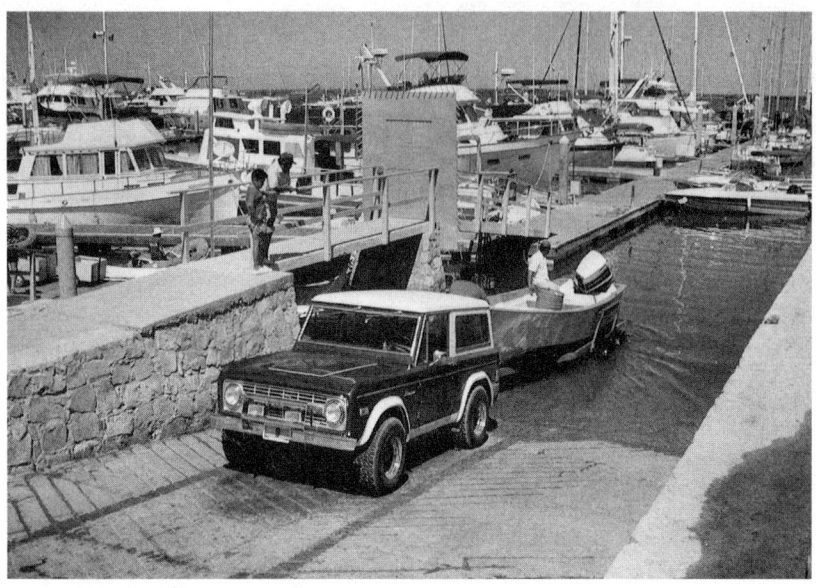

The modern Marina de La Paz at La Paz. Photo JW.

Cortez at right angles to these winds puts one's boat in the belly of the seas, a dangerous and uncomfortable exercise. Any of these trips should best be undertaken in April through July. The winter months are windy.

Boaters interested in small boat cruising should consider membership in the Vagabundos del Mar (see notice in Chapter 1 of this book). This club frequently organizes such events in the Sea of Cortez and at Bahia Magdalena on the Pacific side of the Peninsula.

stopping points. Also, increasing numbers of small boat owners are launching at the ramps in Bahia de los Angeles and cruising south along Baja's eastern coast. The return trip is made by hauling the boat north on the Transpeninsular Highway.

I strongly advise that no one undertake any of these ventures in a small boat without having tested it in sea conditions similar to those encountered in the Sea of Cortez. Keep in mind that the prevailing wind during the cruising season is from the north and blows down the long axis of the peninsula. Crossing the Sea of

OCEAN-CRUISING — Records at the office of the port captain at Cabo San Lucas show that over 1,000 foreign yachts check in at that port each year. Most of these vessels arrive from the United States and Canada and return north after the winter cruising season. Some overwinter at protected spots in the Sea of Cortez. A few are making longer passages to the South Pacific or are en route to or from the Panama Canal.

Most readers will not be fortunate enough to make an ocean voyage to Baja. Nevertheless, this section on ocean-cruising is presented for two reasons. First, many of you who visit Baja by land will see the cruisers' vessels at various locations. They are part of the Baja scene and you may be interested in their way of life. More importantly, this brief exposure might encourage some of you to seek an opportunity to make such a voyage. Twice in my life I simply quit work for four months and sailed south to sweep away the cranial cobwebs. These two trips motivated me to give up the office entrapment altogether

A heavy trailer boat (class 3) at a natural surface ramp. Very few boats larger than this one are towed to Baja. Photo JW.

BOATING IN BAJA

San Diego

Ensenada

San Felipe

Isla San Martin

Punta Banda

Enchanted Islands

Bahia de los Angeles

Bahia Kino

San Carlos (near Guaymas)

Isla Cedros

SEA OF CORTEZ

PACIFIC OCEAN

Bahia Tortugas

Asuncion

Abreojos

Bahia Concepcion

Puerto Escondido

La Paz & Islands

Los Muertos

N

100 Miles

CRUISER CONCENTRATION POINTS

MAIN ANCHORAGE POINTS FROM SAN DIEGO TO LA PAZ

BEST BOATING AREAS

THE BAJA PASSAGE

La Paz

Los Frailes

Bahia Magdalena

Cabo San Lucas

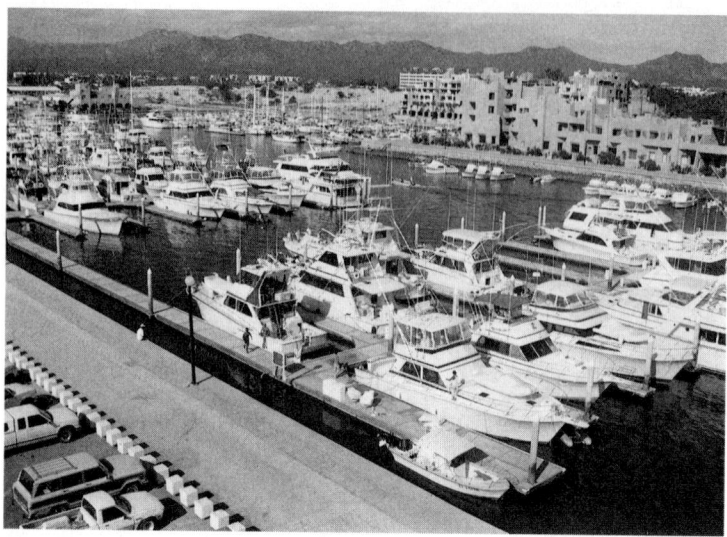

The Cabo San Lucas marina in the inner harbor. The harbor is now largely lined with hotels and condominiums as can be seen in the upper-right corner. Photo JW.

to Cabo San Lucas is 460 miles. For this reason the rule of thumb is that you should not make the Baja Passage in a powerboat that carries fuel for less than 600 miles. This allows a reasonable margin of safety for the passages to and from Bahia Tortugas. You frequently see large, gas-guzzling sportfishing boats with 55-gallon drums lashed in their cockpits to stretch their tankage for the passage. This fuel situation is one of the principal reasons why many mid-sized powerboats (class 2) should not be cruised to Baja. Those broad, open-to-the-sea aft cockpits are another. It is easy for a following sea to invite itself aboard.

Keep in mind that the prevailing wind is northwest along the west coast of Baja during the entire cruising season. With energy from both wind and swells coming from this direction, more or less parallel with the coast, the *downhill* voyage south is usually a delight. The return trip north is *uphill* into the wind and swells. Even sailboats make this return trip almost entirely under power. The pounding the boat and crew takes on the way north is the price to be paid for a sunny winter in Baja. Crews to make this uphill run are often in demand, and skippers with Captain Bligh tendencies may find themselves without help.

and return for two more voyages completely around the peninsula.

There is no set way to make the passage from San Diego to Cabo San Lucas. Some cruisers simply make their way many miles offshore where the winds are stronger, and don't touch land until rounding the cape. However, the majority stay closer to land following the *Baja Passage* shown on the BOATING IN BAJA Map.

The BOATING IN BAJA Map shows several points that provide the principal anchorages along the Baja Passage. At two, there is no possibility of obtaining fuel except from other boaters. At most of the other places, fuel can be obtained only by carrying it over the beach in cans if you can persuade the local inhabitants into giving up some of their own hard-earned supply. The only reliable fueling point, and the only one actually in the business of servicing the cruiser, is Bahia Tortugas. This well-protected port and community lies approximately midway between San Diego and Cabo San Lucas. Even here, you must anchor off the pier while fuel is gravity fed from barrels.

Bahia Tortugas is 340 miles south of San Diego. The journey from Bahia Tortugas

Ocean-cruisers, like the trailer court folks are often a gregarious breed. Thus, it is a bit ironic that people who have the transportation capabilities to visit anywhere they wish tend to congregate at certain ports once they reach the Sea of Cortez. These places are:

Cabo San Lucas, La Paz, Puerto Escondido, and across the Sea of Cortez at San Carlos.

The two last mentioned ports host large numbers of cruising boats whose owners have decided to spend the hot summer in Mexico. Both are well protected and are north of the tracks of a great majority of late summer hurricanes. Because of these intense tropical storms most sensible cruisers will not venture into southern Mexican waters during summer. The safe cruising season in Baja is from December to May.

Please consult the *Baja Boater's Guide* for more details on ocean-cruising. *Volume I, The Pacific Coast*, contains extensive background material on the subject.

MARINAS AND FUEL — Until about ten years ago the subject of marinas in Baja could have been covered in three words: "there aren't any." Now there are six locations in Baja that offer marina facilities. These are:

<u>LA SALINA</u> -- A new marina was being dredged from the coastal lowlands at Playa La Salina at Km A-72 between Tijuana and Ensenada during our 1997 survey.

<u>ENSENADA</u> — Three small marinas are in place at the northern end of the harbor. One of these is operated in conjunction with a small craft shipyard.

<u>CABO SAN LUCAS INNER HARBOR</u> — The entire inner harbor has been constructed by dredging. After a wait of over a decade an excellent marina was constructed about 1990. The harbor, well protected from winter weather and Pacific swells, provides easy access to the open sea.

<u>LA PAZ AREA</u> — Prior to 1985, there were no marinas in La Paz and obtaining fuel was not a simple task. There are now three fully functional marinas at La Paz with fuel docks and launching ramps. An additional marina lies at Pichilingue a few miles to the north. Many large vessels are now docked all year in this area. An additional dredged harbor has been completed at La Paz for several years but as yet it contains no marina facilities.

<u>PUERTO ESCONDIDO</u> — The area immediately inside the entrance channel to the natural harbor at Puerto Escondido has been dredged and reformed and a major resort area with hotels, condominiums, and marina awaits construction. Unfortunately it has been waiting now for over nine years

with no sign of anything new happening. In 1997 the only boating facility completed was the launching ramp.

<u>SANTA ROSALIA</u> — There is a small, but very adequate marina inside the breakwater lined harbor at this community. Plans call for it being enlarged in the future.

There are long range plans for marinas at many other places. In 1989 the Mexican Director of Tourism announced that marinas will be constructed every 150 miles along the Pacific coast of the country. By 1997 nothing new had occurred except at La Salina as noted above. My only recommendation is "Don't hold your breath."

It must be clear by now that obtaining fuel for your boat in Baja is not a simple matter of gliding alongside the nearest fuel dock. This is particularly true along Baja's Pacific coast. Therefore, with the exception of a few of the above noted marinas, the boater must obtain fuel from the land-based PEMEX stations and transport it to the launching site. Serious fishermen carry a drum of gas in the back of their pickups.

BEST BOATING AREAS — The BOATING IN BAJA Map in this chapter shows the locations of what I believe are the eight best boating areas in Baja California. See the *Baja Boater's Guide* for details.

OTHER WATERSPORTS

SURFING — I encountered a party of surfers during my 1995 field trip who complained that there was almost no published information about surfing in Baja. What is available provides the names of many surfing spots but was produced prior to 1980 and gives almost no directional material. It occurred to me that nearly all of these reported surfing locations are already included in the pages of *The Magnificent Peninsula*. All that would be needed to turn the book into a useful surfing tool would be to provide a linkage between the book's existing information and a listing of surfing spots. The accompanying SURFING AREA MAPS and SURFING AREA TABLE are designed to fill this need.

The SURFING AREA MAPS utilizes five charts -- greatly reduced and simplified -- taken from Volume I of the *Baja Boater's Guide* (See the BAJA BOOK-SHELF in the Appendix). In many cases this publica-

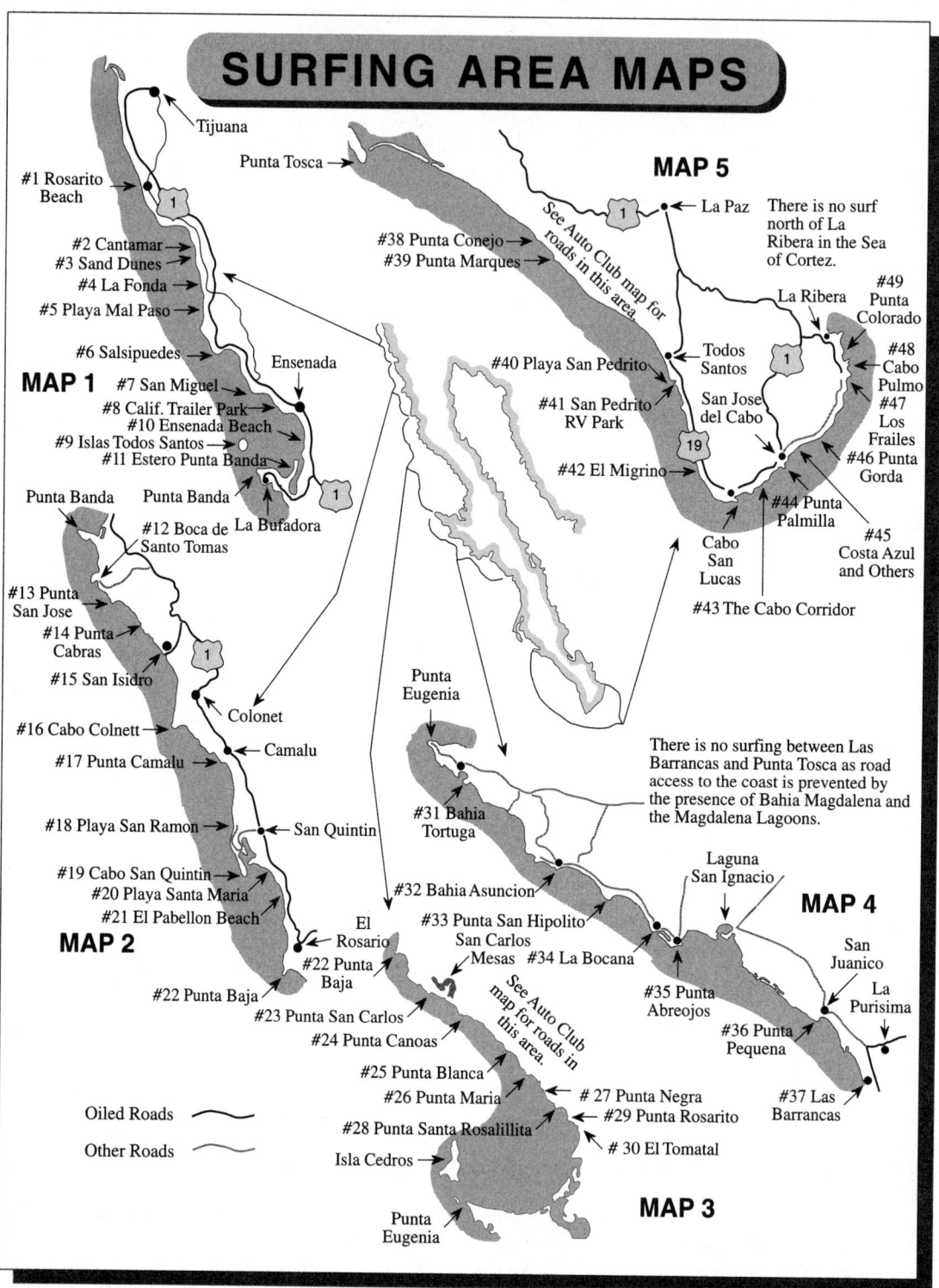

SURFING AREA MAPS

MAP 5

There is no surf north of La Ribera in the Sea of Cortez.

Tijuana

Punta Tosca

#1 Rosarito Beach

#2 Cantamar
#3 Sand Dunes
#4 La Fonda
#5 Playa Mal Paso

#6 Salsipuedes

Ensenada

MAP 1 #7 San Miguel
#8 Calif. Trailer Park
#10 Ensenada Beach
#9 Islas Todos Santos
#11 Estero Punta Banda

Punta Banda   Punta Banda
#12 Boca de   La Bufadora
Santo Tomas

#13 Punta San Jose

#14 Punta Cabras

#15 San Isidro

Colonet

#16 Cabo Colnett
#17 Punta Camalu   Camalu

#18 Playa San Ramon   San Quintin

#19 Cabo San Quintin
#20 Playa Santa Maria
#21 El Pabellon Beach

MAP 2

#22 Punta Baja

#22 Punta Baja

#23 Punta San Carlos
#24 Punta Canoas

#25 Punta Blanca
#26 Punta Maria
#28 Punta Santa Rosalillita

Isla Cedros

El Rosario
#22 Punta Baja

San Carlos Mesas

#33 Punta San Hipolito
#34 La Bocana

#32 Bahia Asuncion

#31 Bahia Tortuga

Punta Eugenia

See Auto Club map for roads in this area.

27 Punta Negra
#29 Punta Rosarito
30 El Tomatal

Punta Eugenia

MAP 3

#38 Punta Conejo
#39 Punta Marques

See Auto Club map for roads in this area.

La Paz

La Ribera   #49 Punta Colorado

#48 Cabo Pulmo

#47 Los Frailes

#46 Punta Gorda

#40 Playa San Pedrito   Todos Santos

#41 San Pedrito RV Park   San Jose del Cabo

#42 El Migrino

Cabo San Lucas

#44 Punta Palmilla

#45 Costa Azul and Others

#43 The Cabo Corridor

There is no surfing between Las Barrancas and Punta Tosca as road access to the coast is prevented by the presence of Bahia Magdalena and the Magdalena Lagoons.

Laguna San Ignacio

MAP 4

San Juanico

La Purisima

#35 Punta Abreojos

#36 Punta Pequena

#37 Las Barrancas

Oiled Roads

Other Roads

SURFING AREA TABLE
Numbers conform to those shown on the Surfing Area Map.

NO	NAME	CHAPTER	COMMENTS
1	Rosarito Beach	17	Miles of beach fronting the town of Rosarito. Km A-34.
2	Punta Santa Rosalillita	17	Town of Cantamar. Use Km A-53 exit from Hwy 1-D.
3	Sand Dunes	17	At S end of El Descanso. Km A-53 exit from Hwy 1-D. Cantamar La Mision Area Map.
4	La Fonda	17	Beach adjoins the La Fonda Hotel. Km A-66. Cantamar La Mision Area Map.
5	Playa Mal Paso	17	2 1/2 mile beach running S from the Rio Guadalupe. Cantamar La Mision Area Map.
6	Salsipuedes	17	Believe this is the coast accessed at the Saldamando Campground. Km A-94.
7	San Miguel	17	Coast adjoins the San Miguel Village Campground near the tollgate at Km A-99.
8	Calif. Trailer Court	17	Coast adjoins the California Trailer Park near Km A-105 north of Ensenada.
9	Islas de Todos Santos	17	Islands lie 12-miles offshore from Ensenada. Hire boats at Ensenada or La Bufadora.
10	Ensenada Beach	18	7 miles of beach S of Ensenada to Estero Beach Resort. Access at resort Km-B-15.
11	Estero Punta Banda	18	The barrier beach fronting Estero de Punta Banda. Hwy 23. Punta Banda Area Map.
12	Boca de Santo Tomas	18	Beach at mouth of Rio Santo Tomas. See Puerto Santo Tomas Side Trip Km B-48.
13	Punta San Jose	18	Road leaves for Punta San Jose from the town of Santo Tomas. Km B-51.
14	Punta Capras	18	Point lies N of Puerto San Isidro. See Puerto San Isidro Area Side Trip Km B-78.
15	San Isidro	18	See Puerto San Isidro Area Side Trip Km B-78.
16	Cabo Colnett	18	See Bahia Colnett Side Trip Km B-129. Road from bay extends S to Punta Camalu.
17	Punta Camalu	18	See Punta Camalu Side Trip Km B-157.
18	Playa San Ramon	18	12 mile long beach best accessed on road running W from Colonia Viciente Guerrero.

tion contains aerial photos and more detailed charts of the places in question. The names of the surfing spots are sometimes changed from previous publications to better conform with place names currently in use.

I should note that I hae never been surfing in my life. My closest encounter with the sport was with a surfboard projecting from the side window of a car on the narrow Transpeninsular Highway where its owner almost forced me off the road. However, I have been to almost all of the places noted in the above referenced table and these places represent about half of the spots noted in previous publications. I have excluded many others as it is difficult to match their names with locations with which I was familiar or that are shown on any available maps. Most of those omitted lie along the heavily urbanized coast between Tijuana and Ensenada or in the Cape Area at the peninsula's tip. Many places

SURFING AREA TABLE

Numbers conform to those shown on the Surfing Area Map.

NO	NAME	CHAPTER	COMMENTS
19	Cabo San Quintin	18	See San Quintin Area map.
20	Playa Santa Maria	18	Beach lines the bay in front of Cielito Lindo RV Park. See San Quintin Area Map.
21	El Pabellon Beach	19	Accessed at the El Pabellon Beach RV Park. Km C-15.
22	Punta Baja	19	See Punta Baja Side Trip C-55 and the El Rosario Area Map.
23	Punta San Carlos	19	A 38 miles dirt road leaves Hwy 1 at Km C-78, 16 miles S from El Rosario.
24	Punta Canoas	19	A remote Pacific point. See Pacific Coast Loop. Km C-128 & D-38.
25	Punta Blanca	19	A remote Pacific point. See Pacific Coast Loop. Km C-128 & D-38.
26	Punta Maria	19	A remote Pacific point. See Pacific Coast Loop. Km C-128 & D-38.
27	Punta Negra	19	A remote Pacific point. See Pacific Coast Loop. Km C-128 & D-38.
28	Punta Santa Rosalillita	19	At fishing village of Santa Rosalillita, Km D-38.
29	Punta Rosarito	19	From Santa Rosalillita village drive S about 9 miles on coastal road.
30	El Tomatal	19	See Km D-68 for 2.9 mile trip to El Tomatal and nearby Miller's Landing.
31	Bahia Tortuga	20	See Punta Eugenia Area Map & Side Trip. Km E-144 to E-98.
32	Bahia Asuncion	20	See Punta Eugenia Area Map & Side Trip. Km E-144 to E-98.
33	Punta San Hipolito	20	See Punta Eugenia Area Map & Side Trip. Km E-144 to E-98.
34	La Bocana	20	See Punta Eugenia Area Map & Side Trip. Km E-144 to E-98.
35	Punta Abreojos	20	See Punta Eugenia Area Map & Side Trip. Km E-144 to E-98.
36	Punta Pequena	22	Drive 45 km north from Km 107 on Hwy near La Purisima town of San Juanico.

in these areas are now difficult to access because of recent hotel and residential construction.

Heavy swells traveling from NW to SE are a daily occurrence along the entire Pacific coast of the Baja peninsula except under storm conditions when swells come from the SW. These swells, which are the cause of coastal surf, refract around the Cape Region as far north as Punta Colorado. There is no usable surf farther north

in the Sea of Cortez. Surfing hotspots that have been reported to me are the Islas Todos Santos, Punta Rosarito, Punta Santa Rosalillita, Punta Pequena, and Punta San Carlos. Should you be able to provide additional input concerning surfing in Baja I will be happy to include it in future editions of this book.

WINDSURFING — The sport of windsurfing has rapidly gained in popularity in Baja in recent years.

SURFING AREA TABLE

Numbers conform to those shown on the Surfing Area Map.

NO	NAME	CHAPTER	COMMENTS
37	Las Barrancas	22	Las Barrancas lies 5 miles W from Km-87 on Hwy N of Ciudad Insurgentes.
38	Punta Conejo	22	See location on Ch 22 Map. See Auto Club Map for raod details.
39	Punta Marques	22	See location on Ch 22 Map. See Auto Club Map for raod details.
40	Playa San Pedrito	25	See Ch 25 Map. Hwy 19 Km-57 & K-59.
41	San Pedtrito RV Park	25	See Ch 25 Map. Hwy 19 Km-64.
42	El Migrino	25	Beach is accessed by El Migrino Loop Road. See Ch 25 Map. Hwy 19 Km-94.
43	The Cabo Corridor	24	There are several beaches. See the Cabo Corridor in Ch 24.
44	Punta Palmilla	24	At Hotel Palmilla Km J-28.
45	Coast Azul and Others	24	Beaches line coast from Pt. Palmilla to town of La Playa. See San Jose del Cabo Map.
46	Punta Gorda	24	Lies 10 miles E of town of La Playa on secondary road. New highway anticipated.
47	Los Frailes	23	See East Cape Loop Side Trip. New highway anticipated.
48	Cabo Pulmo	23	See East Cape Loop Side Trip. New highway anticipated.
49	Punta Colorado	23	See East Cape Loop Side Trip. New highway anticipated.

Windsurfers crave strong winds in the 15-30 knot range that blow parallel to the takeoff area. As noted in Chapter 2, northerly winds that meet these requirements are common along the entire Sea of Cortez coast in the winter season. When the breeze is uncomfortably strong and cool for most campers, it is just right for the windsurfers.

Individual windsurfers will be seen at many locations on the Sea of Cortez and windsurfing equipment is often for rent at the hotels on the outer harbor at Cabo San Lucas, at Nopolo and La Paz. There are, however, two areas of special interest.

THE EAST CAPE — The Buena Vista-Los Barriles area along Baja's East Cape has become one of the most popular windsurfing destinations in North America. The area has long sandy beaches impacted by the wind conditions noted above, and being near the peninsula's tip, air temperatures are warmer than farther north. Even so,

many sailors prefer to wear shorty or full summer wetsuits when spending much time on the water.

Starting about 1987, U.S. windsurfing groups organized an annual Baja International Boardsailing Regatta at the East Cape each January. This event attracts hundreds of young enthusiasts who camp on the beach north of Los Barriles where I rather suspect things get a little wild. These same organizations set up headquarters at the Hotel Playa Hermosa and Hotel Palmas de Cortez during the entire winter season. Rental equipment, instruction, and repair services are thus readily available.

It has also been reported to me that the small town of El Sargento SE of La Paz is becoming a windsurfing mecca. Its growth has no doubt been encouraged by the oiling of the highway to the town about 1995. Strong winds are common at El

A surfer off the San Pedrito RV park along Highway 19. See Chapter 25. The swell shown here is typical of those that occur along Baja's Pacific shore in non-storm periods. Photo BW.

Here in the protected waters of the Bahia Coyote portion of Bahia Concepcion a windsurfer has sufficient wind to move along nicely without any wave action. Photo BW.

Sargento as they funnel down the channel between the peninsula and the nearby Isla Cerralvo.

PUNTA SAN CARLOS — The Sea of Cortez offers windsurfing with surf-less seas. On the Pacific shore, Punta San Carlos attracts the expert surfers with its high winds and breaking seas. I am advised by these hardy souls that it offers the best and most challenging area for their sport on the North American coast. There are no facilities at Punta San Carlos and the trip in from Highway 1 is a rough 40 miles. The access road leaves Highway 1 about 16 miles SE from El Rosario.

KAYAKING — Ocean kayaking is a sport of rapidly growing popularity in Baja. My own observations indicate that there are far more kayaks on the Sea of

Cortez at any one time than there are cruising sailboats.

Ocean kayaking enthusiasts can cruise within feet of Baja's rock-bound coast, and camp, fish, and explore at small idyllic coves and beaches that are too confining for use by larger boats. Kayaks can easily be cartopped on conventional vehicles and launched almost anywhere. The small single seat vessels weigh a scant 50 pounds while two person, 20-foot-long models weigh about 75 pounds. They are quite stable.

Experienced kayakers have traversed the full length of both Baja coasts. The trip from San Felipe to La Paz in the Sea of Cortez is frequently accomplished in 25- to-30 days. The most popular areas for shorter trips are the Bahia de los Angeles, Puerto Escondido, and the Bahia Concepcion areas. On the Pacific side, kayakers use Puerto Lopez Mateos as a base for trips into the Magdalena lagoons for whale-watching expeditions. Also, the BAJABOOKSHELF offers a recent book entitled *Sea Kayaking in Baja*. It offers details concerning 15 kayak trips. See notice in this chapter.

Kayaks can carry sufficient food and gear for extended voyages, but many kayakers take advantage of package tours offered by various outfitters. In these instances supplies are transported to prearranged camping sites by pangas which also provide added safety for trips to islands a bit beyond the range of kayakers alone. Contact Sea Trek, P.O. Box 561, Woodacre, CA, (415) 488-1000. Sea Kayak South, 2803 Morningside Terrace, Escondido, CA 92025 (619) 747-3615, or Baja Expeditions, 2625 Garnet Ave., San Diego, CA 92109, (619) 581-3311. This latter organization also runs other types of boat trips. Kayaks may be rented for trips in Bahia Concepcion from Baja Tropicales, 3065 Ste. C, Clairemont Dr., San Diego, Ca 92117, (619) 275-1836.

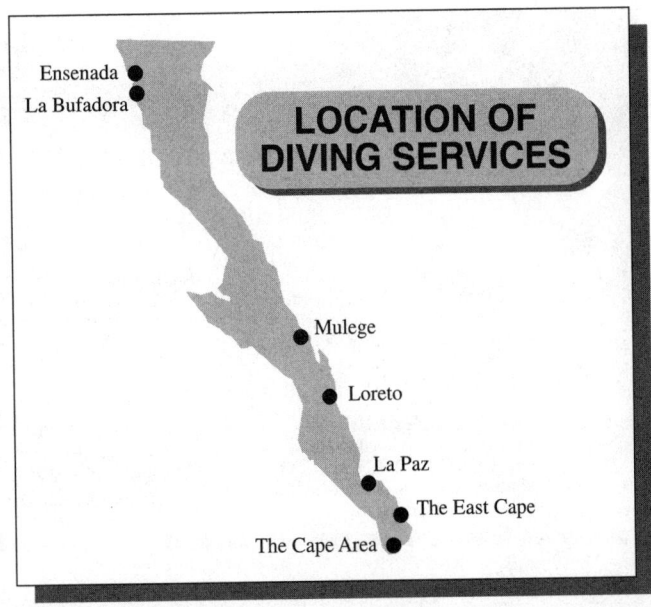

LOCATION OF DIVING SERVICES

DIVING — Many locations around the Baja peninsula offer excellent sites for scuba diving. Reference to the WATER TEMPERATURES Illustration later in this chapter will show that subtropical waters occur off the Pacific coast while those in the Sea of Cortez are tropical. Kelp beds extend southward from the international border to about Bahia Tortugas. Whales, and other marine mammals are common inhabitants off both coasts. The Sea of Cortez is host to giant whale sharks, manta rays, schools of hammerhead sharks, marlin and other large pelagic fish. These and other variables result in a wide variety of diving conditions that are difficult to duplicate anywhere in the world.

Water temperatures along the northern Pacific coast are cool enough to require wearing a 1/4" wetsuit year-round. Similar conditions prevail in the northern portions of the Sea of Cortez while temperatures farther south range upwards of 90-degrees.

The authoritative manual for diving in Baja is Dive Baja California by Susan Speck. It pinpoints and describes the best diving locations. These same spots are also identified by diving symbols in both volumes of the Baja Boater's Guide. Both books are available from the BAJA BOOKSHELF in the Appendix.

Much of the diving along Baja's Pacific coast is done aboard charter vessels based in San Diego. They range as far south as Isla Cedros. Many of these outfitters are based at the Commercial Basin adjacent to the Shelter Island Yacht Harbor in San Diego. Diving stores and outfitters in Baja are located at the places shown on the LOCATION OF DIVING SERVICES Illustration. Following is a listing of those services which came to our attention during our recent field investigations.

LA BUFADORA -- Dale's La Bufadora Dive, APDO #102 Maneadero, B.C., Mexico, 011-52-617-32092. The office is near the waterfront.

MULEGE -- Mulege Divers, On Madero St., 011-52-115-30059.

LORETO -- Deportes Blazer, Hidalgo No. 23, Col. Centro, Loreto, B.C.S., Mexico, 011-52 113 50911; Villas de Loreto & RV Park.

LA PAZ -- Baja Diving & Service, A. Obregon 1665.2 La Paz, B.C.S., Mexico, 011-52-112-21816, FAX 011-52-112-28644. Other locations: La Concha Beach Resort and Marina Palmira; Baja Expeditions 2625 Garnet Ave., San Diego, CA 92109, (800) 843-6967, (619) 581-3311, FAX (619) 581-6542.

THE EAST CAPE -- Vista Sea Sport, APDO #42, Buena Vista B.C.S., Mexico 23580, Tel & FAX 011-52-114-10031.

THE CAPE AREA -- Cabo Acuadeportes, S.A. de C.V. Apartado Postal #136, Cabo San Lucas, B.C.S., Mexico 23410, Telephone & FAX 011-52-114-30117. Two locations: Hacienda Beach and Chileno Beach; Cabo Diving Services, Boulevard Marina esq. Hidalgo, 011-52-114-30150 FAX 011-52-114-31110; Dolphin's Head, Located at Hotel Plaza Las Glorias, Local A-6, Cabo Santa Lucas, B.C.S., Mexico, 011-52-114-33400; Land's End Divers, Located at Hotel Plaza Las Glorias, Local A-5, Cabo San Lucas, B.CS., Mexico, Tel & FAX 011-52-114-32200.

FISHING

One rarely encounters reports concerning fishing that do not extol the virtues of the area being discussed. Certainly this is true for Baja California. The advertisements for the Cape, and East Cape hotels claim the "world's finest big-game fishing." One peninsular fishing book maintains that fishing "is unequaled anywhere in the world," and everything else one can read boasts of the outstanding qualities of the catch in a particular area. In preparing this book, I endeavored —with limited success — to determine if all of this were true. What follows results from readings in the scientific and popular literature, and my own observations.

RATING BAJA'S FISHING — I have been unable to find any author who makes direct qualitative comparisons of the world's fishing areas. I suspect those who claim the *world's best* for Baja may be on shaky scientific ground and could be guilty of what is known in the advertising world as *puffing* (an over-emphasis

of a product's good points). Nevertheless, there are several sound reasons for believing that the fishing in the waters surrounding the Baja peninsula is of high quality. Here they are:

UPWELLING — There are several relatively isolated sections along the western coasts of the world's continents where the prevailing winds have the effect of forcing the surface waters offshore. The result is an upwelling of colder waters from below that bear rich concentrations of nitrates, phosphates, and other nutrients. Their presence allows the development of enormous quantities of microscopic plants and animals known as plankton. Plankton, in turn, is the base of the food chain that results in large numbers of game fish.

This condition exists off the north-central portion of Baja's Pacific coast. The nutrient qualities of these waters are not as high as in similar areas adjacent to Peru and at the tip of South America, but they are considerably better than average. Cool water upwelling also occurs off Baja's East Cape and in the Midriff island area east of Bahia de los Angeles due no doubt to the islands forming a constriction to the flow of tidal currents in the narrow Sea of Cortez. Upwelling conditions rarely occur on the eastern coasts of the world's continents.

WATER TEMPERATURE — The world's oceans are classified into several temperature zones. Those adjoining the coasts of North America are shown on the WATER TEMPERATURE ZONES Map. As can be seen, tropical waters are found in the Sea of Cortez and at the tip of the Baja peninsula. Tropical seas represent the most ideal environment for life on earth. Fish tend to be larger, more abundant, and of different species than those found in cooler waters. Baja's Pacific waters are classified as subtropical and represent a transition between the tropics and the temperate area to the north. Near the shore, they are often cooled by the upwelling noted above. And, in terms of numbers of fish, these cold Pacific waters probably out produce the warmer Sea of Cortez. As a result of these temperature factors, the Sea of Cortez offers the abundance of sea

Some sportfishermen have purchased Mexican pangas made in La Paz. Here one is being launched at the Fisherman's Landing launching ramp at the mouth of the estuary at Mulege. Photo JW.

life common to tropical waters. It is the closest body of such waters to people living in much of western Canada and western United States. At the same time, the presence of cooler, subtropic and upwelling conditions on the Pacific side result in a wide variety of fish species being available to the Baja fisherman.

COASTAL HABITAT — Many species of smaller game fish thrive only where they are protected by

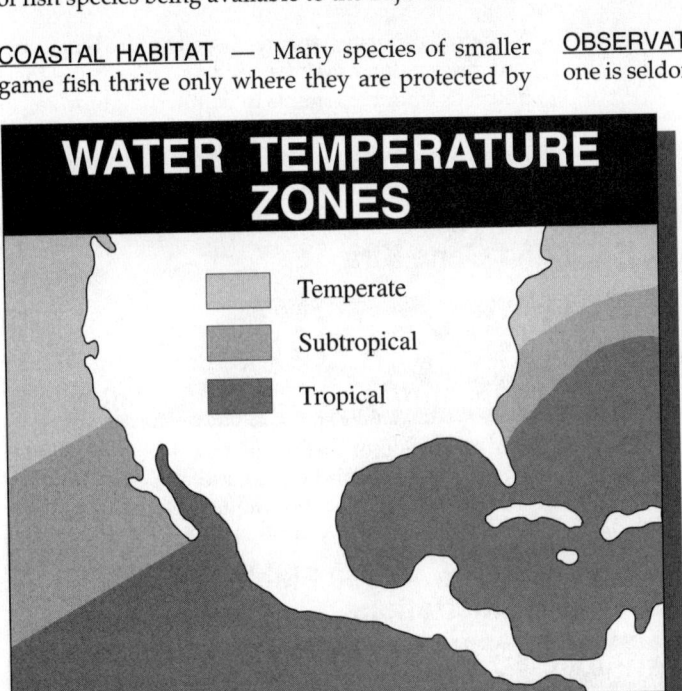

WATER TEMPERATURE ZONES

Temperate

Subtropical

Tropical

rocky shores and reefs. As previously noted, much of Baja's coastline is mountainous and rocky. In addition, there are a considerable number of coastal islands with similar shoreline characteristics. The peninsula thus offers favorable marine environments for those who fish from, or close to, the shore.

OBSERVATION — In cruising off the coasts of Baja, one is seldom out of sight of a Mexican fishing vessel of some type. These boats do not fish hundreds of miles out to sea but near the land. There are fishing camps and villages in scores of locations. Fish processing plants are to be found in most larger communities. It is a simple matter of observation to conclude that there is abundant marine life in the surrounding waters.

OVERFISHING — Sadly, this heavy commercial fishing has significantly decreased the quality of sportfishing in Baja waters in many locations. The heaviest impact has come from Mexico's own fishing vessels based at Ensenada and La Paz on the peninsula, and at Guaymas, Topolobampo, and other ports on the Mexican mainland. Mexican officials have even licensed foreign fleets to fish in Baja waters sacrificing long-term good for quick profit.

Neil Kelly laments the adverse effects of commercial fishing in his book *The Baja Catch*, noting particularly the areas around San Felipe, Bahia de los Angeles, Loreto, Mulege, and Ensenada. The sportfishing fleet operators at La Paz readily concede that the waters immediately adjoining their city have been fished-out, and several resort owners have asked me if there is anything I can do about the heavy commercial fishing. In spite of all this, sportfishing in Baja is still outstanding although it is not as good as it once was in some places.

During our 1997 survey we became aware of the recent establishment of *Parque Marino Bahia de Loreto* (Marine Park of the Bay of Loreto). The park embraces many of the islands in the central portion of the Sea of Cortez and maintains an office near the Loreto harbor. The local grapevine hopes that this development will result in the restriction of heavy commercial fishing in this area.

FISHING ALTERNATIVES — Fishermen have a wide range of alternatives for enjoying their sport in Baja waters as indicated in the outline below.

LARGE CHARTER BOATS
    Party Boats
    Sportfisher Charters
    Extended Trip Charters
MEDIUM CHARTER BOATS
PANGA CHARTERS
FISHERMEN OWNED BOATS
    Ocean-Cruisers
    Trailer Boats

<u>LARGE CHARTER BOATS</u> — Vessels in the 40-60 foot range.

Party Boats — At many Pacific coast ports in the United States, individual fishermen may pay to join 15-to-30 others for a day's sport. Fishing gear may be rented, or you may bring your own. The advantage of such trips is their relatively low cost made possible by the large number of fishermen making each trip.

Many party boats are based in San Diego at the Commercial Basin on the north side of Shelter Island. Some of these fish in Mexican waters surrounding the Coronado Islands. Others offer more extended trips farther south. Ensenada is the only port offering true party boat service in Baja. Fishing, here, is in Bahia Todos Santos and around the Islas Todos Santos. Mexican fishing licenses are usually included in the cost of the Ensenada trips. Many species caught off Ensenada are seldom taken farther north.

Sportfisher Charters — "Sportfisher" is the name applied to any number of fast, open-transom powerboats in the 40-60 foot range. They normally accommodate only 2-4 anglers at a time who sit in fancy chairs in the boat's stern and haul in the large glamour fish. Trips are normally on a day basis only as overnight accommodations are limited.

Numerous sportfishers are based at Cabo San Lucas and reservations may be made at any of the local hotels or from U.S. agents in Southern California. In the past, many of these craft have been operated by U.S. skippers without formal authority from the Mexican government. I am advised that this practice may be coming to an end, but certainly sportfishing boats will be available at Cabo through one means or another. A smaller number of sportfisher vessels operate out of La Paz.

Extended Trip Charters — There are three ports in Baja that offer ocean-going vessels large enough to provide overnight accommodations for multiday fishing, whale-watching, and general enjoyment adventures. These are <u>ENSENADA</u> contact Ensenada Clipper, 8194 Havasu, Buena Park, CA 90621 (714) 994-1872 — <u>SAN FELIPE</u> Tony Reyes Fishing Tours, contact The Long Fin, 4010 E. Chapman Ave. Suite D, Orange, CA 92669 (714) 538-8010, or The Poseidon, P.O. Box 974, Calexico, CA 92231 (619) 239-6123. The Tony Reyes trips are 6-day adventures to the Midriff Island area. — <u>LA PAZ</u> Baja Yacht Charters, contact Frazer Charters Inc, P.O. Box 60099, San Diego, CA 92106 (619) 225-0588. The Tony Reyes vessel is moved from San Felipe to La Paz during January and February.

MEDIUM CHARTER BOATS — Most of the larger vessels discussed above were manufactured in the United States. Dozens of smaller flybridge cruisers in the 25-35 foot range have been produced by small Mexican boatyards in the southern portion of the peninsula. They are less sumptuous than the U. S. products.

The majority of these boats make up the fishing fleets of the hotels from Cabo San Lucas to San Jose del Cabo and the Buena Vista-Los Barriles area. Another fleet operates out of the Hotel Los Arcos in La Paz. Chartering these vessels is usually less expensive than the larger vessels. Contact any of the major hotels in the areas noted.

PANGA CHARTERS — No discussion of boating in Baja would be complete without reference to the panga, a heavy fiberglass open boat powered by an out-

board motor. They are made in La Paz and were designed by Mac Shroyer a former math teacher from the United States who now manages the Marina de La Paz in La Paz. They range from 18-to-24 feet in length. There is hardly a Mexican fisherman in Baja who does not operate from such a boat. About 2,500 have been constructed (see picture in this chapter). You will see them everywhere Mexican fishermen gather.

Most pangas are used for commercial fishing by the members of fishing cooperatives. However, more and more they are being offered for charter to sportfishermen. At La Paz, pangas make up the fishing fleet operated by Bob Butler. Contact the Hotel Los Arcos, or P.O. Box 6688, Crestline, CA 92325. In Bahia de los Angeles a small fleet is maintained by Guerrmo's Trailer Court. In most other places one contacts the individual operators of the pangas who will be waiting by their boats.

Concentrations of pangas available for hire may be found in the inner harbor at Cabo San Lucas, at the fisherman's landing at the small town of La Playa 1 mile east of San Jose del Cabo, near the trailer courts in Loreto, immediately south of the lighthouse in San Felipe, at the mouth of the river in Mulege, and in scores of other less visited locations. Even if a panga fishermen is not normally in the sportfishing busi-

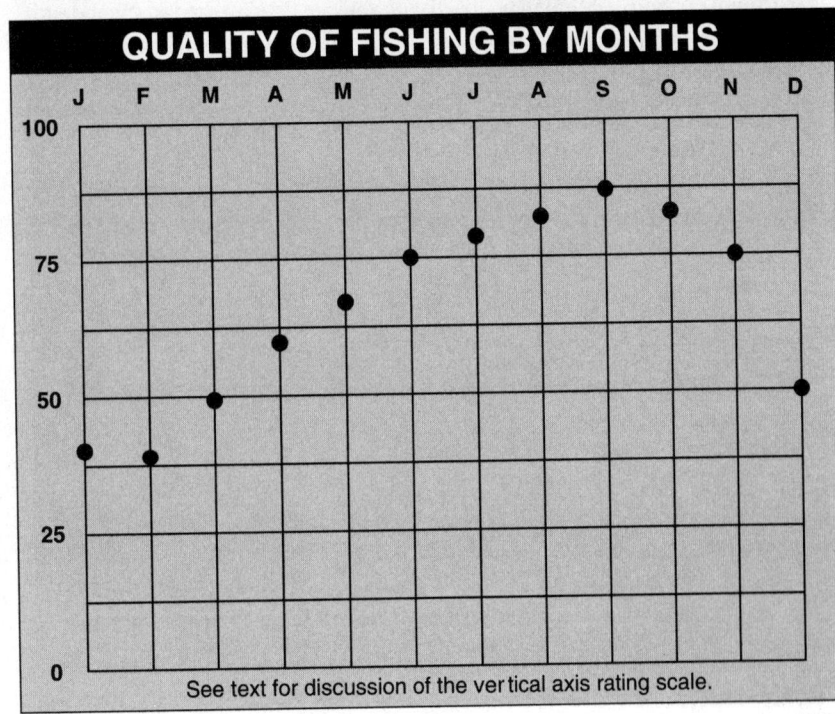

QUALITY OF FISHING BY MONTHS

See text for discussion of the vertical axis rating scale.

ness, his boat can usually be hired for that purpose. Hard cash is hard to turn down.

FISHERMAN OWNED BOATS — We will now discuss the three classes of boats brought south by tourists. The three classes are the same as presented earlier in this chapter.

Ocean-Cruisers — The people coming to Baja on ocean-cruising sailboats usually engage in sportfishing. Some of this is simply bottom fishing from the boat when it is at anchor. More often the ship's tender is used for trolling away from the anchorage. When this occurs, the ocean-cruiser has the advantages attributable to the small class 4 boats described below, plus the range provided by the larger mother vessel.

Trailer Boats — Small car-top and trailerable boats are taken south to Baja by the thousands. They are the class 3 and 4 vessels noted earlier in this chapter. They range in size from small 13 foot aluminum craft to the heavy vessel on the three-axle trailer shown in the photo in this chapter. The larger boat has significant range but lacks maneuverability for fishing in shallow and restricted areas. The 13 footers have maximum maneuverability and can be launched at hundreds of places where there is no ramp. The fisherman's range is thus expanded by moving the boat around on land. The small boat's disadvantages are that it cannot be used in even moderately rough weather and they cannot safely venture far from land.

FISHING LITERATURE — Past books about fishing in Baja waters have been long on fish-stories but short on specifics, even though they have been instrumental in drawing large numbers of fishermen to the peninsula. Fortunately, a fishing manual worthy of the name is now available. This is *The Baja Catch*, now in its 2nd edition.

Coauthored by Neil Kelly and Gene Kira, the book documents the extensive fishing exploits of the first named author. Kelly fishes almost exclusively from a small 13 foot aluminum boat. This craft is easily launched over the beach and provides the maneuverability necessary to fish over reefs and close to shore where Kelly believes the best habitats are found. Most of his fishing involves trolling over zigzag courses at 3-to-6 knots using jointed, artificial lures.

The book's subtitle, *An Inshore Fishing Manual for Baja California* alerts you that it is devoted largely to the above described method of fishing. The coastal areas described are necessarily limited to only a small percentage of the Baja shore, and only a few of its many islands, as these are the areas safely accessible in Kelly's small vessel. However, what is covered is presented in great detail. Explicit recommendations on boats, tackle, fishing tactics, best fishing seasons, and descriptions and drawings of the fifty most common fish species are also included. One of the books best features are its numerous fishing maps. One of these maps for *Estero de Coyote* area on Baja's Pacific shore is included in this chapter. Another map of the Bahia Gonzaga area in the Sea of Cortez is presented in Chapter 15. My thanks to Gene Kira for allowing use of these maps here in *The Magnificent Peninsula*. I wander if he thought of the possibility that his generosity is also good advertising?

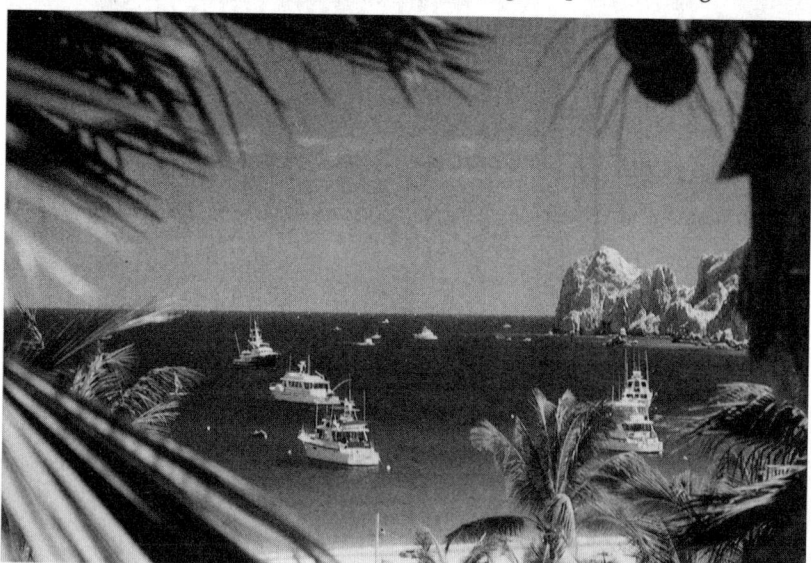

Large sportfishing vessels lying at anchor in front of the Hotel Hacienda at Cabo San Lucas. Scores of such boats make the run from southern California to Cabo each winter. Photo JW.

Acquire *The Baja Catch* if fishing is one of your primary objectives in visiting Baja. Many of the fishing areas it recommends are shown in the aerial photos in the *Baja Boater's Guide*.

FISHING OVERVIEW — By way of background I present the following overview material.

<u>WHEN TO FISH</u> — There are hundreds of varieties of game fish in the waters surrounding the Baja peninsula. They range in size from giant marlin to small rockfish and triggers. There is considerable variation in the time of year when any given species is present, and this availability also differs from section-to-section of the coast.

Please refer to the graph entitled QUALITY OF FISHING BY MONTHS. It is based on a composite of information for common game fish for all areas of the peninsula. The rating index in the chart's vertical axis is my own invention and has no significance other than to show the relative fishing quality by months of the

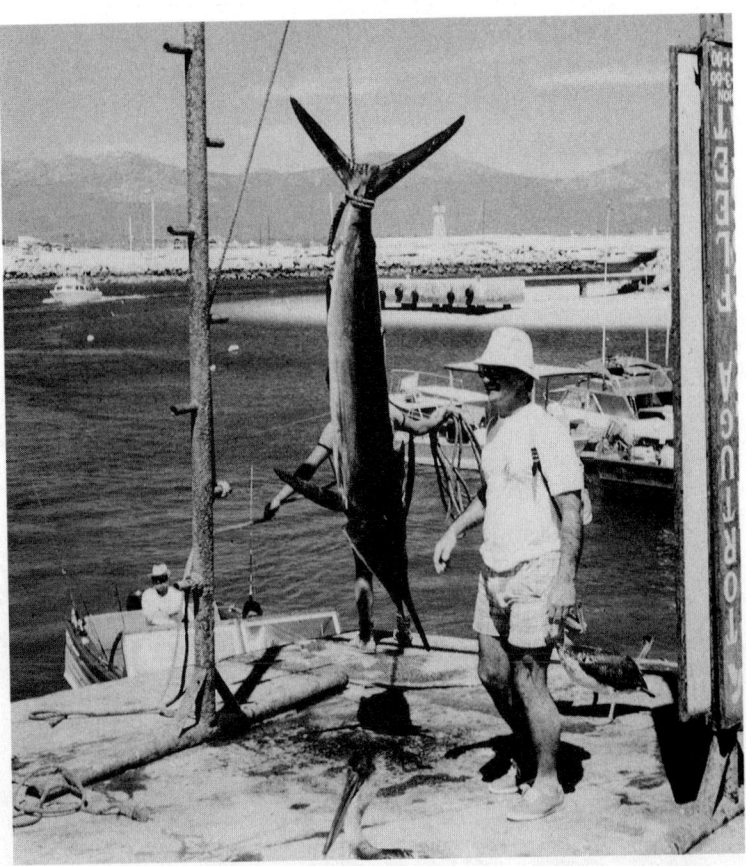

Landing one of the mammoth glamour fish is commonplace at Cabo San Lucas. Photo JW.

year. It is designed to show that (1) fishing in Baja is never poor, (2) the best fishing is during the summer and early fall, and (3) the least productive months are during the winter.

In general, the peninsula-wide yearly trend shown in the chart is also encountered in most individual sections, particularly in the tropical waters of the Sea of Cortez. Clearly, the presence of many species increases as the waters become warmer during summer. However there are numerous seasonal variations, particularly if you are interested in one particular species of fish. More data on when to fish are noted in the area summaries below.

<u>UPPER SEA OF CORTEZ AREA</u> — This is the area from north of Santa Rosalia to the mouth of the Rio Colorado. While the waters here are still classified as tropical, there is upwelling of cooler waters near the Midriff Islands lying off Bahia de los Angeles and

some of the tropical fish species such as sailfish, amberjack, snappers, and needlefish do not migrate this far north. By way of compensation, the northern area has several species not found farther south. These include the spotted bass and many of the mullet, tortuava, croker, and corvina that spawn in the shallow waters south of the Rio Colorado.

In much of this area fishing is good year-round, but fishermen are faced with two practicalities posed by the weather. The chilly, winter, northerly winds present throughout the Sea of Cortez are particularly strong north of Santa Rosalia. Fishing in small boats can thus be both cold and dangerous during these months. In the summer, air temperatures are excessively hot, even more so than areas to the south. Thus, from a practical standpoint, the spring and fall months constitute the best fishing periods. Boat launching is also complicated by the extreme tide fluctuations and severe currents present in these waters.

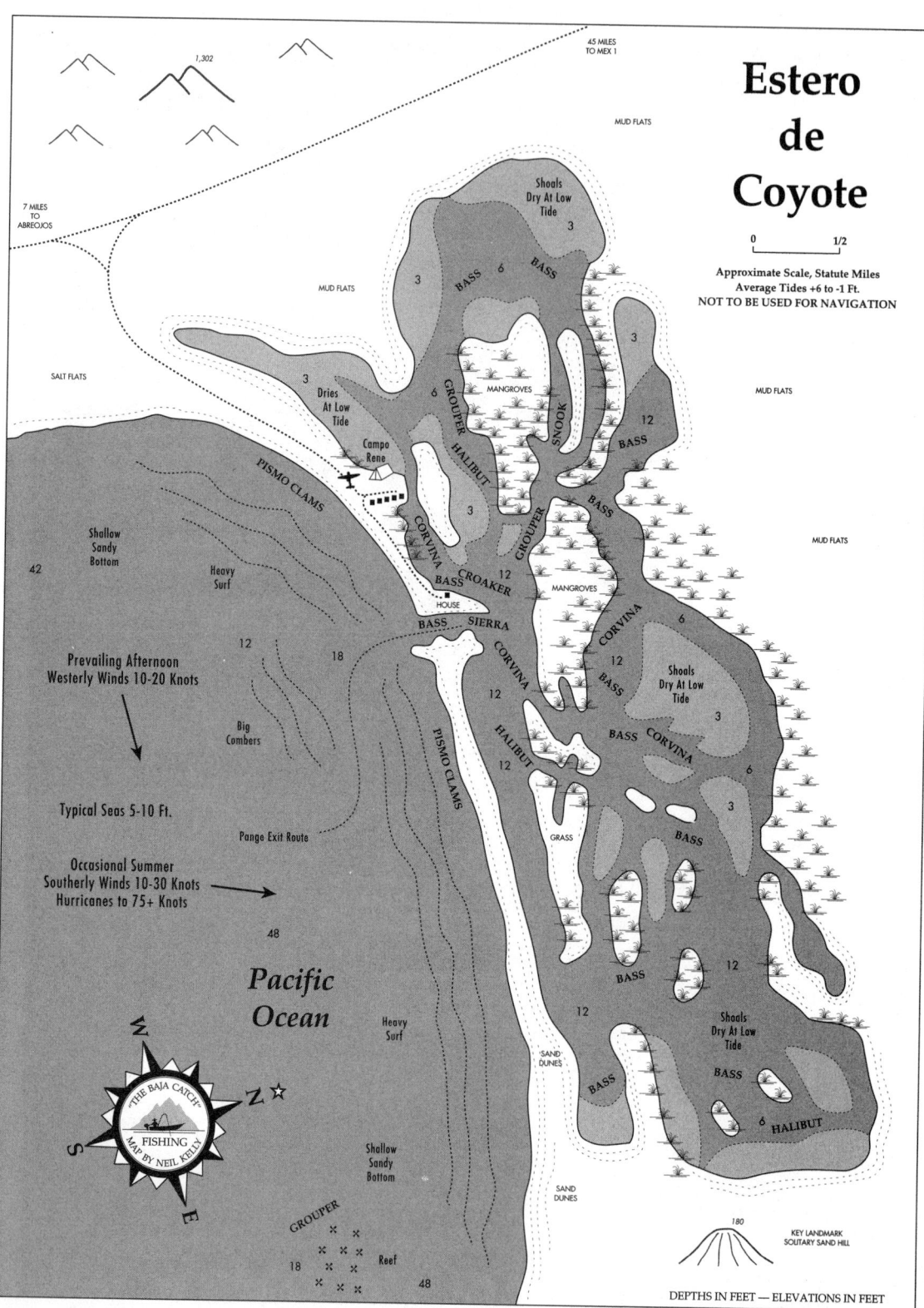

Estero de Coyote

0   1/2

Approximate Scale, Statute Miles
Average Tides +6 to -1 Ft.
NOT TO BE USED FOR NAVIGATION

45 MILES
TO MEX 1

MUD FLATS

Shoals
Dry At Low
Tide
3

BASS   6   BASS

3

3

6   GROUPER   MANGROVES   12   BASS

Dries
At Low
Tide

Campo
Rene

3   HALIBUT

SNOOK   BASS

3

MUD FLATS

MUD FLATS

SALT FLATS

MUD FLATS

7 MILES
TO
ABREOJOS

1,302

PISMO CLAMS

CORVINA   GROUPER

BASS

CROAKER   12   BASS

HOUSE   BASS   SIERRA   CORVINA

BASS   6

MANGROVES

CORVINA

12   BASS   Shoals
Dry At Low
Tide

3

Shallow
Sandy
Bottom

Heavy
Surf

42

12

18

BASS   CORVINA   6

HALIBUT   BASS   3

Prevailing Afternoon
Westerly Winds 10-20 Knots

Big
Combers

12

GRASS   BASS

Typical Seas 5-10 Ft.

Pange Exit Route

Occasional Summer
Southerly Winds 10-30 Knots
Hurricanes to 75+ Knots

48

BASS   12

PISMO CLAMS

12   BASS

*Pacific
Ocean*

Heavy
Surf

SAND
DUNES

BASS   Shoals
Dry At Low
Tide

BASS

6   HALIBUT

Shallow
Sandy
Bottom

SAND
DUNES

W
N
Z ☆
S
E

"THE BAJA CATCH"
FISHING
MAP BY NEIL KELLY

GROUPER
× ×
× ×
18   × ×   Reef   48
× × ×

180

KEY LANDMARK
SOLITARY SAND HILL

DEPTHS IN FEET — ELEVATIONS IN FEET

MULEGE-LORETO AREA —

Several of the extremes which confront the fisherman in the upper Sea of Cortez are less of a problem farther south. Winter temperatures are milder and winds, while present, are less severe. And summer temperatures, while hot, are less so than farther north. Tides and currents are not serious problems as they are to the north. However, fisherman need to be alert to the possibility of severe tropical storms that occasionally reach into this area. U. S. Naval Weather Service records indicate the danger period is from mid-August to mid-October.

This photo was taken from the beach at Hotel Melia at Cabo San Lucas. There was so much watersports activity taking place that one could think the scene was staged. It wasn't. Photo BW.

While fishing is good year-round near Caleta San Lucas, it is more seasonal in such other popular fishing areas as Punta Chivato, Mulege, Bahia Concepcion, and the area around Puerto Escondido. This is because several of the most sought after species are migrators that come and go with the seasons. As examples, yellowtail are prevalent in the winter while July is the big month for dorado and marlin. Consult *The Baja Catch* for details.

LA PAZ AREA — The fishing fleet advertisements in

La Paz stating that their city is Baja's all-season fishing grounds are a bit deceptive. First, fleet operators readily concede that the waters immediately off the city are badly depleted. For this reason they transport their clients either to the northern end of the East Cape area (access to the water at Bahia de los Muertos) or to the waters around the southern end of Isla Espiritu Santos. In this latter area they can meet the large migratory species moving north into the Sea of Cortez around June.

Thus, La Paz has to reach somewhat far afield to tap good fishing waters and the area is only lightly visited by fishermen in small trailerable boats.

THE EAST CAPE AREA — The East Cape is that

section of coast from the southern end of Isla Cerralvo south to Bahia los Frailes (see map in Chapter 23). The areas hotel operators boast it is the finest fishing grounds in the world, and Neil Kelly's *The Baja Catch* rates it as the *best-of-the-best* in Baja. There are four basic reasons for this high praise.

(1) While Cabo San Lucas is recognized as the marlin capital of the world, this species is also one of the big draws along the East Cape. (2) The most sought after species of fish along Baja's east coast are migrators which include marlin, tuna, dorado, roosterfish and wahoo. They move north into the Sea of Cortez in the spring and back south again in fall. Most of this migration takes place close to the Baja shore rather than on the mainland side. It passes on either side of Isla Cerralvo.

(3) Ocean waters over 1,000 feet deep lie only a few miles offshore along much of the East Cape shoreline, and it is in such deep, blue-water areas that marlin thrive. Thus, lengthy trips to sea are not required to reach the large glamour species in this area. The best season is short, however, centering around six-week periods in late May and October, although some of the large species persist in some areas through the summer. (4) While the main marlin periods are limited, the East Cape also has a sizeable population of top-flight resident species so that fishing of some variety is always available.

THE CAPE AREA — There are fewer resident fishes at

the tip of the Baja peninsula than in other areas, but fishing for striped marlin and other billfish is unexcelled. They are catchable throughout the year with the best seasons centering around April and November.

As in the East Cape, the deep waters favored by marlin come close to shore at Cabo San Lucas. They may thus be caught only a few miles off the Cape, although many charter vessels take their customers to various *banks* that lie some 20-25 miles offshore. During the winter months the marlin are found on the Pacific side of the Cape and along the Sea of Cortez shore in the summer.

Small boats may be launched at the excellent ramp in the inner harbor at Cabo San Lucas, but surf conditions greatly limit over the beach launching in the Cape area. Each morning there is a mass exodus of sportfishing vessels leaving the Cabo San Lucas harbor. Some are small fishermen owned boats but most are various sizes of charter vessels catering to the areas hotel clients. There is considerable fishing action at San Jose del Cabo, but simple observation will disclose that Cabo San Lucas is the fishing capital of Baja California. Additional information of Cape Area fishing is given in Chapter 14.

PACIFIC LAGOONS — Much of Baja's Pacific shore consists of the extremely low-lying terrain of the Continental Borderlands Province (see map in Chapter 9). Saltwater lagoons lie behind the barrier-beaches in many places and most have entrances to the sea protected by breaking bars. The larger lagoons support Mexican fish camps and receive light visitation from sportfishermen using small car-top boats.

The lagoons most frequently visited are Puerto San Quintin, Laguna Manuela, Laguna la Bocana, Estero Coyote (See map in this Chapter), Laguna San Ignacio, and Bahia Magdalena and the extensive lagoons north of its main bay. Fishing in these places is rated from fair to excellent. See this books Index for the location of these lagoons, and consult *The Baja Catch* and *Baja Boater's Guide* for more details.

With the exception of Bahia Magdalena, these places are mostly accessed by washboarded secondary roads over level but poorly vegetated planes. Camping sites are austere and often windswept, but avid fishermen will find the lagoons a special and rewarding challenge.

PACIFIC ROCKY SHORES — The GEOLOGIC PROVINCES Map in Chapter 9 shows the mountainous, and rocky portions of Baja's Pacific coast. There is little sportfishing data on these areas as road access is poor and the launching of small boats into the heavy Pacific surf is very difficult. I expect that the Punta Eugenia and Punta Abreojos area will become popular fishing areas when oiling of the highway to Bahia Tortugas is completed.

For now, sportfishing is concentrated in the Bahia Todos Santos area at Ensenada, and at various reefs and Islands to the south which are accessed by three and four day charter trips out of San Diego and Ensenada. The Coronados Islands may also be reached by larger fisherman-owned boats out of San Diego.

SHRIMP — Tourists at San Felipe and Bahia Concepcion in the Sea of Cortez will frequently observe Mexican fishing vessels in the 40-to-60 foot class. These, in most cases, will be *shrimpers* and may be distinguished from more conventional fishing boats by the large array of often colorful nets hanging from booms when the boat is not actually working. Many shrimpers work at night so you will see them anchored during the day.

Dragging for shrimp takes place in relatively shallow waters along both coasts in the northern half of the Sea of Cortez. I have also seen shrimpers working the waters of Bahia de La Paz. On the Pacific coast shrimp boats will also be seen in Bahia Magdalena and in the shallow waters along the sandy beaches north of this bay.

Because of Mexico's economic problems, the government has decreed that shrimp must be sold on the international market in order to produce foreign currency. Many fishermen will sell shrimp to tourists, but you should recognize the illicit nature of these transactions. There are reports of shrimp being sold to tourists, who are then approached by the salesman's accomplices posing as federal officers looking for *la mordida*.

Here is a typical scene in the Sea of Cortez where small tourist owned boats are hauled up on the beach near camping spots. Photo by BW.

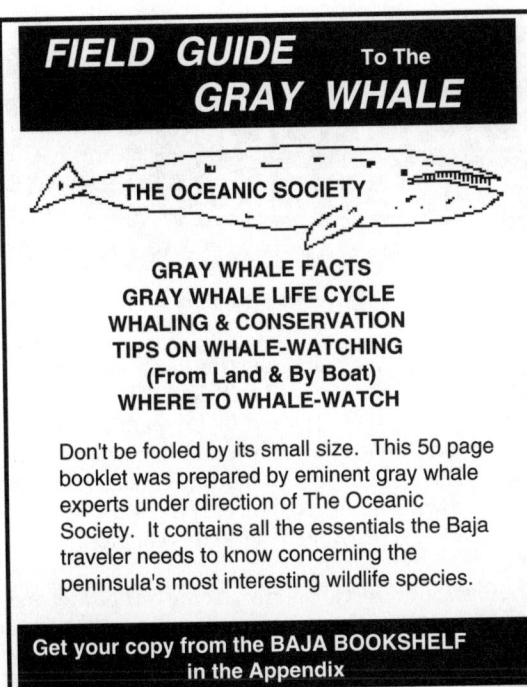
mitted and, again, they may not be legally sold to tourists.

FISHING LICENSES — All tourists 12 years or older must obtain a Mexican Sport Fishing License to fish in Mexican waters. They are issued by the day, week, month, or year. Fees depend upon the length of time involved and fluctuate widely according to the current exchange rate. All persons aboard a tourist's boat must have a license if the vessel is carrying fishing gear or any kind of fish or fish parts. This can become expensive for yachts carrying numerous people on extended voyages.

A fishing license must also be obtained for any boat used for fishing. Here, the fee is based on the length of the vessel. Some guidebooks mistakenly refer to this license as a boat permit. To be on the safe side, it may be prudent to get a boat fishing license if your boat is of the type commonly used for fishing even if you do not intend to use it for fishing purposes. Clearly, you do not need a permit for a surfboard, wind surfer, or similar small craft. A license is also required to fish from the shore in Mexico. These licenses are issued at no charge.

Licenses covering all types of sportfishing are issued by the federal government (*Secretaria de Pesca*) and are thus valid throughout Mexico. They may be obtained at the offices of the Mexican Department of Fisheries in San Diego and Ensenada. Several of the travel clubs noted in Chapter 1 sell licenses through the mail as a service to their members.

LOBSTER — Lobsters abound in the waters along the rocky sections of the Pacific coast and its islands. Bahia Magdalena is at the southern end of the lobstering area. Boaters must be continually alert for small buoys attached by line to a lobster trap resting on the ocean floor. As with shrimp, the taking of lobsters by other than Mexican nationals is not per-

CHAPTER 6
RESORT AREAS, GOLF COURSES and HOTELS

This chapter was simply entitled *Hotels* in early editions of this book. *Resort Areas* were added starting with the 5th edition as it was obviously necessary for people seeking a hotel vacation to first choose a resort area before selecting a specific hotel. One must also be aware that the ambience of Baja's resort areas vary markedly, one from the other, and that several new, or heavily altered areas have emerged within the last few years. Starting with this 6th edition *golf courses* have been added to the mix as they have become one of the principal attractions for Baja's hotel visitors.

RESORT AREAS

An accompanying map shows the locations of the ten resort areas that are described below. These descriptions are obviously flavored by my personal judgements and biases. Nevertheless, I hope they are of some value. The map also indicates the locations of Baja's growing number of golf courses. More detailed information is provided later in this chapter.

The first four resort areas are near the U.S. border and receive much of their use from Southern California residents escaping the jungle on weekends. They are not the places I would recommend for one's prized yearly vacation. Having said this, I am well aware that many of the hotel visits throughout Baja are limited to brief weekend and holiday-weekend visits. The flying time to the peninsula's southern resort areas is little different than that spent driving to the border areas. I have included the names of my favorite hotels in each area for what it is worth.

TIJUANA -- A large bustling city with few waterfront attractions or other amenities normally associated with a resort town. There are several good hotels that serve mostly business people, visitors to the golf course and bull rings, or those looking for a quick taste of Mexican culture. The *Hotel Lucerna* offers a restful atmosphere and is

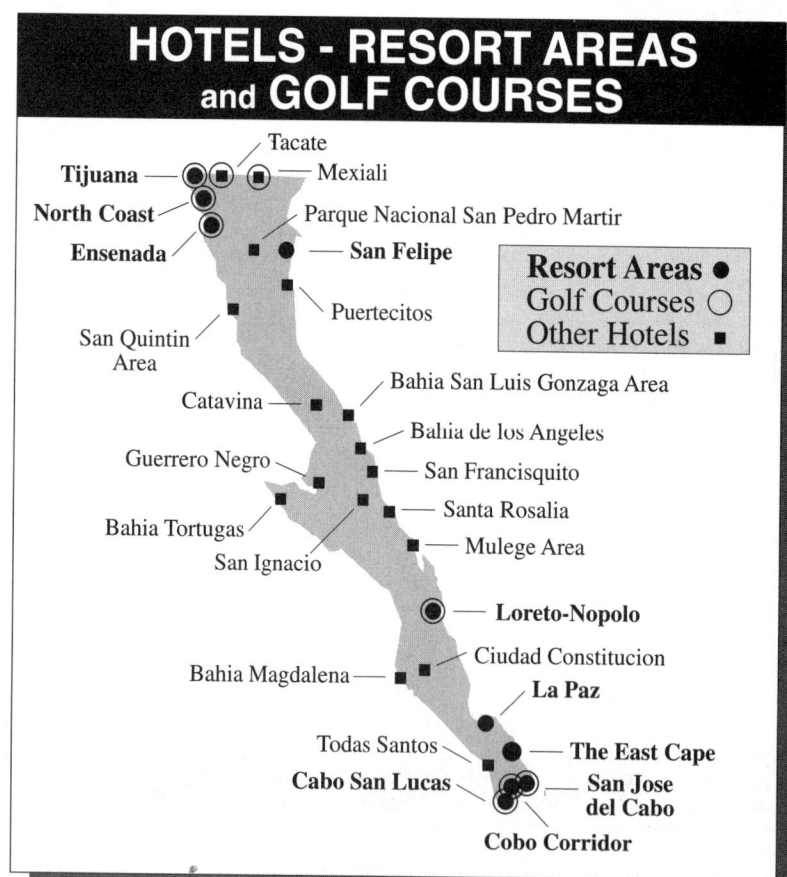

HOTELS - RESORT AREAS and GOLF COURSES

Tacate
Tijuana
Mexiali
North Coast
Parque Nacional San Pedro Martir
Ensenada
San Felipe

Resort Areas ●
Golf Courses ○
Other Hotels ■

Puertecitos

San Quintin Area

Catavina
Bahia San Luis Gonzaga Area

Bahia de los Angeles

Guerrero Negro
San Francisquito

Santa Rosalia

Bahia Tortugas
Mulege Area

San Ignacio

Loreto-Nopolo

Ciudad Constitucion

Bahia Magdalena
La Paz

Todas Santos
The East Cape

Cabo San Lucas
San Jose del Cabo

Cobo Corridor

my favorite. The *Grand Hotel Tijuana* is more grandiose for those seeking a skyscraper atmosphere.

SAN FELIPE -- A modest sized town on the upper end of the Sea of Cortez that is a major RV park haven for northern snowbirds. There are a few nice hotels but they serve mainly the weekend visitor. While the appearance of the community has improved considerably in recent years, it is still far from a world class resort area and its vegetation is a bit sparse for my tastes. The *Hotel Las Misiones* is the pick of the hotel crop in my view.

NORTH COAST (Rosarito to Ensenada) -- The town of Rosarito has long been the home of several good hotels. But in recent years, several luxury establishments have been constructed along the coast to the south. One of them has a golf course. Of the four border resort areas, this is my recommendation as the best for those looking for a pleasant, coastal hotel experience. The other three are better for those wishing to explore a Mexican community. The *Rosarito Beach Hotel* would be my choice in part because of its historic background. The new ones to the south are also very nice.

ENSENADA -- As with Tijuana, Ensenada is a large, busy community. It is not a beach resort but has now turned a once shabby waterfront into an attractive promenade inside the breakwater lined harbor. Nearby is a clearly defined tourist area which attracts thousands of tourists. Most visitors to its hotels are using them as a base for seeing the city and its night life. A few miles south of town is the *Estero Beach Resort Hotel* which lies on a beach within a protected lagoon. This is the best hotel in the area in my view. The *San Nicolas Resort Hotel* is probably the best in Ensenada proper although the *Mision Santa Isabel* is my personal favorite.

LORETO-NOPOLO -- For years, the small town of Loreto was a relatively sleepy fishing village. Then in 1977 the Mexican government chose it and a nearby beach called Nopolo for development of a major resort area. This effort has met with only limited success and tourism has

been modest. But, a fine medium sized hotel, golf course and tennis courts were constructed at Nopolo along with a nearby international airport. Loreto itself has now been spruced up considerably and there are several fine, small hotels. To me, the failure of the big development plans has been a blessing as Loreto and Nopolo retain there small town atmosphere. I recommend them to your attention. Any of the hotels noted later in this chapter offer good Mexican ambience. The *Eden Loreto Resort* at Nopolo is the fanciest, but the others offer the advantage of being directly within the community.

LA PAZ -- La Paz is a city of 160,000 people with an international airport. It is my favorite city in Mexico. There are several very good hotels located near a protected bay off the Sea of Cortez. I recommend it to your attention, keeping in mind, that one visits its hotels primarily as a means of enjoying the city. While on the waterfront, it is not primarily a beach resort as are the four resort areas noted below in this listing. The *Hotel Los Arcos* is my personal favorite but others prefer *La Concha Beach Resort*.

THE EAST CAPE -- The East Cape shares the stage with Loreto-Nopolo as being Baja's low-key resort areas. Many tourists prefer its small, often isolated, beach-front hotels to the bigger, more urbanized settings of the Cape Area's three resort areas. It is served by the international airport at Los Cabos. My favorite is the *Hotel Palmas de Cortez* but all the facilities noted in this chapter are high quality.

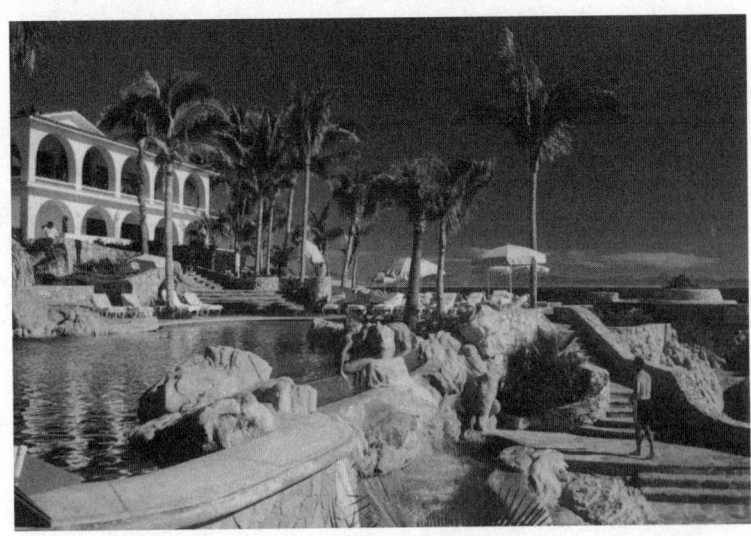

Fine architectural style and great seaside location make Hotel Palmilla one of Baja's best hotels. Photo BW.

SAN JOSE DEL CABO -- Government development started here at the same time as that at Loerto-Nopolo but was far more successful. A very fine, hotel, now the *Presidente Inter-Continental,* was constructed on the beach. The town of San Jose was considerably modernized and a previously vacant area was developed into a golf course and major residential area for investing North Americans. The new developments are largely separated from the old Mexican town and thus are all modern and uniformly pleasing. Several other medium-sized hotels were constructed on the same beach but they have not been overly popular. They appear to be the victims of poor lot design. I can recommend the San Jose del Cabo area but strongly advise the above noted hotel, the *La Jolla* at the western end of town or the popular *Tropicana Inn* in the old section of town. The small *Huerte Verde* offers a delightful retreat in the nearby community of Santa Rosa.

CABO SAN LUCAS -- The fishing village at the peninsula's tip was the prime target for the government resort development that started in 1977. Here at Cabo San Lucas the central feature was a dredged inner-harbor. Development was agonizingly slow but the harbor is finally finished. It is now filled with a high quality marina and is lined with hotels and condominiums. Other hotels and condos stretch eastward along the beach. Unlike San Jose del Cabo, the tourist attractions here are somewhat intermixed with less attractive older developments. This can be either unattractive or charming, depending on one's frame of mind. Cabo contains several world class hotels and is regularly visited by large cruise liners. I believe the best water front hotels are the two that were there long before the government development, the *Hotel Finisterra* and the *Hacienda Hotel.* The *Malia San Lucas* is probably the best of the newer places. The *Mar de Cortez* offers a good off-the-beach inn for the economy minded. Scattered about are a variety of *let-it-all-hang-out* night spots.

Many Baja old timers, myself included, disparage the new Cabo and regret the passing of the old. It took so long to mature that it became fashionable to report that the place was a mess. In spite of this negative comment, I am now forced to recommend it to you. It has finally reached a reasonable stage of respectability and thousands of people visit and seem to enjoy themselves.

CABO CORRIDOR -- The coastal area between San Jose del Cabo and Cabo San Lucas is known as the Cabo Corridor, although there are no sharp denotations as to where it begins or ends. It is served by a 24-kilometer long four-lane highway. It has long been home to three of Baja's very best hotels, the *Hotel Palmilla, Hotel Cabo San Lucas,* and *Hotel Twin Dolphin.* Then, starting about 1990, some of the intervening space began to fill with a wide range of tourist oriented developments. The largest of these are *Cabo Real, Cabo del Sol* and the area adjoining the *Hotel Palmilla.* Each of these three is hundreds of acres in size and combines luxury hotels, golf courses, and various residential developments. Much construction is still going on, but all development is uniformly first class. In this regard these areas are clearly superior to any other resort area in Baja, and to

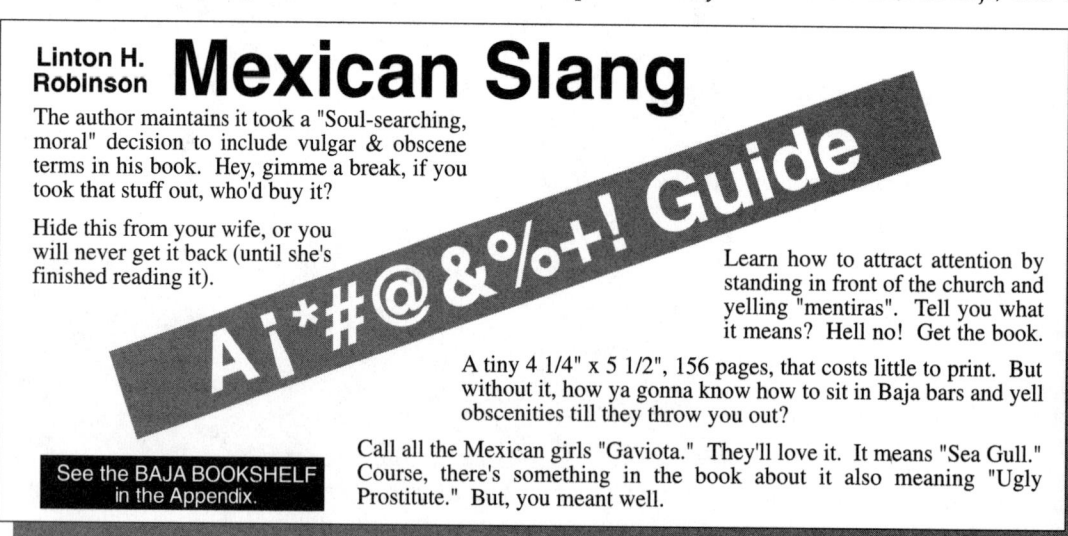

anything I have seen in the entire world. While they may lack the third-world charm of other places in Baja, they are undeniably world-class. In spite of all this grandeur, my favorite hotels in the Corridor are the original three noted above.

FONATUR

In the above descriptions of Baja's resort areas it was noted that the Mexican government was the initial developer of resort facilities at Loreto-Nopolo, San Jose del Cabo and Cabo San Lucas. The government agency responsible for this effort is FONATUR, the acronym for *Fondo National de Formento al Turismo* (translated into English as *National Fund for Tourism Development*). FONATUR was created by the federal government in 1969. Its primary function is to encourage and channel the government and private investments needed to establish new centers of tourist activities with the objectives of increasing domestic employment, generating foreign exchange, and promoting regional development.

FONATUR'S initial activities were on the mainland at Cancun on Mexico's Caribbean coast and at Ixtapa on the Pacific coast north of Acapulco. Here, two essentially deserted sections of coast were converted into rows of high-rise hotels, condominiums, and tourist-oriented facilities. International airports were constructed nearby.

During the mid 1970s FONATUR initiated work in the Baja peninsula. Actual construction started at Loreto in 1977, and at San Jose del Cabo and Cabo San Lucas in 1978. At all sites, early work consisted of developing such essential facilities as water and power supplies, sewage systems, and offices and housing for employees. New hotels soon followed, along with extensive networks of streets for vacation homes and condominiums. Golf courses were largely complete by 1989. So far, these developments have not included high-rise buildings; one would hope that this remains true for the future.

It is interesting to note that the newest resort developments along the Cabo Corridor are the result of private, rather than government activities. This is in keeping with Mexico's marked movement away from socialism in recent years.

HOTELS

I must alert you that I am in love with Baja's hotels. They are one of her major tourist attractions and provide excellent examples of the blending of man-made features with outstanding natural surroundings. The destination of most of my travels north of the border has usually been an interesting city, a National Park or other enticing outdoor attraction. With few exceptions, the hotels and motels in which I have spent the night offer little more than a place to stay. When you visit Baja's fine hotels, I hope you will come to agree that they provide an end in themselves.

The logo of Baja's La Pinta Hotels

I am not a world traveler, but I have been fortunate in recent years to visit most of the Caribbean islands, the major South American cities, England, Spain, Portugal, Switzerland, Turkey and parts of France, Italy and an assortment of lesser spots. Baja's resort hotels are better than anything I have seen in these places (I will concede to some excellent hotels in Hawaii). I will now briefly explain why I hold this view.

1. LOCATION — Except in the larger cities, most of Baja's better hotels are situated directly on the water's edge, thus taking full advantage of mankind's love affair with the seacoast. In some cases, the front yard of your room will be an extensive white sand beach as at San Felipe, Buena Vista, and San Jose del Cabo. In others, the setting blends the hotel with craggy cliffs as at the tip of the peninsula.

Hotel locations run the gamut from busy downtown La Paz to complete isolation. In some cases, there are no other man-made features for miles in any direction. If you are less than enchanted with visiting such sardine-packed resort centers as Acapulco, Honolulu, and the Florida coast, Baja will provide a welcome change.

2. ARCHITECTURAL STYLE — The designers of Baja's fine hotels have achieved an outstanding blending of structural and landscape architecture. Perhaps most importantly, almost all of Baja's fine hotels are low rise. Three stories are usually the limit. These buildings blend with the natural environment. That Wall Street feeling is left behind. North of the border, the hotel guest is greeted by steel, lumber, and sheetrock; in Baja, it is brick, native stone, and tile, with palm thatching in the patio areas. These building materials, combined with the archways, tile corridors, and other trappings of Colonial architecture, provide a charming change for the northern visitor.

Completing the picture are swimming pools, fountains, and attractive desert landscaping. Baja's desert plants seem amazingly tolerant to being transplanted for domestic purposes. They provide peninsula hotels with instant oasis of greenery and shade. If you cannot relax in such a setting you may be beyond relaxation.

3. UNCROWDED SETTING — Only a few of Baja's hotels have as many as 250 rooms. The majority are much smaller. The overall ambiance is usually one of freedom and spaciousness. There is no need to rise at dawn to reserve one's lounge chair from among all the others packed at the rim of the pool, as in many other parts of the world.

Even the best hotels are seldom full except during three-day weekends and immediately prior to Christmas and Easter. (This observation spans all of my travels in Baja. It is as true today as it was 20 years ago when Baja was far less popular than it is presently.) Reservations should be made well in advance for these peak periods. They are advisable at other times but are usually easily obtained. While this light use is not good news for management, it is pleasant for the patron who benefits by receiving better service under less hectic conditions. It seems all too obvious that there are more hotel rooms than the supply of tourists and more are being built. While this would seem to make very little economic sense for the hotel operators, it results in a relaxed and uncrowded atmosphere for the tourist.

THE LA PINTA CHAIN — In tandem with the completion of the Transpeninsular Highway in 1973, came the construction by the government, of a series of paradors and nearby hotels. (*Parador* is derived from the Spanish word *parada* meaning stopping place.) The paradors originally offered fuel, cafeteria-style restaurants, restrooms, and trailer courts. Many of these facilities have been abandoned, but the hotels are all still in operation, all bearing the name *Hotel La Pinta* (see the hotel logo in this chapter).

It is clear that the Mexican government wished to provide modern, first-class facilities for the deluge of tourists that were expected after completion of the highway. The paradors were to fill this need from Ensenada to the Sea of Cortez where there were then few tourist accommodations. The onslaught came, but in the form of recreational vehicle users hellbent on making it south to the beaches in the shortest possible time. Relatively few visitors arrived in automobiles, and as a result, there was only light demand for restaurants and hotels along the highway.

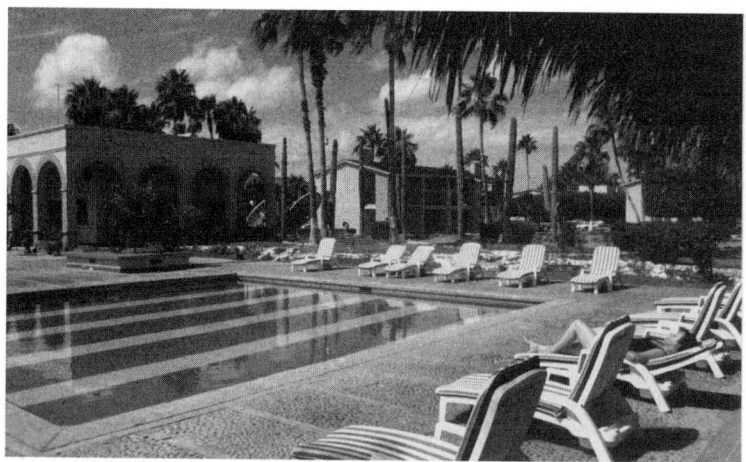

The La Pinta hotel at Loreto. Note the lack of "Maddening Crowds" a common occurrence at Baja's hotels except on peak weekends. Photo BW.

More recently there has been a significant increase in the number of tourists traveling Highway 1 in automobiles and the La Pinta hotels are thus enjoying better business. They are located at, or near, San Quintin, Catavina, Parallelo 28 near Guerrero Negro, San Ignacio, and Loreto. These hotels are modest in size (25 to 65 rooms). and they were being well maintained during my most recent visit. I recommend them to you for an overnight stop.

In recent years small to medium-sized motels have been developed in many of the towns along

Highway 1. They are clean and fully usable for an overnight or longer stay but are too numerous to include in the HOTEL DESCRIPTIONS presented in this chapter.

FLY-IN HOTELS — Long before completion of the Transpeninsular Highway, private hotel operators were catering to the North American tourist trade; however, many facilities south-of-the-border cities had to be reached by air. The hotels at La Paz have long been served by an airport suitable for large commercial aircraft in addition to ferry service from the mainland. Most of the other hotels had

The rustic dining room of the famous Meling Ranch near the Parque Nacional San Pedro Martir. Photo BW

to provide their own dirt-surface landing strips. Their patrons were thus almost exclusively people who arrived in small, privately-owned aircraft.

These hotels were scattered along the coast of the Sea of Cortez from Bahia Gonzaga, on the north, all the way to Cabo San Lucas. The majority were isolated from the outside world. Some were very modest, having only a few cabins and a central dining and lounging facility. Others were, and still are, among the most luxurious resorts in all of Baja. Most of these hotels are still in operation, but many are in locations now served by main highways, and in some cases their airstrips have been closed by the Mexican government to deter drug traffic or the land has been utilized for other purposes. The principal hotels that still have nearby airstrips and cater to the general aviation flyer are; The *Meling Ranch, Hotel Punta Chivato* north of Mulege, *Hotel Serenidad* at Mulege, *Hotel Palmas de Cortez* at Los Barriles, *Huerte Verde* near San Jose del Cabo, *Hotel Pescadero* north of Los Barrilies.

OFFBEAT HOTELS — Finally, lets get down to some places most people have never heard of and which offer a special charm at reasonable prices. I hate to mention these hideouts because their owners may get the *bighead* and raise their prices; and then, where am I going to stay? But here they are from north to south:

The *Meling Ranch* (Parque Nacional San Pedro Martir), *La Fonda Motel & Restaurant* (Old Highway 1), Bay-

side Motels (Bahia San Quintin), *Las Casitas* (Mulege), *Hotel Oasis and Villas de Loreto* (Loreto), *Hotel Gardinas* (La Paz), *Hotel California* (Todos Santos), *Hotel Palomar* (Santiago), and *Hotel Mar de Cortez* (Cabo San Lucas).

In addition, I recommend that you take advantage of the services of a travel agent. Many Baja hotels offer discount rates for stays of more than two or three days, and lower air fares can frequently be obtained if travel is combined in a package with hotel reservations. These and other advantages can easily be missed if you make your own reservations. Unfortunately, travel agencies will not help you with some of the smaller, charming hotels that do not have toll free numbers or pay agency commissions.

Finally, brace for the fact that some Baja hotels change their names and phone numbers with great regularity. You may have to do some detective work to match what you find here with what appears at your travel agency.

GOLF COURSES

Commentary by Rex Crabtree & Barbara Williams.

Only a few years ago the only golf courses in Baja were in a few locations near the international border. Then about 1989 modest courses were constructed as part of the FONATUR projects at Nopolo and San Jose del Cabo. In the late 1900's several fancy new links joined the scene along the North Coast between Tijuana and Ensenada and in the Cape Area far to the south.

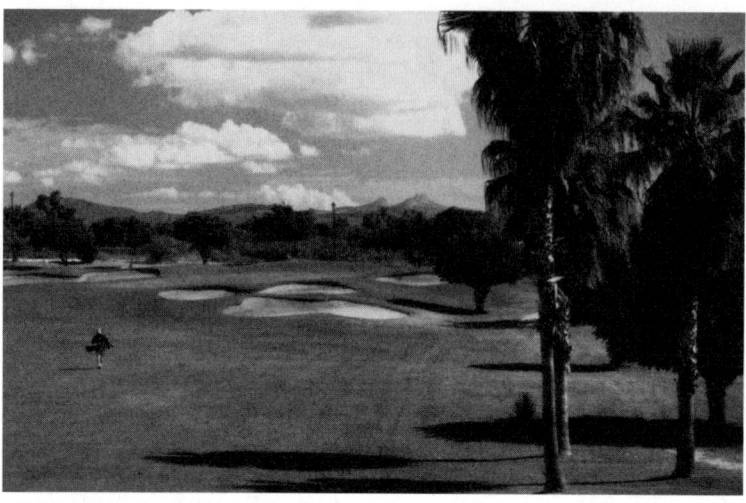

The pleasant fairway at the Campo de Golf in San Jose del Cabo. Photo by BW.

All toll there are twelve golf courses in Baja, most of them in two relatively compact clusters. The first group of six are in the northeastern corner of the peninsula where they are within easy reach of the Los Angeles - San Diego metropolitan areas. These are accessed almost exclusively by highway. At the tip of the peninsula the second group of five courses cater largely to hotel guests who arrive by airplane or to people staying for more extended visits in RV parks and private residences. The lone remaining course is all by itself as part of the Nopolo development near Loreto. Most of those playing there arrive by air.

I have visited all of these twelve courses but must note that I am of that class of folks who would rather invest his funds in fine wine than in paying green fees. To me, the highest and best use of a golf course is for walking the dog, a practice, I am advised, that is frowned upon north of the border. But in Baja, my dachshund is such a novelty that everybody loves him and we get along just fine. Fortunately, I have been accompanied in these visits by several golfers who have contributed to the following reports. Principal among these is Rex Crabtree of Lake Shastina, California who has played all five of the courses in the Cape Area.

Two overall statements can be made about Baja Golf courses. (1) Some times construction and maintenance standards in Mexico are not of the highest quality. However, in all cases we found Baja's golf courses to be of top quality and as good or better than many in the United States. Rex Crabtree rates three of the courses in the Cape Area as world-class. (2) I am advised by land developers that developing a golf course is at best a break-even venture financially and that any profit lies in selling residential and commercial property adjoining the course. Thus, ten of Baja's twelve courses adjoin real estate ventures. Those in Tijuana and Mexicali appear to stand on their own. ------ Here is our report on Baja's golf courses. I should note that the Spanish words "club campestre" mean "country club." ------ The descriptive material for each course has been provided by Rex Crabtree and Barbara Williams.

TIJUANA

Club Campestre Campo de Golf Tijuana -- 18 holes. -- West of the Agua Caliente race track in Tijuana on Blvd. Agua Caliente. See *Tijuana and Vicinity* map in Chapter 14. Phone (66) 817855 -- There is a large parking lot in front of the course which is important in busy Tijuana. -- Hotels Plaza las Glorias and Grand Hotel Tijuana are within walking distance. -- A par 72, 18 hole course surprisingly tucked into the busy city next to the Grand Hotel Tijuana. The course is semiprivate, with Wednesday and Saturday mornings reserved for members-only. The club also features a pool, spa, tennis court, pro shop and clubhouse. Private and clinic lessons are offered by the resident pro. We have not yet played this course and thus cannot offer a description of course play.

TECATE

Rancho Tecate Resort and Country Club -- Planned for 18 holes if sufficient water becomes available. In November 1997 3 holes were completed with 6 under construction. The second 9 holes will use the same greens, but with different tee-boxes. -- At Km 10 on west side of Hwy 3 south of Tecate. See Highway 3 map in Chapter 16. -- First class clubhouse, 45 room hotel and excellent dining room frequently used for weddings, conferences and other functions stemming from southern California. -- Several high standard residences under construction. -- This entire operation appears first class with good landscaping. Green fee $10.00 all day. No carts as yet. The course is still a long way from providing great golf, but the very friendly resort is worth a visit.

MEXICALI

Club Campestre de Mexicali -- 18 holes. -- West of Hwy 5 at Km 2.5 in the southern outskirts of Mexicali. Sign on Hwy 5 reads Fracc Campertre. Drive 0.4 miles west and then 0.7 miles north on Aveneda Camprestre. -- Phone 63-61-70, FAX 63-61-71, or write 233 Paulin Ave, Box 8515, Calexico, CA 92231. -- This facility, Club de Golf at the Club Deportivo Campestre de Mexicali (Sport and Country Club) has been a member of the Southern California and US Golf Associations since 1978. It sells memberships to many Southern Californians who can frequently come to play. We spoke to some regular players who rated it as "better than good, but not great." They reported that the abundance of trees, sand and water provide plenty of challenge, and that one uses every club in one's bag. The club has a pool, other sports facilities and a children play area but there are no nearby hotels. Lifetime membership is $625 while green fees with carts are $45-$55.

NORTH COAST

Real del Mar Golf Resort -- 18 holes. -- East of Hwy 1-D at Km 19.5. The resort is served by its own highway interchange. -- The golf course clubhouse is adjacent to the Real Del Mar Golf Resort and Spa by Marriott. -- Call 1-800-803-6038 in Mexico 1-800-331-3131 in USA or 011-526-631-3406. US address is 4492 Camino de la Plaza #1246, San Ysidro, CA 92173-3097 -- The course consists of two 9 hole courses, one in each of two small canyons that extend up-slope from the ocean and offer views of Islas Coronados offshore. Ponds, swimming pool, a nice pro shop and home sites are also available. An additional nine holes and an elementary school are planned for the future. We have not played this course yet, but the large crowd of North American golfers interviewed in the pro shop reported they loved the course.

Bajamar Ocean Front Golf Resort -- 27 holes -- West of Hwy 1 at interchange at Km A-78. -- The golf course is served by a Hacienda style hotel and restau-

rant. -- The resort area is located on a relatively level bench adjacent to the Pacific Ocean -- Hotel reservations direct 011-52-615-501-51, Tee Time Direct 011-52-615-501-61, San Diego Office (619) 299-1112. 1-800 BAJA-4-18 -- Amidst three housing and condo developments lie the three 9 hole courses that make up Bajamar. A fourth canyon course is planned for the future. The development includes a driving range, putting green, and a very nice two-story clubhouse which overlooks the Pacific Ocean and golf course. We haven't played this course yet so I have no report on playing conditions.

ENSENADA

Baja Country Club -- 18 holes. -- Access road leaves Hwy 1 1.7 miles north of Hwy 23 (The Punta Banda highway). Drive east 5.5 miles through farm land. Drive several additional miles along edge of the golf course to clubhouse facility. -- Plans for a much improved clubhouse and residential development surrounding the course are on hold due to lack of financing. -- This quiet par 72 course fills a broad valley south of Ensenada. As it is not associated with

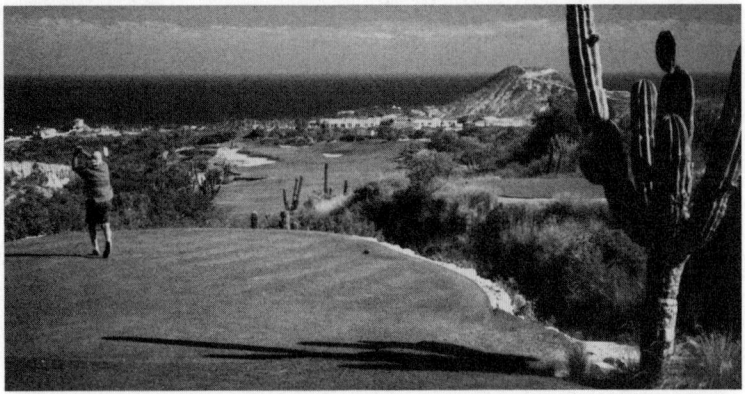

The 7th tee at the Pamilla Golf Club. Centuries old giant cactus plants and other desert vegetation provide an outstanding setting for the Cape Area's golf courses. Photo BW.

any resort or hotel facilities, it seems to be often overlooked, or used by Southern Californians who come down for the day. We have not yet played here but folks we have interviewed who have played all the courses in Baja describe it as "outstanding." The sixth green is on an island in a small lake. Greens fee and cart is $45.00. The pro shop is minimal and construction on the clubhouse has never been completed.

LORETO-NOPOLO -- 18 holes -- Golf course is part of the FONATUR development at Nopolo. See the Nopolo map for access directions. -- The Eden Loreto

18th Tee at the World class Cabo del Sol Golf Course. Photo BW.

Campo de Golf - San Jose del Cabo -- 9 Holes -- Located within the FONATUR development at San Jose del Cabo. See the San Jose del Cabo map in Chapter 24 for specific location. -- There are no on site hotels but the Howard Johnson Plaza Hotel is across the street and several others are nearby. -- This is a great course for beginners or those wanting an inexpensive golfing experience in the Cape Area. Its 2900 yard, par 35 nine holes offer a more casual atmosphere than the larger, more sophisticated courses along the corridor. It is the only Los Cabos course suitable for walking. The course is situated on gently rolling terrain, amidst scattered condo and hotel developments. It is landscaped with a mixture of palms, citrus and native vegetation, and provides views of granite hillsides, the historic San Jose cemetery, and occasional glimpses of the Sea of Cortez. While not in the world-class league, this is an enjoyable, fun-filled little course.

Resort hotel lies nearby and offers golf packages. -- The golf course is surrounded by residential lots but so far only a few have been built upon. -- Not world-class, but a good, challenging 18 holes. The course plays over flat terrain, but ever-present views of the looming Sierra Giganta on one side, and the Sea of Cortez on the other, provide an outstanding golf setting. The Nopolo course features two unique arched bridges over course water, and picturesque Punta Nopolo at the 14th green. The club house and pro shop facilities are minimal, but most golfers return to the Eden Loreto Resort which has several restaurants and bars. Course play is not managed with the organization usually found at most North American courses (there are no marshals and play can get quite backed up during busy times of year) but if you are there to relax and take things easy, you'll enjoy this course.

SAN JOSE DEL CABO

CABO CORRIDOR

Notes applying to the four Cape Area courses noted below. Carts are mandatory as there are long distances between holes in many cases. While it is often hotter in the afternoons there are fewer players during this time and views of the sea are more spectacular due to the angle of the sun. Each course sells memberships and may eventually become a private facilities but all are currently open to public play. All have state of the art water reclamation facilities, and use water-conscious course design and landscaping that features the unique native vegetation of the area. This is most spectacular in the fall weeks following heavy rains. Fairways and greens are soft and slower than many northern courses due to the use of warm-climate grasses such as Bermuda. All have only modest clubhouses facilities and most golfers do their dining, drinking and socializing in local hotels, restaurants and bars.

The 8th hole at the outstanding golf course at Cabo Real with views of the ocean. Photo BW.

Palmilla Golf Club -- 18 holes Jack Nicklaus design -- Interchange on Hwy 1 between Km J-26 & J-27. -- The golf course lies above (north) of the highway. Most holes have ocean views. -- The golf course is part of a 900 acre Palmilla resort community which features the famous Hotel Palmilla. Golf reservations (800) 386-2465 Http://www/kollresorts.com - Hotel reservations (800) 637-2226. -- There are nearby residential developments. -- An outstanding par 72 course with exciting diversity in setting, scenery and play. Jack Nicklaus designed the front Arroyo Nine and back Mountain Nine that wind through scenic hills and deep arroyos overlooking the Sea of Cortez. Every hole offers something new and different. While offering numerous challenges, Palmilla is potentially the most enjoyable of the Cabo corridor courses for the average golfer. Within a fairly straightforward course layout, its fairways are the most forgiving, and its greens are generally flat and true. This course was the favorite of many of the Baja golfers we interviewed. Look forward to the planned Ocean Nine course sometime in the next few years.

Cabo Real -- 18 hole Robert Trent Jones II design. An additional 18 holes designed by Jack Nicklaus is planned to open in 1999. -- Access at Km J-21 on Hwy 1. Fifteen holes lie above (north), and three below Hwy 1 with the club house and 1st tee in the upper NE portion above the road. -- Phone 011-52-144-40050 FAX 011-52-114-40155 -- The 2,600 acre Cabo Real resort development has three hotels with others planned. All offer golf packages. Casa del Mar - (800) 221-8808 - Melia Cabo Real - (800) 336-3542 - Western Regina (800) 228-3000. There are nearby residential developments. -- This beautiful course is a classic, serious player's course, offering the most challenging golf in Baja. It boasts ocean views from every green as play proceeds up and down a rolling hillside, eventually reaching the Sea of Cortez. This par 72 course is typical of Jones's designs, with numerous bunkers along the fairways and a generally clear visually layout but the hilly topography does add some blind shots. Cabo Real has many long holes and challenging green designs, and provides a true test of golfing skill. Its expansive views

provided the setting for the 1996 PGA Tour Senior Grand Slam tournament.

Cabo del Sol -- 18 holes Jack Nicklaus design. Two additional 18 hole courses are planned. Includes an excellent practice facility. -- Interchange on Hwy 1 between Km J-9 & J-10. -- The golf course is part of the 1,800 acre Cabo del Sol resort community which eventually will have four oceanfront hotels. -- Phone (800) 833-3030 or 011-52-114-33990. Golf reservations (800) 386-2464. http://www.wotw.com/koll -- Playing this par 72, Jack Nicklaus course is a fantastic experience. Play is through a diversity of hills, arroyos, and beautiful native vegetation before reaching seven ocean-side holes. The designer boasts that the course has the three best finishing holes in the world and playing them provides a breathtaking thrill which includes vistas of historic Shipwreck Beach, and the Punta Cabeza Lighthouse. If one is looking for a Pebble Beach setting in Los Cabos, this is the course to choose. It offers the perfect level of challenge for every level of player, and every hole has a unique feel and character. Cabo del Sol has hosted the PGA Tour Senior Grand Slam tournament in 1995 and 1998 and has been rated as one of the top 100 golf coursed in the world.

CABO SAN LUCAS

Cabo San Lucas Country Club -- 18 holes Dye Corporation design -- Access is at Km J-3 of Hwy 1 at

Signs of Distinction

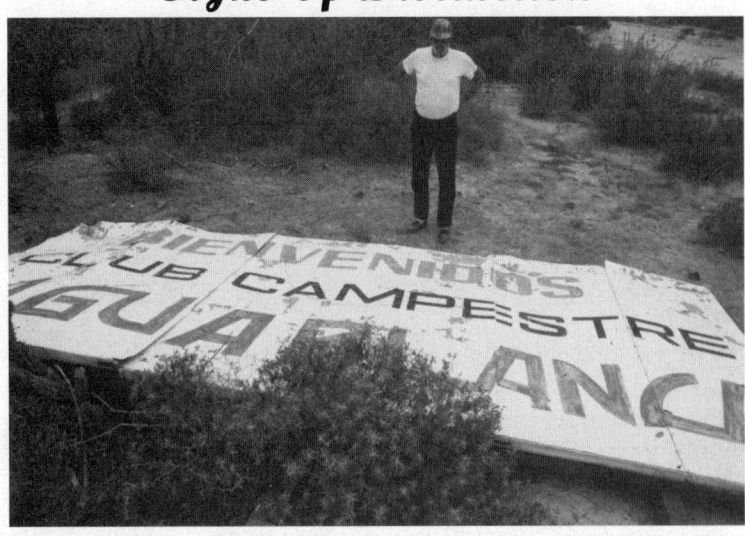

The Agua Blanca Country Club south of La Paz. This photo offers living proof that you can always get at least one sucker to go look at your real estate venture. Photo BW.

Signs of Distinction

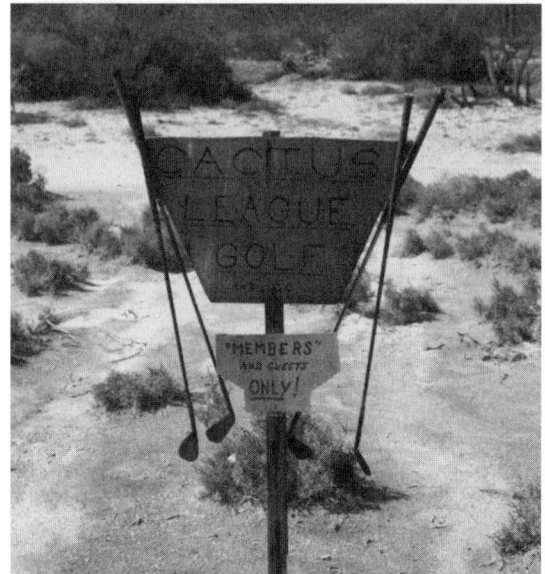

The Cactus League Golf and CC -- Finding a member of the club who is not fishing or drinking beer may be the most difficult part of acquiring permission to play on this course. Photo BW.

the eastern edge of Cabo San Lucas. The course is entirely on the north side of the highway. -- The course occasionally sufferers flood damage at its lower end. -- There are no on-site hotels but extensive residential development is planned. -- Phone (800) 854-2314 or 011-52-114-31922. -- This is a very nice course with some excellent features, but it is not on the same level as the three Cabo Corridor courses noted above. It does, however, provides Baja's only golf course views of promontory at Land's End. The course features many ponds, where one may watch osprey and other diving sea birds. Play is over relatively level terrain, with fairways that are soft and forgiving. It offers the longest par 5 hole in Los Cabos, but does not provide as much playing diversity or challenge as do the other three Corridor courses.

OTHER COURSES -- In our efforts to be comprehensive about our coverage of Baja's golfing scene we must mention three other facilities. They are featured nearby in several *Signs of distinction* photos.

We had heard several reports about a golf course at La Paz and I recalled seeing a sign along Highway 1 some 10 miles south of town announcing a country club. So we found the sign and headed west some 15 miles into

the desert. After a frustrating and bumpy drive we located a second sign lying flat on the ground around a sea of lot boundary markers announcing "Welcome, Club Campestre". There was nothing else in sight for miles around. I have seen many failed real estate ventures in my day, but this one takes the prize.

The other two courses appear to be the work of Gringo types who have excessive time on their hands, a sense of humor and a desperate need to play golf. On the dirt road accessing the Punta Arena camping area (See *Bahia Coyote Area* map in Chapter 21) lies the Cactus League Golf and CC. Three holes, each about 75 feet long best suited for your trusty putter. If you tire of lying in the sun, this is your sports alternative. -- At Pete's Camp a few miles north of San Felipe a sign announces "Golf Course." And there it was, a full 9 holes carved out of the desert with rusty tin cans for holes. And, we encountered two golfers in Mexicali who had actually played it. It abounds in tongue-in-cheek signs one of which is shown nearby. The parking lot alluded to in the sign is the edge of the road.

Signs of Distinction

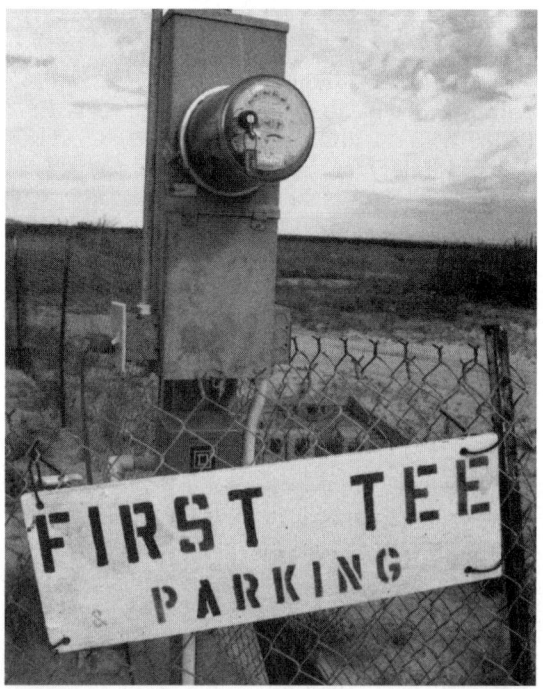

Here is where you park at the Pete's Camp golf course. Anouther sign announces "No Off Road Vehicles Allowed on Golf Course. At Pete's camp that eliminates everybody. Photo BW.

HOTEL DESCRIPTIONS

Towns are listed as encountered from north to south (See map on page 84).

TIJUANA

PLAZA LAS GLORIAS — 200 rooms, pool, Jacuzzi, convention center for 400 people. Blvd Agua Caliente No. 11553 adjacent to the Tijuana Country Club. PO Box 43-1588, San Ysidro, CA 92173. (888) 748-8785. An 8-story modern hotel.

HOTEL HOWARD JOHNSON CONQUISTADOR — 110 rooms, pool, sauna, convention center for 300 people. Located near the Tijuana Country Club at 1777 Blvd Agua Caliente. PO Box 434421, San Ysidro, CA 92173. (800) 569-6161. An attractive 2-story motel with old world charm.

GRAND HOTEL TIJUANA — 422 rooms, pool, sauna and tennis courts. Convention center for 1,200 people. Agua Caliente Blvd # 4500. (800) GRAND TJ. Hotel is part of the Plaza Agua Caliente on Blvd Agua Caliente adjacent the Tijuana Country Club. For a skyscraper view of Tijuana, this is the place, as there are 27 floors of rooms in this westerly segment of a modern twin-towered building. Hard to tell it apart from hotels in the major cities north of the border.

HOTEL LUCERNA — 168 rooms and suites, pool convention facilities. NW corner of Paseo de los Heroes and Ave Rodriguez. PO Box 437910, San Ysidro, CA 92143. 011-52-663-42000 or (800) LUCERNA. A modern 6-story hotel in the developing Rio Tijuana area. As a result, the overall atmosphere is less crowded than that in the older sections of town and the interior court is well landscaped.

TECATE

RANCHO TECATE RESORT & COUNTRY CLUB — 45 rooms, spa, pool, dining room. Gym, tennis courts & golf course under construction in 1997. Located on grounds of turn of the century vineyard & winery.

MOTELS — There are two motels on the north side of old Highway 2 entering Tecate from the west. These are the Motel El Dorado and the Hotel Hacienda. The latter establishment has a restaurant and disco-bar. Its rooms face inward toward a central courtyard. There are no trailer courts in Tecate.

MEXICALI

HOTEL LUCERNA — 200 rooms, pool. 2151 Blvd Benito Juarez. 011-52-656-61000 or (800) LUCERNA. A very nice 6-story hotel with well-landscaped inside courtyard.

SIESTA INN HOTEL — 70 rooms, restaurant, bar, pool, meeitng room for 50. 011-52-656-82001. Calzada Justo Sierra 899.

ARAIZA INN MEXICALI — 120 rooms, pool. On Blvd Benito Juarez. Toll free (800) 456-4329. A multi-storied hotel with pleasant internal courtyard. (Formerly the Holiday Inn)

SAN FELIPE

MOTEL EL CORTEZ — 78 rooms, pool, and boat launching ramp. PO Box 1227, Calexico, CA 92232. 011-52-657-71055. A pleasant motel located on the beach about 1/2 mi. south of the center of town.

HOTEL LAS MISIONES — 120 rooms, tennis court, meeting facilities. PO Box 120637 Chula Vista, CA 92012. In California (800) 664-7466, Nationwide (800) 336-5454. A very nice modern 3-story hotel directly on the beach about 1 mi. south of town. Well-landscaped courtyard area.

COSTA AZUL — 140 rooms, pool. Av. Mar de Cortez and Calle Ensenada. Mail Address; 233 Pauline Ave., P.O. Box 6252, Calexico, CA 92231. 011-52-657-71548.

SAN FELIPE MARINA RESORT & SPA — Newest and finest resort. Rooms, 60 luxury beach front suites some with kitchenettes, restaurant, bar, pool, tennis courts. KM 4.5 Careterra San Felipe Aero Puerto. (800) 291-5397, (619) 558-0295, 011-52-657-71435.

ADDITIONAL MOTELS — There are 5 other very adequate motels within a few blocks of, and south of, the center of town. They are the Motel Capitan, Motel

95

Chapala, Hotel Truncha Vagabundo, Hotel Riviera, and Motel Villa del Mar.

PUERTECITOS

POSADA DE OROZCO — Six rooms. This facility is located near the PEMEX on the beach at the head of the cove.

THE NORTH COAST (Tijuana to Ensenada)

REAL DEL MAR — 76 suites, 18 hole golf course, tennis, pool spa, restaurant, piano bar. Hwy 1-D at KM 19.5. US address: 4492 Camino de la Plaza #1246, San Ysidro, CA 92173. (800) 803-6038 or 011-526-631-3406. Very fancy.

OASIS — 100 suites, pool, convention center. Hwy 1-D KM 25 (off ramp south lane only). P.O. Box 158, Imperial Beach, CA 91933. (800) 462-7472, 011-52-661-33252. A new modern faciltity.

ROSARITO BEACH HOTEL — 275 rooms, 128 suites and apartments, pool, entertainment. On Old Hwy 1 at the south Rosarito exit from Hwy 1-D. P.O. Box 430145, San Diego, CA 92143-0145. (800) 343-8582. Area code (619) call 498-8230. A former gambling casino dating from the 1930s. Many of the rooms have been remodeled and the public rooms are also well kept. The hotel is on the POINTS OF SPECIAL INTEREST Tour because of its historic interest.

LA FONDA — 25 rooms, plus apartments, entertainment. On Old Hwy 1, 0.3 mi. south of the La Mision exit from Hwy 1-D. P.O. Box San Ysidro, CA 92073, no phone. A famous old road-house with great food located on the bluffs overlooking the Pacific. The restaurant is more of the attraction than the motel.

HOTEL LAS ROCAS — 26 suites & 46 rooms, conference facilities, pool, tennis court and Jacuzzi. P. O. Box 189003 HLR, Coronado, CA 92178. (800) 733-6394. Area (619) call 425-2682. A new (1991) modern, 5-story hotel on cliffs overlooking the ocean. All rooms with terraces and ocean views. Located on old Highway 1 at Km 37.5. Fancy.

HOTEL NEW PORT BEACH — 150 rooms, tennis courts, gift shop, pool and Jacuzzi. P. O. Box 139 Plaza Patria 22441, Tijuana. (800) 582-1018. A new (1991) modern 3-story hotel on cliffs overlooking the ocean. All rooms with ocean views. Located on old Highway 1 near Km 45. Fancy.

HACIENDA LAS GLORIAS (Bajamar Ocean Front Golf Resort) — 81 rooms 7 suites, pool, Jacuzzi, golf, tennis, restaurant, bar. Hwy 1-D Km 77. (800) BAJA-418, 011-52-615-50151. San Diego, CA office (619) 299-1112.

ENSENADA AREA

ESTERO BEACH RESORT HOTEL — 110 rooms, tennis court. PO Box 86, Ensenada, B.C., Mexico. 011-526-176-6235. At this location on the shores of Estero Punta Banda are combined an attractive and well-landscaped hotel, trailer court and shops. It is the only Ensenada area hotel which fully meets my standards for a destination resort. Located 6 mi. S of Ensenada's tourist center.

HOTEL AGUA CALIENTE — 50 rooms. Large swimming pools heated by nearby hot springs. Adjoining camping area under large live oak trees. The hotel is a bit run-down. A pleasant spa, 5.1 mi. by dirt road south of **Km 26** on Hwy 3 east of Ensenada.

HOTEL MISION SANTA ISABEL — 58 rooms, pool. An older, charming, colonial-style hotel at the east end of the *Tourist Row* area. Completely remodeled in 1989. Isabel Travel, 011-52-617-83616. P.O. Box 76, Ensenada B.C., Mexico.

HOTEL LA PINTA ENSENADA — 52 rooms, pool. Blvd Los Bucaneros. (800) 262-4500 or (800) 542-3283. The northernmost of Baja's chain of La Pinta hotels. Built around a central courtyard.

SAN NICOLAS RESORT HOTEL — 150 rooms, pool, restaurant, bar, convention facilities for 500 people. Ave Lopez Mateos and Ave Guadalupe. PO Box 437060, San Diego, CA 92143-7060. 011-52-617-61901. This is the fanciest of the hotels in downtown Ensenada. It is close to the tourist area shops and has a pleasant internal atmosphere.

CASA DEL SOL — 46 rooms, pool. (800) 528-1234 (Best Western reservation system) or 011-52-617-81570. A motel directly on Tourist Row.

EL CID HOTEL — 52 rooms, pool, restaurant bar. Reservations (800) El Cid 05 A motel directly on Tourist Row.

ENSENADA TRAVELODGE — 52 rooms, pool and enclosed parking. Ave. Blancarte # 130. P. O. Box 1467, Ensenada. (800) 578-7878 or 011-52-617-81601. A motel directly on Tourist Row.

CORONA HOTEL — 93 rooms, pool. Blvd. Costero #1442. US address 482 W. San Ysidro Blvd., Suite 303, San Ysidro, CA 92173. 011-52-617-24800. A 4-story hotel at the edge of the harbor area a few blocks from the tourist area.

BAJA INN — 50 rooms, 4 suites, restaurant, bar, pool. Blvd. Lazaro Cardenas No. 1536. 011-52-617-72255. The newest hotel in town.

The Cape Area's Hotel Twin Dolphin. **Photo JW.**

JOKER — 40 rooms, pool, convention center. Hwy 1 KM 12.5. Across from the airport. (800) 2 JOKER 2. A small hotel built like a castle.

BAJA BEACH RESORT — Rooms, 2 & 3 room cabanas with kitchens, pool, tennis, restaurant. Approx. 20 minutes south of Ensenada off the road to La Bufadora on Ensenada Bay. Reservations (619) 426-8576 or 011-52-615-40230.

PARQUE NACIONAL SAN PEDRO MARTIR

MELING RANCH — The Meling Ranch is a working cattle ranch but with very pleasant accommodations for about 12 guests. There is a dining room and swimming pool. The ranch lies 32 miles east of Hwy 1 on the road to Parque Nacional San Pedro Martir, and 19 miles west of the park boundry. There is a nearby air strip. Mailing address: PO Box 1326, Ensenada, BC, Mexico.

SAN QUINTIN AREA

HOTEL LA PINTA SAN QUINTIN — 60 rooms, tennis court restaurant, bar. (800) 262-4500. One of the original parador hotels. See Chapter 19 for directions. All rooms have a private terrace facing the ocean. Winter season often cool and windy. There is an airstrip nearby.

RANCHO CIELITO LINDO MOTEL — 13 rooms. Write Santa Maria, Valle de San Quintin, B.C.N. Mexico. (619) 593-BAJA. A modest but pleasant motel operated with the nearby Cielito Lindo Trailer Court. Rooms are grouped in several buildings facing

a central grassy courtyard. It is a relatively short walk to the beach. Located away from other developments. See Chapter 19 for directions. The lounge has a band and dancing on Saturday nights, and from the way it looked on Sunday morning, a good time is assured. An airstrip is located 200 yards to the east.

BAY-SIDE MOTELS — There are three motels which lie on the low bluff near the water's edge along the east shore of Bahia San Quintin. They are used primarily by fishermen and bird hunters. These are Ernesto's (Baja Ron's), (909) 765-9522 or (909) 929-3883, Old Mill Motel, (800) 479-7962 or (619) 428-2779, (619) 428-6946, and Muelle Viejo Motel. Each has a restaurant and bar, that touch of rural Mexico flavor, views of the bay and the cinder cones to the west. See Chapter 19 for directions. The *Old Mill Motel* has been greatly improved in recent years and its owners hope it will become a destination resort in addition to a sportsman's haven.

CATAVINA

HOTEL LA PINTA CATAVINA — 28 rooms, pool, tennis court. (800) 262-4500. One of the original parador hotels. A pleasant hotel located adjacent to Hwy 1 at Catavina. Perhaps its most appealing feature is its location within the fascinating granite boulders and outstanding desert vegetation present in this area. The nearby airstrip was closed in 1997.

BAHIA SAN LUIS GONZAGA AREA

ALFONSINA'S — 6 rooms, restaurant (order in advance). A line of very modest rooms along the beach at the north end of the residential development and dirt airstrip at Bahia San Luis Gonzaga. Fronted by an outstanding sand beach.

PUNTA BUFEO TOURIST CAMP — 10 or more stone houses for lease or rent. Small restaurant and 3 small rental rooms. Owned by Francisca Fernandez and sons. This is the northernmost of the fly-in facilities on the Sea of Cortez. It has a dirt landing strip parallel to the beach. A really isolated location with little vegetation, as is typical of the San Felipe Desert. Located near Punta Bufeo, 6 mi. north of Punta Willard. See US nautical chart 21008 for location.

PAPA FERNANDEZ — Cabins and refreshments. A very modest facility located near the north end of Bahia Gonzaga. The founder, Papa Fernandez, was 100 years old in 1995. The resort is now run by his son, who bears the same name.

BAHIA DE LOS ANGELES

VILLA VITTA HOTEL — 40 rooms, pool, boat rental. Write Jimsair, 2904 Pacific Hwy, San Diego, CA 92101. (619) 298-4958. A very nice modern facility located adjacent to the paved highway as one enters the village. They have an excellent boat launching ramp.

CASA DIAZ — 15 rooms, restaurant, store, boat ramp, rental boats. Write Antero Diaz, PO Box 579, Ensenada, B.C. Mexico. Not quite as fancy as the Villa Vitta, but this is the original, family-operated, fly-in resort at Bahia de los Angeles and is well liked. Make reservations in advance for the restaurant, where meals are served family style.

SAN FRANCISQUITO

PUNTA SAN FRANCISQUITO RESORT — 11 cabins with cots, restaurant, central restroom, shower facilities. Write 2004 Newton Ave, San Diego, CA 92113. (619) 239-8872. A modest fly-in facility with poor road access. Also caters to boaters crossing the Sea of Cortez from Bahia Kino. Some visitors fly in, camp on the beach, and use the resort's restrooms and other facilities.

GUERRERO NEGRO

HOTEL LA PINTA GUERRERO NEGRO — 28 rooms, restaurant, bar. (800) 262-4500. Another of the original parador hotels. Located adjacent to Hwy 1 next to the eagle monument at the 28th parallel. The

hotel is modern and comparable to the other La Pinta facilities, but its setting in the flat, relatively barren desert is less attractive than those of its sister hotels.

There are several small motels on the right side of the road entering the town of Guerrero Negro. Of particular note is the Malarrimo restaurant and motel.

BAHIA TORTUGAS

VERA CRUZ MOTEL — 8 rooms, restaurant, bar. A modest motel near the PEMEX station. After having driven so many miles even a modest establishment looks good.

SAN IGNACIO

HOTEL LA PINTA SAN IGNACIO — 28 rooms, restaurant, bar, pool. (800) 262-4500. My favorite of the original parador hotels, due in part to its setting in the palms and other vegetation at the edge of the charming town of San Ignacio.

LA POSADA MOTEL — 8 rooms. Write La Posada Motel, San Ignacio, B. C. S. Mexico. A small but pleasant motel on a San Ignacio back street 2 blocks from the civic plaza.

SANTA ROSALIA

HOTEL EL MORRO — 21 rooms, restaurant, cocktail lounge, pool. PO Box 76, Santa Rosalia, B.C.S. Mexico. 011-52-115-20414. A modern motel with attractive stone buildings. Built on a bluff overlooking the Sea of Cortez. Some rooms have patios with water views. Adjacent to the Transpeninsular Highway at the southern edge of Santa Rosalia.

HOTEL FRANCES — 17 rooms, pool, restaurant-bar. Calle Jean M. Cousteau # 15 Col. Mesa Francis, C.P. 23920 Santa Rosalia, B.C.S., Mexico. 011-52-115-22052. This old historic hotel has been refurbished and reopened and is operating as a Bed & Breakfast. However, the historic photos of the mining and shipping days of Santa Rosalia that used to adorn the walls were stolen when the hotel was closed for several years.

MULEGE AREA

HOTEL PUNTA CHIVATO — About 30 rooms, restaurant, bar, pool, beachside camping and RV park. Write Apartado Postal 18, Mulege, B.C.S., Mexico (706) 853-0188. The secondary road leading to the hotel joins Highway 1 near **Km F-156**. The dirt surface access road is graded frequently and is easy to travel.

HOTEL SERENIDAD — 32 rooms including 2-bedroom cottages, pool. Write PO Box 9, Mulege, B.C.S. Mexico. (706) 853-0111. This is one of Baja's longstanding fly-in hotels. The airstrip is directly adjacent to the hotel. An attractive facility readily accessible from Hwy 1 near **Km F-132** over 1/2 mi. of dirt road. Located at the mouth of the river with an adjoining boat launching ramp. Considering the ease of access and its overall attractiveness, it is probably Mulege's best hotel.

HOTEL TERRAZAS — 35 rooms. 011-52-115-30009. This is a clean but basic motel in the center of the Mulege business district.

Loreto's Hotel Oasis. This small modest hotel pleasantly blends desert landscaping and the use of native building materials with its beach side location. Photo JW.

HOTEL LAS CASITAS — 8 rooms, restaurant. Write Las Casitas, PO Box 3, Mulege, B.C.S. Mexico. (706) 853-0019 OR 011-52-115-30019. This is a small, older, inexpensive, and charming hotel near the center of town. It is the kind of place you would expect to find in a sleepy Mexican town. Mulege, of course, is no longer sleepy. The restaurant is a favorite with the local tourist community.

SAN BUENAVENTURA — A very nice small hotel with restaurant and RV park located on the shores of Bahia Concepcion south of Mulege at KM 94.5. The workmanship of the facilities are exceptionally good and much better than at Baja's other rural hotels.

LORETO-NOPOLO AREA

HOTEL LA PINTA LORETO — 30 rooms, pool. (800) 262-4500. Another of the original parador hotels. Large rooms with private patios or balconies. It is located on a great beach at the north edge of Loreto.

HOTEL MISION DE LORETO — 36 rooms, pool. Blvd. Lopez Mateos No. 1, Apartado Postal 49, C.P. 23880 Loreto, B.C.S., Mexico. (800) 777-2664 or 011-52-113-50048. A very nice 3-story hotel. It has no

beach but fronts on an attractive waterfront street and breakwater facing the Sea of Cortez.

HOTEL OASIS — 35 rooms, tennis court, pool. Apartado Postal #17, C.P. 23880 Loreto, B.C.S., Mexico. (800) 662-7476 or 011-52-113-50211. This small attractive hotel has its one floor of rooms along the beach toward the south end of Loreto.

PLAZA LORETO — 18 rooms, a new 2 story downtown hotel. (800) 777-2664 or 011-52-113-50280.

VILLAS DE LORETO — 6 rooms, pool and adjoining RV park. Antonio Mijares y Playa, Colonia Zaragosa. PO Box 132, Loreto, B.C.S., Mexico C.P. 23880. 011-52-113-50586. A charming facility facing the Sea of Cortez.

EDEN LORETO RESORT — 236 rooms with 9 suites, restaurants, bars, 2 pools, tennis, golf, disco. (888) 282 EDEN. This adults only all inclusvive vacation resort is Loreto's finest resort, although it is not in Loreto but 6 mi. south at Nopolo. It is well-landscaped and located on the beach across the street from the international tennis center.

CIUDAD CONSTITUCION

HOTEL MARIBEL — 39 rooms. Write Maribel, Guadalupe Victoria 156, Ciudad Constitucion, B.C.S.

Mexico. (706) 832-0155. A 3-story concrete building at the corner of the main street of town (Hwy 1) and Olachea St. This corner is 2 blocks south of the junction of Hwy 1 and Hwy 22. A clean spot for overnight, but nothing fancy.

HOTEL CASINO — 37 rooms. Write Casino, Ciudad Constitucion, B.C.S. Mexico (706) 832-0004. Located 2 blocks east of the Hotel Maribel on Olachea St. A basic motel, perhaps a bit more quiet than the Maribel, being 2 blocks from the traffic on the main highway.

BAHIA MAGDALENA (San Carlos)

HOTEL ALCATRAZ — A small hotel entering San Carlos from Highway 22. Phone 011-52-113-60017, Fax 011-52-113-60086. A pleasant place in a town that otherwise leaves a bit to be desired.

LA PAZ

VILLAS DEL MAR BEACH CLUB — 50 suites, pools, convention facilties for 700. Marina Fidepaz, P.O. Box 482, La Paz, B.C.S, Mexico. 011-52-112-40830. One of La Paz's newest hotels, located south of the city at the outer edge of the FIDEPAZ Marina. Very fancy.

LA POSADA DE ENGELBERT — 25 rooms, restaurant, bar, pool. Nueva Reforma and Playa Sur. PO Box 152, La Paz B.C.S. Mexico C.P.23000. 011-52-112-24011. It is a well-landscaped, and very pleasant spot on the beach. Its chief disadvantages are that it is located some distance from the downtown area and its access route leaves something to be desired. For those who are not concerned with doing the town, La Posada is a charming place to stay.

HOTEL LOS ARCOS — 150 rooms, pool. Baja Hotel Reservations, 6 Jenner St., Suite, 120, Irvine, CA 92618. (800) 347-2252, (714) 450-9000. The Los Arcos is the only top hotel located in the downtown area and within walking distance of stores and restaurants. It faces the beach but is separated from it by the city's main waterfront street. The 3-story structure is built around 2 inner courtyards containing the pool, fountain, and greenery. The downtown location, moderate prices, and excellent food make it a favorite. One often encounters guests who have moved from other hotels.

CABANAS DE LOS ARCOS — 55 rooms, pool. Other information is the same as for the Los Arcos.

Located on an adjoining corner from the Los Arcos and operated by the same organization. A group of 16 Tahitian-style cabins in a tree-shaded area plus an adjoining 3-story building. It has its own pool but shares its other facilities with the Los Arcos.

HOTEL PERLA — 102 rooms, pool, 1570 Malecon Alvaro Obregon. Write Hotel Perla, 1570 Obregon, La Paz, B.C.S., Mexico. 011-52-112-20777. A top location on the main waterfront street near the heart of town. Greatly enlarged and upgraded in 1989. The adjoining sidewalk cafe La Terraza is a good place for breakfast or lunch.

ARAIZA INN PALMIRA — 120 rooms, pool, convention center for 600 people. (800) 929-2402, 011-52-112-24000. A resort hotel located 2 mi. north of downtown La Paz on the highway to Pichilingue. It has a very nicely landscaped pool area, but the hotel is located on the side of the highway away from the beach.

LA CONCHA BEACH RESORT — 109 rooms plus condominiums, pool, meeting and banquet facilities. Km 5 Carretera a Pichilingue. (800) 999-BAJA, 011-52-112-16161. A resort hotel located 4 mi. north of downtown La Paz on the highway to Pichilingue and next door to the governor's mansion. This very pleasant hotel has what I believe is the best beach location of the La Paz hotels but it is rather far from the downtown area.

CLUB EL MORO — 22 apartments, restaurant, bar, pool. Km 2 Carretera a Pichilingue. P. O. Box 357, La Paz B.C.S., Mexico. 011-52-112-24084. It is La Paz's best apartment complex with an attractively landscaped pool area. Units contain 1 or 2 bedrooms, sitting-room and cooking area.

HOTEL GARDENIAS — 56 rooms, restaurant, bar, pool. P.O. Box 197 La Paz B.C.S. Mexico. Corner of Aquiles Seroan and Querrero. Not as plush as some of the others, but nice and less than half the price. Located in a residential neighborhood about 8 blocks from downtown. Plenty of parking. If you are just passing through town and need to rest-up, this is the place.

HOTEL MARINA — 70 rooms & 23 suites, reaturant, pool. North of town at KM 2.5 on the highway to Pichilingue. (800) 826-1138 or 011-52-112-16254. Located on the bay in conjunction with the Marina Palmira.

TODOS SANTOS

HOTEL CALIFORNIA — 16 rooms, restaurant, pool. On Calle Juarea, between Morelos & Marquez de Leon. (800-736-8636 or 011-52-114-4002. A thick-walled, 2-story masonry building that looks like a hotel in a small Mexican town ought to look. Not built with today's fancy tourist needs in mind, but upgraded in 1988 to include a well landscaped pool area. A real charmer in a charming small town.

THE EAST CAPE

HOTEL LAS ARENAS — 40 rooms, restaurant, bar, pool, fishing fleet. Rooms have balconies facing the ocean. It is a high-quality facility located on a remote section of the coast some 30 air miles southeast of La Paz and west of Punta Arena de la Ventana. It is also reachable by 40 mi. of highway and roads from La Paz. The route is described in Chapter 23 in relation to the side trip to Bahia de los Muertos. .

PUNTA PESCADERO — 21 rooms, with patios and ocean views, restaurant, bar, pool, tennis court, fishing fleet and paved airstrip. Write 24831 Alicia Pky #C-320, Laguna Hills, CA 92653 or PO Box 362, La Paz, B.C.S. Mexico 23000. (800) 426-BAJA, 011-52-114-10101. A remote location some 9.3 mi. by dirt road east from Hwy 1 at **Km J-111** near Los Barriles. See Chapter 23 for route description.

HOTEL PLAYA DEL SOL — 26 rooms. PO Box 9016, Calabasas, CA 93172. (800) 368-4334, (818) 591-9463. A pleasant spot on the beach at Los Barriles. I rate this as the most modest of the 4 hotels in the immediate Los Barriles-Buena Vista area but it could be just the one that suits you best. Popular with the younger set and is headquarters for windsurfing fans.

HOTEL PALMAS DE CORTEZ — 32 rooms and 10 suites, pool, fishing fleet. PO Box 9016, Calabasas, CA 91372. (800) 368-4334, (818) 591-9463 or 011-52-114-10050. One of the long-established fly-in hotels that

The Eden Loreto Resort, the first, and up to now the only hotel to be constructed at the FONATUR resort community at Nopolo. Photo JW

now finds itself easily reached via the Transpeninsular Highway. This very nice destination resort has improved with age. It adjoins a fine, sand beach with its airstrip paralleling it on the inland side.

RANCHO BUENA VISTA — 57 rooms, pool, tennis courts, fishing fleet. P.O. Box 1408, Santa Maria, CA 93456 (800) 258-8200, (805) 928-1719. Easily reached over a short side road from Highway 1 at Buena Vista. This is a very charming facility.

HOTEL BUENA VISTA BEACH RESORT — 80 rooms, pool, tennis court, hot mineral bath, fishing fleet. 110 West 35th St., Suite V, National City, CA 91950., (800) 752-3555. Original building is a converted mansion near the beach at the south end of Buena Vista. Many new rooms have now been developed.

HOTEL PUNTA COLORADO — 29 rooms, restaurant, bar, fishing fleet. PO Box 9016, Calabasas, CA 91372. (800) 368-4334. Located at an isolated spot overlooking the beach south of Buena Vista. Can be reached by road over the East Cape Loop (See Chapter 23). Not as fancy as some others, but very nice with a relaxing isolated location.

RANCHO LEONERO — 25 rooms, restaurant, bar. This is the areas newest hotel. (800) 696-2164 or (619) 428-2164. Located on a rocky cliff overlooking the sea with dirt road access.

HOTEL BAHIA LOS FRAILES — A small resort/ bed & breakfast with luxury accommodations. Apartado Postal 230, San Jose del Cabo, BCS, Mexico. 1 (800) 762 BAJA Located on a great beach at Bahia los Frailes and near the coral reefs at Cabo Pulmo.

SAN JOSE DEL CABO

HOWARD JOHNSON PLAZA HOTEL — 192 room & suites, (suites with dining & living room &1 to 3 bedrooms), restaurant, bar, Olympic size pool. (800) 446-4656 or 011-52-114-20999. Paseo Finisterra # 1. The 12 low-rise Mediterranean style buildings are located across the street from the Los Cabos Golf & Tennis Club. Hotel is not located on the beach but provides free transportation to the La Concha Beach Club & downtown area..

LA JOLLA — Rooms and suites, restaurant, bar, pools. Hwy 1 KM 29. (800) 455 CABO, 011-52-114-23000. A very nice newer hotel on the beach near the western edge of town.

PRESIDENTE INTER-CONTINENTAL LOS CABOS — 250 rooms, restaurants, bars, pools, tennis courts. An all inclusive resort. (800) 327-0200 or 011-52-114-20211. A very good 3-story destination resort on the beach. Adjoins a pleasant coastal lagoon.

HOTEL POSADA REAL — 150 rooms, pool, tennis court, meeting facilities, on the beach. PO Box 51, San Jose del Cabo, B.C.S. Mexico. (800) 528-1234, a Best Western affiliate.

HOTEL AGUAMARINA — 99 rooms, pool, on the beach. US (800) 544-4686, Mexico 91 (800) 90229.

FIESTA INN — 157 rooms, restaurant, bar, pool, on the beach. 011-52-114-20211, FAX 011-52-114-20232.

TROPICANA INN — 40 rooms, restaurant, bar, pool. Heart of downtown San Jose del Cabo on Boulevard Mijares # 30. 011-52-114-20907 or 21580, US FAX # (510)-939-2725. Not on the beach but this is a popular and charming place.

HUERTA VERDE B&B INN — 7 suites, pool, a pleasant garden setting for your special get-away. Light lunch & chef's choice dinners available. From Los Cabos Inter'l Airport, 5 miles south to Santa Rosa, left (east) 1.3 miles to Huerta Verde. Reservations: 7674 Reed St., Arvada, CO 80003. (303) 431-5162, FAX (303) 431-4455 or 011-52-114-80511.

CABO CORRIDOR

HOTEL PALMILLA — 62 rooms, 7 suites, 2 villas with verandas, restaurant, pool, fishing fleet, golf, tennis courts, croquet. 4343 Von Karman Ave., Newport Beach, CA 92660. (800) 637-2226. Located on a point of land overlooking the sea 0.8 mi. south of Hwy 1 near **Km J-28.5.** This is one of the top hotel-resorts in Baja, if not the best.

WESTIN REGINA RESORT (Cabo Real) — 295 rooms & suites all with private balconies & 62 villas overlooking the Sea of Cortez, restaurants, bar, pools, spa, tennis, golf nearby, meeting facilties for 500. Hwy 1 **J-Km 22.5.** (800) WESTIN-I or 011-52-114-29000. This is a large, elongated, eight-story structure. It's rated 5 stars, but somehow this isn't my idea of Baja.

MELIA CABO REAL (Cabo Real) — 302 rooms & suites and everything else imaginable. This is the first of the mega-hotels at the major Cabo Real resort development between San Jose del Cabo and Cabo San Lucas. Hwy 1 **J-Km 19.5.** Golf course nearby. (800) 336-3542, 011-52-114-40000. If you like your resort hotel done on a grand scale, this is the place. It is one of Baja's largest hotels.

CASA DEL MAR GOLF & SPA (Cabo Real) — 25 rooms & 6 suites, restaurant, bar, pool, spa, tennis. Hwy 1 **J-Km 19.5.** (800) 221-8808, 011-52-114-40030. A 5 star hotel near the water front but with only 32 rooms. Exclusive but nice.

HOTEL CABO SAN LUCAS — 125 rooms, multi-bedroom villas, restaurant, bar, pool, fishing fleet, tennis court, dive shop. 6523 Wilshire Blvd., Los Angeles, CA 90048. (800) 733-2226 or (213) 655-2323. Built around a small picturesque cove with dense palm trees and other landscaping. One of Baja's top hotel-resorts. Located 1/4 mi. south of Hwy 1 near **Km J-15.5** between San Jose del Cabo and Cabo San Lucas.

MARIA GAVIOTA — Suites, restaurant, bar. Hwy 1 **Km J-17.** P.O. Box 257, La Paz, B.C.S. Mexico 23040. 011-52-684-33377. Resort is built on the theme of a small Mexican town with tropical landscaping.

HOTEL TWIN DOLPHIN — 50 rooms with terraces, restaurant, bar, putting green, pool, tennis court, overlooking the Sea of Cortez. (800) 421-8925. The twin Dolphins has made a special effort to use native desert plants in its landscaping. It is one of Baja's best hotels. Located a short distance south of Hwy 1 near **Km J-12.**

CABO DEL SOL — New luxury hotels were under construction at this developing resort area in 1997 including a 550 room Grand Hyatt.

CALINDA BEACH — 125 rooms with balconies, restaurant, bar, 3 pools. (800) 221-2222, 011-52-114-58044. It is located south of **Km J-4.5.** This resort offers a fine view of the rocky tip of the peninsula with its famed arched rock. The 2 and 3-story buildings remind one of a SW Indian pueblo.

CABO SAN LUCAS

HACIENDA HOTEL — 114-plus rooms, suites & townhouses with private balconies or patios,

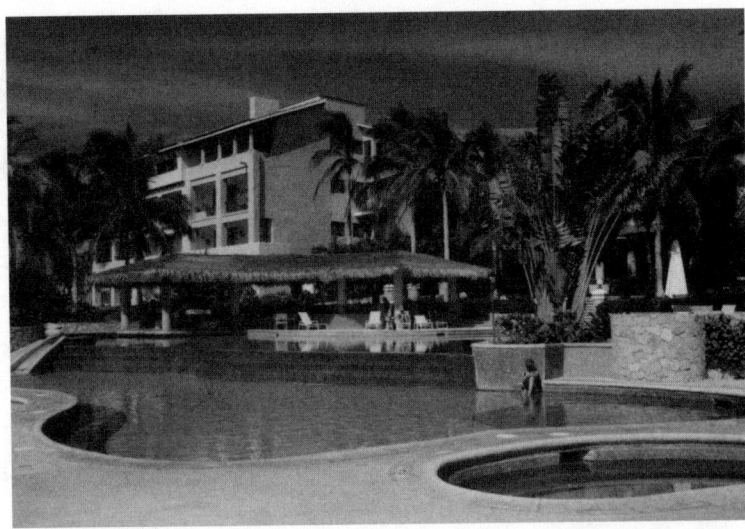

The luxury Casa del Mar Hotel at the Cabo Real development along the Cabo Corridor. Photo BW.

restaurants, bars. pool, paddle tennis, variety of watersports. 6523 Wilshire Blvd., Los Angeles, CA 90048. (800) SEE CABO or (213) 655 2323. One of the very best Baja resorts. It is located within the broad bay at Cabo San Lucas at a point where the beach is well protected from Pacific swells. It advertises the only safe swimming beach in the area.

SOLMAR SUITES HOTEL — 125 suites with patios, restaurant, bar 3 pools. PO Box 383, Pacific Palisades, CA 90272. (800) 344-3349 or (310) 459-9861. The Solmar has the distinction of being the southernmost development in Baja. This destination resort is all but surrounded by the beach on the Pacific side of the peninsula's tip. The ocean surf is heavy at this point, but if you crave the beach, this is the place.

MAR DE CORTEZ HOTEL — 72 rooms, pool. 011-52-114-30032. Reservations: 17561 Vierra Canyon #99, Salinas, CA 93907, (800) 347-8821 or (408) 663-5803. This is the best of the moderately priced hotels at Cabo San Lucas. It is located on the main street (Lazaro Cardenas) of town about 1/2 mi. from the ocean. The rooms are built around a pleasant pool area. A place to savor the charms of "Cabo" without the fancy prices of the fancy resorts.

MELIA SAN LUCAS — 190 rooms with terrace, restaurants, bars, pool, Jacuzzi, tennis center. Three convention facilities for 100. (800) 336-3542 or 011-52-114-34444. On the beach of the Bahia San Lucas which is well protected from Pacific swells. A first class hotel

although not quite as large and fancy as the Melia in Cabo Real.

HOTEL SANTA FE — 42 studios with fully equipped kitchenettes. restaurant, bar pool. This new four-story building is located approx. 6 blocks from the marina. Corner of Alvaro Obregon & Ignacio Zaragoza. (800) 366-2291 or 011-52-114-34401.

THE BUNGALOWS BREAKFAST INN — Ten 1 & 2 bedroom suites, six 2 bedroom bungalows with kitchenettes, pool. Five blocks to downtown on Libertad. Reservations: 011-52-114-35035 or write 9051-C Siempre Viva Rd., Suite 40-497, San Diego, CA 92173.

SIESTA SUITES HOTEL — Suites with kitchens. Centrally located, 2 blocks from the marina and the Los Glorias Hotel. Moderately priced. Daily & weekly rates. Reservations: 9051-C Siempre Viva Rd., 40-273, San Diego, CA 92173. (909) 945-5940, FAX 011-52-114-32773.

HOTEL FINISTERRA — 197 rooms, suites & villas with private balconies, restaurants, bars, pools, gym. Baja Hotel Reservations, 6 Jenner St., Suite 120, Irvine CA 92618. (800) 347-2252 or (714) 450-9000, 011-52-114-31090. What better place to end this tour of Baja's hotels than at the one called Finisterra, "Lands-end." But last is not least as the Finisterra is one of Baja's finest. Its stone architecture and ocean views are the best of any of its competitors. The Finisterra has been substantially increased in size in recent years.

CHAPTER 7
BORDER INFORMATION

In preparing this chapter it has been necessary to interview numerous government officials and visit many offices involved in entrance requirements. All too often it developed that there are differences between what the official regulations and the guidebooks say will happen and what, in fact, takes place. For this reason, be sure to read the WHAT ACTUALLY HAPPENS Section later in this chapter. The saving feature is that, in practice, traveling in Baja is an extremely simple process for most people.

One overall item of advice is appropriate. Do everything possible before entering Mexico, unless your previous experience tells you to do otherwise. This includes fulfilling the various entrance requirements

IMPORTANT NOTICE

In considering the recommendatons for entering Mexico offered in this book, please be aware that your choice of ports-of-entry and travel routes in and approaching Baja may be significantly altered when, and if, the surfacing of Highway 5 is completed south of Puertecitos.

See the discussions presented in the "BAJA'S OTHER ROADS" section of Chapter 2, and at the beginning of Chapter 15.

and obtaining auto insurance, Mexican currency, foodstuffs, and other supplies. In doing this, you can minimize peak-period crowding at the border and the complications always inherent with unfamiliar surroundings.

ENTERING MEXICO

TRAVEL ZONES — The requirements for United States and Canadian citizens who travel to Baja California differ depending on the areas to be visited. There are three travel zones:

BAJA BORDER ZONE — In 1952, the United States and Mexico reached an agreement that citizens of its respective border cities could visit the other nations' border cities for up to 72 hours without permits. The Mexican regulations refer to such visitors as *visitante locales* (local visitors) and define the area in question as the *ciudades fronterizos* (city limits).

As tourism increased, the Mexican regulations changed unofficially. A local visitor became anyone visiting the border area regardless of place of residence. On the Pacific side, the "city limits" expanded to include Ensenada and the nearby towns of La Jolla and Maneadero. For many years the tourist card checkpoint lay adjoining Highway 1 at Maneadero, about 60 miles south of the border. As a result, some older travel books referred to a 60-mile-wide border zone. Now even the Maneadero checkpoint has disappeared. On the east coast, San Felipe is considered part of the border zone even though it is 120 miles south of the border.

Requirements in this elastic border zone are the least restrictive of the three travel zones.

<u>REMAINDER OF BAJA</u> — Travel requirements for the remainder of the Baja peninsula are more restrictive than for the border area but are not as complex as those for the Mexican mainland.

<u>MAINLAND MEXICO</u> — Requirements for entering mainland Mexico are the most restrictive and must be anticipated by travelers (1) entering Baja by first passing through the mainland or (2) by those planning to transport their vehicles from Baja to the mainland on the ferry system or by driving them easterly on Highway 2.

ENTRANCE REQUIREMENTS — The requirements for entering Mexico will vary depending on how you travel, and on what vehicles and other equipment you take with you. I experimented with presenting this material in narrative form but found that something was always omitted or confusing. The end result resembled Mark Twain's incomprehensible description of how to harness a team of horses to a buggy, except that there was no humor in my product. Instead, I offer the ENTRANCE REQUIREMENTS Table.

It summarizes the regulations for the three travel zones discussed above. The numbered text sections, below, provide additional material relating to the corresponding blocks in the table.

BLOCK #1 — Over 30 million people cross the border at Tijuana each year, making it the world's busiest international port-of-entry. Millions more use the other five border crossing points serving Baja. Requiring any type entrance permit for such large numbers of people would create a nightmare of paperwork. No permits of any type are required for tourist visits of up to 72 hours within the Border Zone. A tourist card is needed when one stays over 72 hours.

BLOCK #2 — Mexican regulations define a tourist as "any foreigner who enters the country temporarily for up to six months for recreation, health, scientific or sports activities provided they are neither *remunerative* or *lucrative*." Every tourist who visits the Border Zone for more than 72 hours, or who travels beyond this zone into Baja or the Mexican mainland, must carry a validated tourist card. You need a tourist card even if you have a passport. If your trip is for business you must apply for a business visa at a Mexican Consulate. As with all visas, you must have a valid passport.

BLOCK #3 — No vehicular permits are required for tourist travel within the Baja peninsula. (See further comments under CUSTOMS REGULATIONS later in this chapter.)

BLOCK #4 — A *Temporary Import Permit* must be obtained if you plan to take any motorized vehicle to mainland Mexico. This includes transporting such a

ENTRANCE REQUIREMENTS

ITEM	BAJA BORDER ZONE	REMAINDER OF BAJA	MAINLAND MEXICO
PEOPLE	1 No permits required for tourist travel up to 72 hours. Passport & visa needed for business.	2 For tourist travel, obtain a TOURIST CARD and have it validated after entering Mexico. A passport and visa are required for business travel.	
MOTORIZED VEHICLES	3 No permits required for cars, campers, motor homes, motorcycles or other motorized vehicles.		4 Validated permits are required. Must obtain prior to boarding any mainland-bound ferry.
TRAILERS	5 No permits required for recreational or boat trailers unless they exceed 8 feet in width or 40 feet in length. Obtainable only in Tijuana.		6 Validated permits are required. Must obtain prior to boarding any mainland-bound ferry.
BOAT BY HIGHWAY	7 No permit is required to trailer or otherwise transport a boat into Baja by highway. A fishing license is required for the boat if it is used for fishing.		8 Validated permits are required. Must obtain prior to boarding any mainland-bound ferry.
BOAT BY SEA	9 Obtain a validated CREW LIST at the Mexican Consulate in San Diego. Also obtain TOURIST CARDS for all persons aboard. Port Captain check-in required in Mexico. A fishing license is also required for the vessel.		
COMMER. AIRCRAFT	10 No special requirements. Obtain TOURIST CARDS in advance for airports beyond the border zone. Cards will be validated by officials at the international airports. This is the easiest way to enter Mexico as the validating officals are waiting at the airports and you do not have to search for them.		
PRIVATE AIRCRAFT	11 Must land and obtain a GENERAL DECLARATION at one of Mexico's international airports and file flight plans as required by both Mexican and American authorities. Also obtain TOURIST CARDS for all persons aboard.		

Port-of-entry station at Tecate. The single lane U.S. station is on the left with the Mexican gate on the right. Photo BW.

person's name. Thus, a married couple may obtain permits for two vehicles if they are registered in both their names. Also, another person in the party may obtain a permit for the second vehicle by using a notarized affidavit of authorization from the owner. In any case, all applicants must be qualified drivers. (Red tape is international.)

American and Canadian Automobile Association members can obtain their Temporary Import Permits through association offices. Otherwise the permit is obtained and validated at offices inside Mexico at the border crossings or at the ferry terminals. In Tijuana, permits are obtained at the office of the Registro Federal de Vehiculos, which is located next to the immigration office.

vehicle to the mainland via the Mexican ferry system. There is no charge for these permits. To obtain one you are required to have:

1. Proof of citizenship (the same as for obtaining a tourist card).

2. The current registration certificate (original document, not a copy) or a notarized bill of sale for each vehicle. A notarized affidavit of authorization is also required if the vehicle is registered to a person or company other than the person applying for the permit. (See additional information on this subject in the box in this chapter.)

3. If you are purchasing your vehicle under a finance contract from a bank or other lending institution, you must obtain written notarized permission from the lien holder (the legal owner) authorizing you to take the vehicle into Mexico.

4. A valid driver's license.

There is a complication if you have more than one motor vehicle, such as a motorhome pulling a small car or carrying a motorcycle. One person may obtain a permit for only one vehicle. A second person in the party may obtain a permit for the second vehicle if it is registered in that

BLOCK #5 — Permits are required for trailers only if they, or their load, exceed 8 feet in width or 40 feet in length. These are obtainable only in Tijuana at the

Early in 1992, the Mexican government announced new regulations concerning vehicles brought into Mexico from the United States. These regulations DO NOT apply to vehicles brought into Baja California. However, they will be enforced when vehicles are taken to mainland Mexico from Baja using the ferry system or when driving east on Highway 2. They are designed to deter the large numbers of vehicles that are stolen in the United States and illegally transported into Mexico.

The basic rule is that all imported vehicles must be covered by a current Mexican insurance policy or the driver must post a bond equal to the value of the vehicle. In addition, the driver must provide two photo copies of the following documents to customs inspectors: Title document, driver's license, vehicle registration, insurance policy, car rental contract in the case of rental cars.

It is the opinion of some people that this system will shortly collapse of its own weight. In that my own crystal ball is at the repair shop, I can only advise that you ask your insurance agent for the current state of affairs when you are ready for your visit.

office of the federal highway police. Permits are issued at the discretion of the officials.

BLOCK #6 — The requirements for taking a trailer into mainland Mexico are the same as for a motor vehicle (see BLOCK #4). The trailer is included on the Temporary Import Permit of the towing motor vehicle and is obtained at the same time and place, as for a motor vehicle.

BLOCK #7 — See the FISHING LICENSES Section in Chapter 5.

BLOCK #8 — The Temporary Import Permit covers a boat along with the vehicle that brings it into Mexico.

BLOCK #9 — The crew list must be validated at all ports visited where there is a Mexican Capitan del Puerto (Port Captain). Check-in with the immigration office is also required. The paperwork needed from a yachtsman is considerably more complex than that required of other visitors.

BLOCK #10 — The table says it all.

BLOCK #11 — Private pilots must land at one of Mexico's international airports, fill out an application form, and receive an approved document known in aviation circles as a *General Declaration*. Tourist cards may be obtained at the same time and place. It is recommended that private pilots contact The Baja Bush Pilots for more detailed instructions concerning these and other procedures (See PRIVATE FLYING in Chapter 3).

TOURIST CARDS — Obtaining a tourist card is a simple matter, but do not be dismayed to find that the document in question is not a card, nor does it bear the title tourist card, although it is universally referred to by that name. It is in fact a 5 1/2" by 7", two-copy form that asks you in Spanish, English, or French to provide the answers to eleven easily answered questions.

The tourist card may be obtained north of the border at any Mexican Consulate, offices of the Mexican Government Department of Tourism, offices of Mexican airlines, car insurance companies, and at many travel agencies. It may also be obtained at the immigration offices at the ports-of-entry inside Mexico.

Cards are issued free upon showing proof of one's nationality. This requires that you have any of the following documents: birth certificate, passport, voter registration, naturalization letter, certificate of discharge from the armed forces, or a declaration sworn before a notary public. (Married women relying on a birth certificate also need a sworn declaration to support their change in names.) You are normally given a blank tourist card and asked to fill it out at leisure.

Children under 18 years of age who enter Mexico without both parents must obtain a notarized copy of the form *Permission For A Minor Child to Travel In Mexico* in order to obtain a tourist card. These forms are available at Mexican Government Tourism Offices and Consulates and must be signed by the absent parent or parents.

The regulations require that the tourist card be presented for validation to Mexican immigration authorities *upon entering the country*. The proof-of-citizenship papers will again be required for validation and should be carried with you during your stay in Mexico.

Obtaining your tourist card before entering Mexico gives you a head start, but obviously the entire process of acquiring the card, filling it out, and obtaining validation may be combined in one stop at the ports-of-entry offices.

WHAT ACTUALLY HAPPENS — Prior to 1980, obtaining and validating tourist cards took place at a roadside office at Maneadero on Highway 1. This station disappeared about 1980, reopened briefly a few years later, but was nowhere in sight during our last several visits. As a result of this station being closed, many people entering Baja by highway do not have tourist cards.

Then about 1997 up jumped the devil. Baja travel clubs circulated reports that travelers were being asked to produce their validated tourist cards at the agricultural check point at the 28th parallel state line and that stiff fines were being imposed for failing to have the required cards. During our 1997 survey we were asked for our cards at this point by a uniformed officer. He seemed most disappointed when we had them ready. Then in the nearby town of Guerrero Negro we discovered a new immigration office and sought out an interview. We asked about the reports that people were being fined. The question was evaded with the comment that they were simply present to help tourists acquire their cards. When I left I noted that "The honey moon is over". The officer smiled and agreed. This check point may be a form of

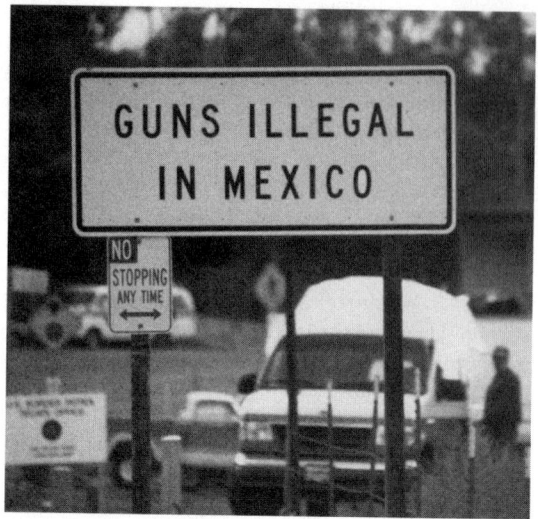

One of the biggest cultural differences between Mexico and the United States is Mexico's opposition to fire-arms. This sign near the international border says it all. Photo BW.

legalized banditry, but its their country and the rule says you need a tourist card. Best obtain one.

Currently there is no check station on Highway 5 from Mexicali to San Felipe, and few people in San Felipe have tourist cards. I am also advised that the various complications noted above concerning tourist cards and car permits rarely cause a problem. In contrast to this relaxed attitude toward tourist cards for highway travel, cards are always checked and validated at international airports during both arrival and departure.

I should also note that Mexican authorities have become strict in their enforcement of the rules concerning foreigners doing work that could be preformed by a Mexican. I have heard of several persons being deported for doing home repairs and other simple tasks.

CUSTOMS REGULATIONS — The Baja peninsula is classified as a *Free Zone,* and in the past, baggage and vehicles were searched only under special circumstances. You were normally waved across the border at all points of entry. But, conditions have changed. At the Tijuana port-of-entry, a special lane is signed for vehicles carrying commercial products. A sampling of those using the regular lanes is stopped and inspected. RVs seem to be a prime target for this treatment. I escaped serious damage in 1995 as the only contraband I had showing was a dachshund that took after the inspector. He laughed, slammed the

door and moved on to more fertile ground. In 1997 at Tecate most recreation type vehicles were stopped and given a once-over-lightly inspection.

Why the change? I will venture a guess. In past years, Mexican tariffs were so high that American goods were rarely seen in Baja stores. Anything smuggled in and placed on sale would be easy to spot. In more recent years, trade agreements have significantly lowered, but not eliminated, these import duties, and American products are much in evidence. Thus, enterprising people smuggle small quantities of *this-and-that* into Baja in their car trunks and under the sleeping bags. (I of course would never do such a thing; at least not anymore.) The store keeper not only escapes the import duty but the Mexican sales tax, as such products leave no tracks entering the country.

One American told me his RV was inspected entering at Tecate where it was discovered that his liquor supply exceeded the one liter legal limit by about 50 bottles, but that this was easily taken care of by a small bribe. Thus, the inspection system is no doubt curtailing small time smuggling by Mexican merchants while at the same time keeping alive the mordida trade between tourists with the customs inspectors.

In recent years there have been two agricultural check stations on Highway 1, one a short distance north of La Paz and the other at the line between Baja's two states. They stop north bound traffic looking for citrus fruit.

In any case, keep in mind that a tourist is one whose purpose of visit is neither remunerative nor lucrative. You should not sell items that you take to Mexico or carry supplies obviously in excess of your personal needs.

DRUGS AND GUNS -- Possessing firearms is contrary to Mexican law, and they are serious about it. The requirements for taking in firearms for hunting is a cumbersome process that is described in Chapter 11. Possessing and using narcotics is also against the law. There is no quicker way to get into trouble in Mexico than by violating these statutes. Mexico welcomes tourists and they are very obliging in their enforcement of the various immigration and customs laws, but they draw the line with firearms and drugs.

Preventing the transportation of drugs has become a priority objective for both the United States and Mexico. During a trip to Baja in 1989 I passed through five drug checkpoints. On my 1992 trip there were none while in 1995 there were two. 1997 disclosed a significant change. We were stopped some 15 times. A full battalion of Mexican soldiers now occupy a permanent base at the parallel-28 state line. At several other points there were small permanent looking military outposts but most check points were simply soldiers standing along the road with temporary barriers. Signs usually announce that they are looking for guns, drugs and explosives

Conventional wisdom believes this greatly increased surveillance is a Mexican response to pressure from the United State government to stop the northern flow of drugs through Mexico. How long it will last is anybody's guess. In any case, all inspections were brief and courteous. When our vehicle was boarded, the inspectors always asked for permission to enter. It is my judgement that these military inspections, while an annoyance, are nothing to be concerned about unless your dog wants to eat the inspector.

PETS — Most tourists don't take their pets to Baja. The potential for inconveniencing one's neighbors in camping areas is considerable, and hotel operators may not permit them in their establishments. However, pets are often encountered in RV parks. If you take your pet to Baja you will need (1) a rabies vaccination certificate from a veterinarian and (2) a veterinarian-validated *Certificate For Interstate and International Health Certificate for Dogs and Small Animals*. This is the title of the appropriate State of California form. The name may vary in other states.

I am advised that the above forms are valid only for 30 days from issuance and that one needs to obtain a similar document from a Mexican veterinarian to clear U.S. Customs. I asked several pet owners in Baja what actually happens and was universally advised they are always admitted home with no questions asked. This is what happened to us in both 1995 and 1997. A U.S. customs inspector advised us that the key to getting your pet back into the United States is having proof of rabies vaccination. If your dog is wearing a dog license tag it is a good indication that you have complied with this requirement.

Heartworm is an internal parasite that can be fatal to small animals. It is transmitted to pets by mosquitoes. There are relatively few such insects in Baja, but they are frequently encountered in the Mulege area where I am advised that heartworm is a problem. Heartworm may be prevented by having pets eat an inexpensive chewable medication. I recommend you consult a veterinarian concerning the proper course of action.

MEXICAN INSURANCE — You need to give special consideration to insurance for vehicles, boats, and private airplanes.

<u>AUTO INSURANCE</u> — Mexican law does not recognize any insurance except that written by companies licensed in Mexico. A Mexican insurance policy guarantees that you are able to pay any potential damages and fines. If you are involved in an accident in Mexico and do not hold a policy issued by such a company, you may be held by authorities pending investigation and determination of fault. Spending time in a Mexican jail can ruin one's day.

Licensed companies are located on both sides of the border near the ports-of-entry. Watch for signs along the highways on the United States' side. Such companies also have offices in several of the larger cities in the United States. By far the least expensive insurance is obtainable through membership in one of the travel clubs listed in Chapter 1.

Coverage may be purchased by the day, month, or on a annual basis. Daily rates are high by United States

Signs similar to this one are placed at military drug and firearms checkpoints along Baja's Highways. It reads "Say No to Drugs." Photo BW.

standards. You can hold down the amount of your premium by covering your vehicle only for the time when you will be traveling and excluding lengthy stays in trailer courts, etc. Obtaining annual insurance from one of the above noted clubs is usually the best course of action for any visit to Mexico for more than a few days.

TRAILERS AND BOATS — If you are towing a trailer, it must also be insured by a Mexican company or your vehicle insurance will be invalid. This coverage must also include your boat if one is being trailered.

Hull and liability insurance for seagoing yachts is a different matter. Some yacht policies issued in the United States include travel as far south as Ensenada as part of their regular coverage. Other companies will issue riders for longer trips at no additional charge. In other cases, riders may involve a considerable additional premium, and some companies simply will not provide coverage for Mexican waters. The skipper's cruising experience may play a considerable role in the insurance company's decision. No additional insurance is required from a Mexican company.

PRIVATE AIRCRAFT — Liability insurance for a private aircraft must be acquired from a Mexican-licensed company in the same manner as for a motor vehicle. In contrast to boat and auto insurance policies, many aircraft policies issued in the United States cover damage to the plane in Mexico. Aircraft insurance is issued by most Mexican insurance companies.

FISHING AND HUNTING LICENSES — Obtaining Mexican fishing licenses is discussed in Chapter 5 WATERSPORTS, while hunting licenses are included in Chapter 11 WILDLIFE.

RETURNING TO THE UNITED STATES

Your vehicle will be required to stop at the United States Customs Service port-of-entry located at the border. A uniformed officer is normally stationed curb-side and will ask you several questions concerning your visit to Mexico. If this officer believes that all is in order you will be allowed to proceed with little delay and without leaving your vehicle. If he/she should determine that checking your vehicle is required, you will be asked to proceed to a secondary parking area where another officer will perform the inspection. This process normally takes very little

time, although you may experience considerable delay waiting your turn in line.

Mexico requires that tourist cards be surrendered when you leave the country. Pilots of private aircraft and the skippers of ocean-going vessels normally check out at their last point of landing in Mexico and return the cards. The United States customs inspectors may check for compliance and become suspicious if these requirements have been ignored. In sharp contrast, persons driving or walking home from Mexico normally retain their cards; there is no apparent effort made to enforce the rule by either government.

CUSTOMS REGULATIONS — The U.S. Customs Service enforces over 400 laws for some 40 different agencies, but they are particularly concerned with (1) preventing the importation of illicit drugs, (2) enforcing the immigration laws, (3) preventing the importation of plant and agricultural products that may harbor dangerous pests, and (4) collecting import duties on foreign goods imported for commercial use and over specified values.

To comply with these requirements, returning tourists should carry proof of citizenship. Also, wise travelers will have exhausted their supply of fresh food supplies, or they may have to be given up at the border. The most common prohibited items are (1) raw and cooked pork, (2) raw meat of both domesticated and game foul, (3) potatoes, and (4) many fruits, including all citrus fruits. The full list of specific items that may not be brought into the United States is extensive and beyond the scope of this book. Write "Quarantines," U.S. Department of Agriculture, Federal Building, Hyattsville, MD 20782 for full details.

Each returning resident of the United States may bring back up to $400 worth of personal and household goods obtained in Mexico. These goods may not be for business purposes or for someone else. Their value includes repairs or alterations to articles taken to Mexico and being returned. You are also limited to one liter of alcoholic beverage provided you are 21 years of age or older. The exemption from duty may be used only once every 30 days. For further information, obtain Publication # 512 "Know Before You Go" from U.S. Customs, P.O. Box 7407, Washington, DC 20229.

DRUG INTERDICTION — At the U.S. ports-of-entry checking for drugs has clearly become the priority concern. Recreation vehicles may be requested to stop at secondary checkpoints on a random basis and trained dogs used to sniff out violators. Customs officers also occasionally stop tourists prior to entering Mexico to inquire about guns, ammunition, and large sums of cash (over $10,000). All of these are related to the drug trade.

Possession of illicit substances is a minor crime (misdemeanor), but importing them into the United States is a felony. If your vehicle is found to contain "any measurable quantity" of illegal drugs, such as one marijuana cigarette, you risk the confiscation of your vehicle and its contents. If young Junior is back there on the weed, best eject him south of the border and air out your rig.

Should you be able to pass on any helpful information to the Customs Service concerning drug trafficking, please phone them at 1(800) BE ALERT.

CANADIAN CITIZENS — Canadians visiting Mexico must pass through both United States and Canadian customs on their way home. The $400 duty-free exemption made available to U.S. citizens is not available to Canadians. U.S. regulations permit Canadians to bring in $200.00 worth of goods purchased in Mexico duty-free. However, I am advised that U.S. officials will normally permit Canadians to import Mexican goods if they are to be transported promptly through the country to Canada. The Canadian's declaration comes at the Canadian border. At press time, the personal exemption was $300.00.

PRIVATE AIRCRAFT — The U.S. Customs Service has identified general aviation aircraft as the highest-risk vehicles for narcotics smuggling. Pilots of such planes are thus required to land at specified U.S. airports near the border for customs inspections. Brown Field SE of San Diego, Calexico International Airport, and Yuma International Airport are directly across the border from Baja. Customs officials must be notified at least one hour prior to the inbound crossing of the U.S. border. Pilots should obtain Customs Publication 513 *U.S. Customs Guide for Private Flyers* for full information.

RETURNING BY SEA — Skippers of yachts returning to the United States from Mexico must check in with U.S. Customs at the Harbor Police dock in San Diego.

PORTS-OF-ENTRY

There are 7 ports-of-entry serving Baja California. These are described in the PORTS-OF-ENTRY Table. One of these, at San Luis, is in the mainland state of Sonora, but tourists may pass in either direction from Baja California to San Luis without the extra paperwork normally required to visit the Mexican mainland.

Usually it takes little time going from the United States into Mexico; however, there can be lengthy delays returning north. Keep in mind that the vast majority of this traffic consists not of tourists but of people from the border area who live in one country and work, or shop, in the other. There is thus heavy border congestion from these *commuters* from 2:00 or 3:00 AM until mid-morning.

Aside from this commute period, U.S. customs officials at Tijuana and nearby Otay Mesa report that

PORTS-OF-ENTRY

LOCATION	DESCRIPTION	HOURS
TIJUANA	This is the busiest port-of-entry. OK for entering Mexico but usually heavily congested when returning to the U.S.	24 HOURS
OTAY MESA	Built to relieve congestion at Tijuana. No adjacent communities so traffic is usually much lighter than at Tijuana.	6:00 A M to 10:00 PM
TECATE	A Mexican town of 85,000 people. Adjoining U.S. community is small. Traffic is usually light.	6:00 AM to Midnight
MEXICALI	Large Mexican city. Two ports-of-entry, one in and one east of town. The latter has eased the wait time going north.	24 HOURS
ALGODONES	A small Mexican town with no adjoining U.S. community. Light traffic.	6:00 AM TO 8:00 PM
SAN LUIS	A Mexican town of 175,000 south of Yuma, Arizona. Moderate traffic.	24 HOURS

overall peak traffic periods are often un-predictable. However, on the average, Sunday traffic is the heaviest, followed in order by Saturday, Monday, and Friday. The lightest traffic occurs on Tuesday, Wednesday, and Thursday. I strongly advise that you obtain the small book entitled *Crossing the Border Fast and Easy* if you plan of using the Tijuana port-of-entry (See notice in this chapter).

Peak traffic periods at <u>Mexicali</u> are also often unpredictable, but generally the busiest days are in descending order, Sunday, Saturday, Wednesday, Monday, Friday, Thursday, and Tuesday. The first and fifteenth days of each month are also generally busy regardless of the day of the week. A second port-of-entry was opened in 1997 near the eastern side of Mexicali. It has greatly lessened the wait time returning north. In fall 1997 we passed through here with almost no delay.

<u>San Luis</u> reports the heaviest traffic between 10:00 AM and 8:00 PM on Sundays when delays of from one-to-two hours may be encountered. November thru April are the busiest months, but even here non-Sunday traffic is light except from 2:00 AM until 7:00 AM when commute workers from Mexico cross to work in agricultural fields on the U.S. side. The

ITEM	POINT OF ORIGIN	
	U.S. & Canadian Pacific Coast	**Other Parts of U.S. and Canada**
ENTERING BAJA	**1** Enter at Tijuana.	**4** Enter at Tijuana, Tecate or San Luis.
MEXICAN TOURIST PAPERS	**2** Acquire at Ensenada. Tijuana best for car permits.	**5** Acquire at Ensenada, Tecate or San Luis.
LEAVING BAJA	**3** Leave at Otay Mesa or Tecate. Avoid Tijuana.	**6** Tecate, San Luis, or Algodones. Avoid Tijuana and Mexicali.

busiest months at nearby <u>Algodones</u> are similar to those at San Luis with weekends bringing the most traffic.

At <u>Tecate</u> the busiest times occur on Sundays and holidays and on days with special events such as races and the August bull run.

We have been advised that license plate scanners are now in place at Tijuana and some of the other ports-of-entry. These devices which detect plates involved in car theft and other violations have considerably shorten the time spent waiting in line.

The United States freeway system tends to funnel Baja-bound tourists living along the Pacific coast to the San Diego area. Persons living east of the coastal area more readily flow towards Yuma, Arizona. The POINT OF ORIGIN Table, provides border crossing recommendations for these two groups. In both cases, it is assumed that the traveler plans to visit the main portion of the peninsula south of Ensenada via Mexico Highway 1. (NOTE — Expect significant changes in traffic patterns when and if Mexico Highway 5 is ever completed from Mexicali to Laguna Chapala. See discussion at the start of Chapter 15.) The following numbered sections in the text refer to the corresponding blocks in the POINT OF ORIGIN Table.

Of late in the USA, the word bimbo is used to describe a lady inclined toward promiscuous behavior, especially in and near the nation's capital. Relax gentlemen, this is not a truck load full of young ladies. In Baja, "Bimbo" is the leading brand of bread (Pan). Photo BW.

BLOCK #1 — There is normally little delay in entering Mexico at Tijuana although the spot inspections noted under MEXICAN CUSTOMS REGULATIONS may slow you down. It is also very important to note that the Highway 1-D route around Tijuana avoids most of the city traffic.

BLOCK #2 — Car permits can be obtained, and tourist cards validated, on a 24-hour basis at Tijuana; however, there is less congestion in Ensenada. The office hours there are 8:00 AM to 8:00 PM Monday through Friday; 8:00 AM to 3:00 PM Saturday. They are closed on Sunday.

BLOCK #3 — Avoid Tijuana at all costs. I have never returned to the U.S. at Tijuana and never intend to do so. If you simply must cross at Tijuana, be sure and acquire the great little book *Crossing the Border Fast and Easy*. It could save you hours of time (See notice at the end of this chapter). Crossing at Tecate is the best choice. There are several twists and turns on the way to the the San Diego freeway system north from Tecate so it is best to have a highway map of the San Diego area on hand.

A somewhat easier return to the United States freeway system is provided by returning home at Otay Mesa, but the port-of-entry is a bit hard to find from the Mexican side of the border. Directions are provided in Chapter 14.

BLOCK #4 — Many travelers will choose to take Interstate 8 from Yuma to San Diego and enter Baja at Tijuana along with their West Coast brethren. The distance from Yuma to Ensenada via San Diego is approximately 260 miles; however, one can see more of Baja and avoid the San Diego traffic by entering Mexico at San Luis and proceeding to Ensenada via Highways 2, 5, and 3. This route is only 30 miles longer, but does involve traveling over the winding mountain highway east of Ensenada on Highway 3, as noted in Chapter 16. As an intermediate alternative, enter at Tecate and drive to Ensenada via scenic Highway 3.

BLOCK #5 — Tecate and San Luis offer relatively congestion-free points to take care of the paperwork. Also see block #2 concerning Tijuana.

BLOCK #6 — It is really senseless not to return home via Tecate, Algodones, or San Luis and avoid Tijuana and Mexicali. The new (1997) eastern port-of-entry at Mexicali has initially proven to be much faster than the old downtown gate, but this may change with time and the eastern gate is somewhat hard to find for first time travelers.

CHAPTER 8
LIVING AND
TRAVELING IN BAJA

The pages to follow discuss a variety of subjects about which you need to know when living and traveling in the Magnificent Peninsula.

HEALTH CONSIDERATIONS

You will find that health conditions in Baja are good. It is widely reported, and it has been my experience, that tourists suffer considerably less from common intestinal disturbances (*turistas*) in Baja than on the Mexican mainland. Nevertheless, I shall pass on the standard fare offered to tourists everywhere in relation to this malady. Avoid overindulgence in food, beverage, and exercise, and get plenty of rest, at least until your system adjusts to its changed environment. In general, avoid tap water by obtaining your needed liquids from bottled water, carbonated beverages, beer, and wine. Avoid unpeeled fruits and uncooked vegetables that are the essential ingredients in salads. It is also advisable to inquire if the hotel swimming pool contains chlorinated water and avoid those that do not.

Having fulfilled this duty I report that I know that this advice is widely ignored in Baja with few ill effects. Travelers and retirees in Baja regularly drink the tap water from many of the towns, large and small, and produce acquired at the markets is treated no differently than it would be north of the border. My best advice is to ask current residents what they do and follow your own best judgement.

SPECIAL PROBLEMS — The requirement for having had a smallpox vaccination to enter Mexico and to return to the United States was discontinued many years ago. The Anopheles mosquito, which transmits malaria, has also been eradicated from the peninsula; Baja is classified as malaria free by the United States Public Health Service. This is not true for the mainland west coast from north of Mazatlan to the Guatamalan border. While there are no special medical requirements for visiting Baja, many doctors recommend vaccination for tetanus and hepatitis prior to visiting certain parts of the world. Contact your personal physician for advice.

MEDICAL FACILITIES — There are well-equipped hospitals in Baja's larger cities. In recent years government medical clinics have also been established in many of the smaller towns. These facilities prominently display the letters I.M.S.S. (Instituto Mexicano de Seguro Social) on the front of the building. All are equipped with radios so that air evacuation or other assistance can be summoned. In addition, two organizations in San Diego operate 24-hour, critical-care, air transportation service throughout Baja. These are

Air-Evac International, Inc. (619) 278-3822, and Critical Air Medicine, Inc. (619) 571-8944. If you have special health problems it may be wise to make prior financial arrangements with one of these services so that there are no delays caused by credit considerations.

The Red Cross is much in evidence in Baja. It operates ambulances and provides emergency medical treatment throughout the peninsula. Roadside volunteers are often encountered soliciting funds for this work.

INSECT PESTS — Troublesome insects are not usually a problem in dry desert climates. I have found this to be the most common situation in Baja. However, there are some important exceptions.

Desert insects achieve enormous increases in numbers following rain. During these periods you may be plagued by large numbers of flies, mosquitos, gnats and no-see-ums. The latter are particularly painful and can make life miserable. Our 1997 trip to Baja followed torrential rains caused by a hurricane that crossed the peninsula in late October. The resultant moisture made mosquitos a severe problem in several places. This is the first time I have experienced these conditions in all my travels in Baja. Mosquitos can also be a problem year-round at hotels and a few RV parks where landscape areas are kept continually moist. For these reasons it is advisable to take insect repellant and spray to Baja. A small section of mosquito netting used to throw over your head at night will help defeat that last buzzing pest that avoids your best efforts at extermination.

CURRENCY

For decades the Mexican peso was an extremely stable currency, and from 1954 to 1976 the exchange rate was 12-1/2 pesos per United States dollar. In September 1976, the country's *spendful* economic policies forced a series of peso devaluations. By the end of 1992 the exchange rate was over 3,000 pesos per U.S. dollar.

Then, in January 1993, Mexico produced a new series of banknotes and coins which removed three zeros from the old peso and created the "nuevos pesos" (new pesos). It is abbreviated N$. As with the old peso, the new peso is divided into 100 centavos, but the smallest coin now minted is five-cents. Cash purchases are supposed to be rounded off to the nearest multiple of five-centavos. In practice, most grocery bills and similar transactions are quoted to the nearest peso.

The new peso started off with something approaching a one-to-one relationship with the U.S. dollar, but the Mexican peso crisis of early 1995 quickly reduced this to about six pesos per dollar. What you will find when you arrive in Baja is anybody's guess. The most recent quote I have seen is about 8.5 New Pesos per U.S. dollar.

I offer the following comments and suggestions that reflect my most recent experiences.

1. — Mexico needs United States and Canadian currency. You can exchange dollars into pesos at any Mexican bank for the going rate. If you try to change these same pesos back into dollars two minutes later the bank may be regrettably out of dollars. If you pay a bill in dollars, you will usually get your change in pesos. In other words, once you exchange your dollars for pesos it is often difficult to reverse the process. Prudent tourists plan ahead and spend all of their pesos before leaving Mexico. Stopping for fuel

Signs of Distinction

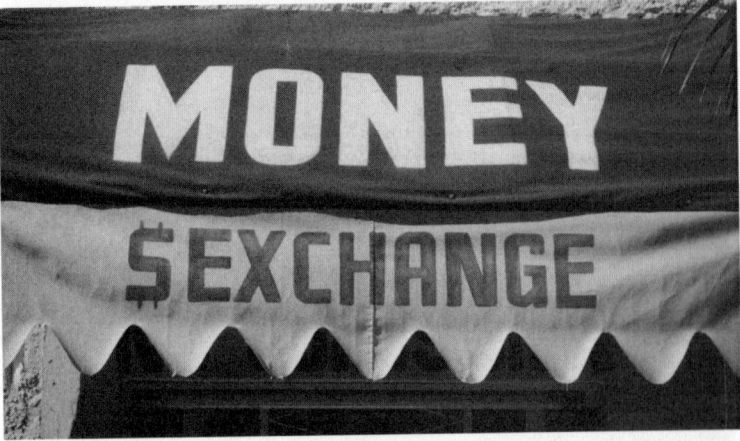

San Jose del Cabo is the place to go to get altered if you are dissatisfied with your present gender. Signs like this are everywhere. Oh! Am I wrong? Is that actually a dollar sign and not an S? Well, I saw several ladies lined up at the window below the sign with money in their hands. So what was I to think? Photo BW.

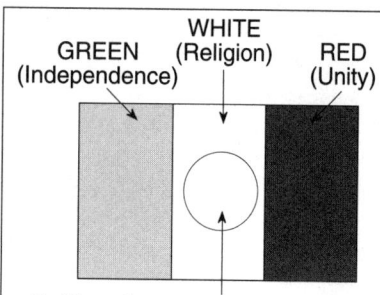

GREEN
(Independence)

WHITE
(Religion)

RED
(Unity)

Emblem shows an eagle on a cactus with a snake in its beak. The cactus grows on an island in the middle of a lake.

MEXICO'S FLAG

The national emblem of Mexico is adapted from the Aztec symbol for their capital, now Mexico City, but originally TENOCHTITLAN, meaning Cactus Rock. Legend says that the wandering Aztecs could not settle until they found a place on an island in a lake upon which grew a cactus. On the cactus there would be an eagle holding a snake in its beak. This place they discovered about 1325. There they established the empire which was later to be conquered by Cortez in 1521. ------ The design has varied through the years. The present configuration was made official in 1968. Each state has an "ARMS" but no flag.

near the border, placing all your remaining pesos on top of the pump, and asking the attendant to dispense that much gasoline is one way to take care of the last centavo.

2. — There is no problem in exchanging or spending dollars or travelers checks in places that are practiced in dealing with tourists such as banks, money exchange offices, hotels, and stores in the border towns. It is often harder to use these same dollars at gas stations, food stores, and other small businesses. For this reason, you should obtain a supply of pesos at a bank near your home, or at one of the border towns.

3. — There are often long lines at bank teller's windows. You can easily spend twenty minutes waiting only to find you are at the wrong window. Service is usually much quicker at an exchange dealer (Casa de Cambio). You will receive slightly fewer pesos for your dollars at these places so first check out the exchange rate at the bank and decide whether time or money is your current priority. In finding a bank, look for signs with the word *Banco* (bank) or such trade names as *Banamex*, or *Bancomer*.

4. — Canadians can exchange Canadian dollars for pesos at the major banks, however, this may not always be the case in the smaller towns. Canadian dollars also may not be as acceptable to business men and individuals. The U. S. dollar is the universal solvent in Mexico and will dissolve any problem. Wise Canadians will carry some of their resources in greenbacks.

5. — Always having pesos available will allow you to use them to purchase an item that is priced in pesos and to receive your change in pesos. Most of us can deal with the mathematics involved in such a transaction. Using dollars in the same situation may give rise to *creative change making* and awakens memories of grade school math tests where some of us received D-'s for not knowing how much change Johnny should receive in pesos when paying in dollars for a watermelon worth 4.5 pesos, when the exchange rate four days earlier was 3.75 pesos to the dollar and is increasing 0.22 pesos per day.

6. — It is always wise to carry a pocket calculator in case you find yourself at a gas pump where the peso gauge is broken or covered-over with tape and you are being told what to pay by a 12 year old kid who is probably playing hookey from school. I have had experiences where the presence of a calculator prevented mistakes in currency transactions. Have one in your hand and punch it even if you don't understand its use. Its mere presence makes everyone more careful.

7. — Many businesses and hotels will also exchange dollars into pesos. My experience is that the rate at stores will be a little better than the official rate. Their managers wish to attract your business. The rates at hotels are usually lower than bank rates as most often you are paying your bill and the hotel's proprietors have already enjoyed your trade.

SPANISH (ESPANOL)

Although most of us know that the language of Mexico is Spanish, it comes as a bit of a shock to find that nearly all road and other signs immediately abandon the English language south of the border. There is no weaning area. However, even if you don't understand Spanish, you will have little trouble getting along in Baja. Almost all tourist-oriented stores in the border area employ someone who speaks English. English-speaking Mexicans rapidly diminish south of Ensenada, but there is rarely a language problem at the hotels and other tourist facilities. Menus are frequently printed in both English and Spanish and will help you to become familiar with frequently used words. What better way to learn that eggs are *huevos* than when ordering breakfast (*desayuno*).

One of the first things you learn upon entering the publishing business is that almost all books have a total number of pages that is divisible by 8, 16, or 32 as the large sheets of paper used in printing presses are divided into this number of sections. If an author has nothing more to say, and is several pages short, or if the book looks too thin to market well, the shortfall is frequently met with an appendix of ornaments *borrowed* from other sources. A list of foreign language words and phrases is one common appendix item.

There is no such section in *The Magnificent Peninsula*. Its appendix does present (1) a GLOSSARY of Spanish words, trade names, and acronyms and (2) a display of ROAD SIGNS. Both contain Spanish words that you will actually see in print in Baja. These two references, along with the bilingual restaurant menus, will meet your minimal language needs.

I suggest that you obtain a English-Spanish dictionary and a simple Spanish textbook. These items are not essential, but you can enjoy your trip more by becoming familiar with simple Spanish. Most Baja citizens are eager to help, and knowing even a little Spanish gives you common ground.

I also recommend a simple but highly effective little book on Spanish and Latin American customs en-titled *Spanish Lingo for the Savvy Gringo* (See notice in this chapter).

SHOPPING & PRICES

Baja's border cities owe much of their rapid growth to the allurements they have provided over the years to residents of southern California in the United States. In the past, gambling, prostitution, and alcohol (during prohibition) were the big sellers. Today, things have calmed down and just plain shopping has become a big money gainer. Each port-of-entry border town has clusters of shops and stores that cater to the shopping tastes of the tourist. The same is true for Ensenada and San Felipe, farther south. The only other shopping centers of significance are La Paz and Cabo San Lucas.

These cities offer a variety of goods ranging from inexpensive baskets, and similar tourist eye-catchers to more expensive silver, porcelain, perfumes, leather goods, and clothing. Much of this merchandise can be obtained at prices lower than in the United States. This is particularly true for products such as tooled belts, shoes, hand bags, and other items that involve considerable hand labor.

Prices are normally fixed, and marked on the merchandise, at the department stores and larger shops, but bargaining is the name of the game in many smaller establishments. This practice is a bit unfamiliar to many tourists, but you are simply paying too much if you don't participate. While there is money to be saved, bargaining often takes extra time as one needs to compare prices at different shops and engage in a sometimes protracted battle of wits with the proprietors. Having dollars rather than pesos will enhance your bargaining position. I normally despise shopping, but the sporting aspects of the bargaining process actually can make it enjoyable.

Liquor stores (Signed Vinos and Licores) are plentiful. There is a wide selection of Mexican brands of beer (cerveza) as well as tequila, rum, brandy, gin, and vodka at prices near, or below, those in the U.S. Bourbon and Scotch are scarce and expensive. Santo Tomas and other brands of wine bottled in Ensenada and the wineries along Highway 3 north of this city are also available at reasonable prices.

Now THE BAD NEWS. In early 1989 (after the election of President Carlos Salinas de Gortari), it was apparent that prices for many commodities had roughly doubled from one year ago. This was particularly true for food. The rates paid by businesses for various government services such as power and water also rose sharply. Finally, the sales tax rate in Baja rose from six to fifteen percent as it has long been on the Mexican mainland.

These price increases were the result of Mexico facing the reality that it could no longer subsidize much of what it provided for its people. Similar price escalations have occurred in other countries around the world as they back away from heavily socialized economies and move toward capitalism. And I believe there is a relationship between these policies and the recent decrease in inflation. But, for what ever reason, living in Mexico is not nearly the bargain it once was. But some items still cost very little. Tortillas and beer both come to mind. The essentials of life are still a bargain.

At times the peso looses much of its value in relationship to the U.S. dollar as occurred early in 1995 and

tourists believe they can travel to Mexico and secure great shopping values. This is in fact true if one is shopping at retail stores and other places frequented by the Mexican people. However, almost all establishments dealing primarily with tourists peg their prices in American dollars and the traveler experiences no bargains. This is true at everywhere from luxury hotels to the smallest RV parks. These folks are the true Mexican bandits.

PROBLEMAS

One of the most common Spanish expressions that a tourist will hear in Mexico is "no problema," meaning that there is no problem, or that one's request will be complied with promptly. However, occasionally a traveler may in fact encounter a real problema and need assistance. Away from the larger towns, authority rests with the Delegado, an appointed official whose office will bear the name Delegacion Municipal, and there are uniformed police in all but the smallest communities. Consult these officials in case of need.

Should you encounter legal difficulties, including those with public officials, contact an office of the State Tourism Department. The State of Baja California also operates the *Procuraduria General de Protection al Turista* (Office of the Attorney General for the Protection of Tourists). Call in Tijuana (706) 684-2138 or the 24-hour hotline (706) 685-0302; in Ensenada (706) 676-3686; in Mexicali (706) 562-5744; and in San Felipe 7-11-55. They act as public defenders and render free legal service.

The laws of Mexico are based on the Napoleonic Code used in much of Europe and Latin America. In these countries, one is held to be guilty until proven innocent, a somewhat frightening prospect to those of us accustomed to the opposite foundation of English law. This legal difference is a key reason why you should carry Mexican insurance for your vehicles. Failure to do so could result in your being detained pending determination of responsibility in case of an accident.

Tourists may occasionally encounter the need to part with a small bribe or tip called *la mordida* (the death bite) to avoid a problem with a public official. The Mexican government has been making a considerable effort to eliminate this practice, but it still prevails on occasion. My personal familiarities with the practice all involve situations where tourists were in violation of Mexican regulations, or wished to avoid full compliance with such requirements. Conforming fully with Mexico's way of doing things would seem to be the simplest means of avoiding the need for la mordida.

TELEPHONING

Baja California has a modern telephone system but the number of individual telephones is relatively small. For example, there are less than 100 pages of phone numbers in the single phone book covering all of the state of Baja California Sur. Each phone book also has a yellow pages section which you may find useful in locating specific services. The phone systems for the various towns and cities are linked together by microwave radio; you will see the *microondas* towers at many places along the main highways.

CALLING MEXICO — You may dial directly to telephones in Baja from many places in the United States and Canada. Consult the International Calling instructions in the front section of most phone books. The following examples utilize the phone number for the Estero Beach Hotel near Ensenada.

(1) 011 + 52 + 617 + 6-6235
(2)   (526) 176-6235

In areas served by International Direct Distance Dialing (IDDD) 011 is the *International Access Code*, 52 the *Country Code* for Mexico, and 617 the *City Code* for Ensenada. 6-6235 is the hotel's phone number as it appears in the Mexican phone book.

The second example lists the same series of numbers in the format familiar to U.S. and Canadian citizens.

This is how the numbers are shown in most travel brochures and in this book. Many of the *City Codes* in Baja start with 6. Thus, for practical purposes, 52 + 6 or (526) is what we would call the *area code* for these cities.

CALLING HOME — It is possible to dial directly to the United States and Canada from Baja by using a private telephone. Most tourists do not have access to such a telephone and will need to utilize one of the following alternatives.

1 -- There are phone booths on the streets in the major cities. Place a coin in the slot at the top of the phone to activate the circuit. Dial 95 for calls to the U.S. and Canada. I have always found that an operator answers and speaks sufficient English to complete a collect or credit card call. This is an inexpensive way to call home.

2 -- Most hotels place calls for their patrons but there is often a fee. If you are not a guest you may be refused assistance.

This photo is of one of the telephones discussed in item #4 under "Calling Home" in the text. Photo BW.

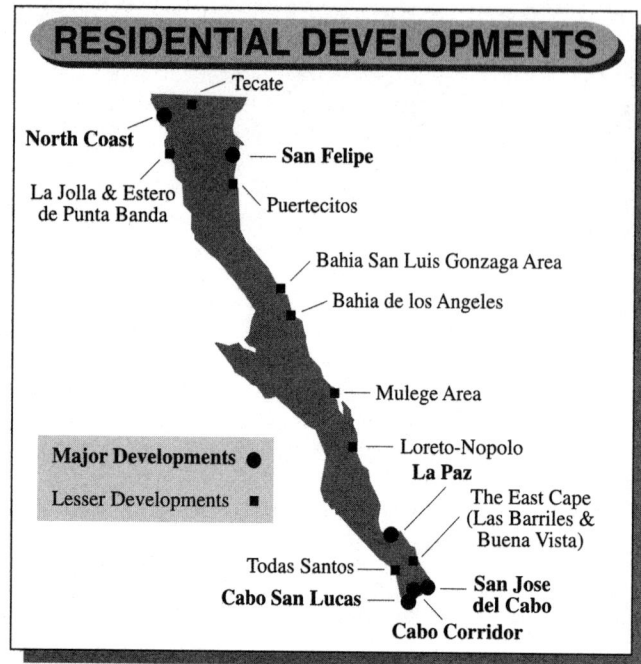

RESIDENTIAL DEVELOPMENTS

- Tecate
- **North Coast**
- **San Felipe**
- La Jolla & Estero de Punta Banda
- Puertecitos
- Bahia San Luis Gonzaga Area
- Bahia de los Angeles
- Mulege Area
- Loreto-Nopolo
- **La Paz**

Major Developments ●
Lesser Developments ■

- The East Cape (Las Barriles & Buena Vista)
- Todas Santos
- **Cabo San Lucas**
- **San Jose del Cabo**
- **Cabo Corridor**

I am occasionally asked my views about starting a business in Baja. I wish to make it very clear that this subject is not within my field of expertise. However, I offer the following comments.

1 -- I made a quick count of non-Mexicans (mostly Americans) that I have observed with tourist-related business in Baja. The number was 25. There are no doubt others. Almost all of these people are married couples where one spouse is a Mexican. Obviously one's nationality is an important business factor. I met one Canadian who has invested a great deal of money in his business but periodically has to renew his right to remain in Mexico. On the last occasion he was granted only a six months extension as the immigration official was peeved over the anti-immigration movement in the U.S.

3 -- In the larger towns you will find long-distance offices staffed with one or more operators who will place calls for a fee. Be alert for the *larga distancia* sign.

4 -- During our most recent field trips we encountered scores of phones located in the open at all prominent tourist facilities. They contain prominent signs reading "TO CALL THE USA -- Collect or With Credit Card." You simply dial 0, an operator answers promptly and makes your call. Then when you get home your phone bill reads like the national debt. Our calls averaged over $5.00 per minute and we paid $10.00 each time we got a busy signal. This service was efficient but outrageously expensive.

5 -- Upon returning home from the above disaster, we contacted AT&T and were given a code number to use in direct dialing. The other long-distance companies apparently each have their own codes. You also need a credit card (calling card) from your company. We will try this method next time.

6 -- On our most recent field trip we found many phone booths bearing the words LADA and Ladatel. These are modern facilities replacing the older phone booths referred to in item 1 above. The facilities noted in items 5 and 6 will almost certainly replace the offices noted in item 3. In other words phoning north from Baja is becoming very simple.

2 -- Some of the above noted people have been in business for years and seem to be quite happy and successful. Others have suffered disasters of one sort or the other that relate, not to the failure of the business itself, but to the business environment in Mexico. In several cases a land lease expired and could not be renewed at a reasonable price, and there went ten years of hard work. The very successful Serenidad Hotel in Mulege was invaded and shut down by members of an ejido claiming the land was theirs. It took a lengthy and expensive court battle to get the ejido ejected. I have taken many risks in my life, but following in these people's tracks will not be one of them.

3 -- If you can survive these negative comments and are still interested in business opportunities in Baja, consider acquiring one of the books advertised in this chapter. Also acquire the book *Distant Neighbors* (See notice in Chapter 13) and read the chapter on *The System*.

Thousands of people from north of the border have purchased residential real estate in Baja. Some units are used for the buyers personal use, and others are intended to be investment properties. I will limit my counsel in this regard to noting the locations of the most prominent real estate developments.

The places shown as "Major Developments" on the map offer relatively-recent modern units. Some are very fancy and expensive, others more modest. The three locations at the peninsula's southern tip are the most rapidly growing. The "Lesser Developments" are for the most part older less auspicious places. These include the lease of space in some RV parks where the investor moves in a mobile home or trailer and adorns it with various ornaments.

Remember that buying residential real estate is a form of business enterprise, and that business in Mexico is not the same as it is north of the border. Thus, I again strongly recommend you obtain one of the business related books advertised in this chapter before investing in real estate in Baja. I will also note that the selling of time-share and other residential real estate in the Cape Area is a very high pressure enterprise conducted mostly by American salesmen. If you visit the area you will have a hard time escaping their attention.

ROADSIDE MEMORIALS

An article in the San Francisco Chronicle by Christopher Heredia notes that roadside memorials honoring accident victims are commonplace in the United States and other parts of the world. But, *you ain't seen nothing yet* until you drive Baja's highways. A few years ago I recall seeing numerous white crosses along the road. I thought they were the highway department's way of warning drivers about danger points. I now know that they are placed there by families honoring persons killed in highway accidents. Heredia quotes anthropologist Ricardo Alegria as hearing stories of souls wandering the roads in Latin America because accident victims are unable to receive the blessings of a priest. People apparently believe that without the blessing the roadside memorial will help.

But in Baja, the simple white crosses are now a thing of the past and roadside memorials have become an art form. Even the simple memorials are reasonably complex and some are approaching being small landscaped buildings. One cannot but sense that a spirit of competition has developed and that out doing the other guy has become as important as honoring the departed. I am sure folks don't want to loose a loved one but "if your going to kill yourself Jose, do it on the highway so we can show off a little." In any event, be alert to Baja's roadside memorials as illustrated in several nearby photos.

EL MALO Y EL BUENO
(The Bad and the Good)
By KEN REIMER

This arid land, so hot and so dry,
*   Where the sun always shines in a bright azure sky*
On rough ragged rocks and on scorching sand,
*   Offering to humans a most desolate land*
Covered with cacti and thickets of thorn,
*   A prickly jungle, dense and forlorn;*

Where the coarse cardon commands and at its feet
*   The pin-cushion cholla and the ocotillo meet;*
The ridiculous roadrunner hurries about
*   Pursuing a lizard that skitters in rout;*
The merry mockingbird sings in his bower,
*   The promiscuous hummingbird kisses each bright cactus flower*
And along the shores within easy reach
*   The snowy white surf caresses a golden beach.*

ROADSIDE MEMORIALS

Here is shown a selection of the roadside memorials you will see along Baja's main highways. <u>Bottom Left</u> - This one is about as simple as they get. The old wooden, white crosses are gone. <u>Top Left</u> - Getting much bigger and more complex. - <u>Top Right</u> - The man-made part here is fairly simple but this one embraces a living cardon cactus which has been painted white and topped with crosses. <u>Bottom Right</u> - The deluxe model. The building is at least five foot square and is fully enclosed by an ornate fence complete with landscaping.

PART II
HIGHER NEEDS

THE PAUPER PENINSULA

At an occasional oasis or in a sheltered bay
Small Spanish settlements managed to stay.
Loreto...Santiago...La Paz with the precious pearls,
San Ignacio...Todos Santos...Mulege...vital streams in the world;
Meanwhile Manila galleons with rich Philippine cargo
Which came to provision at San Jose del Cabo
Were often plundered by Cavendish and Drake
Who burned the ships and the treasures did take;
And although Mexico finally won freedom from Spain
Poor Baja California greatly neglected remains.

Ken Reimer

Ken's poem introduces us to a land which is perhaps poor in worldly goods but is rich in scenic beauty, vegetative variety, wildlife, and history. Viewing these features together with the people and culture of a land different from our own will provide enrichment for the visitor. PART II focuses on fulfilling these HIGHER NEEDS.

Adobe ruins of the Dominican mission at Santo Domingo. Here Baja's rich past lies next to the poor dwelling of a present-day Mexican farmer.

CHAPTER 9
GEOLOGY

PLEASE READ THE
FOLLOWING PARAGRAPH

Few people have training or knowledge concerning geology. Others may believe that they will have little interest in this subject. For these reasons, I am fearful that many readers may be inclined to pass over this chapter. *I implore you not to do so.* I make this pledge: everything presented in this chapter is essential background material concerning features which you may readily see from the peninsula's main highways. Ex-

cluded are lengthy descriptions of geologic history and the unnecessary use of technical terms which, for the average tourist, do little more than occupy space. If technical language is necessary, straightforward definitions are provided, enhanced where possible by sketches or tables.

I sincerely hope you have been persuaded to read on and savor Baja's geologic panorama. Making such a decision would be less important were you contemplating traveling through the vast plains and prairies of central and eastern United States and Canada where there is relatively little geologic story to be told. Even in areas such as the Appalachian Mountains in eastern United States, where there is much of geologic interest, the humid weather conditions and resultant dense forest vegetation tend to round over the landscape and mask the rocks and other structural features.

In contrast, geologic features are plentiful, varied, and easily seen in areas such as Baja that are both mountainous and arid. Perhaps the most outstanding such region in North America is the southwestern portion of the United States. I would rate this latter area as superior to Baja in both scenery and geologic interest, although the comparison may be unfair due to the tremendous size and diversity of southwestern United States. Regardless of its relative rank, the Baja peninsula is a place of fine, and at times outstanding scenery.

In presenting this picture, I will begin with the peninsula itself and then proceed through more specific elements. As in all the chapters of PART II, the material presented here will be further amplified as individual features are encountered in PART III. The book *The Baja Highway* (See notice in this chapter) is an

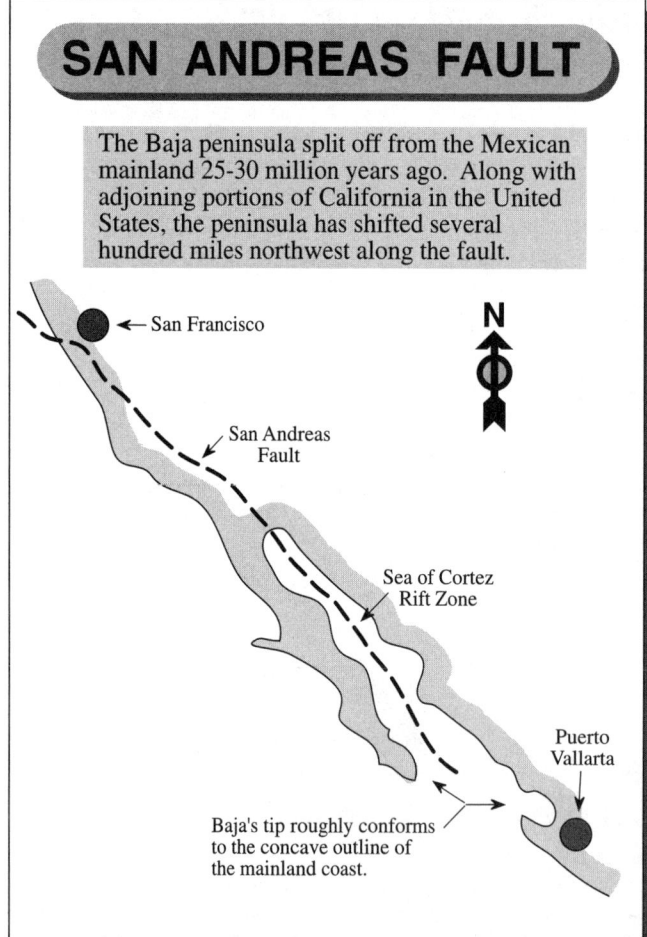

SAN ANDREAS FAULT

The Baja peninsula split off from the Mexican mainland 25-30 million years ago. Along with adjoining portions of California in the United States, the peninsula has shifted several hundred miles northwest along the fault.

N

← San Francisco

San Andreas
Fault

Sea of Cortez
Rift Zone

Puerto
Vallarta

Baja's tip roughly conforms
to the concave outline of
the mainland coast.

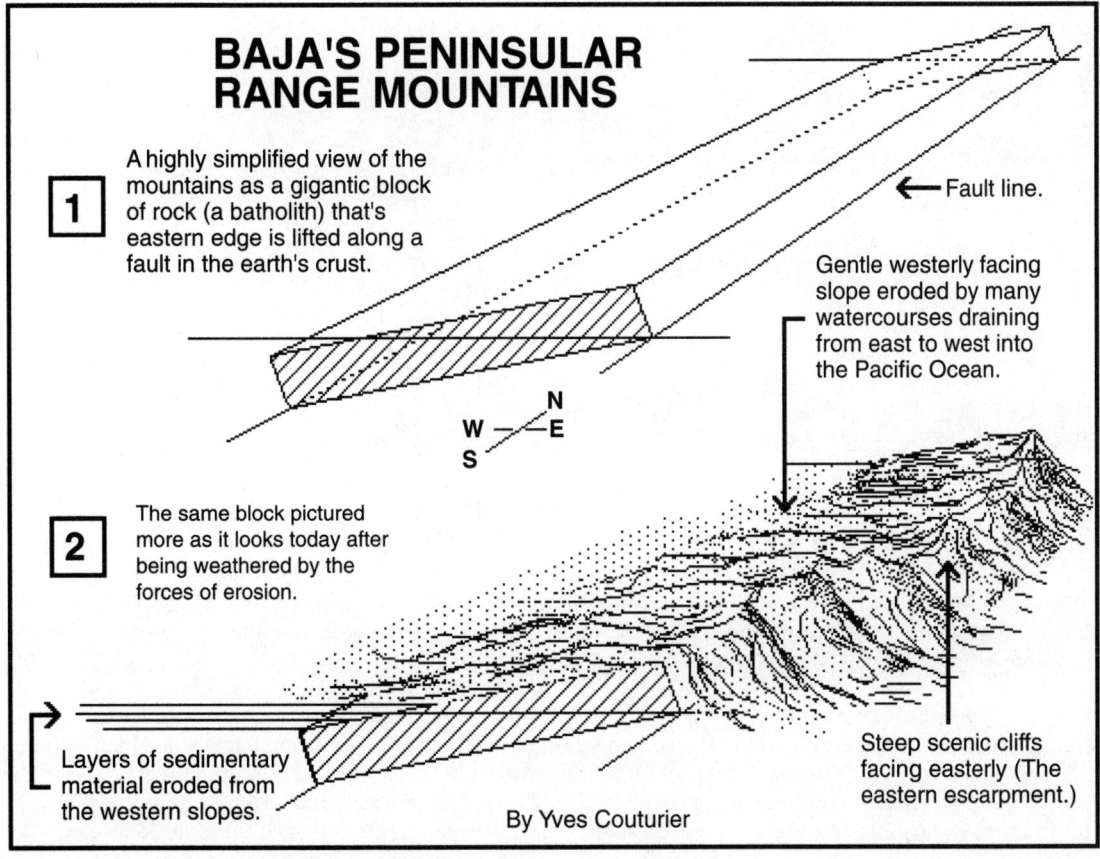

BAJA'S PENINSULAR RANGE MOUNTAINS

1 A highly simplified view of the mountains as a gigantic block of rock (a batholith) that's eastern edge is lifted along a fault in the earth's crust.

← Fault line.

Gentle westerly facing slope eroded by many watercourses draining from east to west into the Pacific Ocean.

2 The same block pictured more as it looks today after being weathered by the forces of erosion.

Layers of sedimentary material eroded from the western slopes.

Steep scenic cliffs facing easterly (The eastern escarpment.)

By Yves Couturier

excellent resource for those desiring more detailed information about the geology of the Baja peninsula.

THE PENINSULA IS BORN

Scientists estimate that the earth is some 4.5 billion years old. In comparison to this incredible age, the geologic story of Baja California is a recent one, with reliable dating going back only some 150 million years. But even at this relatively recent time, there was yet to be a peninsula. The birth of the present jagged finger of land was not to begin until 25-30 million years ago as a byproduct of the formation of the famous San Andreas Fault and its undersea extensions both to the north and south. (See SAN ANDREAS FAULT Map.)

The San Andreas Fault is a deep, linear fracture extending from the floor of the Pacific Ocean some 25 miles north of San Francisco, south through Alta California to the mouth of the Rio Colorado, and then into the Sea of Cortez. On the floor of this body of water it continues southward as a zone of sea floor spreading called the Sea of Cortez Rift Zone.

Most geologists now ascribe to the theory of plate tectonics wherein the earth's crust is believed to be made up of a number of massive plates which move more or less independently from each other. The San Andreas Fault and the Sea of Cortez Rift Zone are part of the boundary between the two gigantic plates that form the North American Continent to the east and the Pacific Plate to the west.

Millenniums ago the Pacific Plate began to slide up the California coast in a northwesterly direction. The total displacement is estimated at approximately 450 miles and is still occurring at the rate of about one inch per year. The southern portion of the plate gradually separated from the continent to open up the area now occupied by the Sea of Cortez. There is a more westerly movement toward the southern portion of the sea which explains why it is wider there than to the north.

As a result, the Sea of Cortez is one of the world's youngest seas and it, and the Red Sea to the east of Africa, serve geologists as classic examples of tec-

In the background of this photo one can see the dramatic east-facing escarpment of the Sierra Giganta Mountains west of the camping area at El Juncalito. These steep cliffs may be seen in the area from Loreto south to Ligui. Photo BW.

INTEREST Tour stop in the mountains north of La Paz. This vista point overlooks the low-lying Llano de La Paz, the gap which separates the lagging mountains of the Cape region from the Sierra Giganta to the north. It would take very little rise in sea level to convert the lethargic southern tip into an island.

BAJA'S BACKBONE MOUNTAINS

Perusing the topographic maps of the world will readily show that most of our planet's mountains occur in ranges or chains rather than as isolated peaks. In western North America, many of these ranges are the result of linear masses of molten minerals welling up from below the earth's crust and solidifying into gigantic structures called *batholiths*. The main backbone mountains of the Baja peninsula, the Peninsular Range, are formed from part of a chain of such batholiths which stretch along the west coast of the North American continent. It is thus a close cousin of similar ranges in British Columbia, Idaho, and the Sierra Nevada of Alta California.

tonic interaction. And because of all this, the American residents of southern Alta California are cast together with their Mexican neighbors in a slow and rocky boat to China. The former can take heart in knowing that the latter seem to get along quite well being separated from the mainland. It also appears that those northern California politicians who yearn to separate California into two states may eventually get their way.

The splitting and northerly movement of the peninsula has been a slow and complex event. It would appear that the journey has not been uniform and that the peninsula has been stretched in the process. In particular, the mountains at the southern tip have lagged behind the northern portion. This situation may be clearly observed at the POINTS OF SPECIAL

The Sierra Nevada and Baja's Peninsular Range are similar in two basic respects. They are both formed from *fault block batholiths,* and in both cases the block has been tilted upward unevenly to create a steep face, or *escarpment*, along the eastern edge. Knowledge of these very basic circumstances will allow the

San Diego

Sierra de Juarez

Laguna Salina

Rio Colorado

GEOLOGIC PROVINCES
AND PROMINENT TOPOGRAPHIC FEATURES

Valle de Camalu

San Quintin Cinder Cones

Valle de San Quintin

Punta Baja

Catavina Boulder Fields

Sierra San Pedro Martir

Scammon's Lagoon

Barrier Beaches

Las Tres Virgenes Volcano

Lava Flows

Punta Eugenia

Desierto Vizcaino

N

Sierra Vizciano

Punta Abreojos

Barrier Beaches

Sierra Giganta

An underwater range of mountains connects the Sierra Vizcaino and the Sierra Magdalena

Barrier Beaches

Llano de Magdalena

Sierra Magdalena

Llano de La Paz

Barrier Beaches

Sierra de la Laguna

**PENINSULAR RANGE PROVINCE **

BASIN AND RANGE PROVINCE

CONTINENTIAL BORDERLANDS PROVINCE

** Plus isolated mountain ranges.

Las Tres Virgenes volcano north of Santa Rosalia. Note the organ pipe cactus on the left. Photo JW.

fracture or fault occurred along the eastern edge of the plank.

Over millions of years this eastern edge was raised up along the line of the fault to form a steep cliff, or escarpment. What was formerly the top of the plank now becomes the gently sloping west face of a range of mountains. The forces of erosion carve the upper eastern edge into a linear series of peaks. These same processes of erosion also dissect the westerly face,

traveler to observe and to understand the most prominent topographic features of the peninsula.

sometimes creating quite rugged topography marked by scores of watercourses running from east to west.

To comprehend the makeup of a fault block batholith, see the accompanying illustration and visualize the basic structure of these mountains as a gigantic piece of lumber sawn so that it is much wider than high. A 2" x 10" plank will do nicely. Then, because of tremendous forces developed within the crust of the earth, a

In the United States, the situation just described is readily apparent in the Sierra Nevada to travelers crossing the range from east to west on Interstate 80. At Reno, Nevada, the steep eastern escarpment may be seen stretching majestically both north and south. A few miles west of the city the highway climbs steeply and in a short distance crosses over the crestline at Donner Summit. The descent over the more gentle western slope extends a much longer distance, and it involves several ups and downs resulting from the forces of erosion. The highly scenic eastern escarpment of the Sierra Nevada and its series of 12,000-to-14,000-foot peaks are in clear view for hundreds of miles to the south of Reno and east of Highway 395. This situation in the United States has been described because many visitors to Baja will have traveled in this area and will now be able to relate the two geologically similar circumstances.

This photo shows a rock formation named El Pedregoso (The Rocky One). It lies at **Km C-206** along Highway 1. The formation illustrates how granite rock erodes into rounded, yellowish boulders. Such boulders are apparent in the Cativina Boulder Fields (**Km C-157 to C-179**) and in many of the granite mountain outcroppings in northern Baja. Photo BW.

The geologic story of the Peninsular Range has been complicated by the linear stretching previously described, by substantial volcanic activity, and by other factors; yet the dominant element is the fault-block mountain building just described. The traveler to Baja can see many evidences of this process and other related geologic events. Here is a list of the principal phenomena.

1. — In general, the highest mountain peaks lie along the main crestline divide in the eastern portion of the peninsula. In many places, this divide lies so close to the Sea of Cortez that the eastern escarpment falls directly into the ocean and there are no coastal roads. For this reason, some of the peninsula's most scenic areas are not readily accessible to the tourist. They may be viewed only by the boater sailing close to the rocky coast and by passengers of small private planes flying overhead.

2. — The scenic eastern escarpment of the Peninsular Range may be best seen by the land-based tourist in two places: (a) from the San Felipe area where Highways 2 and 5 traverse the flat desert lands east of the escarpment and (b) along the Sea of Cortez coast between Santa Rosalia and a point about 20 miles south of Loreto. This southerly portion of this section is the most scenic area along the Transpeninsular Highway.

Rugged mountainous areas may of course be visited in many other places by use of secondary and more primitive roads. Journeys to the National Parks in the Sierra de Juarez and Sierra San Pedro Martir are particularly rewarding. These side trips are described in Chapters 16 and 18.

3. — The Peninsular Range mountains are crossed by the main highway system in several places, thus affording the traveler the opportunity to experience the steep eastern escarpment. A classic example lies south of Loreto. After a steep climb of some 10 miles up the steep eastern slope, the traveler might well ask "where is the other side of the mountain?" For all practical purposes, there is none. The crestline of the mountain range falls gently to the west and eventually blends into the Llano de Magdalena and the Pacific Ocean.

4. — The lands lying to the west of the crestline divide are of fairly gentle overall topography. The large volumes of sediments caused by the erosion of this broad slope have been deposited to the west of the mountains resulting in the formation of some of the largest flat plains found along the west coast of the North American continent. The major areas are the Desierto de Vizcaino near the center of the peninsula, and the Llano de Magdalena in the south.

Much of the Transpeninsular Highway has been located in the western and central portion of the peninsula to take advantage of this relatively gentle topography. However, the highway must cross, at right angles, the hundreds of watercourses that have been cut in an east-west direction down the west facing slope of the mountains.

5. — While the eastern side of the peninsula has risen over time to form the steep eastern escarpment, the western side, south of the 28th parallel, has been subsiding for millions of years. This may be the result of the weight of erosion-deposited

ROCK CLASSIFICATION

1 - IGNEOUS - All of the earth's rocks originate as igneous rocks formed by the cooling of molten material at or near the surface of the earth.

    PLUTONIC - **Intrusive** rocks cooled slowly **below** the earth's surface, resulting in **coarse grain**, with **identifiable crystals** of various minerals. **Light color**. The most common rock is GRANITE.

    VOLCANIC - **Extrusive** rocks cooled rapidly at or near the earth's surface, resulting in **fine grain**, with **no identifiable crystals**. **Darker color**. The most common rock is BASALT.

2 - SEDIMENTARY - Rocks made-up of (1) fragments of preexisting igneous or metamorphic rocks worn down and deposited elsewhere by the forces of erosion (running water, wind, ice flows, freezing temperatures, and gravity) or (2) by the accumulation of various organic materials. Common rocks are CONGLOMERATE, SANDSTONE, SHALE, and LIMESTONE.

3 - METAMORPHIC - Preexisting igneous or sedimentary rocks which have undergone change by being subjected to intense heat and pressure under the surface of the earth. Individual rocks are frequently banded or stratified.

sediments that in places are 10 miles thick. Evidence that the land is sinking into the sea is provided by the large numbers of coastal lagoons lying between Scammon's Lagoon on the north and Bahia Magdalena on the south. Seaward from these lagoons lie long sand bars known as barrier beaches. The major areas of such beaches are shown on the map in this chapter.

GEOLOGIC PROVINCES

Geologists have divided the North American continent into a large number of provinces. Each of these is an area of relatively homogeneous geologic features, and the dividing lines between the different provinces are in most places readily apparent to the traveler. Such geological provinces as the Sierra Nevada Mountains, the California Central Valley, the Cascade Mountains, the Willamette Valley, and the Colorado Plateau are well-known to the citizens of western United States.

For the Baja peninsula, the situation is relatively simple as there are only three provinces: the Basin and Range, the Peninsular Range Mountains and the Continental Borderlands. They are shown on the GEOLOGIC PROVINCES Map in this chapter. This map also shows the location of various other geologic and topographic features. Most of these features, and the dividing lines between the provinces, will be pointed out during the GRAND TOUR in PART III.

BASIN AND RANGE PROVINCE — The Basin and Range province is that vast area of the United States and Mexico which lies roughly between the Rocky Mountains on the east, and the Sierra Nevada and Cascade Mountains on the west. It is characterized by terrain which is quite flat overall although it is dissected by numerous, relatively short, ranges of mountains almost all running in a generally north-south direction. Highways through the province traverse flat terrain but usually curve to skirt the edges of the mountain ranges.

The southern extremity of this large province extends into the northeastern portion of the Baja peninsula, an area referred to as the San Felipe Desert. As in the province as a whole, the terrain is flat with a scattering of mountain ranges running north and south. While much of the floor of the province in the United States is thousands of feet above sea level, in Baja it is only a few hundred feet in elevation.

PENINSULAR RANGE PROVINCE — This province encompasses the Peninsula's backbone mountain range as previously discussed. Remember that the entire range is characterized by a precipitous east-facing escarpment and a much wider, overall gently sloping western portion. In the United State the Peninsular Range Province extends into northern San

Diego and western Riverside counties in southern California. Its northern boundary roughly follows Interstate 10 through San Gorgonio pass east of San Bernardino.

The range has been divided into numerous sections, each with its own name. These are the names that are frequently shown on the maps available to travelers. The more important ones in Baja are shown on the GEOLOGIC PROVINCES Map.

One other point must be noted concerning the Peninsular Range Province. The mountains in Baja's northern half, and the Sierra de la Laguna at the southern tip, are composed primarily of *granite*, a plutonic rock. In contrast, the Sierra Giganta in the peninsula's southern half is made up of a volcanic rock named *basalt*. The differences between these two rock types will be readily apparent to the traveler. They are described in more detail in the final section of this chapter.

CONTINENTAL BORDERLANDS PROVINCE — While sailing along the Pacific coast of the United States and Canada, one is impressed by the fact that virtually the entire shoreline is steep and mountainous. This situation begins to change south of the United States-Mexican border where much of the western shoreline is backed by flat, or gently sloping, plains. These plains are located in four more or less separate areas. (See the GEOLOGIC PROVINCES Map.)

In the north, a relatively small area surrounds the towns of Camalu and San Quintin. To the south, the Desierto de Vizcaino, Llano de Magdalena, and the Llano de la Paz are names given to sections of what is actually one, continuous, largely level area. These lands are composed of deep layers of sediments eroded over geologic time from the Peninsular Range mountains to the east. The tremendous weight of these sediments is causing the western edge of the province to sink below sea level as evidenced by numerous saltwater lagoons and barrier beaches along the Pacific shore.

Along the western edge of this province lie two relatively minor mountain ranges, the Sierra Vizcaino and the Sierra Magdalena. Oceanographic investigations have disclosed that the two are actually linked together by a ridge of mountains lying beneath the surface of the ocean. Taken together, this system comprises a rather significant range of mountains paralleling the main Peninsular Range.

ROCK TYPES

The discussion of the Peninsular Range Mountains introduced several geologic terms relating to different types of rocks. We now need to pause briefly to examine this subject. At the outset, it should be noted that the terminology being presented has worldwide application. Knowing these few facts can thus be used to enhance traveling experiences anywhere on earth.

Geologists have classified the world's rocks into three great classes, *igneous*, *sedimentary*, and *metamorphic*. The igneous class is further divided into two subgroups, *plutonic* and *volcanic*. Please refer to the ROCK CLASSIFICATION Chart to learn the basic elements common to these classes of rock. Each of the classes will be encountered frequently while traveling through the peninsula and many will be pointed out in the course of the GRAND TOUR in PART III.

By now you know that you will be encountering igneous-plutonic rocks (granite) in the northern portions of Baja's Peninsular Range mountains and in the Sierra de la Laguna in the extreme south. One of the most interesting points will be the Catavina boulder fields south of El Rosario. Igneous-volcanic rocks (basalt) will dominate the scene in the Sierra Giganta. You will also see the massive Las Tres Virgenes volcano and nearby recent lava flows. Volcanic cinder cones will be in evidence near San Quintin. While traveling through the various sections of the Continental Borderlands, sedimentary rocks prevail and are easily seen in the highway cuts and other places.

CHAPTER 10
VEGETATION

I have promised to be judicious in my use of superlatives, but it would be ignoring reality not to note that the desert vegetation of the Magnificent Peninsula is in itself magnificent. I have traveled extensively in the desert areas of the United States and mainland Mexico and they offer nothing compared to the desert plant communities in Baja. (The best the United States has to offer occurs in the Organ Pipe Cactus National Monument in Arizona.) In one of my botanical readings I encountered the author's view that Baja's desert vegetation was the best in the world. I cannot personally verify this position but can report that the deserts of the Jordan Rift in Israel and Egypt's Sinai area (which provide much of the setting for the Judeo-Christian Bible) area essentially barren.

As in so many other fields, appreciation of vegetative beauty can be significantly improved by understanding something about what one is viewing. With this in mind Chapter 10 provides material concerning the desert itself, its various plant communities, and the common characteristics of desert plants. Photographs and descriptions of many of the more interesting species are also included.

VEGETATIVE REGIONS AND PLANT COMMUNITIES

Botanists have classified the world's vegetation into easily recognizable plant communities. The Douglas fir forests of the Pacific Northwest, various areas of grasses in the Great Plains, and the chaparral brushlands of southwestern United States are examples of such communities.

Norman Roberts discusses a total of eight plant communities in his *Baja California Plant Field Guide*. These are grouped into three broad regions: (1) The California Region, (2) The Sonoran Desert, and (3) The Cape Region.

The three regions may be easily distinguished from each other. They are shown on the VEGETATIVE REGIONS Map. Identifying all of the communities is a more difficult task. The map points out only the two communities that stand out best in the field.

Regional and community boundaries are distinct where there are sharp geographical changes but are

---

BAJA CALIFORNIA PLANT FIELD GUIDE

BY NORMAN ROBERTS

Norman Robert's book is THE definitive work on the plants of Baja California for the amateur plant enthusiast. The present edition is a heavily revised version of the original volume which has been out-of-print for many years. This 309 page guide describes 550 plant species with color photos of 275 of them.

BRILLIANT COLOR PHOTOS MAKE PLANT IDENTIFICATION EASY

Get your copy from the BAJA BOOKSHELF in the Appendix

more gradual where this is not the case. The map and an accompanying table point out places where boundary changes, or other regional distinctions, are easily detected.

The Sonoran Desert Region, lying in the central portion of the peninsula, is part of a far larger area classified as a true desert. The other two regions receive too much precipitation to rate this distinction. Delineating the three regions is thus basically a matter of knowing what is desert and what is not. Let us look briefly at the three regions, progressing from north to south.

The Arid Tropical Forest near Highway 1 in the Rancho Verde RV Park **(Km J-141)** where the normally dense undergrowth has been cleared. A great place to view this relatively rare plant community. Photo BW.

CALIFORNIA REGION — This

region is a continuation of the vegetational communities found to the north in Alta California. The principal plants are a number of densely growing species of shrubs, commonly referred to as chaparral. At the higher elevations the shrub community gives way rather sharply to forests of pinyon and Jeffrey pine and other conifers.

The California Region will be passed over rather swiftly because it is not unique to Baja, and you may visit similar areas in the United States with relative ease. The coniferous forests in Baja are little different from those that clothe the higher lands in any of southern Alta California's four National Forests.

SONORAN DESERT REGION — There are a dozen
or so major areas of desert and near-desert lands throughout the world. One is the North American Desert located in southwestern United States and northwestern Mexico. This area of over one-half million square miles is divided into four sections, one of which is the Sonoran Desert. Approximately two-thirds of the Baja peninsula falls within the Sonoran Desert, and this area constitutes the largest of the three vegetative regions.

Here, in the central portion of the peninsula, are located Baja's most intriguing plants. Included are a wide variety of cacti and other succulents along with the bizarre cirio, elephant tree, and a host of others. Many of the more prominent plant species have made special adaptations to arid conditions. Their physical

characteristics are thus clearly different from plants living in the California Region and other moist areas. There is also a great deal of space between the individual plants in marked contrast to the dense brush fields to the north.

Botanists recognize four plant communities within this region. One of these, the San Felipe Desert, provides a sharp contrast to the glowing description I have just painted for the region as a whole. This community lies in the rain shadow east of the peninsula's tallest mountains along the shore of the Sea of Cortez. As a result, it is one of the driest areas in Baja and supports only low, sparse vegetation. It is easy to separate this region from its more entrancing neighbors.

THE CAPE REGION — The vegetation of the Cape
Region is also far different from what we are accustomed to north of the border. Here, there are two plant communities. One of these, the *Oak-Pinyon Woodland*, is rarely seen by tourists as it is located at high elevations in the mountains where there are no roads. These peaks receive considerable rainfall as the result of high-intensity tropical storms, and they support stands of oaks, pinyon pine, and other small trees.

The plant community through which the Cape Region highways pass is the *Arid Tropical Forest* . Because these highways are at relatively low elevations, you will still see many plants to which you have become accustomed in the Sonoran Desert. However, the hallmarks of this community are (1) vegetation that is far more densely spaced than in the Sonoran Desert and (2) the presence of a variety of low spreading trees. It has been referred to by one leading botanist as an impoverished tropical forest.

As our next step, let us take a closer look at the desert and near-desert lands of the Baja peninsula.

AGRICULTURE -- There is relatively little commercial agriculture in Baja because of its arid climate. However, the five principal areas devoted to crops are crossed by the peninsula's main highways and they are thus readily apparent to the traveler. These four areas are: (1) The Valle de la Calafia and other valleys traversed by Highway 3 midway between Tecate and Ensenada. This is Baja's largest area of vineyards and the location of two large wineries. These vineyards add a pleasant element to the area's scenery. (2) The Valles de Camalu and San Quintin. They constitute the isolated northern section of the Continental Borderlands Province shown on the *Geologic Provinces*

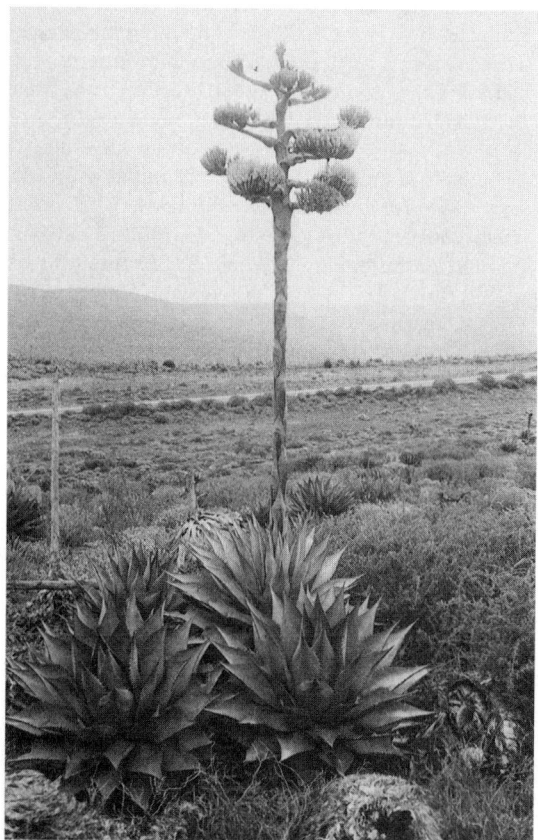

Century plant in full bloom in the sparsely vegetated Sonoran Desert Region. Photo JW.

map in Chapter 9. Water is obtained from wells located so as to tap underground reservoirs fed by several intermittent streams in an area that receives considerable winter precipitation. (3) A portion of the Desierto Vizcaino centered around the community of Ejido Vizcaino (See *Punta Eugenia Area* map in Chapter 20). (4) A portion of the Llano de Magdalena centered around the communities of Ciudad Insurgentes and Ciudad Constitucion. This is Baja's largest agricultural area. The latter two areas obtain their water from deep wells in areas that normally receive little rainfall. (5) The San Juan de los Planes area traversed by Highway 286 SE of La Paz.

BAJA'S DESERT LANDS

CLIMATE — Deserts are characterized as areas receiving less than ten inches of annual rainfall and which have generally high temperatures. Their low humidity allows the sun's rays to penetrate the atmosphere easily and heat the ground far more than in moister areas. Ground temperatures 30-to-50 degrees warmer than the air are common. This same low humidity allows daytime heat to dissipate quickly; nighttime temperatures may decline as much as 50 degrees. The nighttime coolness is a key factor in the survival of both plants and animals and allows campers to enjoy cool, restful sleeping. The cheer and warmth of an evening campfire is always welcome in the desert.

It seems appropriate to ask why much of a long, narrow peninsula surrounded by water should be a desert. The answer lies in a combination of factors. At the broadest level, we find that Baja lies within a worldwide belt of high air pressure. Air is generally descending in such places, and because falling air increases in temperature it is able to absorb, rather than give up, moisture.

Perhaps of more importance is the continual presence of a cell of high pressure, called the Pacific High, off the west coast of the North American continent. It shields the peninsula from most of the moisture-laden air masses arriving from the Pacific Ocean. As this high shifts south during the winter months it allows considerable rain to fall along the west coasts of Canada and the United States; however, this air retains little moisture when, and if, it arrives over Mexico.

Finally, we find that the ocean off Baja's west coast is cold as the result of the upwelling of water from the depths of the sea. Air passing over these waters is chilled, and cool air can carry little moisture. As this air is warmed by contact with the land, it is able to retain, rather than dispose of, its moisture; therefore, there is little rain. These circumstances combine to make Baja a very dry part of the world.

The exception to these conditions occurs near the peninsula's tip due to tropical storms which are formed in the summer over the warm waters off the Mexican mainland to the south. Many of these storms dissipate in the Pacific Ocean, but others veer to the north and cross the southern and central portions of the Baja peninsula. Torrential downpours can occur, and scientists have reported witnessing continuous sheets of water one-half inch thick flowing over hundreds of acres of land.

Unfortunately, the desert's normally dry soils can absorb little water during such storms. As a result, areas in the Cape Region which receive considerable rainfall still support only semiarid types of vegetation. For deserts as a whole, it is estimated that only about three percent of their rainfall penetrates any distance into the soil.

POINTS OF VEGETATIVE SIGNIFICANCE
(See Vegetative Regions Map)

1 The segment of Highway 1 between the two arrows passes through the most impressive and picturesque vegetation in the Baja peninsula. The transition between the California Region and the Sonoran Desert is distinct near the upper arrow where Highway 1 rapidly gains elevation south of the Rio del Rosario.

2 The two squares indicate the location of Baja's two National Parks. Secondary roads may be driven to these parks which lie in the coniferous forest plant community. The boundaries between this community and lower elevation chaparral are evident as you enter both parks.

3 At this point on Highway 3 is the most dramatic elevation change in all of Baja's highways. At the base of the grade to the east is the sparsely vegetated San Felipe Desert. At the top of the grade lies the northern fringe of the pinyon pine and juniper portion of the coniferous forest community. To the west the chaparral brush fields dominate.

4 Highway 3 again crosses the eastern escarpment of the Peninsular Range Mountains as it did at point #3. This time the crossing is at a lower elevation so there is no coniferous forest. The boundary between the San Felipe Desert community and the chaparral of the California Region is very apparent. There is an outstanding area of barrel cactus at this point.

5 Here is another crossing of the mountain's eastern escarpment. At the base of the grade is, again, the sparse vegetation of the San Felipe Desert. To the west lies one of the most picturesque sections of the Sonoran Desert Region with an outstanding stand of Baja's most unique plant, the cirio tree. The boundary between the two is easily seen.

6 In this section of the Transpeninsular Highway lies another fine area of Sonoran Desert vegetation. The plant life is enhanced by the presence of the Tres Virgenes Volcano and the lava flows emanating from its southern flank. The elephant tree is the most interesting species here.

7 Look for dense growth of lichens and ball moss on the larger desert plants along Highway 22 and the secondary roads between Highway 1 and the Pacific coast. Also seen along Highway 1 in some places.

8 The section of Highway 1 in the mountains on either side of the town of El Triunfo provides the best view of Cape Region vegetation. Both the denseness and presence of several species of low, spreading trees characteristic of this region's vegetation are very apparent in this area.

9 The dense Cape Region vegetation is present along Highway 19 at the two places indicated by the arrows, although the stands are not as picturesque as those noted at point number 8.

VEGETATIVE REGIONS

Tijuana

Mexicali

3

2

Ensenada

2

4

San Felipe

POINTS OF VEGETATIVE SIGNIFICANCE

#

See comments in the box on the adjacent page.

N

100 Miles

1

5

6

1

PACIFIC OCEAN

SEA OF CORTEZ

REGIONS

7

CALIFORNIA REGION
That portion of the region in the coniferous forest plant community.

SONORAN DESERT REGION
That portion of the region in the San Felipe Desert plant community.

THE CAPE REGION

La Paz

8

9

Cabo San Lucas

Ocotillo. Note the wide spacing of the other plants as is typical in the desert. Photo JW.

In desert areas, *water* becomes the critical element in plant competition. As little moisture penetrates more than a few inches into the soil, most plants have a broad network of roots near the surface to quickly collect what rain does fall. They cannot survive if other individuals are competing in their collection area. As a result, you will see that there is only one plant in a given spot and there is *no layering* as is common in moister areas. (You will see some degree of layering in the Cape Region due to its more humid environment.) If desert vegetation is destroyed it tends to be replaced with the same species of plants that were displaced and there is no *succession* of plants as in humid areas.

Finally, desert plant communities are made up of a wide *variety of species and life forms*, a factor that contributes significantly to the enjoyment that can be gained from studying desert vegetation.

SOILS — When you arrive in the desert area, look at the soil beneath your feet. There will be almost no

HUMID VERSUS DRY ENVIRONMENTS — There are marked contrasts between the plant communities found in humid versus dry environments. In moist areas of the world, *space and light* are the key factors in competition between different species of plants and among individuals within a species. These communities are frequently *layered* with tall trees that form a canopy over smaller trees or shrubs. The lower layers are often of a different species. Below all this vegetation will be grasses and other ground-loving plants.

With the passage of time there is often a *succession* of plants. Shade-tolerant species will gradually grow through the canopy of the more light-requiring varieties that preceded them. In this manner, a stand of aspen trees will gradually be replaced by conifers, but should the latter stand be destroyed by fire or disease the succession will be repeated and aspen will return.

Finally, humid plant communities are frequently dominated by *one life form* such as coniferous or hardwood trees. All of these characteristics are different for desert plant communities.

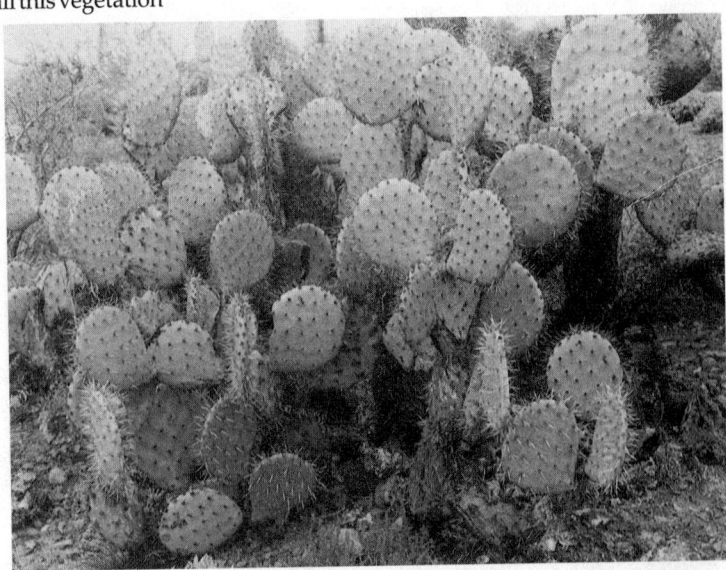

Prickly pear. Bright flowers grow on the ends of the pads after rain. Photo JW.

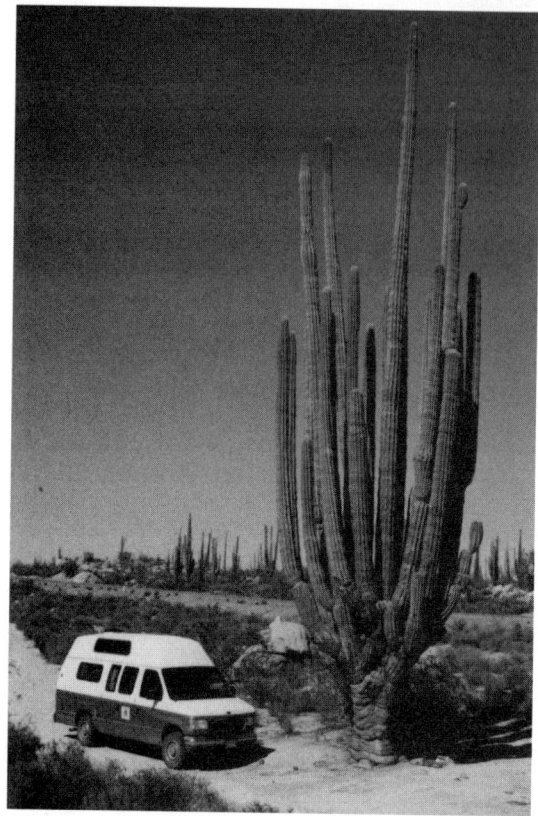

Cardon. Pictured here is the largest cardon I have seen in Baja. It is located on a short loop road off Highway 1 in the Catavina Boulder Fields at **Km C-169**. A great photo opportunity. Photo BW.

Candelabra Cactus. Photo JW.

organic material such as the deep layers of duff found in coniferous forests or the matting of dead grass in meadow areas. There are relatively few desert plants in a given area in comparison to plant communities in moister areas, and these individuals shed very little in the way of leaves and flower parts. Much of what little organic material is produced is washed away in the high intensity storms that are typical of desert areas. Desert soils tend to be high in salt content as there is little rainfall to dissolve and carry away these materials.

DESERT PLANT ADAPTATIONS

It is gratifying to be able to identify specific species of plants when you see them in your travels. Material to help you do this is presented further along in this chapter. However, in the desert, it is of equal, if not greater, interest to study and observe some of the common characteristics of all desert plants.

Most living things are segregated into either the plant or animal kingdom. Each kingdom is further subdivided by phylum, class, order, family, genus, and species. Individual species are named in the scientific world by combining the genus and species names. Thus, the galloping cactus must suffer through eternity being referred to as *Machaerocereus gummosus*, although you would perhaps call it something else should you be so unfortunate as to fall into one.

It would seem logical to suspect that most species of plants living in an environment as harsh as the desert would belong to a limited number of closely related genera and families. Reasoning in this way, one would assume that some particular characteristic of these select genera and families provided the key to dry-land survival. In many cases, it did not happen this way.

Ira Wiggin's classic *Flora of Baja California* notes that there are 2,705 species and 884 genera of plants in Baja California. The 179 most common species described in Norman Robert's original *Field Guide* belong in 64 different plant families. One can speculate that a wide variety of vegetative types were surviving contentedly in a moist environment, then, over time, they were confronted with drying climatic conditions. Those species that were to survive made certain physical and reproductive adaptations which permitted their living under desert conditions.

This process of change is termed *convergent evolution* and is defined as "the evolution of unrelated or distantly related groups of organisms along similar lines, resulting in the development of similar traits or features in the unrelated groups." The different types of adaptations which allow survival under dry conditions are amazingly few. As a result, many species of desert plants that look very much like each other are only distantly related.

Galloping Cactus. Photo JW.

All plants that live in the desert have to deal with surviving drought. Some species have solved the problem by simply avoiding it; they are called the *evaders*. Others have made the various adaptations mentioned above. These plants are the *resisters*. We will now examine these two groups.

EVADERS — These are the grasses, forbs and other annual plants. They quickly germinate from seed following a rain, grow to maturity in a few weeks, produce a new crop of seed, and die. They survive in the form of millions of seeds cast on the desert floor to await the next cycle. This method of existence is little different from that of annual plants in more humid regions. Because desert annuals have not made any pronounced physical adaptation to resist drought, they resemble annual species in moister climates. Grass in Baja looks much like grass in Oregon, although it may not be as tall.

Desert annuals produce a seed crop far in excess of that needed

for their own reproduction. This allows many desert animals to utilize seeds as a basic source of food.

How do seeds that survive the foragers know when to germinate and when to remain dormant? The survival of the species hangs in the balance. The answer

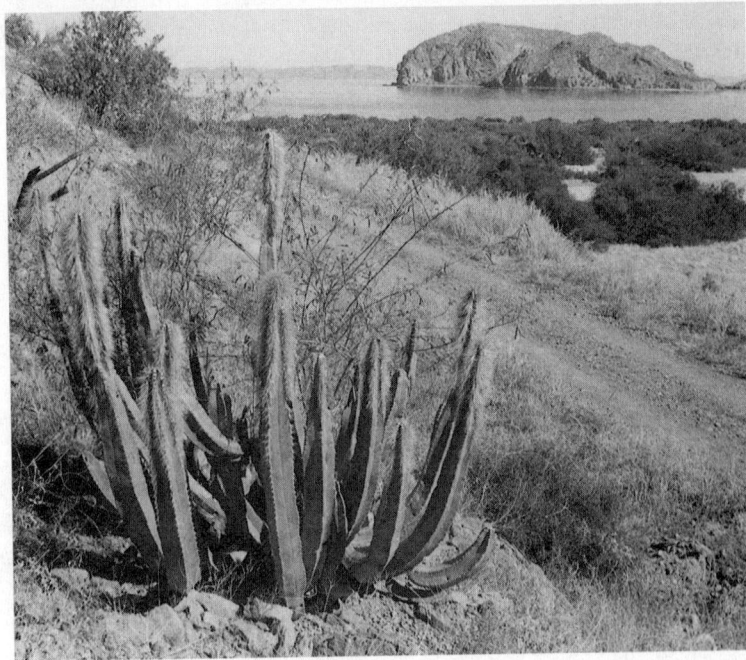

Old Man Cactus. Note the clusters of spines at the tops of the stems which give the plant a bearded look. It is easy to recognize. Photo JW.

Barrel Cactus. The base of the cardon cactus to the right is growing straight up from the ground. Almost all barrels lean to the south as can be seen with this individual. This no doubt gives them minimum exposure to the sun. Photo JW.

tainers as part of their roots. The wide-spreading and shallow root system of the commonly seen cardon cactus is capable of soaking up hundreds of gallons of water following a rain, after which four-fifths of its weight may consist of water.

ACCORDION STRUCTURE —
A common characteristic of many species of cactus is the accordion-like structure of the stem. As the plant takes in water, the fleshy stem expands quickly. It subsequently contracts slowly as the supply is utilized. Note the stem condition of the cacti you examine.

If you are traveling south on Highway 1, following winter rains, you will observe that the water-filled cacti in the northern portion will display broad, U-shaped spacing between their ribs. Only a few days later, you may arrive near the peninsula's tip and see that the pleats are deeply indented and V-shaped. These southern plants normally receive their moisture as the result of summer, rather than, winter storms.

is generally believed to be that seeds have a growth-inhibiting chemical in their coats which is dissolved away when exposed to sufficient quantities of rainfall. When they do germinate, the traveler is treated to the colorful spectacle of the desert in bloom.

RESISTERS — Perennial plants live continually from year to year and gradually grow larger. They are the trees, shrubs, cactus, and other species with woody superstructures which have made special adaptations to resist dry conditions. Look for evidence of these methods of adaptation in studying Baja's desert vegetation.

WATER STORAGE — Perhaps the desert's most interesting plants are the *succulents*, which have developed the ability to store water. The best known are the cacti, which use their stems as reservoirs. Species such as the century plant have adapted their leaves for this purpose. Others have underground con-

Cholla Cactus. The most recent season's growth is lighter in color than the rest of the plant. Photo JW.

Creosote Bush. An uninspiring picture of this uninspiring but common plant. Photo JW.

ing significant rainfall, you will see that the ocotillo, cirio and similar plants are greenish in color, but you will have difficulty distinguishing any leaves from a distance. The leaves are there, but they are tiny affairs no more than an inch long. Small leaf size reduces the amount of water lost through transpiration. In addition to having leaves of such small size, these species quickly shed their foliage when the ground dries. The production of leaves is not a phenomenon one can count on at a particular time of the year but is clearly the result of recent rainfall, whenever it occurs.

The characteristic of having small, and even minute, leaves is typical of much of Baja's perennial vegetation. Even sizeable trees have small leaves. The most conservative of all are the cacti, which have no leaves except for a short period in youth. Their chlorophyll is located in the main stem of the plant as evidenced by their green color.

ARMAMENTS — A high proportion of the perennial plants in desert areas have developed thorns, leaves with sharpened points or toothed edges, and other similar armaments. Plants in other environments also contain thorns, but they are so prevalent in desert species that it is clear that they are an important adaptation for survival under arid conditions.

These armaments protect plants from browsing animals. They cannot afford to lose the food producing foliage that took up precious water to create. It is interesting to note that very few plants in the great desert in western Australia have thorns, and that this is the only one of the world's major arid areas that does not have, or has not once had, hooved, browsing animals. (Kangaroos do little browsing.) Also intriguing is the fact that some desert species that bear thorns in the wild produce no such protection when grown in the humid environment of a greenhouse.

LEAF CHARACTERISTICS — If you are fortunate enough to visit Baja's desert areas follow-

WIDE SPACING — As already noted, desert vegetation is widely spaced so that each individual plant has a water collecting area sufficient for its survival. Even

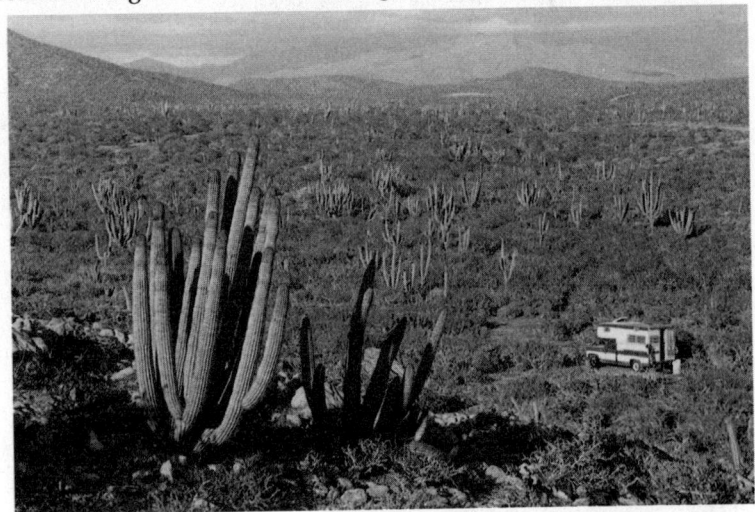

Organ pipe cactus close to our campsite near Playa los Cerritos near Highway 19. Note that the vegetation is far more dense here in the Cape Region than in the Sonoran Desert Region. Photo JW.

A clump of datilillo in full bloom. Photo BW.

These means of vegetative reproduction allow plants to avoid the costly water and energy-consumptive process of producing seeds and permit spreading of the species in years when seed production is not possible. If you visit the FONATUR nursery at Primer Agua, near Loreto, you will see a large number of species that are being propagated by vegetative means.

TRUNK FORM — Many species of low trees and shrubs in Baja have a trunk or main stem that is very thick in proportion to the size of the plant. The elephant tree is the most prominent example. There are in fact two different species of plants, both commonly called elephant trees. They are so similar that close inspection is required to distinguish one from the other, yet they are members of two distantly related families. (See POINTS OF SPECIAL INTEREST Tour stop No. 11.)

OTHER ADAPTATIONS — To resist drought conditions, desert plants have made a variety of other adaptations which are difficult to observe during a casual visit. Some species simply surrender and die back to ground level after each rain-induced period of above ground growth. Food and water are stored in a wide variety of underground structures related to the plant's roots. Other species have developed thick or waxy outer skins to reduce water loss, and they have fewer skin pores than their related wetland cousins. Still others are found to have developed poisonous or repulsive juices to ward off browsing animals.

ENDEMISM — An endemic species is one which is found in only one area of the world. Endemism is common in Baja because plant species have adapted to their harsh environment on an isolated peninsula. Almost 75 percent of the cactus species are endemic, as are many of the other easily observed plants. This uniqueness contributes to its aesthetic quality.

It can also be the cause of some frustration to those who are well versed in plant identification in other areas. For many years I referred to the abundant large cactus in Baja as a saguaro only to find that it was really the cardon. In a similar manner, the datilillo may be confused with the Joshua tree common in Alta California.

EPIPHYTES — Epiphytes are plants which gain physical support from other plants, poles, wires, and other objects. It is unusual to find epiphytes in deserts as they have no roots and must obtain their water from the air. But while the atmosphere in most

in relatively dense areas of vegetation, it is possible to walk between the plants without being impaled by thorns. The open spaces are not filled with young plants, because they are unable to compete with their parents for moisture. Some species also seem to practice chemical warfare as their roots give off toxic substances which prevent the growth of other plants. Be particularly alert for the wide, uniform spacing of the creosote bush if you visit the San Felipe and Bahia de los Angeles areas.

VEGETATIVE REPRODUCTION — It is possible to reproduce many plants by placing cuttings from their stems in moist soil or water. Many desert plants routinely reproduce in this fashion without human assistance. Look at the several species of cholla cactus common in Baja. Their stems are made up of numerous segments. The terminal segments frequently fall to the ground and take root, often producing dense cholla thickets. Also, study the galloping cactus and other species of spreading plants; notice that they are able to produce new roots at places where their stems touch the ground.

deserts is extremely dry, fog and moist air overrun much of Baja's level Pacific coastal areas. Thus the larger desert plants growing here are often heavily festooned with such species.

The traveler may observe two basic types of epiphytes in Baja. Most common are lichens. These are associations of separate and distinct species of algae and fungi which live together in an intimate relationship called symbiosis. The algae provide the nourishment for the symbiotic pair, as they contain chlorophyll, and can make food using the sun's energy. The fungi, which have no chlorophyll, provide mechanical support and aid in the absorption of moisture.

While lichens are not a moss, they can best be described as looking like linear strands of moss. The Spanish moss which hangs from trees in SE United States is a lichen. Sometimes the lichens are so dense as to almost obscure the branches of the host plants, making them appear quite different than they would in dryer areas.

Ball moss also is not a moss, but a perennial herb. It forms spherical clumps about six inches in diameter. This rounded shape makes for easy identification. Neither ball moss nor lichens harm the plants from which they gain support.

COMMON PLANTS

It is well beyond the scope of this book to present extensive material on the identification of individual species of plants. Included are photographs and brief descriptions of only sixteen. These are all in view from the highways and can be identified with reasonable certainty when they are called to your attention in the GRAND TOUR in PART III.

Should your interest in vegetation extend beyond this level, I highly recommend Norman Roberts' *Baja California Plant Field Guide*. This book has excellent color photos and amplifies the material on plant communities presented in this chapter. It is available from the BAJA BOOKSHELF in the Appendix (see notice in this chapter). Also be sure to visit the botanical garden at **Km-57** on Highway 19 south of Todos Santos (See Chapter 25).

CIRIO
Photo - Page 17 & 144

Idria columnaris — For once, a plant's scientific name imparts some information, even to the amateur. In English, *columnar* means having the shape of a column; in Spanish, *cirio* means candle. So, in whatever language, the cirio is a plant shaped like a tapering column, although it often branches several times near the top. It can grow up to 60 feet high but is usually considerably shorter. Along the trunk are numerous branches smaller than the diameter of a pencil and totally out of proportion to the plant as a whole. These bear the tiny leaves that clothe the cirio in green following rain.

If Baja California had a state plant, this would have to be it, as most people would concur that it is Baja's most unique species. It is endemic to Baja except for a small colony across the Sea of Cortez along the coast south of La Libertad. The cirio is present in groves along Highway 1 from immediately south of the Rio del Rosario to the northern edge of the Vizcaino Desert (Geographic Section No. 8). It also grows along the highway to Bahia de los Angeles.

CARDON
Photos - Page 2 & 138

Pachycereus pringlei — While cirio may be Baja's most unique plant, the cardon, or giant cactus, is the most widespread of the peninsula's larger plants. Cardon is a very large cactus with one main trunk, which

Palo Blanco. Note the light bark. Photo JW.

Here a curved and branching cirio frames a portion of the Transpeninsular Highway south of El Rosario. Photo BW.

branches from one to numerous times as the plant grows older. The branches have from 11-to-17 vertical ribs. It is a good cactus in which to check the state of expansion of an accordion structure.

Don't confuse the cardon with the organ pipe which is also many branched but has no main trunk. It is also possible to confuse the cardon with the saguaro cactus of southwestern United States, but we amateurs are blessed by the fact that the saguaro does not grow in Baja. Like the cirio, the cardon is visible immediately south of the Rio del Rosario, but unlike the cirio, it is present all the way to the tip of the peninsula. Extensive stands of cardon are called *cardonals*. An outstanding cardonal covers many square miles along the southern and eastern shores of Bahia Concepcion.

CENTURY PLANT
Photo - Page 134

Various species — Throughout the Sonoran Desert Region and in the southern portion of the California Region, you will begin seeing a variety of plants that are composed of a cluster of bayonet-like leaves.

There are many species of such plants in Baja and throughout the world. Some species common to Baja bear the generic name Agave, while others are in the genus *Yucca*.

The specimen in the picture is *Agave Shawii* commonly called the century plant. This and similar species grow slowly for years, finally pouring forth all their reserves of energy in producing an amazingly luxuriant flower stalk. After blooming, the plant dies. You can see these stalks at many places in the desert; fine samples are present immediately south of the Rio del Rosario.

The century plant is a succulent because its leaves have become adapted for the storage of water. (Squeeze the leaves near their base to test the quantity of their water content.) A large number of distantly related species have developed leaves similar to the century plant, providing an excellent example of convergent evolution, and making species identification a difficult task for the amateur.

OCOTILLO
Photos - Pages 137 & 226

Fouquieria splendens — The ocotillo is easily identified. It consists of numerous whip-like branches that spread out from its base. There is no main trunk. Each branch is covered with thorns, thus providing an excellent example of the extreme protective armament which has been developed by many desert plants. Using ocotillo for firewood is a challenge.

The ocotillo is in the same family as the cirio and, like its cousin, produces a myriad of tiny leaves following rain. The plant is very sensitive to soil moisture and drops its leaves promptly at the first hint of drought. Several different crops of leaves may be produced in a given year in response to rainfall. The ocotillo is a good indicator of recent weather conditions and local soil moisture. Ocotillo is most common in the San Felipe Desert and along Highway 1 within Geographic Section No. 8. As one drives south, it comes into view shortly after crossing the Rio del Rosario.

PRICKLY PEAR
Photo - Page 137

Opuntia Spp. — The plant in the photo is an example of the many species of cactus which bear the name prickly pear. They are probably the most familiar cactus to tourists as they also grow in many locations north of the border. The common feature of all species is their flat, thin, pad-like stem segments, which resemble a beaver's tail.

Prickly pears grow throughout Baja but are most common in the north. The flat stem, a popular food source, may be cut up and cooked as one would prepare green beans. You will find them fresh or canned in many Mexican food stores. The Spanish name for this cactus is Nopal, with the canned product bearing the name *Nopalitos*. Many excellent specimens of this cactus are located immediately south of the Rio del Rosario.

At one point in reviewing the literature for this chapter, I was seeking out what might be the common feature of all cacti. One author proudly announced, with no warning, that almost all species have no glochids in their areoles. Should you care, the areoles are the small depressions from which thorns project on the flat surface of the prickly pear stem (see photo). *Glochids*, tiny barbed hairs, are of course missing. Knowing all this will make you the hit of the evening at tonight's campfire.

CANDELABRA CACTUS
Photo - Page 138

Myrtillocactus cochal — This is one of Baja's endemic species. There are many excellent specimens along Highway 1 south of the Rio del Rosario.

The candelabra's thick, woody branches are all nearly uniform in size and curve inward in graceful arcs toward the center of the plant. If hung upside down, it would resemble the outline of an enormous chandelier. There are six-to-eight ribs within each branch. Now that you are an expert in areoles (see the prickly pear cactus), note that they are spaced along the ridge lines as is the case with many other species of cactus.

This cactus blooms yearlong, often during the nighttime hours. So, if you and the love of your life just must go for an evening walk in the desert, here is the perfect excuse.

GALLOPING CACTUS
Photo - Page 139

Machaerocereus gummosus — The galloping cactus is one of the most widespread species seen throughout the Sonoran Desert and Cape Region and is often present along the highways. Its individual branches are essentially the same size as those of the candelabra cactus but look like members of the latter species who have been mixing growth hormones with their margaritas. The galloping cactus branches grow randomly in all directions, often touching the ground and taking root. They can form impenetrable thickets as large as 30 feet in diameter. The galloping cactus flowers in July and August and produces a fleshy edible fruit.

OLD MAN CACTUS
Photo - Page 139

Lophocereus schottii — Old man cactus branches near the base with each stem having five-to-seven ribs. The tip of each branch is crested with large numbers of coarse, hairlike, gray spines giving it a whiskered look, and providing the basis for its name. It is common in the area south of the Rio del Rosario.

BARREL CACTUS
Photo - Page 140

Ferocactus Spp. — The barrel cactus is lower growing than many of the more prominent species, but it is

Elephant trees growing from the sterile lava flows east of San Ignacio along Highway 1. Part of PSI stop #11. Photo JW.

easy to recognize, provided you are content with identifying only the genus. There are over a score of species in Baja.

Their common feature is one cylindrical stem that resembles a barrel or similar container. Occasionally they will branch. The spines are often flattened and hooked at the end, and the upper portion of the barrel is often reddened. Notice that most plants lean to the south.

CHOLLA CACTUS
Photo - Page 140

Opuntia Spp. — Here is another cactus genus represented by over a score of species. They are widespread throughout the Sonoran Desert and Cape Regions. The cholla stems are not flat like the prickly pear, or ribbed as in many other species. In contrast,

Tree Lovers -- Here in the Arid Tropical Forest two plants appear to be embracing. It is probable that a bird once perched in the tree after eating a cactus seed, and well, you know the rest. Photo BW.

the stem is made up of numerous linearly attached segments or joints. Each joint is further divided into many, small, rounded subsections called *tubercles*.

One of the most common species is the teddy bear cholla shown in the photo. Its silvery spines are so dense that they resemble fur at a distance, an illusion that can be promptly corrected by closer inspection. These spines are barbed at the ends and will catch on anything passing by. Joints readily break off, and if you are snared, a veritable pincushion of spines will attach themselves to your skin or clothing. Removing these with a bare hand is not recommended. You may see some of these joints lying about on the ground or rooted in vegetative reproduction.

CREOSOTE BUSH
Photos - Page 141 & 226

Creosote bush is one of the most common of Baja's desert shrubs. Most other shrubs are light green or grayish in color. The deep olive green of the creosote bush stands out in sharp contrast. Its small leaves are often coated with a shiny, sticky substance. Small, five-petaled, yellow flowers are present throughout the year.

Creosote bush is one of the most drought-tolerant of desert plants. When the more interesting vegetation disappears, creosote bush often becomes dominant. Botanists believe its roots emit a toxic substance that prevents seedlings from growing too close to the parent plants. However, the intervening spaces are usually occupied by other species.

DATILILLO
Photos - Page 142 & 257

Yucca valida — The datilillo is a yucca, but it becomes a small tree in contrast to other ground-hugging plants of the same genus. The leaves are bayonet-like, although they do not store water as does the succulent century plant. The species is similar to the Joshua tree of southwestern United States. Individual plants grow in clumps and branch along the trunk.

ELEPHANT TREE
Photo - Page 145

Pachycormus discolor — Elephant tree, endemic to Baja, is one of its most interesting species. Its principal characteristics are (1) the grayish-white to yellowish

A CONSERVATION ETHIC FOR BAJA CALIFORNIA

There are very few natural resource managers in Mexico, and most of the environmental constraints imposed on us north of the border are not readily apparent. Also, on occasion, we tourists will see Mexican citizens conducting their affairs in ways which are not in keeping with sound conservation practices. These conditions may influence us to forget our environmental manners in Baja.

To complicate matters, Baja California is largely a desert. Deserts are particularly sensitive to disruptive man-made change. Arid lands do not heal themselves nearly as rapidly as would be the case in areas with more moisture, as is the case where most of us live.

The conditions just noted place an added responsibility on the visitors. If we are to preserve the features about Baja California which we find attractive, we must act responsibly, and do so on a voluntary basis. I recently heard a church sermon where the minister posed the question "How does one avoid doing what is wrong?" His answer was, "Just don't do it."

Avoiding environmental damage is largely a matter of using good common sense. It should be obvious that digging up sensitive plants, destroying tide-pool organisms, picking up artifacts, walking about in seabird nesting areas and throwing trash in the sea will cause long-term damage. Something inside ought to say "Just don't do it."

bark which peels off in papery layers and (2) the tree's overall shape with the trunk and main branches thick in proportion to the plant as a whole. Although found in many places along Highway 1, it is most prominent in the lava flow area east of San Ignacio.

The two principal characteristics noted above are also shared by other peninsular species, some of which are only distantly related. This appears to be an example of convergent evolution, discussed earlier in this chapter. *Bursera microphylla,* also called elephant tree, or torote, is a principal example. Its twigs and branch ends are reddish brown in contrast to the gray color of pachycormus discolor, and its leaves are also much smaller.

ORGAN PIPE CACTUS
Photos - Page 128 & 141

Lemaireocereus thurberi — The organ pipe is a large, erect cactus which at first glance may be confused with the cardon. Note, however, that the organ pipe branches near ground level and has no main trunk as does the cardon. It occurs only in the southern half of the peninsula.

This species produces a sweet globular fruit, about the size of a tennis ball, which was the prized food of the original Indian population. Apparently they were well fed only when it was available. It is reported that once the supply was exhausted, the Indians would gather their own dried feces and collect the seeds that had passed through the intestinal tract. These were ground into meal.

Ball Moss -- This fairly large ball moss plant was growing on the branch of a bush from which it was easly stripped away. Photo BW.

PALO BLANCO
Photo - Page 143

Lysiloma candida — Palo, meaning stick or pole in Spanish, has become the first name of a large number

147

of small trees. Many are quite common but the palo blanco (white) is the one most easily identified from the highway. The trunk is quite straight, with smooth, silvery-white bark which is its identifying feature. Except for one locality across the Sea of Cortez, this species is endemic to Baja.

BALL MOSS
Photo - Page 147

Tillandsia recurvata -- A round, densely-branched herb (not a moss) that clings by aerial roots to the branches or sides of other plants and even to telephone wires and rocks. It is about the size of a grapefruit or larger. It is classified as epiphytic, which means it does not invade the tissues of, and sap nutrients from, the plants on which it grows as does mistletoe. As ball moss takes its moisture from the air, it is common in Baja only where fog and moist air from the Pacific Ocean flows over the land.

PALMS
Photos - Page 271, 289 & 336

There are over 1,100 species of palms worldwide in warm climates. The chart below will allow you to identify Baja's three basic types based on leaf and trunk characteristics.

PALMS		
TYPE	**LEAVES**	**TRUNK**
FAN	FAN SHAPED -- Individual leaflets radiate from the ends of the stems.	EXTREMELY ROUGH -- The bases of the dead stems remain attached to the trunk. This is true even if most of the stems have been pruned off.
DATE	PINNATE -- Individual leaflets project along both sides of the stem, similar to a birds feather.	
COCONUT		SMOOTH -- The entire dead stem falls from the trunk leaving a smooth surface.

CHAPTER 11
WILDLIFE

Accounts of wildlife frequently evolve around an array of animals that people rarely view. In this vein, I will present a few nonspecific introductory remarks about desert animals, but the major portion of this chapter relates to a relatively few animals which you should actually see in your travels in the Baja peninsula.

DESERT ANIMALS

As noted in the previous chapter, desert plants have made substantial physical adaptations as a means of surviving in the harsh living conditions of the desert. Such modifications are far less pronounced in the animal kingdom. Most desert birds and animals are quite similar to their cousins living in more humid areas. Also, the wildlife species found in Baja are essentially the same as those living in the Mexican mainland or farther north, in the United States. As is the case for many desert animals, they do tend to be smaller in size and paler in color.

Insect life in the desert is robust and peaks with the culmination of plant growth following rains. The immense supply of eggs and dormant pupae left behind by these creatures combine with the seeds of annual plants as the basic food for birds and animals. The majority of desert mammals are seed-eating rodents. (See discussion of Insect Pests in Chapter 8.)

The traveler will see relatively few land animals in Baja's deserts because most of them feed and move about only at night. Also, most species make their homes in burrows in the ground, or in large plants, where they can escape the rigorous environment.

For this reason, I suggest that you pay a visit to the zoological garden located in the small town of Santiago south of La Paz. It is stop No. 21 on the POINTS OF SPECIAL INTEREST TOUR. The unlikely location of this facility may lead the traveler to expect very little. Surprisingly, this very pleasant zoo, constructed in 1983, is well shaded and contains many different displays of living animals. Most are species of local Mexican mammals, birds, and reptiles. Here may be your only chance to see these animals. (Every cage had occupants in my most recent visit, including, believe it or not, a tiger.)

When you walk about in the desert you will see a variety of lizards darting about on the desert floor. Their scaled skin, which is highly resistant to drying, allows them to move about in the daytime. You will also see considerable bird life during the daylight hours, particularly near the coast. A discussion of several of the most common large birds is presented below. The concluding section describes the California gray whale, sea turtles and other marine mammals.

HUNTING

Hunting by tourists is permitted in Baja. Doves are taken throughout the peninsula. The Valle de Mexicali SE from Mexicali produces a variety of dove and pheasants in the areas irrigated pastures. Waterfowl hunting along the lower Colorado River and Laguna

PRINCIPAL SEABIRDS THAT BREED IN THE SEA OF CORTEZ

black storm petrel	yellow-footed gull
least storm petrel	elegant tern
brown pelican	royal tern
double-crested cormorant	sooty tern
Brandt's cormorant	noddy tern
red-billed tropicbird	American oystercatcher
magnificent frigatebird	osprey
blue-footed booby	great blue heron
brown booby	reddish egret
Craveri's murrelet	black-crowned night heron
Heermann's gull	yellow-crowned night heron

List courtesy of Daniel W. Anderson

Securing permission to hunt in Mexico is a complicated process due in part to the country's strict laws concerning gun possession. The hunter is required to obtain a multiple-entry tourist card and several other documents from different Mexican agencies including the military. A character reference also must be obtained from the hunter's local law enforcement agency.

The process is sufficiently complicated and so subject to change that I will not pass on further details but instead refer you to an organization that's basic function is processing the documents needed to hunt in Mexico for it members. It is the Mexican Hunting Association, 6840 El Salvador St, Long Beach CA 90815, (310) 430-3256. The association also publishes a newsletter concerning game regulations and other matters.

Salada was excellent in the past but is now greatly reduced by low water levels resulting from upstream reservoirs. There are ongoing efforts underway to restore these lost wetlands. The Pacific coast chaparral region from Ensenada south to El Rosario produces some of the largest quail populations in North America. The Bahia San Quintin area is famous for black brant and other sea-duck hunting.

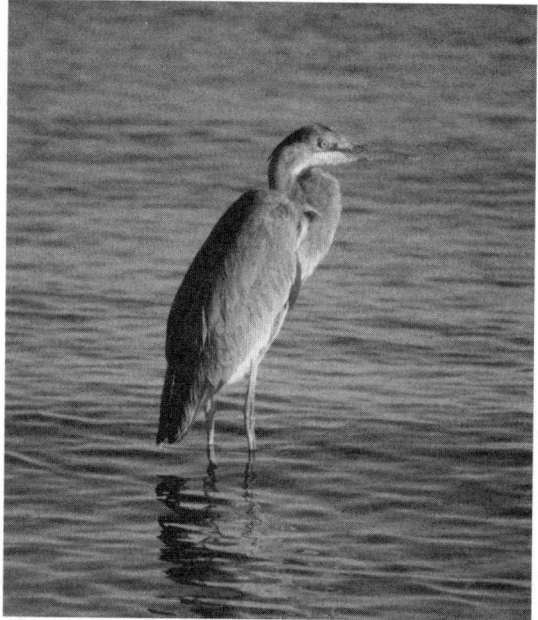

Travelers in Baja will often see great blue herons like this one in shallow waters offshore or in coastal lagoons. Photo BW.

BIRDS

BIRD WATCHING — Baja is an excellent place to visit for those interested in observing and studying bird life. Desert vegetation supports little of the dense foliage common in humid climates. As a result, birds have relatively little cover and are easily viewed. You will often see hawks and other large birds perched on the top of giant cactus plants. The seashore and marsh areas are alive with bird life.

The serious observer should obtain Peterson's *A Field Guide to Mexican Birds*. Unfortunately, the illustrations of many of Baja's birds are omitted as they would duplicate those already included in previous Peterson volumes on Texas and eastern and western United States. As a minimum, the western guide is needed to augment the Mexico book. The National Geographic Society's *Field Guide to the Birds of North America* also describes much of the peninsula's bird life.

WATERBIRDS — Many North American waterbirds (ducks, coots and similar species) breed during the summer in Alaska, Canada, and northern United States. They then winter in southern United States and Mexico. These birds travel south in fairly well defined paths called *flyways*. Birds using the Pacific Flyway spend the winter in Alta and Baja California and along the west coast of the Mexican mainland. A few birds migrate to the delta of the Rio Colorado, but the majority of the marsh habitat here has been destroyed by the regulatory effects of upstream reservoirs.

An exception to this Rio Colorado situation can be found along Highway 5 where the main river is joined by the Rio Hardy. During wet years, bird life is abundant here and at the nearby southern end of Laguna Salada (See Chapter 15).

The principal waterbird wintering areas in Baja are along the Pacific coast from Ensenada south to Bahia Magdalena. If you are even remotely interested in bird life, I recommend that you drive the Puerto Venustiano Carranza side trip starting at the town of Guerrero Negro. It is described near the beginning of Chapter 20. The road to the abandoned port facilities passes through several miles of outstanding saltwater marsh which provides a home for thousands of egrets, pelicans, cranes, gulls, and many other species of marsh and seabirds. The roadbed is elevated some ten feet above the sea level so you may look down upon the many birds.

FRIGATEBIRD

SEABIRDS — The Sea of Cortez area offers the most spectacular concentrations of nesting southern seabirds on the west coast of North America. The specific species involved are given in a table in this chapter. The majority of these birds nest primarily on the offshore islands. A few, the shoreline group (osprey, herons, and terns), are more frequently found along the peninsular shore. There are a variety of other seabird species that visit the Sea of Cortez but which do not breed in the area. Likewise, many of the breeding varieties migrate to both north and south after the breeding season. These birds will be seen principally by those who participate in boating.

The interface of seabirds with the boating public presents a special problem in the Sea of Cortez. The adverse effect of human disturbance on nesting seabirds is well documented by the scientific fraternity. There is clear evidence that the brown pelican has abandoned its former nesting sites on Islas San Martin and Todos Santos along Baja's Pacific shore due to human disturbance. Visiting scientists have also observed damaging effects following such widely divergent visitations as; individual sightseers on their own, American tourists guided by Mexicans, curious Mexican fishermen, commercial egg collectors, and even American scientists and educational tours.

Regardless of who causes the disturbance, here are the destructive results when nesting seabirds are flushed from their nests.

1 — Eggs and chicks may be knocked from their nests by frightened adults.

2 — Unprotected chicks and eggs may die from excessive heat or cold.

3 — Predators, mainly gulls, may eat unguarded eggs and chicks.

4 — Nests, and eventually entire nesting sites, may be abandoned.

If you should come upon nesting seabird colonies please observe them with binoculars from a distance. Stay at least 100 yards off when in a boat, and 300 yards away when onshore. Those desiring to seriously study seabirds should obtain a competent book on the subject.

FIVE COMMON BIRDS — Following is a brief discussion of five of the common large birds seen in Baja.

<u>FRIGATEBIRD</u> — The frigatebird, or man-o-war bird, is unmistakable in flight. Their wingspan can exceed seven feet and is greater in proportion to the body than that of any other seabird. The wings are swept back like a WW II navy Corvair fighter plane. The tail is deeply notched. Those with white breasts are the female.

While the pelican is a master fisherman, the frigate is basically a thief. They cannot swim or dive but make a living largely by forcing other seabirds to disgorge or drop food that they have captured. You will see the frigate soaring over-head in coastal areas in the southern portion of the peninsula.

<u>BROWN PELICAN</u> — There are pelicans north of the border, but only people who live near the sea coast

The brown pelican is commonly seen on Baja's beaches and marinas. Frequently, as here, they are accompanied by sea gulls ever hopeful that one of the pelicans will drop a portion of its catch. Photo JW.

erless head is small in proportion to the body and is red in color. The rest of the body is black. They will usually be observed feeding on a dead animal, which of course does not contribute to the artistic setting. You will also frequently see individuals sitting on the top of a cardon cactus.

Most commonly, the turkey vulture can be seen soaring overhead. Look for the small head, and two-toned wings which are held aloft clearly above the horizontal. The outer portions of the wings are lighter than the rest of the bird. It rocks unsteadily as it soars along.

will have seen them. In Baja the species is common along all coastal areas and if you don't see many of them, you simply aren't looking. The pelican is an unmistakable bird (see photo in this Chapter).

Breeding takes place locally on offshore islands. During the summer, many individuals migrate north into the United States, but their numbers greatly decreased in recent decades. Studies conducted during the 1970s in the breeding areas of Baja's Islas de los Coronados, south of San Diego, showed that the bird's egg shells contained concentrations of D.D.T. insecticide. The result was shell walls too thin to survive the reproductive process. Since D.D.T. has been banned there has been a dramatic increase in pelican birthrates.

TURKEY VULTURE — The turkey vulture, or buzzard, is not unique to Mexico, but most people do not have the opportunity to study this bird near their homes. In Baja, you will sometimes have the opportunity of seeing groups of vultures at close range, particularly if your travels take you to a garbage dumping area. They are not pretty birds. The feath-

ROADRUNNER — Bird guidebooks note that the roadrunner's call is a dove-like *coo*, but we all know they really go *beep beep*. Baja is a good place to observe this escapee from the movie cartoons. In the films, they seem to run up and down the roads, but in the wild they emulate the chicken and always seem to be crossing the road. They are more commonly seen on the secondary and dirt roads than on the main highways.

Senorita
Beep Beep

Roadrunner

The roadrunner is 20-to-24 inches in length, heavily streaked, has a long, narrow tail and a shaggy, roosterlike crest on the head. If a large bird runs across the road, what else can it be?

CARACARA — The caracara is a large, long-legged, long-necked, dark bird whose white head is topped with a rooster-like crest. The bill is yellowish. In flight they display white markings on the wings and tail. They are a bird of prey like the turkey vulture. They are commonly seen in dry desert areas in the southern half of the peninsula.

MARINE MAMMALS

SEA LIONS AND DOLPHINS — My experience in cruising the Pacific coast clearly indicates that there are far more dolphins, and sea lions in Baja's waters than in those north of the border. Unfortunately, they are infrequently seen by the tourist unless one ventures out to sea. Seeing a dolphin is simply a matter of chance, but sea lions live in colonies well known to Mexican fishermen. You can arrange for sightseeing trips at Loreto, Cabo San Lucas, and other places. Ask to be shown the *lobos del mar*.

Baja's Pacific waters also provide a home for the elephant seal, but the known colonies are all on offshore islands. If you wish to see this fascinating marine mammal, the best place to do so is at the Ano Nuevo State Reserve north of Santa Cruz in Alta California. An excellent booklet on the elephant seal is available from the BAJA BOOKSHELF in the Appendix of this book.

CALIFORNIA GRAY WHALE — In recent years, there has been wide public interest concerning whales in general and the California gray whale in particular. Whale-watching has become a popular pastime in many areas along the Pacific coast. The Baja penin-

sula plays a prominent part in this gigantic animal's life history as it is Baja's Pacific lagoons that are the primary destination of the whale's annual southern migration. The gray's basic characteristics are described in a nearby insert.

ANNUAL MIGRATION CYCLE — It was recently estimated that there are 21,000 gray whales. This population spends the summer months feeding in the Bering and Chukchi Seas off Alaska. Starting in October, they begin their annual southern migration to the subtropical waters of several coastal lagoons along Baja's south-central Pacific coast. Here the calves are born.

The whale's migration route is close to shore as the gray is a bottom feeder. As a result, whale spouts are easily seen from shore. Ocean-cruisers sail in these same waters and are frequently in company with the migration.

Reference to the ANNUAL MIGRATION Chart will disclose that the several migration phases overlap

PELICAN RESEARCH PROJECT

Brown pelicans have been leg-tagged by University of California Davis researchers to study their movements, migrations, and interactions with man. Tags vary from plain aluminum bands to bands plus colored plastic markers. Each configuration has a meaning. If you see a tagged bird, please report the following information:

1 -- The configuration (what is on what leg).

2 -- The color (and number if possible).

3 -- Date and location of sighting.

4 -- The situation. How did you come to see the bird, was it sick or injured, was it being a nuisance, etc.

5 -- Your name and address so that you may be sent information on the bird's origin, age, etc.

6 -- Do not remove the tags or bands unless the bird is dead. In this instance please send the tags along with the other information.

BAND

TAG

REPORT FINDINGS TO:

Daniel W. Anderson
Pelican Research Project
Dept. of Wildlife and Fisheries
University of California
Davis, California, 95616

Your help will be much appreciated.

CALIFORNIA GRAY WHALE CHARACTERISTICS	
THE ANIMAL	A true mammal. Air breathing. Warm blooded. Nurse young on milk.
ADULTS	Length, 30 to 50-ft. Weight 20 to 40-tons. Avg. age 30 to 40-years, occasionally 60.
CALVES	Length 15-ft., weight 1.5-tons at birth. Consume 50-gal. of milk, gain 60 to 70-lb. daily.
MIGRATION	Travel 20-hours & 100 miles per day. Trip of 6,000-miles takes 6 to 8-weeks.
COLOR	Slate gray caused by natural pigments, barnacles, and barnacle scars.

1. Viewing by boat — Many Pacific coast ports in the United States offer one-day whale-watching trips in the same type of vessels normally used for sportfishing. You can frequently get close-up views of the whales on these ventures. The various fishing charter organizations noted under fishing in Chapter 5 also provide whale-watching trips.

2. Viewing from the air — Passengers in small private aircraft can get fine views of whales both in the ocean and in the lagoons. The Baja Bush Pilots *Airports of Baja California* reports that landing at the dirt airstrip adjoining Laguna San Ignacio provides a ringside seat.

3. Viewing from land — Seaward views of Pacific waters are offered at numerous points along the southern portion of the highway between Tijuana and Ensenada. Take Highway 1, rather than 1-D, so you may easily pull off onto the side roads accessing the coastal bluffs. Also visit the MIRADOR vista point, which is stop No. 3 on the POINTS OF SPECIAL INTEREST Tour.

There are several good vantage points along the road to La Bufadora on the Punta Banda peninsula. Punta Banda projects well out into the ocean, and the road is a considerable distance above the water. See Chapter 18 for directions. Another point is Punta Baja, but its elevation is not nearly as high as at Punta Banda. See Chapter 19 for the side trip to this area.

each other. Some individuals are still arriving in Baja while others are already heading back north. Pregnant females, well into their 12-month gestation period, leave Alaska early with their mission clearly in mind. Others lag behind while males and in-season females court and mate on the way south.

By December, the whales begin arriving in the waters off northern Baja. By mid-January, most females have arrived at their destinations in the backwaters of the lagoons where most of the calving takes place. The return north occurs in somewhat reverse order. The newly pregnant females and other *single* whales begin north, starting in February, while the new mothers and their calves linger behind, occasionally as late as May and June. As a result, there are whales in Baja waters from December to June.

An excellent booklet concerning the California gray whale is available from the BAJA BOOKSHELF in the Appendix.

WHALE-WATCHING — The whale may be observed in a variety of ways. They are summarized as follows.

1. Viewing by Boat.
    a. Day Trips.
    b. Long-range Trips.
2. Viewing from the Air.
3. Viewing from Land.
    a. Coastal Observation Points.
    b. Baja Lagoons.

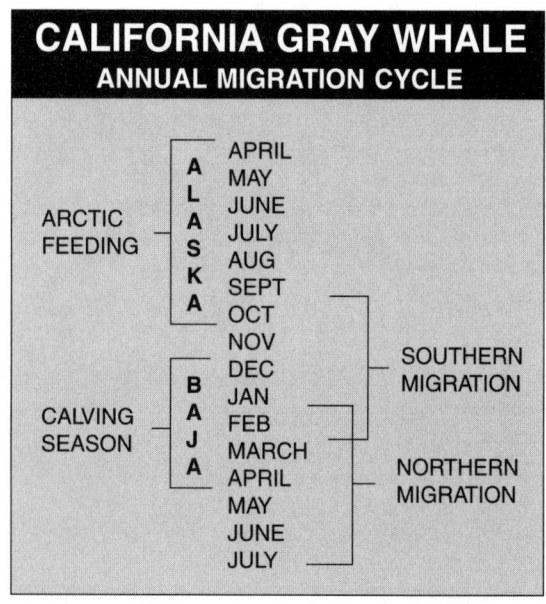

CALIFORNIA GRAY WHALE ANNUAL MIGRATION CYCLE		
ARCTIC FEEDING	A L A S K A	APRIL MAY JUNE JULY AUG SEPT OCT
		NOV
CALVING SEASON	B A J A	DEC JAN FEB MARCH APRIL MAY JUNE JULY

SOUTHERN MIGRATION

NORTHERN MIGRATION

During the winter of 1988-89 numbers of California gray whales migrated to the shallow waters immediately outside the harbor at La Paz. The spouts of these animals could easily be seen from many of the coastal areas described in Chapters 23 and 24.

Finally, the land-based traveler can drive to the edge of the calving lagoons at several places. In Bahia Magdalena, whales can be seen from the docks at San Carlos and boats may be rented to travel to the bay's opening into the Pacific where whales are more com-

The massive back of the gray whale. Photo BW.

mon. Today the easiest place in all of Baja to visit the whales at close range is at Puerto Lopez Mateos which can be reached by oiled highway. Boats may be rented to visit the calving grounds inside Boca de Solidad (see Chapter 22.)

There are two additional sites in the vicinity of Guerrero Negro. The first is the abandoned salt dock at Puerto Venustiano Carranza. In some years there are no whales here as the lagoon's entrance to the sea is blocked with sand. In others, they are present and may be seen from a tour boat advertised in the area's hotels (see Chapter 20). The most famous site is Scammon's Lagoon, which will now be discussed in more detail.

SCAMMON'S LAGOON — Scammon's Lagoon (Laguna Ojo de Liebre) is the largest lagoon in Baja. Its easternmost segment is called The Nursery. This area has been designated as the *Refugio Natural de la Ballena Gris* (Natural Refuge of the Gray Whale). You may camp on the shore of the lagoon in an area administered by one of the local ejidos. See Chapter 20 for access details.

I recommend you visit this area not solely to see the whale, as obviously the great majority of the creatures' bodies will be below the water's surface. What you do absorb is an overall impression of a desolate area where nature is playing out the climax of a 6,000-mile journey. You will see and hear four signs of the whale:

1. The backs of the whales break the surface as they move about. From your vantage point on the six-foot-

high sand bar at the edge of the lagoon, you see only a small portion of the whale.

2. Occasionally, the upper 8-10 feet of a whale's head projects vertically from the water. This behavior is called *skyhopping*. Apparently the animal is simply looking about.

3. Perhaps the most common sign of the whales are the spouts which rise up to 15 feet. What you see is largely condensation caused when a whale's warm breath cools in the sea air.

4. Accompanying the spout is an explosive "whoosh." The sounds of this breathing create an eerie feeling as evening falls at Scammon's.

If you make the trip to Scammon's, I recommend you spend the night at the lagoon's edge. Nothing that you will see is spectacular, and it takes some time to absorb what is occurring. Be sure to take your field glasses.

THE WHALE'S FUTURE — Because populations of whales hunted by European and Yankee whalers became depleted during the early years of the 19th century, it became necessary for them to turn to the gray whale to fill their holds. By 1845, the migration route and the Baja calving lagoons had been discovered, and in 1857 Captain Charles M. Scammon first entered Laguna Ojo de Liebre. Fifteen whaling stations were eventually established along the Alta and Baja California coasts. Hunting continued until 1890,

Sea turtle tracks in the sand near the El Migrino Loop on the Pacific Coast. The right hand photo shows that the animal approached from one direction, laid her eggs near some rocks and then left by a different route. The other photo shows a close-up view. Photos BW.

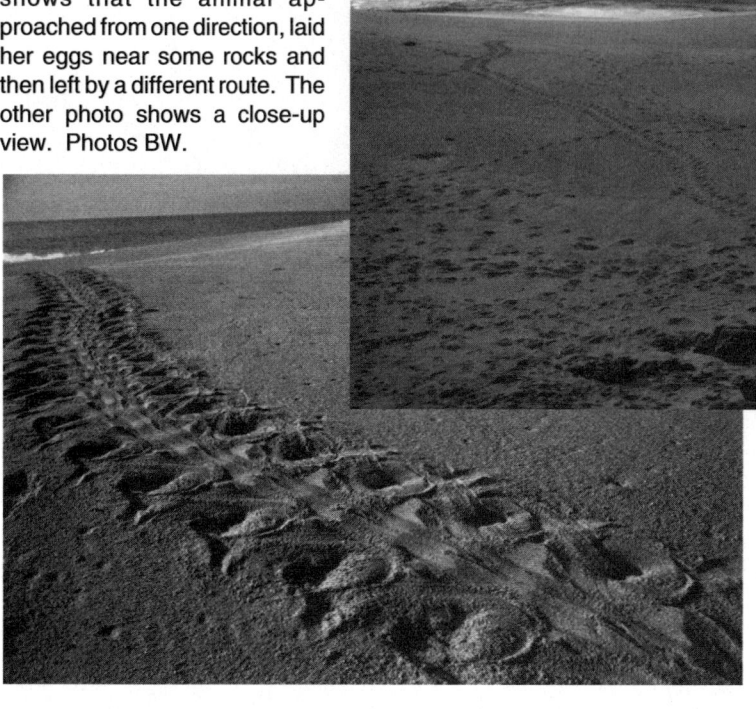

able environmental success story.

SEA TURTLES

Five species of sea turtles inhabit Baja's coastal waters. For years these giant amphibians were hunted by Mexican fishermen for their meat and shells. As recently as 1988 I observed dozens of turtles being driven to market by fishermen along Baja's Pacific coast. Finally, a total ban on these activities was declared by the Mexican government in 1990. It will no doubt be some time before it is fully honored.

WHY DON'T YOU GO TO HELL? It is not to many authors who can tell their readers to "Go to Hell," but this is just what you should do if you want to see thousands of sea turtles at the turtle farm near the community of Hell on Grand Cayman Island in the Caribbean Sea. But, if you will settle for a smaller number of turtles, visit the Sea Turtle Research Station at the government RV park near the village of Bahia de los Angeles (See map in Chapter 19). Three species of turtles are usually kept here in concrete tanks where they are open to public viewing. The small station is managed by Mexican biologist Antonio Resendiz. Antonio and his helpers gather biological information about the turtles, educate local fisherman about the need for their protection, and take various steps to enhance turtle survival in the local area.

when it was abandoned because the population had been reduced to only a few thousand.

Today, the gray is protected under the auspices of the International Whaling Commission. In 1972, the Mexican government established sanctuaries at Scammon's Lagoon and the other principal breeding areas. As a result, the gray whale has experienced a remarkable recovery.

In the past, the animal's predictable migration pattern made it an easy mark for the hunter. These same habits have now worked to save the species because mates are easily found. As a result, breeding has flourished. By 1991, the total population was estimated to be 21,000, a number probably higher than prior to commercial whaling activities. Late in that year the U.S. National Oceanic and Atmospheric Administration proposed removing the whale from the U.S. Endangered Species list and this action has now been taken. However, the whale is still off-limits to hunting and is protected by a variety of other statutes. The whales recovery represents a remark-

Please see notices for books about the gray whale and elephant seals on page 83

CHAPTER 12
HISTORY

Remote, isolated, arid, and little known. This is Baja California. One might expect to find little of historic interest in such a place. It is just the opposite. Our Magnificent Peninsula boasts an amazingly rich and fascinating history beginning a scant 42 years after Columbus's first voyage to the new world in 1492 and almost a full century before the pilgrims landed at Plymouth Rock in Massachusetts. It employs a cast of characters no novelist could have devised: Hernan Cortez, Juan Cabrillo, Francis Drake, Thomas Cavendish, Padres Francisco Kino and Junipero Serra, and the notorious filibuster, William Walker.

In addition to many persons of Spanish origin, Baja's soil has witnessed the coming and going of Jesuit missionaries from Italy, English adventurers, Dutch pirates, French miners, war with the United States, internal revolution, and incredible land fraud. The broad aspects of this enticing drama are presented in this chapter. Details will be interwoven as the many easily visit-ed sites are encountered along the GRAND TOUR in PART III.

But first this historic stage must be set with a brief review of Baja's pre-Hispanic inhabitants. I must also note that much of the material presented in this chapter is based on an English Translation of *A History of Lower California* by Pablo L. Martinez.

THE PREHISTORIC CALIFORNIANS

A sharp contrast existed between the Indian in habitants of the Baja peninsula and the native populations that the Spanish conquistadors encountered in main-

land Mexico and much of South America. In these latter areas, the Aztecs, Mayas, and Incas had developed highly advanced civilizations with large cities and complex religious and cultural institutions. The Indians of southwestern United States also had well developed, although somewhat less advanced, civilizations. As a result of their isolated location on the Baja peninsula, the Baja California Indians were found to be among the most primitive in the Americas. This situation was to have important impacts on their interrelationships with Spanish conquerors in the centuries to come.

The early Spanish encountered three well defined tribal groups. The most southerly were the *Pericues*. They inhabited the peninsula's tip north to a line drawn south of present-day Todos Santos and San Bartolo. They were to interface with the Spanish during the important early day events at San Jose del Cabo.

North of the Pericues were the *Guaycuras*. Their domain stretched from the line mentioned above north to Loreto. From a historic standpoint, these people were the most important as it was they who were destined to greet the early Spanish landings in the La Paz and Loreto areas, and they were to be the objects of the earliest missionary activities.

The balance of the peninsula was home to the *Cochimies*. The three tribal areas are shown on the SPANISH EXPLORATIONS Map.

In keeping with their primitive nature, the peninsula's Indians had no written language and only the most

---

BAJA MUSEUMS

What follows is a brief summary of five museums in Baja that deal with history and prehistory. More details are given where the facilities are encountered in PART III.

<u>La Paz</u> -- History and Anthropology Museum. See map of La Paz in Chapter 22.

<u>Loreto</u> -- History of the Baja California missions. See map of Loreto in Chapter 21.

<u>Mulege</u> -- A small museum containing items of local interest in front of the famous Mulege penitentiary. The prison itself is the most interesting exhibit.

<u>San Ignacio</u> -- Museum features the cave paintings of Baja. See the map of San Ignacio in Chapter 20

<u>Santa Rosalia</u> -- Museum & exhibits along nearby street feature mining history of Santa Rosalia. See Santa Rosalia map in Chapter 20.

BAJA CALIFORNIA HISTORY

	EVENTS IN BAJA	DATES	OTHER EVENTS

Spanish Conquest of New Spain (42 Years)

Columbus lands in the West Indies → 1492

· **1500**

Jimenez discovers Baja peninsula ↘ 1533-34

Cortez lands at La Paz ↗ 1535

1565 ↙ Start of the Manila galleon sea route from the Philippines to Acapulco.

1588 ← Defeat of the Spanish Armada.

Exploration and Failed Colonization (162 Years)

1600

1620 ← Pilgrims land at Plymouth Rock.

Atondo-Kino expedition. ↘ 1683-85

1697 ↗

AMERICAN

COLONIAL

· **1700**

Jesuit Missionary Period (71 Years)

Jesuits found Loreto mission.

PERIOD.

Jesuit expulsion ↘ 1768

Padre Serra's Journey to San Diego. ↗ 1769   1776 ← United States Declaration of Independence.

Franciscans and Dominicans (53 Years)

· **1800**

Oath of allegiance to Mexico signed in Loreto. → 1822   1821 ← Mexican Independence from Spain.

1846-48 ← Mexican-American War and signing of the Treaty of Hidalgo in 1848.

The Mexican Nation

· **1900**

1910-1917 ← Period of revoluation in Mexico culminating in the Constitution of 1917.

Baja California becomes a state. ↘ 1952

Baja Californa Sur becomes a state. → 1974

(World War I -- 1914 to 1918)

elementary of religious beliefs. They lived in communal groups in the vicinity of fresh water and slept on the bare ground. Shelter was provided by holes dug in the earth, crude arrangements of branches, and occasionally by a cave. More commonly, the Indians slept within a low circle of stones without any roof. A fire would be kept burning during the night in the winter. They cultivated nothing and lived from their native environment by hunting, fishing, and gathering.

In spite of stone age conditions, these Indians were described by the early Spaniards as strong, tall, and healthy. They were good runners and swimmers. The men went totally nude, if one discounts their habit of painting the body in various grotesque patterns. The women normally wore some form of garment made from native materials.

Their possessions were limited to a few crude cups, bowls, baskets, and simple implements for fishing, hunting, and warfare. For these latter activities they had mastered the use of the bow and arrow, boomerang, and wooden lances. This mention of warfare leads to a discussion of several attributes of the Indians which were of particular importance in their future relationships with the Spanish.

TRIBAL WARFARE — There appears to have been a more or less continuous state of warfare between the tribes; the males were practiced in this art. On the whole, the Indians did not transfer their hostilities toward the Spaniards. There were few organized attempts to eject the intruders. The Spaniards did not have to conquer California with force of arms as was necessary on the mainland. Nevertheless, there were armed encounters between the two parties, and the Spanish possession of firearms was all important. In addition, the Indians' warlike behavior toward each other frequently cast the Spaniards in the role of referee. It also led in part to the next point of importance.

POLYGAMY — As a result of battlefield mortality, there were considerably more women than men. The natural outcome was that the surviving males acquired more than one wife. Multiple wives also contributed considerably to the husband's standard of living in a culture requiring the constant gathering of food. This polygamous lifestyle was to lead to considerable conflict with the missionaries, who endeavored to enforce Christian morality.

SHAMANS — The California Indian had little in the way of a tribal hierarchy, except during periods of warfare. However, there was the universal presence of the *shaman*, or witch doctor. These individuals, usually elderly men, had considerable influence over the Indian. They functioned as healers and exercised their authority during the frequent public dances and at funeral ceremonies. The coming of the Spanish missionary was to threaten their authority. As a result, the shaman became the principal obstacle to the work of the missionaries.

LANGUAGE — The missionaries found the Indian languages inadequate to use for instructing their charges in Christianity and the arts of civilization. The native tongues were very basic, and there were significant dialect differences between the tribes and subtribes. The Indians were thus taught Spanish, a process which was duplicated in many other areas and had far-reaching consequences for the Americas. It explains, in part, why Spanish is the native tongue in most of Mexico and South America.

HISTORIC OVERVIEW

The historic pageant of Baja California is summarized in a full-page chart. It commences with Columbus's landing in the West Indies in 1492 and ends with the achievement of statehood by Baja California Sur in 1974. It is divided into five historic periods that correspond to the five remaining sections in this chapter. Each section begins with a small chart summarizing additional dates and events. The full-page chart also indicates the chronological relationship of Baja's history to several other well-known world events.

It is perhaps a natural tendency for those of us who live in the highly developed areas of the United States and Canadian Pacific coast to surmise that the historic events in these areas must surely have preceded those in a land as remote as Baja California. As can be seen, it was just the reverse. Civilization on the Pacific coast was to flow from south to north. The founding of the Loreto mission on the east coast of the Baja peninsula preceded the first Alta California mission by 72 years.

SPANISH CONQUEST OF NEW SPAIN (42 YEARS)

Columbus's discovery of the islands of the Caribbean Sea promptly engendered Spanish colonization. The first colony was on the island of Haiti, then called Espanola. By 1511, there were settlements on the

Chapter 12

```
┌─────────────────────────────────────────┐
│  ● SPANISH CONQUEST OF NEW SPAIN ●       │
│                                          │
│  1492--1502-------  COLUMBUS's 4 voyages to │
│                     the West Indies.     │
│                                          │
│  1519 -------------  CORTEZ lands at Vera Cruz to │
│                     conquer New Spain (Mexico). │
│                                          │
│  1522 ------------  CORTEZ conquers the Aztecs │
│                     and founds Mexico City. │
│                                          │
│  1532 ------------  Failed MENDOZA expedition. │
│                                          │
│  1533--34 --------  Baja peninsula discovered by │
│                     mutineer FORTUN JIMENEZ. │
└─────────────────────────────────────────┘
```

The world was aware that Magellan had circled the globe in 1522, passing through a strait at the southerly tip of the South American continent. Cortez longed to explore to the northwest along the recently discovered Pacific Ocean in order to discover a similar passage above the North American continent. However, he was blocked from doing this by land by the presence of Guzman.

Cortez thus reached agreement with the Spanish crown that he would, at his own expense, undertake seaborne explorations of the Pacific coast. To this end, Cortez established a ship building station on the Pacific coast near the mouth of the Rio Balsas about 100 miles north of present day Acapulco. Native porters endlessly transported all of the rigging, iron work, and similar materials needed for the ships across the mountains of Mexico from Vera Cruz.

islands of Jamaica, Cuba, and Puerto Rico. Among the earliest settlers was the nineteen-year-old Hernan Cortez, who arrived in 1505. He proceeded to earn his living from ranching and mining.

In time, reports of golden cities in the interior of Mexico reached the islands, and Cortez resolved to lead an expedition of conquest. After many intrigues, he boldly sailed for the mainland in 1519 leading a force of 11 ships, more than 800 Spaniards and Cuban Indians, 16 horses, and 14 cannons. Upon landing, he founded the first Spanish city in Mexico at Vera Cruz. He promptly scuttled his ships to prevent the desertion of his forces. In a series of adventures that would fill a novel, he brutally captured the Aztec capital of Tenochtitlan in 1522, with the estimated loss of 100,000 of its inhabitants.

In the decade to follow, Cortez and his men ravaged the land in all directions, accumulating great wealth and enslaving the native populations. Mexico City was constructed on the site of Tenochtitlan. During this period, Cortez operated largely on his own initiative, with his own resources, and only marginally within the auspices of the Spanish government.

This same methodology was also employed by Cortez's bitter rival Nuno de Guzman, a fellow Spaniard who had amassed great wealth by illegal slave trading in the Caribbean Islands. During 1530-31, Guzman conquered vast areas of land northwest of Mexico City and established a personal empire. This action established Guzman as the master of the lands on the Mexican coast opposite the southern tip of the Baja peninsula.

During this same period, the King of Spain gradually moved to gain control of the actions of his freewheeling conquistadors.

The stage was thus set for the discovery of the Baja peninsula. In 1532, Cortez dispatched the first of four expeditions into the Pacific. The first was under the command of Diego Hurtado de Mendoza, Cortez's cousin. Mendoza sailed north and penetrated the Sea of Cortez; however, the expedition was never to return. It met its end at the hands of Indians, Guzman, or both.

Undaunted, Cortez sent forth a second group of two ships which departed from present-day Manzanillo on October 29, 1533. The two ships soon parted company. The first discovered the Revilla Gigedo Islands, which lie some 400 miles off the Mexican coast, and then returned to the mainland at Acapulco.

The second vessel was placed under the command of Diego de Becerra, a captain of tyrannical nature. As a result, Becerra was soon set upon and killed by many of his crew under the leadership of the pilot Fortun Jimenez. After depositing the non-mutinous crew members on the Mexican mainland, Jimenez and the others fled to the north and stumbled upon the Baja peninsula. They became the first Europeans known to have set foot on this land.

The Magnificent Peninsula was thus discovered through accident by a group of mutineers. The date of the discovery is unknown as journals are rarely kept on such adventures. It was either late 1533 or early 1534. The spot of the landing was subsequently determined to be Bahia de La Paz.

It is reported that Jimenez and most of his crew were killed by the Indians as a result of their attempts to violate the Indian women. The survivors sailed across the gulf to the mainland, where they fell into the hands of Guzman. There they passed on stories of their discovery of what was then believed to be an island. Of equal importance was their report of the abundance of pearls. This news would increase Cortez's desire to continue with his exploratory efforts.

EXPLORATION AND FAILED COLONIZATION (162 YEARS)

Angered at the interference of Guzman and by the failure of the two expeditions he had dispatched, Cortez chose to lead the next effort himself. This expedition differed from the previous two in that Cortez was aware of his destination, the Island of California. It was to be the only serious effort to actually conquer and colonize the new land until 162 years later.

Three new ships were constructed and loaded with 300 men and 130 horses. Many of the men took along their families, among them 37 women. In May 1535, Cortez landed at Bahia de La Paz and named it Santa Cruz. There he was to find evidences of the Jimenez mutineers and the pearls that they had reported. It is now believed that the actual location of Santa Cruz was at Pichilingue, 14 miles north of present day La Paz.

Cortez's colonization efforts were to prove unproductive. He did build a church and houses for the colonists. It has also been reported that he made exploratory trips into the interior of the peninsula. However, there were apparently no efforts made to raise crops, and the colony had to be supplied by ship from across the gulf. After a year of failure and the death by starvation of many of the colonists, Cortez returned to Mexico and shortly ordered the others to follow.

In Mexico, Cortez encountered Antonio de Mendoza, the first of a long line of Viceroys of New Spain appointed by the King. From this time forward, adventurers like Cortez and Guzman were to have far less of a free hand, and decisions affecting the Baja peninsula would emanate largely from the Viceroys at Mexico City.

FRANCISCO DE ULLOA — For his part, Cortez remained obsessed with the desire to press forward by sea to the northwest. Without the approval of the Viceroy, he dispatched his fourth and final expedition under the command of Francisco de Ulloa. Ulloa's orders were to press as far north as possible. He left Acapulco in July 1539, and accomplished an amazing feat of navigation. (See the SPANISH EXPLORATIONS Map in this chapter.)

Ulloa sailed the full length of the Sea of Cortez exploring both coasts, stopping at La Paz going and coming. He anchored at the mouth of the Rio Colorado and established that the Baja peninsula was not an island, although the island myth was to persist for centuries. Finally, the expedition rounded the peninsula's southern tip, and explored the Pacific coast to north of Isla Cedros. From there Ulloa sent one of his ships south to report to Cortez concerning his findings, a most fortunate decision, as nothing further was ever heard from this intrepid explorer.

ORIGIN OF THE NAME CALIFORNIA

The name "California" was first encountered in the diary of one of the people who accompanied Francisco de Ulloa on his exploratory voyage. For centuries its origin was a mystery. It was surmised that it had been derived from the Latin words "calida formax" meaning hot furnace. Then in 1862 a New England clergyman, Edward Hall, came upon a Spanish novel "The Adventures of Explandian," which was known to be popular during the years of the conquest of Mexico. It describes a fantastic island inhabited by Amazons: "It is known that to the right of the Indies there exists an island called California very near the side of the Terrestrial Paradise... and was peopled by black women, among whom there was not a single man.... Their weapons were all of gold... because in all the island there was no metal except gold."

This story flourished along with other legends of golden cities in the unknown lands beyond New Spain. It is now the opinion of most historians that the seafarers of the day came to mix these prevailing legends with the tale of California from the "Adventures" and applied the name to the newly discovered "island" to the west. In any event, from then on, the land from the tip of the peninsula north was to be known as California.

SPANISH EXPLORATIONS

THE FOUR EXPLORATIONS SHOWN ON THIS MAP TOOK PLACE WITHIN 50 YEARS OF THE DISCOVERY OF THE AMERICAS BY COLUMBUS IN 1492.

To Latitude 44 (Oregon)

San Francisco Bay

Monterey Bay

Point Conception

San Miguel Island

San Diego Harbor

Rio Colorado

Harbor at Ensenada

TRIBAL GROUPS OF BAJA CALIFORNIA INDIANS

A -- PERICUES

B -- GUAYCURAS

C -- COCHIMIES

PACIFIC OCEAN

Isla Cedros

C

N

NEW SPAIN

Chiametla

B

Bahia Magdalena

La Paz

A

FORTUN JIMENEZ -- 1533-34

Leader of a group of mutineers. The first Europeans known to have set foot in Baja California. Landed in Bahia de La Paz.

HERNAN CORTEZ -- 1535

The conqueror of New Spain. He and 100 men and women spent one year in an unsuccessful attempt at colonization at La Paz.

FRANCISCO DE ULLOA -- 1539-40

Explored both coasts of the Sea of Cortez and the Pacific Coast to north of Isla Cedros. He disappeared at sea north of the island after having sent his report to Cortez.

JUAN RODRIGUEZ CABRILLO -- 1542-43

Explored the Pacific north to mid-Oregon. Cabrillo was killed in an accident at the Channel Islands but his ships returned after 292 days of navigation.

Navidad

Santiago (Manzanillo)

Acapulco

At this point it may be well to reflect that the humble California peninsula was discovered, explored, and first colonized under the auspices of one of the most renowned men in the history of the new world. But although Cortez was the conqueror of Mexico, he was, in turn, largely conquered by the Magnificent Peninsula. He secured little of the riches he sought and spent a significant part of his personal fortune in the process.

While other explorers were to push even farther north, up the Pacific coast, the route they discovered was not to be the one used in the northern expansion of New Spain. In the years after Cortez, great land expeditions under Coronado and others pressed north along the western edge of New Spain and into what are today the states of Arizona and New Mexico in the United States.

By the year 1600, over 160,000 Spaniards had migrated to the New World. There were over 200 chartered towns in New Spain. The path of this movement was on the mainland, not along Baja's Pacific coast. The Baja peninsula was not to be settled by Europeans for more than 150 years after the era of Cortez.

It is apparent that the peninsula acted as a massive barrier in the path of the northerly march of European civilization. With the help of a margarita or two, it would be interesting to speculate on what would have occurred along the west coast of the United States if the *Baja barrier* had not existed. Certainly Alta California would have been heavily colonized by the Spanish at a far earlier date, and the course of history would have been greatly altered.

JUAN RODRIGUEZ CABRILLO — After the Ulloa expedition, Cortez returned to Spain and faded from the new world scene. In New Spain, Viceroy Mendoza was faced with the reality of the California coast and not our margarita-induced speculation. As a result, he dispatched a new expedition under the command of Juan Rodriguez Cabrillo. It was to prove to be one of the most remarkable in the history of navigation.

Cabrillo left the Mexican mainland on June 27, 1542, from the well-protected harbor at Navidad. He arrived at the tip of the Baja peninsula in early July and took on water at San Jose del Cabo. His ships were to join the hundreds that were to make this open roadstead a key stopping point along the Pacific coast. Today, the hotel *Presidente Inter-Continental* has been

EXPLORATION AND FAILED COLONIZATION	
1535	CORTEZ lands at La Paz.
1539--40	ULLOA expedition.
1542--43	CABRILLO expedition.
1565	Start of the galleon sea route from Manila to Acapulco.
1578	DRAKE circles the world.
1586	CAVENDISH in Baja.
1596-1602	VISCAINO expeditions.
1615	PICHILINGUE pirates.
1644	GONZALEZ expedition.
1663	BERNAL expedition.
1683-85	ATONDO-KINO expedition.

constructed adjacent to the stream-fed estuary that provided water to these mariners.

After this brief stop, Cabrillo rounded Cabo San Lucas and on the 13th of July sailed by the magnificent harbor at Bahia Magdalena. In August, he arrived at Isla Cedros, the farthest point north known to have been reached by Ulloa two years earlier. From here, Cabrillo inched his way north, anchoring each night. He reached the broad, protected bay at present-day Ensenada in September; a few days later he stepped ashore near what is now San Diego. On September 28, 1542, he claimed this land in the name of Spain and became the first European known to have set foot on the west coast of what was to become the United States.

In the months to come, Cabrillo beat his way through the notoriously bad weather off Point Conception and reached as far north as Fort Ross on the California coast. After retreating south, Cabrillo met his death on San Miguel Island as the result of an accident. His second-in-command took charge, fought his way north again during winter weather, and eventually reached latitude 44 off the Oregon coast.

From there, the expedition returned to the point of origin, in Navidad, after an absence of nine and one-half months. Tragically, the results of Cabrillo's voyage were considered of little importance by the Spanish officials and no further formal efforts at exploring the peninsula were undertaken for more than 50 years.

PIRATES AND THE MANILA GALLEONS — The Viceroy of New Spain was ordered to shift his efforts to the Philippine Islands, which had been discovered by Magellan during his circumnavigation of the globe. Ships sent from the coast of Mexico sailed west to the islands and developed trade with the countries of the Far East. Starting in the spring of 1565, Spanish ships voyaged northeasterly from the Philippines almost to Japan to reach the prevailing westerly winds. These winds blew them west to the California coast along the northern part of the Baja peninsula and then south to Acapulco. The following winter, the galleons would return to the islands with the aid of the southeast trade winds. The ships making these circuits became known as the *Manila Galleons,* and their annual trips were to continue for an incredible 250 years.

The development of this important trade route was to be of special importance to the California peninsula. The long voyage east from the Philippines was a difficult undertaking requiring six to eight months (twice the time of the westerly leg). By the time the galleons reached the waters off California their food and water supplies were nearly exhausted, and the crews often suffered from scurvy. There was obviously a pressing need for a coastal supply point. While this need was to go unmet for many decades, it did strongly influence future activities on the Baja peninsula.

The presence of the Manila Galleons also resulted in the Baja California cape region becoming the hiding place of pirates who would lay in wait for the annual passage of the richly laden ships. In 1578, Francis Drake entered the Pacific through the Straits of Magellan and became the first to prey on the Spanish galleons. Drake's prizes were seized in waters to the south of Baja, but he and the *Golden Hind* touched at San Jose Del Cabo to take on water, joining the illustrious ranks of those who would visit the peninsula at this point.

Drake was followed eight years later by his fellow Englishman, Thomas Cavendish. After ravaging the South American coast, Cavendish arrived in the protective shelter of the harbor of Cabo San Lucas to lie in wait for the annual trip of the Manila Galleons. On November 4, 1587, he attacked the 700-ton *Santa Ana*, which was so heavily laden that her guns had been left behind. After a fierce defense with small arms, the *Santa Ana* was captured and taken to the anchorage off San Jose del Cabo and the Spanish survivors were cast ashore.

On the 17th of November, Cavendish hosted the Spanish on board his vessel to celebrate the seventeenth anniversary of the coronation of Queen Eliza-

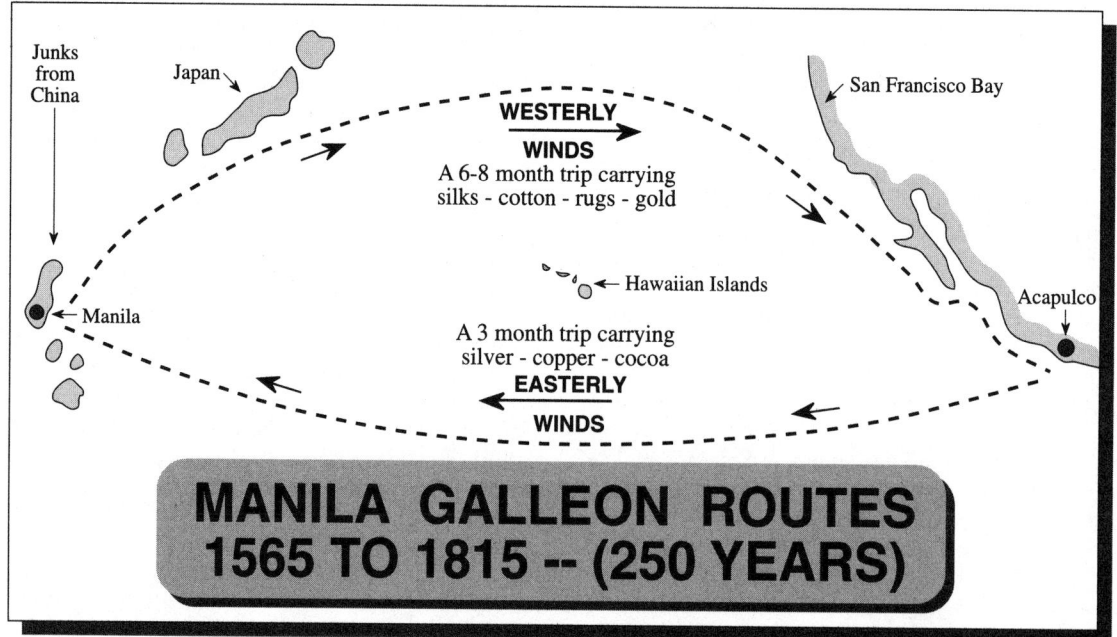

MANILA GALLEON ROUTES
1565 TO 1815 -- (250 YEARS)

beth. Two days later, he set fire to the *Santa Ana* , promptly weighed anchor, and arrived in England after circling the globe.

Remarkably, the stranded Spaniards, headed by Sebastian Vizcaino, were able to extinguish the fire. After performing makeshift repairs, they sailed their ship to the Mexican mainland.

Today, the site of the burning of the *Santa Ana* is in plain view from the swimming pools of the hotels that line the beach at San Jose del Cabo. From the balconies of the Hotel Finisterra, on the cliffs at Cabo San Lucas, one may look over the harbor where Cavendish lay in wait for his prey.

The lure of the Manila Galleons and Spanish shipping along the South American coast also attracted Dutch pirates in the years after the adventures of Drake and Cavendish. Sizeable fleets of these raiders entered the Pacific through the Straits of Magellan starting in 1598. The year 1615 was to witness the coming of a Dutch armada of eight well-armed ships commanded by Boris van Spilbergen. Following a victorious battle with a Spanish fleet to the south, the Dutch fleet infested the waters of the Baja peninsula in hope of capturing ships from Manila.

The men of these ships came to be known as the *Pichilingues*. This name was left behind on the excellent natural harbor north of La Paz, which today is the terminal for the La Paz-to-Mazatlan ferries. This obviously non-hispanic name has become a tongue twister for today's tourists.

Spanish authorities became concerned with the losses incurred at the hands of these adventurers. The need for reliable supply points on the peninsula became clearly apparent. However, these distant events were overshadowed by the defeat of the Spanish Armada in European waters the year following the sacking of the *Santa Ana*. It was thus several years before the Viceroy of New Spain obtained authority to press forward with exploration and colonization in Baja, and it was stipulated that few public funds were to be expended.

SEBASTIAN VIZCAINO — Further authorization for exploration was then awarded to Sebastian Vizcaino. This intrepid seaman made two expeditions. The first, in 1596, resulted in an effort of several months to colonize La Paz. The second, in 1602, was to see Vizcaino sail as far north as Cape Mendocino in Alta California. He visited the sites of present-day San Diego and Monterey and described the latter port as an excellent possibility for establishing a supply station for the Manila Galleons. Plans were actually made to put these recommendations into action but they were not carried out.

Vizcaino had essentially duplicated the path that Cabrillo had taken 60 years earlier, and with similar results. Little occurred as the result of either voyage. Monterey and San Diego faded from memory. They were not colonized for more than 160 years, but many of Vizcaino's geographic place names have survived. The extensive Vizcaino Desert surrounding present-day Guerrero Negro is named in his honor.

Following the expedition of Sebastian Vizcaino, more than 80 years were to pass with only an occasional attempt at colonizing California. Brief efforts were made in 1644, under the command of Alonzo Gonzalez, and again, in 1663, under Bernardo Bernal. While these ventures seem to have been in response to various royal decrees, they do not appear to have been vigorously pursued. As in the past, little in the way of public funds was allocated to these projects; in reality they were little more than pearl fishing ventures.

It was not until 1683 that an expedition was mounted that was to have lasting effect on the colonizing of the Baja peninsula. The Spanish authorities came to realize that public funding was going to be required if colonization was to be achieved. They thus provisioned a small fleet of three ships and gave command to Isidro de Atondo y Antillon.

ATONDO AND KINO — In January 1683, Atondo crossed the Sea of Cortez in four days and arrived at La Paz with some 200 men. With him was the Jesuit padre Francisco Kino. In Kino's hands was to lie the future of the peninsula.

The first event of importance occurred within a short time. The Indians in the La Paz area had grown accustomed to the temporary presence of ships engaged in pearl fishing. In contrast, Atondo and his party obviously intended to stay. The Indians became restive. In due course, Atondo invited the native leaders to a feast and used the occasion to fall upon, and kill, ten of their number.

This event made matters worse. Atondo was forced to abandon La Paz and return to the mainland. As a

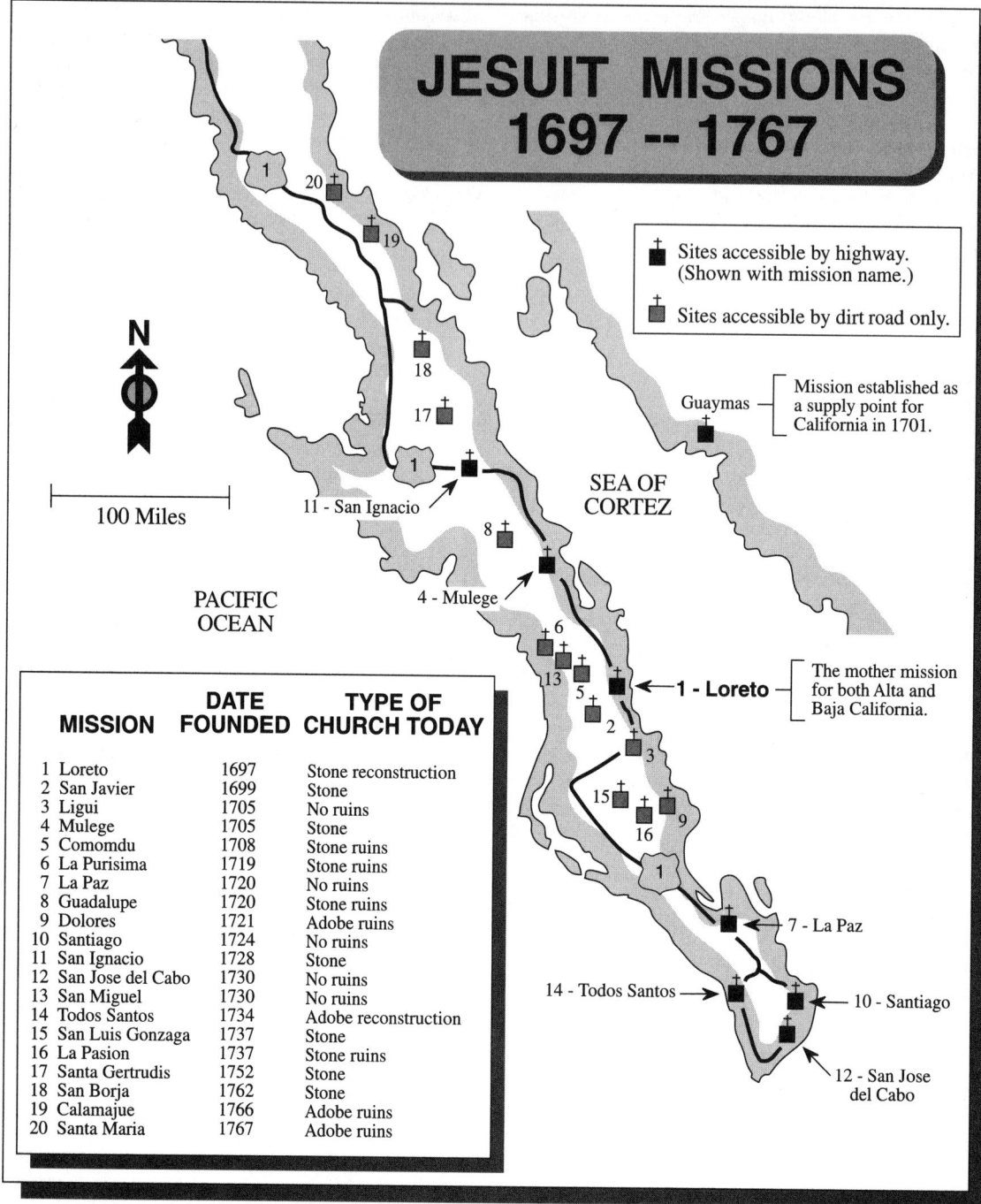

JESUIT MISSIONS 1697 -- 1767

† Sites accessible by highway.
(Shown with mission name.)

■ Sites accessible by dirt road only.

Guaymas — Mission established as a supply point for California in 1701.

SEA OF CORTEZ

PACIFIC OCEAN

N

100 Miles

11 - San Ignacio

4 - Mulege

1 - Loreto — The mother mission for both Alta and Baja California.

7 - La Paz

14 - Todos Santos

10 - Santiago

12 - San Jose del Cabo

MISSION	DATE FOUNDED	TYPE OF CHURCH TODAY
1 Loreto	1697	Stone reconstruction
2 San Javier	1699	Stone
3 Ligui	1705	No ruins
4 Mulege	1705	Stone
5 Comomdu	1708	Stone ruins
6 La Purisima	1719	Stone ruins
7 La Paz	1720	No ruins
8 Guadalupe	1720	Stone ruins
9 Dolores	1721	Adobe ruins
10 Santiago	1724	No ruins
11 San Ignacio	1728	Stone
12 San Jose del Cabo	1730	No ruins
13 San Miguel	1730	No ruins
14 Todos Santos	1734	Adobe reconstruction
15 San Luis Gonzaga	1737	Stone
16 La Pasion	1737	Stone ruins
17 Santa Gertrudis	1752	Stone
18 San Borja	1762	Stone
19 Calamajue	1766	Adobe ruins
20 Santa Maria	1767	Adobe ruins

result of this tragic but important event, the center of colonization efforts on the peninsula was to shift to the north.

After refitting their ship, Atondo and Kino set out again and in October 1683 landed at a place far to the north of La Paz which they named San Bruno. This site is 12 miles north of present-day Loreto. At San Bruno they erected a small triangular fortification surrounding a church and other buildings. Some ten miles inland they found better water and established a livestock farm at a site they named San Isidro. From these bases of operations Atondo and Kino mounted four expeditions into the interior. On one, Padre Kino reached the Pacific coast and became the first European known to have crossed the peninsula on foot.

The San Bruno colony was to last for 19 months. In May 1685, supplies were exhausted and the colonists returned to the mainland. However, the aborted San Bruno colony was to give rise to the permanent settlement of the Magnificent Peninsula within a few years.

JESUIT MISSIONARY PERIOD (71 YEARS)

THE JESUITS — The driving force behind the permanent colonization of the Baja peninsula was the Company of Jesus, the Jesuits. (They are also known today as the Society of Jesus.) Because of the importance of the missionary system in general, and the Jesuits in particular, it is necessary to examine them both briefly.

As the result of the Catholic Counter Reformation in Europe, members of several religious orders accompanied the conquerors of new lands to many parts of the world. Use of the missionary system became a hallmark of Spanish colonization. It was to become an effective and economical tool for accomplishing the purposes of the kings, for the orders had their own internal administrative systems and access to sources of revenue other than the royal treasury.

Ignatius Loyola founded the Company of Jesus in 1534. Members of the order came to Mexico in 1572 and soon established extensive missions in the northwestern region. Their members were university-trained men of good family from many European countries. By the time of the Atondo colonizing effort at San Bruno, the Jesuits had over 100 years of missionary experience in Mexico.

The *mision* was to become an institution under Spanish law along with the *pueblo* and the *presidio*. Each mission was planned to last only ten years. It was then to be replaced by the pueblo, with the mission lands divided between communal acreage, town site areas, and individual plots for each Indian. As we shall see, this transfer process was a long time coming in Baja. The presidio was the headquarters of the military establishment that accompanied the missionaries.

In Baja, each mission consisted of a central village where the missionary and any accompanying sol-

diers lived. Each had a number of outlying *visiting stations* which are sometimes mistakenly referred to as missions.

Establishment of a mission was not done at the whim of the local priest but required following well-established rules and sequences. After securing approval for a new mission, the padre would bless the chosen site and erect the necessary buildings. Indians were attracted through gifts of food and other items. Children and any dying adults were baptized. The receptive Indian was required to give up his wandering ways and settle down in the vicinity of the mission. The teaching of Spanish and the tenets of Christianity were to follow.

Each mission aimed at becoming self-supporting through farming and grazing, but this was difficult because of Baja's arid conditions. Heavy reliance had to be placed on supplies shipped from the mainland.

Padre Francisco Kino was of Italian birth and had been educated in mathematics at German universities, a strange background for his assignments in spreading Christianity in remote areas of the world.

JESUIT MISSIONARY PERIOD

1697	Salvatierra founds Loreto mission.
1717	Salvatierra dies -- succeeded by Ugarte.
1734	Pericue Indian revolt.
1742-48	Epidemics kill many Indians.
1768	Jesuits expelled from Baja.

Upon returning to the mainland from the failed effort at San Bruno, Kino and Atondo found the Viceroy unwilling to expend additional funds in colonizing the arid lands across the Sea of Cortez.

As a result, the Jesuits assigned Padre Kino to missionary efforts in the mainland northwest, where he was to become one of the most successful and famous figures in the history of Mexico and the American southwest. But before moving to these tasks, he was to transfer his enthusiasm for missionary work in California to a visiting Jesuit, Padre Juan Maria de Salvatierra. The two made a mutual promise to work toward establishing missions on the distant peninsula.

The burden of pursuing this effort was to fall to Salvatierra, but he was to meet with continual frustration. Neither the Spanish authorities or the leader of the Jesuits in Mexico would undertake the project. Finally, help came from none other than Father Santaella, the General of the Jesuit order, who visited Mexico in 1696. His support resulted in the order giving Salvatierra permission to enter California.

But frustration was to continue because the Viceroy would not provide financial support for such an enterprise. It became necessary for Salvatierra to solicit contributions from private sources. Accomplishing this, he finally secured a license to proceed on February 6, 1697. Because they were to provide the funding, this document gave the Jesuits almost complete control over the peninsula. After additional delays, Salvatierra and his followers finally arrived on the California shore in October of that year. The Baja peninsula was never again without settlers from the old world.

FOUNDING OF LORETO — San Bruno was the site of the Jesuit landing. Little remained of the fortifications that had been constructed fourteen years earlier. Salvatierra decided to search for a better location for his mission because San Bruno was situated more than a mile from the coast and the water supply was brackish. In a few days a suitable place was found to the south.

On October 19, 1697, supplies from the ship began to be unloaded on the beach at the present location of Loreto. This was to be one of the most momentous events in the history of the Californias as Loreto was to become the mother mission for all those to follow in Baja and Alta California.

The settlers were able to converse with the Indians because the elements of their language had been documented by one of the padres who had accompanied the Atondo expedition. A porridge of corn meal was shared with those who had helped in the work as was the missionaries' practice. This act of charity was soon to cause the Indians to covet the limited food supplies.

After more than three weeks of tension, the Indians attacked the meager fortification, which consisted of a wall made up of the expedition's supplies. It was finally necessary to resort to firearms and the death of several Indians to save the day. One cannot help but compare the Loreto Indians' reaction to the missionaries' generosity with the feelings of outrage often encountered in today's world when the accustomed benevolences of church and state are threatened with reduction.

During the next seventy years, the Jesuits established twenty missions (see *Jesuit Missions* Map) and many more visiting stations from the tip of the peninsula north to the vicinity of Catavina. Certain missions were to be used as bases from which new ones were founded. This stepping stone sequence was eventually to lead to the establishment of a chain of missions with its northern limit at Sonoma, north of San Francisco, in Alta California.

ADDITIONAL JESUIT MISSIONS — By the end of the first year, there were twenty-two Spaniards at Loreto, and the situation with the Indians had quieted to the point where Padre Salvatierra set forth in search of new mission sites. The initial efforts at expansion were located in the mountains to the west of Loreto and north along the coast to Mulege. Father Salvatierra was also called to cross to the mainland and establish a mission at Guaymas

The stone church at San Javier. It is the best preserved of the missions established by the Jesuits in Baja. Photo JW.

for use as a supply point for the peninsula. By the time of Salvatierra's death in 1717, a total of five peninsula missions were in operation.

Salvatierra's successor was Padre Juan Ugarte. Considerable progress was made under his leadership; eleven new missions were established during the next twenty years. But while there was continual progress, there was also the never-ending need for additional financial support. Arid conditions on the peninsula resulted in very little food being raised, and the missions did not become self-supporting as was usually the case in better agricultural areas. It was continually necessary to bring supplies across the Sea of Cortez by ship.

Over the years, the peninsula's leaders wrote letters and even made trips to the mainland to plead their case with government authorities. The response was always negative. The padres' only alternative was to continue to seek out contributions from wealthy citizens on the mainland.

In the long run, they were very successful in this effort. The money and lands that were acquired were to become known as the Pious Fund. It was this fund that later became the financial basis for the founding of the future chain of missions in the United States.

The founding of the mission at San Jose del Cabo in 1730 was to be an important, although tragic, event. Within a short time of its establishment, one of the great ships inbound from Manila dropped anchor nearby. Fearing hostile Indians, the captain sent armed men ashore in search of water. To their astonishment, they were met by the padre and his charges and were provided with fresh supplies. At long last, after 165 years, the Manila Galleons had a supply point on the California coast. This good news was carried to Mexico City and Manila, and the order was given for all future sailings from the Philippines to stop at San Jose del Cabo. Sadly, this state of affairs was to be short-lived.

INDIAN UPRISING — As previously noted, the peninsula Indians were polygamists. It was with the Pericue Indians at the southern missions that the padres' efforts to change this system was most resented. Many came to conspire against the missionaries under the leadership of the shamans. By 1733, the rebellious individuals felt they had sufficient strength and plotted to eliminate the few soldiers who guarded the missions - only one at La Paz, two at

Santiago, and three at Todos Santos. There were no soldiers at San Jose del Cabo.

The Indians made their move the following year by killing the soldier stationed at La Paz. Within a short time they killed the padre, two soldiers, and an Indian at Santiago, and the padre at San Jose del Cabo. The padre and other surviving mission personnel from Todos Santos fled first to La Paz and then to the mission at Dolores.

Upon receiving news of the uprising, soldiers from the presidio at Loreto moved south to La Paz. They were joined by Indian soldiers from the mainland. Military action was taken against the peninsula Indians with little success. In January 1735, a ship from Manila arrived at Cabo San Lucas in search of the padre and the warm reception they were told to expect. Instead, they were greeted with violence at the hands of some 600 natives who almost succeeded in taking over the vessel.

Upon arrival in Acapulco, the galleon captain traveled to Mexico City and advised the Viceroy of the situation on the peninsula. As a result, the authorities were finally moved to provide greater assistance to the struggling missionaries. As is so often the case, it was economically related events that were to be the motivating factor. None other than the governor of mainland Sinaloa was ordered to the peninsula. Although his initial efforts were ineffective, the rebellious Indians were finally crushed by the end of 1736.

In response to all this unrest, a new presidio was established at San Jose del Cabo with a complement of thirty soldiers. Little by little, modest buildings rose to replace those destroyed in the rebellion, but conditions would never be the same. While the Manila galleons brought silks and jewelry to the mainland, they left smallpox, measles, and venereal disease in California.

During the years 1742 to 1748, epidemics spread throughout the peninsula, particularly in the south. Almost the entire Pericue tribe was wiped out. Some missions were abandoned, and the few remaining Indians concentrated at other points. The port of La Paz was abandoned and bore no sign of life for many years.

With the curtailment of activities in the south, the Jesuits began to push toward the north. In the final fifteen years of their reign they were to establish four new missions in the mountains north of San Ignacio. The previous missions were located where concentrations of Indians and the best sites for agriculture and grazing were found. The majority were in places which today support substantial communities. To the north, such favorable conditions were located near the crest of the peninsular divide, which lies to the east of the Transpeninsular Highway and far from the path of today's activities.

In founding these new missions, the padres were endeavoring to establish stepping stones linking the peninsula missions with those on the Mexican mainland. Although this was never to occur, the new outposts were eventually to serve as the supply route for the founding of a new empire of missions in Alta California.

These final years for the Jesuits were to be restless ones in other ways. The increase in support from Mexico City brought with it conflict between civil and Jesuit authorities. The Indians began to petition the government authorities to grant them the lands they were cultivating. Diseases continued to cause many deaths particularly among the women, who suffered disproportionately from venereal disease. Men who had only recently ceased the practice of polygamy were now unable to find even one wife.

JESUIT EXPULSION — While the Jesuit situation on the peninsula was in a deteriorating condition, the ultimate blow was to be delivered from the outside. The military-like Company of Jesus had attracted many enemies throughout the years, and there was world-wide resentment of their power and wealth. Even in Baja, it was believed that the Jesuits had accumulated and concealed a sizeable treasure.

These resentments peaked in Europe where the Company was expelled from Portugal in 1759, France in 1764, and finally from Spain in 1767. The Viceroy of New Spain was to receive a double-sealed package from Charles III to be opened June 24, 1767. In this message, the king ordered all Jesuits to be arrested and sent to the port of Vera Cruz for deportation to Spain.

On the peninsula, the unhappy task of carrying out this order fell to Captain Gaspar de Portola. He and fifty soldiers arrived in San Jose del Cabo that same year and proceeded to arrest sixteen padres from the fourteen remaining missions. On February 3, 1768, the missionaries met in front of the church in Loreto,

where the image of the virgin was draped in black. There the weeping inhabitants watched as the Jesuits departed for the mainland with only a few personal possessions. By July, they were imprisoned in Spain in company with Jesuits from other regions.

To the Jesuits goes the credit for bringing civilization to California. Each mission had a school. Primitive roads were constructed which were to ultimately connect Baja and Alta California. There was even a regular postal service linking the missions. The first garden plants were introduced at Loreto, and in 1730 date palms were brought to San Ignacio, Loreto, Mulege, and other locations.

Most of the buildings were constructed of adobe and have not survived. The principle exception is the stone church at San Javier built between 1744 and 1758. It is located some twenty-four miles from Highway 1 by secondary road. Tourists staying in the Loreto-Puerto Escondido area will be well rewarded with a visit to this historic spot.

Tragically, through no fault of the padres, contact with the outside world during this period brought the diseases that were soon to almost exterminate the Indian. Estimates of the pre-Hispanic population range from 40,000 to 50,000 persons. By the end of the Jesuit period, only some 7,000 remained.

FRANCISCANS AND DOMINICANS (53 YEARS)

THE FRANCISCANS — Prior to the expulsion of the Jesuits, the Franciscan order had been responsible for missionary activity in northwestern Mexico. Now they were pressed to also take over the area vacated by the Company of Jesus on both the mainland and the Baja peninsula. There was to be little lapse in authority because the Franciscan padres sailed for California on the same ship which had just delivered their expelled predecessors to the mainland.

FRANCISCANS & DOMINICANS

1768	Franciscans arrive in Baja.
1769	Expedition to San Diego.
1772	Dominicans take over Baja missions.
1780-82	Severe Indian epidemics.
1810-22	Revolution against Spanish rule.
1822	Baja swears allegiance to Mexico.

FRANCISCAN & DOMINICAN MISSIONS

Franciscan Missions

† Dominican Missions
(Accessible by highway)

† Dominican Missions
(Accessible by dirt road or trail)

FRANCISCAN MISSIONS

MISSION	DATE FOUNDED	TYPE OF CHURCH
A San Fernando	1769	Adobe ruins
B San Diego	1769	Restored

DOMINICAN MISSIONS

	MISSION	DATE FOUNDED	TYPE OF CHURCH
1	El Rosario	1774	Adobe ruins
2	Santo Domingo	1775	Adobe ruins
3	San Vicente	1780	Adobe ruins
4	San Miguel	1787	Adobe ruins
5	Santo Tomas	1791	Adobe ruins
6	San Pedro Martir	1794	Adobe ruins
7	Santa Catalina	1797	Adobe ruins
8	Descanso	1814	No ruins
9	Guadalupe	1834	No ruins

Fifteen priests landed at Loreto on April 1, 1768, under the leadership of Padre Junipero Serra. Each of Serra's charges was assigned to one of the fourteen missions remaining in service at the time of the expulsion.

During the Jesuit period, the missionaries had been the virtual masters of life on the peninsula, which included authority over military personnel. They had discouraged the settlement of lands by immigrants from the mainland, so there was little activity outside the missions. All of this was to change dramatically. Captain Portola, who had expelled the Jesuits, had been appointed governor. He met the Franciscans

and advised them that he and his soldiers would dispense justice and administer farming, grazing, and other economic activities.

The missionary system had remained in effect for over seventy years rather than the ten-year period that had been anticipated. The change to civil authority was now to come, even though conditions on the peninsula had not advanced to the point where the transformation was fully justified.

Shortly after the arrival of the Franciscans, there came to the peninsula one Jose de Galvez, a personal agent of the King of Spain. He established himself at Santa Ana, a silver mining center near the present towns of San Antonio and El Triunfo south of La Paz. Mining, here, was one of the few economic activities carried out on the peninsula outside the administration of the missionaries. It is a very interesting area to visit, and El Triunfo is included in the POINTS OF SPECIAL INTEREST Tour.

Galvez carried royal orders to organize an expedition aimed at colonizing Alta California and to make changes in operations on the peninsula. From Santa Ana, he issued numerous decrees to which little attention was paid once he departed the region. However, he was successful in giving birth to the new missionary venture.

The padres had been pressing for the establishment of settlements in San Diego and Monterey for over 150 years since these sites were discovered by Cabrillo and Vizcaino. However, the Spanish authorities showed no interest in expending effort in this direction until it became known that Czarist Russian fur trappers and explorers were working their way down the northwestern Pacific coast. They had set up outposts as far south as the Farallon Islands off San Francisco.

From his headquarters at Santa Ana, Galvez summoned Padre Serra and Captain Fernando Javier de

Rivera y Moncada, commander of the Presidio at Loreto. There, in this obscure hideaway in the mountains south of La Paz, the plans were drawn up for the settlement of what was to become the homes of millions of people in today's southern and central California in the United States.

Governor Portola was placed in command of the venture. He was delighted to be relieved of the political obscurity of his post in Loreto. Padre Serra was also eager to join and quickly secured release from his peninsular duties. The expedition was to be divided into four units, two by land and two by sea. In January 1769, the packet *San Carlos* weighed anchor at La Paz and sailed for San Diego. (Six years later, this same *San Carlos* became the first European ship to sail into the harbor at San Francisco.) A second vessel, the *San Antonio,* followed a month later. Both arrived at San Diego in April.

The first land party was led by Captain Rivera y Moncada. It was his assignment to visit the missions north of La Paz and collect everything that he could in the way of livestock, food, and other supplies and to proceed with these to the northernmost mission at Santa Maria. This task was successfully accomplished, although he was forced to move northwest from Santa Maria to obtain better pasturage. This was found at a place to be named Velicata. After recouping there, Rivera y Moncada set out for San Diego where he arrived on May 14, 1769, after a journey of fifty days.

Portola and Serra led the last party and proceeded to Velicata where Rivera y Moncada had rested. Here, Padre Serra founded Mission San Fernando, the only mission to be established on the peninsula by the Franciscans. It was to stay in operation for forty-nine years providing one more link in the chain of missions stretching north from Loreto.

The ruins of this mission lie three miles west of the Transpeninsular Highway (Highway 1) midway be-

Ruins of the Dominican mission at Santo Domingo. Several similar sites may be visited within a few miles of Highway 1. Photo JW.

tween the towns of El Rosario and Catavina in what is a very remote area even today. Its location will be noted during the GRAND TOUR in PART III. It is hoped the traveler will pause briefly to honor the passage of Portola, Serra and their men on their historic journey.

The two leaders arrived in San Diego on July 1, 1769. While both land parties had suffered great hardships, the crews of the ships which had arrived earlier in April were in worse condition. Scurvy had claimed the lives of over one-third of the crew on each vessel.

From this base in San Diego, Father Serra and his successors were to found twenty-one missions and to give birth to western civilization in what has become California in the United States. It is clear that the success of what has taken place in the north was predicated on events preceding it in the Baja peninsula. It is certainly ironic that the mighty giant of the north owes such an enormous debt to a place that most of its citizens know virtually nothing about.

THE DOMINICANS — While Padre Serra labored to advance the cause of Christianity in Alta California, the reign of the Franciscans to the south was to be brief. Following the Jesuits' expulsion from the Spanish domain, the Dominican order petitioned the King of Spain to obtain missionary territory in California. This request was soon granted, and the King ordered the peninsula to be divided equally between the Dominicans and the Franciscans.

The Franciscans, who had originally resisted their assignment to California, soon found that they were in continual disagreement with the peninsula's civil authorities. Various epidemics caused the death of some 2,000 Indians in only three years, and the missions in the south were in a state of complete deterioration. Thus, it is not surprising, that after some initial disagreement, the issue was resolved by providing the Dominicans with the entire peninsula, while the Franciscans received Alta California. We prideful U. S. citizens would no doubt maintain that the latter order negotiated a very favorable settlement. Avoid playing poker with a Franciscan.

Dominican friars arrived in Loreto on October 14, 1772. There had been only four and one-half years of administration by the Franciscans. Inspection of the existing missions and their Indian charges made it clear to the Dominicans that their future lay to the north. Within two years, they established a new mission on the banks of the Rio del Rosario at the present town of El Rosario. The site of the buildings was to be moved down river some twenty-eight years later. The crumbling ruins may be easily visited in a short side trip from the Transpeninsular Highway. They are included in the POINTS OF SPECIAL INTEREST Tour.

Within twenty years of their arrival on the peninsula, the Dominicans responded to royal order by establishing a total of five new missions between Velicata and San Diego. These served as stepping stones along the road pioneered by Junipero Serra. The linkage with Alta California was complete. In the years to follow, four additional missions were founded in the northern portion of the peninsula.

It should be noted that the churches which may be visited by today's travelers were built some years after the original missions were founded. Several stone buildings were built by the Dominicans, but the only one still standing is the beautiful church at San Ignacio. More recently, reconstruction at other sites has been sponsored by the Mexican government and private groups.

Epidemics also followed the northward march of the Dominicans. Smallpox struck the northern missions in 1780 to 1782. Indians who were moved from the north to populate the decimated southern missions often met prompt death from disease.

A report prepared in 1786 paints this horrible picture. "The missions of San Jose, Santiago, Todos Santos, San Javier, Loreto, Comondu, Cadegomo, Guadalupe, and Mulege are on the way to total extinction. The reason is so evident that it leaves no doubt. Syphilis has taken possession of both sexes to such a degree that mothers do not conceive, and if they do conceive, the fetus is born with little hope of living. There are three times as many adults who die as there are babies born." By 1800, there were no more than 4,000 to 5,000 Indians still living in the entire peninsula, only ten percent of the original population.

Changes in the peninsula's civil administration under Governor Portola also led to the decay of the entire missionary system. These same adjustments did bring about small increases in the number of Spaniards and *Mestizos*, and in their hands rested the future of Baja and all of Mexico. In 1800, the estimate of their number was 700 to 800. They gained a living from cattle raising and farming. Historic accounts also frequently refer to the mining of silver at Santa Ana (near present-day San Antonio and El Triunfo) as well as the salt deposits on Isla Carmen. These salt mines had been worked from the early days of the Jesuits and may be visited today by boat from Loreto or Puerto Escondido.

There were also important administrative changes made during the reign of the Dominicans. Shortly after their arrival, a 1776 royal order separated the provinces of Texas, New Mexico, New Viscays, Coahuila, Sinaloa, Sonora, and the Californias into a new *Internal Province* to be governed from Arizpe rather than Mexico City. The capital of the Californias was also to be changed from Loreto to Monterey. Under this arrangement, peninsular business matters had to travel from Loreto to Monterey and then to Arizpe.

THE MEXICAN NATION

1822	Baja swears allegiance to Mexico.
1830	Capital moved -- Loreto to La Paz.
1846 -- 48	Mexican-American war in Baja.
1853	William Walker invades Baja.
1864	Baja leased to the Americans.
1883	Law to Colonization passed.
1885	Copper mining at Santa Rosalia.
1901	Founding of Mexicali.
1911	Revolutionary activity in the north.
1933	End of the Law of Colonization.
1952	Baja California becomes a state.
1974	Baja California Sur becomes a state.

It is a matter of considerable wonder that the great state of California in the United States was once governed from what is now a small Mexican town (Arizpe) located on a side road northeast of present-day Hermosillo on the Mexican mainland. Twenty-eight years after the capital was moved to Monterey, the seat of peninsula government was to return to Loreto as the result of Baja and Alta California being separated into two provinces.

Of far more importance to Mexico were the events which took place from 1810 to 1822. Mexico was to rise in revolution against the authority of Spain, as were peoples throughout the Americas. Action began September 16, 1810, now Mexico's Independence Day. Independence was finally achieved in 1821; however, there remained some hesitancy by the peninsular people to accept the rule of the new Mexican nation. As a result, they were to come under attack from an amazingly unlikely source.

Almost two and one-half centuries after Francis Drake and Thomas Cavendish had left Baja's waters, another English adventurer appeared in the Sea of Cortez. Lord Thomas de Cochrane arrived off San Jose del Cabo with two ships on February 17, 1822. This seaman was the archenemy of Spain and had arrived after pillaging along the South American coast wherever any vestiges of Spanish authority were to be found.

A ship in the roadstead off San Jose del Cabo still flew the Spanish flag, and Cochrane used this as an excuse to sack the town. From there he turned to Loreto where fifteen days later he made a similar attack. The governor and other citizens fled, but Cochrane was repulsed by fifteen men led by Ensign Jose Maria Mata. Mata took command and felt that the time had come to swear allegiance to Mexico. An official ceremony took place in July of that year at Loreto; the peninsula formally took its place in the Mexican nation.

The dominance of the mission system and the authority of Spain had come to an end. In the years ahead, events on the peninsula would reflect the political aftermath of the revolution. Civil rather than religious matters would dominate, and war would come with the United States.

THE MEXICAN NATION

Many aspects of life were to change on the Baja California peninsula and throughout Mexico following independence from Spain. Mexican officials arrived from the mainland to rule in Loreto. In time, all the missions were converted to pueblos, many lands distributed to those who worked them, and religious affairs turned over to the secular clergy. The peninsula was divided into four municipalities, each under the authority of a mayor. In 1828, the town of Loreto was largely destroyed by heavy rains and flooding. The capital was transferred briefly to the silver mining town of San Antonio and then, in 1830, to La Paz. Loreto was to languish in obscurity for many years.

Guaymas

San Ignacio →

Mulege →

7

Comondu

5

SEA OF
CORTEZ

N

50 Miles

6

8

#
Numbered squares indicate key
events occurring between June
1846 and March 1848. The
numbers correspond to similar
numbered sections in the text.

PACIFIC
OCEAN

4

La Paz

3

San Antonio

10

9

Todo Santos →

San Jose
del Cabo →

1

2

WAR BETWEEN
MEXICO AND
THE UNITED STATES

Mazatlan →

Political passions rose in the peninsula. There were Indian uprisings in the north. Uprising of citizens and soldiers occurred at La Paz, and small battles were fought. Clearly, economic factors and the press for land ownership were becoming important issues to the peninsula's people as the influence of the clergy dissipated. Finally, as the midpoint of the 19th century approached, the peninsula was to be caught up in the fringes of war between Mexico and the United States.

THE MEXICAN-AMERICAN WAR — Momentous events were occurring in the outlying Mexican lands that are today a part of southwestern United States. Texas had declared itself a separate republic in the 1830s, and Mexico's General Santa Ana was defeated by the forces of Sam Houston. In Alta California, there were only scattered Mexican forces and settlers along the coast. English-speaking peoples from the east were migrating west and taking up lands.

It became clear that both England and France coveted possession of Alta California and its fabulous harbor at San Francisco. By 1837, the United States was making proposals to Mexico for the purchase of Mexican lands in the west. A mood of expansionism, *manifest destiny* prevailed in the United States. In 1845, James Polk was elected president, standing on a political platform advocating the annexation of Texas and the purchase of Alta California from Mexico.

As a result of the election mandate, the United States issued, and received acceptance of, an invitation for Texas to join the Federal Union. This *annexation* infuriated Mexican authorities and resulted in armed conflict along the border. In addition to the issue of Texas, the United States had various grievances against Mexico and also feared the potential takeover of California by England or France. As a result, the United States declared war on May 11, 1846.

Prior to the outbreak of hostilities, the United States had been prepared to pay approximately $25 million for California, depending on the inclusion or exclusion of Baja California. This *either/or* proviso would seem to indicate that obtaining possession of Baja California was not a primary goal of the United States government. However, once war started, specific military steps were taken to bring the peninsula under United States authority.

The decisive battles of the Mexican-American War took place in mainland Mexico. Invading United States forces under the command of Zachary Taylor and Winfield Scott conducted successful campaigns. The latter general captured Mexico City on September 14, 1847. Lesser actions took place in New Mexico and Alta California. Perhaps the least known of all were the battles that took place in the Baja peninsula, where the fighting was actually heavier than it was to the north. These peninsular events are depicted on a

Aerial view of the estuary forming the mouth of the Rio Santa Rosalia at Mulege This area was the site of the Mexican-American War battle between the U. S. sloop Dale and Mexican patriots. Photo JW.

map and are amplified below. The item numbers in the text correspond to similar numbers on the map.

1. — A squadron of eight United States navy ships and their marine contingents had been stationed in Pacific waters for some time. They were commanded by Commodore John D. Sloat, who was under instructions to occupy San Francisco and other Alta California ports in the event of war with Mexico. Sloat stationed his fleet at Mazatlan, where there was a United States consul; it was apparently the best site along the entire Pacific coast for him to receive instruction from Washington.

On May 16, 1846, he received word that fighting had begun along the Rio Grande. While he did not know that war had been declared several days earlier, he moved his ships north along the California coast and during July took possession of Monterey, San Francisco, and San Diego - without resistance.

2. — After completing this assignment, some of the American ships returned south to blockade the Mexican coast and take possession of additional ports. In September 1846, these ships arrived in La Paz. The United States commander told local authorities they were under American control and secured an agreement that they would remain neutral. The United States forces were under orders to utilize this *neutrality* approach to pacify the Mexicans and to make them more receptive to a change in authority.

3. — On March 29, 1847, the United States sloop *Portsmouth* sailed to San Jose del Cabo and imposed the same arrangement.

4. — Prior to the declaration of war, the United States Congress had authorized the formation of battalions of volunteers as backup forces to the regular army. The first was to be the First Battalion of Volunteers from the State of New York. It was composed mostly of young boys eager for adventure and was referred to in New York newspapers as the Baby Regiment.

The battalion was placed on ships and transported around Cape Horn to Alta California, where it arrived in spring 1847. The boys were assigned to guard the various towns in the region. Subsequently, two companies were ordered to La Paz, where they went ashore without incident on July 20, 1847.

5. — Word reached the Mexican government of the neutral position taken by their small military force that was stationed at La Paz. In anger, they dispatched Captain Manual Pinada and a small group of officers and arms to take over military matters in the peninsula. Pinada had previous knowledge of the terrain and people of Baja. He crossed the Sea of Cortez from Guaymas and arrived at Mulege in September 1847. Here, he organized the local people into a force to defend the peninsula.

6. — Hearing of Pinada's arrival, the Americans dispatched the sloop *Dale* to Mulege, where it arrived in October. The sloop's commander sent a message ashore demanding that the inhabitants preserve neutrality. Pinada responded with a prideful message that he and his soldiers would defend their country until the last drop of blood was shed.

Hearing this, the United States commander sent boats ashore with some 60 men and a small artillery piece. This force was fired upon by Pinada and his small group of men. There followed a considerable exchange of gun fire, including some 135 canister shots from the *Dale* lying offshore. The proud Mexicans held fast, and by afternoon the Americans returned to their ship.

Having met with resistance, the *Dale* left Mulege leaving a smaller ship behind to provide a blockade. All this action took place at the mouth of the Rio Santa

NO MAN'S LAND

When Cortez and the conquistadores
To Baja California came,
They discovered a poor land
That they could not tame;

Then the missionaries tried
With the same short success,
They found very little
And they left even less;

The "civilization" they brought
For the Indians' release
Killed most of the natives
With the white man's disease.

No treasures were gained
When Spain's flag was unfurled
And the souls converted
Soon departed this world.

So Baja was abandoned,
Like a poor bastard child,
To shift for itself
and revert to the wild.

Ken Reimer

Rosalia near El Sombrerito, a small but conspicuous peak that now bears the Mulege lighthouse. It is in plain view from Highway 1 and is within a few yards of the Serenidad Hotel.

7. — The heroic defense of Mulege gave rise to considerable public spirit. Pinada was able to recruit a force that Mexican historians say numbered about 300 men. They came from the pueblos of San Ignacio, Mulege, and Comondu, and later from San Antonio and Todos Santos.

8. — Pinada marched his soldiers south. Part of the force was detached and sent to San Jose del Cabo. On November 16, 1847, the main body of some 180 men under Pinada attacked the New York Volunteers who had fortified themselves in buildings within La Paz. There was to follow 12 days of fierce fighting, with the Americans defending themselves with cannon fire and by tearing down buildings which were providing the Mexicans with cover. At one point these forces penetrated to within 100 feet of the fortified Americans, but Pinada finally had to withdraw due to lack of ammunition. After the fighting was over, American reinforcements arrived by sea.

9. — After hearing of the Mexican successes at Mulege, the citizens of San Jose del Cabo tore down the American flag and declared an end to American rule. As a result, American ships arrived and left a detachment of twenty-four men. As at La Paz, this force was required to fortify itself in the town buildings when they were attacked by the Mexicans from Pinada's forces that had marched south from La Paz. The assault failed, and the Mexican leader, Naval Lieutenant Jose Antonio Mijares, was mortally wounded. A monument to this fallen hero may be seen in the town plaza at San Jose del Cabo.

As at La Paz, American ships arrived, and the garrison was reinforced with 46 additional men. The Mexican forces were also reinforced by Pinada's soldiers from the north. When the American ships left, the Mexicans renewed the attack in mid-January 1848. They surrounded the American position and cut off all sources of water and supplies.

By mid-February, surrender seemed inevitable; but reinforcements again arrived by sea. The Mexicans attacked these newcomers. Fierce fighting and artillery fire was to occur on the way from the sea to the pueblo. In the end, the arrival of these reinforcements required the Mexicans to retire to the north.

10. — During March, the American forces from La Paz conducted several campaigns to put an end to the Mexican resistance. On March 27, 1848, they captured Captain Pinada in San Antonio. A few days later, a force of more than 200 Americans surrounded and captured the remaining Mexican defenders north of Todos Santos and fighting came to an end.

Much of the fighting at San Jose del Cabo and the final actions at San Antonio and Todos Santos were to take place after the signing of the peace treaty on February 2, 1848, but this information had not been received in the peninsula.

Having been victorious in the major land battles on the Mexican mainland, the United States was in a position to demand a harsh settlement. However, their proposal was not to differ greatly from that made prior to the war. Under its terms, Mexico ceded Alta California and New Mexico. In return, they received $15 million, and the United States agreed to pay various claims held by its citizens against Mexico.

The original draft of the treaty presented by the United States included the Baja peninsula within the lands to be ceded by Mexico. In its counter-proposal, Mexico asserted "The cession of Lower California ... offers great embarrassment to Mexico, considering the position of that peninsula, facing our coast of Sonora, which is separated from it by the narrow Gulf of Cortez." The United States negotiator bowed to the Mexican position. As a result, the Baja peninsula together with sufficient territory to tie it to the mainland was retained in the Mexican republic.

One can readily draw the conclusion that the principal objective of the United States occupation of the peninsula was that of obtaining a bargaining chip. If so, this posture was apparently not conveyed to the American military commanders, who assured the Mexican citizens in the south that United States administration was there to stay. With these assurances, many Mexicans placed themselves openly on the side of the invading forces. After the peace treaty, these people were branded as traitors. When the American military left the peninsula in September 1848, more than 300 of these people were taken to Monterey in Alta California to prevent their being killed by their outraged fellow Mexicans.

While they were not to prevail in the military actions on the peninsula, the Mexican forces obviously conducted themselves with valor. This is particularly impressive when one considers that most of them were not professional soldiers but only citizens gathered from far-flung towns where there was little knowledge of the overall motivations of the war. Hopefully, today's tourists will stop at the sites and monuments relating to this conflict and pay homage to the combatants.

FILIBUSTERS AND FRAUDS — Turbulent years lay ahead for Baja. The decade following the war was to give rise to a period of filibustering. Filibusters were lawless military adventurers who entered Mexico and Central American countries with the intent of overthrowing the national authorities. Americans involved in these activities in Mexico had as their objective the annexing of the *conquered* areas into the United States, as had occurred with Texas.

The most notorious of these individuals was William Walker. He gathered forty-eight armed followers in San Francisco and sailed for Mexico. On November 3, 1853, he landed at La Paz, seized control from the local authorities, and declared the establishment of the Republic of Sonora. Within a few days, he was attacked by Mexican forces and lost six men. He retreated to Cabo San Lucas and eventually to Ensenada.

Near Ensenada there were several armed conflicts and deaths. During the weeks to follow, Walker's men were to assert their authority at San Vicente, San Quintin, and El Rosario, all towns visited by today's traveler along the Transpeninsular Highway. From this area, Walker moved east to conquer mainland Sonora but in turn was defeated by the rigors of the Sonoran desert. He was forced to return to the United States, where he was captured and tried.

In the years to come, William Walker was to move his operations to several Central American countries. He was put to death in 1860 by Honduran authorities, bringing to an end the era of filibustering.

These same years were to see civil war within Mexico between groups with opposing liberal and conservative political views. Baja California was firmly on the liberal side. There was some fighting in the peninsula. The year 1857 was to see the establishment of a new constitution for Mexico and Benito Juarez became president in 1861. Statues and other references to Juarez may be seen throughout Mexico.

In 1862, new silver mines were discovered in the historic mining district of San Antonio in the moun-

tains south of La Paz. The area became a bonanza, and many miners came from the United States. The ruins of the smelters and other facilities may be seen at the town of El Triunfo and San Antonio and are included in the POINTS OF SPECIAL INTEREST Tour in PART III.

In the years to follow, some twenty-five to thirty mining and colonizing land frauds were known to have been perpetrated on North Americans using the claimed resources of the Baja peninsula as bait. The most outrageous of them all was instigated by none other than President Juarez himself.

As a means of obtaining badly needed funds, Juarez actually leased some two-thirds of the entire peninsula to a United States citizen named Jacob P. Leese. In 1864, Leese sold out to a group of New York capitalists whose object was to raise $25 million, through fraud, on a massive scale. Announcements in California newspapers read "Free lands, free commerce, homes for the poor, riches for the wealthy. For

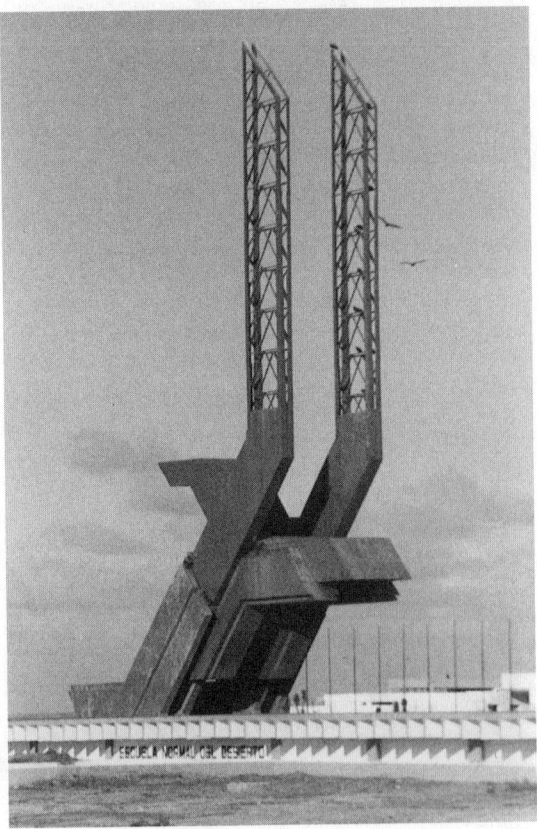

The towering eagle statue at the 28th parallel. The buildings at the base of the monument have now been taken over as part of an army base. Photo JW.

the first 1,000 colonists who acquire land in Lower California a lot of 160 acres is offered absolutely free." Colonists were actually transported to the Bahia Magdalena region to till the "pure black humus soil where the grass was higher than the shoulders of a horse." The lease was cancelled within a few years because the company was unable to meet some of its near-impossible terms.

Twenty years after issuance of the lease to Jacob Leese, Mexico passed a Law of Colonization as a means of raising foreign capital. Under this 1883 law, some thirty land concessions covering vast areas of the peninsula were granted to foreigners. Few were aggressively pursued, but as a result Mexican citizens were prohibited from developing the land of their own country and economic growth was impeded. This era of concessions was not to end until 1933. Because of its unsuccessful background in foreign concessions, the Mexican government today, understandably, maintains stringent control on private ownership of businesses and foreign ownership of land.

At least one of the Law of Colonization concessions was to be aggressively pursued. This concession was issued on July 17, 1885, for the mining of the large copper deposits found some years earlier at Santa Rosalia. It came into the hands of a French syndicate that operated the mine and smelter until 1954. Coal and coke were shipped from northern Europe in square-rigged ships to the smelter at Santa Rosalia, one of the last world ports used in the age of sail. The smelter, French buildings, port facilities, and machinery provide a must stop for the traveler along the Transpeninsular Highway.

Santa Rosalia's copper operation was also to be of importance to the peninsula's history in another way. Labor conditions there have been described by one Mexican historian as nauseating. This situation was to contribute to labor unrest and revolutionary uprisings in the future.

ACTIVITIES IN THE NORTH — As can be seen, historic events were concentrated in the southern portion of the peninsula up to this point. At the time of passage of the Law of Colonization in 1883, there were some 30,000 people in the entire peninsula. Only a few hundred lived in the northern portion. In this region, all of the missions had been abandoned. Ensenada was little more than a ranch, and Mexicali did not exist. But conditions were to change rapidly as the result of the land concessions issued by the federal government.

In 1884, large acreages of land in the north came under the control of New York capitalists who organized the International Company of Mexico. The usual land-promotion schemes were soon to follow, with the objective of selling land to gullible persons north of the border. However, the developers were required to make some investment in Mexico.

The town site of Ensenada was laid out, and various business enterprises sprang up. Within four years it had a population of approximately 1,400 people. Government inspectors issued such a glowing report that in 1887 the peninsula was formerly divided into two parts; and the *District of the North* was to have its own government, independent of La Paz.

In 1899 gold was discovered at El Alamo southeast

Steam engine monument at Santa Rosalia. A remnant of this historic town's heyday as a copper mining center. Other old mining machinery is also on display nearby. Photo JW.

of Ensenada. Thousands of miners poured in from north of the border. In the United States an irrigation project was undertaken to bring water from the Rio Colorado to the Imperial Valley. Small communities sprang up along the border as an indirect result of activities in the United States. One of these was Mexicali, which was founded in 1901 and was destined to become the capital city of the state of Baja California. Within a few years after the turn of the century, it became apparent that few projects of the International Company of Mexico were to flourish, but life in the north had taken root.

POLITICAL TURMOIL — In the minds of some North Americans, Mexico is a land of revolution and political unrest. Actually, the country has had a remarkably stable government for many decades, but its reputation in this regard suffers from its inaccurate association with revolutionary activities in countries in Central and South America, and from its own previous political turmoil in the years surrounding the turn of the century. This period will now be briefly reviewed.

There were small armed conflicts in the south in 1865, 1875, and again, in 1880. More serious unrest was to follow in both the north and south after the turn of the century. These activities reflected political turmoil in the nation as a whole, arising from the thirty-year dictatorial reign of President Porfirio Diaz and from various socialist and labor-oriented movements that were present in many parts of the world. Revolution was to force Diaz to resign in 1911, and his successor also was overthrown, and assassinated.

Also in 1911, revolution broke out in the newly populated areas in Baja California along the United States-Mexican border. This conflict was led by Mexican citizens based in the United States. Small armies of Mexicans were organized, and battles were waged with Mexican federal troops in the general area around Mexicali, Ensenada, and Tijuana. For a time, the latter town was controlled by the revolutionary forces. Additional federal troops from the Mexican mainland were sent to quell the uprisings. As a result of this unrest, some 30,000 United States troops were sent to the international border to protect their country's interests.

The revolutionary forces may be labeled *socialist*, although historians also utilize the terms *liberal* and *anarchist*. Their leaders clearly associated themselves with labor movements in the United States that advocated strikes, boycotts, and sabotage.

There was also added intrigue spawned by the political activities of foreigners who owned or controlled most of the land in the peninsula. There were always the threats, some real and some invented, that a popular uprising would be used as the rationale for the purchasing, or otherwise annexing, of the peninsula by the United States as had occurred with Texas some sixty-five years prior. Such an event would of course have been favored by the U.S. landowners.

Revolutionary action in the south was to follow that in the north by two years. It was to be more purely Mexican without the overtones of involvement by foreigners. The leader of this "Constitutionalist Revolution" was Felix Ortega, who organized a band of armed men who fought with federal troops in many battles at La Paz and in the mountains and towns to the south. During these campaigns, in 1913 to 1915, Ortega's forces frequently took refuge in the cape region mountains. Today's tourists drive through this same terrain on the Transpeninsular Highway between La Paz and San Jose del Cabo.

The size of the forces engaged in these battles was often considerably larger than those involved in the war with the United States sixty-five years earlier and thus represents the largest military operation ever to take place on the Baja peninsula. While the federal forces were to prevail, as in the north, Baja's citizens are proud that their efforts contributed to the civil liberties and land reforms gained on a national level from these revolutionary activities. The Constitution of 1917 was to be the result.

A very brief review of historic events that took place in the north and south, following the revolutionary period, will now be presented.

SUMMARY OF ACTIVITIES IN THE SOUTH — There were to be continuing revolutionary activities on the mainland, but a relative calm prevailed in the southern peninsula. Various public works projects were undertaken starting in 1920, including the beginning of construction of the Transpeninsular Highway between La Paz and Bahia Magdalena.

One of the most important events in the history of the peninsula took place in 1933, when the national government recovered the lands that had been encumbered for fifty years in various foreign-dominated concessions. It is from this very late date that the citizens of the peninsula were able to take up the colonization and development of their own land.

Agricultural settlement was started at Santo Domingo north of the highway junction at Ciudad Insurgentes. The extensive farming activities resulting from this early effort are clearly evident to the traveler. A second agricultural effort was started at San Juan de Los Planes in 1946 and may be visited on Highway 286.

During this period of agricultural development, the peninsula was to suffer the tragic loss of its pearl and oyster fishing industry. Between 1936 and 1949, the oysters in the Sea of Cortez were attacked by an unknown disease. The pearl, which had lured the original explorers and which had been a source of wealth for 400 years, was to disappear.

In its place, as a source of revenue, hotel and other tourist facilities came into being in the 1940s and tourism is now the region's principal industry. The population gradually increased, and in 1974 the southern territory proudly entered the Union. It, and Quintana Roo in the Yucatan peninsula were the last two Mexican states.

SUMMARY OF ACTIVITIES IN THE NORTH -- Following the revolutionary activities of the early 1900s, the northern territory was to see a period of spectacular development. Two progressive and skilled administrators were to govern during most years between 1915 and 1929. The second of these, Abelardo Rodriguez, was later to become President of the Mexican Republic. Roads, schools, and extensive other public works were developed.

Much of this activity was financed by astute taxation on gambling houses, prostitution, and drug traffic centering largely in Tijuana. In 1920, the Mexicans struck it rich with the coming of prohibition in the United States. The saloons and restaurants of Tijuana contributed on a massive scale to the prosperity of the territory. Its greatest natural resource was its location adjacent to the international boundary. As in the south, the inefficient land concessions were recaptured in the 1930s, but here the process was not as simple.

Most land in the fertile Valle de Mexicali west of the Rio Colorado was owned by foreign interests under the name of the Colorado River Land Company. These lands were not farmed, as existing irrigation systems served only the Imperial Valley to the north in the United States. Company lands were used only for grazing, with the labor performed by imported Chinese and other Asians.

It required protests by local Mexicans and action by the progressive President Lazaro Cardinas to bring about removal of the foreign interests and placement of the lands in the hands of Mexican farmers. This action was completed in 1937. New villages promptly sprung up, and the population rapidly increased.

Large-scale irrigation of the valley lands was to follow as the result of a water treaty with the United States in 1945, and the construction of the Morelos Dam on the Rio Colorado three years later. During these same years, construction work on Baja's only railroad was to take place. After its completion in 1948, for the first time in history there was a land transportation link between the Baja peninsula and the Mexican mainland that did not pass through the United States.

The Mexican constitution requires that a territory must have a population of 80,000 to merit admission into the national union. By 1950 there were actually more than 225,000 people. For this and other reasons, the northern territory became Mexico's twenty-ninth state on January 16, 1952.

CHAPTER 13
OUR DEVELOPING COUNTRY NEIGHBOR

This chapter is concerned with Baja's people and her political, economic, and social systems. Much of what is presented is of a positive nature and should provide encouragement to those interested in beneficial social change. And, I hope you might concur that acquiring an understanding of a country's people may, in the final analysis, be the most important benefit derived from travel to a foreign land. It is the objective of this chapter to assist in bringing this about.

In recent years there has been much reference in the news to the *third world* and to *developing countries*. Many of us may have a vague conception as to where these countries are located. We are perhaps most likely to think of nations in Africa, South America, and Southeast Asia. We may overlook the fact that the United States has such a country on its southern doorstep, and in visiting the rural areas of Baja California we are viewing some of the last sections of Mexico to experience modernization. The states of Baja California Sur, along with Quintana Roo in southeast Mexico, were the last to receive statehood in Mexico.

Mexico and Baja California are considerably more advanced than the average third world country. They nevertheless share many characteristics and problems in common with these nations. As a result, there is much to learn about the developing world through a trip not very far from home.

In other portions of this book, the material presented is founded on some degree of my personal experience or training. In the present chapter, I clearly tread beyond my fields of expertise. A friend once told me that I know just enough to be dangerous. Perhaps that will be the result here.

It will also be difficult to discuss the subjects of sociology, economics, and politics with complete objectivity. I apologize in advance for the almost certain bias of my personal convictions. Conversely, one rarely finds two economists or politicians who agree with each other, so perhaps I am after all on sound ground. I believe that the worst course of action I could take would be to omit discussion of these subjects.

MEXICO'S PEOPLE

Some seven-to-nine million Indians lived in what is present day Mexico when Cortez arrived in 1519. (A century later, their numbers were reduced to only 1 million by disease and warfare.) These various Indian nations had developed some of the most brilliant civilizations in the world. Today's Mexican is the end product of the intermarriage of these people with Europeans, almost all of Spanish origin. The result has been the emergence of a new race, the *Mestizos*. These are the people you will meet in Baja. There are millions of Indians still living in Mexico, but few of them reside in Baja. The only concentration of these people about which I am aware is in the Valle de San

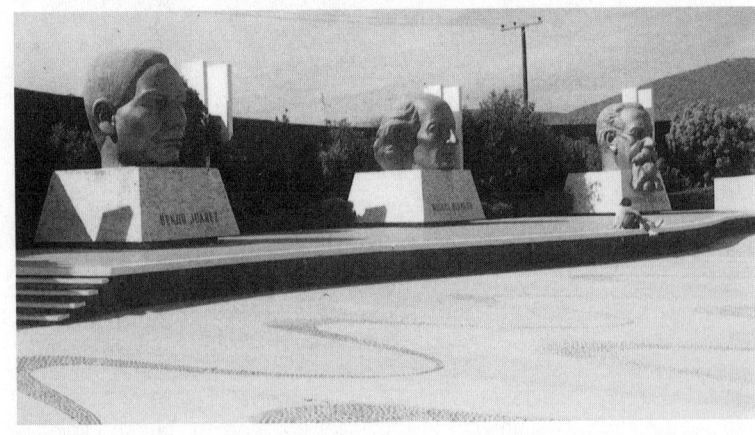

Statues of three of Mexico's famous men in the civic plaza in Ensenada. On the left is Benito Juarez the symbol of Mexico's nationhood and a full-blooded Zapotec Indian. He was a leader in the reform movement that resulted in the Constitution of 1857. Photo JW.

Quintin where they have migrated from southern Mexico to work in the area's farms (See Chapter 18).

POPULATION GROWTH — Although Mexico begat a new race of people, a case can now be made that they have made too much of a good thing. Mexico's exploding population is a serious national problem which tends to cancel out the country's significant economic advances.

The population of Mexico was 13.5 million in 1900. It grew slowly during the revolutionary period and was only 15 million in 1920. Continued slow growth brought the population to 19.6 million in 1940. Then after World War II the explosion began. There were 35 million in 1960, 46 million in 1970, 67 million in 1980 and 76 million by 1884. During these latter years, Mexico's population growth rate was 3.4 percent, one of the highest in the world.

During most of this period, the law, public policy, individual inclination and the influence of the Roman Catholic Church favored population growth. Perhaps influenced by the results of the 1970 census, the government came to realize that Mexico had a population problem. 1973 saw passage of the General Population Law which began a series of steps aimed at *Integrated Family Planning*. The result has been one of the most successful state-coordinated programs of family planning in the world.

Today, free contraceptives are supplied at government clinics; population and sex education are included in the public education system, and there is dissemination of material on these subjects on radio and television. Although abortion is prohibited by law, one in six pregnancies ends in this manner, often resulting in serious harm to the woman. The overall result of these actions has been a reduction of the population growth rate to 2.4 percent by 1984, and the national goal is to reduce it to *1.0 percent* by the year 2000.

The United Nations reports that many developing countries have achieved substantial reductions in birth rates and that the most important factors involved relate to improvements in (1) family planning, (2) health, and (3) education. (We will examine Mexico's progress in the last two areas in the pages to come.) Ironically, a byproduct of improvements in these areas is a marked increase in life expectancy, a factor that counteracts lowering of the birth rate. This has occurred in Mexico and accounts for much of the population explosion.

In Baja, my personal observations can attest to substantial population increases in nearly all communities, both large and small, although there has been no detectable increase in the number of communities themselves. Baja is still largely a thinly populated land although the traveler on Highway 1 must pass south of El Rosario to realize that this is true.

IMMIGRATION — Mexico's population growth is also of concern to the United States. Prior to World War II, the vast majority of immigrants into the United States came from western Europe. A quota system established by U.S. law had the effect of maintaining this European ethnic composition while minimizing the influx of peoples from other countries. Since the war, the law has changed and the

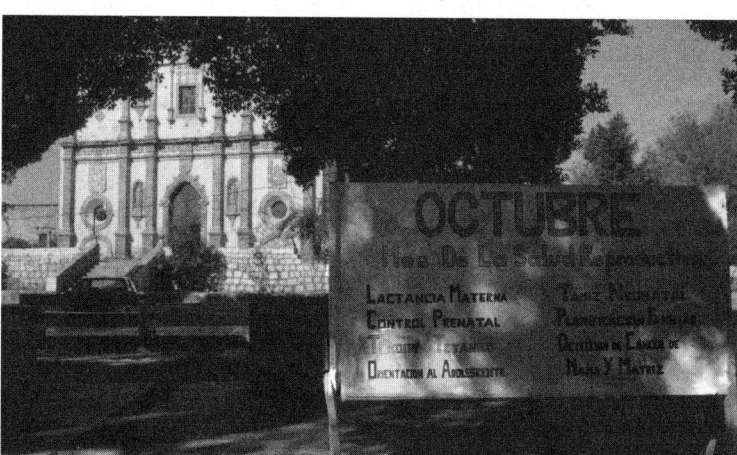

My Favorite Photo -- It is taken in the shady and peaceful civic plaza in the rural town of San Ignacio. In the background is the famous Dominican-built church where Roman Catholicism holds sway. To the right, across the street in the park, stands a sign reading "Octubre - Mes de la Salud de Reproductiva." (October - Month of Reproductive Health) Among the services offered, presumably at the local government health clinic, is "Planification Familiar" (Family Planning). The opposing views of Church and state on the issue of birth control could not be better illustrated. The photo was taken near the end of October and the sign was still standing proudly and unmolested. Photo BW.

country again is experiencing a wave of immigration, but this time consisting largely of peoples from Asia and Latin America. Approximately 40 percent of the total inflow comes from Mexico.

In the past a great majority of this immigration from Mexico entered the United States without permission. This situation aroused national concern and the U.S. Immigration Reform Act was passed in 1988. Then, Proposition 187 was placed on the November 1994 ballot in California. It called for widespread reductions in the expenditure of government funds received by persons residing in the state illegally. It passed by an overwhelming majority but much of it was overturned as the result of court appeal. U.S. border surveillance has been greatly increased, and national legislation aimed at preventing illegal immigration was passed into law in 1996.

Press reports indicate that activist groups representing Latino people in the United States look on this anti-immigration movement as also being anti-Latino -- more simply put, they feel it is racist. I thus anticipated that I might encounter backlash anti-American sentiment on the part of Mexicans in Baja during my recent visits. This was clearly not the case. I suspect that most Mexicans have far more pressing personal concerns on their minds than American politics. I might also note, that I personally have no trouble in distinguishing between my support for control of illegal immigration and my affection for the Mexican people. In other words, support for enforcement of the law does not translate into racism. Perhaps you might wish to test your owns views on these issues as you travel in Baja.

Birth rates in the United States have declined in recent years reaching a record low in 1977 and immigration now accounts for much of the country's population growth. Of every 100 new U.S. residents, only 64 are born is the country with 34 arriving as legal immigrants. If the present trends continue, a time will come in the next century when all population growth will come from immigration. I make no judgements as to whether this situation is good or bad, but it does raise questions about the future size and ethnic proportions of the United States.

GOVERNMENT AND POLITICS

Although Mexico freed herself from Spanish rule in 1821, the new nation continued to be dominated by the institutions of the past. The country was ruled by authoritarian leaders. The Catholic Church controlled from one-third to one-half of the national wealth and owned nearly one-half of the land. All but 3 percent of the remaining land was vested in the hands of a mere 830, mostly absentee owners.

The *Mestizos* gradually grew to dominate the racial composition of the country and became the core of various liberal movements which culminated in the revolution of 1910. The Constitution of February 5, 1917 resulted from this struggle. Almost all of Mexico's current political and economic institutions and progress stem from this date and constitution. The Mexican citizen's civil rights guarantees are contained in the first 29 articles. Mexico's Indian, rather than her Spanish, heritage predominate after 1917.

The new constitution also severely limits the position of the Catholic Church. Today the church may not own property and priests are not permitted to vote or wear clerical garb in public. (NOTE - Press reports in early 1992 indicate that the Mexican congress has given preliminary approval to a series of constitutional reforms that would give the Church formal recognition by the government. I am sorry that I cannot update this report.)

The ninety-six years between Mexico's independence from Spain (1821) and enactment of her present constitution (1917) were filled with upheaval. There were wars with other nations, civil war, the loss of one-half the nation's territory to the United States, and political, economic, and social degeneration. It can be seen that while western civilization was well established in Mexico far earlier than in Canada and the United States, Mexico's modern era was to get a very late and tumultuous start. Its underdeveloped status is a product of its history.

THE GOVERNMENT — Although the Constitution of 1917 establishes a tripartite division of power between the executive, legislative, and judicial branches of the government, the authority of the executive far exceeds that of the latter two. The President is elected by universal suffrage for a six-year term. (Minimum voting age is 18.) An individual may serve only one term. The most recent presidential election was held in 1994. The election campaign received widespread press coverage in the United States as one of the leading presidential candidates was assassinated in Tijuana. The President appoints a cabinet to oversee more than twenty ministries, or *Sectetarias*. You will see this word and the names of the various ministries in numerous places in your travels in Baja California.

There are two houses of the national legislature. The Senate is composed of two individuals elected for six-year terms from each of the thirty-one states and the Federal District. The Chamber of Deputies is made-up of over 200 members elected for three-year terms. Each member represents a specific number of citizens. The members of both houses are barred from reelection, so there is an often disruptive turnover in both the legislature and the ministries following elections.

The state governments consist of an elected Governor and a Chamber of Deputies, but the autonomy of the states is limited. The federal system is not the result of a merging compact between independent states as in the United States. In Mexico, the states have been created by the national government. Federal financing and administration of programs dominate at all levels, and the states are expected to enforce federal law. While traveling in Baja, you will see the names and acronyms of federal agencies on signs and government construction projects throughout the peninsula. (NOTE - My most recent travels in Baja indicate a reduction of a least the outward signs of the federal government. Perhaps this is merely because I have grown accustomed to Mexican conditions, but I believe it reflects the countries steady move away from socialistic tendencies over the last decade.)

Each of Baja's two states is divided into municipalities similar to those of counties in the United States. The cities do not incorporate and establish separate governments. Thus, the official that tourists may refer to as the Mayor of Ensenada is in fact the *Presidente Municipal* of an area of hundreds of square miles which includes many communities other than

PAN - The symbol of the National Action Party. In Spanish, the word pan means bread. Photo BW.

Ensenada. The municipalities of the peninsula are shown in an accompanying table. Look for the *Palacio Municipal* (municipal palace) when you visit the towns which are the *Cabacera Municipal* (the seat of government). The municipal boundaries are also marked by signs along the Transpeninsular Highway.

In other towns, the government building will bear the name *Delegado Municipal*. The *Delegado* (delegate) is an official appointed by the *Presidente Municipal* to represent him in the area in question. In the smallest communities, there are *subdelegados*. Thus, the citizens of a small town find themselves governed by a Subdelegado, Delegado, Presidente Municipal, Gobernador, and finally, El Presidente.

POLITICS — A common characteristic of developing countries throughout the world is the presence of one dominant political party. Mexico has been no exception. Since 1929, the country's government has been dominated at all levels by the *Partido Revolucionario Institucion* (Institutional Revolutionary Party). You will see the PRI symbol in many places in Baja.

In reading of the immense powers of the Mexican president, and the domination of the PRI, one could easily come to the conclusion that the country's government should be classified as a dictatorship. Certainly, one party dominance has resulted in substantial government corruption. Nevertheless, the PRI

MUNICIPALITIES

MUNICIPIO*	CABACERA** MUNICIPAL
BAJA CALIFORNIA	
Tijuana	Tijuana
Tecate	Tecate
Mexicali	Mexicali
Ensenada	Ensenada
BAJA CALIFORNIA SUR	
Mulege	Santa Rosalia
Comondu	Ciudad Constitucion
La Paz	La Paz
Los Cabos	San Jose del Cabo

* MUNICIPIO -------- Municipality
** CABACERA MUNICIPAL --- Seat of government

has provided Mexico with a stable administration for decades. There is a minimum of domination by the military, and social programs aimed at providing a better life for the masses are in evidence everywhere.

In the past the PRI party's nominees for president, governors, and other officials was tantamount to their being elected. They often received some 90 percent of the vote although it has been alleged that vote fraud was widespread.

The principal opposition party has been the *Partido de Accion Nacional* (National Action Party). Its acronym is PAN. PAN's agenda can best be described as "conservative" and it is supported by the business community and the Catholic Church. However, emerging in 1988 was a coalition of several liberal-leaning parties who adapted the name Partido de la Revolucion Democratica or PRD, who along with the PAN, mounted a serious challenge to PRI. Vote counting fraud was again charged by the opposition parties, and the PRI candidate was eventually announced to have won by a narrow 50.5 percent. It is widely alleged that PRI actually lost the election.

Reading the American media one is lead to believe that the current PRI administration has made some significant modifications in the rules of the political game in Mexico. Perhaps as a result, the midterm election of 1997 saw the two opposition parties, PAN and PRD, amass sufficient delegates so that together they represented a majority of one of Mexico's two legislative bodies. Even though their respective political positions are at the two opposite extremes of Mexican politics, they can for the first time combine to force political compromise upon the PRI. The American press widely reported this event as a watershed change in Mexican politics.

It would thus appear that Mexico is now on the threshold a multiparty political system and sev-

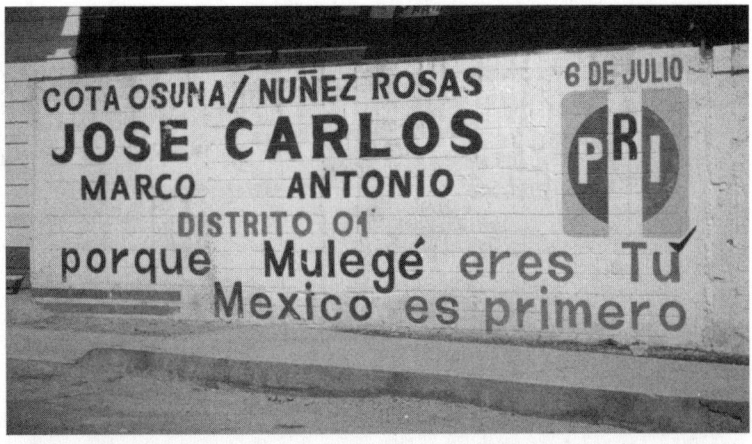

Here we see a notice for PRI candidate Jose Carlos painted on a wall in a rural Baja town. Note the PRI symbol on the right. Signs such as this one usually remain in place long after the election is over. Photo BW.

eral state's governors are now from opposition parties. Some may conclude that traveling in Mexico is unwise because of this political situation. I firmly believe this to be untrue. In my view the political changes occurring in Mexico are positive and will have no direct effects on foreign visitors. My travels in Baja after the 1988, 1994 and 1997 elections have been no different than they were in past years.

THE MILITARY — Those who keep abreast of current events in developing countries are well aware that many nations' military establishments dominate and often overthrow the civilian authority. This was true in Mexico in the distant past, but it is generally conceded today that the military has only modest influence on the government. The last president who was also a general left office in 1942.

Here is the office (oficina) of the Revolutionary Democratic Party in the town of Ciudad Insurgentes. The PRD symbol is painted to the right of the door. Photo BW.

Chapter 13

The Mexican army, air force, and navy are assigned the responsibility of defending the independence of the country, but from a practical standpoint, their most significant mission is the preservation of internal order. The navy patrols the coastline and in general assumes the duties assigned to the Coast Guard in the United States. Over the years, the army has been called on to suppress riots and other forms of civil unrest, to control illicit drug traffic, to register firearms, and to undertake similar activities. In effect, the army is assigned duties that citizens of Canada and the United States would normally associate with the civil police.

Because of their policing responsibilities, the army and navy are much in evidence to the tourist in Baja, which, from a public relations standpoint, is unfortunate. These people normally carry automatic rifles and those of us from north of the border tend to associate such weapons with trouble. A blue-uniformed policeman with a sidearm in the United States is one thing; a soldier in brown combat fatigues and helmet carrying a machine gun, in a country where the traveler is a bit squeamish to begin with, is quite another.

This situation was observed to be considerably enhanced during our 1997 survey as the military were manning large numbers of drug and gun checkpoints along Baja's highways. In addition, a full battalion of soldiers is now housed at a base striding the highway at the 28th parallel state line. There were in fact so many soldiers and checkpoints in evidence that one could readily become accustomed to them and emotionally move from fear to being annoyed.

My messages here are that you will frequently see the *militar*, that their role is keeping the peace, and that you should not be concerned. However, the Mexican government would be well advised to prevail upon the military to put their weapons out of sight in the vicinity of tourists and to provide them with public relations training. My observations would indicate that they have done the latter but not the former.

You will see the military at their encampments in many peninsula communities. There are also small detachments at recreation spots such as Puerto Escondido and Santispac. Usually there is an enlisted man on guard duty who speaks no English and who has an exaggerated view of the importance of his assignment. I have found them almost universally brusque, quick to wave their rifle about, and obviously wanting me to depart. I have also found that if you can arrange to see an officer, only courtesy and helpfulness prevail. My counsel is to avoid the military unless you have a particular need, and then ask for the brass.

MEXICO'S ECONOMY

A DEVELOPING COUNTRY — A majority of the countries in the world are considered developing countries. They are endeavoring to improve the quality of life of their people through industrialization and other means. From an economic standpoint, such a country is defined as "one that has not yet reached a stage of economic development characterized by the growth of industrialization, and a level of national income sufficient to yield the domestic savings required to finance the investment necessary for further growth." This complex definition simply means that a developing country must rely on foreign investment and international borrowing to fuel its economic growth. During the 1970s and 80s, Mexico, along with Brazil, led the world in such borrowing. Mexico made rapid industrial growth and is now classified by the World Bank as a *Newly Industrialized Country* and as a *Middle Income Developing Country*.

This situation was clearly apparent in Baja during the mid 1980's. The initial field work needed to produce this book was done from about 1984 to 1988. The dominant impression that lingers in my mind from this period was that government developmental activities were everywhere. There were new roads, water lines, schools, tourist facilities and everything imaginable. And on one's next trip, many of these projects were abandoned or had received little maintenance. One had to ask, "Mexico is supposed to be a poor country, where is the money coming from for all this development?" International borrowing was no doubt the answer. But, by this same period, borrowing became Mexico's curse, and the country's payments on its immense national debt threatened to collapse its economy. The situation was known as *La Crisis* (the crisis).

Mexico apparently learned from the crisis. Developmental activities in much of Baja have clearly slowed down, and the emphasis has shifted from government to private projects. Private developments have proceeded rapidly in the last several years in the Cape Area at the peninsula's southern tip and in the industrial areas along the U.S. border. But, the balance of Baja has experienced more moderate growth, and in some cases, little at all.

DISTANT NEIGHBORS

USA

Perhaps nowhere in the world do two neighbors (the USA and Mexico) understand each other so little. The purpose of Alan Riding's Book is to bridge this gap and make Mexico more accessible to non-Mexicans. Great coverage on: the Mexicans; a concise historical summary; the political system; economic, social, and population problems; Mexico City; foreign policy; and much more.

By ALAN RIDING

NO MAPS, NO PHOTOS. JUST 564 PAGES OF THE MEATIEST TEXT YOU WILL EVER READ

A FOREIGN AFFAIRS BEST SELLER

Author Alan Riding was born in Brazil and educated in England. He has spent 12-years as a journalist in Mexico for various publications including 6-years as the New York Times bureau chief. I learned more about Mexico in a few hours with this book than I had in years of travel in the country. Its simbly **the best book I have ever read about Mexico.**
Jack Williams

Mexico

FOREIGN INVESTMENT — In 1973, Mexico enacted the Foreign Investment Law. It was designed to *promote foreign investment*, while at the same time ensuring the *government's autonomy and control over the country's economy*. Under this law, a foreign investor's interest in a commercial enterprise was limited to 49 percent while a Mexican national was required to own the controlling 51 percent. Mexico coveted foreign assistance, but on its own terms.

In addition, a foreigner could not own real estate within 100 kilometers of the border or 50 kilometers of the coastline. That very well blankets the desirable locations in the Baja peninsula. Foreign interest in land was secured through a trust arrangement which required that after thirty years the trust must be sold to *persons or entities capable of acquiring legal title*. It is understandable why Mexico would not wish to engender a recurrence of the land frauds and other negative aspects of past foreign control of its assets, but many feel that these rules inhibit, rather than encourage, investment.

As of 1991 some of Mexico's landownership laws have been changed or are in the process of change. Then 1994 saw passage of the North American Free Trade Agreement. How all of these developments will effect development in Mexico is beyond my field of expertise. What little I know about these matters leads me to suggest caution to potential investors and to advise that they seek the counsel of a competent attorney not connected with persons offering land for

sale or lease. Also note the two business related books offered in the BAJA BOOKSHELF.

A unique form of foreign investment, the *maquiladora* program, occurs at Baja's border cities. It started two decades ago when the Mexican government permitted these cities merchants to import U.S. goods duty free so that local citizens would not do their shopping north of the border. In due course, U.S. manufacturers established hundreds of assembly plants across the border where finished products are produced by cheap, nonunionized Mexican labor from U.S. raw materials imported duty free. When shipped back north, the U.S. tariff is paid only on the value added. The two chief maquiladora cities in Baja are Tijuana and Mexicali but Tecate has also grown significantly.

SOCIALISM — A great majority of the world's developing nations look on their economies as *socialistic*. Mexico has fit this mold. Certainly, they have not been *communistic* as there is much private land and thousands of small private businesses, but major enterprises have been government owned or controlled. During La Crisis the banks were nationalized as was one of the countries airlines.

However, the winds of change have been blowing. During the last several years hundreds of government businesses have been moved into the private sector. Mexico, along with the countries of Eastern Europe, the former Soviet Union and much of Latin America that experimented with socialism are finding it prudent to move rapidly toward a capitalistic

The extensive port facilities at Ensenada built by the Mexican government. Photo JW.

economic system. These changes appear to be meeting with success. The Inter-American Bank recently reported that Mexico and other Latin American countries had made impressive economic gains in 1991 after the "lost decade" of the 1980.

But while change is occurring, much of socialism remains. The CONASUPO stores are government owned as is much of the land with tourism potential brokered by FONATUR. The entire fishing industry is based on government-controlled and financed cooperatives, and its modern fishing fleet has been constructed with federal funds. Government planning and control is evident to the traveler in most aspects of Mexico's social and economic systems.

It is my understanding that Canada can be classified as somewhat more socialistic than the United States, but Mexico is clearly far more socialistic than either. Travel to Baja thus gives citizens of these two countries an opportunity to view a nation different from their own. Talk to the Mexicans; see how they view their socialist country and how they view the changes that are taking place. How would you change Mexico if, suddenly, you were president? After all, you have to think about something while lying there in the sun.

LAND REFORM — Since the 1910 revolution, much of Mexico's land has been distributed to the people. In Baja, one principal method of accomplishing this has been the *ejido*. You will see this word on maps and on countless road signs along the highways, and it is easy

to arrive at the conclusion that it means village or town. This is not the case. An ejido is a landholding institution established under Mexican law. There were over 28,000 of them in Mexico in 1990.

It is the ejido rather than the individual that has been made the legal proprietor of the land. Land may be worked on a cooperative basis or may be distributed to individuals who acquire what are called usufructuary rights. Land may be passed on through inheritance, but it is lost if not worked for two consecutive years. The ejido is administered by elected officials. Here, again, is another Mexican institution which has skirted the private land and capitalist systems we are accustomed to in Canada and the United States.

But the ejido system has recently undergone change. In the past, ejido farmers had been unable to secure credit for seed and machinery because they did not own the land they farmed. And as farmers divided their plots among their children, the average acreage of an ejido holding dwindled to an unprofitable size. In Baja, there is clear evidence of areas that have been cultivated that are submarginal for such purposes.

In 1992, the Mexican constitution was amended so that ejido members could obtain title to their lands, and could in turn sell or lease them to others. Apparently prior law strictly prohibited the sale or lease of ejido property. The fact that sizeable hotels, trailer courts and residential improvements in Baja have been leased from ejido's by American investors for many years is no doubt an indication that Mexicans also trade in the old adage that "A sucker is born every minute."

Ejidos engage in enterprises other than farming. Members of ejidos work in the CONASUPO stores; there is a mining ejido in the town of El Triunfo on Highway 1, south of La Paz; and ejidos run camping areas on the highway to La Bufadora, near Ensenada, and at the whale-watching site at Scammon's lagoon.

DEVELOPMENTAL ACTIVITIES

Publications by the United Nations and the World Bank discuss common problems which must be addressed by all developing countries. Of these, family planning, the need for industrialization, and land reform have already been discussed. This section briefly reviews several others. An effort has been made to emphasize items that will be of interest to the tourist and can be seen while traveling in the Baja peninsula.

In reading about Mexico and other developing countries, it is often noted that progress has been made but that its benefits have not spread to the rural areas. While I am sure this is true to some extent in Mexico, I can attest that there are clear evidences of government-sponsored improvements in even the smallest and most remote of Baja's villages. Even at isolated fish camps the fishermen's boats are modern fiberglass pangas provided by government-sponsored cooperatives, and access may be over a newly modernized road.

The distribution of income in Mexico is held to be amongst the most inequitable in the world and the press reports that this gap is widening as the result of the governments economic policy of privatization, free markets and integration into the global economy. But it is also evident, at least to this observer, that some degree of social improvement is being shared by most of Baja's citizens. It is a simple matter of observation to note that there are far more late model cars and trucks on Baja's streets and highways than there were only a few years ago. The stores in all the towns are full of merchandize and they are filled with Mexicans not just tourists. It is widely reported that Mexico's government officials are corrupt and amass sizeable personal fortunes. All I can say is that they seem to be letting some of the country's wealth slip through their fingers and trickle down to a growing middle class. Perhaps Baja is somewhat better off

than other parts of Mexico as there is considerable industrialization, it benefits from its position adjacent to the United States and it enjoys considerable tourism.

AGRICULTURAL PRODUCTION — The development of Baja's agricultural lands was almost totally prevented until 1933 due to the presence of various foreign land leases. (See Chapter 12 HISTORY.) Today you will see substantial farming areas in (1) the Valle de Mexicali near the mouth of the Rio Colorado, (2) along the Pacific coast from Ensenada to south of San Quintin, (3) in the desert surrounding Ciudad Constitucion and Ciudad Insurgentes, (4) in the desert around the community of Vizcaino south of Guerrero Negro, and (5) in the plains near San Juan de los Planes southeast of La Paz. Water for irrigation comes from deep wells.

EDUCATION — You will see recently constructed school buildings in many locations. Often they are clearly the newest buildings in town. Sometimes there is even a school building and no community. Look for one-room school houses at crossroads along the highways.

Be alert for the *Jardin de Ninos* (kindergarten) where attendance is optional for three years for children from ages four to six. Most of the *escuelas* (schools) will bear the name *Primaria* (primary). Here, attendance is mandatory from ages six to fourteen, or until six grades are completed. Middle schools, *Secundaria* (secondary), *Secundaria-Tecnico* (secondary-technical), and *Tecnico* (technical) are less in evidence to the traveler but are frequently seen if you drive off the main roads.

The number of new schools is impressive, as is the fact that the children are frequently well dressed. There is an obvious pride taken in the children. Sadly, you must keep in mind that many of the people you will meet have no more than a sixth-grade education, but progress is clearly evident.

MEDICAL SERVICES — There are private doctors in Mexico, but most people receive medical attention at clinics and hospitals operated by the *Instituto Mexicano de Seguro Social* (Mexican Social Security Institute). Look for the large letters IMSS on the front of the buildings. Most of them are new facilities in the smaller towns. Social security refers to health services in Mexico rather than to retirement pensions as in the United States.

WATER AND SEWAGE — A major water pipeline was constructed early in the 1970s from water sources in the mountains north of San Jose del Cabo, all along Highway 1 to Cabo San Lucas. FONATUR has developed a new water system from wells for Loreto and the tourist facilities at Nopolo. On a recent visit to Mulege, I saw roads being torn up for new pipelines. In 1986, a large water line was constructed to serve the coastal towns south of Guerrero Negro. This line will replace salt water conversion plants which are themselves only a few years old. The ocean-cruisers always fill their tanks from city water lines at La Paz and with no ill effect. These and other signs of safe water and sewer systems are in clear evidence throughout the peninsula.

ELECTRIC POWER — There are three major diesel-fueled electric power plants in Baja, all in clear view to the traveler. The northern plant is located between Highway 1-D and the coast near Rosarito, south of Tijuana. The southern plant is adjacent to the highway between La Paz and Pichilingue. The most recent plant lies a few miles inland from San Carlos near Bahia Magdalena.

COMMUNICATIONS — Baja's telephone system has been described in some detail in Chapter 8 (TRAVELING IN BAJA). The system is founded on modern microwave radio techniques. Watch for the numerous microwave radio towers along the main highways. A major new communications cable was observed being buried along the main highways in southern Baja during our 1997 survey.

CONSERVATION -- About 1990 I attended a lecture by an American biologist who looked upon Mexican conservation activities as a joke. In his view, Mexican politics and economic concerns held sway over environmental matters. I cannot say to what degree this is still true, but I can report the following positive observation. (1) There is a modern biological center (Centro de Investigaciones Biologicas de Baja California Sur located near La Paz (See La Paz Area Map in Chapter 22). Much of the center's work is concentrated in the Sierra de la Laguna mountains east of Todos Santos and in the Vizcaino Desert (La Reserva de la Biosfera el Vizcaino) region of Baja California Sur. (2) There are two long standing National Parks in the state of Baja California and a new park has now been established covering the islands in the Sea of Cortez east of Loreto. (3) The American manager of the manganese processing operation at Santa Rosalia informed me in 1995 that the environmental regula-

tions he must follow differ little from those encountered in the United States.

TRANSPORTATION — Hundreds of miles of new roads were constructed in Baja during the 1980s. (See Chapter 3 TRANSPORTATION.) More recwnt road building has been largely limited to improvement of the streets within existing communities, converting Highway 1 to 4-lanes from the Los Cabos Airport to Cabo San Lucas and development of a 4-lane limited access highway along the U.S. border from Tijuana to Mexicali.

Although the standards of Baja's roads are considerably lower than those encountered north of the border, they meet the needs of the Mexican people and are an immense improvement over what was available only a few years ago. In addition, the past two decades have seen the construction of several international airports, numerous smaller airfields, and port facilities at Ensenada, San Carlos, La Paz and several other places.

DISTANT NEIGHBORS

Since producing *The Magnificent Peninsula* I have had to guard against the tendency of being overly critical of the works of other writers, particularly when their subject is Mexico. Professional jealousy strikes us all. I note this shortcoming to add extra weight to my uncompromising praise for Alan Riding's 1984 best-selling *Distant Neighbors*. It is must reading for anyone seriously interested in understanding Mexico and Mexicans.

Here in *The Magnificent Peninsula* I have endeavored to enhance your ability to interpret and enjoy what you see in Baja California. *Distant Neighbors* presents a remarkable account about the things in Mexico that you can't see. If this chapter on OUR DEVELOPING COUNTRY NEIGHBOR has aroused your interest, you need to know that it has merely scratched the surface. *Distant Neighbors* plows far deeper.

Distant Neighbors is available from the BAJA BOOK-SHELF in the Appendix. But trust me, I am not making this endorsement to make money. Alan's book sells for so little that my profit is not worth the promotional effort. It is offered for sale because I believe it is the best book I have ever read on Mexico, that you will enjoy it, and that it will help in achieving mutual understanding between those of us who have been cast together on the North American continent.

SUMMARY

What is set forth here are my personal views about my observations concerning social and economic progress in Baja. They were largely written for editions of this book. See the NOTE at the end of this summary for my current observations.

First, it is evident that there has in fact been substantial economic and social progress. Much has been accomplished between my first visit to Baja and my most recent, but perhaps progress has been a bit too swift. The leaders of developing countries are under tremendous pressures to produce progress rapidly. If they don't, they face political upheaval. In Mexico, as in other nations, much of this progress has been financed through the borrowing of foreign capital and with the vehicle of deficit federal spending. The result in the mid 1980s was a near collapse of the Mexican economy.

The hand of the federal government is everywhere. It has built hotels and airfields that simple observation indicates are financial liabilities. The creation of jobs, not profitability, seems to be the objective. I have observed dozens of government projects, ranging from the ferry terminal at Puerto Escondido to the buildings in the center of the highway at the state line, that lie unused and unrepaired (The latter facility has now been taken over by the Mexican army). The major airport between Santa Rosalia and Mulege lies with little use.

The Mexican people must come to grips with the question of how many non-income-producing government services they can afford to provide for themselves. We, in Canada and the U.S., also face this same question, but I believe it is more aggravated in Mexico. Perhaps what we observe while traveling in Baja can offer an insight into addressing such problems in our own countries.

It is my personal view that the administration of President Salinas (1988 to 1994) recognized the shortcomings that have been noted above and moved very early in his administration to make major economic changes. Mexico also pressed hard to secure the passage of the North American Free Trade Agreement with the United States and Canada. Unfortunately, many recent changes designed to produce long-term benifit have more immediate negative impacts on working people. This is occuring all over the world as countries move away from socialism to market-oriented economies.

A final observation. I have come to the conclusion that one of Mexico's most pressing problems involves the construction and maintenance standards of almost everything one sees. Often the traveler can observe partially completed buildings and other structures lying unused. Concrete is often mixed by a shovel in a small depression in the sand pile with little concern for the proportions of its ingredients. The use of reinforced concrete construction in multi-storied buildings, and the total lack of structural steel, is frightening, as the country found to its sorrow in the 1985 Mexico City earthquake. Fortunately, there are few such buildings in Baja.

Much of what is completed appears to receive little maintenance. The doors of public buildings hang from their hinges, windows are broken and not repaired, letters fall from signs and are not replaced. It is as if no one in the community possesses a screwdriver, wrench, or other simple hand tools, and that the most common repair items from a hardware store are unavailable. Alan Riding's *Distant Neighbors* notes that Mexican's have little desire to contribute to the upkeep of such public improvements. This lies in sharp contrast to the obvious pride they take in their persons and their own homes. Perhaps their lack of concern for public property lies in the "cradle to the grave" philosophy inherent in socialism.

NOTE -- Much of the above summary material was written for previous editions of this book. I have left it largely in tack, if for no other reason than to form a basis for reporting that conditions in Baja have improved in recent years. I do not recall seeing any new governmental white elephants in the past several years. Road maintenance is considerably improved over the past, particularly in Baja California Sur. The new four-lane highway from Tijuana to Mexicali appears to be of excellent quality. The major new resort developments in the Cape Area are first class in appearance and are well maintained. The move from government to private ownership of businesses may be having its effect. Many conditions experienced in Baja are still substantially below what one encounters North-of-the-Border, but clearly they are improving.

PART III
THE GRAND TOUR

The pages ahead will guide the reader along more than 3,100 miles of the Magnificent Peninsula's roadways. Road log information is tied to kilometer post signs which adjoin all the principal highways.

BAJA DISTANCE TABLE

Top line is distance in miles
Bottom line is distance in kilometers
Figures based on use of Highway 1-D between Tijuana and Ensenada.

All distances are over Highway 1 except for the last line which utilizes the Highway 1 and Highway 19 route between La Paz and Cabo San Lucas.

From \ To	Tijuana	Ensenada	Colonet	San Quintin	El Rosario	Catavina	Bahia de los Angeles Junction	State Line	San Ignacio	Santa Rosalia	Mulege	Loreto	Ciudad Insurgentes	La Paz
Ensenada	68 / 109													
Colonet	145 / 234	77 / 125												
San Quintin	185 / 299	118 / 190	39 / 61											
El Rosario	223 / 360	156 / 251	78 / 126	38 / 61										
Catavina	297 / 479	239 / 370	157 / 245	112 / 180	74 / 119									
Bahia de los Angeles Junction	363 / 585	295 / 476	218 / 351	177 / 286	140 / 225	66 / 106								
State Line	442 / 713	374 / 604	297 / 479	257 / 414	219 / 353	145 / 234	79 / 128							
San Ignacio	533 / 860	466 / 751	388 / 626	348 / 561	310 / 500	236 / 381	171 / 275	91 / 147						
Santa Rosalia	579 / 934	512 / 825	434 / 700	394 / 635	356 / 574	282 / 455	216 / 349	137 / 221	46 / 74					
Mulege	617 / 995	549 / 886	472 / 761	432 / 696	394 / 635	320 / 516	254 / 410	175 / 282	84 / 135	38 / 61				
Loreto	701 / 1131	634 / 1022	556 / 897	516 / 832	478 / 771	404 / 652	339 / 546	259 / 418	168 / 271	122 / 197	84 / 136			
Ciudad Insurgentes	776 / 1251	708 / 1142	631 / 1017	590 / 952	552 / 891	479 / 772	413 / 666	334 / 538	242 / 391	197 / 317	159 / 256	74 / 120		
La Paz	924 / 1490	856 / 1381	778 / 1256	738 / 1191	701 / 1130	627 / 1011	561 / 905	482 / 777	391 / 630	345 / 556	307 / 495	223 / 359	148 / 239	
Cabo San Lucas Via Highway 1.	1059 / 1711	993 / 1604	916 / 1477	875 / 1412	838 / 1351	764 / 1232	698 / 1126	619 / 998	528 / 851	482 / 777	444 / 716	360 / 580	285 / 460	137 / 221
Cabo San Lucas Via Highway 1 & 19.	1003 / 1618	936 / 1509	858 / 1384	818 / 1319	777 / 1254	706 / 1139	604 / 1033	561 / 905	470 / 758	424 / 684	386 / 629	302 / 487	228 / 367	79 / 128

GASOLINE STATIONS (PEMEX) ALONG HIGHWAY 1

KILOMETERS TO MILES

Kilometers	Miles	Kilometers	Miles
1	0.62	30	18.6
2	1.24	40	24.8
3	1.86	50	31.0
4	2.48	60	37.2
5	3.10	70	43.4
10	6.20	80	49.6
15	9.30	90	55.8
20	12.40	100	62.0

1 mile = 1.61 kilometers. To convert kilometers to miles divide by 2 & add 25%.

LITERS TO GALLONS

Liters	Gallons		
1	0.26	40	10.57
2	0.53	50	13.21
3	0.79	60	15.85
4	1.06	70	18.49
5	1.32	80	21.14
10	2.64	90	23.78
20	5.28	100	26.42
30	7.93	150	39.63

1 gallon = 3.78 liters.

INTRODUCTION TO PART III

Now that you have completed the background and introductory materials in PARTS I and II, you are ready to begin your PART III - GRAND TOUR of the Magnificent Peninsula.

What is the GRAND TOUR? It has three basic objectives. These are to provide:

1. Essential travel directions needed for use of the main highways and secondary roads. The maps found in each chapter will be principal tools. The material presented has been kept from becoming an all-inclusive road log of everything one encounters. This has been done because such an exhaustive treatment simply is not necessary. It is possible for the first-time traveler to become temporarily disoriented within the larger cities, but on the open road it would really take special effort to become lost. There are very few paved side roads, and I submit that most people could find their way from Tijuana to Cabo San Lucas by adhering to only one instruction, "Stay on the blacktop and follow your nose."

2. *Travel directions on recommended side trips off the main highways. The symbol* SIDE TRIP *will alert you to this information. This material is printed in Italics type as is this paragraph. The text will frequently be supplemented by large-scale local maps.*

3. Special information concerning local history, vegetation, geology, etc., which builds upon the background material presented in PART II - HIGHER NEEDS. In this regard, don't forget to consult the **GLOSSARY** found in the appendix. Many of the words and acronyms it presents are seen along Baja's highways, and in the towns you will visit. It can be a substantial help in increasing your understanding of the Spanish language.

The GRAND TOUR is presented in twelve chapters. The first three cover the border towns along Highway 2, Mexicali to Highway 1, and Highway 3. The eight that follow relate to the Transpeninsular High-

way. The concluding chapter describes the region accessible by Highway 19, the Pacific coast highway to Cabo San Lucas via Todos Santos.

Several other techniques are also used throughout the GRAND TOUR. These are as follows:

KILOMETER POSTS AND HIGHWAY SECTIONS — To many of us, *milepost* is a common word. Unfortunately few roads in the United States have them. Most U.S. highways are marked with long numbers that give the distance to the one-hundredth of a foot from the initial point of the construction survey, a place known only to God and the highway department. In Baja, the road engineers have shared their secret with travelers. Along all main highways you will find numbered white signs every kilometer. Outside of the cities, hotels and other businesses will use the nearest kilometer as their mailing address.

The Mexican highway department has divided the Transpeninsular Highway into nine sections. For the purposes of this book, these sections have been desig-

KILOMETER POST SIGN

Km
4
7

Originally the kilometer numbers were painted on stubby concrete posts. These have now been replaced with metal signs as shown.

nated by the letters **A** through **J**. The kilometer post numbers begin with zero in each section. The location of each section, along with its distances in kilometers and miles, is shown in an accompanying map. In the northern state of Baja California, the numbers run consecutively from north to south. To add zest to your travels, they proceed from south to north in Baja California Sur. In this state, the south-bound traveler encounters the numbers in reverse order.

The eight chapters of this book that cover the Transpeninsular Highway begin and end at the same places as the highway sections, except that in two cases, two sections are combined in one chapter. (See the *Kilometer Post Sections* map.)

If you need to be alerted to look for some particular point of interest, the GRAND TOUR will reference it to the *nearest* kilometer post. All you need to do is watch for the proper kilometer post without the necessity of keeping track of your odometer readings from some obscure reference point. Canadian drivers should be particularly pleased with this system as their highways and odometers utilize the metric system.

Knowledge of sectional breakpoint locations also allows you to use the posts to assess your progress all along the way. Kilometer post numbers will be printed in **BOLD TYPE**. Thus **Km D-14** refers to the 14th kilometer in section **D**. Travel distances for some of the SIDE TRIPS are given in miles when there are no kilometer posts.

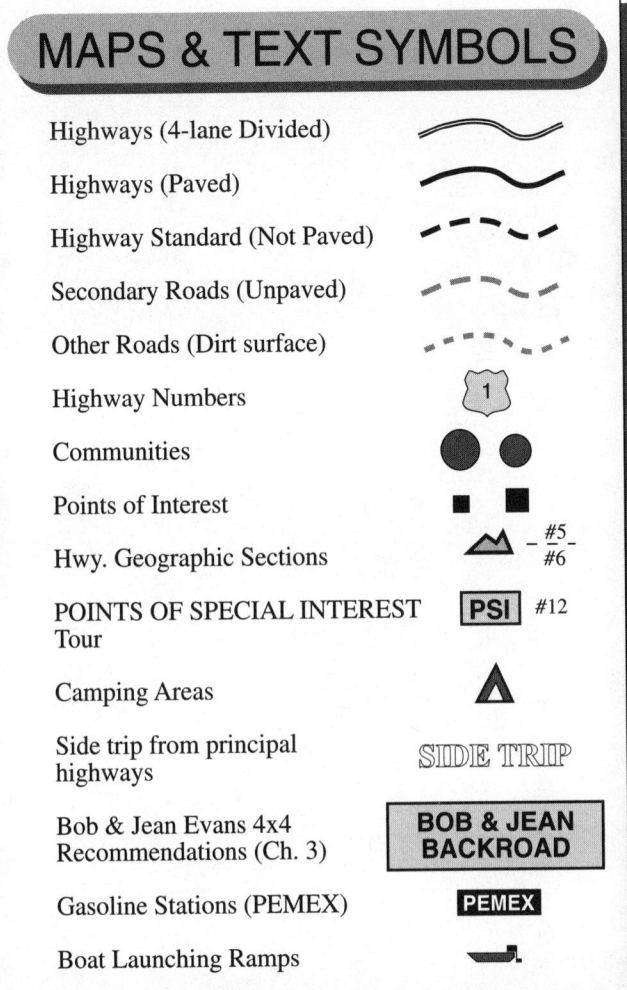

MAPS & TEXT SYMBOLS

Highways (4-lane Divided)	
Highways (Paved)	
Highway Standard (Not Paved)	
Secondary Roads (Unpaved)	
Other Roads (Dirt surface)	
Highway Numbers	1
Communities	
Points of Interest	
Hwy. Geographic Sections	#5 #6
POINTS OF SPECIAL INTEREST Tour	PSI #12
Camping Areas	
Side trip from principal highways	SIDE TRIP
Bob & Jean Evans 4x4 Recommendations (Ch. 3)	BOB & JEAN BACKROAD
Gasoline Stations (PEMEX)	PEMEX
Boat Launching Ramps	

TRANSPENINSULAR HIGHWAY GEOGRAPHIC SECTIONS — This book segregates the Transpeninsular Highway into nineteen geographic sections based on geologic and topographic aspects of the land through which it travels. There are ten odd-numbered sections of gentle terrain, and nine even-numbered ones with steeper topography. These gentle and steeper areas alternate.

The ten gentle sections gross 956 Km (595 miles) or 56 percent of the total length of the highway. The nine steeper areas account for the remaining 748 Km (464 miles) or 44 percent. These figures demonstrate that the highway is basically level and straight for over onehalf of its length, even though Baja as a whole is a mountainous land. Also, large portions of the steeper sections follow valleys or cross gently rolling plateaus which provide relatively easy driving conditions.

The nineteen geographic sections are shown on a map and described in a table in this Introduction. Kilometer post starting and ending points and the length of each section also are included. By using these aids you can look ahead to the kind of terrain through which you will be driving and also will be more aware of the peninsula's geological story. The symbol of the mountain, shown above, will alert

Continued on Page 204

TRANSPENINSULAR HIGHWAY KILOMETER POST SECTIONS

Total Length of Highway is 1,704 Km (1,059 Miles)

Tijuana

A

Ensenada

B

San Quintin

STATE OF BAJA CALIFORNIA

A	109 Km	68 Miles	(Chap. 17)
B	196 Km	122 Miles	(Chap. 18)
C	280 Km	174 Miles	(Chap. 19)
D	128 Km	76 Miles	

Kilometer post numbers in each section start from zero and progress from NORTH to SOUTH.

C

Hwy. Junction to Bahia de los Angeles

D

STATE LINE

Santa Rosalia

N

100 Miles

Guerrero Negro

PACIFIC OCEAN

E

F

Loreto

SEA OF CORTEZ

STATE OF BAJA CALIFORNIA SUR

E	221 Km	137 Miles	(Chap. 20)
F	197 Km	122 Miles	(Chap. 21)
G	120 Km	74 Miles	(Chap. 22)
H	239 Km	149 Miles	
J	221 Km	137 Miles	(Chaps. 23 & 24)

Kilometer post numbers in each section start from zero and progress from SOUTH to NORTH.

G

Ciudad Insurgentes

La Paz

J

H

Cabo San Lucas

TRANSPENINSULAR HIGHWAY GEOGRAPHIC SECTIONS

Numbers refer to the tables on the following two pages.

Tijuana

1

2
Ensenada

3
Colonet

4

5

San Quintin

6

7

8

9
San Ignacio

PACIFIC
OCEAN

Guerrero
Negro

Santa
Rosalia

10

11

 # Sections of GENTLE Topography
956 Km (595 miles)
56 Percent of the Highway

This symbol accompanies
all references to the Geographic
Sections throughout the book.

1

SEA OF
CORTEZ

Loreto

N

100 Miles

13

12

15

16

14

17

La Paz

18

San Jose del Cabo

Cabo San Lucas

19

 # Sections of STEEPER Topography
748 Km (464 miles)
44 Percent of the Highway

199

GEOGRAPHIC SECTIONS ALONG THE TRANSPENINSULAR HIGHWAY

NO.	FROM	TO	DESCRIPTION	GENTLE		STEEPER	
				Km	Mi	Km	Mi
1	International Border at Tijuana.	Km (A-75) 21 mi. N of Ensenada.	Limited access freeway (Hwy.1-D) near sea level. Traverses flat areas and gentle hills along the coast.	75	47	--	--
2	Km (A-75) 21 miles N. of Ensenada.	Km (A-99) Tollgate 6 mi. N of Ensenada.	Limited access freeway (Hwy.1-D) Low mountainous section. Good views of the Pacific Ocean along southern portion.	--	--	24	15
3	Km (A-99) Tollgate 6 mi. N of Ensenada.	Km (B-25) 16 mi. S of Ensenada.	Flat lands around Ensenada. Some agriculture in southern portion. Narrow 4-lane hwy. from Ensenada to Maneadero. 2 lanes to south.	35	22	--	--
4	Km (B-25) 16 mi. S of Ensenada.	Km (B-125) at the town of Colonet.	Moderately steep mountains with numerous intermountain valleys.	--	--	100	62
5	Km (B-125) at the town of Colonet.	Km (C-41) 28 mi. S of San Quintin.	Mtns. move inland at Colonet. Highway passes over wide coastal plain. Southerly 17 Km. (11 mi.) is within 1/4 to 1/2 mi. of the ocean.	112	70	--	--
6	Km (C-41) 28 mi. S of San Quintin.	Km (C-55) at the town of El Rosario.	A short mountainous section involving a moderate climb to a plateau, and then a steep descent into El Rosario.	--	--	14	9
7	Km (C-55) at the town of El Rosario.	Km (C-63) at the Rio del Rosario bridge.	A short flat section along the north edge of a valley through which flows the Rio del Rosario.	8	5	--	--
8	Km (C-63) at the Rio del Rosario bridge.	Km (D-70) North edge of the Desierto de Vizcaino.	High dissected plateaus, ridges and mountains. The gentle west slope of the Peninsular Range Mtns. The longest mountain section of Hwy. 1.	--	--	287	178
9	Km (D-70) North edge of the Desierto de Vizcaino.	Km (E-84) SE edge of the Desierto de Vizcaino.	Hwy. straight & level, but narrow. The most dangerous section of hwy. E of Guerrero Negro, hwy. climbs slowly to a pass through the mtns.	192	119	--	--

NO.	FROM	TO	DESCRIPTION	GENTLE		STEEP	
				Km	Mi	Km	Mi
10	Km (E-84) SE edge of the Desierto de Vizcaino.	Km (E-8) Highway 1 meets the Sea of Cortez.	Hwy.1 passes over the Peninsular Range Mtns. through a gentle pass. Eastern 27 Kms. (17 miles) has steep descent to the sea.	--	--	74	46
11	Km (E-8) Highway 1 meets the Sea of Cortez.	Km (G-83) Highway 1 leaves the Sea of Cortez.	Coastal benches and low hills between the coast and the Sierra Giganta. Near sea level in most places. South portion very scenic.	241	150	--	--
12	Km (G-83) Highway 1 leaves the Sea of Cortez.	Km (G-45) Mtns. blend with Llano de Magdalena.	Highway 1 again passes over the main Peninsular Range Mountains. Eastern 10 Km fairly steep with many curves. A scenic section.	--	--	38	24
13	Km (G-45) Mtns. blend with Llano de Magdalena.	Km (H-120) Llano de Mag. blends with plateau lands.	Highway 1 is straight and level through the Llano de Magdalena. Passes through agricultural lands near Ciudad Constitucion.	164	102	--	--
14	Km (H-120) Llano de Mag. blends with plateau lands.	Km (H-31) Plateau lands end. Start Ll. de La Paz.	A section of relatively level plateau lands formed by the gentle western slopes of the Peninsular Range Mountains.	--	--	89	55
15	Km (H-31) Plateau lands end. Start Ll. de La Paz.	Km (J-170) End Ll. de La Paz. Start Sr. de la Laguna.	Highway 1 passes over the level Llano de La Paz. This is the peninsula's lowest and narrowest section.	82	51	--	--
16	Km (J-170) End Ll. de La Paz. Start Sr. de la Laguna.	Km (J-112) Hwy. 1 meets the sea near Los Barriles.	Section through the granitic Sierra de la Laguna and its "Arid Tropical Forest" plant community.	--	--	58	36
17	Km (J-112) Hwy. 1 meets the sea near Los Barriles.	Km (J-93) Junction with the road to La Ribera.	Section along coastal flat lands. Northern portion adjoins the Sea of Cortez coast near the resort towns of Los Barriles and Buena Vista.	19	12	--	--
18	Km (J-93) Junction with the road to La Ribera.	Km (J-35) Hwy.1 meets the sea at San Jose del Cabo.	Highway 1 passes over low hills and plateaus lying between the Sierra de la Laguna to the west and a lesser range to the east.	--	--	60	37
19	Km (J-35) Hwy.1 meets the sea at San Jose del Cabo.	Km (J-0) Highway 1 ends at Cabo San Lucas.	A section of coastal benches and low hills at the peninsula's southern tip.	33	21	--	--

TRANSPENINSULAR HIGHWAY
POINTS OF SPECIAL INTEREST TOUR
Points 29 and 30 are along Highway 19.

NO.	POINT OF INTEREST	HRS	PTS	KM	COMMENTS
1	International boundary monument.	0:20	3	A-9	Historic monument near Bullring By-the-Sea at Tijuana. Photo Ch. 17.
2	Rosarito Beach Hotel.	0:20	2	A-34	Historic hotel, wall decorations, etc. Former 1930s gambling casino.
3	El Mirador (the vista point).	0:10	1	A-84	Fine views of coast and Islas Todos Santos. Adjoins Hwy 1-D.
4	Ensenada -- Tourist Row.	1:00	4	A-109	One of Baja's best shopping areas, plus a taste of a large Mexican city.
5	La Bufadora.	1:00	5	B-14	Intriguing ocean blowhole and fine coastal views. 14-mile side trip.
6	Adobe ruins of mission at El Rosario.	0:30	4	C-55	1.6-mile side trip to ruins overlooking Rio del Rosario. Photo Ch. 19.
7	Excellent desert vegetation.	0:30	3	C-63	Northern edge of Sonoran Desert vegetation region. First cirios.
8	Catavina Boulder Fields.	0:15	2	C-157	Geologically interesting boulder fields and fine desert vegetation.
9	Scammon's Lagoon -- Whale-watching. **	3:00	8	E-208	Major whale calving area. 16-mile side trip. Consider overnight stay.
10	San Ignacio.	0:45	3	E-74	One of Baja's most charming towns. Historic church, square, and palms.
11	Tres Virgenes Volcano and lava flows.	0:15	2	E-42	Lava flows adjoining hwy. Excellent specimens of elephant trees.
12	Santa Rosalia.	2:00	6	E-0	Historic church, copper smelter, French buildings, hotel, and harbor.
13	Mulege.	2:00	6	F-136	Savor the town and visit the historic prison and restored mission church.
14	Microwave radio tower and fine scenic view.	0:30	4	F-124	Excellent views of the Sea of Cortez. A 3/4-mile side trip.
15	Loreto	1:00	5	F-197	Historic town -- Site of the mother mission. Visit church and museum.

** A drive, and boat trip at Puerto Lopez Mateos (Chapter 22) may be substituted.

TRANSPENINSULAR HIGHWAY
POINTS OF SPECIAL INTEREST TOUR
Points 29 and 30 are along Highway 19.

NO.	POINT OF INTEREST	HRS	PTS	KM	COMMENTS
16	Nopolo.	0:30	2	G-111	Visit the hotel and tennis courts in this developing resort area.
17	Puerto Escondido.	0:30	2	G-94	Baja's best natural harbor. Trailer court and developing resort area.
18	Vista point north of La Paz.	0:10	1	H-35	Views of La Paz, Llano de La Paz, Sea of Cortez, and islands.
19	La Paz.	4:00	6	H-0	Tour the downtown area and waterfront. Good shopping and hotels.
20	El Triunfo.	1:00	4	J-162	Historic silver mining town. Visit old smelter and cemetery.
21	Santiago.	1:30	5	J-85	Pleasant town and site of a Jesuit mission. Visit the zoological garden.
22	Tropic of Cancer monument.	0:05	1	J-82	Stop and stretch your legs as you enter the tropics. Photo Ch. 23.
23	San Jose del Cabo.	2:00	4	J-33	Tour the town square, church, and developing resort area.
24	Hotel Palmilla.	0:30	2	J-26	One of Baja's finest hotels. Walk in from highway if driving large RV
25	Hotel Twin Dolphin.	0:30	2	J-11	Another of Baja's fine hotels.
26	Cabo San Lucas Vista from the Hotel Calinda Beach.	0:20	2	J-6	Celebrate arrival at "Cabo" by viewing the cape from the hotel pool area.
27	Hotel Finisterra.	0:20	2	J-0	A fine hotel plus excellent views of the Pacific and inner harbor.
28	Boat trip to the tip of Cabo San Lucas.	2:00	4	J-0	Hire a glass-bottomed boat to visit the Cabo arch and view tropical fish.
29	(Hwy 19.)	1:00	3	Hwy 19	A charming historic town and farming area. Jesuit mission site.
30	Botanical Garden.	0:30	2	Hwy 19	Excellent garden of labeled desert plants. Adjacent to the highway.

you to textual material relating to these geographic sections.

POINTS OF SPECIAL INTEREST TOUR — As noted earlier, I sincerely hope that you will decide to savor your trip through the Magnificent Peninsula and will not choose to drive through it in the shortest possible time. With this in mind, a thirty-stop POINTS OF SPECIAL INTEREST Tour has been prepared to guide you along the Transpeninsular Highway. These stops are listed in a table and are described in more detail in the text.

Look over the brief comments presented in the table to obtain an overall impression of the attractions included and the time involved in paying them a visit. Some of the points are adjacent to the highway. A majority require stopping and visiting a town or other feature just off the highway. A few require a more lengthy side trip, the longest being 16 miles to visit the whales at Scammon's Lagoon. Many stops on this POINTS OF SPECIAL INTEREST Tour also are logical places to spend the night. Thus, paying them a visit may not significantly increase your travel time.

In both text and maps, the POINTS OF SPECIAL INTEREST Tour will be identified by the **PSI** symbol shown above. The text will alert you to a few of the stops that provide special problems for the larger RV's. And finally, to add a bit of sporting challenge, a specific number of points have been assigned to each of the POINTS OF SPECIAL INTEREST. The more time and effort involved in visiting a site, the more points allotted. The top score is 100 points. Rate yourself as follows:

90	to	100	— Grande Baja Buff
70	to	89	— Baja Buffito
50	to	69	— Baja Amigo
30	to	49	— Posiblemente Manana
0	to	29	— Speed Merchant

No fair saying "There it is!" and roaring by. You have to stop and at least stretch your legs. There is no prize for scoring 100 points, but you know I will want to shake your hand, and should we chance to meet, the cerveza is on me. We have received a letter from one couple who made it from Portland, Oregon, to Cabo San Lucas and back in two weeks and scored 100 points on the tour. They are Grande Baja Buffs who also qualify as Speed Merchants. Hopefully you can proceed at a more leisurely rate.

A typical kilometer post marker along the Transpeninsular Highway. Every fifth marker includes the Mexican shield containing the number of the highway, in this case, Highway 1. Photo BW.

CHAPTER 14
THE BORDER AREA
AND HIGHWAY 2

This initial chapter of your GRAND TOUR of the Magnificent Peninsula begins with an examination of Highways 2, 2D and the Mexican communities lying along the international border. It is divided into eight sections:

    1 -- Tijuana
    2 -- Hwy 2 and 2D, Tijuana to Tecate
    3 -- Tecate
    4 -- Hwy 2 and 2D, Tecate to Mexicali
    5 -- Mexicali
    6 -- Hyw 2 and 2D, Mexicali to San Luis
    7 -- San Luis
    8 -- Algodones

Highway 2 extends from east to west a short distance south of the international boundary. It is a two-lane roadway little different in design standards from most other highways in Mexico. Construction started about 1990 on Highway 2D which roughly parallels the old road. It is a four-lane, divided, limited access tollway. Those portions that were completed in 1995 are shown on the Chapter 14 Map. In 1997 we ob-

served construction of Highway 2D immediately east of Tecate and other construction between Tecate and La Romorosa were observed in 1995.

Large numbers of tourists enter Mexico at the Tijuana-San Ysidro port-of-entry and simply wish to pass through Tijuana as quickly as possible to head south on Highway 1. If you are one of these, I suggest you read the first two items in the Tijuana section and then proceed to Chapter 17. The two items in question concern entering and leaving Mexico in the Tijuana area.

TIJUANA

We North Americans mispronounce the name of many Mexican communities, but our reference to the city of Tijuana as Tia Juana heads the list. I thought the blame could be laid at the door of the Tijuana Brass (A mariachi band from my younger days), but reference to their music labels shows the name spelled correctly, and travel books of the 1950s note that the problem already existed for many years. In deference

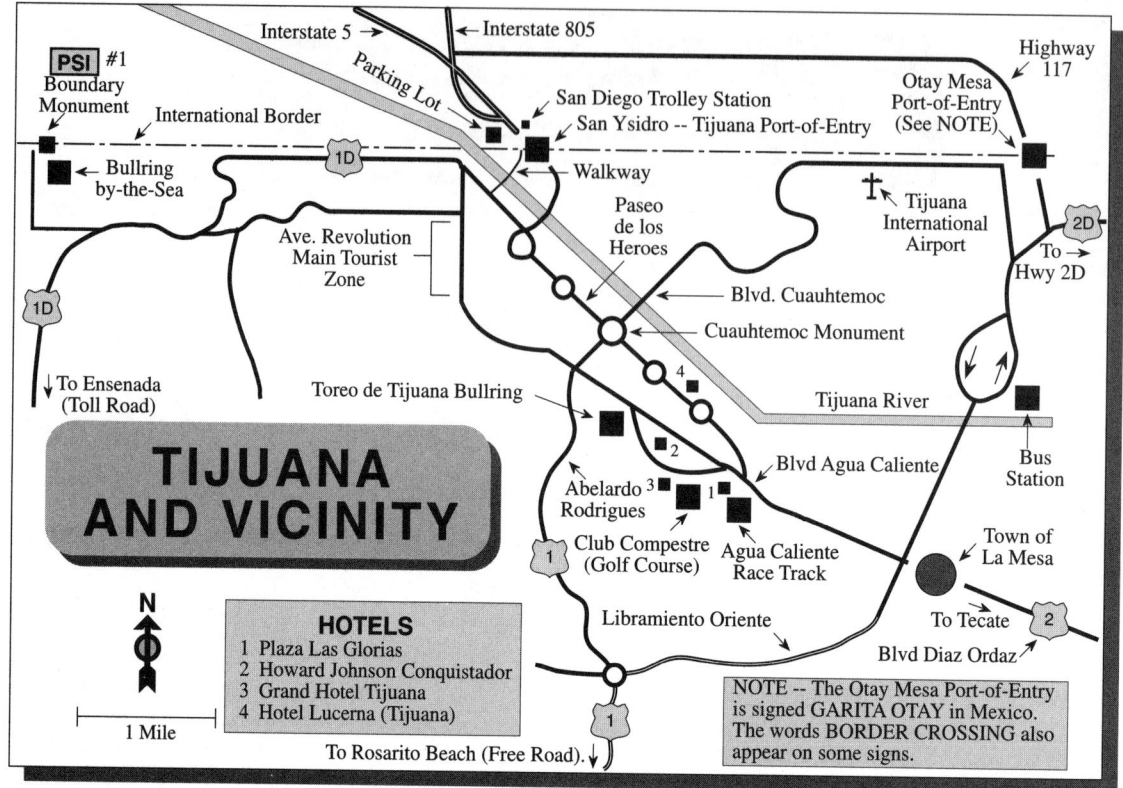

Interstate 5 → ← Interstate 805 — Highway 117

PSI #1 Boundary Monument
International Border
Parking Lot
San Diego Trolley Station
San Ysidro -- Tijuana Port-of-Entry
Otay Mesa Port-of-Entry (See NOTE)
1D
Walkway
← Bullring by-the-Sea
Ave. Revolution Main Tourist Zone
Paseo de los Heroes
Tijuana International Airport
To → Hwy 2D
2D
1D
Blvd. Cuauhtemoc
Cuauhtemoc Monument
↓ To Ensenada (Toll Road)
Toreo de Tijuana Bullring
4
Tijuana River
Bus Station

TIJUANA AND VICINITY

2
Blvd Agua Caliente
Abelardo 3 Rodrigues
1
Town of La Mesa
Club Compestre (Golf Course)
Agua Caliente Race Track
1
Libramiento Oriente
To Tecate
2
Blvd Diaz Ordaz ↗

N

HOTELS
1 Plaza Las Glorias
2 Howard Johnson Conquistador
3 Grand Hotel Tijuana
4 Hotel Lucerna (Tijuana)

1 Mile

1

To Rosarito Beach (Free Road). ↓

NOTE -- The Otay Mesa Port-of-Entry is signed GARITA OTAY in Mexico. The words BORDER CROSSING also appear on some signs.

to our long suffering Mexican friends, let us proceed to the blackboard with chalk in hand and try to get it right.

The town of Tijuana did not come into existence until the 1870s, almost three and one-half centuries after the Baja peninsula was discovered, and 175 years after the founding of the first Jesuit mission at Loreto in 1697. Today, it has a population of well over one million, is the fourth largest city in Mexico, and is reportedly the fastest growing city in North America.

The portion of Chapter 12 HISTORY concerning the years after the Mexican-American War will provide the community's background. Its rapid rise to prominence came in the 1920s as the result of prohibition in the United States. Tijuana led the way in attracting visitors from the north interested in gambling, prostitution, and the drowning of sorrows in unnumbered saloons. This *wicked* past is now largely replaced by a modern metropolis with much business activity and more conventional tourist attractions.

Please refer to the TIJUANA AND VICINITY Map. Depicted are the main points of interest and principal travel routes of concern to the first-time visitor. Hun-

dreds of lesser streets are omitted. This *highlight approach* will be used for the community maps throughout this book. Detailed maps are available in a variety of publications obtainable at the border and in almost every hotel and other places frequented by tourists.

ENTERING TIJUANA FROM THE NORTH — In approaching Tijuana from the north, you will be led directly into the port-of-entry from either Interstate 5 or 805. A canopy over the Mexican entry station bears directional signs.

In 1995 these signs required some tourists vehicles to pull over to the right for a customs inspection. This could change in the future. Drivers wishing to proceed south on Highway 1-D should bear sharply to the left a short distance after the border as the appropriate route circles over the entrance road, and heads west directly adjoining the border fence. Follow the signs for *Rosarito* and *Ensenada*. This route skirts Tijuana and most of its traffic, and in a few miles delivers its users to the Pacific coast in the vicinity of the *Bullring by-the-Sea* . (Follow the Rio Tijuana signs if you wish to access Paseo de los Heroes and Tijuana's better hotels.)

If you are heading south on Highway 1-D in this manner, you will now wish to move to Chapter 17; but first read the following item if you plan to return to the United States in the Tijuana area.

RETURNING TO THE U.S.A. — In returning north on Highway 1-D, you may enter the United States at San Ysidro or Otay Mesa. The decision on which crossing point to use must be made at the Highway 1-D offramp at the north end of the town of Rosarito. (See the map in Chapter 17.) Here are the advantages and disadvantages of these two alternatives.

SAN YSIDRO — Returning home this way is essentially a retracement of the south-bound Highway 1-D route described above and in Chapter 17. It is largely a sea level route with few hills. Traffic is modest, as most of the route is on a limited access toll road. Then brace yourself for lengthy delays while waiting your turn in line at United States customs. I am advised that all of the U.S. entry gates are now manned, rather than only some as in the past, and that license plate scanners are in use. The time spent in line should thus be reduced. (See additional comments concerning the ports-of-entry in Chapter 7.) I have never returned to the United States using this port-of-entry and never intend to. There is a limit to the misery I am willing to endure for my readers. I strongly recommend you obtain the book *Crossing the Border Fast and Easy* (See the BAJA BOOKSHELF) if you wish to return north here.

OTAY MESA — This station was opened in 1985 to help alleviate the lengthy delays experienced at San Ysidro. This route to the border is steeper and a bit more complex than that to San Ysidro, but the crossing delays are usually less. I recommend it for everyone. (Travelers with large RVs and trailers will experience heavy traffic in places but this is the price to be paid for the lesser wait at the port-of-entry.) Proceed as follows from Highway 1-D to Otay Mesa.

1. — Exit Highway 1-D at the north end of Rosarito. The exit sign reads "Tijuana Libre." Drive north on four lane Highway 1 through hilly terrain. (In the past this road was only two lanes and lengthy delays were caused by slow moving trucks).

2. — Exit Highway 1 at the top of the grade onto Libramiento Oriente, a four-lane freeway. The exit sign reads "Garita Otay Mesa / Border Crossing." From this exit, it is 3.8 miles to Boulevard Agua Caliente (Highway 2) and an additional 1.7 miles to the bus station turnoff. The freeway ends about one-half mile

south of Boulevard Agua Caliente, and heavy city traffic may be encountered from here north to the vicinity of the bus station. Follow signs for the "Aeropuerto" along the way.

3. — From the bus station, climb up the mesa on a one-way highway to an intersection. Turn right here. The sign reads "GARITA DE OTAY." After 0.6 miles turn left at a similar sign. From this last turn it is 1.2 miles on a six-lane divided boulevard to the border. This all sounds a bit difficult, but try it, you'll like it, and once you have it down, you will never use San Ysidro again.

VISITING TIJUANA — If you plan to visit Tijuana for only a short period, why not leave the car behind? There is a 500-car commercial parking lot immediately adjoining the border west of the port-of-entry on the United States side. From the lot, it is about one-half mile over a pleasant walkway to the north end of the Avenida Revolution tourist zone.

As at all the ports-of-entry, the walking circulation is counter-clockwise, so you will return to the United States on the east side of highway. There are elevated pedestrian walkways over the highway on both sides of the border. Customs delays are usually minimal.

Better yet, take the San Diego Trolley to the border and walk into Mexico. The trolley station is adjacent to United States customs on the east side of the highway. By leaving the car at home you escape the need for Mexican insurance, greatly diminish U.S. Customs delays, and avoid traffic and parking problems. There are plenty of taxis, and the distances to most of the tourist attractions are minimal. Consult the map to locate the following places.

AVENIDA REVOLUTION — A seven-block stretch of Ave. Revolution is the main tourist zone. There are many shops, restaurants, and nightclubs. Its northern end is easily reached by the walkway from the border. A few blocks to the west is the principal shopping and business district.

BOULEVARD AGUA CALIENTE — The Tijuana Bullring, Country Club, and Agua Caliente Race Track are all located on the south side of Blvd. Agua Caliente. This same segment of the boulevard also is the location of most of the city's better hotels and motels.

PASEO DE LOS HEROES — This broad boulevard and several other similar thoroughfares lie south of

TECATE

Highway 94
Port-of-Entry

United States
Mexico

Calle Cardenas

Avenida Juarez

Bus Depot

Bank

2

2

To Tecate Motels
and Tijuana

Parque Hidalgo

Oritiz Rubio

Tourist Bureau

Tecate Brewery

3

N

0.2 Miles

Rio Tecate

Fonart
Centro
Artesanal

To
Ensenada

Interchanges to Hwy 2D lie east &
west on Hwy 2, and south on Hwy 3.

west of Tecate from Highway 2 and south of Tecate on Highway 3.

(Km-166) — Here Highway 2 crosses the narrow crest of the concrete Rodriquez Dam (Presa Rodriques). Natural runoff captured by this structure was Tijuana's principal source of water prior to 1960. The reservoir ran dry in 1961 as the result of rapid population growth and a series of dry years. Runoff is now supplemented by water piped in from La Mision, south of Tijuana on the Pacific coast, and from the Rio Colorado to the east.

From Presa Rodriquez to Tecate, Highway 2 passes through pleasant rolling hills. There is some urbanization, with the flatter lands utilized for farming, grazing and olive orchards. The underlying rock is granite. Note the many hills that are being fractured and eroded into large, light-colored, granite boulders. When these boulders occur adjacent to the highway, they create natural billboards used to advertise political parties and their candidates.

(Km-163) — Highway 2 is joined at this point by an expressway that bypasses the towns of La Mesa and La Presa. Its western terminus is a short distance south of the Tijuana bus station.

(Km-140) -- At this point lies an interchange between Highways 2 and 2D. Much of Highway 2 between here and Tecate is four-lane.

(Km-133) TECATE — Between Tijuana and Tecate, Highway 2 has slowly climbed the western slopes of the Peninsular Range Mountains. A sign at the western edge of Tecate marks the 500-meter (1,650 feet) elevation point.

the Rio Tijuana and are centered around the statue of Cuauhtemoc (the last king of the Aztecs, defender of Tenochtitlan, and for many Mexicans, the original patriot). This is the newest section of the downtown area. There are many businesses, government offices, and grassy open areas.

HIGHWAY 2 & 2D — TIJUANA TO TECATE

Tijuana's principal east-west street is Agua Caliente. It is also Highway 2. The route crosses Presa Rodriquez (Rodriquez Dam) 14 miles east of downtown Tijuana. Between these two points there is considerable traffic as the highway is also the main four-lane artery for this city and the communities of La Mesa and La Presa. In La Presa, the highway becomes two-lane. East of the dam, traffic is lighter but is utilized by many heavy trucks escaping the tolls required on Highway 2D.

Highway 2D is completed between the eastern edge of Tijuana and Tecate. The Tijuana entrance to this toll road is about 2 miles east of the Otay Mesa port-of-entry access road (See TIJUANA AND VICINITY Map). Highway 2D may be accessed both east and

TECATE

Tecate's population of 85,000 is supported by agriculture and growing numbers of assembly plants operating under the maquiladora program. It is also the home of the Tecate Brewery. As with other communities in Mexico, it is amazing how a town with this many people is compressed into such a relatively small area.

The community contains several tourist-oriented stores, but its chief attributes for the traveler are the port-of-entry and the Tecate Brewery. One way to visit the brewery is by traveling on vintage trains departing from the U.S. town of Campo located a few miles to the northeast on California Highway 94. It is reported that spirits are considerably higher on the return trip after passengers have sampled the brewery's output. Tecate is also located at the junction of Highways 2 and 3. Highway 3 is described in Chapter 16, but it should be noted here that it is a very pleasant way to travel south and is the recommended route for tourists returning to the United States from Ensenada.

The town sguare in the pleasant town of Tecate. Photo BW.

There is little adjoining community on the United States side of the border; thus, there is little commuter traffic and usually little time is spent waiting in line at the U.S. port-of-entry. Mexican customs and immigration offices are found immediately on the right when entering Mexico. There are also several auto insurance offices within one block of the crossing. Parking is usually available on the city streets. The Motel El Dorado lies 0.8 miles west of the Highway 2 and 3 junction on the north side of Highway 2. The Motel Hacienda is found 0.7 miles farther along, in the same direction. An excellent hotel is part of the Rancho Tecate Resort and Country Club at Km 10 south of Tecate on Highway 3. The Rancho Ojai RV Park lies 10 miles east of town on Highway 2 while the Barrett Lake RV Park lies some 7 miles north of Tecate east of Highway 94 in the United States.

The presence of the above noted motels, hotel and RV parks make the Tecate area an attractive place to enter Mexico using a combination of California Highway 94 and Mexican Highway 3. Both of these roads offer pleasant, although rather winding routes to Ensenada which avoid the congestion of the Tijuana-Rosarito Beach areas. It is my preferred way to enter Baja.

A few years ago I was advised by a reliable source that Tecate is the only Baja border town that does not support prostitution, a notable distinction. It may be the only one in the world. I must hasten to add that this bit of information does not reflect my own personal observations. On to Mexicali.

HIGHWAY 2 and 2D -- TECATE TO MEXICALI

A sizeable industrial park lies along the highway east of Tecate no doubt spawned by the North American Free Trade agreement. East of Tecate, Highway 2 continues to climb gradually upward. Most of the agricultural land has been left behind, to the west. The land becomes steeper and is vegetated largely with chaparral.

(Km-126) -- Here is an interchange with Highway 2D near the eastern outskirts of Tecate. There was much road construction in this area in 1997 meaning that a new section of Highway 2-D will be opened in the near future. In 1995 additional construction of Highway 2D between Tecate and La Rumorosa was limited to overpass structures. The new highway's route roughly parallels Highway 2.

(Km-112) -- Located here adjoining the north side of the highway is the attractive Rancho Ojai RV Park and campground. Look for the stone archway. There are newly planted trees along with older live oaks. The RV park is part of an active cattle ranch.

(Km-109) — At approximately this point the steeper lands are left behind, to the west, and the highway enters a broad plateau with views of the main peaks of the Peninsular Range Mountains to the east.

(Km-97) -- The town of El Hongo lies south of the highway at this point.

(Km-80) VEGETATIONAL CHANGE — Starting near this point and continuing for the next 20 Km (13 miles), you will see a scattering of Parry pinyon pine trees and low-growing California junipers. This is the best location for observing these species from Baja's highway system. More extensive stands may be viewed by taking the side trip noted below at **Km 72**. Pinyon pine produces cones containing large nut-like seeds which are easily gathered when they mature in May. They make good eating and may be found marketed as *Indian Nuts* .

SIDE TRIP

(Km-72) ROAD TO NATIONAL PARK - *A secondary road leaves Highway 2 to the right (south) 0.1 miles east of this point. Immediately west of this junction is a CONASUPO store. This road provides the backdoor route to the Parque Nacional Constitucion de 1857, one of Baja's several National Parks. It passes through excellent stands of Parry pinyon pine and numerous unimproved places to camp. Be extremely careful with fire in this area. Pinyon*

but is of little other interest to the tourist. Its chief claim to fame is that it lies at the top of the grade. What grade? You will shortly discover: At the eastern edge of La Rumorosa lies the tollgate-interchange for that portion of Highway 2D which was completed in 1995.

THE CANTU GRADE — East of La Rumorosa you will be making a 15-mile-long descent of the eastern escarpment of the Peninsular Range Mountains. It is the most dramatic segment of highway in the Baja peninsula. This steep and rapid drop, combined with the lengthy and gradual grade to the east, is the peninsula's best demonstration of its fault block mountain structure. (See Chapter 9 GEOLOGY.)

Although the highway is well constructed, careful driving is required. Slow moving vehicles and high winds can be a problem, and snow may be encountered during winter storms. On the positive side are the excellent views to be had of the United States, to the north, and Laguna Salada and the San Felipe Desert, to the east. Also, note the light blue pipeline north of the highway. It brings water from the Rio Colorado to Tijuana. Pumping stations are in view at the base of the grade and near the conduit's midpoint.

The Cantu Grade. Baja's most dramatic segment of highway. Its eastern end lies in the desert while there are high elevation pinyon pines at its western terminus. Photo JW.

pine burns with great intensity and is very slow to regenerate as its heavy seeds cannot be spread by the wind.

It is 38 miles to Laguna Hanson, the park's principal attraction. This route is recommended only for pickup and van-type vehicles. See full description and map of the park in Chapter 16. End SIDE TRIP.

(Km-68) LA RUMOROSA — Here, at over 4,000 feet in elevation, lies the small town of La Rumorosa. It contains a modest restaurant and a PEMEX station

In 1995 the westbound lanes of Highway 2D were completed from the northern end of Laguna Salada near **Km-23** to the above noted tollgate-interchange at the eastern edge of La Rumorosa. Eastbound traffic was limited to using old Highway 2, while westbound traffic could select either route.

SIDE TRIP

(Km-27) CANYON GUADALUPE — *A secondary road leaves Highway 2 to the south a short distance west of Km-27. It provides access to one of Baja's hidden hot spring oasis, Canyon Guadalupe. Nestled in a canyon near the foot of the majestic Sierra de Juarez's eastern escarpment, it has long been a favorite of offroad vehicle fans. In 1987 most of the route into the spring was upgraded to secondary road standards.*

The road roughly parallels the western edge of Laguna Salada for <u>26.7 miles</u>. At this point take a branch road to the right through agricultural fields for an additional <u>7.7 miles</u> to the campground. The last 1.5 miles is steep and rocky and crosses an arroyo several times among granite boulders. This final section of road is clearly not suited for larger RVs. (See **Km-25** below concerning an alternate route over the lake bed of Laguna Salada.)

Hot spring waters (105-degrees) are piped to rock tubs at each campsite among native fan palms and other desert vegetation. There is also a small store and hot water pools for swimming. The per night fee

Daughter Barbara poses with the Green Angels at La Rumorosa at the western edge of the Cantu Grade. Note the pinyon pine trees behind the building. Photo JW.

in 1995 was $15.00 per night. Call (714) 673-2670 for reservations. The area is very crowded on weekends and looses some of its ambience. Otherwise, its a delightful spot. Indian petroglyphs and a small waterfall may be visited by hiking up the canyon further into the mountains. End SIDE TRIP.

SIDE TRIP

(Km-25) LAGUNA SALADA — A sign for Playa Laguna Salada marks the junction of a secondary road which leads south for 0.5 miles. to the north end of Laguna Salada. Here are located a modest cafe and camping area at the edge of the lake bed. It is a pleasant spot on those few occasions when there is water in the lake. Otherwise, it leaves much to be desired.

From the above described point one may proceed over "The Laguna Salada Freeway" (See CHAPTER 14 Map) for a flying 26.2 mile trip over the level lake bed toward Canyon Guadalupe. This route is far smoother and faster than the often washboarded road noted under **Km-27** above. It joins this latter road near the last 7.7 mile road section into the hot springs. Avoid this trip if there is the slightest hint of recent rain. End SIDE TRIP.

VALLE DE MEXICALI — Approximately halfway between Laguna Salada and the city of Mexicali on Highway 2 lies the agricultural community of Colonia Progreso. This town marks the western edge of the vast Valle de Mexicali agricultural area which stretches

east to the Rio Colorado. It is Baja's largest farming area. The history of its development is contained in the closing section of Chapter 12 HISTORY. Much of the the area along the highway was urbanized in 1995.

HIGHWAY 5 JUNCTION — Highway 2 joins Highway 5 near the southern edge of the city of Mexicali. (See MEXICALI Map)

MEXICALI

Tourism statistics indicate that Mexicali is the final destination point for 15 percent of the foreign visitors who enter the state of Baja California. The comparable figure for Tijuana is 34 percent and 23 percent for Ensenada. In spite of Mexicali's reasonably high share of total visits, the city has a definite non-tourist flavor. One can only speculate that most of her visitors are from farming communities in the nearby Imperial Valley and are bent on activities not usually associated with tourism. The economic well-being of Mexicali's 600,000 people rests on industry, agricultural activities in the Valle de Mexicali, and on its being the capital of the state of Baja California.

Mexicali's principal business district adjoins the international border generally SE from the port-of-entry. Most of its newer development is taking place in the Centro Civico-Comercial some two miles south of the border. Here are located state and federal office

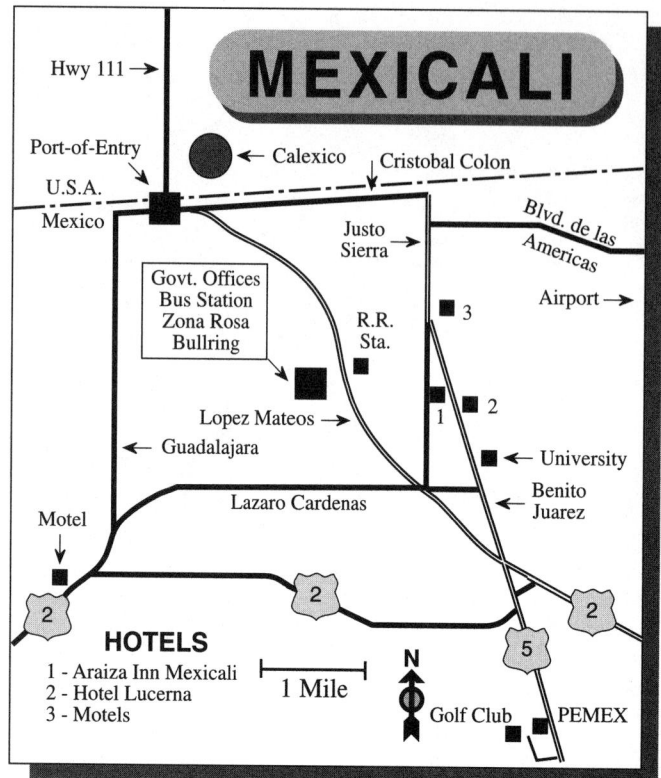

MEXICALI

Hwy 111 →

Port-of-Entry
U.S.A.
Mexico
← Calexico   Cristobal Colon

Govt. Offices
Bus Station
Zona Rosa
Bullring

Justo Sierra →
Blvd. de las Americas
Airport →

R.R. Sta.

Lopez Mateos →
← Guadalajara

University ←
Benito Juarez ←

Lazaro Cardenas

Motel

HOTELS

1 - Araiza Inn Mexicali
2 - Hotel Lucerna
3 - Motels

1 Mile

N

Golf Club   PEMEX

record time. I found it by driving east along the Blvd. de las Americas but their has to be a better way. Until I can give the matter more study, you're on your own.

HIGHWAY 2 MEXICALI TO SAN LUIS

The junction of Highways 2 and 5 is near the southern outskirts of Mexicali. The nature of the intersection is shown on the MEXICALI Map. This is a busy industrial area so drive with care.

It is 65 km (40 miles) from the above referenced junction to the Rio Colorado and an additional 3 km (2 miles) to San Luis. From the junction to the river, the entire highway is four-laned, straight, and level. In terms of roadside activity it may be divided into three sections:

1. — The westerly 6 miles is adjoined by numerous industrial buildings. The railroad paralleling much of this section serves these facilities. (I was unable to visit this area in 1995 and industrial development has no doubt spread farther east.)

buildings, bus station, bullring, and the pink zone (shops, theaters, restaurants, etc). The city's hotels and motels cluster around the intersection of Boulevard Benito Juarez and Boulevard Justo Sierra.

Tourists entering Mexico at Mexicali and heading south to San Felipe need merely follow Calzada Lopez Mateos (a multilaned boulevard) SE through town. The railroad lies in the median strip for the first two miles and will serve to keep you on *track*. Follow the signs for San Felipe. See Chapter 15 for a full description of the Highway 5 route from Mexicali to the San Felipe area.

Motorists waiting their turn to enter the United States using the older or western port-of-entry line up east of the port-of-entry on Avenida Cristobal Colon. This street directly adjoins the border fence and carries one-way, west-bound traffic. Travelers returning north might best enter Cristobal Colon at its eastern end (via Benito Juarez and Justo Sierra) to most judiciously assume their place in line. A new port-of-entry (Garita Oriente - Eastern Gate) was opened in December 1996 about 5 miles east of downtown Mexicali. I was the only vehicle in line and cleared customs in

2. — East of the industrial area, Highway 2 passes through the heart of the Valle de Mexicali agricultural area but, initially, the highway is lined with scores of farm dwellings and garden plots reflecting the nearness of the city.

3. — Approximately halfway between Mexicali and the Rio Colorado the city's influence ceases. The highway then passes through pleasant, well-ordered farms watered by extensive irrigation ditches.

Highway 2 crosses the Rio Colorado on a two-lane toll bridge and enters the state of Sonora.

SAN LUIS

San Luis is a town of 135,000 people in the Mexican state of Sonora. Tourists may enter or leave Mexico here, as at any of Baja's ports-of-entry. No Mexican car permit is required to pass through this small section of the Mexican mainland en route to the peninsula.

The main street of San Luis is also Highway 2. At the most westerly traffic light a turn to the north will lead

'THIS
NO MAN'S LAND'

By KEN REIMER

The conquistadores came with their greed
But Baja California would not concede,
Cortez...Mendosa...Cabrillo...Vizcaino...and more
The riches they sought were not on her shores;
Not even enough food could be found
To feed men and beasts on this arid ground,
Native Pericues and Guaycuras barely survived
and with white man's diseases too many died.
Then missionaries tried but despite their valiant struggle
Many missions remain only as heaps of old rubble,
Padres Kino...Salvatierra...Serra...Ugarte...
Like the conquistadore bands,
Left only their names on this inhospitable land.

to the port-of-entry only one block away. Cars returning to the United States line up east of the port-of-entry on the street that directly parallels the border fence. Drivers should access this street several blocks to the east of the above referenced light to most conveniently locate the end of the line.

San Luis is visited by many tourists from the large city of Yuma, Arizona, 23 miles to the NW. It thus contains many shops and other tourist-oriented activities. Mexican immigration offices and insurance outlets are present near the crossing.

ALGODONES

Algodones is a small farm community located on the international border directly west of the Rio Colo-rado. It has the most lightly used of Baja's ports-of-entry. We have been advised, however, that thousands of tourists sometimes park on the United States side of the International border and walk to Algodones for a quick visit to Mexico. The station is open from 6:00 AM to 8:00 PM. Immigration and insurance offices are adjacent to the crossing.

Algodones may be reached from Highway 2 over a level, paved highway that parallels the Rio Colo-rado. Travel distance is 18.1 miles through pleasant agricultural country. The junction of the two highways is 2.0 miles west of the Rio Colorado near **Km-3**. Travelers may stop and look at the Morelos Dam a short distance south of the community. It diverts all of the water used to irrigate the Valle de Mexicali.

CHAPTER 15
HIGHWAY 5

Chapter 15 describes the Highway 5 route from the international border at Mexicali to its junction with Highway 1 at Laguna Chapala 267.5 miles to the south. Most of this road is constructed to highway standard, but at press time the oiled surface terminated at the community of Puertecitos 180.1 miles south of the border. The southerly 87.4 miles remains to be paved.

In previous editions of *The Magnificent Peninsula* I noted that it was reported that this unpaved section of highway would be completed by 1989. In the eight years that have transpired since, nothing new has occurred. For now, this section is heavily washboarded and should be traveled only by pickups, vans and other vehicles designed to take rough treatment. It was in poor condition following the hurriucane which crossed the peninsula in fall 1997.

If, and when, the new highway is completed, it will provide a major alternative to Highway 1 for accessing the southern half of Baja California. People approaching the peninsula from Arizona, Nevada, and other states to the north and east will no longer have to travel to, and through, the Tijuana-Ensenada area to head south. The new highway joins Highway 1 near **Km C-229** a point approximately 324 miles south of Tijuana. Almost 1/3 of the Transpeninsular Highway, and the congestion of the two metropolitan areas can thus be bypassed.

And travelers heading south to Baja from northern California, Oregon, Washington, and Canada along U.S. Interstate 5 might choose to route themselves from Bakersfield, California to Mexicali through the Mojave Desert and, believe it or not, bypass *The Jungle*, and those delightful monuments to man's insanity, the Los Angeles-San Diego Freeway systems. It is approximately 580 miles from Bakersfield to Lake Chapala via Tijuana and Highway 1, and 607 miles using Highway 5 when entering Mexico at Mexicali. The small additional mileage of only 27 miles should be more than compensated for by safer, easier, faster, and more scenic driving conditions.

Even travelers from the Los Angeles area may choose the Highway 5 alternative by traveling east on Interstate 10 toward Mexicali. Those from San Diego can also easily reach Mexicali over Interstate 8. The completion of Highway 5 should thus bring about a dramatic reduction in the use of the Transpeninsular Highway as a route to southern Baja. Tourism in the towns along Highway 5 will increase accordingly.

HIGHWAY 5 OVERVIEW — Reference to the GEOLOGIC PROVINCES Map in Chapter 9 GEOLOGY will show that the portion of Highway 5 between Mexicali and Puertecitos is within the *Basin and Range* Geologic Province. The western edge of this province is the escarpment of the Peninsular Range Mountains. This steep-faced cliff rises dramatically from near sea level to over 10,000 feet in elevation. The escarpment is in view from this section of the highway, although in most places its base is obscured by lower intervening ranges of mountains. The latter are typical of the north-south ranges found throughout the Basin and Range Province.

From Puertecitos to Laguna Chapala the highway passes through the edge of the Peninsular Range Mountains and moderatly steep terrain is encountered in many places. Much of this section of road is within sight of the Sea of Cortez. Scenic qualities are thus considerably better than along Highway 1 far to the west.

Most of the area traversed by Highway 5 lies in the rain shadow of Baja's highest segment of the Peninsular Range Mountains and is thus its driest area. Reference to the VEGETATIVE REGIONS Map in Chapter 10 shows that the area's vegetation has been classified as the San Felipe Desert portion of the Sonoran Desert Region. Few of Baja's large and attractive species of desert plants are present here. The area's vegetation is thus rather drab. Plant variety improves west of the Highway 5 junction with the secondary road to Calamajue and is comparable with the better plant areas seen along Highway 1.

MEXICALI — It is approximately 6 miles from the old or western Mexicali port-of-entry to the junction of

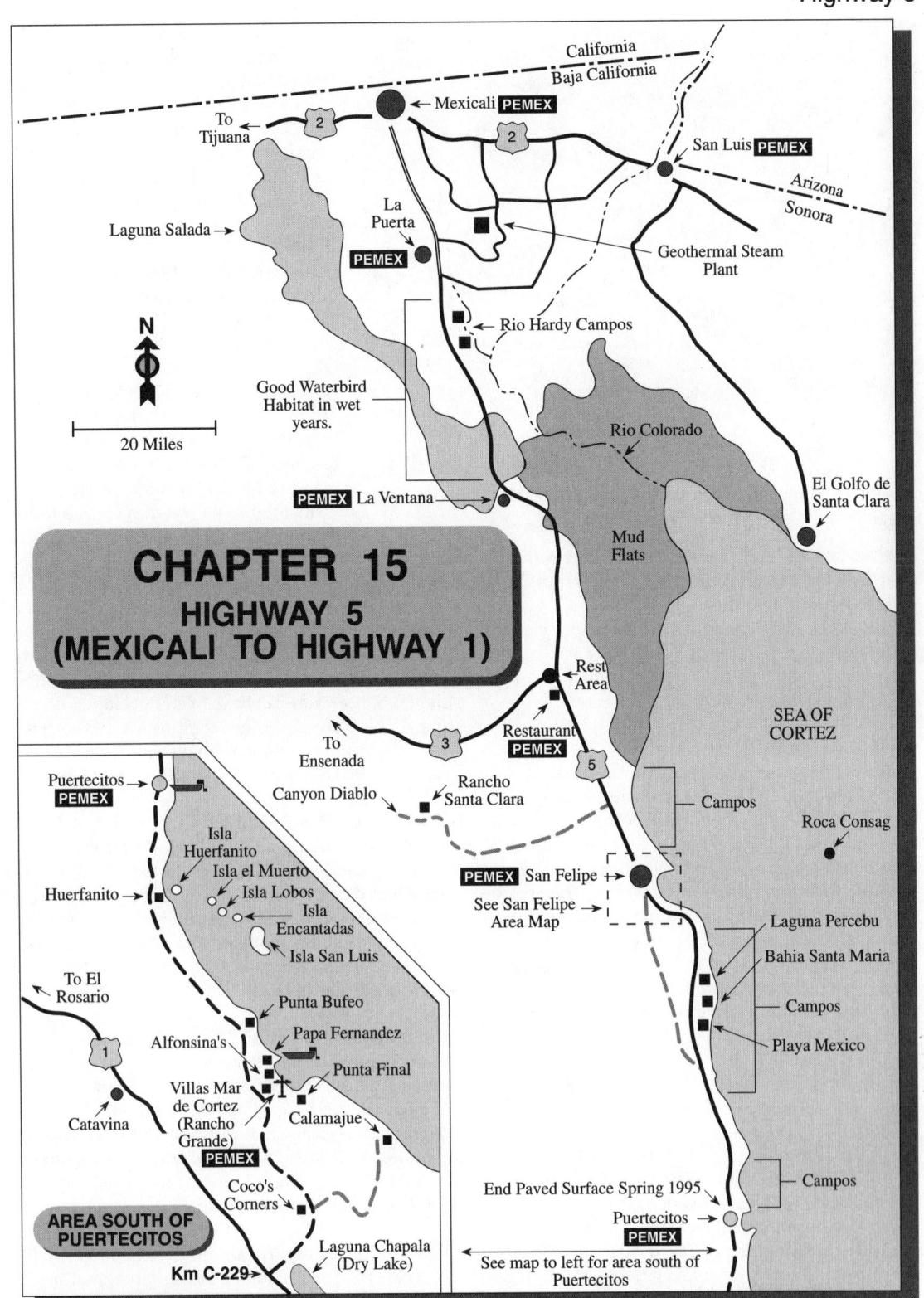

California
Baja California

To
Tijuana ←
2
● ← Mexicali **PEMEX**

2

San Luis **PEMEX**

Arizona
Sonora

La
Puerta

Laguna Salada →

PEMEX ●

■ → Geothermal Steam
Plant

N

■
■ → Rio Hardy Campos

Good Waterbird
Habitat in wet
years.

Rio Colorado

20 Miles

PEMEX La Ventana → ●

El Golfo de
Santa Clara ●

Mud
Flats

CHAPTER 15
HIGHWAY 5
(MEXICALI TO HIGHWAY 1)

Rest
Area

SEA OF
CORTEZ

To
Ensenada
3
Restaurant
PEMEX

5

Campos

Puertecitos →
PEMEX

Canyon Diablo
■ Rancho
Santa Clara

Roca Consag ●

Isla
Huerfanito
○ Isla el Muerto
○ Isla Lobos
○ ○
Isla
Encantadas
Isla San Luis

PEMEX San Felipe → ●

See San Felipe →
Area Map

Laguna Percebu

Bahia Santa Maria

■
■ ← Campos

Huerfanito →

To El
Rosario

■ Playa Mexico

1

Punta Bufeo ■
Papa Fernandez
Alfonsina's ■ ■
■ Punta Final
Villas Mar
de Cortez
(Rancho
Grande)
PEMEX
Calamajue ■

Catavina ●

Coco's
Corners ■

**AREA SOUTH OF
PUERTECITOS**

Km C-229 →

Laguna Chapala
(Dry Lake)

End Paved Surface Spring 1995

Campos

Puertecitos ○
PEMEX

←   →
See map to left for area south of
Puertecitos

Laguna Chapala
; El Faro

A section of the Rio Hardy in the level agricultural plain between Mexicali and San Felipe. Photo JW.

Highways 2 and 5 (Kilomiter posts to the south appear to start from this junction) over the multilaned Calzada (wide avenue) Lopez Mateos. See the MEXICALI Map in Chapter 14. Its accompanying text provides suggestions for approaching the port-of-entry when returning to the United States and other information about Mexicali.

VALLE DE MEXICALI — Highway 5 is fringed by urban activity for many miles south of its junction with Highway 2 and what was formerly a 2 lane road is now a 4 lane divided highway south to **Km-22** with 4 lane construction under way in 1997 south to **Km 39**. The urbanization along the road hides the Valle de Mexicali farm lands from the traveler. The agricultural area extends south to approximately **Km-48**. These lands are irrigated by an extensive series of canals emanating from the *Presa Morelos* (Morelos Dam). This diversion extends across the Rio Colorado just south of the international border near the town of Algodones.

The history of the valley's development is indicated in the final section (SUMMARY OF ACTIVITIES IN THE NORTH) in Chapter 12 HISTORY.

(Km-20) GEOTHERMAL STEAM — Approximately five miles east of the highway at this point lies the Cerro Prieto geothermal steam wells and its related electric generating plant. The facility produces 620 megawatts of electricity, making it the second largest producer of geothermal steam energy in the world. It is exceeded only by the Geysers development north of San Francisco in the United States.

If the air is cool, extensive clouds of water vapor may be seen rising into the air above the wells. These may be visible during the morning hours but often are absent in the afternoon.

(Km-33) LA PUERTA — A small, Valle de Mexicali farming community with a cafe, store, and PEMEX stations at each end of town.

RIO HARDY AND RIO COLORADO — The Rio Colorado and its short tributary, the Rio Hardy, roughly parallel Highway 5 on the east from approximately **Km-52** to **Km-55**. During most years there is no water in the Rio Colorado as it is all diverted for domestic and agricultural purposes. During the early 1980s, SW United States experienced heavy rainfall, and water flowed down the Rio Colorado in excess of the storage capacity of its reservoirs. As a result, most of the older Campo communities along the Rio Hardy were flooded. Now several new campos (including Campo Sonora **Km-52**) have been developed on the river. There are also other campos located easterly from the highway which I have not investigated. These campos advertise bird hunting and fishing.

(Km 71) LAGUNA SALADA — At this point, Highway 5 lies on top of a 9-mile-long levee constructed across the southern end of Laguna Salada. The lake was filled during the flood years referred to above, but in most years there is no water in sight. During wet years, there are many waterbirds and some limited marsh lands along the northern shore. The San Felipe desert vegetation starts south of the lake.

(Km-98-105) MUD FLATS — In this vicinity, the desert vegetation is interrupted and the highway passes over the edge of the extensive mud flats that make up the delta area of the Rio Colorado. They are also closely approached near **Km-111**. These mud areas are up to 15 miles in width and extend easterly from the highway from Laguna Salada to near **Km-174**, a distance of almost 60 miles.

Wildlife experts report that the Rio Colorado delta once consisted of extensive marsh lands that made excellent waterbird habitat. The Auto Club map of

Baja California still identifies these areas with the symbol for marsh lands. Moisture-loving vegetation has now disappeared as a result of the water-regulating effects of the reservoirs upstream along the river. This situation provides another example of mankind's environmental compromises.

SIDE TRIP

(Km-141) JUNCTION OF HIGHWAYS 3 AND 5 — *It is 210 km (130 miles) to Ensenada via Highway 3. See Chapter 16 for a full description. The easterly portion of this route provides an interesting side trip from Highway 5. It is 28-miles to the base of the majestic escarpment of the Peninsular Range Mountains, through terrain typical of the Basin and Range Geological Province. A further 5-mile climb reaches the top of the grade.*

The vegetation of this Highway 3 segment of the San Felipe Desert is considerably more interesting than that in view from most of Highway 5. This is particularly true of the 5-mile section which climbs up the escarpment. An outstanding stand of barrel cactus is present at the top of the grade. End SIDE TRIP.

A fancy rest area, and restaurant were constructed at this Highway 3 and 5 junction in early 1992. At that time I wrote "I can't conceive of why a picnic area is needed at such a place and will make book that it will be in ruins in a few years." I was wrong. In 1997 the area was going strong.

A roadside residence and cafe lie about 0.7 miles south of the Highway 3 and 5 junction. Of particular interest are the antique gas pumps that require pumping fuel into their glass containers by hand. They were still in use in 1992 but have since been replaced by a more modern station.

ROCA CONSAG — After proceeding south of the Highway 3 and 5 junction, start looking to the SE, over the Sea of Cortez, for a view of *Roca Consag* (Consag Rock). It is a steep-sided, isolated pinnacle rising sharply from the sea to a height of 286 feet. It lies approximately due east from San Felipe at a distance of 18 miles offshore. Fishing boats from the town use it as a destination point.

The rock is named in honor of Padre Fernando Consag, one of the most prominent of Baja's Jesuit priests. In 1746 he conducted a maritime exploration of the northern reaches of the Sea of Cortez and the mouth of the Rio Colorado.

(KM 150) -- Also look ahead for several isolated peaks along the coast of the Sea of Cortez. They lie only a few degrees to the east of the line of the highway. These peaks are situated immediately north of San Felipe. They can be used to judge one's progress in the journey to this community.

(Km-172) SAN PEDRO MARTIR MOUNTAINS —At this location, high points on the main ridge of the Sierra San Pedro Martir are approximately due west from the highway. The principal peak is 10,126-foot Picacho del Diablo, Baja's highest point. As at other places along Highway 5, the base of the mountain's eastern escarpment is obscured from view by intervening lower ranges.

Picacho del Diablo (the Devil's Pike) lies near the center of the Parque Nacional Sierra San Pedro Martir. The park and its pine and fir forests may best be reached from Highway 1 south of Colonet. It is described in Chapter 18.

(Km-174) CAMPOS — Near this point is the southern end of the Rio Colorado mud flats. The desert vegetation now directly adjoins the sea. As a result, the coast between here and San Felipe is lined with a series of campos. (See comments under San Felipe below.) Each campo is reached over a short dirt road extending easterly from Highway 5.

The double-arch monument entering San Felipe. Photo JW.

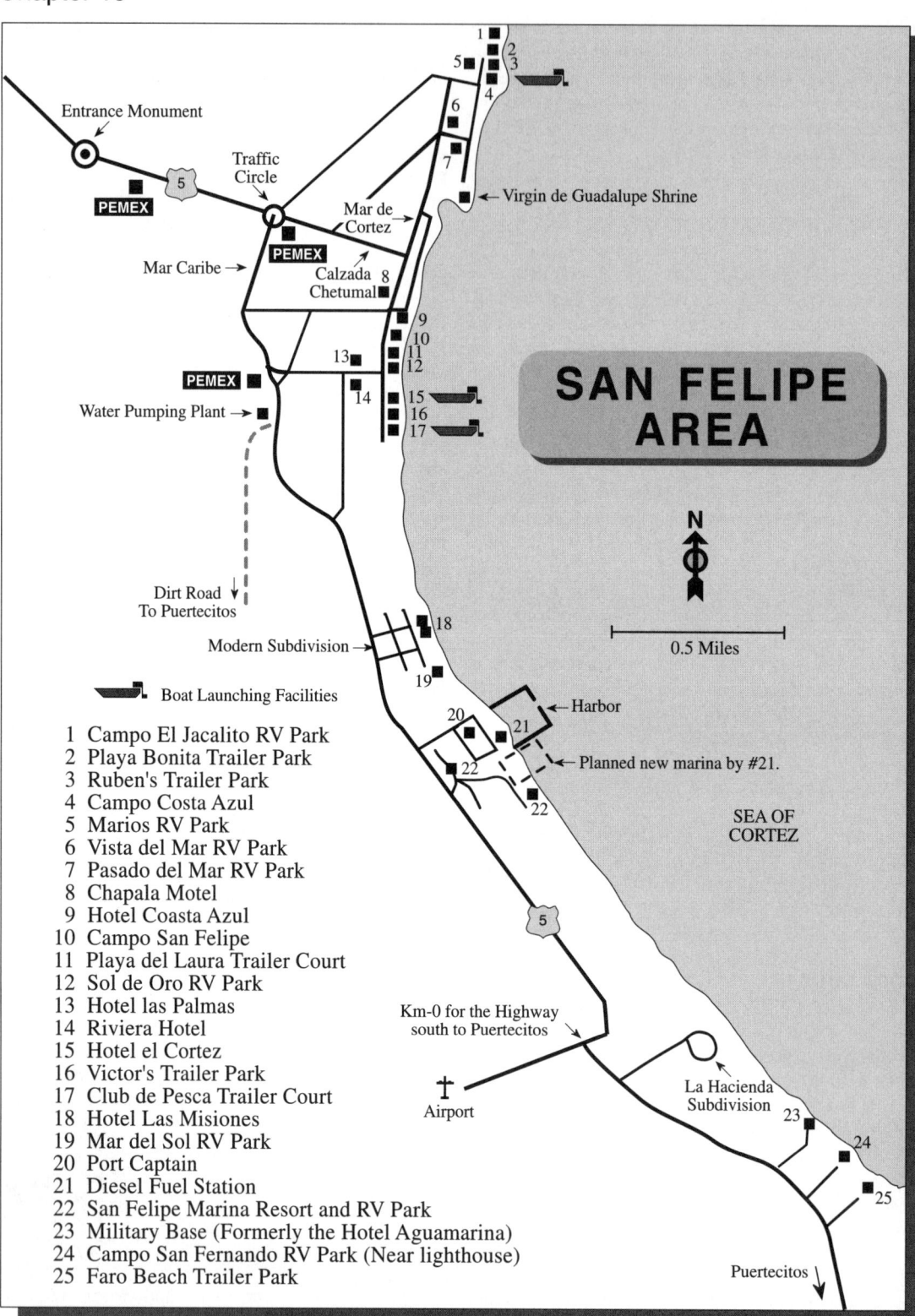

Entrance Monument

Traffic Circle

PEMEX

Mar de Cortez

Mar Caribe →

PEMEX

Calzada Chetumal

PEMEX

Water Pumping Plant →

Dirt Road To Puertecitos

Modern Subdivision →

Boat Launching Facilities

→ Virgin de Guadalupe Shrine

SAN FELIPE AREA

N

0.5 Miles

18

19

Harbor

20

21

22

22

← Planned new marina by #21.

SEA OF CORTEZ

5

Km-0 for the Highway south to Puertecitos →

Airport

La Hacienda Subdivision

23

24

25

Puertecitos ↓

1 Campo El Jacalito RV Park
2 Playa Bonita Trailer Park
3 Ruben's Trailer Park
4 Campo Costa Azul
5 Marios RV Park
6 Vista del Mar RV Park
7 Pasado del Mar RV Park
8 Chapala Motel
9 Hotel Coasta Azul
10 Campo San Felipe
11 Playa del Laura Trailer Court
12 Sol de Oro RV Park
13 Hotel las Palmas
14 Riviera Hotel
15 Hotel el Cortez
16 Victor's Trailer Park
17 Club de Pesca Trailer Court
18 Hotel Las Misiones
19 Mar del Sol RV Park
20 Port Captain
21 Diesel Fuel Station
22 San Felipe Marina Resort and RV Park
23 Military Base (Formerly the Hotel Aguamarina)
24 Campo San Fernando RV Park (Near lighthouse)
25 Faro Beach Trailer Park

The dark hill in the photo's left sector is Punta San Felipe. San Felipe and its harbor are to the right of the point. Photo JW.

BOB & JEAN BACKROAD

SIDE TRIP

(Km-180) CANON DIABLO — *Leaving Highway 5 to the right (west) is the most direct route to Canon Diablo and Canon Diablito. It is trip #1 of the "Bob and Jean Backroad" Recommendations presented in Chapter 3. The two canyons are cut into the steep eastern escarpment of the Sierra San Pedro Martir. They offer year-round streams, pools and waterfalls along with a shady camping spot. The road into the canyons is west from Rancho Santa Clara as shown on the AAA map. This is a trip of about 32 miles.* End SIDE TRIP

(Km-191) SAN FELIPE ARCH — A large, white, double-arch monument is constructed within a traffic circle at this point. It marks the entrance to the community of San Felipe, a town of some 19,000 people.

SAN FELIPE — One mile east of the entrance arch on Highway 5 lies another traffic circle. Highway 5 turns southward at this point. Continue straight ahead for the town's downtown area. Also located at the traffic circle is one of the town's PEMEX stations. Diesel fuel has not been available. It can be obtained at the diesel storage area at the southern end of the harbor south of town.

The community's main shopping area is located on Calzada Chetumal and Mar de Cortez within a few blocks of the junction of these two streets. See the SAN FELIPE AREA Map for the location of the principal hotels and trailer courts. The RV parks in San Felipe and others located south of town are good-to-

excellent facilities and are in sharp contrast to most of the campos described below.

The San Felipe-Puertecitos area is one of Baja's six principal tourist areas. This is due in large measure to its location only a few miles from the United States. It can thus be reached on weekend trips and is particularly busy on holiday weekends. It contains by far the largest concentration of RV parks and campos of any locale in Baja. In this regard it is becoming a southern extension of the "Snowbird" centers located in southern Arizona. Perhaps the word is spreading among these people that it is safe to travel in Baja, and that with only a few more miles of driving, one may spend the winter at the seaside and leave the drab Arizona desert behind. There are long, sandy beaches both north and south of town. These are an inviting environment for the owners of motorcycles, dune buggies, and other types of off-road vehicles.

Adjoining the beaches north of town are dozens of campos. They vary in size but generally consist of a group of modest residences and trailers owned by Norte Americanos. The mandatory decoration for these dwellings appear to be signs appropriated from the highways and other public places north of the border.

It would also appear that ownership of some form of open-air, specially crafted dune buggy is required equipment. Although I am sure that the great majority of the campo people do not fall in the unruly category, the San Felipe-Puertecitos area, without question, has an atmosphere quite different from that found in other parts of the peninsula.

Hotel Las Misiones. Punta San Felipe lies in the background. Photo JW.

damaged when the peninsula was crossed by a hurricane in October 1997. Inquire locally before using this section of road. Low-water crossings (vados) are a common feature along Baja's highways, but, no where are they as abrupt as those in some sections of the highway north of Puertecitos. Be prepared to lower your speed to about 30 MPH in driving through these obstructions. The mileage figures below start at San Felipe.

Lying south of San Felipe is a breakwater-lined harbor. It is the home port for many of the shrimp boats that ply the shallow waters of the northern Sea of Cortez. Conventional fishing is good in the area, but launching small boats is complicated by the high tides associated with the constricted upper end of the Sea of Cortez. These may exceed twenty feet and launching ramps are usable only at high tide. There are currently no marinas but one is planned adjoining the above noted harbor (See SAN FELIPE AREA Map).

San Felipe is home for Tony Reyes Fishing Tours. This firm charters a large sportfishing vessel that travels to the Midriff Islands 200 miles south in the Sea of Cortez. For information contact The Long Fin, 4010 E. Chapman Ave. Suite D, Orange CA 92669 (714) 538 8010.

SAN FELIPE TO PUERTECITOS — Puertecitos is the approximate dividing point between the Basin and Range Geological Province to the north and the Peninsular Range Province to the south. With few exceptions, the coastline between San Felipe and Puertecitos is formed by level terrain with almost continuous sandy beaches and shallow offshore depths. Mountains start south of Puertecitos and a majority of the coast consists of rocky bluffs or shingle beaches with deep water close to shore. Thus, both swimming and the launching of small boats at high tide is far more easily accomplished north of Puertecitos.

It is 56.1 miles (paved) from San Felipe to Puertecitos and an additional 87.4 miles (unpaved) from Puertecitos to Highway 1 at Laguna Chapala (total 143.5 miles). Portions of this latter 87.4 miles were

1.1 Miles — The San Felipe sea water pumping plant adjoins the west side of the highway. An old dirt surface road toward Puertecitos leaves the highway directly in front of this facility. After 35 miles, it joins Highway 5. One may visit an abandoned open-pit sulfur mine along the way.

2.7 Miles — A blacktop road leads to the San Felipe harbor and its adjoining industrial park. Note that most vessels are moored along the outer breakwater. This is because there is no water in the inshore portions of the basin at low tide.

6.5 Miles — Highway junction. An oiled surface highway to the airport runs straight ahead (west). Highway 5 veers to the left (SE). This is the zero point for kilometer posts between here and Puertecitos.

10.8 Miles — A concrete road leads in a short distance to the Faro Beach Trailer Park. Its sign boasts that it is the finest resort in Baja, and it does appear to be an excellent facility. Between here and Puertecitos you will encounter dozens of side roads leading to beach-side campos. The most prominent of these are Laguna Percebu, Bahia Santa Maria and Playa Mexico.

56.1 Miles — Arrive at Puertecitos. The paved road ended here in spring 1995. The road to the south is built to highway standards except for a short segment through the community of Puertecitos. The eventual paved highway will no doubt pass a short distance inland.

PUERTECITOS — This community surrounds a well protected but very shallow natural harbor. There is a boat launching ramp on the north side of the entrance to the cove. Near the head of the cove is the Puertecitos Resort, a cafe, RV park and PEMEX station. I have heard that the PEMEX station appeared abandoned in 1996. This may be because of competition caused by a newer station at Rancho Grande some miles to the south. There is a nearby airstrip.

Puertecitos consists of several hundred homes owned mostly by Norte Americanos. The quality of these structures is generally well above that found in the campos, but the community clearly bears the special flavor of the San Felipe-Puertecitos area. It is no doubt the world's leading depository for stolen road signs. No house is complete without one or more. Dune buggies are also in plentiful supply. Perhaps the highpoint is a very small but prominent outhouse bearing the delightful label "Hoppy's El Stinko House."

PUERTECITOS SOUTH TO HIGHWAY 1 — There are a few small resorts between Puertecitos and Highway 1. New signs announcing lots for rent and new campos began appearing several years ago, no doubt in reaction to completion of the oiled-surface road

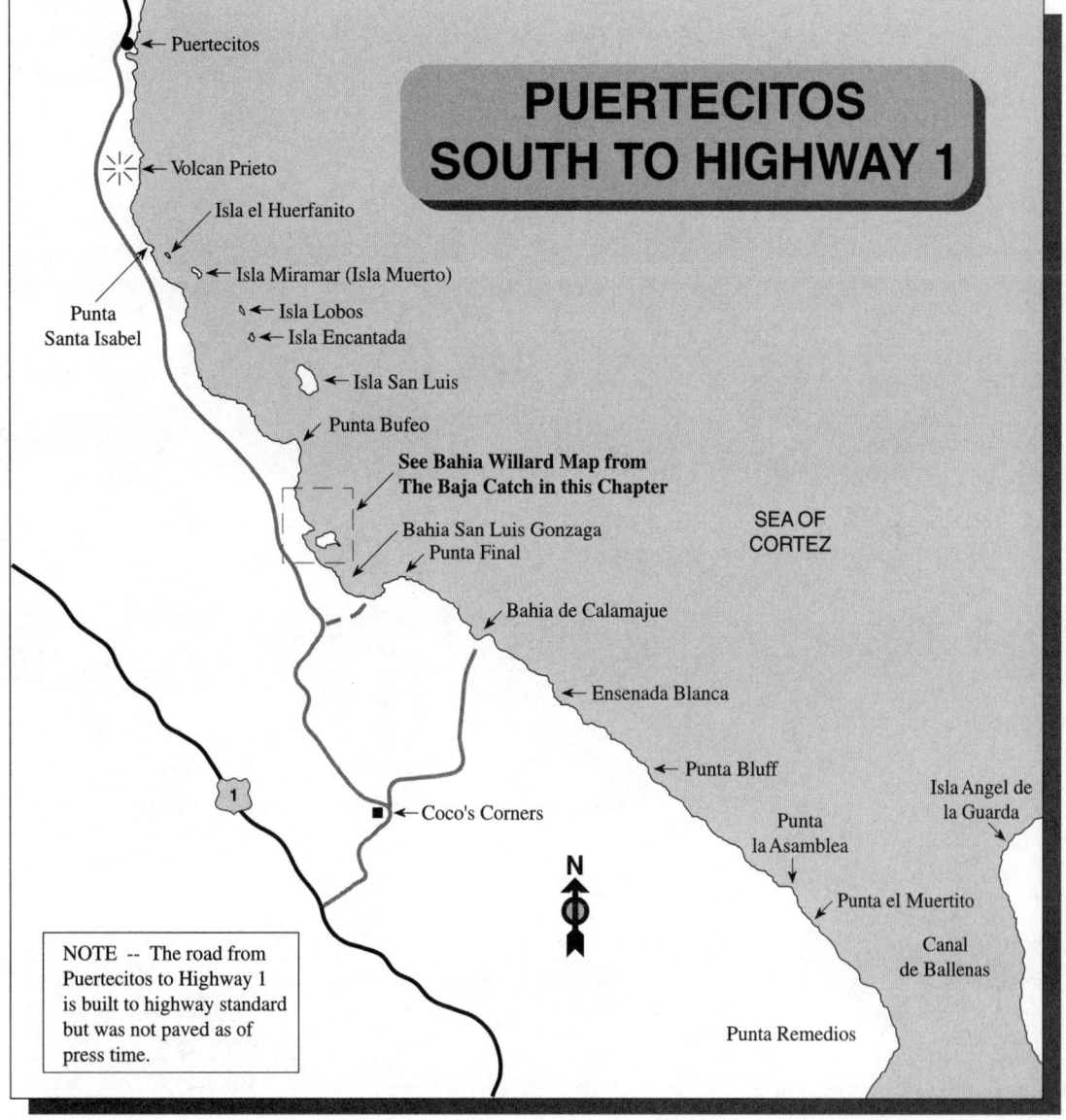

PUERTECITOS SOUTH TO HIGHWAY 1

Puertecitos
Volcan Prieto
Isla el Huerfanito
Isla Miramar (Isla Muerto)
Punta Santa Isabel
Isla Lobos
Isla Encantada
Isla San Luis
Punta Bufeo
See Bahia Willard Map from The Baja Catch in this Chapter
Bahia San Luis Gonzaga
Punta Final
SEA OF CORTEZ
Bahia de Calamajue
Ensenada Blanca
Punta Bluff
Isla Angel de la Guarda
Coco's Corners
Punta la Asamblea
Punta el Muertito
Canal de Ballenas
N
NOTE -- The road from Puertecitos to Highway 1 is built to highway standard but was not paved as of press time.
Punta Remedios

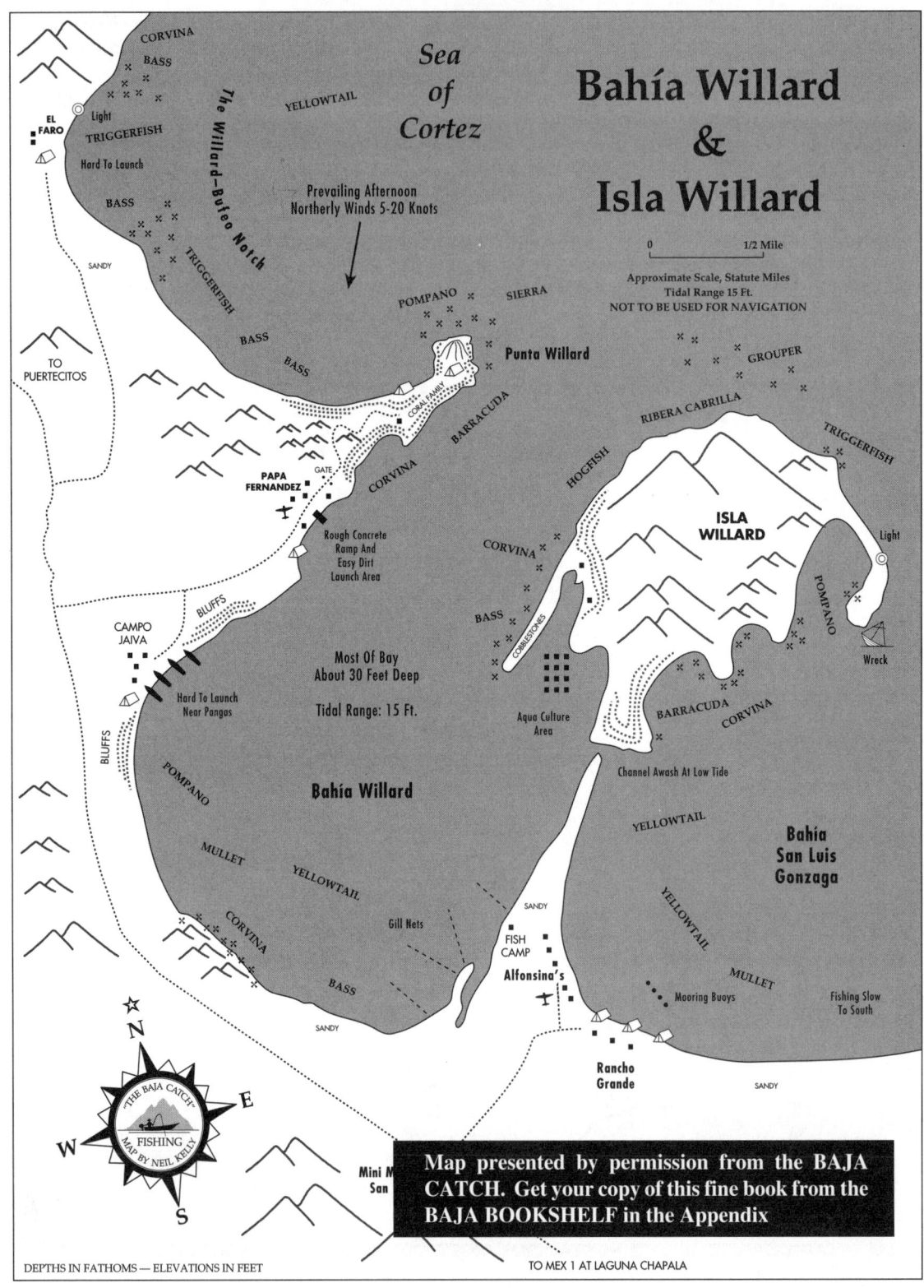

Bahía Willard & Isla Willard

Sea of Cortez

CORVINA
BASS
YELLOWTAIL
TRIGGERFISH

El FARO
Light
Hard To Launch
BASS
SANDY
TRIGGERFISH
BASS
BASS
TO PUERTECITOS

The Willard–Bufeo Notch

Prevailing Afternoon
Northerly Winds 5-20 Knots

POMPANO
SIERRA

Punta Willard
CORAL FAMILY
BARRACUDA
CORVINA

GROUPER
TRIGGERFISH
RIBERA CABRILLA
HOGFISH

0   1/2 Mile
Approximate Scale, Statute Miles
Tidal Range 15 Ft.
NOT TO BE USED FOR NAVIGATION

ISLA WILLARD
Light

PAPA FERNANDEZ
GATE
Rough Concrete
Ramp And
Easy Dirt
Launch Area

CORVINA
BASS
COBBLESTONES
POMPANO
Wreck

BLUFFS
CAMPO JAIVA
Hard To Launch
Near Pangas
BLUFFS

Most Of Bay
About 30 Feet Deep

Tidal Range: 15 Ft.

Aqua Culture Area
BARRACUDA
CORVINA

Channel Awash At Low Tide

Bahía Willard

POMPANO
MULLET
YELLOWTAIL

YELLOWTAIL

Bahía
San Luis
Gonzaga

CORVINA

Gill Nets

SANDY
FISH CAMP
Alfonsina's

YELLOWTAIL
YELLOWTAIL
MULLET
Mooring Buoys
Fishing Slow
To South

BASS
SANDY

Rancho
Grande
SANDY

N
E
W
S
"THE BAJA CATCH"
FISHING
MAP BY NEIL KELLY

Mini M
San

Map presented by permission from the BAJA
CATCH. Get your copy of this fine book from the
BAJA BOOKSHELF in the Appendix

DEPTHS IN FATHOMS — ELEVATIONS IN FEET

TO MEX 1 AT LAGUNA CHAPALA

south to Puertecitos, and anticipation of its furthur extension. Most of these signs were in poor repair in 1995 with little evidence of new development. The road south of Puertecitos is too rough to invite many visitors and this section of Baja will no doubt remain little changed until the road is surfaced. There are many good places to drive to camp sites on the sea-coast over dirt roads from 1/4-to-1/2 miles in length. Some of these will no doubt be taken over by campos but for now this section of coast has little development. Perhaps the extreme shortage of fresh water in the area will keep it that way. Also there are few good sand beaches. Most coastal areas are rocky making boat launching and swim-ming access a bit difficult.

74.6 Miles — Side road to the Huerfanito fish camp and camping area. Fishing boats are for rent.

96.6 Miles — A dirt road leads to the east and in 1.6 miles arrives at the small Punta Bufeo Resort. Most of its buildings are made of stone. Those along the beach are private residences. Inland a short distance is a small but attractive restaurant and several rental cabins.

102.3 Miles — A 0.6 mile long side road leads to the Papa Fernandez Resort. It offers several modest cabins, concrete boat ramp, and fishing pangas for rent. A dirt road leads westerly a short distance to a good camping area at Punta Willard. Papa Fernandez founded his resort many years ago and in spring 1995 was still alive at the age of 100. Stop by and say hello.

106.1 Miles — A 0.8 mile long secondary road leads to Bahia San Luis Gonzaga and the southern end of a long row of vacation homes with an outstanding sand beach on their eastern flank. A dirt airstrip is on the other side. At the north end of the residential area is Alfonsina's, a modest hotel offering five cot-filled rooms and a restaurant. Our 1995 survey also found a higher standard airstrip immediately south of the above noted facilities. A gas station and other build-ings were completed west of the road. This Villas Mar de Cortez (Rancho Grande) development has plans for a fancy subdivision, golf course and marina, aimed at serving the private aviation flyer. They have made a brave start, but only time will tell.

Highway 5 moves inland at this point and leaves the Sea of Cortez behind. The road passes over relatively level terrain southward to the 120.3 mile point noted below.

116.5 Miles — A low standard dirt road branches to the east and arrives at the Punta Final development in 9.1 miles. (I have not driven this road.) When visited by sea in 1984 there were a group of about 30 houses and trailers owned by Norte Americanos most of whom arrive by private aircraft on a nearby dirt strip. There was no resort facility. Small boats can be launched at low tide from a sand spit connecting the peninsular shore with a small nearby island.

120.3 Miles — At this point the highway enters more mountainous terrain. The desert vegetation ahead improves in aesthetic appeal and many granite boul-ders begin to appear. It is similar, but not of as high a quality, as the Catavina Boulder Fields area along Highway 1.

SIDE TRIP

129.9 Miles — Here is a road junction now named Coco's Corners in honor of a small enterprise contain-ing a restaurant, RV parking, sodas, and auto repairs. It is decorated by various items rescued from the area's trash cans. *At this same point a good quality secondary road branches to the left (north) and arrives at the fish camp of Calamajue in 23.0 miles. The camp houses the single male fishermen while families live at a village some 1/2 mile inland. A few camp spots are available on the shingle beach north of the camp.*

My trip into Calamajue provided one of the most pleasur-able experiences I have had in Baja California. The area's metamorphosed rock provides road building material that permits a relatively smooth ride with minimal washboarding. In my view, it is the best secondary road in the peninsula. The surrounding mountains are also very scenic and the soil supports a far greater growth of annual plants than most other places. I hope you might arrive at similar conclusions. End SIDE TRIP.

143.5 Miles — Junction with Highway 1 near **Km C-229**. The dry lake bed of Laguna Chapala lies south of the junction point. There is a small cafe and residence west of Highway 1 near the junction point.

CHAPTER 16
HIGHWAY 3

This chapter describes the two separate sections of Highway 3. They are Baja's most lightly used highways; yet road construction standards are as good as anywhere in the peninsula. Both sections traverse hilly-to-mountainous terrain and offer good scenery.

HIGHWAY 3 OVERVIEW -- Here is a brief overview of the two sections of Highway 3.

<u>TECATE TO HIGHWAY 1 NEAR ENSENADA</u> — This 106 km (66 mile) segment of Highway 3 passes through rolling hills covered with chaparral. Also present are several flat valleys devoted to agricultural. There are no large communities, and in the spring the green countryside is very pleasant. It resembles the area surrounding the cities of southern California in the United States but is without the massive intrusion of urbanization. It has the type of highway scenery one would like to admire on a Sunday drive.

This section of Highway 3 also provides tourists northbound on Highway 1 with the opportunity to cross into the United States at the lightly used port-of-entry at Tecate and of then proceeding north on California Highway 94. I do not understand why anyone who has been to Ensenada -- or farther south -- would return home any other way. (See the port-of-entry discussion in Chapter 7.) Using these same roads traveling south is also my favorite route for entering Baja for travelers living along the Pacific coast or Canada and the United States (See the *San Diego to Ensenada the Pleasant Way* insert map in the *Highway 3* map in this chapter). This routing offers pleasant but hilly terrain and bypasses the busy port-of-entry and city of Tijuana. The pleasant Barrett Lake RV Park in California offers a good place to spend the last night in the USA.

<u>ENSENADA TO HIGHWAY 5</u> — Containing 196 km (122 miles), this section of Highway 3 is almost exactly twice the length of the first segment. It also passes through hilly, and in some places, quite steep terrain. However, most of the route is over relatively gentle plateaus and valleys. There are few communities.

This section of highway offers travelers from the Yuma, Arizona area a means of reaching Ensenada and the area to the south without passing through San Diego and Tijuana. If your purpose is to see Mexico, why not drive through it, and leave the United States freeway system to the less fortunate. (This Highway 3 alternative will become unnecessary if and when oiling of Highway 5 from San Felipe south to Lake Chapala is completed. See Chapter 15).

TECATE — This community and the route to the Tecate port-of-entry are described in Chapter 14. Only about four kilometers of Highway 3 lies within the

The Domecq Winery and its vineyards in the Valle de la Calafia. The hilly terrain in the background displays numerous rounded granite boulders which are typical of the mountains along Highways 3 and 5 in northern Baja. Photo BW.

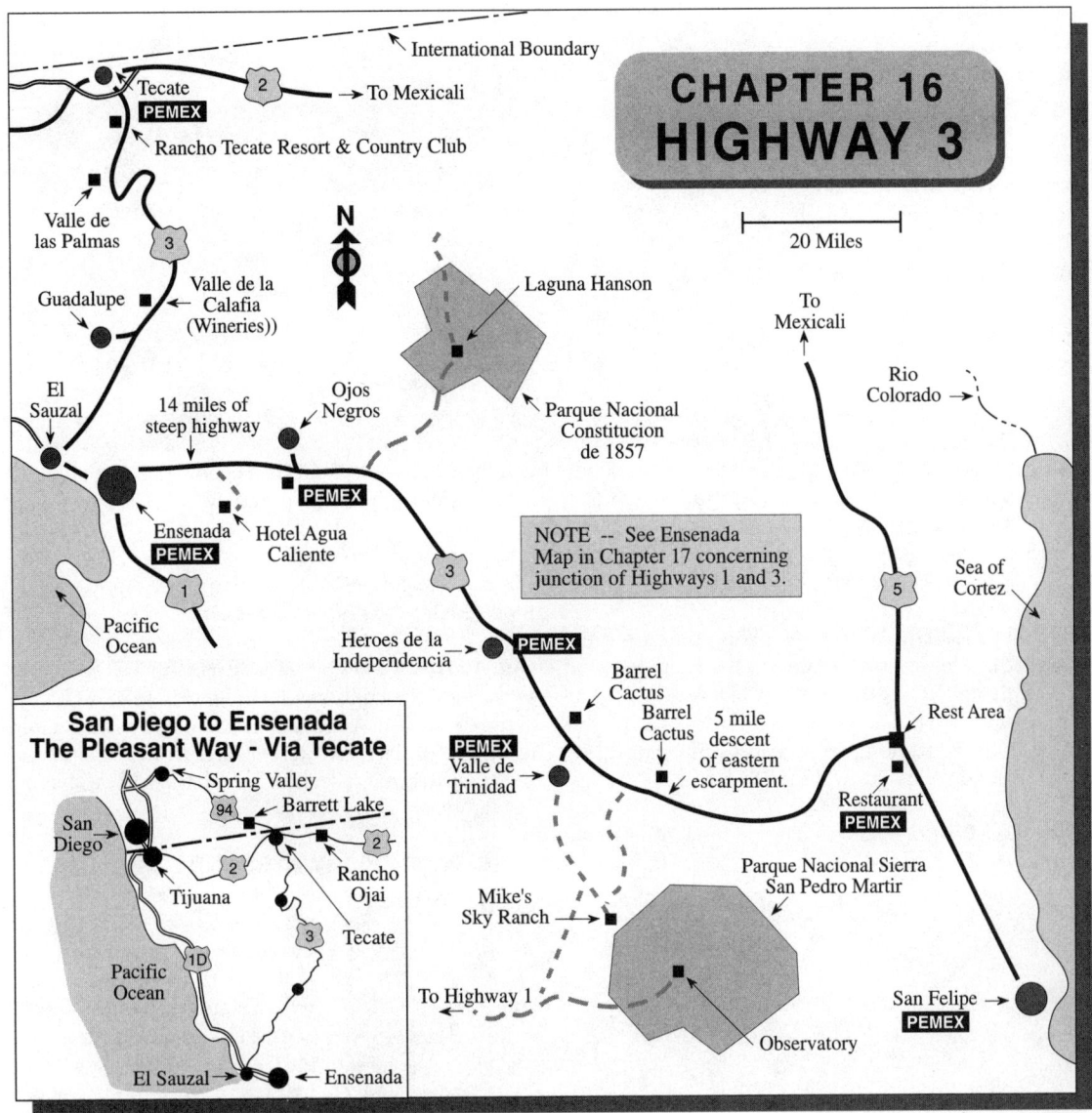

CHAPTER 16
HIGHWAY 3

Tecate
PEMEX
→ To Mexicali
2
International Boundary

Rancho Tecate Resort & Country Club

Valle de
las Palmas
3

N

20 Miles

Guadalupe
Valle de la
Calafia
(Wineries))

Laguna Hanson

To
Mexicali

Rio
Colorado →

El
Sauzal

14 miles of
steep highway

Ojos
Negros

Parque Nacional
Constitucion
de 1857

Sea of
Cortez

PEMEX

3

Ensenada
PEMEX

Hotel Agua
Caliente

5

NOTE -- See Ensenada
Map in Chapter 17 concerning
junction of Highways 1 and 3.

1

Pacific
Ocean

Heroes de la
Independencia

PEMEX

Barrel
Cactus
Barrel
Cactus

5 mile
descent
of eastern
escarpment.

Rest Area

PEMEX
Valle de
Trinidad

Restaurant
PEMEX

San Diego to Ensenada
The Pleasant Way - Via Tecate

Spring Valley
94
Barrett Lake

San
Diego
2

2
Tijuana

Rancho
Ojai

3
Tecate

Mike's
Sky Ranch

Parque Nacional Sierra
San Pedro Martir

San Felipe →
PEMEX

Pacific
Ocean
1D

To Highway 1
←

Observatory

El Sauzal →
← Ensenada

---

community. Traffic is moderate to light. Northbound travelers should have little trouble finding the port-of-entry into the United States. Also there is an interchange with the 2D 4-lane divided highway a short distance south of Tecate so that one may enter the expressway from the south without going into town.

The hills between Tecate and Valle de las Palmas are made-up of granite rock. The surface areas have been fractured and eroded into thousands of light-colored boulders. This coloration and erosion pattern is typical of granitic rock areas. One starts seeing vineyards starting at about **K-8**.

(Km-10) -- On the west side of the highway at this point is the Rancho Tecate Resort and Country Club. The golf course was under construction in 1997 and contained only 3 completed holes. However, an excellent hotel and restaurant were in operation.

(Km-29) VALLE DE LAS PALMAS — Here is a beautiful valley surrounded by hills. It is planted with grain, grapes, and olive and citrus orchards. Farther south, the highway passes through a series of similar valleys.

(Km-74) VALLE DE LA CALAFIA — This broad, flat valley is planted exclusively with vineyards and is home to the Domecq Winery. It is a modern facility and produces *Pedro Domecq* wine. The overall setting is the match for anything available in the wine country north of San Francisco in Alta California. There is a public tasting room and winery tours are available Monday through Friday 10:00 A.M. to 4:00 P.M. and Saturday 10:00 A.M. to 1:30 P.M.

SIDE TRIP

Across the highway from the Domecq Winery a level, natural surface road heads easterly and in 1.5 miles arrives at the L.A. Cetto Winery. This is a very pleasant facility which offers tours, and a nearby picnic and vista area. End SIDE TRIP

Ocotillo and creosote bush thinly vegetate the San Felipe desert along Highway 3 west of its junction with Highway 5. Photo JW.

(Km-77) GUADALUPE — The community of Guadalupe lies a short distance to the right (west) of the highway in another valley devoted largely to vineyards. This pleasant spot is the site of the last mission (no ruins) founded in Baja California. It saw service for only six years (1834-1840).

(Km-99) SCENIC VIEW — The journey from Tecate to the Pacific coast is almost over, and Highway 3 begins its final descent to the sea. In view, ahead, are the Islas Todos Santos. These two rocky islands lie ten miles offshore, SW from Ensenada.

(Km-105) JUNCTION WITH HIGHWAY 1-D — Highway 3 joins the Highway 1-D 4-lane divided highway at the coastal town of El Sauzal. Highway 1-D is a toll road north to Tijuana but is toll-free from this junction point south into Ensenada. See Chapter 17 for details of Highway 1 and Ensenada.

JUNCTION OF HIGHWAYS 3 AND 1 IN ENSENADA — The second section of Highway 3 starts in the heart of Ensenada at a junction point with old Highway 1 marked with a statue of Benito Juarez. See the Ensenada Map in Chapter 17. The statue is a key landmark as in our 1997 survey we saw no signing indicating the start of Highway 3. The initial 4 km of the route proceeds easterly over four-lane Calzada Cortez, one of Ensenada's main business streets. There are several PEMEX stations along the way.

(Km-4) ENTER MOUNTAINS — The flat lands on which much of Ensenada is built terminate near **Km-4,** and Highway 3 begins the longest sustained climb found anywhere

Laguna Hanson is framed in Jeffrey pine foliage in the Parque Nacional Constitucion de 1857. Photo JW.

on the peninsula's highways. The grade winds upward to near **Km-20**, after a brief respite it continues to **Km-26**. This steep and curving area can be taxing for vehicles pulling large recreation trailers. This could preclude their owners from using this otherwise fine highway as a route from the Yuma, Arizona, area to Ensenada.

This steep grade near the Pacific coast provides the exception to all other highway crossings of the Baja peninsula. In these other cases the steep section of highway is encountered near the Sea of Cortez coast where the highway crosses the east-facing escarpment of the Peninsular Range Mountains. In all these other cases the highway climb from west to east is a very gradual one.

PARQUE NACIONAL CONSTITUCION DE 1857

10 Miles

NOTE -- A large segmemt of the forest in the northern portion of the park was destroyed by fire in 1985.

SIDE TRIP

(Km-26) AGUA CALIENTE — *A short distance east of **Km 26** the highway reaches the top of the grade and descends into the Valle de Ojos Negros. Exactly at this high point a dirt road leaves to the right (south) and descends steeply for 5.4 miles to the Hotel Agua Caliente. (See HOTEL DESCRIPTIONS Section in Chapter 6.) The descent is steep but suitable, if recently graded, for most large RVs (other than trailers).*

The hotel has large swimming pools fed by hot springs. Camping is permitted in an area of giant live oak trees adjoining the hotel and the Rio San Carlos. End SIDE TRIP.

(Km-36) VALLE DE OJOS NEGROS — Highway 3 enters the western edge of the broad Valle de Ojos Negros (Black Eyes Valley). A short oiled access road heads left (north) at **Km-39** to the farming community of Ojos Negros. It once had a PEMEX station but it was gone in 1997 while a newer station built on Highway 3 near the road junction appeared abandoned. The flat valley continues to near **Km-50**.

SIDE TRIP

(Km-55) PARQUE NACIONAL CONSTITUCION DE 1857 (LAGUNA HANSON) — *A secondary road leaves the highway 200 yards east of **Km-55**. It is signed for Laguna Hanson 35 Km. This shallow lake (and the extensive stands of Jeffrey pine surrounding it) are the park's main attractions. It is 22.0 miles to Laguna Hanson from*

Highway 3. Although constructed to secondary road standards, the road has some rough spots. The entire route lies in decomposed granite soils and thus is subject to erosion following rain. It is marginal for larger RVs. (See the accompanying map for additional details.)

*One may also drive to Laguna Hanson from the north. See Chapter 14, **Km-72**. This northern road is of lower standard than the route from Highway 3, with the most difficult 2.5 mile segment lying in a granite, boulder area just inside the park's northern boundary.*

Laguna Hanson contains water following rains; when it is full it provides a very pleasant environment. The area surrounding the lake is heavily forested and of gentle terrain. There are minimum facility campsites at the water's edge along the western shore. End SIDE TRIP.

Chapter 16

VEGETATION — The vegetation east of Ensenada is chaparral typical of the California Vegetative Region. (See Chapter 10 VEGETATION.) East of Valle de Ojos Negros the highway slowly climbs over plateau lands. Near **Km-76** the traveler begins to see low juniper trees and an occasional pinyon pine. This is the lower fringe of the coniferous forest that covers the land in the national park to the NW.

(Km-91) HEROES DE LA INDEPENDENCIA -- A small community lies at this point. A PEMEX station (Nova only) is on the east side of the highway.

Along Highway 3 west of Ojos Negros is this rock formation painted to resemble the head of an alligator. North of the border the artists involved would have been thrown in jail for defacing the environment. In Baja they no doubt had a grand time. Photo BW.

(Km-119) DESCENT INTO VALLE DE TRINIDAD -- The highway starts a steep descent into the Valle de Trinidad. This is the start of a two-part drop from the mountains into the San Felipe desert. The second segment takes place east of the valley near **Km-149**. During this first portion notice the numerous barrel cacti growing on the steep slopes, a sign that you are rapidly approaching a change in vegetational types.

Near **Km-123** a secondary road bears right (south) to the farming community of Valle de Trinidad. It reaches the town's main street in about 1 mile. At this junction turn left for 0.5 miles to the PEMEX station. The road to the right leads to one of the backdoor entrances to the Parque Nacional Sierra San Pedro Martir. The preferred access route to this park leaves Highway 1 at **Km B-140** south of Colonet. (See Chapter 18.)

(Km 138) ROAD TO MIKE'S SKY RANCH — A secondary road to the right leads to Mike's Sky Ranch, a resort catering to private flyers. I have not been over this route.

(Km-148) HIGHWAY DESCENT — Highway 3 now starts the 4.9 mile second leg of its descent of the eastern escarpment of the Peninsular Range Mountains. As at the first segment, notice the dense stand of barrel cactus. Nowhere else in Baja are such large numbers of these plants in view from the highway. Also present are ocotillo, agave, cardon, and other species which are common in Baja's desert areas. The descent represents a vegetational transition from the California Region vegetation, to the west, and the San Felipe Desert, to the east.

(Km-157) VEGETATION AND GEOGRAPHIC CHANGE — Here, at the base of the mountains, are encountered two major changes. The chaparral vegetation of the Peninsular Range Mountains is left behind, to the west, and is replaced with the widely spaced species of the San Felipe Desert. Between here and the Highway 5 junction to the east the presence of numerous ocotillo plants gives some degree of character to the landscape; yet overall this San Felipe Desert has relatively drab vegetation due to the extreme dryness caused by its location in the rainshadow of the mountains.

The highway has also entered a typical portion of the Basin and Range Geologic Province. (See Chapter 9 GEOLOGY.) Note that the highway will traverse relatively flat land but that several north-south ranges of mountains project from the plain. Also note the majestic cliffs extending south from the foot of the grade. This is one of the best places in Baja to view the dramatic eastern escarpment of the Peninsular Range Mountains.

(Km-196) JUNCTION WITH HIGHWAY 5 — Highways 3 and 5 meet at this uninspiring point in the desert. Fortunately, the inviting Sea of Cortez has been in view from Highway 3 en route to the junction for several miles to the east. While I feel the place is uninspiring, the Mexican Highway Department was inspired in 1992 to build a picnic area and restaurant at the spot. If anyone ever decides to have a picnic here, please let me know.

CHAPTER 17
TIJUANA TO ENSENADA

Thousands of Baja Buffs find that the Magnificent Peninsula provides a welcome relief from, shall we say benevolently, the hectic conditions of the Los Angeles-San Diego metropolitan areas. Many buffs would also agree that decompression takes place in three stages: (1) Tijuana to Ensenada, (2) Ensenada to San Quintin, and (3) south of San Quintin. Described in this chapter is the first stage of relief. It may be undertaken without a doctor's perscription.

Highway 1-D between Tijuana and Ensenada is one of Baja's best highways. It and the older, more or less parallel Highway 1 are described in this chapter.

OVERVIEW OF HIGHWAY 1-D — Highway 1-D is a four-lane, divided, limited-access toll road. It is signed "Cuota" meaning "fare." A toll is collected to use all but short sections at either end. It may be paid in either pesos or U.S. dollars. (There are three toll-gates as shown on the Chapter 17 Map.) This route is the fastest, safest, and most scenic way to travel between Tijuana to Ensenada.

There are approximately twenty interchanges along Highway 1-D. I say "approximately" in that several of the original interchanges are sometimes closed and new ones are sometimes constructed. In all cases, it is possible to leave the highway and then to reenter at or near the same point to travel in the same direction. In most places, one may also reenter to travel in the opposite direction.

OVERVIEW OF HIGHWAY 1 — There are three distinct sections of Highway 1. All are built to good two-lane standards. There is no toll on this road so it is signed "Libre" meaning "free."

TIJUANA TO ROSARITO — This is the quickest way to travel south for those starting their journey from the vicinity of the bullring on Boulevard Agua Caliente in Tijuana. However, it offers no advantages for the southbound traveler starting at the Tijuana-San Ysidro port-of-entry who should use Highway 1-D. In contrast, it is my recommended route for returning north as it provides access to the Otay Mesa port-of-entry.

The southern most 7.3 miles of this route is a four-lane, divided highway. It is described in the RETURNING TO THE U.S.A. Section in Chapter 14.

ROSARITO TO LA MISION — This section of highway passes along the edge of a series of communities made-up largely of homes, condominium developments, restaurants, and other facilities serving people from north of the border. I estimated that 75-percent of this area was committed to some form of development during our 1997 survey. Unless you are headed for one of these destinations, taking this route offers no advantages to the southbound traveler. This portion of Highway 1 is also heavily used by truckers and others who wish to escape the tolls charged on Highway 1-D. Unless you are short on funds, the latter route is by far the best choice.

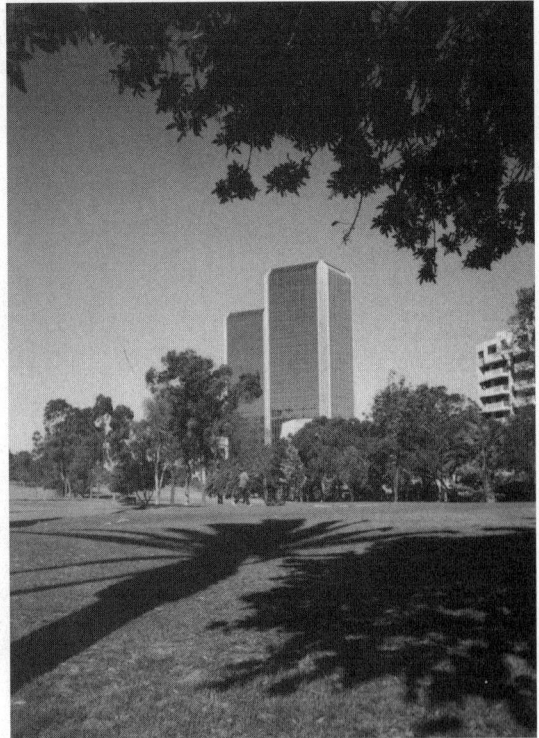

The twin towers of Tijuana's Grand Hotel as viewed from the nearby Tijuana Country Club. Photo BW.

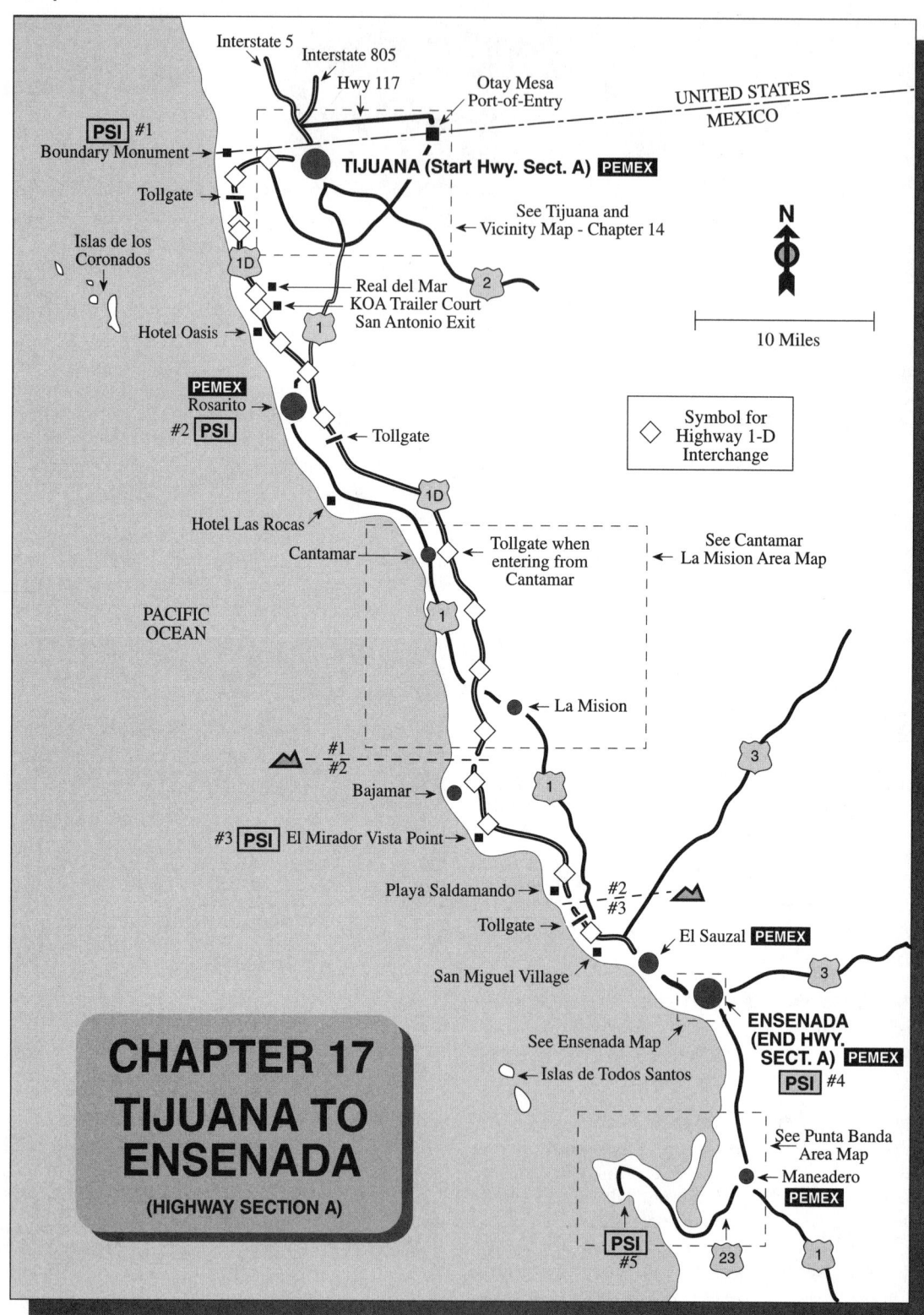

Interstate 5
Interstate 805
Hwy 117
Otay Mesa
Port-of-Entry
UNITED STATES
MEXICO

PSI #1
Boundary Monument →
■

TIJUANA (Start Hwy. Sect. A) **PEMEX**

Tollgate →

See Tijuana and
Vicinity Map - Chapter 14

N

Islas de los
Coronados

1D

2

Real del Mar
KOA Trailer Court
San Antonio Exit

10 Miles

1

Hotel Oasis →

PEMEX
Rosarito →
#2 **PSI**

Symbol for
Highway 1-D
Interchange

Tollgate

1D

Hotel Las Rocas →

See Cantamar
La Mision Area Map

Cantamar →

Tollgate when
entering from
Cantamar

1

PACIFIC
OCEAN

La Mision ←

3

#1
#2

1

Bajamar →

#3 **PSI** El Mirador Vista Point →

Playa Saldamando →

#2
#3

Tollgate →

El Sauzal **PEMEX**

San Miguel Village

3

**ENSENADA
(END HWY.
SECT. A)** **PEMEX**

PSI #4

See Ensenada Map →

Islas de Todos Santos

**CHAPTER 17
TIJUANA TO
ENSENADA**

(HIGHWAY SECTION A)

See Punta Banda
Area Map

Maneadero
PEMEX

PSI
#5

23

1

LA MISION TO EL SAUZAL —
This is an inland road through the mountains. It provides a pleasant drive through undeveloped countryside but does not offer the excellent scenic vistas of the ocean and coast which are available from Highway 1-D.

The balance of this chapter describes the Highway 1-D route from Tijuana to Ensenada.

(Km A-0) TIJUANA — After entering Mexico at the San Ysidro port-of-entry one must drive a circle route bearing left. Follow the signs for Rosarito and Ensenada. After the circle, Highway 1-D proceeds west along the international boundary fence toward the Pacific. See the TIJUANA AND VICINITY Map and the ENTERING TIJUANA FROM THE NORTH Section of Chapter 14 for more details.

PSI #1

(Km A-9) BOUNDARY MONUMENT — Just prior to **Km A-9** one encounters an interchange signed "Playas de Tijuana" as Highway 1-D begins a broad curve from westbound to southbound. The Bullring by-the-Sea is in view near the coast, and its access road is easy to find by taking this offramp.

Immediately north of the bullring and adjacent to the Tijuana lighthouse is the international boundary fence and a twelve-foot obelisk commemorating the establishment of the United States-Mexican boundary which resulted from the Mexican-American War and the February 2, 1848, Treaty of Guadalupe Hidalgo. While the monument itself is not overly impressive, it has been included as stop No. 1 on the POINTS OF SPECIAL INTEREST Tour. It is a good place to pause and reflect on the history of the two countries and also to relax a moment and celebrate your safe arrival in Mexico's Magnificent Peninsula.

The northerly tollgate is located just south of the "Playas de Tijuana" interchange near **Km A-10**.

The international boundary monument a few yards from the Pacific Ocean at Tijuana. Sadly, there has to be a chain-link fence between the two countries. Photo JW.

(Km A-11) ISLAS CORONADOS — Islas Coronados (Coronados Islands) lie about 6 miles offshore. These islands are in view for many miles along Highway 1-D but all four of the two large and two smaller islands can be seen from here, near **Km A-11**.

(KM 19.5) REAL DEL MAR -- On the inland side of the highway lies the very swank Hotel Real del Mar and a 18-hole golf course. The course is described in the *Golf Course* section of Chapter 6.

(Km A-22) SAN ANTONIO DEL MAR — The Rosarito KOA trailer court lies on the side of a nicely landscaped hill 0.2 miles east of the highway after taking the San Antonio interchange. It is the closest trailer court to the international border along Highway 1-D. Most of its sites are rented on a year-round basis but there is always room for overnighters.

(Km A-25) OASIS HOTEL AND RV RESORT --

The hilly Real del Mar Golf Resort with the Pacific Ocean and the Islas Coronados in the background. Photo BW.

The map shows the Cantamar La Mision Area with the following labels:

- Hotel New Port Beach
- Cantamar Interchange
- Greenhouses and Mission Site
- Cantamar
- El Descanso
- San Dunes
- Cuenta Interchange Southbound only (No access to Hwy. 1)
- Rio Discanso
- 5 Miles
- PACIFIC OCEAN
- **CANTAMAR LA MISION AREA**
- Los Alistros Trailer Park
- La Fonda Hotel
- La Mision - Plaza del Mar Interchange
- Beach and Parking Area
- Rio Guadalupe (Tijuana Water Source)
- Mal Paso Beach -- Camping
- La Mision
- Mission Ruins
- Baja Seasons RV Park
- La Salina Interchange
- La Salina Marina Development

Between the highway and beach lies a fancy hotel and RV complex. It is accessible only from the southbound lanes of Highway 1-D.

(Km A-34) ROSARITO — Rosarito is a major center of tourist-orientated shops, motels, hotels and restaurants strung out along a lengthy section of old Highway 1. The town adjoins an excellent sand beach. Government statistics indicate that 11 percent of the tourists entering Baja have Rosarito as their destination point. The most visible facilities are the eight-story Quinta del Mar Resort and other high-rise buildings. In the past, Rosarito was a somewhat shoddy looking town but now its appearance has been greatly enhanced by development of the main street into 4-lanes with palm trees planted along the median strip. Seemingly endless stop signs and traffic lights impede progress, so stay on Highway 1-D unless you particularly wish to visit the town. The middle of the three tollgates straddles this highway immediately south of Rosarito.

PSI #2

The historic Rosarito Beach Hotel lies on the beach near the southern end of town. Portions of the hotel are one of three casinos that operated in the border area during the late 1920s and early 1930s. Many of the rooms have recently been remodeled and a new wing has been added. It is stop No. 2 on the POINTS OF SPECIAL INTEREST Tour. You may leave High-

The Islas Coronados as viewed from Highway 1. Photo BW.

way 1-D at the southernmost of the three exits into Rosarito north of **Km A-34** to visit the hotel without having to drive through all of the town's stop signs.

There are many smaller motels, restaurants, and condominiums from Rosarito south to Cantamar. One must travel on non-toll Highway 1 to access this area. This is also the route to use to reach the Hotel Las Rocas and the Hotel New Port Beach.

(Km A-53) CANTAMAR AND EL DESCANSO — The Cantamar interchange is the place to exit Highway 1-D to visit the towns of Cantamar and El Descanso. At the southern edge of the latter community are situated large coastal sand dunes that provide an excellent dune buggy area.

South of the sand dunes, Highway 1-D crosses the Rio Descanso at **Km A-55**. Just south of this kilometer post look for a large complex of glass greenhouses inland from the highway. Behind the greenhouses can be seen a small church. This church stands on the site of the Descanso mission established here in 1814 by the Dominican Order. It was the next to last of the peninsular missions.

(Km A-58) LA MISION — The La Mision-Plaza del Mar interchange is the place to exit Highway 1-D to visit the La Fonda Hotel, the Los Alistros Trailer Park and to take the side trip noted below. The La Fonda is one of Baja's best Mexican charm road houses with fine food and live music. The trailer court offers minimum facilities and is little more than a parking lot. However, it is a great place to stay for campers wanting to take in the night life at the nearby hotel. Both facilities are located on a bluff above an excellent beach with great views of the ocean.

SIDE TRIP — It is 3.8 miles south and then east on old Highway 1 from the La Mision-Plaza del Mar interchange to the ruins of the San Miguel de la Frontera mission. These adobe remains lie within a chain-link fence in the yard of the La Mision community school. They are directly adjacent to the highway 0.8 miles east from the Rio Guadalupe bridge. In 1997 we observed construction work under way here which we hope will make the ruins more accessible to the traveler. You may also continue south on Highway 1 toward Ensenada. This drive is through pleasant, undeveloped hill-country but lacks the ocean views afforded by staying on Highway 1-D. End SIDE TRIP.

(Km A-69) PARKING AREA AND BEACH — Just north of the Highway 1-D crossing of the Rio Guadalupe estuary is a 50-car parking lot and fine sandy beach directly adjoining the highway. It gets heavy use on holiday weekends.

(Km A-71) PLAYA MAL PASO — Exactly at **Km A-71** is the beach camping area at Playa Mal Paso. It contains mostly old permanent trailers but parking is permitted along the beach. This beach can be reached only from the southbound lanes of the highway. Extra care is needed in reentering the highway as this is not a regular interchange.

(Km A-72) BAJA SEASONS — Located here is one of the finest trailer courts in Baja operated by Outdoor Resorts of Baja (800) 986-Baja. It has 137 units, tennis courts, pool, clubhouse, and related facilities. Rates are expensive. The court is directly on the beach but Pacific waters are cold this far north. Near the RV park is a fancy hotel (villas) establishment. There is no direct access from the northbound lanes of Highway 1-D.

(Km A-73) LA SALINA — A short drive south from the La Salina interchange brings one to Playa La Salina beach. Here a marina with breakwater protected access to the sea is being dredged from the coastal lowlands. The development was only partially finished in 1997 but is eventually planned to have some 500 boat slips, shopping center, hotel and other facilities.

The northernmost of the three tollgates on Highway 1-D.

The view looking south from the El Mirador Vista Point at Km A-84. Highway 1 may be seen descending from left to right. Photo BW.

#1 ⛰ **#2**

(Km A-75) GEOGRAPHIC CHANGE — You have now reached the most northerly breakpoint between the nineteen geographic sections encountered along the Transpeninsular Highway. The relatively flat coastal beaches (Section 1) will be left behind as the highway starts a climb into steeper terrain (Section 2). In a few miles, this increase in elevation will reward the traveler with excellent vistas of the coastline.

(Km A-78) BAJAMAR INTERCHANGE — Immediately west of this interchange lies the Bajamar Resort. It contains 27 holes of golf, the Hacienda las Glorias hotel-condos and surrounding residences. There is a pro-shop with restaurant, and bar. Bajamar is one of the finest residential developments in the Baja peninsula. There is little development between Bajamar and the southernmost tollgate at Km A-99 due no doubt to the absence of a domestic water system.

Great views of the Pacific Ocean are to be had from the Playa Saldamando RV Park. Very few camping spots in Baja have an ocean view of this quality. Photo BW.

PSI #3

(Km A-84) EL MIRADOR VISTA POINT — An interchange a short distance north of **Km A-84** provides direct access to a parking area near the cliffs overlooking the Pacific Ocean. There is a restaurant, bar and gift shop. From here, you will be rewarded with the best views of the Pacific coast that are available from the entire Transpeninsular Highway. Also in view are the Islas Todos Santos which lie 12 miles to the SW. These two small islands guard the outer limits of the broad bay on whose shore is built the city of Ensenada. Because of the excellent view, El Mirador is included as stop No. 3 in the POINTS OF SPECIAL INTEREST Tour.

(Km A-92 to A-94) SEDIMENTARY ROCKS — The majority of the rocks visible in the mountainous areas of the peninsula will be granitic or volcanic. Both of these are igneous rocks. Here, north of Ensenada, the highway cuts clearly display the layering which is the most common characteristic of sedimentary rocks. (See the ROCK TYPE Chart in Chapter 9 GEOLOGY.)

(Km A-94) PLAYA SALDAMANDO — Just past **Km A-94** a dirt road to the west descends steeply to the residence of the operator of a camping area on the bluffs above a rocky shoreline. (There is no access from the northbound lanes of Highway 1-D.) Several camping spots have been carved out along the road for about 1/2 mile south from the residence. They provide excellent views of the ocean but are not well-suited for larger RVs.

(Km A-94.5) Vista Point -- About 200 yards south of the exit to Playa Saldamando is a vista point parking area labeled Vista de Ballenas. It offers excellent views of the Pacific Ocean, where spouts of the gray whale will be in view in the proper season.

#2 ⛰ **#3**

(Km A-99) TOLLGATE AND GEOGRAPHIC CHANGE — Near **Km A-99** is situated the southernmost of Highway 1-D's three tollgates. The remainder of the trip into Ensenada is toll-free. Just south of the toll gate is the junction with old Highway 1. The toll station also marks the end of mountainous Geographic Section No. 2. For the next 22 miles the highway passes over flatlands (Section No. 3) surrounding the city of Ensenada.

Immediately south of the tollgate is San Miguel Village. A minimum facility camping area is present on a level bench near the rocky shoreline.

EL SAUZAL AREA — Approximately <u>1.5 miles</u> south of the tollgate is the junction of Highway 1-D

and Highway 3 and the community of El Sauzal. El Sauzal is one of the largest fishing ports on the Baja peninsula. Note the breakwater-lined harbor that is usually filled with numerous fishing vessels. Adjoining the harbor are a packing plant and related buildings. We tourists can rejoice that most of the fishing business has been established away from the tourist areas in Ensenada. In recent years the packing plant has been closed as the result of a U.S. embargo on Mexican tuna brought about by concerns over the fishermen's taking of dolphin as part of their catch. I believe this dispute has been settled but the plant was still closed in 1997. The harbor itself was quite busy.

POINTS OF INTEREST

1 Bank
2 Hussong's Cantina
3 Food Market
4 PESCA (Fishing Licenses)
5 PEMEX
6 Capitan de Puerto (Port Captain)
7 Servicios Migraorois (Immigration)
8 Shipyard Launch Ramp

9 Sportfishing Docks & Launch Ramp
10 Plaza Civica (Civic Plaza)
11 Park & Flag Pole
12 El Cid Hotel
13 Ensenada Travelodge

14 Casa del Sol Motel
15 Hotel Villa Marina
16 Mision Santa Isabel
17 Riviera del Pacifico
18 Govonors Office & Tourist Info

19 Hotel Corona
20 Baja Inn Hotel
21 Hotel La Pinta
22 San Nicolas Resort Hotel
23 Post Office

Between El Sauzal and Ensenada there are several motels and trailer courts. The latter cater mostly to year-round tenants. This entire section of highway is now almost fully lined with urban developments.

PSI #4

(Km A -109) ENSENADA — Ensenada is Baja California's third largest city with a population of about 170,000. Twenty-three percent of the tourists entering the peninsula have Ensenada as their destination point. It is thus second only to Tijuana as a tourist attraction. It gives the one-day or weekend tourist the feeling of having really been to Mexico that somehow does not result from a visit to Tijuana.

To classify Ensenada as a beautiful city would be inaccurate in my view, but certainly it is a pleasant place with a climate similar to that of San Diego. There are no major beaches but the city is fronted on a busy and interesting breakwater-lined harbor. For years this waterfront was dirty and of little interest to the tourist. However, our 1997 found a lengthy segment of attractive promenade and a new park replacing what had been the naval base headquarters. This park boasts a huge flagpole and enormous Mexican flag. The town's main tourist street, Ave. Lopez Mateos, was also receiving a facelift with sidewalk widening and vehicular traffic restrictions. Future plans call for moving the cruise ship dock from its present location across the harbor to a location along the western end of the promenade. All of this is greatly increasing Ensenada's appeal as a tourist attraction where the pedestrian will be king.

IMMIGRATION -- The Mexican immigration office (signed Servicios Migrarois) is located on the left side of the street as you enter Ensenada from the north. Here is the place to obtain, or validate tourists cards if you are heading south of the city where they are required. A tourist information office is located as shown on the ENSENADA Map.

TOURIST ROW — The city's main tourist area centers in and around the section of Avenida Lopez Mateos shown on the inset map of the ENSENADA Map. Traffic is usually heavy on this street, so the wise visitor will park in other areas. An aerial photo of Ensenada's waterfront area is presented in Chapter 13.

This section of the city is stop No. 4 on the POINTS OF SPECIAL INTEREST Tour. At first glance it may appear to be just another long array of tourist traps. Typical souvenir items are of course in plentiful supply, but there is also much quality merchandise. I have found the selection to be much better than in La Paz. If you are a budget-minded person it is simply foolish not to stock up on Christmas and birthday presents, etc., while in Ensenada. The savings can be substantial.

Also consider visiting the Riviera del Pacifico (former gambling casino), the Santo Tomas winery at 666 Avenida Miramar, and, of course, Hussong's Cantina. You may find the latter establishment a bit lowbrow, but thousands of us less discerning beer drinkers like the place, and the mariachi music is free (unless you are so unwise as to request your favorite song). It was

Ensenada Looking Southeast -- The tall flagpole is erected in the Civic Plaza while the high-rise building to its left is the Hotel Villa Marina. The pleasant promenade can be seen fronting the left edge of the harbor and its pleasure-boat docks. Photo BW.

ENSENADA

Ensenada is an active and colorful place. Top Left - A sidewalk cafe near the Civic Plaza. Top Right - The Ensenada harbor with many anchored small craft and a US-based cruise ship docked nearby. Center Right - A bicycle race along the downtown streets. Lower Left - Ensenada's annual Carnaval celebration. Photos BW.

established in 1892 and is still operated by the same family.

DRIVING THROUGH ENSENADA — It is recommended that the Highway 1-D, Lazaro Cardenas, General Agustin route is the best way to travel through the city. These streets are multilaned all the way and traffic is usually moderate. I see no advantages for the average tourists in taking the old Highway 1 route unless they are interested in increasing the chances of the culturally rewarding experience of becoming lost.

CHAPTER 18
ENSENADA TO SAN QUINTIN

The GRAND TOUR now proceeds from Ensenada south to the town of San Quintin and nearby Bahia San Quintin. This 196 km (122 mile) section of the Transpeninsular Highway is the second decompression step from the Southern California Pressure Cooker. There are far fewer tourist accommodations and travelers than there were north of Ensenada. However, you will still encounter a series of sizeable towns, much agricultural development, many people, and vegetation that still looks much like it does north of the border. You will have to wait until the next chapter to get into the *real* Magnificent Peninsula.

PASSING THROUGH ENSENADA — There is considerable traffic in Ensenada. I recommend that you enter from the north on Highway 1-D and follow the Lazaro Cardenas-General Agustin route to Highway 1 south of the downtown area. See the ENSENADA Map in Chapter 17.

ENSENADA TO MANEADERO — It is 14 km (9 miles) from Ensenada to Maneadero over a four and six-lane highway. This section of Highway 1 provides a transition from the 4-lane divided highway to the north and the two-lane road which starts south of Maneadero. The terrain is level. There is much urbanization from Ensenada to the Estero Beach road. Farther south, there are still some farms and olive orchards. As in other metropolitan sections, the kilometer posts are often missing. Watch for the Joker Motel and Estero Beach turnoff along the way.

(Km B-13) JOKER MOTEL AND RV PARK -- A pleasant RV Park adjoins the Joker Motel on the east side of the highway at this point.

SIDE TRIP
(Km B-15) ESTERO BEACH — *At the 15-km point a paved road leaves Highway 1 to the right. (See PUNTA BANDA AREA Map.) A 0.7 mile drive brings one to an intersection. The road to the right leads to El Faro Beach, a residential subdivision. Take the left fork a short distance to the very fine Estero Beach Resort Hotel, trailer court, shops, and boat launching ramp. They lie on the shore of Estero de Punta Banda. The trailer court here is one of the*

best in the Baja peninsula and is often used as the first nights stop for large RV caravans heading south.

Estero means estuary. Estero Beach is the northern shore of a sizeable saltwater estuary (Estero de Punta Banda). The western side is a wide, 4-mile-long coastal sand spit which protects the estuary from the swells of the Pacific Ocean. Launching small boats is thus an easy matter, but the breaking bar at the mouth of the estero must be negotiated to reach the open ocean. The hotel and its grounds are very pleasant and they are worth a visit even if you don't plan to stay. There is ample parking and turnaround area for the large RV's. End SIDE TRIP.

SIDE TRIP **-- (Km B-18) BAJA COUNTRY CLUB**
-- Just south of Km B-18 a paved road leaves Highway 1 to the east and passes through level farm land and accesses the Baja Country Club. It is 5.5 miles from the highway, around the golf course to the club house. See the Chapter 6 section on golf courses for further details. End SIDE TRIP.

PSI **#5**

SIDE TRIP **— (Km B-21) HIGHWAY 23 AND LA BUFADORA** — *Highway 23 branches to the west from Highway 1 in the town of Maneadero (population 11,600) about 200 yards south of a pedestrian overpass. (See PUNTA BANDA AREA Map.) It is a good standard blacktopped highway of some 20 km's (14 miles). Its first 8 miles cross flat terrain, some of which supports olive orchards and other agricultural fields. The last 6 miles traverse the sides of precipitous Punta Banda, a narrow, rocky peninsula that projects into the Pacific Ocean.*

As the road gains elevation, one is afforded excellent views of the ocean and Ensenada to the northeast. The spouts of the California gray whale also may be seen during the months of its migration from Alaska to Baja's Pacific lagoons. (See Chapter 11 WILDLIFE.)

There are several places of interest served by Highway 23 including the La Bufadora blowhole. The commanding views and intriguing blowhole demand that this side trip be placed on the POINTS OF SPECIAL INTEREST Tour.

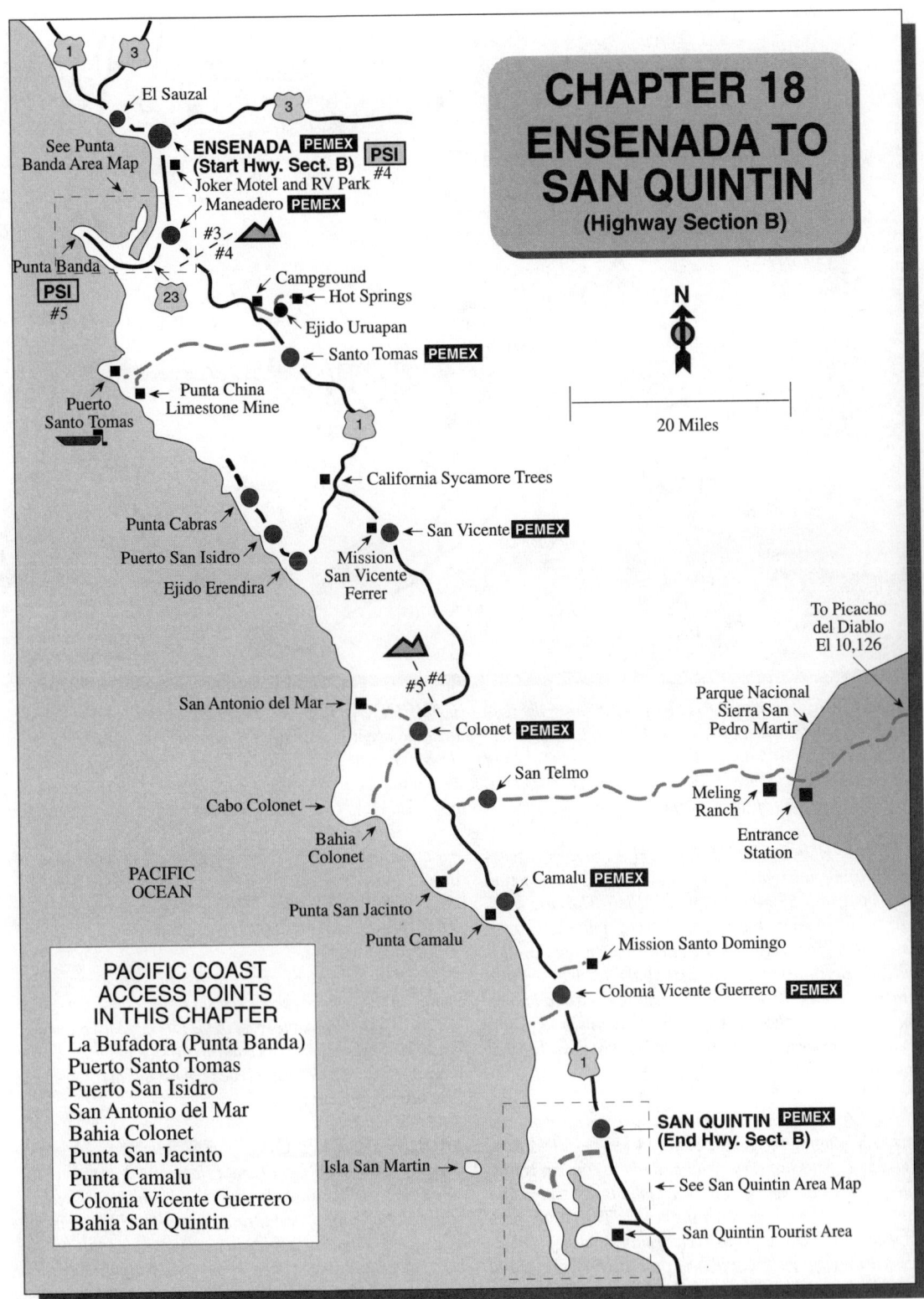

El Sauzal

See Punta
Banda Area Map

ENSENADA PEMEX PSI #4
(Start Hwy. Sect. B)
Joker Motel and RV Park
Maneadero PEMEX

#3
#4

Punta Banda

PSI
#5

23

Campground
Hot Springs
Ejido Uruapan
Santo Tomas PEMEX

Punta China
Limestone Mine

Puerto
Santo Tomas

1

California Sycamore Trees

Punta Cabras
Puerto San Isidro
Ejido Erendira

San Vicente PEMEX

Mission
San Vicente
Ferrer

#5 #4

San Antonio del Mar

Colonet PEMEX

Cabo Colonet

Bahia
Colonet

San Telmo

Punta San Jacinto
Punta Camalu

Camalu PEMEX

Mission Santo Domingo

Colonia Vicente Guerrero PEMEX

CHAPTER 18
ENSENADA TO
SAN QUINTIN
(Highway Section B)

N

20 Miles

To Picacho
del Diablo
El 10,126

Parque Nacional
Sierra San
Pedro Martir

Meling
Ranch

Entrance
Station

PACIFIC
OCEAN

**PACIFIC COAST
ACCESS POINTS
IN THIS CHAPTER**

La Bufadora (Punta Banda)
Puerto Santo Tomas
Puerto San Isidro
San Antonio del Mar
Bahia Colonet
Punta San Jacinto
Punta Camalu
Colonia Vicente Guerrero
Bahia San Quintin

Isla San Martin

SAN QUINTIN PEMEX
(End Hwy. Sect. B)

See San Quintin Area Map

San Quintin Tourist Area

PUNTA BANDA AREA

N

Bahia de Todos Santos

1 Mile

Punta Banda

Ejido Camping Area

Ejido Camping Area

Ejido Camping Area

Numerous Residences

Fish Camp

La Bufadora Blowhole

PSI #5

Community of La Bufadora -- Camping and diving service.

La Jolla (RV Parks)

Proposed Marina

Estero Beach Resort Hotel and RV Park

To Ensenada

Breakers →

Small Boat Channel

Estero de Punta Banda

Baja Beach Resort

Baja Country Club →

Dock

Maneadero PEMEX

Agricultural fields, Olives and other produce for sale at roadside stands.

23

1

Numerous souvenir stands have been built along the road near the blowhole so there is no lack of things to buy. There is parking at La Bufadora, although trailers should not proceed past the restaurant (0.2 miles from La Bufadora) due to the steepness of the parking lot.

PUNTA BANDA BARRIER BEACH — Barrier beaches are low-lying, narrow, spits of sand built by wave action along shallow sections of ocean coastline. They are separated from the mainland by saltwater estuaries. Here at about 8-miles from Highway 1 is such a formation. An oiled road leads north out the barrier to the Baja Beach Resort and numerous private residences. A small marina and launch ramp are located a short distance out along this road. Until recently the resort was a private membership club. In 1997 it was a hotel open to the public.

LA JOLLA — La Jolla is a community made up of several older recreation home subdivisions 14 km (9 miles) from Highway 1. Lots are very small and many contain trailer houses. There are two RV Parks, La Jolla Beach Camp and Villarino RV Park, located on the beach. The former park has a boat launching ramp. The ramp, which provides access to the open Pacific, will pose problems at low tide and would be unusable in heavy swells.

CAMPGROUNDS — There are several gently sloping areas adjacent to the highway near the point where it starts descending to La Bufadora. They provide the sites for minimum facility campgrounds operated by the members of a local ejido (See GLOSSARY). What you receive for your modest fee in these places is little more than a place to park, but there are excellent views of the ocean. Some of these camps may give way to subdivisions which are making their appearance. The parking area for one of my favorite camp spots is obviously a building pad.

There are also RV camping areas and some recreation homes on flat benches above the shoreline cliffs at the head of a cove (Bahia Papalote) east of the La Bufadora blowhole. Because of this cove's rocky nature, it is a popular diving location, and in 1997 was served by a small diving service (See diving in Chapter 5).

LA BUFADORA BLOWHOLE — Highway 23 passes over the top of the Punta Banda ridge and descends to the rocky coast on the slope facing SE. Here you will find a scattering of homes, restaurants, open-air shops, parking areas, and a masonry viewing structure adjoining the blowhole. The area is a popular weekend recreation spot for people of the Ensenada area.

There are occasional points along the Pacific Coast where rock formations cause the incoming ocean swells to cast up a spout of water; but La Bufadora (The Roarer) is a blowhole without rival. It consists of a substantial sea-level cave. After observing it for some time, one can readily imagine that it is a living creature. The rhythmic ocean swells impart a breathing cycle to the cave. Water is first taken in. Then, following a pause, it is sprayed back outside by internally compressed air to the accompaniment of a deep roar. Heavy swells cause a large vertical geyser, but La Bufadora puts on a good performance even in calm seas. End SIDE TRIP.

(Km B 23) INMIGRACION — *Inmigracion is the* Mexican equivalent of the Immigration Service in the United States. Here at the town of Maneadero was the immigration checkpoint where officials issued and validated tourist cards. Their building was 1 mile south of the Highway 1 junction with Highway 23. There has been no checkpoint here for many years but the point is noted in the event it should reappear.

The Transpeninsular Highway has only two lanes from here to the tip of the Baja peninsula except within some of the larger communities and along the Cabo Corridor between the Los Cabos Airport and Cabo San Lucas.

#3 ⏶ #4

(Km B-25) GEOGRAPHIC CHANGE — Here the highway enters Geographic Section No. 4 and initiates a 100 km (62 mile) journey through moderately steep mountains with numerous intermountain valleys. The area and its chaparral vegetation are similar to those in the mountainous areas in southern Alta California. The brush here in Baja is not as dense as that found north of the border due to the occurrence of frequent uncontrolled wildfires.

Although the Transpeninsular Highway begins to curve, its grades are moderate and there are many straight, level sections. Its course through this area is reasonably typical of what lies ahead for hundreds of miles, so if what you see here is acceptable you can relax and enjoy the remainder of your trip.

(Km B-42) Uruapan -- A dirt road leaves Highway 1 just north of **Km B-42.** immediately on the left is a nice picnic and camping area in a grove of old live oaks. Their are picnic tables and stoves and the area is no doubt used by the citizens of the nearby ejido

but overnight campers appear to be welcome.

SIDE TRIP
It is about 1/2 mile on this dirt road to the rural village of Ejido Uruapan and a total of 2 miles to a rustic hot springs area named Banos Termales (Hot Baths). This is a fine side trip to take to get a taste of a rural Mexican village. At the hot springs the hot water is used to supply a decades old laundry facility and adjoining bathing areas utilizing turn-of-the-century bath tubs. To get to the hot springs proceed to the village, turn left on Ave. Francisco Ramero, cross an arroyo and turn right following the north bank of the stream. End SIDE TRIP.

SIDE TRIP
(Km B-48) PUERTO SANTO TOMAS — *A secondary road signed "La Bocana 26 km, and Punta China 28 km" leaves Highway 1 to the right (west). This road is constructed along the foot of the mountains bordering the northern side of the Rio Santo Tomas. It is well constructed but it is not recommended for use by larger RV's.*

16.1 Miles — The road to Punta China forks to the left and crosses the Rio Santo Tomas. A 2.9 mile drive brings one to the workers camp at the Punta China limestone mining operation. A short distance to the south, rock is loaded by conveyor belt into barges for shipment to the cement plant in Ensenada. There are nice ocean views along the way.

17.6 Miles — The road arrives at the small village of La Bocana (boca means mouth in Spanish), appropriately located at the mouth of the Rio Santo Tomas. There is a small store and a camping spot with a good view of the ocean. Another nearby campground is operated on a tree lined meadow adjoining the beach and a marshy lagoon. If the croaking of frogs will keep you awake consider camping elsewhere.

All that remains of the Dominican mission founded in Santo Tomas in 1791. The ruins are visible from the Transpeninsular Highway. Photo JW.

20.3 Miles — *This point brings you to Puerto Santo Tomas, presently the site of a modest fish camp. The small cove provides protection from the ocean swells that crash on the shore only a few yards to the south. Surprisingly, this insignificant cove was a principal port during the missionary period. It served the inland settlement of Santo Tomas. In viewing its waters, picture it containing the ship of Juan Rodriguez Cabrillo, who anchored here during his historic exploratory voyage in 1542.*

Within the fish camp is a small cantina and camping is permitted nearby. There is also a narrow, concrete boat ramp facing the open Pacific. Launching boats in heavy swell would not be possible. End SIDE TRIP.

HISTORIC NOTE — THE MISSIONARY TRAIL Since leaving Ensenada, you have been following the approximate route used by Gaspar de Portola and Padre Junipero Serra on their history-making 1769 expedition north from Loreto to found the first Alta California mission at San Diego. In the ensuing twenty-two years, Dominican missionaries were to establish three new missions along that portion of the route described in this chapter. These were at the present-day towns of Santo Tomas, San Vicente, and Santo Domingo. Directions for visiting these sites are given later in this chapter. The ruin of an additional mission near El Rosario is described in the following chapter.

(Km B-51) SANTO TOMAS — Santo Tomas is a small town located in a broad, fertile section of the Rio Santo Tomas valley. It is the site of a Dominican mission founded in 1791. To view the mission ruins, proceed to the roadside directly across the highway from the PEMEX station. Walk several hundred feet north along the east side of the highway. The fifty-foot-square ruins may be seen in a pasture near several tall fan palms and 250 feet north of the olive orchard which contains the El Palomar Trailer Court.

Grapes were cultivated by the missionaries to produce altar wine. Santo Tomas came to lend its name to one of Mexico's most popular brand of wines, although the winery itself has long been located in Ensenada. In the past, much of the valley was planted to grapes. Today, there are relatively few vineyards and most of the land contains olive orchards or is used

for grazing. Grape production has been moved to the Guadalupe area along Highway 3 NE of Ensenada and the the region south of San Vicente to the south along Highway 1.

Today, Santo Tomas offers the tourist a PEMEX station, and the El Palomar motel, restaurant and gift shop. Across the highway is the El Palomar Trailer Court. It is a pleasant, shady spot surrounded by olive trees. It provides full hookups, swimming pool and toilet facilities. Beware of weekends when it is heavily used by people from Ensenada.

(Km B-72 to B-77) CALIFORNIA SYCAMORE — Highway 1 passes along the stream channel of a moderately steep canyon. Here you can observe numerous California sycamore trees (*Platanus racemosa*), a species commonly found in similar moist locations in Alta California and northern Baja. Note the mottled exfoliating brown and white bark. The broad, sharply lobed leaves fall in the winter months, but many spherical fruiting bodies can be seen dangling from the branches. See the outline of the leaf nearby.

Outline of the leaf of the California sycamore (1/3 actual size).

Many of the canyon walls in this area are composed of granite rocks. They can be identified by their light color. Review the ROCK TYPE Table in Chapter 9 GEOLOGY.

SIDE TRIP

(Km B-78) PUERTO SAN ISIDRO AREA — *Midway between* **Km B-78** *and* **Km B-79** *a blacktop highway leaves Highway 1 to the right (west). It is signed for E.J. Erendira. This is one of the few places where you can drive to within a few hundred yards of the Pacific shore on an oiled highway (there were numerous potholes during our 1995 and 1997 visits).*

10.4 Miles -- *Just prior to entering Ejido Erendira a dirt road branches to the left and crosses an arroyo. A sign indicated that following this road would bring one to the Malibu Beach Sur campground after passing through cultivated fields. In 1997 there was so much runoff from these fields that the road was impassable to our vehicle.*

The hard surface highway proceeds along the Rio San Isidro and ends in <u>12.0 miles</u> at the farming community of Erendira. It contains small grocery stores, cafe, PEMEX (Nova only) and the twelve-unit Motel Erendira near the north edge of town. A secondary road continuing NW up the coast provides access to the small fishing port of San Isidro. It is <u>13.3 miles</u> to the port from Highway 1. A reef of rock that projects from the coast provides protection for a fleet of small fishing boats and a boat launching ramp (concrete surface to the highwater line and then packed sand.). Nearby there is a group of small rental cabins bearing the name Castro's. Boats are available for rent. Across the road is an RV park which in fall 1997 was little more than a place to park.

I have driven 9.0 miles north of Puerto San Isidro on a good secondary road. Starting at <u>1.4 miles</u> north of the port are a series of very nice camping sites on the bluffs overlooking the ocean. At <u>4.2 miles</u> north of the port is the growing village of El Destiladero which is made up largely of Americans. At <u>5.9 miles</u> is a turnoff to the beach-lined cove at Punta Cabras. At 6.4 miles is an excellent beach and many camping spots. The road is a bit rough but large RVs make it to many of these camping locations. End SIDE TRIP.

SIDE TRIP
(Km B-88) MISSION SAN VICENTE FERRER — It
is a <u>0.7 mile</u> drive over a dirt road to the ruins of the San Vicente Ferrer mission. This road leaves Highway 1 to the right (west) <u>0.2 miles</u> south of **Km B-88**. Drive about 200 feet after leaving the highway and take the left fork which leads to a parking area adjoining the ruins.

In the past, the crumbling adobe walls of the mission buildings have been protected by a flimsy thatched shelter always in poor repair. In 1997 we were greeted by extensive archeological work which has revealed the underlying building foundations and a visitor center was under construction. The Mexican government has at long last found the resources to protect and interpret the mission ruins along the Baja peninsula. Hopefully, this effort will spread to other sites. Be sure and visit this site.

Dominican padres founded the mission in 1780, on a low rise a few yards from the Rio San Isidro. It was to become the administrative center for the northern Frontera mission district and headquarters

for a garrison of troops. End SIDE TRIP.

(Km B-90) SAN VICENTE — At this point is the town of San Vicente (population 2,500). The only things of interest to the tourist are several stores, a PEMEX station, and a small motel at the south end of town.

(Km B-90 to B-107) LLANO COLORADO — There was little agricultural development on the Baja peninsula prior to the 1940s as the land was controlled by unproductive foreign concessions. Previous travel guides reported only a few families around San Vicente. In contrast, today's traveler will see extensive vineyards, olive orchards and grain fields in the level valley south of San Vicente. (At **Km B-97** is a sizeable cactus farm where prickly pear cactus is cultivated as noted in chapter 10 under prickly pear). This is the Llano Colorado (the Colorado Plain). It is interesting to note that while these Mexican lands are only now being developed for agriculture, tracts used for similar purposes in southern California in the United States have long since given way to urbanization.

#4 〰️ **#5**

(Km B-125) GEOGRAPHIC CHANGE — Just before entering the town of Colonet, the highway leaves the mountains that started 100 km (62 miles) to the north. You will now be entering Geographic Section No. 5, the northernmost segment of the Continental Borderlands Province. As you can see, this dividing line between provinces is easy to identify and is typical of others you will encounter to the south.

Mission San Vicente Ferrer. In view here are the few remaining adobe walls and far more extensive foundations of this historic Dominican mission. Photo BW.

243

Chapter 18

Highway 1 will now traverse 112 km (70 miles) of rolling coastal plain with the mountains always in view to the east. The northern portion of the plain is called the Llano (plain) de Camalu, and the southern portion the Valle (valley) de San Quintin. The highway is constructed near the inland portion of the plain, so the ocean is mostly out of sight. Many of these coastal plain lands are used for agriculture. These developments extend as far south as El Pabellon Beach at **Km C-15**, much of it occurring since this book was first published in 1986. It is also sad to report that this farming is resulting in serious soil erosion. As many crops are irrigated by drip systems, a majority of the exposed surface soil is relatively dry and easily blown away by strong winds moving onshore from the Pacific ocean. One wonders how long Mexico will be able to continue farming this developing dust bowl?

ROAD CONDITION NOTE Several secondary road side trips to the Pacific shore are described over the level lands of the Continental Borderlands in this and the following chapter. Soils in this area are fine-grained and become muddy following rain. Local traffic continues during such periods and many ruts and short detours are created. Be very cautious about using these roads for up to ten days following heavy rain and expect occasional rough spots long afterwards.

SIDE TRIP
(Km B-126) SAN ANTONIO DEL MAR — *North of the town of Colonet a secondary road bears west to the Pacific shore. It leaves Highway 1 about 100 yards NE of the bridge over the Rio San Rafael (Puente Colonet), between the bridge and a white church. A small group of residences, San Antonio del Mar is reached in 7.0 miles. There is limited camping area here but extensive sand beaches and dunes lie in both directions. A great area for those with vehicles capable of traveling over such terrain. End* SIDE TRIP.

(Km B-127) COLONET — South of the Rio San Rafael bridge lies the small farming community of Colonet and its PEMEX station. A considerable agriculture area can be seen on the lands bordering the river.

After passing through Colonet, look south near the western edge of the inland mountains. Here, on clear days, you will see Isla San Martin and a group of volcanic cinder cones lying west of the town of San Quintin. At other times, these peaks may be shrouded in fog or low clouds.

SIDE TRIP
(Km B-129) BAHIA COLONET — *Near Km B-129 a*

secondary road leaves Highway 1 to the right (west) and in 8.1 miles arrives at the southern end of Bahia Colonet on the Pacific coast. The junction is signed for E.J. Villa Morelos.

The road is constructed along the base of low hills bordering the broad valley of the Rio San Rafael. A lesser standard road continues south, along the coast, accessing numerous places to camp on the bluffs overlooking the Pacific. End SIDE TRIP.

SIDE TRIP
(Km B-141) PARQUE NACIONAL SIERRA SAN PEDRO MARTIR — *Leading to the left (east) is the main access road to the largest of Baja's two national parks (Parque Nacional Sierra San Pedro Martir) and the highest mountains in the peninsula. The park features extensive Jeffrey pine forests mixed with several other coniferous species. There are many undeveloped places to camp. At the end of the road is an observatory with one large and two smaller telescope buildings. The clearness of the air makes this an excellent point for astronomical observations.*

Much of the access road's steep grades pass over mountainous terrain making for a total climb of approximately 10,000 feet. Its construction standards are better than those of most of Baja's secondary roads, but the entire route is through decomposed granite soils that are subject to severe erosion. I have seen this road recommended for use by large RVs and believe that it is suitable for such vehicles (no trailers) if it has been recently maintained. Following heavy storms, this is not the case. There is a road maintenance station near the entrance to the park leading one to believe that the road does in fact receive frequent grading.

0.0 Miles -- There are numerous shops and other buildings at the junction with Highway 1. The road is signed for the villages of San Telmo, and Sinaloa, the Meling Ranch and the observatory.

6.0 Miles — Here lies the pleasant farming community of San Telmo.

11.5 Miles -- The village of Hacienda Sinaloa is at this point.

20.5 Miles — To this point the road has traveled along the edge of broad valleys used for agricultural purposes. The route has been level, with few hills. Here, one passes over a wide arroyo which would become impassable during and after heavy rains. Beyond the arroyo it begins to climb the mountains in earnest.

30.7 Miles — A 0.9 mile dirt road to the right brings one to the Meling Ranch. This is an operating cattle ranch,

Top Left - The park's entrance station amid its Jeffery pine forest. Bottom Left - The steep access road to the park many miles below timber line. Top Right - The largest of the park's three telescope buildings. Note the gnarled Jeffrey pine tree and the snow remaining from a late March storm. Photo BW & JW.

PARQUE NACIONAL SIERRA SAN PEDRO MARTIR

which also provides very pleasant accommodations for overnight guests. It has a nearby airstrip and has long been a favorite hideout for private flyers. An excellent place to get away from it all.

46.1 Miles -- Here at the edge of the Jeffrey pine forest is a small stream and level area suitable for camping. It was the site of the Los Manzanos Camping Area in 1997.

48.5 Miles — Here are located the park's gate, entrance station, and small undeveloped campground. A modest entrance fee is charged when the station is manned.

65.0 Miles — The living quarters and administrative buildings for the observatory are located here. It is possible to camp at this point, although there are no facilities and little flat ground. Visitors are required to walk the remaining *1.5 miles* up to the telescopes. End SIDE TRIP.

SIDE TRIP
(Km B-150) PUNTA SAN JACINTO — *A secondary road branches to the right (west) north of **Km B-150**. After about 1-mile the road standard decreases but arrives with no difficulty in 4.1 miles at Punta San Jacinto on the coast.*

There are endless numbers of places to camp on the low bluffs overlooking the sea in both directions and in 1997 a sign on the highway advertised a commercial camping site. End SIDE TRIP.

(Km B-157) CAMALU — Camalu is a town of little interest to the tourist except as a source of supplies and for its PEMEX station. In addition, Red Cross volunteers are often present in the middle of the highway soliciting donations. A contribution will net you a Red Cross sticker for your window which will save you from a repeat performance on the return trip. Pay-up.

SIDE TRIP
PUNTA CAMALU — *Immediately north of the Camalu PEMEX station a dirt road leads west in 2.3 miles to Punta Camalu. At 1.7 miles along the way, a side road bears left to a fish camp. Keeping right at this point will provide access to numerous good camping spots along the coast.* End SIDE TRIP.

SIDE TRIP
(Km B-169) MISSION SANTO DOMINGO — *About*

200 yards north of the bridge over the Rio Santo Domingo a side road leaves Highway 1 to the left (east). It leads to the ruins of a mission founded by the Dominicans in 1775. Its photo appears on the first page of PART II. The road is poorly constructed but passes over flat terrain. It is not recommended for larger RVs

The trip to the mission site and small village of Santo Domingo is 4.7 miles. The ruins lie immediately west of the town's primary school. The full outline of the mission quadrangle is still in evidence, along with several three-foot-thick adobe walls. As with most other missions, the remains lie fully exposed to the elements although some development work was underway in 1997. A short distance prior to reaching the ruins is a very nice community camping and picnic area. End SIDE TRIP.

(Km B-172) COLONIA VICENTE GUERRERO — Colonia Vicente Guerrero is another small agricultural town. It supports a PEMEX station and two RV parks. The road to these parks leaves Highway 1 to the right (west) 0.2 miles north of **Km B -173**. A sizeable electrical substation lies a short distance south of the junction point. The first park (Don Pepes) is close to the highway. The second (Posada Don Diego) is 0.3 miles to the west in a pleasant orchard setting. Both have restaurants and full hookups.

SIDE TRIP
From the Posada Don Diego park drive west 2.7 miles to an excellent sand beach backed by dunes. Camping behind the dunes will cut the wind. The road is low standard with many twists and turns; but no problema, keep heading west and stop short of the water. End SIDE TRIP.

(Km B-175) ISLA SAN MARTIN AND SAN QUINTIN CINDER CONES — Isla San Martin and the San Quintin cinder cones should now be clearly in view to the right. The island lies some 5 miles offshore. It is the farthest peak to the right (NW). It provides a home for several species of marine mammals and is the site of a Mexican fishermen's camp. An anchorage on its SE shore is a frequently used stopover point for yachts making the passage from San Diego to Cabo San Lucas.

CULTURAL NOTE (FISH CAMPS) — The *fish camp* on Isla San Martin is one of scores of such camps to be found on islands and isolated stretches of coast throughout the Baja peninsula. They consist of one or more shacks made of sheet metal, tar paper, poles, and scraps of other building material. There is little, if any, furniture. These crude dwellings provide permanent or seasonal sites for fishing and lobstering operations which are usually outposts for a headquarters cooperative in the larger towns.

Fishing and transportation to and from supply points is done in open, outboard-motor-powered pangas (See photo in Chapter 5). I have visited dozens of such camps and always found their residents to be friendly, hard working, and usually eager to sell a portion of their catch. The location of other fish camps is noted at many other places. Hopefully, you might take the opportunity to pay some of them a visit and gain an understanding of a way of life quite foreign and primitive to most North Americans.

(Km B-178) -- There is a government operated tourist information station on the west side of the highway at this point.

(Km B-190) SAN QUINTIN — San Quintin and adjoining Colonia Lazaro Cardenas are the southernmost of the towns that dot the coastal plain through which you have been traveling. The area's principal tourist facilities lie to the south off Highway 1 at **Km C-1**, **Km C-4** and **Km C-11**, but you need to make an important decision here in town concerning your vehicle's fuel supply.

The objective is to be able to pass through the remote mountains and desert between El Rosario and Guerrero Negro to the south without exhausting your fuel supply. In past years it was often difficult to obtain fuel within this section (about 400 km or 250 miles in length). In the last several editions of this book I reported that fuel was usually available. Then in 1997 we found that two of the key PEMEX stations were closed and appeared abandoned so what you will find is anybodies guess. This fueling situation has improved somewhat with the installation of a gas pump (Magna Sin only) at the hotel at Catavina. However, in the event of low supplies, the hotel will serve only its guests, and may refuse service to caravans at all times.

Ideally, you would obtain fuel at El Rosario. However, should the station there be closed or out of fuel you may have a problem. The prudent plan is to fuel at San Quintin, and top off at El Rosario if it is available.

SIDE TRIP
(Km B-193) COLONIA LAZARO CARDENAS & PUERTO SAN QUINTIN — *To the highway traveler, the*

town of Lazaro Cardenas (population 7,600) will appear only as a southerly extension of San Quintin. It is, however, the gateway to Bahia San Quintin.

Puerto San Quintin is a large, shallow, almost totally landlocked estuary. (See the SAN QUINTIN AREA Map.) Its northern section is served by a highway standard, but badly washboarded road. If you are heading south toward the peninsula's tip there is no particular reason to pay a visit here. However, it is a good place to reach the water's edge if the San Quintin area is the destination point of your trip.

The road to the bay leaves Highway 1 to the right (west) near the center of Colonia Lazaro Cardenas at a point immediately south of a military base. In the past it was signed for "Bahia Falsa but there was no signing in 1997." Bahia Falsa is the westerly arm of the Puerto San Quintin estuary.

A trip of 14 km (9 miles) over this road will bring you to the shores of the bay. Taking the left fork at this point will bring you in about 2 miles to bay-side camp spots and places to launch small boats over the rocky beach.

The main road continues to the right for 2 more miles and terminates at a fishing village and warehouse facility on the Pacific shore. En route, you pass by an oyster farm (Campo Ostionero) and small restaurant and drive very close to the bases of the cinder cones you have been seeing from Highway 1. Note the reddish color of these volcanic rocks compared with the light-colored granite you have seen in other areas.

There are places to camp at various locations along the bay shore but they are difficult to access with larger RVs. Lightweight class 4 boats can be launched over the beach near the fish camp or at boat ramps at the Old Mill Motel (see Chapter 19) and the Pedregal subdivision. You will have to negotiate the shallow bars at the entrance of the bay to reach the open ocean. This entrance is protected from the prevailing NW swells, but careful attention should be given to the state of the tides and weather. End SIDE TRIP.

(KM B-196 AND C-0) END OF HIGHWAY SECTION

B — The breakpoint between Highway Sections **B** and **C** lies six kilometers south of the center of the town of San Quintin.

CULTURAL NOTE (INDIANS IN THE VALLE DE SAN QUINTIN)

-- Upon returning from our 1997 Baja survey I encountered an article in the San Francisco Chronicle by Sam Quinones. It reported that the labor force farming the extensive agriculture lands in the Valle de San Quintin is composed mostly of Oaxacan Indians that have migrated to Baja from southern Mexico. Many of these people are living in most primitive conditions and their native culture is often at odds with the local Mexicans. These people work in tomato, green onion, strawberry, cucumber and celery fields on some 19,000 acres of drip-irrigated land.

The farming technique involves covering the rows of crops with strips of plastic that when discarded becomes scattered about the landscape and becomes most unsightly. The intervening areas of uncovered soil are blown about adding to the unpleasant environment. These were the conditions that I have noted the past several years not realizing the human "Grapes of Wrath" drama lying behind the workforce. I am not aware of the specific location of the Indian's villages but assume that they center about the town of San Quintin. Perhaps both you and I can be alert for them in the future.

Signs of Distinction

One of the least congested FREEWAY ENTRANCES in North America. Here in the small village of Ejido Erendira on the Pacific coast one can count seven signs liberated from their prior home north of the border. Walking one's dog can be accomplished with minimal risk. Photo JW.

POINTS OF INTEREST

1 Ernesto's (Baja Ron's) Motel
2 Old Mill Motel (Ramp & RV Park)
3 Muelle Viejo Motel (RV Park)
4 Pedregal Subdivision
5 Clelito Lindo Camping Area
6 Rancho Cielito Lindo Motel
and (RV Park)

☀ Location of Volcanic
Cinder Cones

N

2 Miles

San Quintin PEMEX

Campo Militar
Bonito Juarez

Colonia Lazaro Cardenas PEMEX

1

Km C-1 → ■ ← Electric Substation

Sandy Road
(Camp Sites) ☀

1
2

Km C-4

Restaurant

3

Old Pier

Warehouse
and houses

4

Oyster
Farm

Old
Highway

Rio
Santa Maria

Flood
Damage

Bahia
Falsa

Puerto
San Quintin

San Quintin
Tourist Area

Camp sites & over the
beach boat launching

Abandoned
PEMEX

1

5   6 †

PACIFIC
OCEAN

Hotel
La Pinta

PEMEX
(Magna Sin Only)

School

Bahia
San
Quintin

El Pabellon
RV Park

SAN QUINTIN AREA

CHAPTER 19
SAN QUINTIN TO THE STATE LINE

Most North Americans who have traveled the Transpeninsular Highway will agree that you really haven't visited the Baja peninsula until you progress south of San Quintin. Once this is done, most of the larger towns will have been left behind, there are substantial areas of open space, and after a few miles the peninsula's fascinating desert vegetation will begin to dominate the landscape. A new world will emerge. You will have entered the final decompression stage in the escape from the land of the freeways to the north.

Roll down the window of your vehicle and take in the fresh air. To hell with the air conditioner. Wave hello to the Mexicans and stop looking like you expect to be attacked by bandits. This is the Magnificent Peninsula. Enjoy.

COASTAL WINDS -- It was noted in Chapter 18 that strong coastal winds cause considerable soil erosion along the Pacific shore's agricultural areas. These same winds sometimes make conditions less than fully enjoyable in the three San Quintin area recreation spots described immediately below. This is particularly true for those using the RV parks. For this reason most serious Baja travelers head farther south and one seldom sees long term visitors in these areas.

(Km C-1 AND C-4) BAY-SIDE MOTELS —
Several miles to the west there are three motels located on the low bluffs overlooking the eastern shores of Puerto San Quintin. These are Ernesto's (Baja Ron's), the Old Mill and the Muelle Viejo. Each has an accompanying restaurant and bar. The Old Mill has been extensively refurbished and includes a boat launching ramp, boat rental, and RV park. Similar improvements may occur at the adjoining Ernesto's (Baja Ron's) Motel. All three places provide pleasant spots at the water's edge. The Old Mill offers the fanciest overnight accommodations, restaurant and bar but for camping I prefer the small RV park at the Muelle Viego. It is situated on a bluff offering good views of

the water below along with a row of trees to help cut the wind.

The access road leading to these facilities from the **Km C-1** point on Highway 1 has been widened and improved but the area's other roads are low standard affairs running between agricultural fields (See the SAN QUINTIN AREA Map in Chapter 18). These latter roads are not well suited for larger RVs, particularly in wet weather when they become next to impassable.

SIDE TRIP

(Km C-11) SAN QUINTIN TOURIST AREA — *A paved access road leaves Highway 1 200 yards north of Km C-11 and is signed for the Hotel La Pinta. This junction is on a relocated section of Highway 1. After 1.2 miles you will cross the original highway and an abandoned PEMEX station. This highway relocation no doubt throws a slight kink into all the kilometer points to the south and provides the perfect excuse if you find my distance figures slightly in error.*

The area contains the Hotel La Pinta San Quintin (3.1 miles from Highway 1) and the Rancho Cielito Lindo Motel

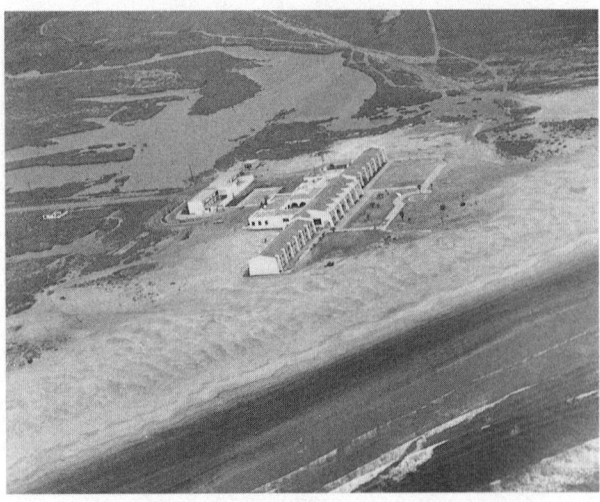

The Hotel La Pinta San Quintin on the beach east of Bahia San Quintin. Photo JW.

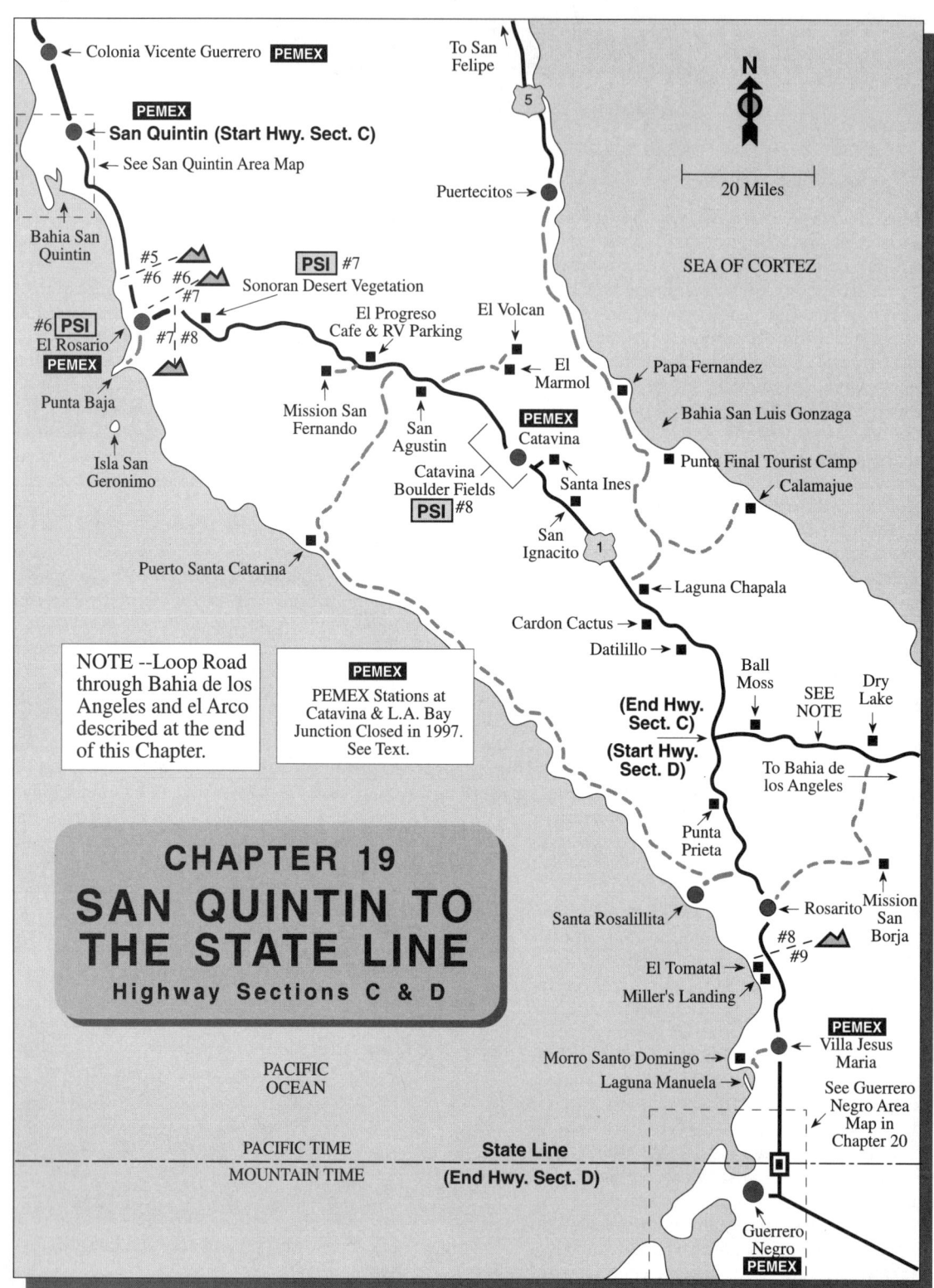

Colonia Vicente Guerrero PEMEX

To San Felipe

PEMEX
San Quintin (Start Hwy. Sect. C)
See San Quintin Area Map

Puertecitos

N

20 Miles

Bahia San Quintin

SEA OF CORTEZ

#5
#6 #6
#7

PSI #7
Sonoran Desert Vegetation

El Volcan

#6 PSI
El Rosario
PEMEX

#7 #8

El Progreso Cafe & RV Parking

El Marmol

Papa Fernandez

Punta Baja

Bahia San Luis Gonzaga

Isla San Geronimo

Mission San Fernando

San Agustin

Catavina Boulder Fields

PSI #8

PEMEX
Catavina

Santa Ines

Punta Final Tourist Camp

Calamajue

San Ignacito

1

Puerto Santa Catarina

Laguna Chapala

Cardon Cactus

Datilillo

Ball Moss

SEE NOTE

Dry Lake

NOTE --Loop Road through Bahia de los Angeles and el Arco described at the end of this Chapter.

PEMEX
PEMEX Stations at Catavina & L.A. Bay Junction Closed in 1997. See Text.

(End Hwy. Sect. C)
(Start Hwy. Sect. D)

To Bahia de los Angeles

CHAPTER 19
SAN QUINTIN TO THE STATE LINE
Highway Sections C & D

Punta Prieta

Santa Rosalillita

Rosarito

Mission San Borja

#8
#9

El Tomatal
Miller's Landing

PEMEX
Villa Jesus Maria

PACIFIC OCEAN

Morro Santo Domingo
Laguna Manuela

See Guerrero Negro Area Map in Chapter 20

PACIFIC TIME
MOUNTAIN TIME

State Line
(End Hwy. Sect. D)

Guerrero Negro
PEMEX

with its two RV parks. They are near an excellent Pacific beach. The Hotel La Pinta is the northernmost of the original parador hotels. I do not find it as nice as the other La Pinta hotels, but it will provide a fair idea of what to expect from its sister facilities to the south. The Rancho Cielito Lindo Motel and its adjoining RV parks are pleasant places to stay. The motel features a live music dance area which adds a touch of night life. The old original RV park (now called Cielito Lindo Dunes) is now little more than a place to park but it is closer to the beach. The access road to Rancho Cielito Lindo has had a coating of gravel but may still be slippery following storms. End SIDE TRIP.

SIDE TRIP

(Km C-15) EL PABELLON BEACH — *Midway between **Km C-15** and **C-16** a dirt road leaves to the right and in 1.2 miles arrives at El Pabellon Beach on the Pacific shore. A 0.3 mile long strip has been graded paralleling the ocean forming the parking area for an RV park. In the process the original coastal dune which once provided some wind protection has been leveled. This is a lovely spot in calm weather but the wind can make it quite uncomfortable. What was once the Honey's Camp RV Park is nearby but has been supplanted by the El Pabellon Beach facility.* End SIDE TRIP.

(Km C-24 to C-41) PACIFIC COAST — After having entered the flat coastal plain at Colonet to the north, you will find that Highway 1 has been constructed some distance inland. Finally, at **Km C-24**, the road approaches the coast and parallels it within 1/4 to 1/2 mile until **Km C-41**. The ocean is in view along much of this section of highway, and there are numerous low standard dirt roads that may be used to reach camp spots on the low coastal bluffs. Sadly, this relatively unimpressive 10-mile section of road is the only place south of Ensenada where the Pacific Coast is in close view from the Transpeninsular Highway. Your next close encounter with salt water will be on the Sea of Cortez, more than 200 miles to the south, near Santa Rosalia.

(Km C-29) PLAYA TRANQUILO -- Located on the level coastal area noted above is the Playa del Tranquilo camping area. Its short access road leaves Highway 1 midway between Km 29 and 30. The area was under development in 1997 and had only a few units built in the shelter of a

dune. Its position on a bluff overlooking a cobblestone beach offers fine ocean views.

#5 #6

(Km C-41) GEOGRAPHIC CHANGE — **Km C-41** brings the traveler to the southern end of Geographic Section No. 5. At this point the highway leaves the flat Continental Borderlands Province and reenters the Peninsular Range Mountains. Lying ahead is Geographic Section No. 6, a short 14 km (9 mile) mountainous segment ending at El Rosario.

At **Km C-41** the highway starts to wind its way uphill to a plateau area which levels out at **Km C-50** at an elevation of some 800 feet. After a few miles, it then descends rapidly to the town of El Rosario.

(Km C-41 to C-55) VEGETATION TRANSITION — Much of the original vegetation north of this point has been replaced or heavily modified by agricultural activities. At **Km C-41** the native chaparral becomes more evident, but it shares the hillsides with various types of cactus, century plants, and other species normally associated with the desert. You are traveling through a transitional vegetational zone between the *California Region* to the north and the *Sonoran Desert* to the south. The full change will become more apparent when the highway crosses to the south of the Rio del Rosario at **Km C-63**.

(Km C-55) EL ROSARIO — At the center of the community of El Rosario (The Rosary), the highway takes an abrupt 90-degree turn to the left (east) and proceeds up the northern edge of the flat valley lands of the Rio del Rosario. At this turn, a secondary road leaves the highway, to the right, and is the starting point for the trip to the mission ruins and Punta Baja. (See the EL ROSARIO AREA Map.)

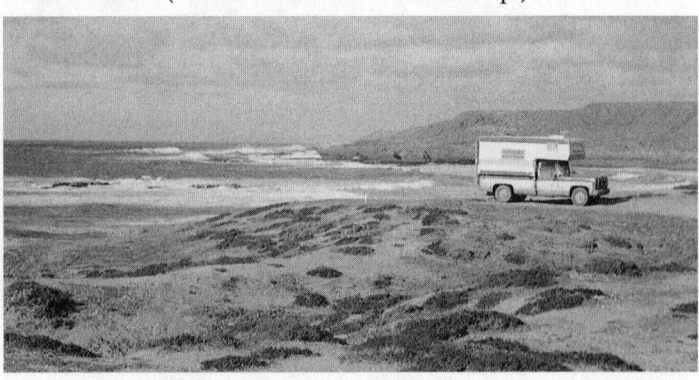

The author's original camper in splendid isolation above the Pacific surf at Punta Baja. Photo JW.

EL ROSARIO AREA

N

To San Quintin

Bridge

Sinai Motel &
RV Park

1

PACIFIC
OCEAN

Km C-57

PSI #6
Mission
Ruins

Rio del
Rosario

Central El Rosario

PEMEX Mama Espinosa's
Restaurant

Motel

Trees

Market

Town of Punta Baja

To Mission Ruins

Punta Baja

Agua Blanca Fish Camp

3 Miles

There is a sizeable PEMEX station on the highway. Be sure to obtain fuel here unless you are positive you can make it through the mountains and desert to Guerrero Negro. (Please note that the PEMEX stations at Cativina and the Bahia de los Angeles Junction were closed and appeared abandoned in 1997.) Near the 90-degree highway turn is Mama Espinosa's restaurant. It is famous for its lobster burritos and is well worth a visit.

As recently as the mid-1960s, El Rosario was portrayed as "the end of the line." Roads to the south could only be described as primitive. Mail service and the weekly bus from Ensenada proceeded no further. The completion of the Transpeninsular Highway in 1973 was to alter El Rosario's place in the sun. Rather than the *end*, the town is now more properly looked upon as the *beginning*; for here the new highway starts its lengthy journey through the interior mountains and deserts of the peninsula.

El Rosario was also the point of beginning for Baja's Dominican friars, for it was here that they established their first mission in 1774, only two years after they took over administration of the peninsula's missionary activities from the Franciscans. It was to be the jumping-off point for the founding of eight additional missions between there and the international border.

The original mission site was up-river from the center of town. In 1882, it was moved about one and one-half miles downstream. Its ruins may be visited as part of the POINTS OF SPECIAL INTEREST Tour. A sign in front of the site notes, "1434 Christian Indians registered between 1774 and 1817. These were supported from products of desert, sea, cattle, sheep, goats, and plantings of cereals imported by the Spaniards." (the sign was unreadable in 1995.) Many of

Pictured here is a sign warning that there is no fuel between Cativina and Villa Jesus Maria. Should either of these stations be closed the fuel-gap will be even greater. The message is, "Don't leave El Rosario heading south without a full supply of fuel." Photo BW.

these Indians were soon to die in the epidemics which accompanied the Spanish wherever they went.

PSI #6

SIDE TRIP

(Km C-55) MISSION RUINS AND PUNTA BAJA — *Start at the 90-degree highway turn mentioned in the first paragraph of the section above and drive west, past the market.*

0.1 Miles - Junction with dirt road marked on the SW corner by two sizeable tamarisk trees. Turn left taking this road. Take the left fork at a junction a short distance ahead.

1.0 Miles - Cross the Rio del Rosario. During my 1992 visit I wrote, "On my last visit in 1992 the river had been bridged with an earthen embankment and culvert, but high water may soon deposit these in the ocean." By 1995 the culvert was gone and one had to ford the shallow river.

1.1 Miles - Junction with another dirt road paralleling the south side of the river. Turn right on this road and drive down-river.

1.6 Miles - To the right, on a bluff overlooking the valley, are the ruins of the mission which was founded in 1774. This is stop No. 6 on the POINTS OF SPECIAL INTEREST Tour. Continue past the mission ruins if you are heading for Punta Baja.

2.6 Miles - Junction with dirt road heading 90 degrees to the left. This road goes to Agua Blanca. For Punta Baja continue straight ahead through agricultural fields.

2.9 Miles - Junction with another dirt road heading 90 degrees to the left. Turn left on this road and promptly begin to climb up the face of a broad ridge.

8.3 Miles - Road breaks out on top of ridge with fine view of Punta Baja and the ocean.

9.6 Miles - Junction with road bearing sharply to the left. Continue straight ahead and remember not to stray onto this road on your return trip.

10.6 Miles - Punta Baja fishing village. Note the one-room school house, which was constructed in October 1980 by the Del Mar Rotary Club and dedicated to the children of Punta Baja.

11.9 Miles - Punta Baja navigation light, and the tip of the point. Almost all of Baja's navigation lights are now reliable and are powered by solar energy. Note the solar panels atop the Punta Baja light.

Punta Baja is one of the most prominent points of land on Baja's Pacific coast. It provides good protection from the ocean's prevailing NW swells. For this reason, it is an anchorage used by Mexican fishing craft and yachts making the Baja passage. Small class 4 boats may be launched over the rocky beach at the village by using a steep road cut through the bluffs by the local fishermen. Because this is the open Pacific, small boats should not stray far from the protection of the point.

From Punta Baja, you can see Isla San Geronimo lying in the Pacific some 8 miles to the SE. It supports a sizeable fish camp. Punta Baja is also a good place to watch for gray whale spouts during the annual migration. End SIDE TRIP.

#6 ⛰ **#7**
(Km C-55 to C-63) GEOGRAPHIC CHANGE RIO DEL ROSARIO VALLEY — This short 8 km (5 mile) section of Highway 1 passes through the valley of the Rio del Rosario (Geographic Section No.7). The highway passes along the northern edge of the valley, which has been cleared for agriculture since the arrival of the missionaries in 1774. It is one of the few places in the peninsula where there is sufficient surface water to support crops. During my 1995 visit it was observed that most of these crops have been replaced by urbanization.

During heavy rain from late fall tropical storms, the river can become a roaring torrent. The Transpeninsular Highway was opened before many of its bridges were completed. The river crossing at **Km C-63** was the burial ground for many vehicles that tried to cross during such runoff periods. The present 0.5 miles of causeways and bridges are safe and the longest anywhere in Baja.

#7 ⛰ **#8**
(Km C-63) GEOGRAPHIC CHANGE — After crossing the Rio del Rosario, the highway enters the longest of its nineteen geographic sections (Geographic Section No. 8). For 287 kms (178 miles), the road passes through the mountains and plateaus that are typical of the gentle, westerly slopes of the Peninsular Range Mountains.

You might care to review the description of this range in Chapter 9 GEOLOGY. To the south, Highway 1 will cross over endless numbers of westerly draining arroyos without the aid of drainage structures. Rain water and debris must pass over the surface of the highway. To drive over these crossings (vados) at high speeds when they contain water or debris is to invite severe tire damage. These places are marked

Adobe ruins of the Mission San Fernando founded by Junipero Serra in 1769. The flat valley behind the ruins provided the pasture which was the reason for founding the mission here. Photo JW.

desert plants persist all the way to the peninsula's tip, you will see no more cirios after leaving Geographic Section No. 8.

At **Km C-80** the desert vegetation is particularly varied and plentiful and by now includes prickly pear cactus, galloping cactus, candelabra cactus, velvet cactus, giant cardon, and cirio. This is stop No. 7 on the POINTS OF SPECIAL INTEREST Tour. Linger here and seek the assistance of Chapter 10 VEGETATION in identifying the more common species and in investigating the characteristics of the desert plants which it describes. It is necessary to look at least 100 feet back from the roadside to locate the larger, more interesting desert plants as they were destroyed in clearing the land to build the highway.

with the VADO sign depicted in the ROAD SIGNS exhibit in the Appendix.

In many places the highway will pass over broad ridges with good scenic views. Also, there are extensive level stretches through intermountain valleys. In summary, the road conditions are not severe and reflect the relatively gentle terrain of the Peninsular Range's western slope. South of the Rio del Rosario bridge, Highway 1 begins to gain elevation rapidly.

The Rio del Rosario crossing also marks a place of climatic, as well as geographic change. The cool coastal lowlands along the Pacific shore are left behind, and the highway to the south passes through warmer air over the interior deserts. This temperature change is often easy to detect and also results in vegetational changes as noted below.

PSI #7
(Km C-63 to C-80) SONORAN DESERT VEGETATION — Sonoran Desert vegetation begins after crossing the Rio del Rosario. The brush species you have been seeing to the north are still present, but true desert plants now become commonplace. Among them are many century plants and several species of cactus. Baja's most unique plant, the cirio, comes into view at about **Km C-69**. From **Km C-70** to **Km C-74** the highway passes through a broad valley where these plants are numerous. Although many of Baja's

SIDE TRIP
(Km C-114) MISSION SAN FERNANDO — *Immediately south of **Km C-114** a low standard dirt road leaves Highway 1 to the right (west). It is level but narrow and is not recommended for larger RVs. A journey of 3.0 miles will bring you to the ruins of the only mission in the Baja peninsula that was founded by the Franciscan order. If you don't make the side trip, you might at least pause and reflect that here in this lonely and desolate place the Portola-Serra expedition passed through in 1769 on its historic journey from Loreto to San Diego. See story Chapter 12 HISTORY.*

The mission site lies on the north side of the Rio San Fernando. This location was selected because it provided good pasturage for the expedition's livestock. It is hard to believe that this remote outpost founded by Junipero Serra was developed by the succeeding Dominicans into the home of some 1,500 Indians. These people were decimated by epidemics in the years 1777-80, and by 1818 the mission was abandoned. A local Mexican has a house here and sells mineral samples, etc. to tourists. He indicated that visitors are welcome to camp nearby. End SIDE TRIP.

BOB & JEAN BACKROAD

(Km C-128) -- PACIFIC COAST LOOP — *Here is trip #2, the longest of the "Bob and Jean Backroad" Recommendations noted in Chapter 3. Leave Highway 1 to the west* just before **Km C-128**. *The road is signed for Puerto Santa Catarina - 33 Km. The route travels about 22 miles south to Puerto Santa Catarina (the former shipping port for the El Marmol onyx mine --- see below) and then some 100 miles SE along the coast to Santa Rosalillita. There are several unroaded gaps shown in this route on the AAA map, but Bob and Jean have driven it many times. Its all there. The return road to Highway 1 from Santa Rosalillita is noted in this chapter at* **Km D-38**.

The Catavina Boulder Field and its impressive Sonoran Desert vegetation. Few places better befit the Norte Americano conception of the Wild-Wild West. Photo JW.

This coastal loop offers numerous outstanding camping spots, deserted beaches, and spectacular vistas of the Pacific. You may find yourself taking a few wrong turns discovering the main road along the coast, but the ever-present coastline will be your guide. Best travel with a buddy vehicle, for breakdowns in this seldom traveled region would mean a lot of walking.

(KM C-140) SAN AGUSTIN — There is an inoperative government-built trailer court at this point. The toilet and related facilities are abandoned and on some of my recent visits the gate was locked shut. On other occasions I have been able to spend the night in its well-landscaped, pull-through trailer spaces. It was closed in 1997.

SIDE TRIP

(Km C 144) EL MARMOL — *It is a 9.8 mile side trip over a good secondary road to the famous open-pit onyx mine at el Marmol (Marble) with its unique onyx block schoolhouse. It was the source of onyx that was hauled over 51-miles of rough dirt road for shipment by sea from Puerto Santa Catarina on the Pacific coast. The market for onyx is now greatly reduced because of the development of plastics. Quarried blocks of onyx may be seen lying about the mine area. Some small scale mining was observed in 1992.*

One would expect a mine to be deep in the mountains. However, el Marmol is at the foot of the hills and the access road is passable even to larger RVs. The initial 6-miles is totally flat with the remainder a bit more rolling. The road surface is easy to drive over in comparison to most of Baja's secondary roads.

BOB & JEAN BACKROAD

NE from the schoolhouse, one can drive about 4.5 miles over rough roads to visit unique El Volcan, a mineral spring

where water oozing from the ground results in new deposits of onyx. It is trip #3 of the "Bob and Jean Backroad" Recommendations presented in Chapter 3. End SIDE TRIP.

PSI #8
(Km C-157 to C-179) CATAVINA BOULDER FIELD — The next 11 km (7 mile) segment of the Transpeninsular Highway is one of its most scenic and interesting. The highway has been constructed through an area of massive granite boulders and the desert vegetation is excellent. In particular, notice the elephant trees growing from the boulders south of **Km C-169**. It is stop No. 8 on the POINTS OF SPECIAL INTEREST Tour. Most vehicles can pull over at many places along the way. Even larger RVs and trailers can pull off and turn around at a side road and blacktop mixing area a short distance north of **Km C-161** and also at **Km C-163**.

The thousands of rounded boulders that you will see are composed of granite rock. Please review the ROCK TYPE CLASSIFICATION Table in Chapter 9 GEOLOGY. Granite is an igneous—plutonic—<u>in</u>trusive rock. All this complicated terminology means that a mass of molten material was cooled <u>slowly</u> beneath (<u>in</u>side) the earth's surface. Because of the slow cooling, <u>identifiable crystals</u> of various minerals were able to form, and the rocks appear <u>light in color</u>. Pick up a piece of granite and you can readily see the individual crystals of quartz, feldspar, and mica. Take a piece with you to compare it with the fine-grained, darker colored igneous—volcanic—<u>ex</u>trusive rocks that you will see to the south.

Observe the soil beneath your feet. It is made up of weathered particles of granite rock. This type of soil is universally known as **D-G**, *decomposed granite*. It is a road engineer's nightmare, as **D-G** soils are subject to severe erosion.

Many tourists ask "Where did the boulders come from?" The answer is that they were manufactured on the spot. Masses of granite rock tend to fracture vertically at the surface. These fractures are weathered by water and freezing temperatures, and the rock mass breaks up into blocks. With further weathering, the blocks are rounded into the boulders that you see.

(Km C-168) -- About 200 yards north of this point a dirt road leaves Highway 1 to the west and in a short distance returns to the highway. Along its path is the largest cardon I have seen in Baja. Its picture is presented in Chapter 10 VEGETATION. Taking this diminutive side trip offers a great photo opportunity.

(Km C-171 & C-175) PALM TREES — Within the Catavina Boulder Field Highway 1 crosses two substantial arroyos near **Km C-171** and **C-175**. Along these water courses you will see groves of native Washingtonia fan palms. Note that the leaves extend fan-like from the end of each stem. While palms are inhabitants of the desert, most species grow in places such as these arroyo bottoms where there is water near the surface.

There are several species of palm that are native to the Baja peninsula. However, most of the trees that you will see are date palms introduced by the early missionaries. They are still found in great abundance in such towns as San Ignacio, Mulege, and Loreto. The leaves of this species project from both sides along the stem.

(Km C-174) CATAVINA — Catavina is a small development located near the highway in the heart of the Catavina Boulder Field. At **Km C-174**, adjoining the highway, are an RV park, PEMEX station and the attractive Hotel La Pinta Catavina. The latter is typical of the original parador hotels.

The RV park is also typical of other government camps built throughout the peninsula. The white masonry structures housing the water and electrical outlets make these facilities look like cemeteries from a distance. Some of these courts have been abandoned. The one here was open during my last visit. The PEMEX station across from the hotel has been a

key link in the gasoline supply in recent years. In 1997 it was closed and appeared abandoned. The smaller station at the La Pinta Hotel was dispensing gas to everyone at that time (Magna Sin only) but they could easily revert to their previous policy of serving hotel guests only.

(Km C-175) SANTA INES — A blacktop road leaves Highway 1 to the left (east) south of **Km C-175**. It is 0.8 miles to an airstrip and the Rancho Santa Ines. The ranch has a small cafe and several low-standard rooms for rent. An area near the cafe has been cleared and is used as an RV parking area. It offers a bit more seclusion than the park at Catavina. There are numerous native palms trees in the nearby arroyo.

The Mission Santa Maria, established to the east in 1767, was the last of the chain of outposts built by the Jesuit fathers. At the time, it was the most northerly point of civilization on the peninsula and was the final jumping-off point for the Portola-Serra expedition to San Diego in 1769.

BOB & JEAN BACKROAD

A 14 mile private road was constructed some years ago from Rancho Santa Ines over the peninsular divide to the mission. This road is now in poor repair. Driving it is trip #4 of the "Bob and Jean Backroad" Recommendations presented in Chapter 3. Only the end walls and foundations of the mission remain, but its lovely palm canyon and the remote beauty of the area make this a rewarding adventure. Ask for directions at the Rancho Santa Ines.

Km C-187) SAN IGNACITO — Here, across the highway from the Rancho San Ignacito restaurant, is a brass plaque marking the point where the two ends of the Transpeninsular Highway came together, and where work on the road was finished in September 1973.

(Km C-206) EL PEDREGOSO — On the right (west) side of the highway can be seen a hill of grotesquely shaped granite boulders. It is named El Pedregoso (the rocky one). It is a boulder field in the process of development.

(KM C-229) HIGHWAY JUNCTION — The southern end of the road from San Felipe joins Highway 1 at this point. It is built to highway standards but only the first 56-miles south from San Felipe are oiled (See Chapter 15 for a full description).

If ever completed, this highway will become a major new access route from the United States to Baja California. It will bypass all of the 324 miles of Highway 1 to the north of this point. The road was signed to Calamajue (60 kms), a Sea of Cortez fishing community at the end of a branch off the main road.

(Km C-231) LAGUNA CHAPALA — Highway 1 passes along the western edge of a large dry lake bed (a playa lake), Laguna Chapala. This topographic depression is similar to many found in desert regions where water collects after heavy rains due to lack of a drainage outlet. Prior to the completion of the new highway, the road ran across the middle of the lake and provided rock-jostled drivers with a rare opportunity to gather speed. Following rain, the lake bed became a quagmire and vehicles had to be detoured around the eastern perimeter.

(Km C-241) A CARDONAL — The Transpeninsular Highway passes through an impressive *cardonal*, or forest of cardon (giant cactus). See Chapter 10 VEGETATION. Also present are numerous ocotillo and cirio.

(KM C-250) DATILILLO — At this point the traveler can see a scattering of datilillo trees. This species will become commonplace south to the state line and along the highway to Bahia de los Angeles. Datilillo means *little date*, although the plant is in the lily family and is not related to the date palm. These multitrunked plants closely resemble the Joshua tree found in the deserts east of the Los Angeles basin and in other places in SW United States.

(Km C-280 & Km D-0) BAHIA DE LOS ANGELES JUNCTION — This is the breakpoint between Highway Sections **C** and **D** and the junction with the highway to Bahia de los Angeles. The government trailer court here was gated shut in 1997 and the PEMEX station was closed and appeared abandoned. Both of these facilities have been open on some occasions in recent years.

SIDE TRIP -- *A loop road leaves Highway 1 at this point and travels 42 miles to Bahia de los Angeles, south along the Sea of Cortez, and then inland through el Arco to rejoin Highway 1 at **Km E-190**. Bahia de los Angeles is an important tourist area. The entire loop is described in a separate section at the end of this chapter.* End SIDE TRIP.

(Km D-13) PUNTA PRIETA — A detachment of army personnel is based to the right (west) at a place named Punta Prieta. The area to the south is sometimes bathed in fog and low clouds rolling in from the Pacific Ocean. Starting at about **Km D-20**, note that many of the cirio trees are draped with flowing lichens which thrive in the often moisture-laden air.

(Km D-29) OCEAN VIEW — From this point on the highway, you will be able to see the Pacific Ocean many miles to the west if it is not obscured by fog. This will notify you that the Transpeninsular Highway is now rapidly approaching the Pacific coast. There will be three opportunities to make side trips to camping spots on the coast between here and the state line.

SIDE TRIP

(Km D-38) SANTA ROSALILLITA — *Midway between **Km D-38** and **Km D-39** a secondary road leaves Highway 1 to the right (west) for the small fishing village of Santa Rosalillita, which is located directly on the Pacific shore. It is 15 km to the coast.*

If you turn left (south) after reaching the town you will find places to camp on the bluffs overlooking the Pacific. A little further along on this same road is a beach where the fishermen launch their boats. Because the waters are very shallow at this point, launching is done with the aid of a trailer made from the rear axle and wheels of a car. It is an

Datilillo is one of the dominant plants along the southern portion of Highway 1 described in this chapter. Photo JW.

interesting operation to watch. You can also work your vehicle over low standard roads to the beach in the cove north of the village. End SIDE TRIP.

(Km D-45) BALL MOSS — For a mile or so south of this point, you will see round masses surrounding the branches of the larger plants. These are ball moss. There is a far larger colony on the highway to Bahia de los Angeles and on numerous secondary roads near the Pacific shore.

(Km D-51) EJIDO ROSARITO — The town of Ejido Rosarito has a restaurant but is otherwise of little interest to the traveler, and its PEMEX station and trailer court are abandoned.

(Km D-68) EL TOMATAL — A low standard road leaves Highway 1 to the right (west) midway between **Km D-68** and **D-69**. It is 2.9 miles to a camp spot in a grove of date palms at the inland edge of a small lagoon and some 100 yards from the beach. Approximately 0.2 miles past the palms and SE along the coast is the El Tomatal fish camp. The road is straight and flat but of low standard and is not recommended for large RVs.

An even lower standard road branches south from the road to El Tomatal 0.4 miles before reaching the palm grove. This leads in 2.0 miles to Miller's Landing. Take the right fork along the way. Miller's Landing was a shipping point for onyx many decades ago. There are a dozen or so blocks of onyx and many smaller pieces lying about near the shingle beach.

#8 ⛰ #9
(Km D-70) GEOGRAPHIC CHANGE DESIERTO DE VIZCAINO — Here, just south of the junction with the road to El Tomatal, is the dividing line between the Peninsular Range Mountains (Geographic Section No. 8) to the north and the Desierto de Vizcaino (Geographic Section No. 9) to the south. The Desierto de Vizcaino is a portion of the Continental Borderlands Province. As in other places, this dividing line between geographic provinces is readily apparent. The highway now leaves the mountains and plateaus and will traverse flat terrain for the next 192 km (119 miles).

(Km D-80) LIVING FENCE — Notice that the fences along the highway starting near here are made of posts cut from the datilillo. Densely packed rows of posts also outline the yards of the dwellings in the upcoming town of Jesus Maria. Many of these take root and form living fences. This is an example of vegetative reproduction common with desert plants.

(Km D-96) VILLA JESUS MARIA — Villa Jesus Maria (population 500) is a small community adjacent to the highway. I have always found the PEMEX station open here and this is a good place to fill one's fuel tank before traveling north on Highway 1. If you look to the west you will see a small mountain, Morro Santo Domingo, the only one present in this otherwise flat area. Keep it in mind for it will guide you to the coast if you choose to take the side trip described in the following item.

SIDE TRIP
(Km D-96) LAGUNA MANUELA — *A secondary road to the Pacific at Laguna Manuela leaves Highway 1 to the right (west) at Villa Jesus Maria, 200 yards north of* **Km D-96**. *Laguna Manuela is a saltwater estuary lying directly south of Morro Santo Domingo. The first 0.8 miles is a two-lane paved, road. At the 0.8 mile-point a wide, straight, gravel road veers off to the left and heads directly to the peak of the mountain. Taking this road for an additional 6.4 miles will bring you to the coast near the edge of Laguna Manuela. (Total 7.2 miles.) This road is straight and flat but with a washboard surface.*

Local fishermen launch their boats into the protected lagoon and have developed its waters into an oyster farm. Tourists can find camp spots along the shore. The lagoon and adjoining ocean bay are protected from the Pacific swells by Morro Santo Domingo.

BOB & JEAN BACKROAD

The camping spots adjoining Laguna Manuela leave something to be desired. Thus, if you have a 4x4 vehicle, you may take an excursion up the steep, sandy road that starts near the masonry buildings at the head of the lagoon and proceed westerly past the lighthouse to Morro Santo Domingo.

This is trip #5 of "Bob and Jean Backroad" Recommendations noted in Chapter 3. This short 3-mile drive traverses the cliffs above the Pacific and offers secluded camping sites with spectacular views of the surf below. End SIDE TRIP.

(Km D-128) PARALELO 28 (THE STATE LINE) — Starting about **Km D-117,** the huge, 135-foot tall Monumento Aguila (Eagle Monument) is in view rising above the desert floor. In 1997 there was also a huge Mexican flag similar to the one flown in Ensenada. They mark *Paralelo 28*, the 28th parallel of north latitude, and the line between the states of Baja California and Baja California Sur.

Here is located another in the chain of parador developments that accompanied the completion of the

Transpeninsular Highway. The Hotel La Pinta Guerrero Negro is well maintained and the adjoining RV park (named the Dunes) is open. For years a series of semi-underground shops built as a tourist attraction between the highway's divided lanes stood abandoned. In 1997 we found them taken over by the military. They and numerous other newly constructed buildings are now the home for a full 1,200 man battalion of soldiers. There is now a gas pump at the hotel and there are gas stations in nearby Guerrero Negro. In 1997, a restaurant called La Espinita just north of the point where the highway divides offered free RV parking in an adjacent graded field.

Paralelo 28 is the division point between highway sections **C** and **D**. In the sections to the south, you will encounter the kilometer posts in reverse order (descending numbers heading south). It is also the dividing point between the Pacific Time Zone to the north and the Mountain Zone to the south. On most of my trips it has been necessary to adjust one's watches one hour here, but both zones had the same time in 1997. Keep alert. There is also an agricultural inspection station where you will be asked if you have any citrus fruit. It is recommended that you answer "No," and that you be telling the truth. Also, in 1997, a uniformed officer checked for our tourist cards at this station. Other travelers have reported they have been fined for not having the necessary form. See comments under *What Actually Happens* in Chapter 7.

BAHIA DE LOS ANGELES - EL ARCO LOOP

This subsection of Chapter 19 will detail the loop road starting at the division point between Highway 1 sections **C** and **D** (**Km C-280** and **Km D-0**) and ending at **Km E-190**. It consists of four substantially different segments with a total distance of <u>181.4 miles</u>.

(1) The initial 68 Km (<u>42 miles</u>) is a paved highway to the village of Bahia de los Angeles on the Sea of Cortez. En route it passes through desert vegetation that is varied and interesting. The old gas station at the Casa Diaz Motel in the village was closed in 1997 but a new station at the entrance to town was under construction. Hopefully it will be in operation when you arrive. The highway has always received less maintenance than Highway 1 and frequently has numerous potholes. In 1997 we found it in better shape than in the past with potholes encountered in only about 10% of its length.

PEMEX ← Abandoned 1997
Km C-280

Isla Angel de la Guarda

See Bahia de los Angeles Map

Bahia de los Angeles →

PEMEX

Bahia de las Animas

N

See text concerning gas station situation.

Playa San Rafael

← Camp Site

BAHIA DE LOS ANGLES - EL ARCO LOOP

Pacific Ocean

1 - San Francisquito Fish Camp
2 - Punta San Francisquito Resort
3 - El Barril
4 - La Cuesta de la Ley
5 - Santa Gertrudis Mission

1
2
4
3
Rancho El Progreso
5

STATE Line
El Arco →

See Guerrero Negro Area Map in Chapter 20

Guerrero Negro
PEMEX
← Km E-190

(2) The second segment is a 1 1/2 lane secondary road with a fairly rough surface. It connects Bahia de los Angeles with the El Progreso Ranch area and provides side trips to several places on the ocean. It is easily traveled by pickups and vans but travel time is slow due to the rough surface.

(3) From El Progreso to the town of El Arco is a narrow, low-standard dirt road. In most places travel speeds are actually faster than on segment (2) because of the smooth, sandy roadbed. With one exception the terrain is relatively level. The exception is La Cuesta de la Ley (Grade of the Law). It poses a segment of steep grades for both directions of travel. My standard drive pickup made it with no trouble going NE, but the opposite direction appeared more formidable. As few Mexicans have 4x4 vehicles it is no doubt passable to standard vehicles in both directions, but be prepared to grit your teeth.

(4) A paved highway was constructed from El Arco to **Km E-190** on Highway 1 when the latter route was completed. This was no doubt a concession to the community for being bypassed by the new highway. Virtually all of the original layer of paving has disappeared leaving a moderately washboarded travel surface. Most traffic uses a closely paralleling and smoother surfaced dirt road.

SEGMENT (1) — The highway to Bahia de los Angeles leaves Highway 1 to the left (east).

(Km-10) BALL MOSS — Starting at this point, you will see hundreds of six-to-eight-inch diameter, ball-shaped masses surrounding the branches of the cirio, datilillo, and other larger plants. This is ball moss (although it is not a moss). The plant makes its own food through photosynthesis and secures moisture from the air. It does not penetrate into the tissue of its host as is the case with mistletoe.

(Km-36) DRY LAKE — At this point, the highway enters the western edge of a dry lake bed some 5 miles in diameter. It is nearly surrounded by high, sparsely vegetated mountains.

(Km-49 to Km-52) CIRIO — Here, near the southern end of the dry lake, is an outstanding array of cirios. The individual plants are large and of many interesting shapes. A good spot for photography.

(Km-52) GEOGRAPHIC AND VEGETATIVE CHANGES — At this point, the traveler is rewarded with a vista of the Sea of Cortez and the highway begins its descent to sea level. From the Transpeninsular Highway to here, the terrain has been gentle, as one would expect of the westerly slopes of the Peninsular Range Mountains. Ahead lies the much steeper grade down the eastern escarpment.

There also occurs a prompt change in vegetation. The interesting and varied species of the Vizcaino Desert community are left behind and one enters the less attractive San Felipe Desert community composed mostly of creosote bush and other low shrubs. This scant plant growth clearly reflects the arid conditions of the rain shadow of the mountains.

(Km-58) OCEAN VIEW — A short distance past **Km 58**, Bahia de los Angeles and its close-in group of protecting islands are arrayed before you. Isla Angel de la Guarda, the second largest island in the Sea of Cortez, is in the background. These islands combine to make Bahia de los Angeles an extensive and well-protected boating area.

An army base, complete with a gigantic Mexican flag, surrounds the impressive eagle statue at the Paralelo 28 state line. Photo BW.

(Km-61) PUNTA LA GRINGA SHORT-CUT -- An old dirt road leaves the highway about 200 yards downgrade (easterly) from Km-61. This is the short-cut route to Punta la Gringa. Its travel surface is smoother than the main secondary road described in the next paragraph.

(Km-64) PUNTA LA GRINGA — To the left is a road junction at the northern edge of the village of Bahia de los Angeles. (See BAHIA DE LOS ANGELES Map.) You will no doubt wish to proceed straight ahead into town. Should you return to this Punta La Gringa road you will travel over it as follows: (A) 0.8 miles. Branch road straight ahead to the airport. Bear right. (B) 1.3 miles. Branch road right to the Brisa Marina and Campo Archelon RV parks). The former area is used as a camping site although its restrooms are not available to the public. It also contains the Sea Turtle Research Station described in Chapter 11 WILDLIFE. (C) 7.8 miles. End of the road near a point of land, Punta La Gringa.

Punta la Gringa has a fine beach where you may camp after paying a small fee. The area has extensive views of the bay and the towering escarpment of the mountains in the background. Many visitors find this a more enjoyable site than the trailer courts in the village.

(Km-64) VILLAGE OF BAHIA DE LOS ANGELES At this point you enter the village of Bahia de los Angeles. Here you will find the Hotel las Hamacas, Casa Diaz Motel and Hotel Villa Vitta. The latter two establishments operate nearby RV parks. Guillermo's Trailer Court lies between these first two. They offer little or no landscaping due to the areas dryness and thus appear a bit austere. Each court offers a hard-surfaced boat launching ramp.

To some people, the Bahia de los Angeles area suffers in charm because of its scant vegetation. To others, its near-barren mountains are beautiful to behold as the sun casts an ever-changing variety of shadow patterns on their slopes. Also on the positive side are its excellence as a boating and fishing area and the rela-

tively short driving distance from the international border (405 miles).

Bahia de los Angeles can be particularly hard hit by the strong northern winds common to the upper Sea of Cortez in the late fall and winter. In addition, gale force winds sometimes flow across the Baja peninsula from the west and strike the village area. Taking to sea in small boats becomes impossible and living conditions become most uncomfortable.

SEGMENT (2) — The Segment (2) secondary road leaves the Bahia de los Angeles village behind (west of) the Casa Diaz Motel. (The mileages noted below

BAHIA DE LOS ANGELES

261

The village of Bahia de los Angeles. The oiled highway can be seen entering town at the top of the photo. The secondary road heading south toward El Arco is visible at the bottom of the photo. Photo JW.

41.6 Miles — Spur road east heading toward the coast. In about 1 mile it becomes very low standard and is best for 4x4 vehicles.

45.6 Miles — A short spur road leads east and in about 0.1 miles arrives at a camping spot at the north end of Playa San Rafael.

47.8 Miles — Spur road east leads in 0.1 miles to a fish camp at the south end of Playa San Rafael.

48.3 Miles — Spur road east accesses camping spots on a bluff overlooking a rocky shore. The San Lorenzo Island chain and the south end of Isla Angel de la Guarda are in view from here.

start at 0.0 from this point.) The initial 3-4 miles parallels the shore of Bahia de los Angeles where tourists homes are being constructed. It then moves inland.

4.6 Miles — A low-standard dirt road heads east at this point, traverses a dirt airstrip and accesses a small group of tourist houses and a good camping area at the SE corner of Bahia de los Angeles in about 5 miles.

27.6 Miles — Junction with side road to Bahia de las Animas. It is 10.7 miles to the first good camping spots on the edge of the bay and an additional 0.3 miles to the first of two fish camps. Most of this road is little more than two tracks in the sand but the terrain is level and regularly traveled by standard-drive vehicles. Portions of the route are in an arroyo bottom which could be impassable following rain. At the 7.1 mile point one has the choice of going straight ahead or turning 90 degrees to the left. The left turn is the proper choice.

There are several good camping sites on a narrow sandy beach. Be alert to numerous small sting rays that inhabit the shallow waters at the head of the bay. I was treated to my first, and hopefully last, sting from one of these *Moving Rocks* while cooling the beer in the ocean (one of the lesser known hazards of alcohol addiction).

73.7 Miles — Junction with low standard road to the right (south) leading to Rancho el Progreso. This spur road is the beginning of Segment (3) of the loop route under discussion. However, the main secondary road continues eastward. Taking this latter route one encounters (1) a junction with another 2-lane road heading SE in 0.3 miles (see note below); (2) the junction with the road into the Punta San Francisquito Resort in an additional 11.8 miles; then arrives at the Bahia San Francisquito Fish Camp in an additional 0.4 miles. It is thus 86.2 miles from Bahia de los Angeles to Bahia San Francisquito.

The Punta San Francisquito Resort offers several modest sleeping cabins, central toilet and shower facilities, and a small restaurant. It caters primarily to patrons arriving at its nearby dirt airstrip. Aviation and regular fuel are available but it is expensive.

NOTE — I have not traveled the 2-lane road mentioned above but it appears to be being constructed to highway standards. It is no doubt heading toward El Barril, a private residential area on the coast about 7 miles distant.

SEGMENT (3) — Return to the Rancho El Progreso junction noted above at 73.7 miles.

74.3 Miles — The Rancho El Progreso and its well of fresh water lies on the south side of the road.

82.7 Miles — A gate in a cattle drift fence is built at the top of the steep La Cuesta de la Ley (See discussion at the start of this subsection). Between here and the rock corral noted below much of the road passes through an extensive burned over area indicating that travelers must be careful with fire even in the desert.

Returning from a days fishing near the Casa Diaz Motel at Bahia de los Angeles. Photo BW.

92.0 Miles — A large rock corral lies adjacent to the road making an unmistakable landmark.

106.5 Miles — At this point one leaves the relatively level terrain and sandy soils prevailing to the NE and enters rolling hills. The travel surface becomes more rocky.

112.8 Miles — El Arco. In approaching El Arco from the reverse direction (west) one is tempted to turn right in the center of town. The correct course of action is to proceed straight ahead crossing an arroyo whereupon the road veers to the NE.

The main peninsular road passed through El Arco prior to construction of the Transpeninsular Highway. Gold was mined in the area by an American company, and during the 1920s over 1,000 people were employed. Gerhard and Gulick's *Lower California Guidebook* describes the town in 1960 as consisting of two groups of shacks on opposite sides of the arroyo with a population of about 150. By 1989 there had been a modest rejuvenation of the mining industry and the community was the base for a small detachment of federal soldiers. A lonely place for such duty.

SEGMENT (4) — It is 26.6 miles from El Arco to Highway 1. The first 6 miles SW from town passes through rolling terrain and one is compelled to drive on the main highway standard road and its washboarded surface. Beyond this point the land is level and the road is closely paralleled by a low-standard dirt road where a smoother surface makes it the most popular route of travel.

139.4 Miles — After many bumpy miles, the loop road joins Highway 1 near **Km E-190**.

Signs of Distinction

Follow the sign to the trayler park at Bahia de los Angeles. We are hunting for the fellow who painted this sign to be an editor for our books. Photo BW.

CHAPTER 20
STATE LINE TO SANTA ROSALIA

Chapter 20 will guide you for 221 km (137 miles) in a journey completely across the peninsula from the Pacific Ocean to the Sea of Cortez. While very few tourists set out to visit this region, it nevertheless contains some of Baja's most intriguing points of interest. These include the gray whale-watching area

at Scammon's Lagoon, the very interesting town of San Ignacio with its famous mission and the major cave painting area at San Francisco de la Sierra. Many of Baja's best cave painting sites are present in the central portion of the Baja peninsula presented in this chapter. For this reason the chapter concludes with a

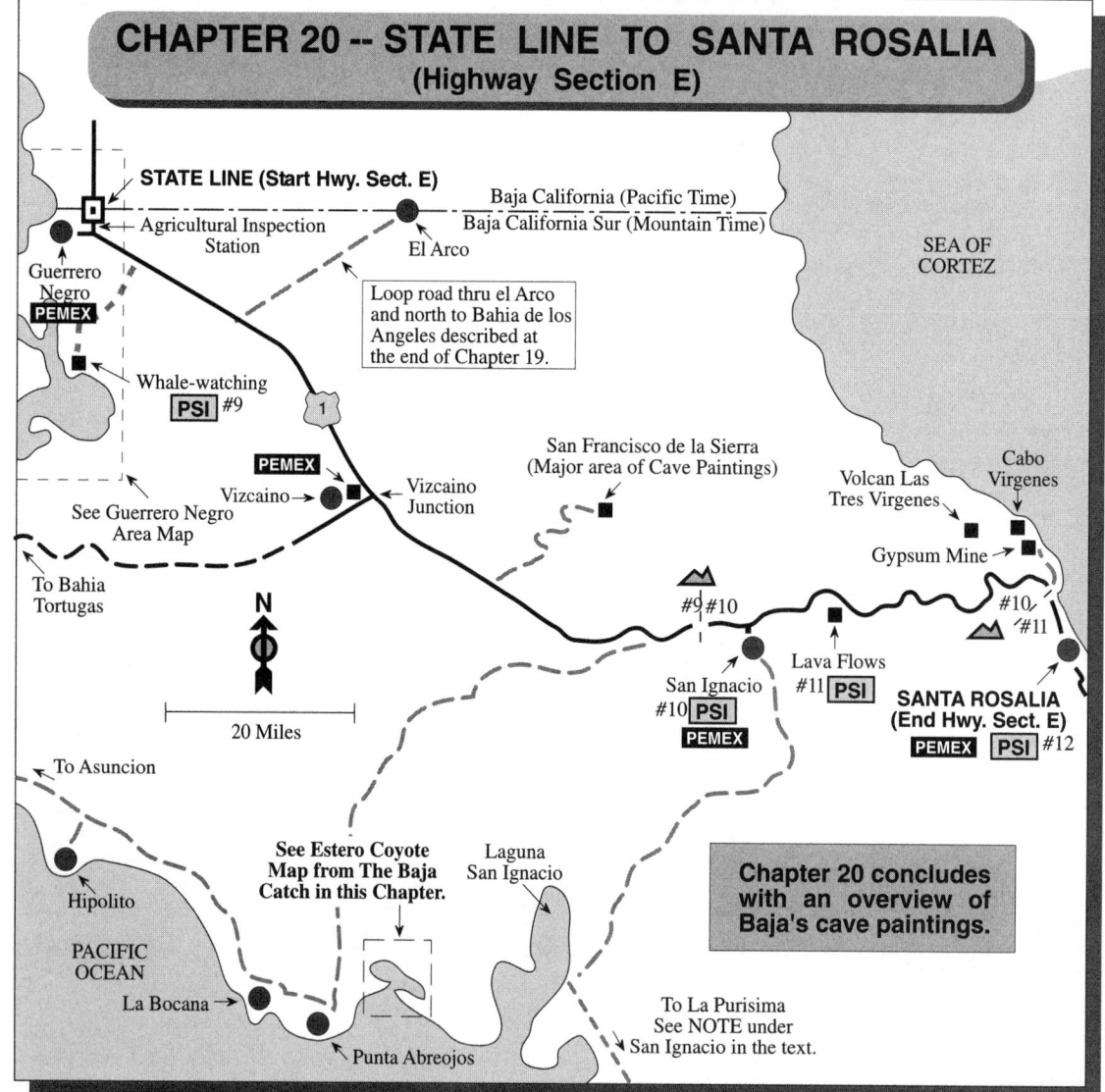

CHAPTER 20 -- STATE LINE TO SANTA ROSALIA
(Highway Section E)

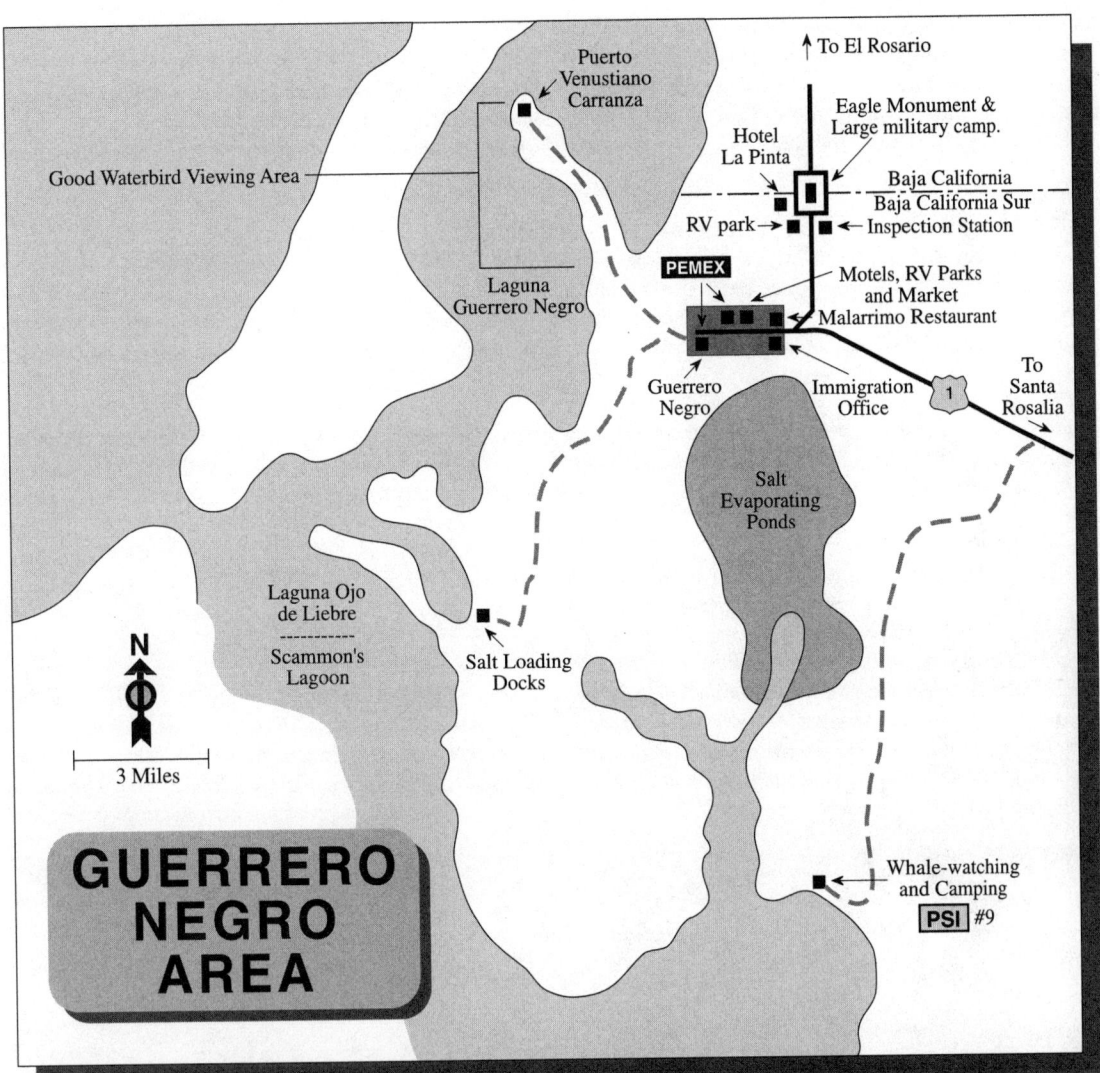

GUERRERO
NEGRO
AREA

brief overview concerning this subject. For these reasons, I hope you will not let the lure of the beaches ahead pull you through this region with undue haste.

(Km E-217) GUERRERO NEGRO — At this point, Highway 1 veers to the left to begin its journey across the peninsula. Turn to the right, at the junction here, to enter the town of Guerrero Negro (Black Warrior) and its 7,200 people. After 1.1 miles you will find the Malarrimo Restaurant and several motels (several with RV parking) all on the right (north) side of the road. The Malarrimo restaurant (tourist hangout with live music) is very nice and the above motels are modest but adequate. Further into town are a supermercado and two PEMEX stations, one on each side of the road. Remember to pay them a visit before

starting the long trip north on your way home. There is also an immigration office across the road from the Malarrimo Restaurant where you can acquire a tourist card if you get caught at the state line without one.

SALT MANUFACTURING — Guerrero Negro is supported largely by the salt-producing industry. Large segments of the land to the south have been converted into salt-evaporation ponds, reportedly the largest such operation in the world. Sea water is introduced into these areas. After the sun has baked out sufficient layers, the salt is trucked to barges waiting at docks located west of town.

The shallow waters of the coastal estuaries near Guerrero Negro are unsuited for large ocean freighters. The barges are thus towed through a channel into the ocean and then to the shores of Isla Cedros some 70 miles away. Here, at a deep-water port, the salt is transferred into gigantic mounds where it awaits reloading into large ore carriers.

SIDE TRIP

PUERTO VENUSTIANO CARRANZA — *A wide, two-lane road with a packed sand surface turns right (north) from the main street of Guerrero Negro in front of the salt company's headquarters near the western edge of town. Travel over this road, as follows:*

1.1 Miles. Another wide, two lane, dirt road leads to the left (SW). Stay straight ahead for Puerto Venustiano Carranza. The road to the left leads in 6.8 miles to the gate of the salt-barge loading facilities on Scammon's Lagoon (visitors are not normally encouraged).

6.9 Miles. Arrive at the long-abandoned port facility that extends into Laguna Guerrero Negro. Mating gray whales may be present in this lagoon, but in some years they are unable to enter because the entrance is blocked with sand. I have not been able to view them from the dock area during my visits as they tend to congregate some distance away near the lagoon entrance. Whale-watching trips by boat are usually available and arrangements may be made at the motels and RV parks in Guerrero Negro.

Bird lovers will wish to take this side trip to Puerto Venustiano Carranza, regardless of the presence of whales, as the road passes through 5 miles of excellent salt water marsh lands. The road lies atop a massive, 10-foot-high fill, so you can look down on the birds. See Chapter 11 WILDLIFE. **End** SIDE TRIP.

SIDE TRIP PSI #9

(Km E-208) SCAMMON'S LAGOON — *Laguna Ojo de Liebre (Scammon's Lagoon) is one of the major breeding grounds for the California gray whale. Visiting the whales is stop No. 9 on the POINTS OF SPECIAL INTEREST Tour.*

The whales are normally present from the end of December to early April. See Chapter 11 WILDLIFE for details concerning the whale, Scammon's Lagoon, and for observational techniques. (Also see the nearby notice for an excellent small book about the gray whale.) Whale-watching boat service usually operates from the Scammon's Lagoon camping area. No reservations are normally required.

A sign on Highway 1 marks the junction with the road to Scammon's Lagoon 100 yards north of **Km E-208***. It reads "Parque National de la Ballena Gris 25 Km. Daily boat tours Jan. 1 - 15 April subject to weather." It is 15 miles to the edge of the lagoon over a flat, natural surface road that*

The fishing village and small cove at Punta Eugenia. Photo JW.

is graded through the desert. The road may be washboarded but it is occasionally graded with equipment owned by the salt company.

Members of a local ejido collect a small fee for camping at the edge of the lagoon and operate the whale-watching boats. Facilities are limited to crude outhouses, but the area is kept clean, and the road from the highway is signed at points where you might go astray.

I recommend that you plan to camp overnight if you take this journey. It is a long trip in and out, and you need to let the sight and sounds of the whales make a proper impression on the senses. I fear you will be disappointed if you rush in and out and allow for only a short stay at the water's edge. End SIDE TRIP.

(Km E-190) ROAD TO EL ARCO — Between **Km E-189** and **Km E-190**, a road branches to the left. This is the southern end of the Bahia de los Angeles - El Arco loop road described at the end of Chapter 19.

The mining town of El Arco is located some 26.6 miles to the east, at the base of the mountains which can be seen in this direction.

SIDE TRIP

(Km E-144) VIZCAINO JUNCTION AND ROAD TO PUNTA EUGENIA AREA -- There is a growing cluster of homes, a PEMEX station and the Kaadekaman RV Park and motel where a blacktopped highway leaves Highway 1 to the right (west) exactly at **Km E-144**. There are several other motels in this area. (See the PUNTA EUGENIA AREA Map.) *It is 5.4 miles to the turnoff to the village of Vizcaino. Vizcaino is surrounded by orderly plantings of grape vines and fig and citrus trees. It is a good place to visit to see the Mexican people turn the desert into a productive farming area.*

West of the Vizcaino junction, the oiled surface continues for an additional 16.5 miles. Further west, to Bahia Tortugas, the road has been constructed to highway standards, but as of 1995 was not yet oil surfaced. (The same

PUNTA EUGENIA AREA

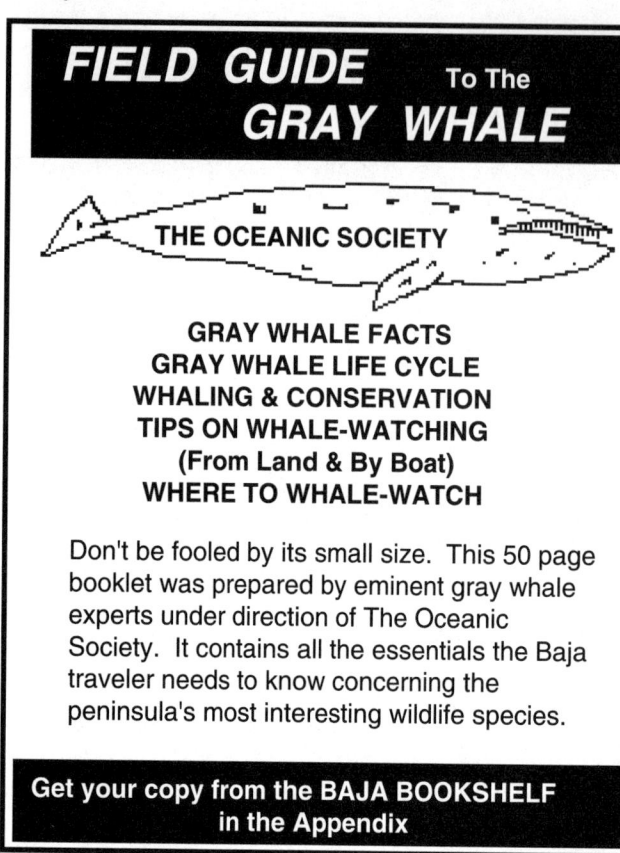

FIELD GUIDE To The GRAY WHALE

THE OCEANIC SOCIETY

**GRAY WHALE FACTS
GRAY WHALE LIFE CYCLE
WHALING & CONSERVATION
TIPS ON WHALE-WATCHING
(From Land & By Boat)
WHERE TO WHALE-WATCH**

Don't be fooled by its small size. This 50 page booklet was prepared by eminent gray whale experts under direction of The Oceanic Society. It contains all the essentials the Baja traveler needs to know concerning the peninsula's most interesting wildlife species.

**Get your copy from the BAJA BOOKSHELF
in the Appendix**

is true of a 23.8 mile branch road leading to Asuncion.) The oiled surface has not been extended on this road for several years and what the future holds is anybody's guess. For now, most of the roads shown on the PUNTA EUGENIA AREA Map are usable by large RVs, although there is some washboarding. But, because of the relatively long distances involved, the area currently receives little vehicular tourist traffic. However, the town of Bahia Tortugas is a major stopping and fueling point for yachts making the Baja passage. Its people are thus well accustomed to American and Canadian visitors.

In my 1992 survey I found that much of the road from Km E-98 on Highway 1 to Punta Abreojos had been completely rebuilt and was about 6-miles shorter than the old route. This road, and most of the others shown on the PUNTA EUGENIA AREA Map, do not have a surface of rough imported gravel as do most other secondary roads in Baja. The travel surfaces are thus relatively smooth.

Each coastal town shown on the map is a sizeable communitiy with schools, fish-packing plants, and power generation facilities. There is a PEMEX station at Bahia Tortugas. A

major water line has been constructed from wells near Vizcaino to all the coastal towns.

While many of the roads pass over flat desert lands, the coastline is mountainous, picturesque, and offers many places to camp. The only tourist facilities are the small Vera Cruz Motel at Bahia Tortugas and the minimal facility resort named Campo Rene on the shores of Estero Coyote. For an extended trip, make a complete loop starting at the Vizcaino junction and ending at **Km E-98** on Highway 1. Also, take the side road to Punta Eugenia. End SIDE TRIP.

PINTURAS RUPESTRES (Cave Paintings) -- Starting in 1995 several signs were noted along Highway 1 south of Guerrero Negro calling attention to Baja's cave paintings. As a result I have included a brief overview of this subject at the end of this chapter. The peninsula's most accessible area of paintings is noted below. Please read this material before taking the side trip to San Francisco de la Sierra.

SIDE TRIP
(KM E-119) SAN FRANCISCO DE LA SIERRA — Just south of **Km E-118** a secondary road leaves Highway 1 to the left (east) and may be seen climbing the mountains to the NE. A sign reads "San Francisco de la Sierra 37 km -- Pinturas Rupestres."

6.0 Miles. After a six mile drive across level terrain, the road moves steeply into the mountains. After about one mile there are several places where one may camp in the rugged mountains with their fine views and desert vegetation. The road ahead was constructed to good secondary standards but was badly eroded by a major storm during the winter of 1993-94. The damage becomes worse as the road gains elevation, with the last 3 1/2 miles being the worst due to steep side-slopes. I made it with little trouble in 1995 in my 19-foot van but caution is clearly in order until such time as repairs are undertaken.

16.4 Miles. At this point is an interpretative sign which notes that the area is administered by the Instituto Nacional de Antropologia e Historia.

21.4 Miles. At this point is Cueva del Raton (Rat Cave). It is located directly along the road but a guide must be

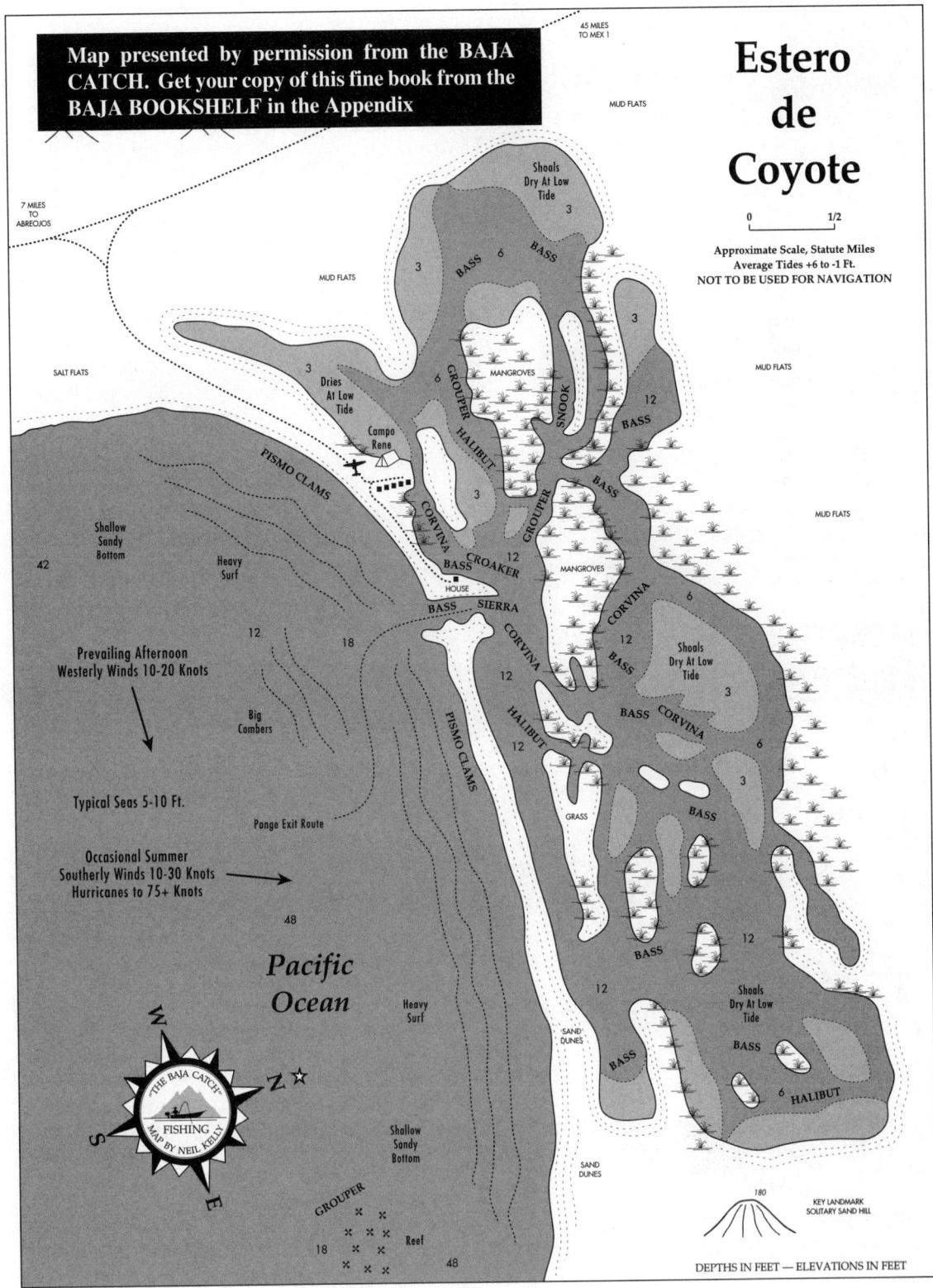

Map presented by permission from the BAJA CATCH. Get your copy of this fine book from the BAJA BOOKSHELF in the Appendix

Estero de Coyote

45 MILES TO MEX 1

MUD FLATS

0   1/2

Approximate Scale, Statute Miles
Average Tides +6 to -1 Ft.
NOT TO BE USED FOR NAVIGATION

7 MILES TO ABREOJOS

Shoals Dry At Low Tide

3

BASS   6   BASS

3

3

MUD FLATS

MANGROVES

SNOOK

BASS

12

3

SALT FLATS

Dries At Low Tide

GROUPER

6

HALIBUT

BASS

MUD FLATS

Campo Rene

GROUPER

3

CORVINA

PISMO CLAMS

BASS

12

MANGROVES

6

Shallow Sandy Bottom

42

Heavy Surf

CROAKER

CORVINA

12

CORVINA

BASS

12

HOUSE

BASS   SIERRA

BASS

CORVINA

Shoals Dry At Low Tide

Prevailing Afternoon Westerly Winds 10-20 Knots

12

18

CORVINA

12

BASS

3

6

Big Combers

HALIBUT

BASS   CORVINA

Typical Seas 5-10 Ft.

12

6

Pange Exit Route

GRASS

3

Occasional Summer Southerly Winds 10-30 Knots
Hurricanes to 75+ Knots

BASS

48

Pacific Ocean

Heavy Surf

PISMO CLAMS

BASS

12

12

Shallow Sandy Bottom

SAND DUNES

Shoals Dry At Low Tide

BASS

"THE BAJA CATCH"
FISHING
MAP BY NEIL KELLY

W N
Z ☆
S E

BASS

6   HALIBUT

SAND DUNES

GROUPER   ✕ ✕ ✕
✕ ✕ ✕ ✕
✕ ✕ Reef
18   ✕ ✕ ✕   48

180
KEY LANDMARK SOLITARY SAND HILL

DEPTHS IN FEET — ELEVATIONS IN FEET

Young men help a diver unload his catch of abalon (abalone) at the cove at Punta Eugenia. Photo JW.

secured from the village ahead. High quality development of the cave was underway in 1995.

23.0 Miles. Here is located the small village of San Francisco and the camp for workers developing the cave painting exhibits. End SIDE TRIP.

(Km E-98) ROAD TO PUNTA ABREOJOS -- Head-ing south at this point is the road to Punta Abreojos and Campo Rene. (See discussion of this road earlier in this chapter under ROAD TO PUNTA EUGENIA AREA.)
#9 ⚠ **#10**

(Km E-84) GEOGRAPHIC CHANGE — Highway 1 has slowly gained in elevation and one may see a red volcanic cinder cone at **Km E-81** and lava flows near **Km E-82**. In the vicinity of **Km E-84** the eastern edge of the Continental Borderlands blends with the beginning of a low pass through the Peninsular Range Mountains. This dividing line between geographic provinces is not as sharp as in other places, but it will soon be apparent that the highway has left the flat plains behind and enters more rugged terrain.

(Km E-77) -- A small but permanent looking military post is located here where you may be asked to stop for an inspection.

PSI **#10**
(Km E-74) SAN IGNACIO — There is a PEMEX station near the junction of the paved side road into the town of San Ignacio. (A "Magna Sin" pump is also present at the Hotel la Pinta.) Directly behind the station is another of the government-constructed trailer courts. I have always found it to be in operation.

SIDE TRIP -- *San Ignacio is one of Baja's most charming towns and is surrounded by date palms introduced by the Jesuits more than 200 years ago. It is stop No. 10 on the POINTS OF SPECIAL INTEREST Tour. Even the largest of RVs can make this trip and head back to the highway by circling the town square. However, to minimize traffic congestion, I suggest that trail-*

San Ignacio's famous Dominican-built church. Photo JW.

Signs of Distinction

SAN IGNACIO -- <u>Upper Left</u> - One of two delightful palm-lined ponds adjoining the community. <u>Bottom Left</u> - The town of San Ignacio lies in a lava rimmed valley filled with palm trees. The town square is in the trees to the left of the church. <u>Right</u> - The economy minded advertiser in Baja uses anything available as sign material. Here a discarded car door announces you are entering Don Chon's Camping area on the approach road into town. Photos JW & BW.

ers be parked near the hotel and their occupants walk the last few hundred yards.

It is <u>1.4 miles</u> from Highway 1 to the town square. En route, you will pass RV parks in the palms, and the Hotel La Pinta. My favorite spot for camping is in the palms near a small pond west of the El Padrino RV Park. Here is one of the few places to go swimming in the desert. In past years the area was operated as an RV park but is now undeveloped. No one has objected to my using it but this could change in the future. You may also camp by the community reservoir at Don Chon's Camping.

The town square is typical of such public places found throughout Spanish America. Here and elsewhere they are called el zocalo (the public square). At the west end of the zocalo is Mision San Ignacio, one of the finest churches in all of Baja. The mission, originally established by the Jesuits in 1728, was for twenty-four years the northern-most mission. At one time it served some 5,000 Indians. The present thick-walled stone church was completed many years later by the Dominicans, in 1786. A very nice cave painting museum is located near the church.

The square is completely shaded by six massive Indian laurel trees (Arbol de la India) with trunks three-to-four feet in diameter. You will find smaller examples of this broadleafed evergreen tree along the waterfront at La Paz and in many other places. End SIDE TRIP.

NOTE — The northern terminus of the rough-surfaced secondary road leading in 59 kilometers to Laguna San Ignacio is shown on the SAN IGNACIO Map. Laguna San Ignacio is then linked by roads of various standards to the town of La Purisima. From here a paved highway leads south to Ciudad Insurgentes. This entire San Ignacio to Ciudad Insurgentes route may eventually be a paved high-

SAN IGNACIO

To Guerrero Negro

RV Court →

PEMEX

1 — To Santa Rosalia

Don Chon's Camping

San Lino

Pond

1 Mile

Manual Quezada RV Park in Palms

N

← Hotel La Pinta

PEMEX

Stream

El Padrino RV Park

Post Office
Markets

Pond

Church →
Museum →

Camping in Palms

PSI #10

Town Square

← School

La Posada Motel
Road to Laguna San Ignacio →

way. Its present southern portion is described at the end of Chapter 21 under the LA PURISMA & CIUDAD INSURGENTES LOOP.

(Km E-71) SCHOOL BUILDINGS — To the right of the highway notice the modern, one-story school building. Most of the schools you will see in Baja offer primary education only. Here is one of an increasing number of secundaria-tecnico facilities built during recent years to improve the educational standards of rural Mexico. See the discussion of education in Chapter 13 OUR DEVELOPING COUNTRY NEIGHBOR.

(Km E-67) VOLCAN LAS TRES VIRGENES — After passing east of **Km E-67**, you will see a massive mountain ahead and to the left of the highway. This is the 6,547-foot-high Volcan las Tres Virgenes (Three Virgins Volcano). It was known to have erupted in 1746 and to have emitted smoke in 1857. When an area's principal mountains are dominant, more or less isolated peaks such as Las Tres Virgenes, it is a good sign that you are viewing mountains of volcanic origin. In this area you are also passing among several lava flows.

Starting near San Ignacio, you pass through an area made up of volcanic rock. Refer to the ROCK TYPE CLASSIFICATION Chart in Chapter 9 GEOLOGY. This igneous-volcanic-extrusive rock is called *basalt* and is formed when molten material is *extruded* at or near the surface of the earth. Because it cools rapidly, the rock is fine grained as no recognizable crystals have time to form. Note the reddish color typical of these formations. In some places, basalt is honeycombed with small holes formed by pockets of gas trapped at the time of solidification. Thus, from a distance, an observer can come to believe that basalt is coarse, rather than fine grained.

(Km E-62) DATILILLO — The datilillo is one of the most characteristic of the plants of the Sonoran Desert. The stand visible here in the mountains is the most robust seen anywhere along the Transpeninsular Highway. It is mixed with other attractive plant species.

PSI #11

(Km E-42 to E-38) LAVA FLOWS AND ELEPHANT TREES — For several miles the Transpeninsular Highway passes through an area of recent lava flows originating on the sides of Volcan las Tres Virgenes. Here, at stop No. 11 on the POINTS OF SPECIAL INTEREST Tour, I suggest that you pullover and take a closer look at these flows. A good turnout is just east of **Km E-41**. There are very few places along the highways of North America where you will have this opportunity. Walk a few feet onto a flow. There are few environments where you will have such a feeling of complete desolation.

Ironically, this most hostile of growing sites provides the preferred environment for the thick-trunked elephant tree (*Pachycormus discolor*). Some individuals growing on these flows are three feet in diameter at the base, and they are the sole vegetation. In nearby deep-soiled areas you will find a species of very similar appearance but which is only distantly related to the trees on the lava flows. This is *bursera microphylla*. (See Chapter 10 VEGETATION for descriptions.) The fact that these two species look so much alike is a dramatic example of convergent evolution, as discussed in Chapter 10.

(Km E-35) GEOGRAPHIC NOTE — It is here that Highway 1 starts its descent down the steep, east-facing escarpment of the Peninsular Range Mountains. Contrast the considerable drop in elevation you will experience on the highway ahead to the almost effortless climb that has taken place over the gentle western slope behind you. See Chapter 9 GEOLOGY.

The dominant, dome-shaped mountain lying ahead is Cabo Virgenes (Virgin Cape). It marks the northern limits of the relatively gentle coastal lands through which you will be passing in the miles ahead and which contain the most extensive tourist area on the Sea of Cortez. The ruggedness of Cabo Virgenes and the mountains to the north forced highway engineers to route the Transpeninsular Highway across the peninsula through the inviting pass over which you have just traveled.

(Km E-17) SEA OF CORTEZ VISTA — Highway 1 renews its steep descent at this point. A section of highway known as The Devil's Grade lies ahead. It is the most dangerous section of mountain highway in Baja. At **Km E-17** the traveler is treated to the first significant view of the Sea of Cortez. In nine more kilometers you will be at its shore.

Directly ahead you can also see the first of many offshore islands that rim the peninsula's eastern shore. This is Isla Tortuga (Turtle Island). Like its mainland neighbors, it is also an extinct volcano, most of which lies below the surface of the sea.

#10 ⛰ #11
(Km E-8) THE SEA OF CORTEZ AT LAST — At long last, after a journey of 920 km (572 miles) from the international border, the Transpeninsular Highway overlooks the shore of the Sea of Cortez and turns south toward Santa Rosalia. This is the end of Geographic Section No.10 and the northern end of the gentle coastal lands lying along the Sea of Cortez.

Prior to reaching **Km E-7** a dirt road leaves Highway 1 to the north. It provides access in 2.3 miles to an open-pit gypsum mining operation. The area is worth a visit only if you are interested in this industrial activity. Visitors must secure a pass from the mine office in Santa Rosalia.

PSI #12
(Km E-0) SANTA ROSALIA — Santa Rosalia has received mixed reviews from previous travel book writers. Some even have said that it has little interest to the tourist. Nothing could be further from the truth, and I have placed this town of 10,200 people on the POINTS OF SPECIAL INTEREST Tour as stop No. 12.

Admittedly, it may not be a pretty place, for this was an industrial town where there is little vegetation and the surrounding hills bear the scars of more than a century of copper and manganese mining. But for uniqueness and historic interest it would be hard to surpass.

I said *was* an industrial town, as the old smelter closed, probably for the last time, about 1990. During my

The town of Santa Rosalia and its breakwater lined harbor. Photo JW.

The Hotel Frances at Santa Rosalia. It is typical of many of the French-built wooden buildings in this historic town. Photo JW.

merous mine tailings in the area so future smelting activity may still occur in Santa Rosalia.)

The town was built by the French (see Chapter 12 HISTORY for Santa Rosalia's background as a mining center) and as a result almost all of its buildings are made of imported lumber rather than masonry. Many have broad verandas, and the houses along the three main streets are closely packed in orderly lines. It is an interesting community. (During my 1992 visit, the town had sprouted two traffic lights. Horrors, the place is going to hell.)

1992 visit it was being extensively rebuilt, but even a retired forester like myself could see that this was probably socialistic nonsense. It was. (During my 1995 visit I interviewed a mining engineer who is investigating the possibility of reprocessing the nu-

Smaller vehicles can be driven into town but trailers and large RVs should be parked along the highway or in the parking lot at the ferry dock. Do your sightseeing on foot. I recommend you proceed as follows:

SANTA ROSALIA

PSI #12

To San Ignacio

Display of old Mining Equipment.

SEA OF CORTEZ

Hotel Frances

Smelter (Closed)

Mesa Frances

Hospital

History Museum

Motel San Victor (11 Rooms)

French Bakery

Church →

Train Monument

1

Marina

Harbor

Park →

Post Office

Municipal Palace

Navy Base

Ferry Terminal and Parking

Mesa Mexicana

Cemetery →

To Motel El Morro, Las Palmas RV Park and Loreto

0.2 Miles

Airfield →

PEMEX

N

1. Walk about on the streets in the main section of town and notice the architecture and wooden construction of the buildings.

2. Visit the unique church designed by Gustave Eiffel (builder of the Eiffel tower in Paris). It was constructed from prefabricated galvanized iron as the building was originally destined for a humid African country where resistance to termites was needed.

3. Starting in front of the church, proceed up the steep road that winds its way up to the Mesa Frances (French Mesa). Here you will find a broad street lined with large wooden buildings. What for decades was the mining company office has now been converted into a museum (Museo Historio de Santa Rosalia). Down the center of the broad street have been placed an array of old mining railroad equipment. Also visit the Hotel Frances which has been remodeled and reopened after several years of being closed. Outside the hotel, note the adjacent brick tunnel leading from the smelter to the smokestack high above town.

4. Look over the breakwater walls that form the harbor. They are made from blocks of slag left over from the smelting process. A small marina was completed about 1987 and attracts boaters most of whom cross the Sea of Cortez from San Carlos near Guaymas on the mainland shore.

5. If you can get inside the old smelter it is worth a visit. It contains an old French clock and loads of decades-old machinery. It should be made into a museum.

Santa Rosalia's famous metal church surrounded by many of the town's old wooden buildings. Photo JW.

The church interior. The prefabricated iron panels are easy to observe. Photo JW.

PINTURAS RUPESTRES (Cave Paintings)

Signs bearing the term *Pinturas Rupestres* began appearing along Highway 1 south of Guerrero Negro starting about 1993. Pinturas is the Spanish word for "paintings," but I have had a bit more difficulty translating Rupestres. My Spanish-English dictionary indicates the word means "rupestrian," a definition that doesn't move one too far along the road to enlightenment. In biology this term refers to "growing on or living among rocks." It is thus likely that Pinturas Rupestres refers to a variety of prehistoric rock art which includes but is not limited to cave paintings. As Baja is most famous for her cave paintings, I will

275

The old mining office on the Mesa Frances at Santa Rosalia has now been converted to a museum but the building itself is as interesting as its contents. Photo BW.

Baja's cave paintings began to be noted in the literature in the late 19th century but they were brought to the publics attention by mystery writer Erle Stanley Gardner. Gardner mounted two expeditions in 1962 and visited several rock art sites including the one that is now considered Baja's best and that bears his name (Gardner Cave or Cueva Pintada). Baja's caves are similar to those hosting the so called cliff dwellings of the Pueblo Indians in southwestern United States. These are generally shallow linear depressions running along the face of near vertical mountain cliffs. Baja's cave paintings are often spectacular and depict human figures and animals. They extend for hundreds of feet in length and are up to 30 feet in height. Colors are red, black, white and occasionally yellow.

equate the two terms in this discussion until corrected by some irate professor.

Examples of rock art may be found the full length of the Baja peninsula but the largest concentration of cave paintings appear to be concentrated in the four areas shown on the PRINCIPAL CAVE PAINTING AREAS Map accompanying this discussion. These areas encompass some of the Peninsular Range's most rugged mountains.

VISITING THE CAVE PAINTINGS -- There are several ways to arrange to visit Baja's cave paintings.

SAN IGNACIO -- Reference to the accompanying map will show that the town of San Ignacio lies near Highway 1 in the heart of the cave painting country. There is a well designed museum related to rock art and other subjects adjoining San Ignacio's famous church. Unfortunately the display labels and handout material are all in Spanish. Perhaps this will change in the future considering the fact that most of the museum's prospective visitors will be English speaking tourists.

In spite of my deficiencies in Spanish it was made clear to me that persons who wish to visit the cave paintings at San Francisco de la Sierra need to first come to the San Ignacio museum to obtain a permit. The fact that one passes the road to this area some 45 kilometers to the north does not appear to alter this rule. Hopefully, the unreasonableness of this requirement will result in its eventual demise.

The center of the main street on the Mesa Frances at Santa Rosalia is now lined with vintage railroad mining equipment. Photo BW.

MULEGE -- My past visits have also indicated that trips to rock art sights could be arranged by contacting the hotels and RV parks in and near Mulege. During our 1997 survey we made inquiries and were directed to a taxi driver who would conduct tourists to nearby cave paintings. He had an impressive looking government license authorizing his service. He was most uncooperative in advising us about the location of the cave sites. Its all hush-hush. A cave painting site may also be visited as noted at **Km 189** CANDELARIA in Chapter 21

SAN FRANCISCO DE LA SIERRA -- Travelers can drive directly to the vicinity of Baja's best cave sites by taking the SIDE TRIP noted earlier in this chapter on page 268. In 1995 guided tours to backcountry sites could be arranged at the village of San Francisco de la Sierra. In this regard see comments about obtaining a permit at San Ignacio as presented above. One of the added attractions of a visit to this area is outstanding desert mountain and vegetative scenery. Trips into the backcountry also feature delightful palm canyons.

Need another copy of **THE MAGNIFICENT PENINSULA** or other books about Baja? See the **BAJA BOOKSHELF** in the Appendix.

CHAPTER 21
SANTA ROSALIA
TO LORETO

Chapter 21 describes the Sea of Cortez central coast, one of the six principal tourist areas introduced in Chapter 2 THE BIG PICTURE. It contains the peninsula's most heavily used beach-side camping areas and the towns of Mulege and Loreto. Highway 1 will pass over a series of coastal benches and low hills lying at the base of the steep eastern escarpment of the Peninsular Range Mountains. This section of the mountains is called the Sierra Giganta (the Giant Range) and will treat you to the best scenery in view from the Transpeninsular Highway.

The fuel situation has improved along the Central Coast in recent years. There are PEMEX stations at Santa Rosalia, Mulege and Loreto. In addition there is an easy-to-access station about 3-miles south of Mulege on Highway 1. Thus, it is no longer necessary to enter the constricted street of this community to obtain fuel at the town station.

(Km F-195) HOTEL EL MORRO — On the bluff overlooking the Sea of Cortez is the Hotel El Morro. It

has a very nice restaurant and features good ocean views from many of the rooms.

Note the navigation light tower on the small rocky islet lying 200 yards offshore from the hotel. You should become familiar with these aluminum towers and their solar-powered lights if you plan to use a boat in the Sea of Cortez. They are to be found in scores of locations and are reliable aids to navigation.

(Km F-193) RV PARK LAS PALMAS — There has long been need for a trailer park near Santa Rosalia as many people like to settle down for the night after the long journey through the desert required to reach the Sea of Cortez. Also it is quite easy to spend many hours prowling about the historically interesting town and an overnight visit is often just what is needed.

This need has now been met a short distance south of Santa Rosalia by the RV Park Las Palmas and cafe. Since its origin about 1992, is has been extensively landscaped and is becoming one of Baja's most pleasant RV parks.

(Km F-190) STATE PRISON — There are no signs on the large building at this point but there is little doubt about its function. There is relatively little crime in Baja California, but obviously there is some.

BOB & JEAN BACKROAD

CANDELARIA — Six miles south of Santa Rosalia (between Km 188 and 189) a secondary road signed for Santa Agueda 13 Km leaves Highway 1 to the west. The village of Santa Agueda is reached in about _7 miles_. The additional 20 miles to the Rancho Candelaria is lower standard road along an arroyo bottom. Ask at the ranch for a guide for a walk to nearby Indian cave paintings. This is trip #6 of the "Bob and Jean Backroad" Recommendations as noted in Chapter 3.

CALETA SAN LUCAS

↑ To Santa Rosalia

San Lucas

↑ San Lucas

San Lucas RV Park

← Rocky Bar

Caleta San Lucas

1

← Airstrip

SEA OF CORTEZ

Km F-180 ↙

Camping in Palms

#10
#11

PSI #12
Santa Rosalia PEMEX
(Start Hwy. Sect. F)
← RV Park Las Palmas

Santa
Agueda

↑
Rancho
Candelaria

See Caleta
San Lucas Map

Isla San
Marcos

San Bruno

Caleta
San Lucas

Palo Verde →

See Punta Chivato Area Map

Punta Chivato

Islas Santa Inez

CHAPTER 21
SANTA ROSALIA TO
LORETO
(Highway Section F)

N

10 Miles

#13 PSI
Mulege →
PEMEX

← See Mulege Map

Punta Concepcion

#14
PSI Vista
Point
Playa Punta Arena →

See Bahia
Coyote →
Map

← Bahia Coyote

SEA OF
CORTEZ

Playa
Buenaventura
El Requeson
Playa la Perla
Playa Armenta

Bahia Concepcion

← San Sebastian

San Nicolas

↘ Punta Pulpito

PUNTA CHIVATO AREA

SEA OF CORTEZ Punta
Chivato

← To Highway 1

Sand
Dunes

RV Park

Hotel Punta
Chivato

Bahia
Santa Inez

Punta
Santa Inez

Old Arroyo de la
Purisima Road

San Bruno
Landing Site

Isla
Coronado

To San
Ignacio

San Isidro →

← San Juanico

↑
La
Purisima

San Jose
← de Comondu

San Miguel
de Comondu

PSI #15
(End Hwy. Sect. F)
PEMEX **Loreto** →

See Loreto
Map
Isla
Carmen

Las Barrancas →

See Nopolo
Map Chapter 22 →

← Nopolo

Steep section at
this point. 4X4
vehicles needed at
times.

San Javier

Puerto
Escondido

PACIFIC
OCEAN

Landing →   ← La Poza Grande

The isolated Hotel Punta Chivato north of Mulege. Photo JW.

be seen faintly north of the mine. Gypsum is one the softest of minerals, and the San Marcos variety is light yellow in color. Many of the town's buildings have been constructed from foot-thick blocks of compressed gypsum despite the fact that you can scratch it with your fingernail. Walking through this almost totally yellow town is an interesting experience.

(Km F-173) SAN BRUNO — The small dirt-street town of San Bruno is in view on the shore to the left (east). A drive of 0.5 miles over a secondary road accesses a small RV park (Coasta Serena) occupied largely on a full-time basis and for this reason I have not included it in the list of RV parks in Chapter 4. The town is fronted by a good sandy beach. It is a good place to wander about and view a small, rural Mexican town that has had minimal impact from tourism.

(Km F-162) SANTA ROSALIA AIRPORT — A jet airport and 1.6 mile oiled access road were completed east of this point in fall 1988. It was designed to serve Santa Rosalia to the north and Mulege to the south but it has seen almost no use. Such projects illustrate one of the characteristics of a centralized, socialistic form of government. The international airport at Loreto and the resort area at Nopolo to the south are vastly underutilized. And yet, here, someone contemplated a repeat performance. Perhaps new hotels and other tourist facilities will follow. Time will tell. In the meantime, the tarmac makes a fine RV parking area if you can negotiate with the military people that guard the strip from being used for illicit purposes. They use the terminal building as their barracks.

SIDE TRIP
(Km F-182) CALETA SAN LUCAS — *A dirt road leaves Highway 1 to the left (east). In 0.4 miles you will reach the shores of a shallow cove protected from the sea by a rocky bar. This is Caleta (little cove) San Lucas. Here you will find the San Lucas RV Park at the water's edge. A small resturant is located nearby to the south.*

*Near the cove's southern end another dirt road leaves Highway 1 at **Km F-180** and accesses many fine palm-shaded camp sites along the shore. See CALETA SAN LUCAS Map. This road is sometimes fenced-off to prevent public assess and sometimes it is open. It was closed in 1997. End* SIDE TRIP.

ISLA SAN MARCOS — Isla San Marcos is in view offshore from this general area. Notice the light color of the land at the south end of the island. This light area is the barren slope of an open-pit gypsum mine. The workers' village, the mill, and port facilities can

SIDE TRIP
(Km F-156) PUNTA CHIVATO — *A sign at this road junction indicates that it is 20 km to Punta Chivato. The small community of Palo Verde lies along the highway. Taking this secondary road left (east) from Highway 1 leads in 4.5 miles to a point where a lesser standard road branches right to Punta Chivato. The very nice Punta Chivato Hotel is reached after a total*

The historic federal prison at Mulege. Photo JW.

MULEGE

El Sombrerito — Restaurant

SEA OF CORTEZ

Former Hotel Vista Hermosa
Now a military barracks.

Port Captain

Rio Santa Rosalia
Estuary

N

Airstrip

Camping

Hotel
Serenidad

0.5 Miles

1

Maria Isabel Trailer Court

Jungle Jim's Resturant

PEMEX

Penitentiary
Museum

Orchard Vacation Village
(See text under RV parks)

To Loreto →

Hotel Terrazas

Post Office

Motel La Siesta

Hotel Las Casitas

Visit the Mulege
Dive Shop if you
need another copy of
The Magnificent Peninsula

Mulege Dive Shop

PEMEX

Hotel Hacienda

NOTE -- The Rio Santa Rosalia
Estuary is usable for boating
only at high tide.

Highway Sign Reads "Mission."

1

Highway
Bridge

Rio Santa
Rosalia

Mission Church

---

of 12.8 miles with an RV park at the water's edge being an additional 0.6 miles (See inset map on the CHAPTER 21 Map). In the past the access road suffered from chronic washboarditis, but as of my 1995 trip the hotel had acquired a grader and the entire road was being graded every two weeks. Large RVs and trailers make it on a regular basis. End SIDE TRIP.

(Km F-136) MULEGE — Again, as at Santa Rosalia, I suggest that you take an hour or two and visit another of Baja's historic and intriguing communities. It is stop No. 13 on the POINTS OF SPECIAL INTEREST Tour. The two towns have little in common except that the river along which Mulege is built bears the name Rio Santa Rosalia. Santa Rosalia is also the name of Mulege's famous mission.

TOWN CENTER — The center of this community of 3,100 people is reached from a road leaving Highway

The restored mission church on the banks of the Rio Santa Rosalia at Mulege. It was founded in 1705 by the Jesuits. The church was originally built in 1766 and has been remodeled many times. The small hill to the left of the steeple is a good vista point. Photo JW.

1 west of the highway bridge shown on the MULEGE Map. The town's streets are narrow so it is best to leave the big RVs and trailers near the highway. There is a gas station in town but it is usually more convenient to obtain fuel at the PEMEX station 3-miles south of town on Highway 1.

> NOTE -- See aerial photo of the Mulege area on page 176.

If you drive into town, I suggest you park near the Hotel Las Casitas and savor the community on foot. Keep in mind that you are viewing a place that was founded sixty years before the first Europeans discovered San Francisco Bay. Be sure to visit the massive thick-walled federal prison. It looks like a structure you would find in the Sahara Desert manned by the French Foreign Legion. It is no longer an active prison and is maintained as a museum. The prison was famous for being operated on the honor system. The inmates worked or visited in town during the day but were required to return for the night. Misconduct by one prisoner was considered an infraction by all, and all were punished. It was no doubt a very orderly place.

If you have a small vehicle, drive down the dirt road along the palm-lined north bank of the river and visit the area near a small hat-shaped hill which could only be named El Sombrerito (The Little Hat). In October 1847 it witnessed a battle during the Mexican-American War between local patriots and forces from the U.S. sloop *Dale*. See Chapter 12 HISTORY. Along the

way is the former Hotel Vista Hermosa which is now used as a military barracks.

RV PARKS — The SE side of the Rio Santa Rosalia is the main tourist area at Mulege. It may be reached by driving under the highway bridge at the SE end of the main section of town, or directly from the highway. There are two large RV parks among the palms along the river. They have boat ramps usable at high tide only. There is another smaller RV park adjoining the Hotel Serenidad.

MISSION — From under the highway bridge, drive upstream for 0.4 miles on a dirt road through palm groves along the SE bank of the river to the restored Mission Santa Rosalia de Mulege. (The towers of the church can be seen while crossing the bridge and from the highway entering town from the north.) Here, Jesuit missionaries founded their fourth mission in 1705, only eight years after they established themselves on the peninsula in 1697. It originally served an Indian population of some 2,000 persons.

Walk to the vista point on top of a small hill located a few feet behind the mission. From here you can look over a sea of palm trees, a small reservoir, and the agricultural area upstream from downtown Mulege.

SOUTH OF TOWN — At **Km F-132** a dirt road will bring you in 0.5 miles to the Hotel Serenidad. This attractive facility is located near the mouth of the river and directly adjacent to a dirt surface airstrip. Many of the hotel's patrons arrive by small private aircraft. Adjacent to the hotel is a small RV park.

Near the mouth of the river, and hidden from view by the hotel, is the Fisherman's Landing boat launching ramp. One must drive around three sides of the hotel on a narrow dirt road to arrive at the ramp. Boaters need to time their launching with the state of the tide as there is no water at the ramp when the sea is at low ebb.

About 0.1 miles south of the road to the Hotel Serenidad, another side road leaves to the left (east). After passing through the remains of a former dumping ground, this road arrives in 0.4 miles at a camping spot

The entrance to Bahia Concepcion as seen from the vista point at **PSI** stop No. 14. Photo JW.

on a long sandy beach. It was here that my wife and I camped for ten days on our first trip to Baja and fell in love with the Magnificent Peninsula. We both agreed that we had never had such a relaxing vacation. After returning to the hectic life of the city, it was several days before I was aware that I was no longer smoking a pipe which had been a constant fixture in my mouth. I have never touched it again.

(Km F-131) PEMEX STATION — This station was constructed about 1990 to relieve traffic congestion caused by the old station on Mulege's narrow streets.

(Km F-126) VIEW OF PUNTA CONCEPCION — You are now approaching Bahia Concepcion, the largest protected body of water on the Sea of Cortez. To the SE from this point on the highway, you can see Punta Concepcion, the northern tip of the peninsula which forms the eastern shore of the bay. The channel into Bahia Concepcion lies between this peninsula and the promontory supporting a microwave tower, which is in view ahead and to the left.

Near this same point on the highway, a dirt road leaves to the left and in 0.4 miles arrives at a camping spot on the low bluffs above a shingle beach. There are also several other dirt roads heading toward the Sea of Cortez between the new PEMEX station and the vista point noted below. I have not explored these so help yourselves.

PSI #14

SIDE TRIP

(Km F-124) VISTA POINT — *There are few good vista points directly along Highway 1. I have therefore included a visit to the microwave tower, noted above, as stop No. 14 on the POINTS OF SPECIAL INTEREST Tour. It is signed for "Est. Microondas (Micro-*

BAHIA COYOTE AREA

To Mulege
0.3 Miles
Playa las Naranjos
1.7 Miles
1.6 Miles
Playa Punta Arena (Restaurant & Bar)
Punta Arena

N
1 Mile

Playa Santispac →
Hot Spring →
Posada Concepcion →
Punta Piedrito ←
Reef
Isla Sin Nombre
Playa La Escondita →
Isla Coyote
Isla Blanca
Los Cocos →
BAHIA COYOTE
Playa El Burra →
Isla Guapa
Isla Bargo
RV Park
Village
Hot Spring
Playa Santa Barbara
Playa El Coyote
To Loreto

wave Station) Tiburones." *The last word on each micro-wave sign along the highway is the name of the individual station. In this case Tiburones means sharks.*

The cobblestone road to the tower begins with two moderately steep switchbacks which are in view from the highway. These are the main problem spots on the 0.8 mile drive to the tower. Because of these switchbacks and the lack of places to pass oncoming vehicles, this trip is not recommended for large RVs. If you make the trip, you will find good turnaround spots at the end of the road or in a low saddle about 100 yards before reaching the tower. You will be rewarded with fine views of the entrance to Bahia Concepcion and the coastline. End SIDE TRIP.

(KM F- 121) VILLA DE MULEGE — It is 1.6 miles to the beach and a palapa-type, private subdivision. There is a natural surface boat launching ramp.

(Km F-119) PLAYA PUNTA ARENA — To the left, a dirt road leads to the sandy beach camping areas at Punta Arena (Sand Point). The mileages to the areas two RV parks are shown at the top of the BAHIA COYOTE AREA Map. I recommend that you proceed to the Santispac area at the northern end of Bahia Concepcion if you have not visited this region before. However, should the crowds of people that are normally found there not be to your liking, you can consider Punta Arena as an alternative. There are usually fewer campers and the beach is excellent. Its negative features are the bumpy access road and its

exposed location which provides little protection from the northerly winds that prevail in the early winter months.

(Km F-114 to F-108) BAHIA COYOTE — Bahia Coyote is the wind-protected bay lying at the NW corner of the much larger Bahia Concepcion. It is the most heavily used camping and boating area in the entire Baja Peninsula. During my 1992 and 1995 surveys, the number of tourists visiting Baja was down sharply, but the beach camping areas at Bahia Coyote were packed as usual. Most of these camping areas have no facilities other than crude outhouses. RVs simply line up at right-angles a few feet from the beach.

There are six separate sections of the Bahia Coyote area, each served by a short side road from Highway 1. They are described in the order they are encountered along the highway from north to south. The exact operating conditions of these campgrounds will vary from year to year, but at most beaches you will be charged a daily fee. At some places, this will entitle you to the use of a beach-side shelter called a *palapa*. They are made from poles and grass mats.

PLAYA SANTISPAC **(Km F-114)** — Standing at the beach at Santispac, one can readily come to the conclusion that most weary travelers from north of the border shout "This must be the place!" when they arrive at Santispac, for the beach is usually lined with

Bahia Coyote. The birdlimed island in the foreground is Isla Blanca. The J-shaped beach above and to the right of the island is Playa Santispac. Photo JW.

vehicles of every description during the winter. Many travelers stay here for extended periods, others make it a one-night stopping point, for there is a busy influx of vehicles every evening and a sudden torrent of departees after breakfast. Be careful using the steep approach road and guard against the possibility of tipping over at its junction with the highway. The larger trailer rigs sometimes have to take a run to return to the highway.

Shoreside vegetation has long ago yielded to the onslaught of campers. However, the protected cove is excellent for windsurfing, water-skiing, and swimming and in 1995, one of the beach-front establishments was *Baja Tropicales*, a kayak rental establishment. There are two small restaurants, and your modest camping fee helps keep the area clean. A short walk to the west of the main beach, on a trail along the base of the highway, will bring you to a natural hot spring. Thus, if you enjoy beach bumming in close proximity to many other friendly folks doing the same thing, then your first assessment will prove correct and, in fact, *this must be the place.*

POSADA CONCEPCION (Km F-112) — Posada Concepcion is the domain of those who became enamored with this part of the world and decided to stay. Located here is a subdivision of winter homes and numerous trailer houses supplemented with adjoining grass-mat shelters. (There is also a tennis court and an RV and boat storage area.) You can arrange to park your RV by the day, but the permanent residents have the best locations.

PLAYA LA ESCONDITA (Km F 111.5) -- A 0.4 mile long narrow dirt road leads to a secluded beach lined with palapas. The last portion of the road is a bit steep and I believe it would be marginal for larger RV's and trailers.

LOS COCOS (Km F-111) — The access road from Highway 1 is 0.3 miles in length and leads to a fine beach and camping area with many palapas.

PLAYA EL BURRA (Km F-109) — Another good camp-

ing beach which is in full view from the highway. The access road leaves directly at the **Km F-109** sign.

PLAYA El COYOTE (Km F-108) — The southernmost of the Bahia Coyote camping spots is a beach which bears the same name. A few feet after the side road leaves the highway, turn right and proceed along the water's edge and in 0.5 miles arrive at an excellent beach. At the far (south) end of this camping area, a trail leads some 100 yards to a hot spring near the water's edge. (This is my favorite of the Bahia Coyote camping areas.) There is a sizeable trailer park on the other side of the highway, but it is very lightly used.

Approximately 1 mile SE from Playa el Coyote is another fine beach in a deep cove at Playa Santa Barbara. In the past there was no access road but one seemed to have grown by 1995. This cove provides an excellent picnic or camping site for small boat owners who can load up their gear and escape the crowded conditions at the other camping areas that rim Bahia Coyote. It is only a short distance over the protected waters of the bay from any of these areas.

BAHIA CONCEPCION (SOUTHWESTERN SHORE) -- For many years there were no water-front tourist areas along the shores of Bahia Concepcion south of Bahia Coyote. (Recall that sites at Bahia Coyote are reasonably well protected from the winter wind.)

The restored mission church at Loreto. A fine historical museum is housed in an adjoining building. Photo JW.

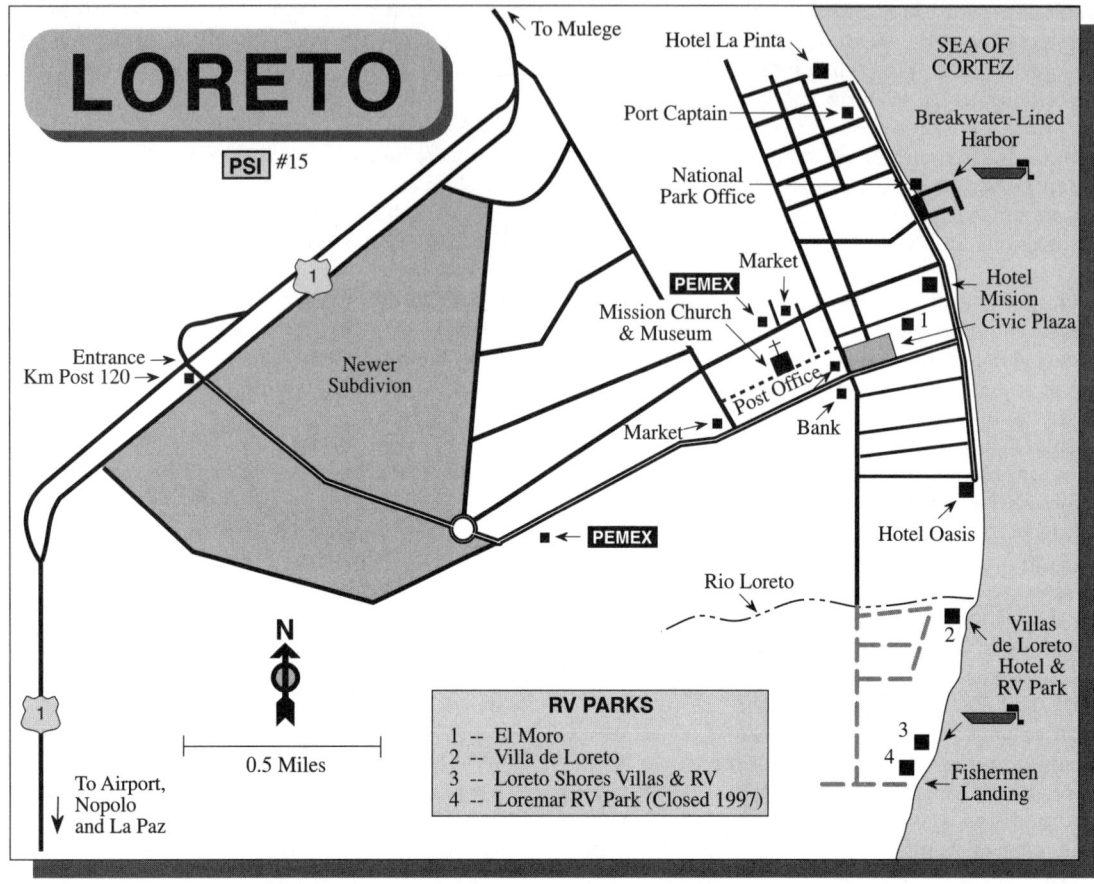

LORETO

PSI #15

To Mulege

Hotel La Pinta

Port Captain

National Park Office

SEA OF CORTEZ

Breakwater-Lined Harbor

Market

PEMEX

Mission Church & Museum

Hotel Mision Civic Plaza

1

Entrance → Km Post 120 →

Newer Subdivision

Post Office

Market →

Bank

PEMEX

Hotel Oasis

Rio Loreto

Villas de Loreto Hotel & RV Park

2

N

0.5 Miles

3

4

To Airport, Nopolo and La Paz

Fishermen Landing

RV PARKS
1 -- El Moro
2 -- Villa de Loreto
3 -- Loreto Shores Villas & RV
4 -- Loremar RV Park (Closed 1997)

There were several reasons for this lack of development including the fact that this southwestern area is subject to brisk northerly breezes funneling down the length of Bahia Concepcion during the winter months. However, the area started to build up early in the 1990's and now contains several of the better tourist areas on Bahia Concepcion. While this section of shoreline can be a bit windy and chilly during the winter, this very condition becomes a blessing as the weather turns hot in spring and summer.

PLAYA BUENAVENTURA (Km F-94) — The development here is probably the nicest on Bahia Concepcion. The owner is an excellent craftsmen who has fashioned a small, low-rise, 22 unit hotel to standards not often found in Baja. Use of the adjoining RV park is restricted to its limited number of developed units thus avoiding the sardine-like conditions often found at Bahia Coyote. There is an adjoining restaurant-bar and a well constructed boat launching ramp. These facilities are directly in view from Highway 1.

EL REQUESON (Km F-92) — El Requeson is a small island lying between **Km F-93** and **Km F-92**. At low tide it is connected to the mainland by an isthmus of sand. The higher portion of this isthmus provides a fine camping spot, and it and the island form a small, well-protected but shallow bay. A good spot for launching class 4 boats over the beach. The entire area is in view from the highway, and the approach road is less than 0.1 miles in length.

PLAYA LA PERLA (Km F-91) -- A short distance north of **Km F-91** a short dirt road leads to a waterfront camping area with palapas.

PLAYA ARMENTA (Km F-91) — Playa Armenta is a small beach lying on the north side of a point of lava rock. It is fully exposed to the prevailing northerly wind but is a good camping spot during calm weather. The approach road is 0.6 miles in length and leaves Highway 1 between **Km F-91** and **Km F-90**. The beach cannot be seen from the junction point, but it and the approach road are in full view from the highway, a short distance to the south, should you care to look it over before driving in.

ADDITIONAL CAMPING SITES — Spur roads lead to several camping sites at (1) 200 yards north of **Km F-88**, (2) north of **Km F-85**, (3) north of **Km F-84**, (4) just south of **Km F-82**, and (5) near **Km F-80**. These are not as good as other areas along Bahia Concepcion, but some of us can suffer some shortcomings in exchange for not being herded into the larger developed areas. Some will no doubt become developed sites in the future.

SIDE TRIP

(Km F-77) BAHIA CONCEPCION (SOUTH AND EAST SHORE) — *A dirt road leaves Highway 1 between **Km F-77** and **Km F-76** and closely follows the south shore of Bahia Concepcion. The terrain at the southern end is extremely low and flat. After a rain, the road in this vicinity becomes slick and impassable, but travel is easy and rapid in dry weather. (After rains in fall 1997 this area was still impassable while all other local roads were dry.) There are numerous spurs that provide access to camping spots at the water's edge. A second, parallel road branches inland about 1/4 mile in from the highway. It traverses higher ground and is preferable in wet weather.*

The area's principal shortcoming is that it is fully exposed to the northerly winds that funnel between the mountains that rim Bahia Concepcion on both sides. Near the junction with Highway 1 lies one of the abandoned cemetery-like RV parks which have been previously mentioned. It was no doubt a victim of these windy conditions. A small group of trees a few yards east of the park is one of my favorite camping spots. As the weather heats up with approaching summer the breeze here makes this a very pleasant location.

At the SE corner of Bahia Concepcion the traveler is offered three choices of travel (see the AAA map). Two roads proceed easterly to San Sebastian and San Nicolas on the Sea of Cortez shore. I have started out on both of these routes but turned back after several miles feeling they were a bit marginal for a standard drive pickup. I have been to both

areas by sea and they are two of the most attractive of Baja's hidden coastal Shangri-las.

BOB & JEAN BACKROAD

A third road runs at the water's edge the full length of the eastern shore of Bahia Concepcion and passes over the divide ridge to the Sea of Cortez. At this point one may explore the extensive ruins of an abandoned manganese mine or take a trail north to Punta Concepcion. This is trip #7 of the "Bob and Jean Backroad" Recommendations presented in Chapter 3. Much of this road is suitable for standard drive vehicles but there are rough spots making extra traction advisable. End SIDE TRIP.

(Km F-77) CARDON — The flat plain lying along the southern and eastern shore of Bahia Concepcion (just

The boat launching ramp and breakwater-lined harbor at Loreto. The open boats in view are different models of the Mexican panga. Photo JW.

south of **Km F-77**) supports one of the finest *cardonals* of giant cardon cactus in view along the entire Transpeninsular Highway. It is a good area for photographing Baja's largest desert dweller.

(Km F-68) SIERRA GIGANTA — The base of the Sierra Giganta has been some distance inland since the Peninsular Range Mountains were crossed north of Santa Rosalia. South of **Km F-68**, the range's steep eastern escarpment is closer to the coast and will provide you with the best mountain scenery in view from the Transpeninsular Highway. Note the characteristic saw-toothed silhouette.

Loreto — An aerial view of Loreto. The town dock has now been expanded into a small breakwater-lined harbor (see photo on page 287). The sizeable three-story building on the shore to the left is the Hotel Mision de Loreto. Photo JW.

SIDE TRIP

(Km F-60) ROAD TO LA PURISIMA — *At this point, a secondary road leads right (west) to the historic towns of San Jose de Comondu, San Isidro (61 Km) and La Purisima (65 Km), and eventually to Cuidad Insurgentes. It provides one of the most interesting backroad adventures in Baja. The full route is described at the end of this chapter.* End SIDE TRIP.

(Km F-21) SAN BRUNO LANDING SITE -- From this portion of Highway 1, the Sea of Cortez is in view about 6 miles to the east. A low section of coast lies between mountains to both the north and south. It is along here that Padre Francisco Kino and Isidro de Atondo made their attempt to found a colony in 1683. This effort lasted only nineteen months but was a key step to the permanent settlement made in Loreto 14-years later, in 1697. (See Chapter 12 HISTORY). The dirt road to the area leaves the highway just north of **Km F-20**.

(Km F-6) SCENIC VIEW — Prior to **Km F-6** one can see the town of Loreto and its thousands of date palms lying along the shore at the eastern edge of a sizeable coastal plain. The large island south of town is Isla Carmen. The smaller island off its SW tip is Isla Danzante, with Puerto Escondido hidden along the peninsular shore to the west. (See map in Chapter 22.) It is apparent, toward the south, that the Sierra Giganta is sweeping to the coast and the offshore islands appear to be its seaward extension.

PSI #15

(Km F-0 and G-120) LORETO — Whenever you have visited a locality long enough ago to be considered an *old-timer*, you must be prepared for the disappointments brought about by change. Much of Baja is changing rapidly, but it is particularly apparent at Loreto (population 7,300). While the town is the oldest permanent Spanish settlement in all of the Californias, in the past it has never been among its most charming. Its flat terrain made it easy to design the town in conventional and uninspiring square blocks.

But for about ten years Loreto has been receiving a considerable face-lifting of new streets, buildings and other facilities. Finally after my 1995 visit, it became apparent that all this effort had finally transformed Loreto into a very pleasant community. At Loreto the changes have been positive. Even its western fringe (shown as "Newer Subdivision" on the LORETO Map) which was planned to be an extensive recreation home subdivision contains a few newer homes. Recent improvement have included construction of a small breakwater lined harbor, boat launching ramp, and parking area which incorporates the old town pier as its northerly leg. In addition the old earth surface waterfront street has been replaced by a handsome hard-surfaced boulevard complete with palm trees.

Loreto finds a place on the POINTS OF SPECIAL INTEREST Tour as stop No. 15. Drive into town and peruse the civic plaza. The mission church and the adjoining historical museum are the most important places you should visit. The present church is the successor to Baja's original mission founded in 1697. During our November 1997 visit the community was celebrating its 300th anniversary.

Loreto is where it all began. It was the base from which Junipero Serra started his expedition to settle Alta California, and Loreto was to serve as the military presidio, the residence of the Father Superior of the peninsula's missions and the seat of its civil government until 1829. In that year, the town was essentially destroyed by a hurricane and the capital moved to La Paz. Loreto was to drift into oblivion but has now been given a new birth by the tourist industry. There are good RV parks and hotels at various locations. See the LORETO Map.

LOOP ROAD TO LA PURISIMA AND CIUDAD INSURGENTES

SIDE TRIP

Described from north to south in this subsection of Chapter 21 is a 111.6 mile loop road from **Km F-60** on Highway 1 to Ciudad Insurgentes. The route is shown on the LA PURISIMA TO CIUDAD INSURGENTES LOOP ROAD Map. The same area is shown in less detail on the CHAPTER 22 Map.

The principal reasons for traveling this loop are: (1) to visit the historic and picturesque towns of La Purisima-San Isidro and San Jose de Comondu-San Miguel de Comondu; (2) to access sites for launching kayaks and other small boats near the north end of the Magdalena Lagoon System; (3) to access Bahia San-Juanico on the Pacific Ocean (the latter area is one of Baja's better surfing locations); and (4) to take advantage of an alternative to Highway 1 in making the round trip journey up and down the Baja peninsula.

The Baja peninsula offers several small communities that affect travelers

as places that look like a Mexican town ought to look. Among the best of these are San Ignacio, Mulege, and Todos Santos. But each of these has been modified to one degree or the other by the presence of highways and the onslaught of tourism. The best advice I can offer is to say "You ain't seen nothen yet" until you visit the four towns noted in the paragraph above.

The road from **Km F-60** to San Isidro-La Purisima is a secondary road through mountanious terrain but it is readily negotiable in pickups and vans. It is not suited for larger RVs. The 70.1 miles of road from La Purisima to Ciudad Insurgentes is a paved highway through level terrain.

(Km F-60) — The loop road leaves Highway 1 to the west 0.1 miles south of **Km F-60**. The sign at this junction indicates it is 65 kilometers to La Purisima. The mountainous peninsular divide of approximately 1,500 feet in elevation is reached in about 8 miles. West from here the roadbed lies in reasonably gentle terrain but can be badly damaged after heavy rains. Another 1,500 foot pass is encountered at the 31.5 mile point whereupon the road descends steeply into the valley ahead. This is the steepest grade on the entire loop.

Approximately 13 miles SW from Highway 1 on the secondary road to San Isidro one encounters the junction with the old canyon road along Arroyo de la

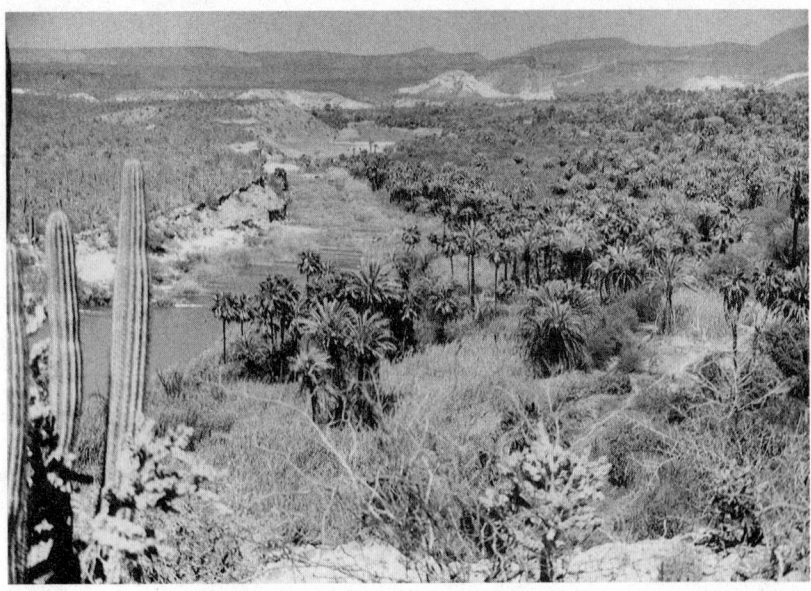

The beautiful valley of the Arroyo La Purisima between the communities of San Isidro and La Purisima. Photo JW.

Purisima to San Isidro. Taking this <u>24 mile</u> long route offers a scenic challenge with numerous arroyo crossings. Near its eastern end the road encounters the Rancho Ojo de Agua which is where the water rises that is eventually channeled into the palm covered valleys at San Isidro and La Purisima.

<u>32.7 Miles</u> — Encounter a T-intersection (straight ahead to San Isidro). The left branch is a single-lane, <u>19.5 mile</u>, secondary road to San Jose de Comondu. It is readily passable to pickups and vans but travel

Taking off to the SE from San Jose de Comondu is a <u>26 mile</u> long road to San Javier which passes through high desert terrain. (San Javier and its remarkable mission church are described in Chapter 22.)

A <u>23.8 mile</u> secondary road runs from San Miguel de Comondu to the highway standard road near La Poza Grande. I have not taken this road but believe it would make a good route for proceeding south and avoiding the return trip to San Isidro. Something has to be left for the adventurous traveler.

LA PURISIMA TO CIUDAD INSURGENTES LOOP ROAD

<u>35.1 Miles</u> — Town center of San Isidro (population 1,000). At the east end of town a road forks to the north and crosses the Arroyo de la Purisima. A short distance further, a second road branches to the right providing access to numerous places to camp in the desert. There are few camp sites in the valley itself that are not a part of someone's home or garden. The road between San Isidro and La Purisima was oil-surfaced in 1995.

<u>37.6 Miles</u> — Center of La Purisima. It is approximately a 6 mile drive through the two towns of San Isidro and La Purisima. The majority of the area is a valley some 1/2 mile in width completely covered with palms and other trees and numerous garden plots. There is surface water running in the stream and the overall atmosphere is most pleasant. During our 1995 trip we observed no tourist-oriented facilities in either San Isidro or La Purisima.

From this point to Ciudad Insurgentes the paved highway is marked with Kilometer post signs and these will be noted during the balance of this side trip.

speed is slow due to its rough, rocky surface. San Jose de Comondu and San Miguel de Comondu lie about 2 miles apart along a palm shaded valley surrounded by steep lava cliffs.

Jesuit padres established their fifth mission in 1708 at Comondu Viejo. It was moved to San Jose de Comondu in 1737. The present stone chapel is reported to have been the missionari's house. San Miguel de Comondu is the site of a 1714 visiting station and cattle ranch for the San Javier mission to the SE.

<u>41.5 Miles</u> (**Km-107.5**) — At this point the paved road bears southward at a junction with a good standard secondary road leading north to San Juanico. I have been informed that this road may eventually be improved to highway standards to San Ignacio but that it is not a high priority project. I have not driven this road.

<u>54.5 Miles</u> (**Km-87**) — A good standard secondary road leads in <u>5.2 miles</u> to a solar experimental area. This sizeable facility built by the Mexican government was abandoned during my last visit.

69.4 Miles (**Km-64**) — A secondary road branches to the NE and accesses San Jose de Comondu in 23.8 miles. I have not traveled this road.

72.4 Miles (**Km-61**) — A two-lane oiled road branches to the west and in 2.0 miles arrives at the community of La Poza Grande. From the extreme southwestern edge of town (at the end of the oiled road) a low standard, but level dirt road leads in 3.8 miles to a good landing and camping site (San Jorge) at the northern end of the Magdalena Lagoon System. Kayaks and small car-top boats may be launched over the shore for trips south through the lagoons. There are a few confusing side roads on the way to the lagoon, but perseverance, and the maintenance of a generally southwest direction will bring one to the water's edge. (San Jorge is shown mistakenly as being northwest of La Poza Grande on the Southern California Automobile Club map.)

92.4 Miles (**Km 27.5**) — A paved road branches to the west and arrives in 2.0 miles at Santo Domingo and its PEMEX station. From this community it is 11.9 miles over a low-standard but level dirt road to a fishing and clamming village near the mouth of Boca de Santo Domingo. A concrete lighthouse marks the spot. Kayaks and car-top boats may be launched here for trips along the Magdalena Lagoon System. There are numerous branching roads along the way so this trip may involve some wrong turns and doubling back.

The community of San Jose de Comondu nestled in its palm filled canyon. Photo JW.

96.0 Miles -- This is the approximate dividing line between desert vegetation to the north and agricultural fields to the south. The farming area extends the remaining 15 miles to Ciudad Insurgentes.

110.1 Miles (**Km 1.5**) — A paved highway to the right leads in 24.6 miles (34 Km) to Puerto Lopez Mateos. Because of this town's importance as a whale-watching center it is described as a side trip from Ciudad Insurgentes in Chapter 22. As of my last visit in 1997 there were no tourist oriented services in this community other than whale-watching panga service.

111.6 Miles (**Km-0**) — Ciudad Insurgentes and the Transpeninsular Highway. End SIDE TRIP.

CHAPTER 22 LORETO TO LA PAZ

Baja's Central Coast Tourist Area continues for 36 kms (22 miles) south of Loreto. It ends near Ligui on the shore of Ensenada Blanca. From this point south to La Paz, there are several interesting and challenging side trips, but the journey along Highway 1 itself is one of the peninsula's least inspiring.

SIDE TRIP

(Km G-118) SAN JAVIER — *To the right (west), a secondary road leaves Highway 1 and crosses the Sierra Giganta to the village of San Javier (32 kms). In the vicinity of this community the Jesuits founded their second mission in 1699, only two years after landing in Loreto. In 1744, they began construction of a stone church at San Javier, which today is a small village of some 300 people. The building's stone masonry and its lava rock ornamentation are truly remarkable considering its location in what was one of the world's most remote and primitive places. Still in use today, it represents Baja's finest and best preserved of the Jesuit missions.*

The access road is well constructed, but because of its steep grades and rough surface it is best suited for lightly loaded vans and pickups. It passes through scenic mountain terrain. (A photo of a portion of the road is presented in Chapter 3.)

9.4 Miles — *Cross stream channel. A good camping spot.*

12.5 Miles — *Rancho Las Parras. A pleasant oasis of grape vines, figs, olives, and citrus trees.*

13.7 Miles — *Top of the divide after having climbed the steep eastern escarpment of the Sierra de la Giganta. The Sea of Cortez has been in sight to the east for some time.*

19.4 Miles — *Junction with a road to San Jose de Comondu. Steep grades and erosion reduced this road to four-wheel-drive status ten miles to the west in 1986 but I have talked with people who made it through with no problem since that time.*

23.1 Miles — *San Javier.* End SIDE TRIP.

NOTE -- See photo of San Javier church on page 168.

(Km G-117) LORETO AIRPORT — An oiled road leaves Highway 1 to the left (east) and arrives at the Loreto airport in 0.7 miles. Here you will find a parking lot, modern waiting room, and an international airfield serving aircraft from the United States and the Mexican mainland. These facilities provide air access to Loreto, Nopolo, and Puerto Escondido. NOTE — Aero California Airlines has had scheduled flights here for several years, (one flight per day in 1997) but at times in the past there has been no commercial air service.

SIDE TRIP

(Km G-114) PRIMER AGUA — *Between **Km G-113** and **Km G-114** is a large electric transformer station. A secondary road leaves to the west, directly south of the sta-*

The Nopolo Golf Course looking over the 14th and 15th holes with the majestic Sierra Giganta in the background. Photo BW.

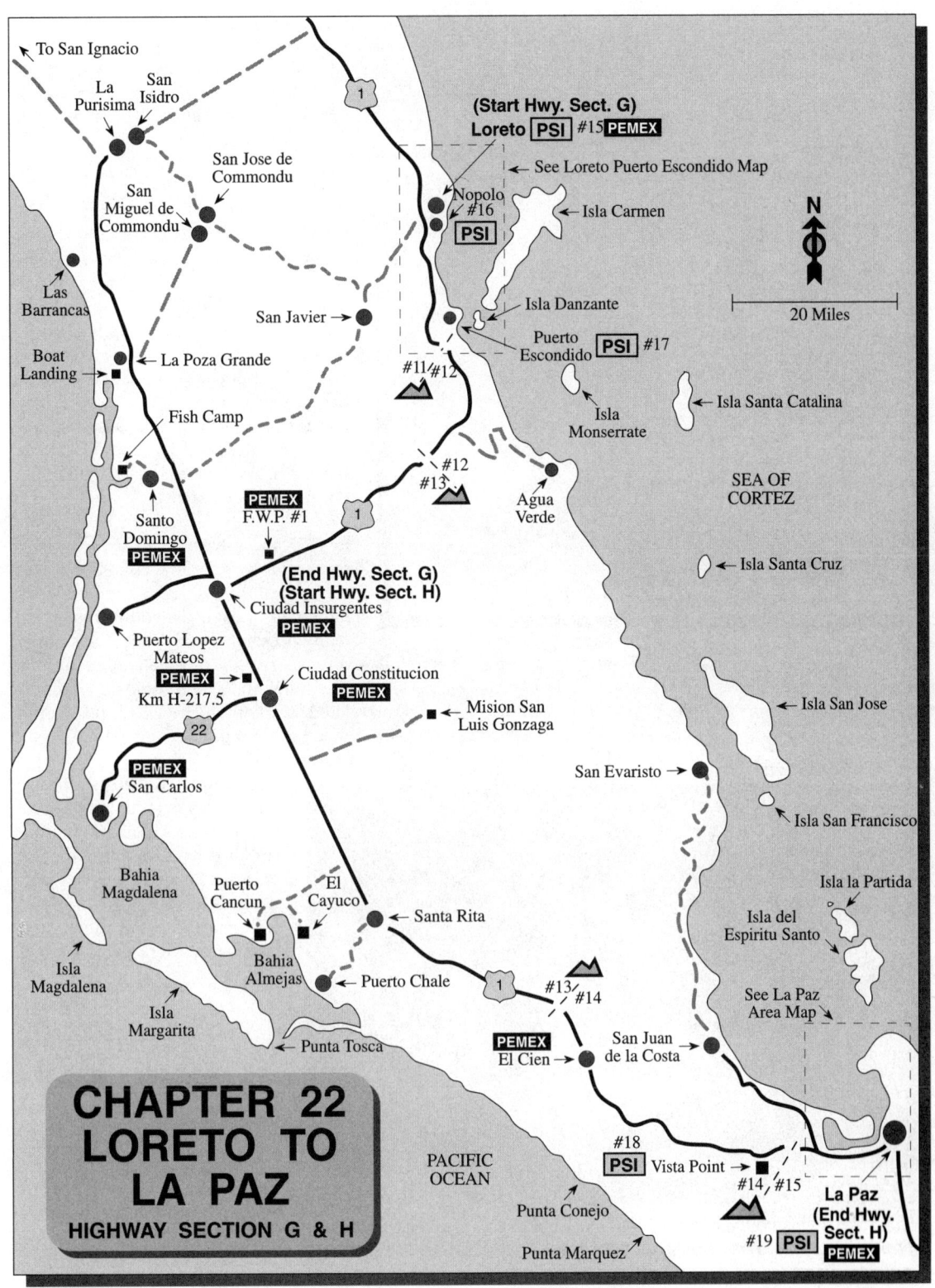

To San Ignacio

La Purisima
San Isidro
San Jose de Commondu
San Miguel de Commondu

(Start Hwy. Sect. G)
Loreto [PSI] #15 PEMEX

← See Loreto Puerto Escondido Map

Nopolo #16
[PSI]

← Isla Carmen

N

Las Barrancas

San Javier

Isla Danzante

Puerto Escondido [PSI] #17

20 Miles

Boat Landing

← La Poza Grande

#11 #12

← Isla Santa Catalina

Isla Monserrate

Fish Camp

#12
#13

Agua Verde

SEA OF CORTEZ

PEMEX
F.W.P. #1

1

Santo Domingo
PEMEX

← Isla Santa Cruz

(End Hwy. Sect. G)
(Start Hwy. Sect. H)
Ciudad Insurgentes
PEMEX

Puerto Lopez Mateos
PEMEX →
Km H-217.5

Ciudad Constitucion
PEMEX

Mision San Luis Gonzaga

← Isla San Jose

22

PEMEX
San Carlos

San Evaristo →

Isla San Francisco

Bahia Magdalena

Puerto Cancun

El Cayuco

Santa Rita

Isla la Partida

Isla del Espiritu Santo

Isla Magdalena

Bahia Almejas

← Puerto Chale

1

#13 #14

See La Paz Area Map

Isla Margarita

← Punta Tosca

PEMEX
El Cien

San Juan de la Costa

CHAPTER 22
LORETO TO
LA PAZ
HIGHWAY SECTION G & H

PACIFIC OCEAN

#18
[PSI] Vista Point

#14 #15

La Paz
(End Hwy. Sect. H)
[PSI] PEMEX

Punta Conejo

#19 [PSI]

Punta Marquez

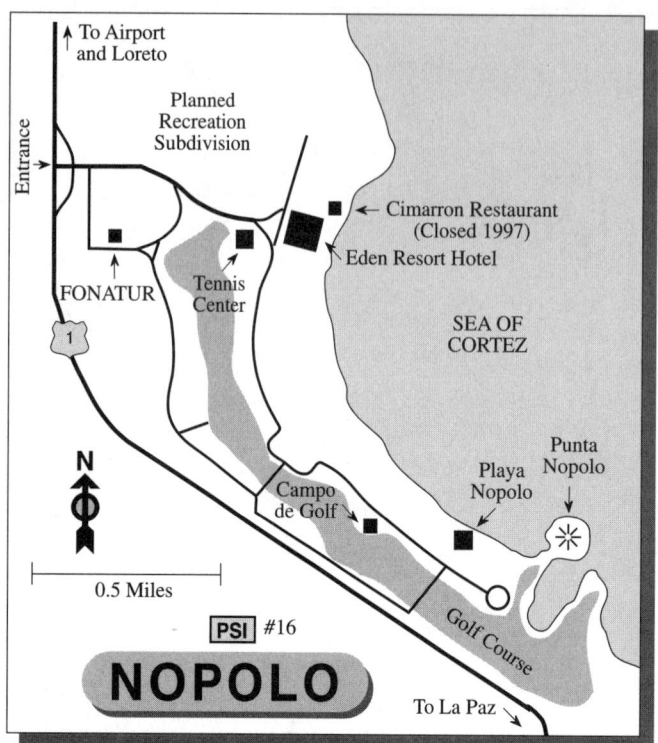

To Airport
and Loreto

Entrance

Planned
Recreation
Subdivision

FONATUR

Tennis
Center

Cimarron Restaurant
(Closed 1997)

Eden Resort Hotel

SEA OF
CORTEZ

Punta
Nopolo

Playa
Nopolo

Campo
de Golf

N

0.5 Miles

PSI #16

NOPOLO

Golf Course

To La Paz

large variety of plants being reproduced from cuttings. There is also a pool of water and an adjoining barbecue area. It is a pleasant spot to visit if you are staying in the Loreto-Puerto Escondido area. It is open to the public on a charge basis. **End** SIDE TRIP.

PSI #16

(Km G-111) NOPOLO — Prior to 1977, this section of coast was a deserted beach providing isolated camp spots for a few people seeking solitude. Now you will find a one-half square-mile area laced with well landscaped roads waiting to serve future tourists. This is the FONATUR development at Nopolo. It has attracted very little attention and lags far behind similar developments at Cabo San Lucas and San Jose del Cabo to the south. For this reason it is a pleasant, unhurried place to visit.

In 1997 there were about twenty very nice residences and the Eden Loreto Resort, one of the peninsula's most charming hotels. I have visited this facility on many occasions, and while it has rarely been full, everyone present seemed quite happy. Across from the hotel are a large number of tennis courts and related facilities which it was hoped would attract international competition. An 18-hole golf course and a fancy club house (Campo de Golf) are also completed. Only the future knows the eventual success of this substantial undertaking, but certainly it will be one of the few places in Mexico where the tourist can enjoy golf, tennis, watersports, a fine hotel, and excellent scenery all at one location.

Nopolo is stop No. 16 on the POINTS OF SPECIAL INTEREST Tour. The hotel is worth a visit, and I believe a circle drive through the area will give you a quick vision of what the future holds for this area. Even the largest of RVs can easily make this tour. On occasion, tourists have been permitted to camp along the excellent sandy beach (Playa Nopolo) at the south end of the

tion, and leads in 4.1 miles (7 Km) to Primer Agua. Here, near the base of the Sierra Giganta, lies a delightful oasis watered by a ditch-diverted stream. FONATUR has developed the area as a nursery to supply ornamental trees and shrubs for its developments. Trails lead through beds of a

There are tennis courts at many hotels in Baja but only here at Nopolo is there a facility devoted specifically to this sport complete with club house and enough courts for tournament play. Phot o BW.

Nopolo development where a cobblestone road built parallel to the beach provides a good parking area. In 1995 a "No Camping" sign had been erected, but each time I visit the camping situation is different.

(Km G-103) PLAYA NOTRI — Playa Notri is a part sand and part shingle beach providing camping spots about 150 yards east of the highway.

(Km G-100) MIRADOR -- About 200 yards south of here is Mirador Frida, a roadside parking area offering excellent views of the nearby islands.

(Km G-97) EL JUNCALITO — A low standard road leaves to the left (east) at this point. This road shortly divides with the left branch leading to the seaside village of El Juncalito. Proceeding straight ahead over a road located largely in an arroyo bottom brings one in <u>0.5 miles</u> to a grove of palms and a fine sandy beach. You may camp among the palms or along the 1/4 mile long beach. (I was advised in 1995 that FONATUR planned some type of development here but it had not occurred in 1997.)

PSI #17

(Km G-94) PUERTO ESCONDIDO — Take the paved side road at this point <u>0.6 miles</u> to Tripui and <u>0.9 miles</u> farther to the inner harbor area. This is **PSI** stop No.17.

The shore of the almost totally landlocked bay at Puerto Escondido (Hidden Port) was long one of Baja's most heavily used camping spots. The area was then taken over by FONATUR for a massive Pueblo Nautico (Nautical Village). Planned for construction were hotels, dockside condominiums, a marina, and other attractions. However, the past 10-years have seen very little progress, and as of spring 1997, the only usable facility was a concrete boat ramp. One could conclude that the balance of the development was an ill-conceived project from Mexico City. (God bless socialism.)

<u>TRIPUI RV PARK</u> — Many tourists regretted the passing of Puerto Escondido's beachside camping area. But at least, here at Puerto

295

Ensenada Blanca and its small off-lying islands. Note the steep face of the mountains directly along the shoreline. Photo JW.

Escondido, an excellent replacement facility was provided. An outstanding, attractively landscaped RV park was constructed nearby and complemented with a swimming pool, showers, restrooms, laundry facilities, restaurant, store, small motel and sports facilities. While not at the water's edge, it offers splendid views of the Sierra Giganta and is surrounded by attractive desert vegetation.

The sad part is that the park has now been totally converted to full-time tenants with a guard at the gate to keep the rest of us out. Short-term RVs are relegated to a relatively small fenced in parking area with a few palm trees next to the road. So depending on your point of view, you will either love Tripui, or hate it.

Should a less expensive beachfront spot be more to your taste, return north to El Juncalito, or drive south to Ensenada Blanca near Ligui.

TRIPUI BEACH -- A good gravel road leaves the oiled highway into Puerto Escondido to the right at the west end of the fence surrounding the Tripui RV Park. In about 1.5 miles this road leads to a secluded camping area near the shore. During our 1995 trip the access road had been gated shut supposedly by orders from FONATUR. Obviously the Tripui RV Park

benefits by this closure. All camping outside established RV parks has been eliminated in the Cape Area for several years and this may be what is occurring here. What the future holds is open to question.

CANYON HIKING — Directly across Highway 1 (and north of an electrical substation) from the blacktopped entrance to Puerto Escondido is a low standard dirt road paralleled by a power line. In 0.9 miles this road will bring you to a water pumping station at the base of the Sierra Giganta. There is a small turnaround area here, but you should leave large vehicles behind. Park at this spot and hike into the steep-walled canyon that dissects the cliffs a few yards north of the pumping station.

There is no developed trail but once you are between the steep cliffs it is impossible to lose your way. It takes 20 to 30 minutes of hiking along a cascading stream to arrive at a point where further progress is impeded by massive boulders. The rocks and canyon walls are of volcanic origin, and the stream bed is an enticing realm of small pools, palm trees, and other vegetation. Take along your bathing suit and enjoy an hour or so in this delightful rock-walled oasis.

(Km G-84) LIGUI (ENSENADA BLANCA) —A small school house and other buildings are located to the left (east) of Highway 1 north of **Km G-84**. This is Ligui. A low standard dirt road leaves the highway and in <u>1.9 miles</u> arrives at the fishing village of Ensenada Blanca located on a fine sandy beach. An even lower standard road continues for some <u>1.1 miles</u> around the edge of Ensenada Blanca to camping spots at the water's edge. There are also several spur roads to similar beach-side hideaways between the highway and the village. These roads are level but unimproved.

Ligui is the southernmost area of level land on the Central Coast Tourist Area that began north of Santa Rosalia. Confronted with this topographic situation, the Jesuit missionaries located the Ligui mission here in 1705, only six years after arriving on the peninsula. It became the jumping-off point for missionary trails leading into the mountains of the interior and south along the coast, but the mission itself lasted only sixteen years.

#11 △ #12

(KM G-83) GEOGRAPHIC CHANGE — The Sierra Giganta's presence at the Sea of Cortez coast forces the Transpeninsular Highway to ascend the steep eastern escarpment (Geographic Section No. 12). The road is winding, but grades are moderate, and the traveler is rewarded with fine mountain scenery, the last to be seen for many miles. This dramatic and rapid climb up the eastern face of the Peninsular Range Mountains, and the level and lengthy descent lying ahead on the western side provides the best examples you will see of the fault-block mountain structure presented in Chapter 9 GEOLOGY.

South of this point **(Km G-83)**, the eastern coastline of the peninsula is steep, rocky, and majestic. It is best viewed by boat or from small private aircraft. However, portions of the area can be enjoyed by taking the side trips to Agua Verde and San Juan de la Costa described in this chapter.

SIDE TRIP
(Km G-63) AGUA VERDE — *A secondary road heads left (south) from Highway 1 between* **Km G-63** *and* **Km G-64** *to the small fishing village of Agua Verde. Taking all or a portion of this 24-*

mile side trip will allow you to enjoy a portion of the dramatic eastern side of the Sierra Giganta, an area which is viewed by very few tourists.

<u>10.9 Miles</u> — You are greeted with an outstanding view of the Sea of Cortez, offshore islands, and the coastal mountains. There is a flat area for camping some 200 yards prior to reaching this vista for those who do not wish to proceed farther. The road to this point passes over rolling desert lands and can be traveled by most RVs.

The road ahead makes a steep, four-mile descent down the face of the eastern escarpment. I recommend that you park your vehicle at the vista point and walk ahead for <u>0.2 miles</u> to a place where the road descending the mountain is in view. From this spot, you can also look to the south and see a large pinnacle rock lying several hundred feet offshore. This is Roca Solitaria. It marks the entrance to the anchorage at Agua Verde. Having located this landmark and looked over the road, you can judge how far you will have to travel to Agua Verde and can make your decision as to whether to proceed. I alert you that it is not a suitable trip for large RVs or any vehicle that tends to be top heavy. However, if the road is in good repair it makes a fine trip for those in pickup trucks, vans, and other smaller vehicles.

<u>14.6 Miles</u> — You have reached the bottom of the grade and can start worrying about the return trip. A short distance ahead, a side road veers sharply to the left and in 200 yards arrives at a camping spot on a bluff overlooking the sea.

<u>16.8 Miles</u> — A side road leads for <u>0.5 miles</u> to a camping spot along the banks of an arroyo near a shingle beach.

Highway 1 passing through the mountains of Geographic Section No. 12 west of Ligui. Photo JW.

There are also several other side roads which I have not explored between this point and the Agua Verde village .

25.4 Miles — Arrive at Agua Verde. You will find this village to be one of the most primitive in Baja, but one most abundantly supplied with goats. The new road built in the early 1980s will no doubt bring much change to Agua Verde. End SIDE TRIP.

(Km G-64 to G-45) VOLCANIC MOUNTAINS —

This section of the highway is relatively flat but passes through massive mountains of volcanic rock. This is a good place to stop and examine these igneous volcanic rocks if you have not done so before. See the ROCK CLASSIFICATION Chart in Chapter 9 GEOLOGY. Note their dark reddish color, fine grain, and the numerous pockets formed by gases trapped in the molten mass as it cooled.

#12 ⛰ #13

(Km G-45) GEOGRAPHIC CHANGE — It is here

that you might ask, "What happened to the other side of the mountain?" You have arrived at the end of Geographic Section No.12, and the western side of the mountains simply blend with the Continental Borderlands Province ahead. This section of the province is the Llano de Magdalena (Magdalena Plain). It is Geographic Section No.13. You will be passing over its flat terrain for the next 164 km (102 miles).

Looking ahead on clear days, you will be able to see the mountains that rim the outer edges of Bahias Magdalena and Almejas on the Pacific coast. At other times, they, and the entire Magdalena Plain, may be shrouded in fog and low clouds. The straight stretch of highway between **Km G-39** and **Km G-32** points directly at this range.

(Km G-17) FEDERAL WATER PROJECT NO.1 —An

easily accessed PEMEX station lies at this point and serves the agricultural area you have just entered. Here, or at Villa Insurgentes, are good places to fuel on the return trip north in order to avoid the congestion often encountered at the stations at Loreto and Mulege.

ZONA DE NEBLINA — At several places along the

highways in this area you will see signs reading "Zona de Neblina" Neblina means fog and you are being alerted to the fact that layers of fog will sometimes restrict visibility. The fog also brings moisture to the desert plants. Many of the larger species become festooned with lichens and ball moss. This situation may be seen along any of the side roads leading from Highway 1 to Bahia Magdalena.

(Km G-0) CIUDAD INSURGENTES — At this point,

Highway 1 makes a 90-degree turn to the south. You have now reached the breakpoint between highway sections **G** (Km-0) and **H** (Km 234) and the edge of the town of Ciudad Insurgentes. A PEMEX station lies on the south side of the highway, a short distance east of this turning point but it was closed in 1997. There is another PEMEX station in town on the west side of the main street.

Cuidad Insurgentes, a town of some 18,500 people, lies near the center of one of the largest agricultural areas in Baja. As noted in Chapter 12 HISTORY, development here was not able to start until 1933. Prior to this time, most of the peninsula's lands were encumbered with various foreign-dominated leases which produced little more than speculation. It is easy to understand why the Mexican government has, until recently, wanted to maintain control over all the country's enterprises.

The highway between Ciudad Insurgentes and Ciudad Constitucion always has considerable traffic. The road itself is often built several feet above the surrounding terrain increasing the risk of turning over if one should stray beyond the oiled surface. Use extra care for these two reasons.

SIDE-TRIP

PUERTO LOPEZ MATEOS — *Cuidad Insurgentes is the starting point for a side trip to Puerto Lopez Mateos on the 70-mile-long coastal lagoon lying north of Bahia Magdalena. It is the most convienient site for viewing the California gray whale in Baja California. (Scammon's Lagoon is also popular but access is over a lenghty dirt road.) See Chapter 11 WILDLIFE for information about the gray whale.*

From the 90-degree turning point in Highway 1 noted above, travel north through Cuidad Insurgentes for 1.5 miles. At this point, a blacktop highway leads to the left (west). It is 24.6 miles to Puerto Lopez Mateos (See PUERTOS LOPEZOS MATEOS Map.) The principal point of interest is the dock where pangas are for hire when gray whales are present in the estuary. They will take you for a close encounter with these marine giants at their calving areas about 5 miles distant. Small boats and kayaks may also be launched over the beach for camping adventures along the lagoon. There is abundant bird life in addition to the whales. (Guided whale-watching trips to Puerto Lopez Mateos are available in La Paz.) End SIDE TRIP.

(Km H-211) CIUDAD CONSTITUCION — Km H-211

marks the center of the largest community in the

Puerto Lopez Mateos on the Magdalena Lagoons. The group of large buildings along the shore is the fish processing plant noted in the text. Whale-watching tours leave directly to the left of the cannery. The community is within the trees further inland. Photo JW.

Llano Magdalena agricultural area. It has a population of 35,000. Upon entering town from the north, look for a small traffic circle on the right with a statue at its center. This is the junction with Highway 22 which leads to Bahia Magdalena and the port city of San Carlos. See SIDE TRIP below.

Also north of town near **Km H-213** is Manfred's RV Park and Austrian Restaurant. It was started by Manfred Roschker and his wife Ida about 1994 and represents a marvel of two people's efforts. The well landscaped park provides a long needed RV rest-stop between the Sea of Cortez coast and La Paz. (The Campestre La Pila noted below leaves a bit to be desired.) The restaurant bears Manfred's name, but lets face it, Ida does the cooking. Come-on Manfred, the lady should have equal billing.

South of the Highway 22 junction the main street of town turns into a palm-lined boulevard. There are two PEMEX stations on the west side of this boulevard plus a station north of town at **Km H-213.5**. Two blocks south of the Highway 22 junction you will cross Olachea street. On the NE corner lies a three-story concrete building housing the Hotel Maribel. Two blocks east on Olachea is the smaller Hotel Casino. These are adequate facilities for an overnight stay but are not of the luxurious variety. There are also other motels along the main street.

At **Km H-209** south of town a road leads to the right (west) and in 0.6 miles arrives at the Campestre La

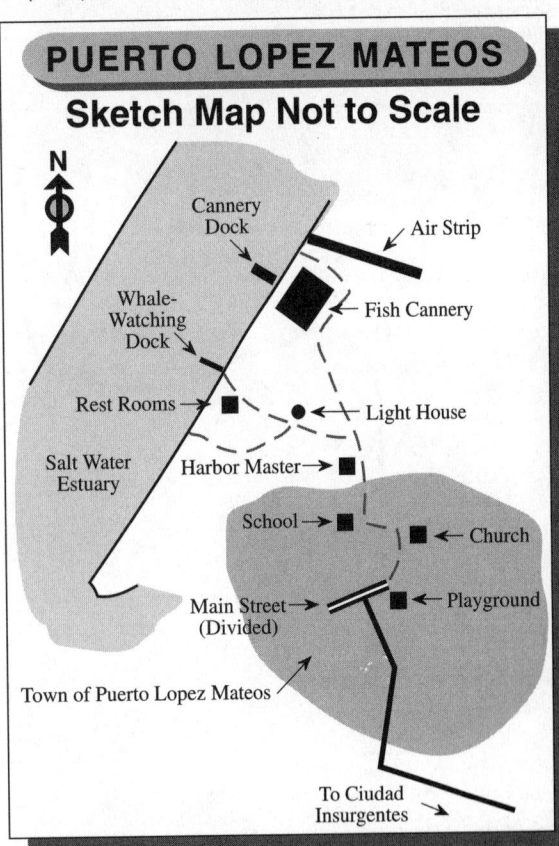

PUERTO LOPEZ MATEOS
Sketch Map Not to Scale

N

Cannery Dock

Air Strip

Whale-Watching Dock

Fish Cannery

Rest Rooms

Light House

Salt Water Estuary

Harbor Master →

School →

Church

Main Street → (Divided)

Playground

Town of Puerto Lopez Mateos

To Ciudad Insurgentes

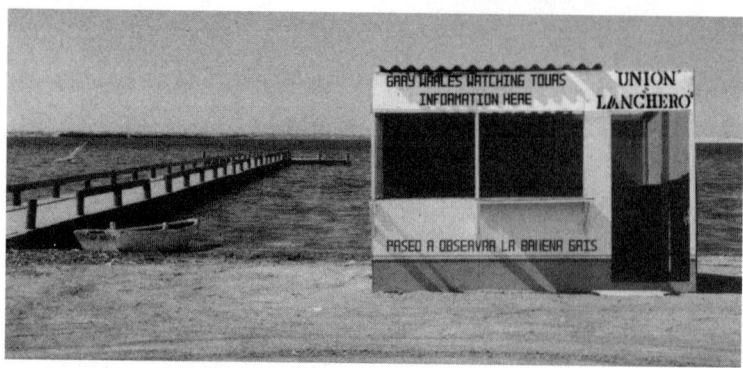

Shown here is the whale-watching boat dock and ticket building on the estuary at Puerto Lopez Mateos. Photo BW.

Pila Trailer Court. (The junction point is marked across Highway 1 by a large electrical substation.) The trailer court has full hookups. It is located adjoining a working farm and a large grassy area with swimming pools, picnic tables, and showers.

SIDE TRIP

SAN CARLOS (BAHIA MAGDALENA) *It is 57 km (35 miles) to San Carlos, a town of some 5,000 people, and the shores of Bahia Magdalena over straight and level Highway 22. (There is a statue within a small traffic circle at the*

junction point.) I recommend visiting this area if your principal aim is to take advantage of the best waters for using small trailer boats on Baja's Pacific coast. If, instead, you are seeking the best camping locations or hotels, you will be better served in other places. In 1997 Highway 22 passes through agricultural fields for the first 17 kilometers from Highway 1.

At Km 52 (about 3 miles prior to reaching San Carlos) is a massive square building from which projects a stubby smoke stack. This is the most recent of Baja's three power generating plants (Central Termoelectrica). Its fuel is delivered by ship to the port of San Carlos, and then through a short pipeline to the plant. The building and its many lights provide a prominent landmark.

As you approach San Carlos you will begin to see marshy areas and the town itself is located on an island. These features are indicative of the fact that the western edge of the Continental Borderlands is sinking into the sea.

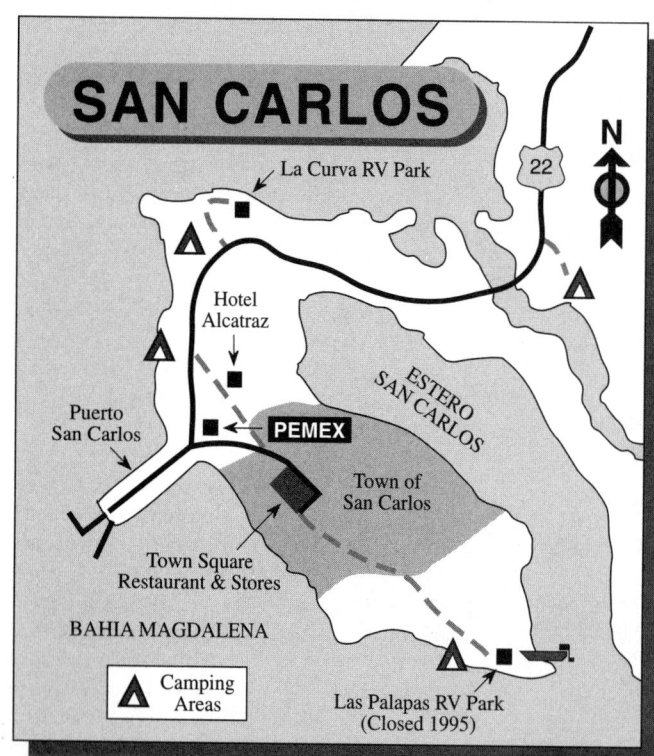

SAN CARLOS

La Curva RV Park

22
US

N

Hotel Alcatraz

Puerto San Carlos

PEMEX

ESTERO SAN CARLOS

Town of San Carlos

Town Square Restaurant & Stores

BAHIA MAGDALENA

△ Camping Areas

Las Palapas RV Park (Closed 1995)

After arriving at the edge of San Carlos, you will see a sizeable wharf that has been built many hundreds of yards into the shallow waters of Bahia Magdalena to a point where deep-draft ships can be accommodated. This dock and its warehouses are the shipping points for cotton, grain, and other agricultural products grown in the interior. San Carlos and Ensenada to the north are the only deep-water commercial ports on the peninsula's Pacific coast. The PEMEX station is near the landward end of the port facility.

Bearing left at the PEMEX station it is 1.7 miles through town to what is indicated as the Las Palapas RV Park on the SAN CARLOS Map. Proceed into town, pass by the eastern side of the town square, and take the road paralleling the shore. The Las Palapas RV Park was originally constructed as a tourist facility many years ago but its former rental cabins have more recently served as homes for Mexican fishermen, a house of ill repute and in 1995 we found them deserted (We were prevented from visiting San Carlos in 1997 because of a accident which blocked the high-

way). Whatever the future holds, the nearby beach is where most RV owners and campers make there headquarters in the San Carlos area. Boats may be launched at mid to high tide at a nearby ramp. Be careful in picking your spot as some high tides will put your vehicle awash. End SIDE TRIP.

BOB & JEAN BACKROAD

(Km H-195) SAN LUIS GONZAGA — Just south of **Km H-195** a secondary road leaves Highway 1 to the east. It is signed for a large dam named La Presa Iguajil which is about 21 miles distant. From the dam a road runs south to a grove of palms sheltering the stone Mision de San Luis Gonzaga and a ranch whose owners serve as caretakers for the mission. This is trip #8 of the "Bob and Jean Backroad" Recommendations (Chapter 3).

San Luis Gonzaga was founded in 1737 and was the fifteenth of Baja's Jesuit missions. Its oasis like setting is a welcome relief from some of the most barren landscape in the peninsula. Numerous other roads proceed easterly into the mountains from here, one of them reaching the Sea of Cortez shore at San Evaristo.

SIDE TRIP

(Km H-173) PUERTO CANCUN — *You may have always longed to take your wife to exciting Cancun in Mexico. Here is your chance. Perhaps she will not notice that this is not the exotic resort area on the Caribbean coast. In any case, she will be consoled knowing that accommodations are a bit less expensive camping here on the shore of Bahia Almejas.*

The secondary road to Puerto Cancun north of **Km H-173** *is straight, wide, level, and washboarded. At the 13.0 mile point a one-lane secondary road leads in 2.5 miles to the El Cayuco fishing village. It is a bit on the dirty side and camping space is limited unless you can negotiate low standard sandy roads along the shore.*

Puerto Cancun is 19.9 miles from Highway 1. There are good camping spots on the bluffs above the beach west of the village. Almejas means clams, and there is no better place to find them than in the extremely shallow waters of Bahia Almejas here at Puerto Cancun. Low tide exposes sandy clamming grounds over 1/2 miles in width. End SIDE TRIP.

(Km H-169) MAGDALENA MOUNTAINS — Here, near a large microwave tower, is an excellent view to the west of the mountains which rim the outer edges

of Bahias Magdalena and Almejas. (On some days they are hidden in fog and low clouds.) A gap in this range is the 2-mile-wide entrance to the bay from the Pacific Ocean. While passing through this rocky portal by boat, one is reminded very much of the Golden Gate at San Francisco. San Francisco Bay and Bahia Magdalena are the two finest natural harbors in the Californias.

SIDE TRIP

(Km H-157) PUERTO CHALE — *Highway 1 makes a 45-degree turn to the left at the very small town of Santa Rita. At this turn is a junction with the secondary road to Puerto Chale. Puerto Chale lies on an estuary at the edge of Bahia Almejas. Here are located a small fishing village and an experimental shrimp farm. It is 14.6 miles to the water's edge over a straight, level road.* End SIDE TRIP.

#13 🔺 #14

(Km H-120) GEOGRAPHIC CHANGE — South of Santa Rita on Highway 1, the totally flat terrain through which you have been passing comes to an end and the land begins to roll. The highway slowly begins to gain elevation, and the Llano de Magdalena merges indistinctly with the gentle western slopes of the Peninsular Range Mountains. Thus, **Km H-120** is only an approximate dividing line between geographical sections. In a few miles, however, it will be apparent that you have left the plains of Geographic Section No. 13 and are in the plateaus of Section No. 14. Here you will be traveling for the next 89 km (55 miles).

The terrain in this section is composed of sandstone, shale, and other sedimentary rocks. Notice the horizontal banding of the rock layers in the highway cuts and surrounding hills.

(Km H-100) EL CIEN — El Cien is a small village whose chief claim to fame for the tourist is a PEMEX station, the only one between Ciudad Constitucion and La Paz. Appropriately, El Cien (cien means 100 in Spanish) lies exactly at the 100-kilometer point.

(Km H-82) PACIFIC VIEW — Near **Km H-82** there is a tall microwave tower. From this point, one can see the Pacific Ocean far to the west. (There will be other such views between here and the Km H-35 Vista Point ahead.) A short distance south, near **Km H-80**, a side road leads to the coast at El Conejo. The coast is relatively uninviting in this area. Beginning south of the Magdalena Mountains and stretching for more than 100 miles to Todos Santos, the shore is basically one long sandy beach backed by monotonous low

A monument bearing a cross lies alongside the highway at **PSI** Stop No. 18. A visit here awards the traveler with fine views of the Sea of Cortez and the Llano de La Paz. Photo JW.

plains. The Pacific swells break heavily, making swimming and boating hazardous activities.

PSI #18

(Km H-35) VISTA POINT — On the right, near **Km H-35,** is a small monument bearing a cross. Even the largest RVs can pull over here at POINTS OF SPECIAL INTEREST Tour stop No. 18 and enjoy a rewarding view.

1. The vista point lies near the edge of the plateau area through which you have just passed. Lying below, to the south, stretches the Llano de La Paz, the southernmost portion of the Continental Borderlands Province. At this narrow point the peninsula is almost divided in half, providing clear evidence to geologists that it has been stretched linearly as noted in Chapter 9 GEOLOGY.

2. South of the plain lie the massive granite Sierra de la Laguna in the Cape Region.

3. To the NE is Bahia de La Paz, a broad indentation in the Sea of Cortez. At the water's edge, near the base of the Sierra de la Laguna, the city of La Paz is in view.

4. Several miles into the Sea of Cortez rest Isla Espiritu del Santo and Isla la Partida. The two islands appear as one. They provide many snug coves frequented by yachtsmen. Here, and on the other Sea of Cortez islands to the north, the ocean-cruisers are free from the activities of the peninsula's road builders.

#14 ⛰ #15

(Km H-31) GEOGRAPHIC CHANGE — At approximately this point, the highway leaves the plateau lands (Geographic Section No. 14) and enters the level Llano de La Paz (Geographic Section No. 15).

(Km H-27) SIERRA GIGANTA — From a slight rise in the highway near **Km H-27**, one may look to the north and see the southern terminus of the escarpment of the Sierra Giganta. This is the end of the steep-faced coastal mountain range that started at Ligui. Visible is a light pinkish band of volcanic ash. This band is not level, as viewed from here. Rather, it slopes downward below the earth's surface at its inland end, providing yet another indication of the downward westerly tilt of the fault-block mountain structure.

(Km H-21) At this point lies a government agricultural inspection station where you will be required to stop. They are looking for citrus fruits, drugs, etc.

SIDE TRIP

(Km H-17) SAN JUAN DE LA COSTA — *A trip to, and beyond, the phosphorus mining community of San Juan de la Costa is your second opportunity to experience the steep coastal section of the Sierra Giganta at close range (the first was at Agua Verde to the north). The road is oiled the first 26 miles into San Juan de la Costa and is constructed to highway standards, but is not yet paved, for an additional 32.7 miles. The route offers some of the best coastal scenery in view from any of Baja's highways.*

1 Mile — In approximately one mile from Highway 1 an oiled road leaves to the right and accesses the Centro de Investigaciones Biologicas de Baja California Sur, a modern scientific facility of laboratories and offices. Their principal interests lie in the high country area of the Sierra de la Laguna south of La Paz, and the Vizcaino Desert region just south of the state line to the north. Of particular interest is the fact that the area on either side of the access road has been fenced for many years and one may see the desert vegetation free from the effects of recent grazing.

<u>12.5 Miles</u> (Km-19) — The oiled road crosses the level Llano de La Paz and arrives at the base of the towering Sierra Giganta escarpment.

<u>14.3 Miles</u> (Km 23) — This point is the end of the flat plain and the site of an abandoned highway work center. Nearby are camp spots behind a coastal dune fronted by a fine sandy beach. There are additional places to reach the coast between here and San Juan de la Costa at points where the road dips to cross arroyos.

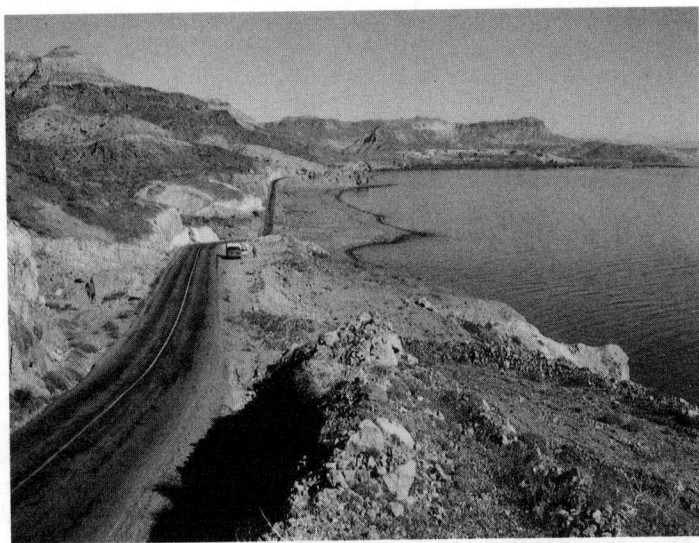

A picturesque section of the highway between Highway 1 and San Juan de la Costa. Photo JW.

<u>25.0 Miles</u> (Km 39) — The main, but unpaved road, veers to the right toward the village of San Evaristo (population 500). The paved road continues straight ahead for one mile into San Juan de la Costa. This community is a mining company town with scores of homes built in neat rows on a level area several hundred feet above the sea. There is a CONASUPO grocery store but no other tourist facilities.

I do not recommend the trip toward San Evaristo for larger RVs. (Mileages continue to be from Highway 1 and do not include the side trip into San Juan de la Costa.)

<u>27.7 Miles</u> — At this point you arrive at the dock and conveyor system used to load ocean-going ore carriers. Inland are the processing facilities where raw earth containing about 10 percent phosphorus is enriched to 30 percent by leaching with sea water. After a fresh water rinse, it is dried for shipping and used as fertilizer.

The road ahead for the next three miles is extra-wide and well maintained but is heavily used by ore carrying equipment except on weekends. Between here and mileage point <u>57.7</u>, the road is constructed to highway standards but is not yet oiled. There are several places to camp on the coast in the shadow of the magnificent Sierra Giganta mountains.

<u>57.7 Miles</u> — End highway standard road. Pickups and vans can readily make it ahead an additional <u>1.2 miles</u> to a camping spot near a shingle beach. Beyond that point the road is best suited for 4x4 vehicles. In the past I have traversed this road in my standard drive pickup complete with camper but when last inspected in spring 1989, the surface had been badly eroded. Look for additional highway standard construction in this area in the future.

<u>73.8 Miles</u> — Arrive on the beach near the small fishing village of San Evaristo, another of the ocean-cruiser's hideaways captured by the road builders. End SIDE TRIP.

(Km H-17) EL COMITAN — Immediately east of the highway to San Juan de la Costa, a dirt road leads to the left (north). In <u>0.8 miles</u> it arrives at a beach-side camping spot at the western end of Ensenada de Aripes.

(Km H-17) ENSENADA DE ARIPES — From the San Juan de La Costa junction to La Paz, Highway 1 passes along the southern edge of a large lagoon (Ensenada de Aripes). It is separated from the Sea of Cortez by a spit of land whose eastern end is a sand bar that is awash only at low tide.

The city of La Paz and all of its tourist facilities are located along this almost fully enclosed body of water. The location protects the area from the open sea, but some tourists find that the lagoon's beaches, the quality of the water, and its overall aesthetic appeal are not as high quality as available in other areas. Please keep this situation in mind when evaluating the La Paz tourist accommodations presented in the

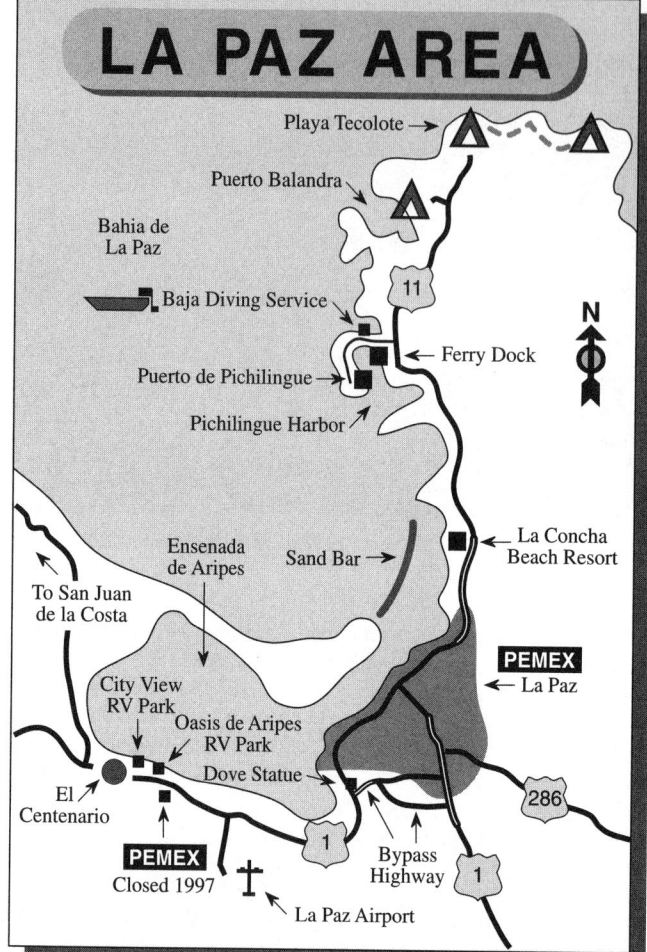

LA PAZ AREA

Playa Tecolote →

Puerto Balandra

Bahia de
La Paz

Baja Diving Service

11

← Ferry Dock

Puerto de Pichilingue →

Pichilingue Harbor

N

Ensenada
de Aripes   Sand Bar →

← La Concha
Beach Resort

To San Juan
de la Costa

City View
RV Park
Oasis de Aripes
RV Park
Dove Statue →

El
Centenario

PEMEX
← La Paz

PEMEX
Closed 1997

286

Bypass
Highway   1

1

La Paz Airport

at the stations in La Paz. Unfortunately it was closed in 1997.

(Km H-9) LA PAZ AIRPORT — A black-topped highway leads to the right for 2.0 miles to the La Paz Airport. This was the first of southern Baja's international airfields. It has modern terminal facilities. (There is almost continual urban development from this junction into the center of La Paz.)

(Km H-7) DOVE OF PEACE STATUE — Just past **Km H-7** is a large, white, concrete statue of a bird. My notes say it's a sea gull, but for a city named La Paz (The Peace) it must be a dove. It marks the junction of the old highway along the La Paz waterfront (to the left), and the newer bypass highway which skirts much of La Paz (to the right). Using this bypass highway is a journey of 2.5 miles from the dove statue to where it joins the old highway south of La Paz at a point south of the Highway 1 junction with Highway 286. I don't know which of these routes is the official Highway 1, but I give the distinction to the old route on the map of La Paz. The bypass highway is by far the best route to take to head for the Cape Area if you have no business in La Paz.

(Km H-6) TOURISM DEPARTMENT — Between **Km H-6** and **Km H-5** is the office of the Coordinador Estatal de Turismo Baja California Sur. Stop here for maps and travel information. There is another office downtown but parking is limited.

(Km H-4) LA PAZ RV PARKS — There are four RV parks in La Paz. The Casa Blanca and El Cardon lie south of the highway near **Km H-4**. The La Paz park and the Aguamarina are located near, but not on the water front close to the highrise Hotel Gran Baja (closed 1997). See the LA PAZ Map.

PSI #19

(Km H-0) LA PAZ — At last, the Transpeninsular Highway arrives at the city of peace, La Paz. It was here that Hernan Cortez stepped ashore on the third of May, 1535, only 43 years after Columbus discovered the Americas. See Chapter 12 HISTORY.

balance of this chapter. In spite of these somewhat negative comments, La Paz is my favorite city in all of Mexico, and I am not alone in this assessment.

(Km H-15) EL CENTENARIO — Adjoining Highway 1 near the shallow western end of Ensenada de Aripes is the small community of El Centenario. At the eastern edge of town are two RV parks. The first bears the name City View Beach RV Park. It is one of the original government constructed parks with desert plant landscaping. As its name implies, it offers a good view of La Paz over the water. On a sandy beach a bit closer to La Paz lies the pleasant Oasis de Aripes RV park and restaurant. These are the only two RV parks directly on the waters edge in the La Paz area. Between **Km H-12** and **Km H-11** east of El Centenario is a PEMEX station with plenty of room for large RVs. It is a good place to avoid the often hectic conditions

La Paz is a clean, modern city of 160,000 people and the capital of the state of Baja California Sur. A walking tour of its waterfront and downtown area is stop No. 19 on the POINTS OF SPECIAL INTEREST Tour. While the city is growing in population, the downtown area is nicely settled down and there is little of the hectic growth apparent at Cabo San Lucas.

There are several fine resort hotels where sun worshippers can hibernate indefinitely. I strongly recommend them as destination

The giant Dove of Peace statue marking a major road junction as one enters La Paz from the west (See Text). Photo JW.

points. However, I submit that if you choose a hotel in La Paz for your vacation, you should do so at least in part to enjoy the city itself; its weather, shopping, culture, and friendly people. If you are more interested in simply relaxing on the beach or around the swimming pool of a fine resort hotel, you probably will be more content at one of the fine hotels at the tip of the peninsula.

Near the heart of the downtown area, and across the street from the beach, is the Hotel los Arcos and its affiliated Cabanas de los Arcos. The restaurant is excellent, and while the Los Arcos is slightly less luxurious than some of the other hotels, it is located where you can readily enjoy the downtown area. The Hotel Perla is also located downtown on the waterfront but is a less auspicious establishment. In addi-

LA PAZ

Hotel La Posada Engelbert
La Paz Yacht Club (Closed 1997)
Hotel Gran Baja (Closed 1997)
Aguamarina Trailer Court
CANAL DE LA PAZ
La Concha Beach Resort
La Paz Trailer Court
V.W. Garage
Marina de La Paz
Marina Palmira
Hotel Marina
Moorings Boat Charters
#19 PSI
Immigration
Commercial Wharf
Tourism Office
PEMEX
Aguina Bus Station
El Cardon RV Park
Casa Blanca RV Park
Tourism Department
Hotel Los Arcos
Cabanas de Los Arcos
Hotel Perla
Araiza Inn Palmira & Convention Ctr
Revolucion de 1910
11
Colima
5 de Febrero
Civic Plaza
PEMEX   G. Prieto
Club el Moro
Church
Ferry Ticket Office (SEMATUR)
Anthropology Museum
Allende
Bravo
5 de Mayo
Ejido
To Dove of Peace Statue
By-Pass Blvd.
CCC Supermarket
Isable La Catolica
0.2 Miles
Forjadores Blvd.
State Government Offices
N
To Cabo San Lucas & Hy 286

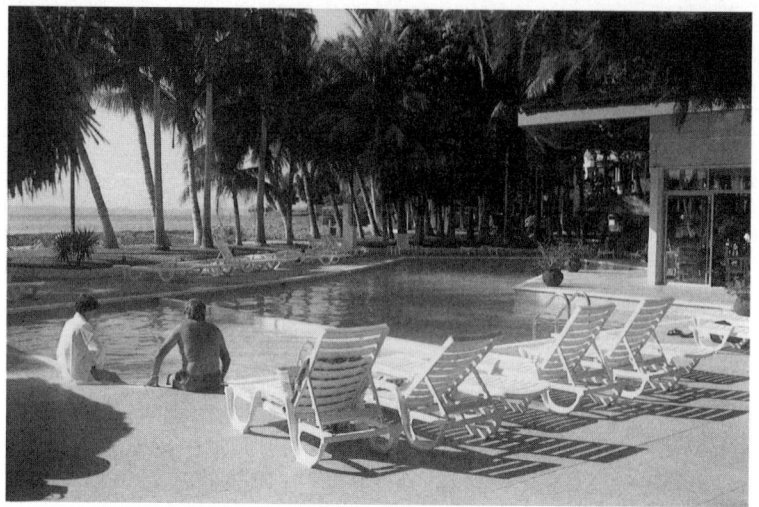

The pool area of the La Concha Beach Resort at La Paz. Photo JW.

miles) north from downtown La Paz to Pichilingue, which derived its name from the Dutch pirates who roamed the area in the 17th century.

As the long and narrow channel leading from the Sea of Cortez to La Paz is not suited for deep draft vessels, port facilities have been developed at the well-protected harbor at Pichilingue. Various industries requiring access to the sea are located in an industrial park surrounding the harbor. Also located here are (1) a new passanger terminal developed to lure ocean-cruise ships into La Paz and (2) the terminal and parking lot for the ferries from La Paz to Mazatlan and Topolobampo. The ferry ticket office SEMATUR is located in La Paz (See La Paz Map).

tion, there are a number of less expensive but fully acceptable hotels in or near the downtown area. The Hotel Gardenias is perhaps the best of these.

The tall building west of the downtown area on the waterfront is the Hotel Gran Baja. It has been closed in recent years but its height makes it an unmistakable landmark. Nearby on the beach is the charming Hotel La Posada de Engelbert. North of town on the highway to Pichilingue are the Club el Morro, the Hotel Marina, the La Concha Beach Resort and the Araiza Inn Palmira. The latter is nicely landscaped but is separated from the beach by the highway.

SIDE TRIP
PICHILINGUE — Highway 11 travels <u>23 km (14</u>

PUERTO BALLANDRA AND TECOLOTE — To the north of Pichilingue there is presently almost no development. Here, facing the open Sea of Cortez are two beach areas heavily frequented by the people of La Paz on weekends. They also make good camping spots for tourists. These places are reached by taking a continuation of Highway 11 which was completed in 1991.

The new highway noted above was obviously constructed in anticipation of the development of a major new resort area (drawing of which adorn the

A view of the Marina Palmira. The large building is the Hotel marina. The white object along the shore in the distance is the La Paz power plant at the north end of the Canal de la Paz. Photo BW.

office walls of the Coordinator of Tourism) but I have been advised by the Coordinator that these plans have now been dropped in favor of lower key facilities for the local citizens. Is it possible one of Baja's great beaches will be spared from the hotel builders?

<u>4.4 Miles</u> — 4.4 miles north of Pichilingue an oiled side road to the left leads in <u>0.3 miles</u> to the inner edge of the cove at Puerto Ballandra. (Continue ahead to Tecolote.) The shallow waters of the cove allow safe swimming, but its waters recede several hundred feet from the road at low tide.

<u>5.7 Miles</u> — At this point you arrive at the beach at Tecolote. It is far superior to the one at Puerto Ballandra although it is exposed to the wind and open sea. It is a fine location in calm weather. A low-standard road parallels the coast, for two miles to the east accessing numerous excellent camp sites. END SIDE TRIP.

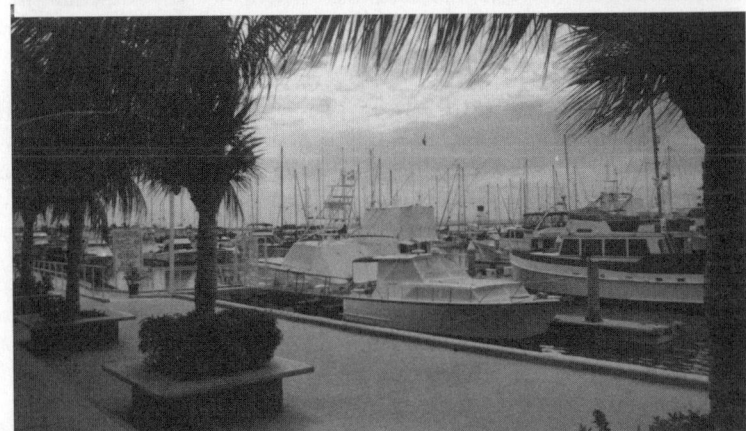

LA PAZ

<u>Top</u> - The pool and outdoor restaurant area at the Hotel Posada de Engelbert. A few feet away is a fine beach on the Canal de la Paz. <u>Middle</u> - A close-up view of the Marina Palmira. <u>Bottom</u> - The main street of La Paz, the Malacone, in front of the Hotel Los Arcos. The walkway on the right follows a long beach along the Canal de la Paz. Anything worth happening in La Paz takes place along the Malocone. Photos BW.

CHAPTER 23
LA PAZ
TO SAN JOSE DEL CABO
VIA HIGHWAY 1

After traveling 1,483 km (922 miles) from the international border, your GRAND TOUR begins the final leg of the journey to the Cape Area at the peninsula's tip. The scenery lying ahead is a considerable improvement over the rather unimpressive plains and low plateaus north of La Paz, as both of the highways to the south pass through or around the Sierra de la Laguna. The vegetation is also some of the most impressive to be encountered on the peninsula.

CAMPING SOUTH OF LA PAZ — Many of the locations along Highway 1 south of La Paz that were once popular beach-front camping areas have been usurped for residential and commercial purposes.

This is particularly true in the "Corridor" between San Jose del Cabo and Cabo San Lucas (Chapter 24) where the last free beach camping area was closed to the public in 1991. It is also true in the Buena Vista-Los Barriles area (Chapter 23). If beach camping is your objective, you need to consider taking one of the side trips described in the present chapter. Excellent beach camping, and beach-side RV parks, are also available along Highway 19 on the Pacific coast (Chapter 25).

PASSING THROUGH LA PAZ — On entering La Paz from the west, keep to the right at the Dove of Peace Statue (See Chapter 22). Taking this route will bypass the downtown section of La Paz.

BAHIA DE LOS MUERTOS AREA

Cerralvo Channel

Isla Cerralvo

← El Sargento

← La Ventana

Hotel Las Arenas (Closed 1995)

Agua Amarga

← To La Paz 286

San Juan de los Planes

N

Bahia de los Muertos

PEMEX San Antonio

1

5 Miles

SIDE TRIP

HIGHWAY 286 — *The residential areas of La Paz are rapidly spreading to the south, so the junction of Highways 1 and 286 falls within the city. Be alert for the highway sign to S.J. de los Planes and position your vehicle to enable you to turn east from the busy, multilaned road. The junction is <u>1.3 miles</u> from the intersection of 5 de Febrero and Forjadores Blvd. It is 58 km (<u>36.5 miles</u>) to Bahia de los Muertos.*

Highway 286 is constructed through highly erosible granite soils. Thus, each side of the road has been provided with concrete-lined ditches to allow rain water to run off without damage to the travel surface.

Km-24 — *Highway 286 climbs through a region of low hills and reaches its maximum elevation near this point. As you descend to the east an excellent view unfolds and you will be able to see the Sea of Cortez and the southern end of mountainous Isla Cerralvo lying 7 miles off the shoreline. For several miles on either side of the summit one may see elephant trees and other diminutive trees that make up the Arid Tropical Forest noted in Chapter 9 VEGETATION.*

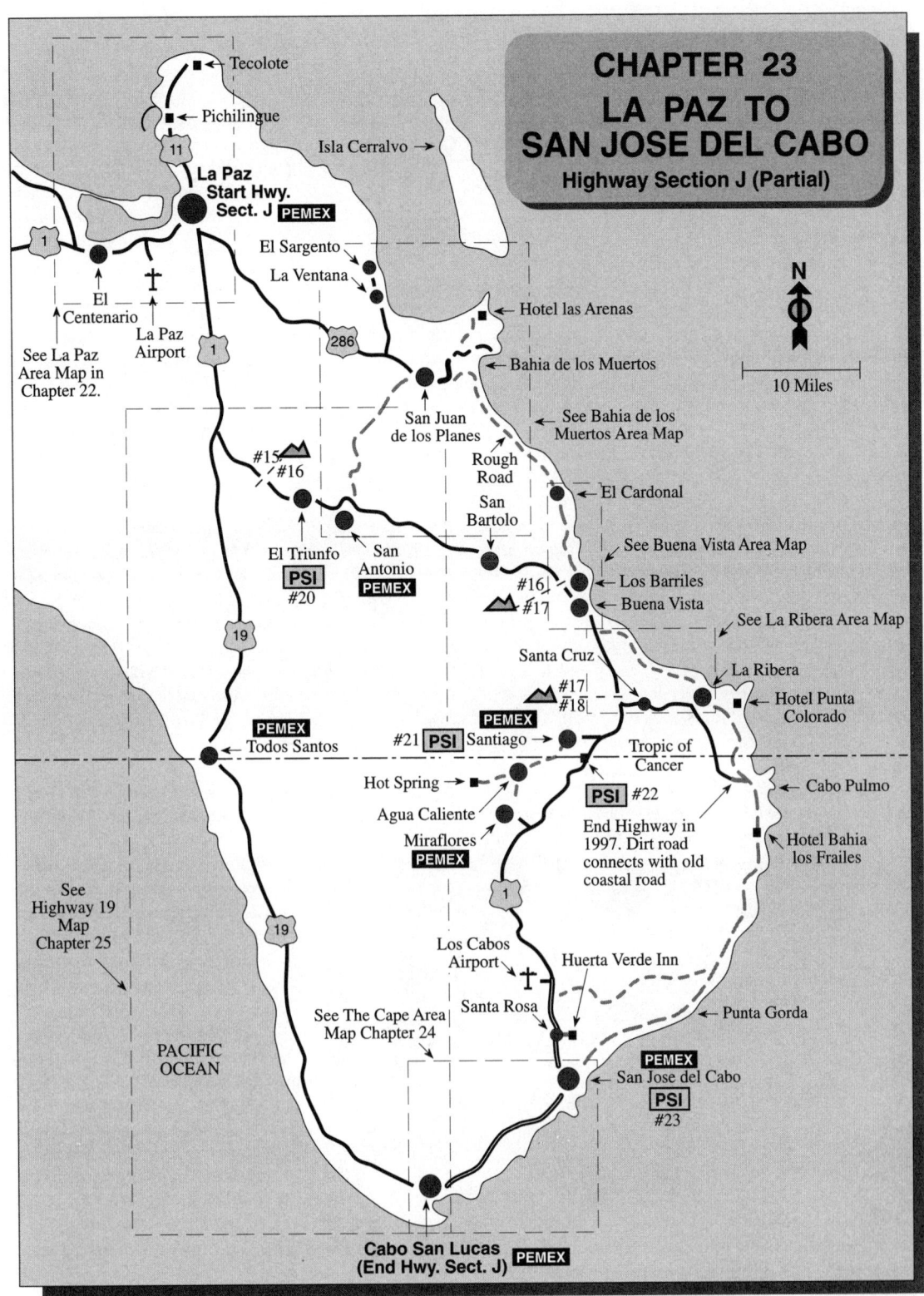

Tecolote

Pichilingue

11

Isla Cerralvo →

**La Paz
Start Hwy.
Sect. J** PEMEX

CHAPTER 23
**LA PAZ TO
SAN JOSE DEL CABO**
Highway Section J (Partial)

1

El
Centenario

La Paz
Airport

El Sargento

La Ventana

286

Hotel las Arenas

Bahia de los Muertos

N

See La Paz
Area Map in
Chapter 22.

1

San Juan
de los Planes

See Bahia de los
Muertos Area Map

10 Miles

#15
#16

Rough
Road

San
Bartolo

El Cardonal

See Buena Vista Area Map

El Triunfo

PSI
#20

San
Antonio
PEMEX

#16
#17

Los Barriles

Buena Vista

See La Ribera Area Map

19

Santa Cruz

#17
#18

La Ribera

Hotel Punta
Colorado

PEMEX
Todos Santos

#21 PSI Santiago →

PEMEX

Tropic of
Cancer

Cabo Pulmo

Hot Spring →

Agua Caliente

Miraflores
PEMEX

PSI #22

End Highway in
1997. Dirt road
connects with old
coastal road

Hotel Bahia
los Frailes

See
Highway 19
Map
Chapter 25

19

1

Los Cabos
Airport

Huerta Verde Inn

Punta Gorda

Santa Rosa

See The Cape Area
Map Chapter 24

PACIFIC
OCEAN

PEMEX
San Jose del Cabo

PSI
#23

**Cabo San Lucas
(End Hwy. Sect. J)** PEMEX

Recreation vehicles line the bluff overlooking Bahia de los Muertos. Photo JW.

Km-37 — *A paved highway leads left (north) to the small towns of La Ventana* **Km-7** *and El Sargento* **Km-11**. *There is a good camping spot on the beach at the north end of La Ventana in a grove of palm and mesquite trees. Now that the access road to this area has been paved, development is occurring between the two communities and eventually they will merge. A low standard road branches to the east between* **Km-6** *and* **Km-7** *(1.2 miles south of the warehouse in La Ventana) and in 0.5 miles arrives at an excellent camping beach. I am advised that this road extends eastward to the Hotel las Arenas but is best suited for 4x4 vehicles due to sandy conditions. During winter all of these locations are exposed to the prevailing northerly winds.*

We have been advised that a concrete launch ramp has been completed at El Sargento, that boat storage is available and

The mining ruins at the town of El Triunfo. Photo JW.

that a future boat dock is planned. Our informant also noted that this area is good for wind-surfing.

Km-41 — *Between* **Km 40** *and* **Km 41** *a secondary road leads right (south) 14.3 miles to the town of San Antonio at Highway 1. It provides the opportunity of traveling south without returning to La Paz.*

Km-43 — *Highway 286 passes through the center of the town of San Juan de los Planes. This community is the center of an agricultural region.*

Km-48 -- *The paved surface ends near the town of Agua Amarga. The road further eastward is constructed to the same standard as the balance of Highway 286 but was not paved in 1997.*

Km 55 — *About 0.1 miles west of* **Km 55** *a 2-lane, level, dirt road leads left (north) for 3.5 miles to the Hotel las Arenas. (At the 2.5 mile point one may proceed straight ahead and in 1.2 miles arrive at good camping spots on a sandy beach near a lighthouse.) Hotel las Arenas has been a first-class resort serving guests who arrive in small private aircraft, however it has been closed for several years. Our 1997 visit disclosed considerable road building and cleanup activity and a report that the hotel would be reopened by December 1997.*

Km-58 — *Arrival at Bahia de los Muertos. The name means The Bay of the Dead, but there could not be a more pleasant spot, with camping along a low bluff overlooking the beach. The beach has reasonable protection from the prevailing northerly winds. My favorite spot is on the floor of a long abandoned warehouse at the northern end of the area.* End SIDE TRIP.

(Km J-185) HIGHWAY19 JUNCTION — Highway 1 from La Paz to its junction with Highway 19 traverses the eastern edge of the Llano de la Paz. It is straight and level. At this junction you have a choice of two paved highways to Cabo San Lucas: 185 km (115 miles) via Highway 1, or 128 km (80 miles) over the shorter Highway 19. If this is your first trip to the area I recommend that you travel south on one route and return on the other. If you simply wish to proceed to Cabo San Lucas in the easiest manner, take Highway 19. It is shorter, does not require climbing over the Sierra de la Laguna, and there are fine views of the Pacific Ocean. See Chapter 25 for details.

A great majority of larger RVs and commercial trucks now travel to the Cape area over Highway 19. This has removed almost all of the slow-moving traffic that once was a problem on Highway 1. The latter route is now far more enjoyable for recreation travel than it was in the past.

#15 ◢◣ #16

(Km J-172) GEOGRAPHIC CHANGE — SE from the Highway 19 junction, the Llano de la Paz (Geographic Section No. 15) begins rising to meet the mountains. At **Km J-172** the plains come to an end and the highway enters the Sierra de la Laguna (Geographic Section No. 16). You will be traveling in the mountains until arriving at the coast at Los Barriles; however, most of the curves and steeper grades are encountered during the first 17 km (10 miles).

DECOMPOSED GRANITE — The Sierra de la Laguna is composed of granitic rocks. If you will remember the discussion about the Catavina boulder fields in Chapter 19, you will recall that granite rock breaks down into a very granular soil referred to as D.G. (decomposed granite). D.G. erodes readily. To complicate matters, the Cape Region receives much of its rainfall from intense storms related to tropical cyclones. The area's roads can suffer heavy damage during such storms. I have always found Highway 1 to be in good repair, but you may encounter washouts and detours when using lower standard roads. Be particularly cautious during and following heavy rains.

CAPE REGION VEGETATION — It is upon entering the Sierra de la Laguna that the characteristics of the Cape Region's Arid Tropical Forest vegetation become readily apparent. In the mountains between **Km J-170** and **Km J-50** several species of low trees become dominant, although many desert species are still present. The white-barked palo blanco is very abundant. This plant community has been described as an *impoverished tropical jungle*. A good place to walk through this vegetation type is at Rancho Verde, an RV park at **Km J-141** a few miles ahead. Here, much of the undergrowth has been cleared and several nature trails are available for your use. South of **Km**

J-50 the trees are replaced by a variety of low shrubs, but the overall amount of vegetation remains far more dense than in the Sonoran Desert to the north.

PSI #20

(Km J-164) EL TRIUNFO — The mining community of El Triunfo (The Triumph - population 400) and its neighboring town of San Antonio lie in one of Baja's most historic areas. El Triunfo was the site of a cattle ranch in the early Jesuit period, and in 1748 silver was discovered in the mountains south of San Antonio. Many years later, in 1862, silver and gold were also located at El Triunfo. Believe it or not, the sleepy little town that you see today soon was to have a population of 10,000, making it the largest community in the southern peninsula.

El Triunfo is stop No. 20 on the POINTS OF SPECIAL INTEREST Tour. Even large RVs can pull off the highway near the church. Take a short walk to the ruins of the old smelter. The smoke stacks are clearly in view from the highway. A few hundred feet SE of the larger stack lies a brick-walled enclosure containing thirteen above-ground crypts. These reportedly contain the remains of American miners.

Be careful as you wander about, because present-day miners are using arsenic to reprocess the old mine tailings, as they seek what little metal remains. These areas are fenced and signed.

(Km J-159) SCENIC VIEW — Between **Km J-159** and **Km J-158** one may look out over the mountains to the plains around San Juan de los Planes. The Sea of Cortez and huge Isla Cerralvo are also in view on clear days. The island is separated from the mainland by a narrow channel. The Arid Tropical Forest vegetation is well developed in this area.

(Km J-156) SAN ANTONIO — San Antonio (population 800) is a pleasant little town lying along the bottom of a sizeable arroyo. The town square and church lie 0.3 miles upstream to the south. There is a PEMEX station on the highway which I have found closed on some of my visits. About 0.1 miles prior to reaching the PEMEX station, an oiled road leaves Highway 1 to the left (north). This is the beginning of the secondary road leading to San Juan de los Planes. After traveling on this road for 0.1 miles it takes first a sharp left, and then a sharp right turn near a high voltage electric tower. Failure to make these turns will place you on the old lower standard road through the northern portion of San Antonio.

Chapter 23

In 1748, silver mining started 5 miles south of here in the mountains at a place called Santa Ana. Look south into the rugged terrain and recall that Santa Ana was the site of one of the most important meetings in the history of the American West. In 1768, Jose de Galvez, personal representative of the King of Spain, made Santa Ana his headquarters. From here he sent for Junipero Serra, the newly arrived head of the Franciscan missionaries, and at this most unlikely of places they drew up the plans for the expeditions that resulted one year later in the founding of the missions in Alta California.

In 1828, Baja California's capital at Loreto was destroyed by flooding. Two years later the seat of power was moved to La Paz. During the brief interim, San Antonio served as the capital city.

(Km J-154) VISTA POINT -- Here is a small mirador vista point overlooking the Arid Tropical Forest.

(Km J-141) RANCHO VERDE -- On the right, only a short distance from Highway 1, is the very pleasant Rancho Verde RV park. I believe it is the only RV park in Baja that is built in the shade of *native* forest vegetation. I suggest you stop here even if you don't wish to camp and walk about on the nature trails that the owner has developed through the Arid Tropical Forest. The park is located at an elevation of 2,500 feet in a small segment of Baja that receives 20 to 30 inches of rainfall per year. Trust us, the vegetation is really dense and lush.

(Km J-128) SAN BARTOLO — The town of San Bartolo (population 550) lies along the highway above the banks of a deep canyon. The area contains numerous palms and a variety of large hardwood trees, a sight that is not often seen in Baja. Note the many light-colored granite rocks in view along the highway and contrast them with the darker basalt found to the north in the Sierra Giganta. Produce stands along the highway are a good place to stock up on fresh fruits and vegetables.

#16 #17
(Km J-112) GEOGRAPHIC CHANGE —Highway 1 arrives at the eastern edge of the Sierra de la Laguna (Geographic Section No. 16) and begins a short journey south along relatively level coastal flats (Geographic Section No. 17). The Sea of Cortez is in full view.

SIDE TRIP

(Km J-110) LOS BARRILES — *A good standard oiled road bears left (east) 0.2 miles north of **Km J-110**, and Highway 1 swings to the south down the coast. Taking the former road brings you in a short distance to the hotels and RV parks in Los Barriles. (See the LOS BARRILES - BUENA VISTA AREA Map.) The oiled surface ends a short distance beyond Los Barriles but the road proceeds further north up the coast as follows:*

9.1 Miles — Arrive at the very pleasant Hotel Punta Pescadero, adjoining recreation homes, and a paved airstrip. The resort's fishing fleet is moored in a shallow bight to the south. There is a steep pitch a short distance prior to arriving at the hotel but it does not pose a major problem.

The Los Barriles-Buena Vista area on the East Cape. Photo JW.

13.7 Miles — *The small village of El Cardonal is located at this point. The town lies on a level plateau above the Sea of Cortez and contains the El Cardonal Resort, a modest motel and RV park. From El Cardonal, the campers on the beach at Bahia de los Muertos to the north are clearly in view. A road continues north from here to San Juan de los Planes but some of those who have used it report that portions are suitable only for the most rugged of 4x4 vehicles. More recently I have been informed that the locals use it with regular vehicles as their short-cut to La Paz. In either case, all agree its a rough road. End* SIDE TRIP.

(Km J-108) BUENA VISTA — The community of Buena Vista lies along the shores of the Sea of Cortez and blends together with adjacent Los Barriles. To the left near **Km J-106** is a short side road to the Rancho Buena Vista. This is a very pleasant resort hotel. A few yards south of the turnoff to the Rancho Buena Vista, a secondary road leads 0.5 miles to the right (west) up the hill to the Flag Monument. From there you can enjoy a good view of the coast in both directions.

A road leaves the highway to the left 0.2 miles near **Km J-105** for the well landscaped Hotel Buena Vista Beach Resort and a subdivision development. One of the residences in this development has a small RV park in its yard. From here south, Highway 1 starts to turn inland. At **Km J-104** another dirt road signed for the Rancho Leonero bears to the left (east) and in 1.6 miles reaches the Capilla RV Park on the beach. It is 4.1 miles on this same road to the Rancho Leonero hotel (see the LA RIBERA AREA Map concerning these developments).

#17 ⛰ #18

(Km J-93) GEOGRAPHIC CHANGE — At this point Highway 1 leaves the flat coastal area (Geographic Section No. 17) and starts a 60 km (37 mile) journey over low hills and plateaus (Geographic Section No.18) between two ranges of mountains. To the right is that section of the Sierra de la Laguna that was the location of revolutionary battles from 1913 to 1915.

(Km J-93) EAST CAPE LOOP — An oiled highway leaves Highway 1 to the left (east) for the small coastal village of La Ribera, which is reached in 7.7 miles. This town is the northern terminus of a 100 km (62 mile) road along the coast leading to

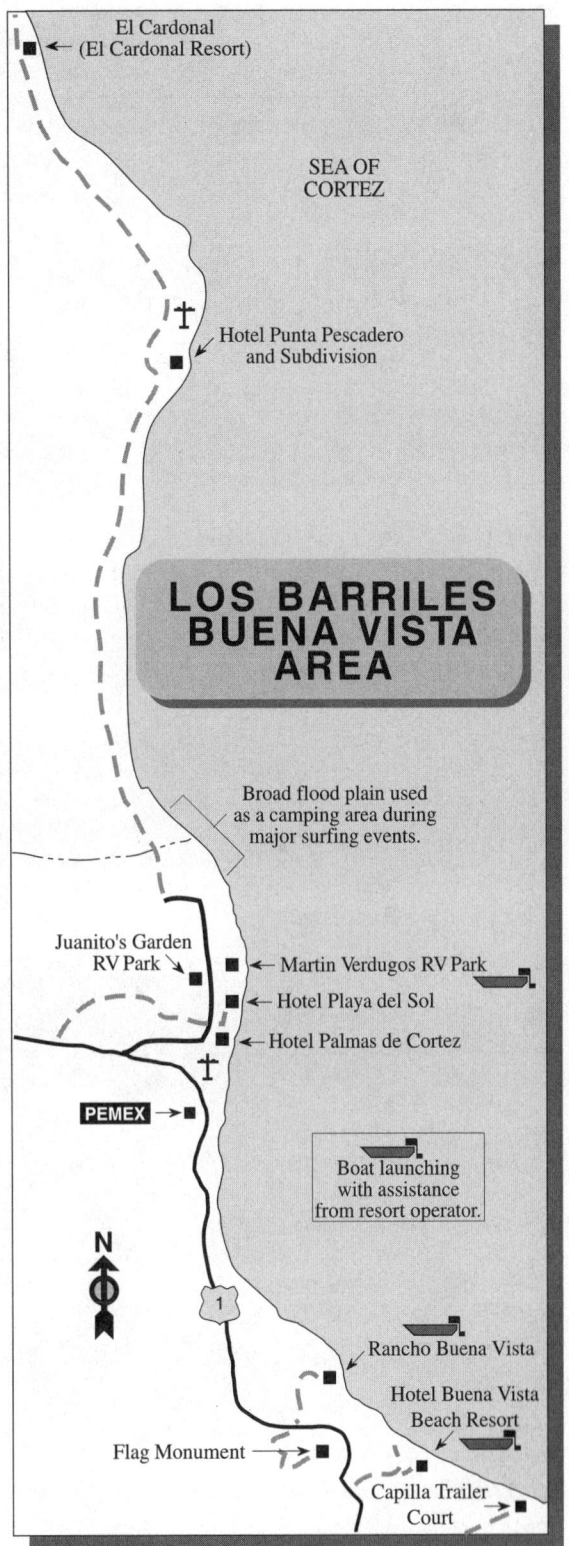

El Cardonal
(El Cardonal Resort)

SEA OF CORTEZ

✝ Hotel Punta Pescadero
and Subdivision

**LOS BARRILES
BUENA VISTA
AREA**

Broad flood plain used as a camping area during major surfing events.

Juanito's Garden RV Park

← Martin Verdugos RV Park

← Hotel Playa del Sol

← Hotel Palmas de Cortez

✝

PEMEX →

Boat launching with assistance from resort operator.

N

1

Rancho Buena Vista

Hotel Buena Vista Beach Resort

Flag Monument →

Capilla Trailer Court

The church at Santiago. Photo BW.

San Jose Del Cabo. This road, referred to in this book as the East Cape Loop, is described in a separate subsection at the end of this chapter.

PSI #21

SIDE TRIP

(Km J-85) SANTIAGO — *A blacktop road joins Highway 1 on the right (west) and leads to the historic town of Santiago, a pleasant village supported by small farms and ranching. It is stop No. 21 on the POINTS OF SPECIAL INTEREST Tour. Here the Jesuits founded their tenth mission in 1724. While the mission was maintained until 1795 (71 years), no traces of it remain.*

Don't miss the pleasant zoological garden at Santiago. Santiago is PSI stop # 21. Photo BW.

Santiago was one of the sites of the 1734 Pericue Indian revolt described in Chapter 12 HISTORY. The missionary padre, two soldiers, and an Indian were killed here, and the uprising caused temporary abandonment of all the missions in the Cape Region and La Paz.

The town square and PEMEX station are 1.5 miles west of the highway. Proceed through the square, bear left, and take the main, tree-lined street to visit the charming Hotel Palomar, a museum, and the only zoological garden in Baja California. (See description in Chapter 11 WILDLIFE.) End SIDE TRIP.

BOB & JEAN BACKROAD

AGUA CALIENTE — Continuing westerly past the zoological garden in Santiago is an 11-mile-long road to the town of Miraflores noted below. Near the midpoint between Santiago and Miraflores is the village of Agua Caliente. Take a dirt road west from Agua Caliente to it's end (about 2.5 miles) where you will be rewarded by a scenic camping spot in a canyon beside a large pool of water. A nearby hot spring fills a cement tub for your soaking enjoyment. There are other roads in this general area accessing the base of the Sierra de la Laguna. This area is trip #9 of the "Bob and Jean Backroad" Recommendations presented in Chapter 3.

PSI #22

(Km J-82) TROPIC OF CANCER — There is nothing fancy about the concrete sphere located by the road on the right (west), but most people from Canada and the United States never have the opportunity to stand exactly on the Tropic of Cancer (23 degrees 28 minutes north of the equator). This is stop No. 22 on the POINTS OF SPECIAL INTEREST Tour. I suggest you pause and stretch. You are now entering the world's tropical

The Bahia los Frailes Area along the East Cape Loop. Cabo los Frailes is the prominent point of land in the top-right portion of the photo. Photo JW.

zone. The sun moves in its yearly course between the Tropic of Cancer and the Tropic of Capricorn in the southern hemisphere.

(KM J-71) MIRAFLORES — A PEMEX station is located here at the junction of Highway 1 with a blacktop road that leads in 1.4 miles to the small town of Miraflores. The town has a grocery store but no other tourist facilities.

(Km J-44) LOS CABOS AIRPORT — The southern-most of Baja's international airports is reached in 0.6 miles over a blacktop road leading right (west). This is the entry point for airborne tourists bound for the Cape Area and the Buena Vista area. There is a modern terminal, parking, ample ground transportation including numerous car rental agencies. The airport has been expanded so as to accommodate jumbo jets. The airport is accessed by an overpass structure over Highway 1 and the remainder of the road to Cabo San Lucas is a four-lane divided highway with numerous traffic lights and continuous urban development. The Cape Area has entered the Big-Time.

(Km J-36) HUERTA VERDE INN -- A few miles north of San Jose del Cabo is the community of Santa Rosa. Turning east on to the town's main dirt street will lead you in about 1 mile across the wide Arroyo de San Jose to the Huerta Verde Bed and Breakfast Country Inn. This is an extremely pleasant facility which you should pay a visit. See notice at the end of this chapter.

#18   #19

(Km J-33) SAN JOSE DEL CABO -- San Jose del Cabo marks the last geographic breakpoint. The highway remaining ahead passes along a section of coastal benches and low hills. The community of San Jose del Cabo is one of Baja's most interesting and is well worth a visit. It is described in more detail in the next chapter (Chapter 24).

The roadside monument at the Tropic of Cancer between Buena Vista and San Jose del Cabo. Photo JW.

EAST CAPE LOOP

This subsection of Chapter 23 describes the roads that closely follow the SE coast of the Cape from Highway 1 south to San Jose del Cabo. The loop is an oiled highway from Highway 1 to the town of Ribera, and then a secondary, often badly washboarded, dirt road from there to San Jose del Cabo. The northern portion of this secondary road is now more-or-less paralleled, and in effect replaced by, a new paved highway that extends south for 10.4 miles from the outskirts of La Ribera.

0.0 Miles — The East Cape Loop begins at the Transpeninsular Highway just south of **Km J-93.**

7.0 Miles — Highway junction. The new highway noted above bears right a short distance prior to Km-11 at the outskirts of the town of La Libera. Stay straight ahead for La Ribera or turn right to follow the East Cape Loop.

SIDE TRIP

La Ribera -- *Staying straight ahead at the highway junction brings one to the town plaza in the small village of La Ribera. Continue straight ahead and drive down a slope*

toward the sea. At the base of the slope is a T intersection with the road to the left (north) leading to Buena Vista. At 0.4 miles along this road on the right is the La Ribera RV Park nestled in a mangrove orchard. It is one of Baja's more pleasant RV parks and a short walk from the beach. Turning right (south) at the T intersection will bring one in about 1 mile to a road junction near a grove of tamarisk trees. Taking a 90-degree turn left from here toward the coast provides access in 2.6 miles to an excellent camping area along the northern edge of a lagoon bordered with low

trees. A sand dune separates the camping area from an excellent sandy beach. End SIDE TRIP.

12.3 Miles -- At this point after turning right at the highway junction at the outskirts of La Ribera you will find a dirt road leading left to the very nice Hotel Punta Colorado.

13.9 Miles -- Here another dirt road leads left to the Faro Punta Arena. Faro means lighthouse and this one is constructed on a low lying point of land a few miles to the east with excellent sand beaches nearby.

17.4 Miles -- At this point the oiled surface highway abruptly ends in the middle of nowhere. It would appear that the road builders ran out of resources short of joining up with the old coastal road some 0.3 miles ahead. The gap is filled with a low standard dirt road.

17.7 Miles -- Junction with the old coastal road. Turn right here to continue south along the East Cape Loop. I have not been along this road for several years and was prevented from proceeding south in 1997 due to wet road conditions. Thus the road mileages presented below are approximate.

20 Miles — Arrive at spur road to Cabo Pulmo. There is a large area for RV parking at this point. The waters of Bahia Pulmo to the south of Cabo Pulmo support the only live coral reefs in the Sea of Cortez. It is thus a popular diving area.

23 Miles — A 0.9 miles spur leads to a ranch and camping area at the south end of Bahia Pulmo. This is the windy side of Cabo Frailes during the winter season.

25 Miles — A short spur road leads to the fine sandy beach at Bahia los Frailes. The point of land to the north (Cabo los Frailes) provides some protection from northerly winds. Located here is the small but very comfortable Hotel Bahia los Frailes. It is used as a headquarters for those interested in acquiring a home in the nearby residential subdivision, but transient visitors are also welcome.

The old secondary road south of this point is built through an area of decomposed granite. There are no steep grades but the road is subject to severe erosion damage in the event of storms. In some years I have had reports that it was open to 4 wheel drive vehicles only.

40 Miles — A side road leaves the East Cape Loop here and joins Highway 1 near the Los Cabos Airport in 23 miles. From here to the lighthouse at San Jose del Cabo I have observed over thirty places to camp near the water's edge, every one of them with one or more groups of people. Most of these are relatively small areas located by the sea below where an arroyo crosses the road. Some are on fine sand beaches, others on the bluffs overlooking the water. Access to these sites is most often over low standard "trails" where one can become mired down in the sand. Freedom has its price.

57.0 Miles — The East Cape Loop formally ends here, only a few feet from the lighthouse on the hill south of San Jose del Cabo. The road forks at this point, but either branch takes you through the small community of La Playa that lies on the east bank of the Rio San Jose. It is 2.0 miles from here, across the riverbed, to the boulevard south of the civic plaza at San Jose del Cabo. The junction is near the fire station and a tall microwave tower. If you plan to drive from San Jose del Cabo north on the East Cape Loop and have some difficulty getting started, look for the lighthouse and work your way to it as your point of departure.

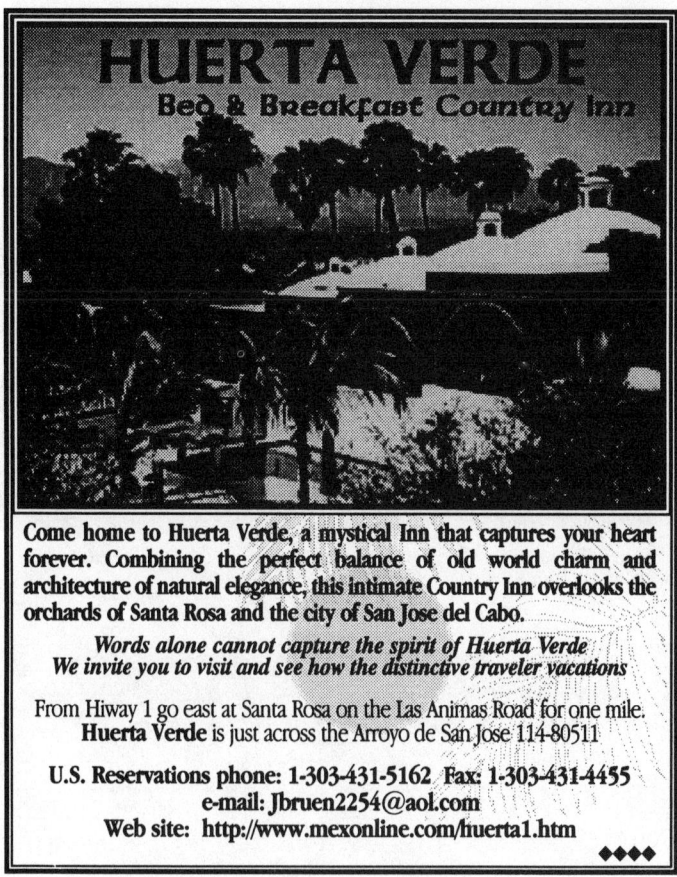

CHAPTER 24
THE CAPE AREA

CAPE AREA SUMMARY -- That portion of the Baja peninsula lying along its southern tip is known in English as "The Cape Area." A cape is defined as "A piece of land projecting into a body of water; promontory; headland." Thus, a good case can be made that the cape in question here is the entire southern end of the peninsula. However, in Spanish the region is referred to as "Los Cabos", that is, The Capes (plural). Are we to believe that there is more than one cape?

The famous Cabo San Lucas is the only really dramatic promontory in the area, with Punta Palmilla to the east being far less dramatic. More likely the plural term "Los Cabos" refers to the two towns of Cabo San Lucas (Cape Saint Luke) and San Jose del Cabo (Saint Joseph of the Cape). If I am not correct, I will no doubt be firmly corrected prior to this book's next edition.

In any case, The Cape Area has undergone more change from a recreational standpoint than any area

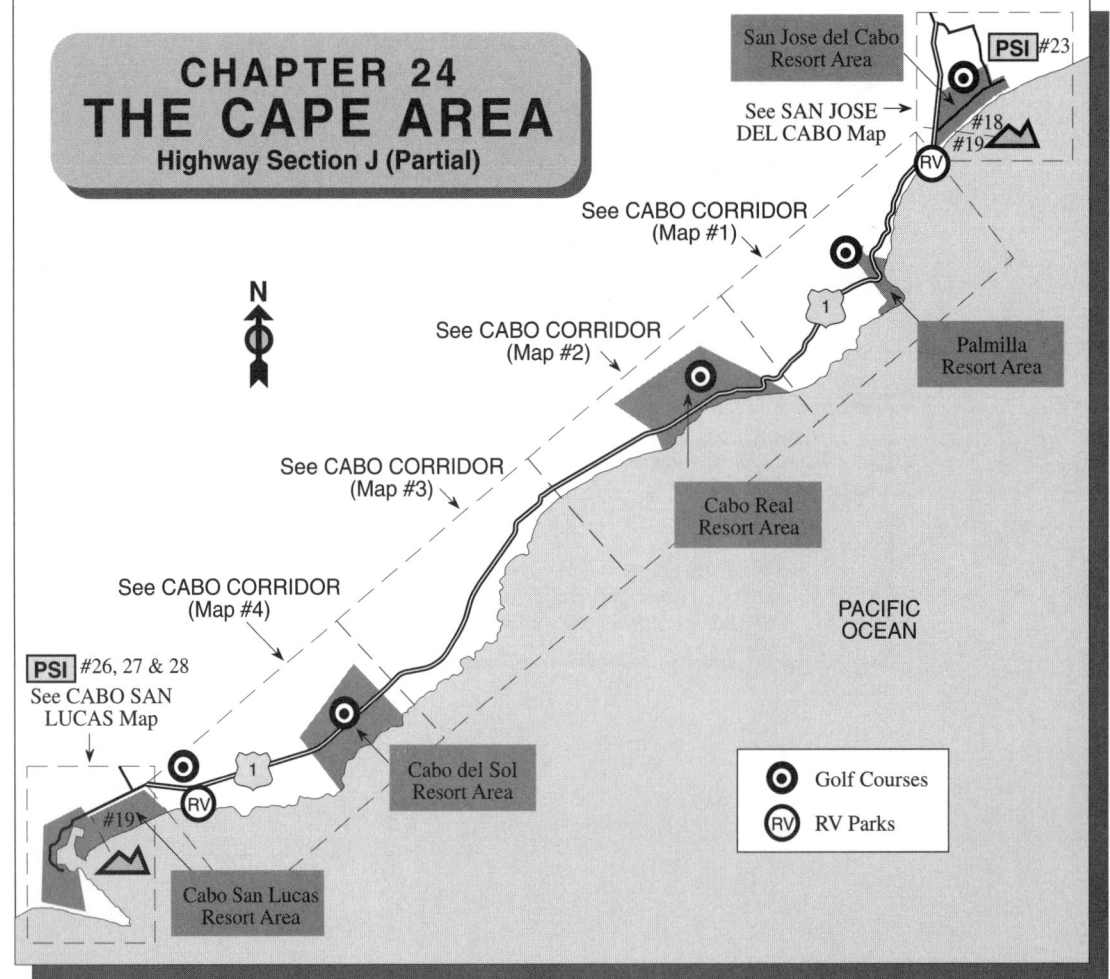

CHAPTER 24
THE CAPE AREA
Highway Section J (Partial)

N

San Jose del Cabo Resort Area
PSI #23
See SAN JOSE → DEL CABO Map
#18 #19
RV

See CABO CORRIDOR (Map #1)

See CABO CORRIDOR (Map #2)

Palmilla Resort Area

See CABO CORRIDOR (Map #3)

Cabo Real Resort Area

See CABO CORRIDOR (Map #4)

PACIFIC OCEAN

PSI #26, 27 & 28
See CABO SAN LUCAS Map

Cabo del Sol Resort Area

Golf Courses
RV Parks

#19
RV

Cabo San Lucas Resort Area

SAN JOSE DEL CABO

in Baja. During the first few years following completion of the Transpeninsular Highway in 1973 the region contained several first class hotels catering largely to the general aviation flyer. But the camper was king, and people like myself lined the beaches under conditions that often were disgraceful from a sanitation standpoint.

Now, camping outside of developed RV parks is a thing of the past. In its place, The Cape Area has become one of the world's finest resort and hotel meccas. I believe that portions of the French and Italian Riviera are superior in overall esthetic appeal, in part because Baja's desert vegetation is a bit austere. But I have never seen the equal of The Cape Area Hotels. Perhaps with another decade or so of development and landscaping,

the southern tip of the Baja peninsula will be unrivaled as the world's best resort area.

To complete this summary, I refer you to the comments made in the Resort Areas section of Chapter 6 concerning San Jose del Cabo, Cabo San Lucas, and the intervening area known as the Cabo Corridor. The points of interest presented in the balance of this chapter are shown on six maps as depicted on the Chapter 24 Map. Keep in mind that the four Cabo Corridor maps are not aligned in a true north-south direction as are most of the maps in this book.

PSI #23

(Km J-33) SAN JOSE DEL CABO — San Jose del Cabo is a town of 10,000 people and the last geo-

CABO CORRIDOR
(Map #1)

La Jolla de los Cabos
Hotel & Condominiums

To San Jose del Cabo
(See San Jose
del Cabo Map)

Terra Cotta B & B

Km J-29

Brisa del Mar
RV Park

Km J-28

Off Ramps

Km J-27

Playa Coasta Azul

PALMILLA DEVELOPMENT
Long Existing Hotel
(Golf Course & Residential Areas Under Development)

Km J-25

Km J-26

To Cabo San Lucas
(Move to Map #2)

Km J-24

Pepe's
Restaurant

Playa Palmilla

Hotel Palmilla

PACIFIC OCEAN

Punta Palmilla

To Cabo San Lucas
(Move to Map #3)

CABO REAL
Hotels - Golf Courses - Residential Property
(In Operation But Construction Continues 1997)

Km J-21

Hotel Casa
del Mar

Hotel Melia Cabo Real

Playa Bledito

Km J-23

Playa Cabo Real

Playa Buenos Aires

Hotel Westin Regina Resort

CABO CORRIDOR
(Map #2)

PACIFIC OCEAN

CABO CORRIDOR
(Map #3)

Maria Gaviota
Suites & Villas

Km J-15

Hotel
Cabo
San Lucas

Dive Shop

Reef

Playa El Tule

Playa Chileno

To Cabo San Lucas
(Move to Map #4)

Km J-11

Km J-12

Cerro
Santa Maria

Cerro
La Cruz

PSI #25

Hotel Twin Dolphin

Playa Viudas

Playa Santa Maria

PACIFIC OCEAN

CABO CORRIDOR
(Map #4)

To Cabo San Lucas
(See Cabo San Lucas Map)

El Arco
RV Park

Km J-4

Km J-5

Vista Bonita
RV Park

Km J-6

CABO DEL SOL
Hotels - Golf Courses - Residential Property
(Under Construction 1997)

Km J-9

Highway
Interchange

Km J-10

Missions del Cabo
Subdivision

Cabo
Bello

Hotel
Calinda Beach

Villa Serena RV Park

Santa Carnela

Hacienda del Mar

Hotels under Construction

Cabo
del Sol

PACIFIC OCEAN

Punta Cabeza
de Ballena

The church at the civic plaza at San Jose del Cabo. Take a close look at the mosaic over the entrance which depicts the 1734 Indian uprising in which a priest was killed. Photo BW.

(See the SAN JOSE DEL CABO Map). San Jose del Cabo is stop No. 23 on the POINTS OF SPECIAL INTEREST Tour. This hard-surface loop will bring you back to Highway 1, near the coast, with no problems. Along the way visit the town's principal area of tourist shops centered near the Civic Plaza and walk the pathway along the Estero de San Jose.

The town's history is one of the richest in the peninsula and includes the activities of the early Jesuit mission, visitations by numerous ships and famous captains, and an intensive battle in the Mexican-American War. The statue in the civic plaza is that of Naval Lieutenant Jose Antonio Mijares, who died here in 1847 while defending the town from takeover by the United States. Visit the church on the west side of the plaza. It was built in 1940 on the final site of the mission originally founded in 1730. A tile mosaic over its entrance depicts the slaying of the mission priest during the Indian uprising in 1734.

graphic breakpoint. If you are approaching from the north on Highway 1 and are in a rush to reach the coast and Cabo San Lucas, stay straight ahead on the divided highway which passes west of the center of town. However, I suggest you turn left at the PEMEX station and take the three-sided loop through town.

The Cape Area coastline. The Hotel Palmilla lies on the prominent point of land (Punta Palmilla) at the left edge of the photo. Cabo San Lucas can be seen in the distance at the photos's top right corner. Photo JW.

Most of the town's major hotels are located along an outstanding beach south of town. The Hotel Presidente Inter-Continental Los Cabos is at the western edge of the coastal lagoon lying at the mouth of the Rio San Jose. There can be no more historic spot on the Magnificent Peninsula. The original 1730 mission was located between here and the cemetery, and the fresh water entering the lagoon was of critical importance to the crews of ships plying Pacific waters.

To the west of the Presidente are three additional hotels. Inland from these is a golf course and residential and condominium area. All of this is a part of FONATUR's San Jose del Cabo development. A major marina project is planned for the estuary between San Jose del Cabo and the small community of La Playa. (Hold not your breath.)

I should note that the major new, privately-owned hotel and resort complexes being developed to the west along the Cabo Corridor, appear to be having a dampening affect on FONATUR's San Jose del Cabo project. There have been no new hotels constructed in this latter area in over three years and some of the existing ones are suffering from lack of maintenance. The activity level here is in marked contrast to the feverish pace in evidence along the Cabo Corridor and at Cabo San Lucas.

THE CABO CORRIDOR — The section of highway between San Jose del Cabo and Cabo San Lucas is referred to as "The Cabo Corridor", or simply "The Corridor." Within as recently as ten years ago there was very little development in this area. It is now probably only a matter of a few more years until it will be solid buildings of some variety. Highway 1 was upgraded to a four-lane divided highway through The Corridor about 1993 thus easing what was becoming a serious traffic congestion problem. The road's right-of-way is fenced in most places, so there is limited access to the waterfront. There are now no areas where the parking of RVs or camping is possible along what is the finest stretch of coast in all Baja.

In conducting my 1997 survey it became apparent that there were often discrepancies between the kilometer addresses noted for various hotels, etc. in locally available literature and the kilometer markings which were present along Highway 1. Perhaps the markings are being changed as part of the roadway upgrading project. The kilometer references given below, and on the accompanying maps, reflect my personal observations. My apologies for the fact that you will necessarily have to join me in suffering through some confusion.

(Km J-29) -- On the beach SW of San Jose del Cabo, near **Km J-29.5**, is the Brisa del Mar, one of Baja's most popular RV parks. There are approximately 100 sites complemented by a bar, restaurant and pool. This is the only RV park on the beach in the Cape Area. All the rest are at the western end of the Cabo Corridor near Cabo San Lucas and are some distance removed from the water's edge. Farther to the west along the beach at **Km J-29** is the very nice Hotel La Jolla.

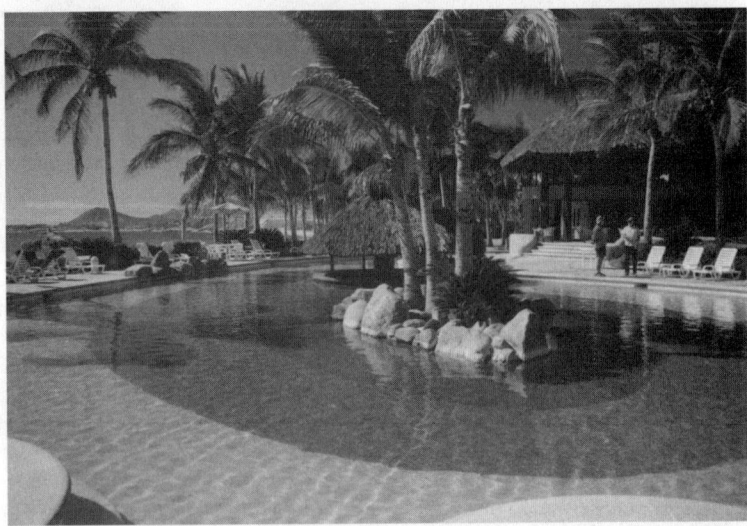

The pool area at the Hotel La Jolla along the beach at San Jose del Cabo. Photo BW.

The next stop on the POINTS OF SPECIAL INTEREST Tour is the Hotel Palmilla. Its buildings may be seen near the end of the point of land projecting to sea several miles to the south. This promontory provides the only protection from Pacific Ocean swells in the San Jose del Cabo area.

PSI #24

(Km J-27) HOTEL PALMILLA — Each time I visit the Magnificent Peninsula I am impressed that a different

A view of the ocean from one of the open-air dining rooms at the Hotel Palmilla at the western edge of San Jose del Cabo. Photo BW.

excellent landscaping. There is a sizeable parking lot, and the road is suitable for even large RVs. A very picturesque, small cove (Puerto Chileno) lies westerly from the hotel. Near the beach at its head is a large palm covered structure offering diving services. The road to this facility leaves Highway 1 a short distance westerly from the hotel access road.

PSI #25

(Km J-11) HOTEL TWIN DOLPHIN — Here is another very fine hotel which may be easily visited by even the larger RVs. Its landscaping was designed to feature native desert plants. It thus offers a unique atmosphere and has been placed on the POINTS OF SPECIAL INTEREST Tour as stop No. 25. Immediately east of the hotel is Bahia Santa Maria, a small idyllic cove with a fine sandy beach.

(KM J-10) CABO DEL SOL -- A highway interchange lies just east of **Km J-10** and provides access to the Cabo Del Sol resort development. In 1997 much construction was under way at this 1,800 acre property. Also envisioned are three additional oceanfront hotels, three golf courses, a colonial village center, 3,400 residences and assorted other amenities.

(Km J-7) VILLA SERENA RV PARK — At this point in time the Villa Serena is the most easterly of several RV parks lying between here and Cabo San Lucas. The access road is 0.4 miles in length. When first developed several years ago many of the sites offered fine ocean views and a pool area fit for a fancy hotel. Unfortunately the best spots have now been converted to permanent status and the transient sites leave a bit to be desired.

(Km J-7) HOTEL CALINDA BEACH — A blacktop road leads left for 0.5 mile to the hotel. Most of the times I have paid it a visit its name has been changed, so be prepared for something different. From the hotel you may look westerly across the outer harbor at Cabo San Lucas and see the peninsula's rocky tip. The pool area is also very nice and one can argue with considerable validity that it has the best view of any hotel in Baja. The Missions del Cabo subdivision lies

hotel seems to be the finest in all Baja, but the Hotel Palmilla is always in the competition. I include it as stop No. 24 on the POINTS OF SPECIAL INTEREST Tour. The drive in from the highway is about one-half mile. There is a small parking lot but the road is narrow and unsuited for large RVs. This hotel has been here for many years and thus has excellent landscaping.

The Palmilla development is now being greatly expanded and the area is served by a full-fledged interchange over Highway 1. A 27 hole golf course is present north of the highway and many condominiums are scattered about. The area is truly world class.

CABO REAL — The advertised address for the Cabo Real resort area is **Km J-19.5**. However this 2,500 acre development lies along several kilometers of Highway 1. At the eastern extremity near **Km J-24** is the grandiose Hotel Westin Regina Resort. Farther west an interchange near **Km J-21** serves the Hotel Melia, the smaller Hotel Casa del Mar and a nearby golf course. The area north of the highway will eventually contain numerous roads and residential developments. Everything is world class and is being done on a grand scale.

(Km J-15) HOTEL CABO SAN LUCAS — By now you must be aware that I believe my readers will be charmed, as I am, by Baja's fine hotels. Here is another one which is among the very best. The Hotel Cabo San Lucas was completed in 1962 and is surrounded by just to the west of the hotel on a promontory of land called Cabo Bello.

PSI #26

(Km J-6) CABO SAN LUCAS VISTA — At this point there used to be a simple concrete monument on the left side of the road. I designated this as POINTS OF SPECIAL INTEREST Tour stop No. 26 and recommended that you stop here for an excellent view of Cabo San Lucas. Nowadays its worth your life to stop along this busy highway, but you are still permitted to admire the view and congratulate all hands on having arrived within sight of the Magnificent Peninsula's most famous landmark. (Better yet,

View from the hot tub area at the Hotel Calinda Beach. The famous Lands End tip of the Baja peninsula is visible to the left of the buildings at the top left. Photo BW.

visit the Hotel Calinda Beach noted above and enjoy a relaxed view of the Cape.) Let me add my own salute. Congratulations, you have arrived within site of *Finisterra* (Land's End). I hope you have not been led too far astray along the way.

(Km J-6 to J-3) RV Parks — There are five RV parks with full hookups adjoining the highway between here and Cabo San Lucas. Take your pick

There is one additional RV park, Club Cabo, tucked in along the eastern edge of the Vagabundos del Mar park. It is reached by turning left (south) of the highway onto a dirt road just west of **Km J-3**. After a short distance again turn left and in about 1/4 mile, there you are. This park is a bit more secluded than the others and caters to tent campers.

(Km J-3.5) CABO SAN LUCAS COUNTRY CLUB - - On the right side of the highway across from the Vagabundos del Mar RV Park lies the Cabo San Lucas Country Club. This 746 acre development is planned to include a 36 hole golf course and approximately 1,600 home sites. Hotels do not appear to be part of the picture here and there is no ocean frontage.

(Km J-3) ENTERING CABO SAN LUCAS — Upon entering Cabo San Lucas note the junction with Highway 19 on the right (north). This highway skirts the community on its eastern edge. A PEMEX station may be found along Highway 19 near the northern

edge of town. Another easily accessible PEMEX station adjoins Highway 1 on the right at **Km J-2**.

(Km J-0) CABO SAN LUCAS — The zero kilometer post for the Transpeninsular Highway lies across from the town square. Let us hope that some of our gringo friends don't steal it. The latest town entrance sign claims 14,000 people, and the town is experiencing an enormous expansion of hotels, condominiums, and tourist oriented shops. In spring 1989 I described the place as hectic and bathed in construction activities. It has settled down quite a bit, but it will never again be the simple fishing village it once was.

There are many places of interest to the tourist in the Cabo San Lucas area. The main center of tourist oriented shops, restaurants, etc. is located in the area generally northwest of the marina along Boulevard Marina and around the Hotel Mar de Cortez. Included here are several establishments which may be classified under the title of nightclubs. Mexicans are famous for permitting their visitors to let their hair down over a margarita or two and here is where that may be accomplished. Following are some of the other more important places:

THE INNER HARBOR — It took over a decade to convert the waterfront area of Cabo San Lucas into a dredged, concrete-walled inner harbor. And now it has finally secured a first-class marina filled with the world's fanciest yachts. (Note - The aerial photo in

To Todos Santos

PEMEX

19

Cabo
San Lucas
Country Club

Km J-2

Leona Vicario (One Way)

Hotel Villa la Paloma

2 ©

Vagabundos
del Mar
RV Park

PEMEX

1

Club
Cabo
RV Park

Jose Morelos (One Way)

(One Way)

Immigration
Office

Km J-2

Club
Cascades

Port Captain

Lazaro Cardenas

Paseo del Pescador

RV Park

Villas del
Palmar

Hotel Mar de Cortez

5 ©

Plaza Bonita Mall

3
©

1

Pueblo
Bonita

Playa El Medano

Bank →
Town Square
(Zocalo)

Boat Launching
Marina
Office

©

Hotel
Melia

Plaza Nautica

Marina

Boulevard

Church →

Marina

Marina Fiesta &
Marina Cabo Plaza
Hotel Hacienda

© RESIDENTIAL DEVELOPMENTS ©

1 - Bahia Condominums
2 - Coromuel Condominums
3 - Marina Sol Condominums
4 - Pedregal de Cabo San Lucas
5 - Roca Vista Condominums

4
©

Pedregal de
Cabo San Lucas
(Subdivision)

Hotel Plaza
las Glorias

Ferry Dock
Ferry Terminal

Sport Fishing Dock

Bahia San Lucas

Hotel
Finisterra →

PSI
#27

Boat
Launching

N

NOTE -- The Cabo San Lucas
to Puerto Vallarta ferry service
was discountinued in 1989.

Rock Pinnacle
(Tropical Fish)

Solmar Suites Hotel

Terrasol
Beach Resort

Cabo
San Lucas

Playa del Amor

Playa Solmar

CABO SAN LUCAS

PACIFIC
OCEAN

El Arco
(The Arch)

#28

PSI

Sea Lions

The Cabo San Lucas Area. The famous Cape itself is at the right side of the photo. Additional developments have been made in several areas since this photo was taken. Photo JW.

this chapter was taken prior to development of this marina.) At the harbor's southern end are open-air gift shops.

HOTEL FINISTERRA — Perched high on the cliffs south of the inner harbor is the Hotel Finisterra. It is stop No. 27 on the POINTS OF SPECIAL INTEREST Tour. The hotel offers intriguing rock-masonry architecture, and from its entrance way the entire Cabo San Lucas community and harbor area are in view. Be sure to visit the Whale Watcher's Bar where the vista changes to the south and provides a commanding panorama of the Pacific Ocean The men's restroom is also one-of-a-kind.

SOLMAR SUITES HOTEL — If you love the beach, the Solmar is the place. It is in view from the Whale Watcher's Bar at the Finisterra, and its access road starts opposite the ferry terminal.

HACIENDA HOTEL — Yet another of Baja's very finest hotels adjoins the beach fronting the outer harbor. Its access road circles the inner harbor on its eastern side. If you like to swim in the ocean, this is the best place, as the beach here is protected from the main force of the Pacific swells.

HOTEL MELIA — One of Cabo's newest hotels all done in a "grand style." It lies immediately northeast of the Hotel Hacienda. Again the beach is readily used for swimming.

MAR DE CORTEZ HOTEL — A more modest, smaller, but very charming hotel lying in the business area of the community.

OUTER HARBOR TOUR — You have arrived at the town of Cabo San Lucas and have gazed seaward at the jagged finger of rock that forms the cape itself, but you haven't actually been there. The next challenge of the POINTS OF SPECIAL INTEREST Tour (stop No. 28) is to visit the natural arch and spires of rock at Land's End. (Stops No. 29 and 30 are along Highway 19 described in Chapter 25.)

There is also a pinnacle of rock in the bay near the cliffs some 0.3 miles south from the inner harbor entrance. Most of this formation lies underwater and attracts thousands of colorful tropical fish that are easily viewed with snorkeling equipment or from a glass-bottom boat. Small boats are for hire in the harbor or along the beach so you may accept this final challenge. Rent one with a glass bottom to see the fish.

CAPE AREA BEACHES

As recently as about 1980, anyone could leave Highway 1 at almost any point where there was a side road and make one's way to the shoreline to camp and use the Cape's numerous beaches. Rapid development of the area's private land has made this practice a thing of the past. During my 1992 survey I noted a sign along the highway at San Jose del Cabo listing 22 beaches that were open to the public. Each was served by an access road of varying standards and its junction with Highway 1 was marked with an "Accesso Playa" (Beach Access) sign. Since then the highway has been upgraded to four-lanes and some of the signs have disappeared. Thus, getting to the beach is more of a challenge than it used to be. To assist in this endeavor the following material lists fourteen Cape

CABO SAN LUCAS

<u>Top</u> - Pool and beach area at the Hotel Finisterra at the tip of the Baja peninsula in Cabo San Lucas. <u>Center</u> - The Giggling Marlin, one of several "on-the-wild-side" bars that cater to your friendly Gringo types. <u>Bottom</u> - Things get really wild at Halloween in Cabo San Lucas. Photos BW.

Area beaches and their location is shown on the six maps presented in this chapter.

From a swimming-safety standpoint, Cape Area beaches can be said to fall into three categories; (1) Dangerous, (2) Normally safe, and (3) In-Between. The <u>dangerous beaches</u> lie westerly from the Cabo San Lucas promontory where they are impacted by heavy swells traveling down the Pacific coast. The breaking swells and undertow can be quite strong and swimming can be hazardous. The <u>normally safe</u> beaches lie immediately easterly from the Cape in the protected portions of Bahia San Lucas. This area offers the best shelter from the prevailing Pacific swells.

Most of the beaches presented below fall easterly from Bahia San Lucas and are in the <u>In-Between class</u>. The prevailing winter season Pacific swells refract around Cabo San Lucas causing breaking swell conditions all the way northeast into the Sea of Cortez to near the town of La Ribera. Swell intensity becomes less the farther one proceeds northeasterly from Cabo San Lucas. However, it must be noted that some of the beaches in this In-Between area have a good degree of local protection from small points of land, or man-made breakwaters. ------- During the summer months the entire Cape Area can be impacted by strong southerly winds and all of its beaches will become unsafe.

LA PLAYA (The Beach) -- This is that portion of a very long beach accessed by road at the town of La Playa where the local panga fishing fleet makes its headquarters. See the SAN JOSE DEL CABO Map.

PLAYA COSTA AZUL (Blue Coast Beach) -- Playa Costa Azul is a miles-long beach extending from the western end of the Estero de San Jose to the eastern edge of the bight northeast of Punta Pamilla. It has long been named Playa Costa Azul. With the advent of the beachfront hotels at San Jose del Cabo, its eastern portion is now referred to as **PLAYA HOTELERA** (Hotel Beach). Access is through the hotels, the Brisa del Mar RV Park and a variety of other places.

PLAYA PALMILLA (Palmilla Beach) -- This is a small section of beach lying in the cove formed easterly from Punta Palmilla. During the winter season it is well protected from refracted swells and is thus one of the safest beaches east of Bahia San Lucas. The beach is reached by road just before arriving at Pepe's Restaurant. Playa Palmilla may be seen in the lower right portion of the Cape Area coastline photo in this chapter.

CABO REAL -- Several great beaches lie along the seaward edge of the Cabo Real resort development. A stone breakwater has been built offshore from the Hotel Melia Cabo Real providing swell protection for **PLAYA CABO REAL** to the east. To the west of the breakwater a small natural cove has **PLAYA BLEDITO** at its head. In both cases access is via the hotel. For several miles easterly from the hotel lies **PLAYA BUENOS AIRES**. This beach is now little used and can be accessed from the hotel. The area is within the Cabo Real resort development property and it is surely only a matter of time before there will be new developments with resulting changes in access. There is also a small beach in front of the Hotel Westin Regina Resort.

PLAYA EL TULE -- A small secluded beach (also known as Surfing Beach) lies near the Maria Gaviota Suites and Villas and is reached over a low standard road at **Km J-16** at the Puente los Tules (Los Tules Bridge).

PLAYA PUERTO CHILENO -- This relatively small beach lies southwest from the Hotel Cabo San Lucas. It is reasonably well protected from refracted swells by a sizeable rocky reef extending at right angles from the coast. The best access is over a road leaving Highway 1 west of the hotel leading to a diving and equipment rental service.

PLAYA SANTA MARIA -- This beach lies at the head of a classic small, horseshoe-shaped cove (Bahia Santa Maria) just east of the Hotel Twin Dolphin. The beach may be reached from a walkway leading from the hotel parking lot or over a nearby dirt road leading to a small parking area. The cove itself is a protected marine sanctuary.

PLAYA LAS VIUDAS (Widow's Beach) -- Playa las Viudas lies on the western side of the Hotel Twin Dolphin. It is reached over a rough 0.4 miles dirt road leaving Highway 1 near **Km J-11**.

PLAYA EL MEDANO -- This is "the" beach at Cabo San Lucas. It stretches from the entrance to the inner harbor easterly for about two miles. It is backed by several major hotels. Access is at the hotels or numerous other places. The farther one proceeds easterly from the inner harbor entrance the more the beach is impacted by refracted swells.

PLAYA DEL AMOR (Lover's Beach) -- This is a small beach which extends completely through the rocky spine that forms Cabo San Lucas. The portion which faces the Pacific side is quite hazardous for swimming. The Bahia San Lucas side is more sheltered. The local propaganda claims that you can only get to Playa del Amor by boat (hiring a ride from the local panga owners is an easy task) but the photo of the Cabo San Lucas area in this chapter would suggest that one can "sneak" around into the beach from Playa Solmar if the tide is right. But, be careful and don't get trapped by a rising tide or increasing swells.

PLAYA SOLMAR -- This is the wide beach facing the open Pacific shown on the Cabo San Lucas area photo. Swimming is dangerous. Access is through the several hotel developments built on or near this beach.

CAPE AREA FISHING

This section is supplemental to the information on fishing in Chapter 5 WATERSPORTS.

FISHING AREAS -- The material presented below relates to the CAPE AREA FISHING GROUNDS Map in this chapter. This map was traced from US Government Nautical Chart 21120 so the relationship between the peninsular coast and the various "banks" is well represented.

1 Golden Gate Bank -- This frequently visited fishing area is 26 nautical miles from the Cabo San Lucas

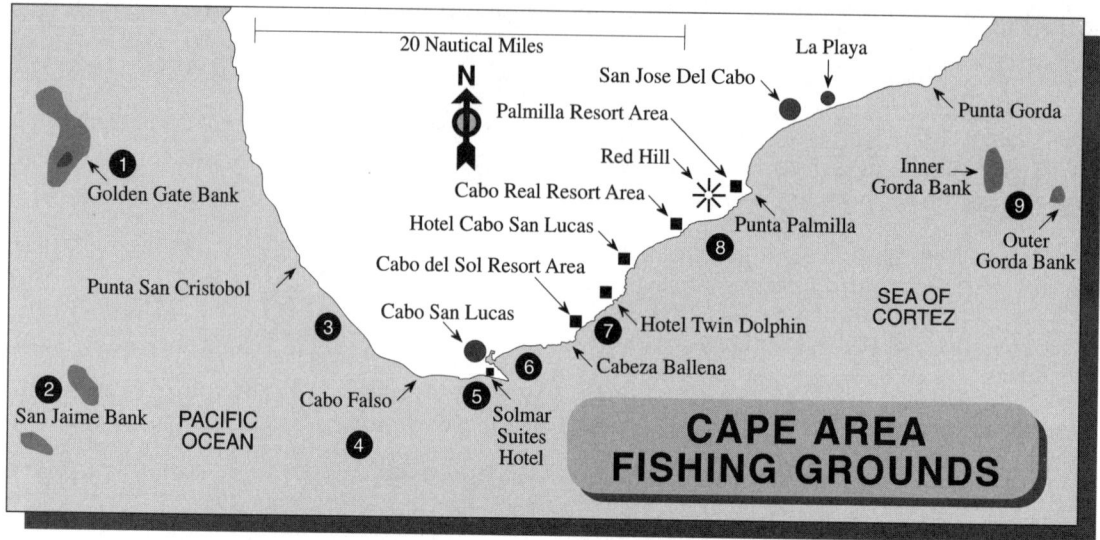

CAPE AREA FISHING GROUNDS

harbor. It is well known for its marlin and other surface game fish. Taking small trailerable boats this far into the open Pacific is a bit risky. Best use one of the larger charter vessels from Cabo San Lucas.

2 San Jaime Bank -- This area is some 20 nautical miles from Cabo San Lucas. It is frequently visited to land marlin, dorado or wahoo. As with the Golden Gate Bank, you are well into the open Pacific.

3 San Cristobol Ranch -- Just north of Cabo Falso a sandy beach extends a considerable distance toward Punta San Cristobol. The area off shore from this beach provides good trolling for wahoo and dorado.

4 Bait Grounds -- This is the area where almost all bait is caught by the charter vessels based at Cabo San Lucas. It is approximately one and one-half miles offshore in water 250-to-350 feet deep. Wahoo and schooling dorado may be found in this area.

5 Playa Solmar -- The waters off the Playa Solmar and the Hotel Solmar are noted for roosterfish and many small boats troll here.

6 Harbor Entrance -- Although most of the better fishing is farther offshore many large game fish are found just outside the harbor entrance. Almost all fish in this area are within easy reach using small boats.

7 Shipwreck Beach -- Just northeast of the harbor is the Cabeza Ballena Lighthouse. In the area offshore from the light and as far east as Santa Maria Bay (east

of the Hotel Twin Dolphin) there is an excellent reef located approximately one mile offshore. This is a productive area for wahoo, dorado, and bottom fish. Water depths vary from 125-300 feet over the reef.

8 Red Hill (Cerro Colorado) -- Red Hill lies just west of Punta Palmilla. Trolling in 200 foot deep waters offshore here often produces good catches of wahoo.

9 Gorda Banks -- It is 26 nautical miles east from the Cabo harbor to the Gorda Banks where one finds excellent bottom fishing along with large grouper and cabrilla. The area is also well known for producing wahoo and many other species of game fish.

FISHING CHARTERS -- Promotional material available in 1995 lists eighteen sportfishing charter fleets based in the Cape Area. One of these is owned by the Hotel Palmilla and is anchored off that hotel at Punta Palmilla. A second is the panga fleet which operates off the beach at the town of La Playa east of San Jose del Cabo. All the rest are based in the harbor at Cabo San Lucas. In the future other fleets may be expected to operate in the protection of new breakwaters at the Cabo Real and Cabo del Sol resort areas. It is a rare Cabo hotel that does not have a sportfishing desk where boat reservations may be arranged.

In 1995 most pangas (22-24 foot open skiffs) could be rented for $125 to 150 per 5-6 hour fishing day. Sportfishing cruiser prices ranged from $235 to $900 per day. Rates include crew, fishing equipment, licenses, ice chest and ice. Food, drinks and tips are normally extra.

CAPE AREA RESIDENTIAL DEVELOPMENTS

For a variety of reasons, I have never been a fan of second home subdivisions, condominiums and their numerous cousins. These developments frequently usurp lands that my sense of values feel might best be devoted to other uses available to the general public, and the vast majority of the resultant residential units seem to lie unused while their owners wait to retire. The world is too full of wonderful places to visit without tying myself down to only one locale at vacation time.

But, regardless of these negative feelings, it is by now obvious to me that Baja's Cape Area is rapidly becoming a major vacation or retirement home capital, with the quality of many of the developments being very high. And it is equally obvious that those who are investing in these developments do not agree with me. For those of you who fall in this category, I offer the following listings (from east to west) of what appear to me to be the most prominent of the modern recreational residence developments. They are good places to start looking if you are a prospective buyer. Also be aware that you will have difficulty escaping sales persons for the time-share and condominium developments in the Cape Area. Their pitches are high pressure and intense. Be cautious.

1 San Jose del Cabo Area -- The land between Valerio Gonzalez Canseco and Paseo San Jose at San Jose del Cabo has been developed to uniformly high standards for second homes and a golf course since about 1985. The Missions Area to the north is largely condominium buildings while the southerly Finnestera Area is single family homes with well developed landscaping. In addition, the Missions de San Jose and Viva Beachfront condominiums are shown on the SAN JOSE DEL CABO Map. Condominiums are also apart of the La Jolla de los Cabos development shown on the CABO CORRIDOR Map #1.

2 Palmilla Resort Area -- Many fancy homes have been built in the vicinity of the Hotel Palmilla for many years. Many more will now be added in the golf club areas on either side of Highway 1.

3 Cabo Real Resort Area -- This 2,500 acre tract is rapidly being developed into a sizeable community built around its expansive golf course.

4 Cabo del Sol Resort Area -- At 1,800 acres, this resort area is slightly smaller than Cabo Real but a community of some 3,400 residences is contemplated. Again a golf course is a central feature.

5 Missions del Cabo -- This is a sizeable area which has been under development for many years. It features lots with views of the nearby ocean waters.

6 Cabo San Lucas Area -- Approximately 1,600 home sites are planned at the Cabo San Lucas Country Club on the eastern edge of Cabo San Lucas. On the western edge of town is Pedregal de Cabo San Lucas. It lies on mountainous ground lying west of the old community and has been in existence for many years. It is without a golf course but features excellent views of the Pacific Ocean and the topographic uniqueness of a hilly area. These and several other condominium developments are indicated on the CABO SAN LUCAS Map.

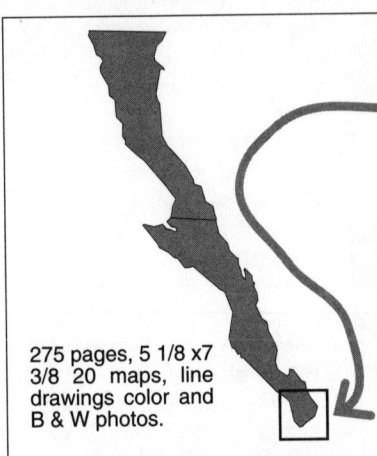

CABO SAN LUCAS
HANDBOOK

BY JOE CUMMINGS

Joe Cumming's book zero's in on the Cape Area of the Baja Peninsula including the Baja Corridor and the towns of Cabo San Lucas and San Jose del Cabo. It provides details on bullfights, local festivals, accomidations, entertainment, beaches, fishing, windsurfing and shopping.

The book also offers great coverage on the Sierra de la Laguna and other lesser-visited sections of the southern Baja peninsula. Covered are hiking trails, remote villages, roadside stands and a many other details little know to most Baja travelers.

275 pages, 5 1/8 x7 3/8 20 maps, line drawings color and B & W photos.

CHAPTER 25
HIGHWAY 19

The northern junction of Highway 1 and Highway 19 is at **KM J-185** on Highway 1. There has long been a road between this point and Cabo San Lucas via Todos Santos and the Pacific coast, but completion of a modern highway took many years. In spring of 1984, the highway was opened to traffic for its full length. Highway 19 is easily traveled by all classes of vehicles and is the shortest and easiest route from La Paz to the tip of the peninsula.

Highway 19 will be described from north to south. Kilometer post numbers proceed in this same direction, with 0 at the Highway 1 junction.

Taking Highway 19 offers the following advantages over traveling to Cabo San Lucas via Highway 1: (A) The 80-mile trip to Cabo San Lucas over Highway 19 is 35 miles shorter. (B) There are no steep mountainous sections such as the Sierra de la Laguna crossing on Highway 1. (C) There are many miles of highway offering fine views of the Pacific Ocean. Water views along Highway 1 are limited. (D) As the Sea of Cortez coast becomes overly hot in the summer the Pacific shore along Highway 19 provides cooler weather.

(Km-10) CAPE REGION VEGETATION — You have now driven well into the area of Cape Region Vegetation, as shown on the map in Chapter 10 VEGETATION. It can be clearly seen that plant growth is far more dense than that encountered in the Sonoran Desert Region. The cardon cactus and many other desert species are still present, but note the dominance now of woody shrubs and small trees. Many of the trees are members of the pea family. They all have very small compound leaves and are armed with numerous spines.

(Km-31) GEOGRAPHIC CHANGE — The northerly 19 miles of Highway 19 crosses the flat southern end of the Llano de la Paz which can be seen stretching endlessly to the NW. In sharp contrast, the lofty peaks of the Sierra de la Laguna rise a short distance to the SW. At **Km-31** the highway begins to enter the low hills at the base of these mountains.

(Km-42) PRESA DE SANTA INES — At this point a secondary road leaves to the left (east) and in 3.6 miles (8 Kms) arrives at the Presa de Santa Ines (Santa Ines Dam). This large concrete dam was completed in 1983 to provide flood control and a more dependable water supply for the town of Todos Santos.

[PSI] #29

(Km-51) TODOS SANTOS — Enter Todos Santos (population 3,400), one of Baja's most entrancing towns. Note the trees and agricultural crops in the flat river valley to the right (west).

Park along the main street near the Hotel California and enjoy the town on foot. Todos Santos is stop No. 29 on the POINTS OF SPECIAL INTEREST Tour. It and Stop No. 30 are the only points not on Highway 1 but

The church and civic plaza at Todos Santos. The mission personnel from here were forced to flee during the 1733 Indian revolt. Photo JW.

they have been included on the assumption that most travelers will use both Highways 1 and 19 in their visits to the Cape Region.

Todos Santos was established as a visiting station for the mission at La Paz in 1724. It became a separate mission in 1734 but was then destroyed in the Indian rebellion that started that same year. The site of this original mission is up the arroyo from the town but no ruins remain. -- I suggest your visit include the following places:

1. Hotel California. The Hotel California was not built with the modern tourist in mind. Rather, it looks like what a hotel in an isolated western Mexican town should look like: thick walls, tile floors, and a balcony rounding its second story. Ownership changed about 1987 and a well landscaped swimming pool was added to provide a touch of moderism to its charms.

2. The village church, civic plaza, and municipal buildings overlook the flat fertile valley of the arroyo. In the 1950s, the valley was reported to be planted almost entirely with sugar cane. Today, the cane is gone and has been replaced with a variety of other crops. It is a welcome change to look out over abundant greenery after driving through many miles of desert.

3. Overlooking the valley are the ruins of one of the town's sugar mills fringed with a few remnants of cane (see TODOS SANTOS Map).

4. Behind the PEMEX station is a well-landscaped RV park which has been converted to all permanent sites. It encompasses another of the town's abandoned sugar mills and is appropriately named El Molino (The Mill).

For the first 20 miles south of Todos Santos, Highway 19 will pass over

CHAPTER 25
HIGHWAY 19

(Km-54) PUNTA LOBOS — The Pacific Coast undergoes a significant geographic change at Todos Santos. North of the village, for over 100 miles, the shoreline is essentially one, long, sandy beach backed by nearly level plains. To the south, the Sierra de la Laguna heavily influences the topography. Here the coast is frequently rocky and steep with mountains towering in the background. It is an attractive region through which to drive.

From Todos Santos, the northernmost of several rocky promontories is in view. This is Punta Lobos. (*Lobo* means wolf in Spanish but refers to sea lions when used in coastal place names.) Here, 200 yards north of **Km-54**, a dirt road to the right (west) leaves Highway 19, and in <u>1.5 miles</u> arrives at a sandy beach. The local fishermen launch their boats over the beach immediately north of the point. The best campsites are at the end of a spur road near an abandoned building a few hundred yards to the north.

(Km-57) PLAYA SAN PEDRITO — Near **Km-57** a dirt road to the right (west) leads in <u>1.5 miles</u> to a fine sandy beach, Playa San Pedrito. The junction point is directly opposite the botanical garden described below. The beach is backed by a large grove of native Washingtonia fan palms mixed with the introduced coconut palm. The combination of sea, sand, and palms makes this one of Baja's most pleasant camping spots. It is one of my favorites. The area is best suited for smaller vehicles as the seaward end of the access road is often badly rutted. Unfortunately, in 1997, the area was signed "No Camping - No Fires." Hopefully these will disappear in the future.

PSI #30

(Km-57) BOTANICAL GARDEN — Opposite the road to Playa San Pedrito is the Campo Experimental Todos Santos. Here has been developed a fine

gently sloping coastal benches, some of which have been cleared for agriculture.

The botanical garden at **Km-57** on Highway 19 south of Todos Santos. A good place to check out plant identification. Photo BW.

array of desert plants from all regions of Baja. Many are marked with signs. This botanical garden adjoins the highway and is open to the public at no cost. This is an excellent place to test whether you have properly identified the plants you have seen along the peninsula's highways. The garden is the final stop on the POINTS OF SPECIAL INTEREST TOUR. I hope you have visited many of the areas it highlights and that they have added to your enjoyment of the Magnificent Peninsula.

(KM-59) SAN PEDRITO RV PARK — A two-lane sandy boulevard leaves the highway to the west 0.2 miles north of **Km-59** and in 1.8 miles arrives at the San Pedrito RV Park. (At the 0.5 mile point a side road branches to the right and travels to Playa San Pedrito as noted at Km 57 above.) This was the first tourist facility built along Highway 19 after it was completed. There is a restaurant, bar, swimming pool, a large number of full hookup units, and an excellent sandy beach. Tent campers are accommodated along the beach immediately south of the RV area. The RV parking area is a bit sterile but it will improve when the recently planted palm trees increase in size. The park's name is a bit confusing, as it is not at Playa San Pedrito. According to the official Mexican government topographic map, Playa San Pedrito is located to the north at **Km-57** as noted above.

(Km-61) EL PESCADERO — At 0.2 miles north of **Km-62** a paved side road leads to the left (east) to the village of El Pescadero (population 1,200). The name means "the fish dealer." There are many palms and other trees in and around the community. It is a pleasant town in the heart of vegetable farming area but is without tourist facilities other than a grocery store and several vegetable stands located along Highway 19.

(Km-64) LOS CERRITOS — A 2-lane secondary road leads to the right (west) 100 yards south of **Km-64** and arrives at a fork in the road in 1.3 miles. The left turn brings one to another of the original government trailer courts. This one is now open and being improved but the restrooms were inoperative in 1997. A short trip on the road to the right terminates at another excellent unimproved camping area near a fine sandy beach. A short point of land provides reasonable protection from both wind and swells. There are fine views of the coastline to the south.

The balcony to the charming old Hotel California at Todos Santos. Photo BW.

(Km-82) GEOGRAPHIC CHANGE — Between here and Todos Santos, Highway 19 has remained within a short distance of the ocean and passed over mostly level coastal benches. At this point 0.2 miles north of **Km-82**, the highway gains elevation and moves inland over rolling plateau lands. The roadside ahead is gradually building up with ranches, homes, cafes and an occasional real estate development.

(Km-94) EL MIGRINO LOOP NORTH END — Leading to the right (west) at a point 100 yards north of Km-94 is the northern end of a section of the old, dirt-surface coastal road. It loops toward the Pacific and rejoins the Highway 1.7 miles ahead. The loop road is about 2.5 miles in length and offers several excellent places to camp on low bluffs overlooking excellent sandy beaches. Near the middle of the loop are several steep dips. Larger RVs should approach these with caution. (To my knowledge this loop area has no name but I call it El Migrino after a ranch bearing this name located near its southern end.)

Ruins of one of the sugar cane mills at Todos Santos. Photo JW.

There are no further coastal camping spots between here and Cabo San Lucas. In the previous edition of this book I wrote "this El Migrino area may become a very popular camping location now that beach sites in the Cabo San Lucas area on Highway 1 are all taken over by hotels and various private interests." To my surprise this has not occurred and this excellent camping area appears to get very little use.

(Km-97) RIO CANDELARIA — About 100 yards north of **Km-97** Highway 19 makes a long, low-water crossing of the Rio Candelaria. While normally dry, this crossing could cause problems during and after storms. One might predict that it eventually will have to be bridged.

(Km-97) EL MIGRINO LOOP SOUTH END — Here, 100 feet south of **Km-97** is the southern junction of the El Migrino loop road. In 1995 a small sign read "Migrino Access a Playa." The last two times I have visited this area this southern end of the loop road has been modified with some of the land placed under agriculture, so you may have to find your way about by trial and error until things settle down. In general try to keep to the right (north) to access the camping areas noted above. Bearing left leads to the edge of a large lagoon area which also offers camping spots.

RIO CANDELARIA TO CABO SAN LUCAS — Highway 19 climbs inland south of the Rio Candelaria, with the Pacific Ocean occasionally in view in the distance. The vegetation you will encounter from about **Km-110** southward is the best example of the Arid Tropical Forest found along Highway 19. In particular, note the cardonals (forests) of cardon cactus and the several species of low-branching trees. Among the largest is the palo blanco. Its light bark makes it easy to identify.

(Km-124) CABO SAN LUCAS — At the northern edge of Cabo San Lucas a new section of Highway 19 turns sharply to the left (east) and skirts the edge of the community. Bearing to the right brings one into the heart of town via Jose Morelos (see Cabo San Lucas Map in Chapter 24). A PEMEX station lies near the junction and offers a fueling alternative to the town's other gas station on

The palm-lined beach and cove at Playa San Pedrito. Photo JW.

Highway 1. See Chapter 24 for details concerning the town's tourist attractions.

VAYA CON DIOS — I always hate books that abruptly come to an end without a parting word. While we have probably never met, we have been companions along the way, and it seems improper to leave without a brief farewell.

The Pacific beach at los Cerritos near Todos Santos. The short point of land noted in the text lies out of sight to the right and provides wind and swell protection. Photo JW.

Former Los Angeles area television personality Ben Hunter wrote a book in 1978 about his experiences in Baja California entitled *The Baja Feeling*. Thousands of Baja visitors join Ben in getting that feeling the minute they cross south of the border.

I sincerely hope you have shared in that feeling with us and that *The Magnificent Peninsula* has enhanced your journey. My wife Patty and I, and in this edition my daughter Barbara, have worked diligently to bring you what we hope is the best guidebook available for Baja California. This 6th edition alone has taken over 8-months of our combined efforts, the same amount of time we spent on the previous two editions. We aren't getting any better at this.

Our greatest joy in producing the book is knowing that we have helped others to more fully enjoy a brief time in their lives. If our paths should cross, please give us a yell so we can say hello. But for now, vaya con dios.

No.	TITLE	AUTHOR	PRICE	AD PAGE
1	The Magnificent Peninsula - 6th Edition	Jack Williams	$18.95	
2	Baja Boater's Guide - Volume I - Pacific Coast	Jack Williams	$24.95	59
3	Baja Boater's Guide - Volume II - Sea of Cortez	Jack Williams	$29.95	59
4	The Great West - A Travelers Guide to Western U.S.	Jack Williams	$19.95	7
WATER SPORTS				
5	The Baja Catch (3rd Edition)	Niel Kelly & Gene Kira	$21.95	29
6	Diving Baja California	Susan Speck	$18.95	74
7	Sea Kayaking in Baja	Andromeda Romano-Lax	$13.95	72
8	Launch Ramps of Baja California	Mike Bales	$ 6.95	61
9	Yachtsmans Chart Book	Mariner's Ink Corp.	$99.95	60
10	Boating Guide to Mexico	John Rains & Patricia Miller	$39.95	340
NATURAL HISTORY				
11	Baja California Plant Field Guide	Norman C. Roberts	$22.95	55
12	The Baja Highway	John Minch & Thomas Leslie	$19.95	126
13	Fileld Guide to the Gray Whale	Oceanic Society	$ 6.95	83-268
14	The Elephant Seal	Burney J. Le Boeuf	$ 4.50	83
15	Marine Animals of Baja	Daniel Gotshall	$20.95	149
FLYING				
16	Airports of Baja California an NW Mexico	Arnold Senterfitt	$49.00	340
17	Fun Flying Baja - 2 Tape Set VCR Video	Rick Roessler	$49.95	44
OTHER GUIDES				
18	Baja Camping (2nd Edition)	Fred & Gloria Jones	$14.95	52
19	Backroad Baja	Patti and Tom Higginbotham	$14.95	39
20	Crossing the Border Fast & Easy	Paula McDonald	$6.95	113
21	Cabo San Lucas Handbook	Joe Cummings	$14.95	331
22	Baja Adventure Book	Walt Peterson	$17.95	340
23	Fun Driving Baja	Rick Roessler	$19.95	213
BAJA RELATED SUBJECTS				
24	Spanish Lingo for the Savvy Gringo	Elizabeth Reid	$14.95	114
25	Back Country Mexico - Guide & Phrase Book	Burleson & Riskind	$14.95	129
26	Distant Neighbors	Alan Riding	$13.00	189
27	Into A Desert Place	Graham Mackintosh	$15.95	148
28	How to Buy Real Estate in Mexico	Dennis John Peyton	$24.95	117
29	Baja Calif Business Opportunities & Retirement Guide	Tom and Mary Lou Magee	$19.95	118
30	Mexican Slang	Linton H. Robinson	$6.95	86
31	King of the Moon	Gene Kira	$21.95	291

Order By Phone (800) 355-8635 book orders only.

(VISA or MASTERCARD)

At the time of publication our business telephone number and FAX is (415) 332-8635 in Sausalito, California. At some point during 1998 we will be moving to Redding, California. Please secure our new phone and FAX number from Information at (530) 555-1212 asking for Jack Williams.

There's a sign over my desk in the back room of our house. It reads, "H. J. Williams Publications -- International Headquarters." The place in question is also U.S. Headquarters, California Headquarters and the only headquarters of our enterprise. In otherwords, we ain't Rand McNally.

With the last two editions of The Magnificent Peninsula, we decided to list our phone and FAX number in the BAJA BOOKSHELF and take credit card orders. Everybody was calling us anyway, so why not go with the flow.

But, keep in mind that if we hire someone to answer the phone, our profits will drop from anemic to hemorrhage. So treat us with kindness and please observe the following Phone Ordering Instructions:

1 -- If nobody answers, we ain't home (or are in bed). Please try again. (We don't use an answering machine.)

2 -- Sometimes we leave town for awhile. If you can't get through by phone, please make your order by mail. Someone is always watching for the mail.

3 -- If you hear a baby crying in the background, you have the wrong number. We're over that.

4 -- If you get me, and I sound grumpy, I'm on the computer and trying to concentrate. Order a book

and I'll cheer right up. If you're lucky, you will get Patty.

5 -- Call anytime 8:00 AM to 5:00 PM except Sun AM and during 49er football games. If they don't win, wait awhile.

6 -- If the phone keeps ringing busy, Patty is talking to her brother in Nevada. Keep trying, they will tire after awhile, and Baja will still be there.

7 -- Ask all the questions you want about Baja, but remember, almost everything we know is "In the Book."

See next page for additional book advertisements.

Shown above is an advertisement about the 17th edition of the AIRPORTS OF BAJA CALIFORNIA book included in the 3rd edition of The Magnificent Peninsula. The Airports book is now in its 19th edition. Unfortunately several of the more recent editions had been reprinted with few modifications despite considerable change in flying conditions in Baja. Our review of the 19th edition discloses that positive revision has been made and the book's loose-leaf format allows for updated material to be obtained from the Baja Bush Pilots. Our humble observations indicate that more revision is still needed but the book is in fact the best and ONLY flying book available for Baja California.

A GLOSSARY
of Spanish words, trade names and acronyms
YOU WILL ACTUALLY SEE
while traveling in the Baja peninsula

ACRONYMS AND ABBREVIATIONS

C and F -- Letters on water faucets made in Mexico. In the poorer establishments they reportedly stand for Cold and Freezing. In the better hotels, C is for CALIENTE (hot) and F for FRIO (cold). Sometimes Mexican faucets may be mixed with those made in the U.S.A. Thus, C (caliente) and C (cold) can be entertaining.

CONASUPO -- COMPANIA NACIONAL de SUB-SISTENCIAS POPULARES. National Company of Popular Subsistences. Government stores selling basic commodities to assure that the public has access to essentials at reasonable prices. Drat, they don't sell beer.

DIF -- DESARROLLO INTEGRAL de la FAMILIA. A government agency concerned with the family. The acronym appears on many public buildings and in parks and playgrounds.

FONATUR -- FONDO NACIONAL de FOMENTO al TURISMO. National Fund for Tourism Development. Federal agency that is developing tourist facilities at Loreto, Bahia Escondido, & San Jose del Cabo.

IMSS -- INSTITUTO MEXICANO de SEGURO SOCIAL. Mexican Social Security Institute. Found on the front of hospitals and clinics.

PAN -- PARTIDO de ACCION NACIONAL. National Action Party. A principal political opposition party to the PRI.

PEMEX -- PETROLEOS MEXICANOS. Mexican Petroleum. The government company that produces all of Mexico's petroleum products and runs the retail gas stations.

PRI -- PARTIDO REVOLUCIONARIO INSTITUCION. Institutional Revolutionary Party. Mexico's dominant political party. Seen painted on buildings, rocks, and other places. It is possible to conclude that he who controls the paint brush controls the political destiny of Mexico.

S.A. -- SOCIEDAD ANONIMA. Literally translated, an anonymous company. It means incorporated. You will see it at the end of many company names. It does not refer to South America

SARH -- SECRETARIA de AGRICULTURA Y RECUSOS HIDRAULICOS. Secretary of Agriculture and Water Resources. The government agency that is developing new farming areas and related water sources.

SCT -- SECRETARIA de COMUNICACIONES y TRANSPORTAES. Secretary of Communications and Transportation. They are in charge of the highway and ferry systems. Look for the symbol on the side of highway maintenance trucks.

SEDUE -- SECRETARIA de DASARROLLO URBANO Y ECOLOGIA. Secretary of Urban and Ecological Development. The agency that adminsters parks, federal beaches, etc. **SRH** -- SECRETARIA de RECURSOS HIDRAULICOS. Secretary of Water Resources. Seen on the side of water tanks.

ALCOHOLIC BEVERAGES

CERVEZA -- Beer. Common brands are:

Bavaria	Bohemia
Carta Blanca	Corona
Modelo	Negra Modelo
Pacifico	Superior
Tecate	XX Dos Equies
XXX Tres Equies	

GINEBRA -- Gin. A common brand is Oso Negro which means Black Bear. Look for the bear's picture on the bottle.

LICOR -- Liquor. Most liquor stores bear the name "Vinos y Licor." "Y" is the Spanish word for "and."

RON -- Rum. A common beverage made from sugar cane which is grown in the tropical southern portion of mainland Mexico. Cuervo (crow) is the principal brand. Look for the picture of the black crow in many advertisments.

TEQUILA -- Tequila.
VODKA -- Vodka
VINO -- Wine. Blanco (white). Tinto (Red). Rosado (Rose)

Appendix

GEOGRAPHIC PLACE NAMES

BAHIA -- Bay. Remember that the letter "H" is always silent in Spanish.

CABO -- Cape. As in Cabo San Lucas.

ESTERO -- Estuary. There is little practical difference between estero and laguna, which means lagoon.

ISLA -- Island.
PLAYA -- Beach.
PUNTA -- Point, or projection of land protruding into the sea.
SIERRA -- Mountain range. The word also means saw. The words **CERRO** or **MONTE** are used to refer to an individual peak or mount.

LICENSE PLATES

FRONT -- FRONT is an abbreviation for FRONTERA, the Spanish word for frontier. It, along with state abbreviations, appears on the plates of the two states in the Baja peninsula and other Mexican states bordering the United States, for cars that are not manufactured in Mexico. Thus: FRONT B. C. indicates a foreign-manufactured car registered in the state of Baja California and FRONT B.C.S. a similar car registered in Baja California Sur.

MEX -- MEX is an abbreviation for Mexico. It and a state abbreviation appear on the plates of any car manufactured in Mexico. Thus: B.C. MEX, B.C.S. MEX, SON (Sonora) MEX, etc.

CALIFORNIA -- Plates from a foreign land to the north, severed from the Mexican Republic in 1848 through the force of arms. It is now being recaptured by the Mexican people through the more socially acceptable processes of nocturnal immigration and the willingness to work for a minimal wage. This latter affliction is readily cured upon obtaining U.S. citizenship or through contact with the civil rights movement.

SCHOOL TERMS

ESCUELA -- School. Escuela is a feminine noun. Feminine nouns usually end in "A." Masculine nouns in "O."

JARDIN DE NINOS -- Kindergarten. Literally, garden of children. The letter "J" in Spanish is pronounced as the English "H."

PRIMERIA -- Primary. The word primeria is an adjective. Spanish adjectives end in A if they modify a feminine noun such as escuela. They end in O with masculine nouns.

SECUNDARIA -- Secondary.

TECNICO -- Technical.

SHOPS AND STORES

ABARROTES -- Groceries or grocery store.

DISTRIBUIDORA -- Distributor. Often the word is followed by the name of the products that are sold.

FARMACIA -- Pharmacy. Mercifully this Spanish word starts with an "F" rather than the insane "Ph" of English. The names of many types of stores end in such letters as "eria" or "cia." Other common examples are:

LLANTERIA -- Tire store or shop.

LUNCHERIA -- A lunchroom or small restaurant. A word obviously derived from English.

MUEBLERIA -- Furniture store.

PANADERIA -- Bakery. PAN is the Spanish word for bread.

TORTILLERIA -- Tortilla shop. A place where tortillas are baked and sold at very low prices.

MERCADO -- Market.

SUPERMERCADO -- Supermarket.

TALLER -- Workshop. You can easily draw the conclusion in Baja that all mechanics are big lanky fellows as there are frequent signs reading TALLER MECANICO. They of course mean "mechanic shop" and not "taller mechanic."

TIENDA -- Store.

NOTE: -- Three words in this list contain a "LL" which is a separate letter in Spanish. In Mexico and much of Latin America, the "LL" is pronounced like the "y" in "yes."

OTHER COMMONLY SEEN WORDS

ABIERTO -- Open. Signs with this word, or CERRADO (closed) hang in store fronts.

ADUANA -- Customs house. Watch for this word at the ports-of-entry and near the ferry docks.

BAJA -- Baja is the feminine form of the adjective BAJO meaning "below."

BANCO -- Bank. Look also for banking company names starting with BANCO or BAN.

BANO -- Bath. Usually the sign reads LOS BANOS and refers to the rest rooms. This is one we all have to know, as we all have to go.

BASURA -- Rubbish. Watch for this word on trash barrels and similar places.

CALLE -- Street. Watch for signs on the sides of buildings at street corners.

CORREO -- Post Office.

CRUZ ROJA -- Red Cross. Most commonly seen on ambulances.

CUENTA -- Restaurant check. This is the one word in this glossary that you rarely see, but if you can't ask for the check, "LA CUENTA." you may be stuck in Baja for the duration. The waiter normally does not bring the check until you request it. You can make believe you are writing on the palm of your hand with an invisible pencil, but that's tacky.

DINA -- Mexico's truck and bus manufacturing company. The name appears on the front of these vehicles.

EJIDO -- Common Land. An institution under Mexican law for the common ownership of land. See Chapter 13. The word, or the abbreviation EJ, is commonly seen as part of place names on road signs and maps.

EMPUJE -- Push. The word appears on doors you are trying to open by pulling. JALE means "pull."

HOTEL -- Hotel. One of several words that are spelled the same in English and Spanish but where the pronunciation is quite different. Remember, "H" is silent in Spanish.

INMIGRACION -- Immigration.

LA PINTA -- The Spot. The trade name of many of the original parador hotels seen along Highway 1. See Chapter 6.

LARGA DISTANCIA -- Long Distance. Look for signs with these words and a picture of a telephone indicating offices where you can make long-distance phone calls.

MICROONDAS -- Microwave. The word is usually pre-ceded by EST, the abbreviation for estacion (station) You will see these words on signs marking the roads to the stations. The additional word or words on the sign name the particular station.

PALACIO MUNICIPAL -- Municipal Palace. Look for these words on the front of town halls in communities that are the seats of local government. In the smaller towns the town hall will bear the words Delagado Municipal, (Municipal Delegate). See Chapter 12.

PALAPA -- A shelter made of palm branches. Usually with no walls.

PANGA -- A flat bottomed fishing boat.

PUENTE -- Bridge. Highway bridges in Mexico are given names. The word Puente followed by the bridge name will be seen on signs on either side of the bridge.

RAMAL -- Branch. The word is commonly seen on road signs and refers to a branch road to the place referred to on the sign.

RESTAURANTE -- Restaurant. One of many words that are spelled almost the same in English and Spanish but where the pronunciation is considerably different. In Spanish the accent is on the "RAN" and the "R's" are rolled.

REGALOS -- Gifts. You will see this word on the front of many stores.

ROPA -- Clothing or clothes. Another word seen on store fronts.

SE VENDE -- Derived from the verb vender (to sell). In effect, it means For Sale. It is frequently followed by the name of the product available.

SECRETARIA -- Secretary. The word will be frequently seen as part of the name of various federal agencies, and in this context means "ministry."

TRES ESTRELLAS -- The full name is TRES ESTRELLAS de ORO. Three Stars of Gold. This is the name of Mexico's largest bus company. Look for the name on all sides of the buses along with the three-star logo.

NOTE: -- Mexicans use a variety of hand and body signals. One of the most common is to hold up the hand with the thumb and index finger separated about one inch. It means "wait a minute." It is often used by waiters or others of whom you are requesting a service. In effect they are acknowledging your presence and indicating that you will be helped soon.

ROAD SIGNS

Some Mexican road signs are pictorially self-explanatory and use the diagonal slash to indicate NO (see the No Parking sign). However, the majority simply spell out their message in Spanish as shown on many of the signs in this exhibit.

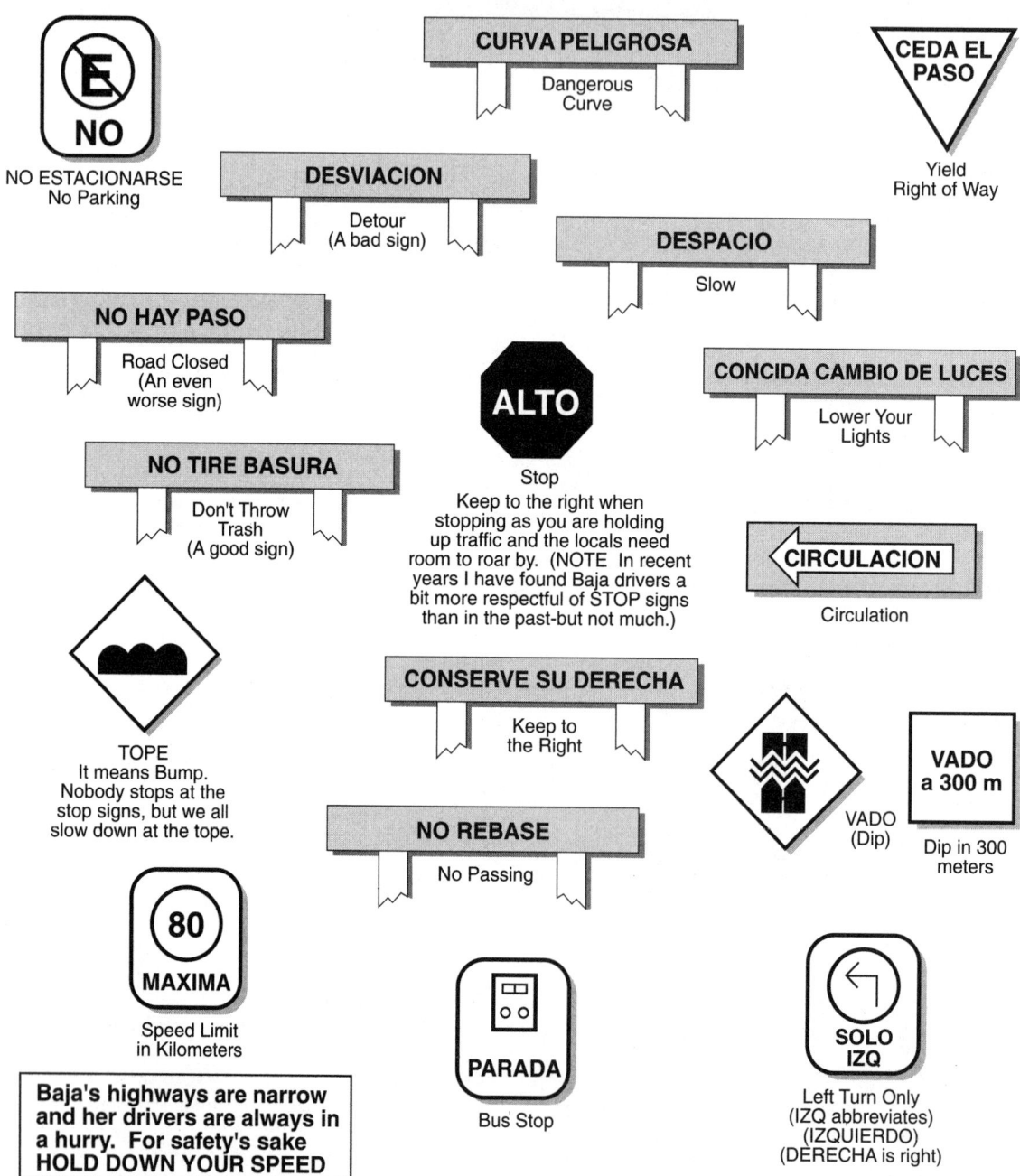

NO ESTACIONARSE
No Parking

CURVA PELIGROSA
Dangerous Curve

CEDA EL PASO
Yield
Right of Way

DESVIACION
Detour
(A bad sign)

DESPACIO
Slow

NO HAY PASO
Road Closed
(An even worse sign)

ALTO
Stop
Keep to the right when stopping as you are holding up traffic and the locals need room to roar by. (NOTE In recent years I have found Baja drivers a bit more respectful of STOP signs than in the past-but not much.)

CONCIDA CAMBIO DE LUCES
Lower Your Lights

NO TIRE BASURA
Don't Throw Trash
(A good sign)

CIRCULACION
Circulation

TOPE
It means Bump. Nobody stops at the stop signs, but we all slow down at the tope.

CONSERVE SU DERECHA
Keep to the Right

VADO (Dip)

VADO a 300 m
Dip in 300 meters

NO REBASE
No Passing

80 MAXIMA
Speed Limit in Kilometers

PARADA
Bus Stop

SOLO IZQ
Left Turn Only
(IZQ abbreviates)
(IZQUIERDO)
(DERECHA is right)

Baja's highways are narrow and her drivers are always in a hurry. For safety's sake **HOLD DOWN YOUR SPEED**

INDEX By Patty

Bold type indicates places found in PART III and plants found in Chapter 10 list of Common Plants.

Appendix

Appendix

Appendix

THE GREAT WEST

A Traveler's Guide To

HISTORY

Of Western United

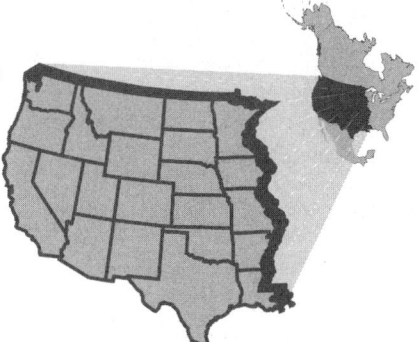

By **Jack Williams & Patty Williams**

author's of two of Baja's great guidebooks

The Magnificent Peninsula and Baja Boater's Guide

Travel Information for 370 Historic Attractions -- 97 Historic Maps -- 32 Photos
288 Pages -- 7"x 9" Format -- Extensive Text About Western History

The Guide that Links History with Places to Visit